Listening to Confraternities

Intersections

INTERDISCIPLINARY STUDIES IN EARLY MODERN CULTURE

General Editor

Karl A.E. Enenkel (*Chair of Medieval and Neo-Latin Literature
Universität Münster*
e-mail: kenen_01@uni_muenster.de)

Editorial Board

W. de Boer (*Miami University*)
S. Bussels (*University of Leiden*)
A. Dlabačová (*University of Leiden*)
Chr. Göttler (*University of Bern*)
J.L. de Jong (*University of Groningen*)
W.S. Melion (*Emory University*)
A. Montoya (*Radboud University Nijmegen*)
R. Seidel (*Goethe University Frankfurt am Main*)
P.J. Smith (*University of Leiden*)
J. Thompson (*Queen's University Belfast*)
A. Traninger (*Freie Universität Berlin*)
C. Zittel (*Ca' Foscari University of Venice / University of Stuttgart*)
C. Zwierlein (*Bonn*)

VOLUME 92 – 2025

The titles published in this series are listed at *brill.com/inte*

Listening to Confraternities

Spaces for Performance, Patronage and Urban Musical Experience

Edited by

Tess Knighton

BRILL

LEIDEN | BOSTON

Cover illustration: Excerpts from Bartolomeo Pellerano (da Camogli), *Madonna dell' Umiltà* (1346), Galleria Regionale della Sicilia in Palazzo Abatellis, Palermo, Sicily. Photo by Eduardo Carrero Santamaría. Image in the public domain.

Library of Congress Cataloging-in-Publication Data

Names: Knighton, Tess, 1957- editor.
Title: Listening to confraternities : spaces for performance, patronage and urban musical experience / edited by Tess Knighton.
Description: Leiden ; Boston : Brill, 2025. | Series: Intersections, 1568-1181 ; vol.92 | Includes index
Identifiers: LCCN 2024033570 (print) | LCCN 2024033571 (ebook) | ISBN 9789004544208 (hardback) | ISBN 9789004702776 (ebook)
Subjects: LCSH: Confraternities—Europe—History—16th century. | Confraternities—Europe—History—17th century. | Music—Social aspects—Europe—History—16th century. | Music—Social aspects—Europe—History—17th century. | Sound—Social aspects—Europe—History—16th century. | Sound—Social aspects—Europe—History—17th century. | Community music—Europe—16th century—History and criticism. | Community music—Europe—17th century--History and criticism. | Processions, Religious—Europe—History. | Church music—Catholic Church—16th century. | Church music—Catholic Church—17th century. | Music patronage—Europe—History. | Counter-Reformation.
Classification: LCC ML3917.E85 L57 2025 (print) | LCC ML3917.E85 (ebook) | DDC 780/.0267—dc23/ENG/20240828
LC record available at https://lccn.loc.gov/2024033570
LC ebook record available at https://lccn.loc.gov/2024033571

Typeface for the Latin, Greek, and Cyrillic scripts: "Brill". See and download: brill.com/brill-typeface.

ISSN 1568-1181
ISBN 978-90-04-54420-8 (hardback)
ISBN 978-90-04-70277-6 (e-book)
DOI 10.1163/9789004702776

Copyright 2025 by Koninklijke Brill BV, Leiden, The Netherlands.
Koninklijke Brill BV incorporates the imprints Brill, Brill Nijhoff, Brill Schöningh, Brill Fink, Brill mentis, Brill Wageningen Academic, Vandenhoeck & Ruprecht, Böhlau and V&R unipress.
All rights reserved. No part of this publication may be reproduced, translated, stored in a retrieval system, or transmitted in any form or by any means, electronic, mechanical, photocopying, recording or otherwise, without prior written permission from the publisher. Requests for re-use and/or translations must be addressed to Koninklijke Brill BV via brill.com or copyright.com.

This book is printed on acid-free paper and produced in a sustainable manner.

Contents

Acknowledgments IX
List of Figures, Music Examples and Tables X
Note on the Editor XVII
Notes on the Contributors XVIII

1   Introduction: Sounds of Body and Spirit – Sense, Space, and Motion in Confraternities 1
    Nicholas Terpstra

PART 1
The Participation of Confraternities in Urban Ceremonial

2   The 'Sensoryscape' of the Good Friday Procession in Early Modern Venetian Bergamo 25
    Emanuela Vai

3   Musical Interactions at the Confraternity of Our Lady of the Rosary in Antwerp in the Seventeenth Century 62
    Ana López Suero

4   Sound and Confraternal Piety in Early Modern Leuven 87
    Henry Drummond

5   Music and Students in the Academy and Confraternity of St. Thomas Aquinas in Barcelona (1588) 116
    Ascensión Mazuela-Anguita

6   The Sonic and Ceremonial Contribution of the Confraternity of Sant Jordi and the *Centenar de la Ploma* to Celebratory Processions in Valencia 152
    Ferran Escrivà-Llorca

PART 2
Devotional Practice and Religious Reform

7   Corporations or Confraternities? Strategies Adopted by Artisan Groups in Response to Pressures Arising from the Catholic Reformation   177
    Noel O'Regan

8   Confraternities and Music on the Eve of the Reformation: Early-Tudor Boston   200
    Magnus Williamson

9   Who was Listening to Oratorio? Lay Confraternities and Patrician Music in Early Modern Italy   225
    Xavier Torres

10 Mustering Troops and Teaching Counterpoint: The Musical Incursions of a Central European Redemption Confraternity   245
    Erika Supria Honisch

11 Confraternities, Congregations and Aural Culture in Counter-Reformation Germany   272
    Alexander Fisher

PART 3
Confraternities as Acoustic Communities

12 Music and Noise: The Sounds of a Youth Confraternity in Renaissance Florence   307
    Konrad Eisenbichler

13 'In parole' and 'in canto': The Songs and Prayers of the Disciplinati in Early Modern Milan   326
    Daniele V. Filippi

14 Performing Poetry at Rouen's Puy of the Immaculate Conception   356
    Dylan Reid

15 Black Dancers and Musicians Performing Afro-Christian Identity in
 Early Modern Sources   381
  Elisa Lessa

16 Devotional Collective Singing and the Construction of Christian
 Indigenous Communities: The Hospital Confraternities of the
 Concepción in Colonial Michoacán   404
  Antonio Ruiz Caballero

PART 4
Mapping the Contribution of Confraternities to the Urban Soundscape

17 Digital Cartography of the Confraternities of Granada and Their Impact
 on the Early Modern Urban Soundworld   435
  Juan Ruiz Jiménez

18 Mapping Post-Tridentine Confraternities and Processions in
 Sixteenth-Century Tarragona   468
  Sergi González González

19 Burying the Bones: Mapping the Sounds and Spaces of the Confraternity
 of the *Verge Maria dels Desamparats* in Early Modern Barcelona   506
  Tess Knighton

  Index Nominum   551
  Index Locorum   581

Acknowledgments

A collection of essays of this kind always involves the support and hard work of a number of people, and I take this opportunity to thank all those who have contributed to its compilation. In particular, I would like to thank Arjan Van Dijk for initiating the process at Brill, the Intersections series editor, Karl Enenkel for his help at every stage of the process, and Ivo Romein and Gera van Bedaf for seeing the volume through the press. I am also very grateful to Nicholas Terpstra for his interest in the idea of listening to the confraternal soundscape. Some of the contributions in this volume, which appear here in revised form, go back to the international conference *Listening to Confraternities* held in Barcelona, 27–29 September 2022. That conference formed part of the research project 'The Contribution of Confraternities and Guilds to the Urban Soundscape in the Iberian Peninsula, ca. 1400–ca. 1700', funded by a Spanish government grant (MINECO, CONFRASOUND PID2019-109422GB-100. I+D+i – PGC TIPO B, 2020–2023) based at the Universitat Autònoma de Barcelona.

Figures, Music Examples and Tables

Figures

2.1 Alvise Cima (attributed), *Veduta di Bergamo a volo d'uccello*, 1693. Oil on canvas, 107.5 cm × 166.8 cm   33

2.2 Enea Salmeggia (Talpino), *Martirio di Sant'Alessandro*, painted 1623. Oil on canvas, 620 cm × 500 cm, Basilica di Sant'Alessandro in Colonna (detail of the City of Bergamo under Venetian dominion)   34

2.3 Basilica of Santa Maria Maggiore, Confraternity of the Misericordia Maggiore, Bergamo (façade and main entrance)   35

2.4 Piazza Vecchia and Palazzo del Podestà, Bergamo   35

2.5 Stefano Scolari, *Perspective Plan of Bergamo*, 1680 (detail). Copper engraving, 77 cm × 104.2 cm   37

2.6 Unknown, *Untitled*. Seventeenth century. Drawing on paper. 107 cm × 166 cm (detail)   43

2.7 Alvise Cima (attributed), *Veduta di Bergamo a volo d'uccello* (detail of a bird's-eye view of Bergamo within the Venetian walls). Numbers on the map mark the locations of buildings, squares and streets along the route of the Good Friday Procession, as mentioned in the archival sources: 1./10. S. Maria Maggiore; 2. S. Grata e Salvecchio; 3. S. Agata; 4. Corsarola; 5. Piazza Vecchia; 6. Gombito Tower; 7. S. Cassiano; 8. Fish market; 9. Cathedral.   44

2.8 Historical GIS (HGIS) analysis of the sixteenth-century map of Bergamo (Esri ArcGIS Education CC BY-SA 4.0). Numbers on the map mark the locations of buildings, squares and streets along the route of the Good Friday Procession: 1./10. S. Maria Maggiore; 2. S. Grata e Salvecchio; 3. S. Agata; 4. Corsarola; 5. Piazza Vecchia; 6. Gombito Tower; 7. S. Cassiano; 8. Fish market; 9. Cathedral. See the QR code on the top right corner of the image for the interactive digital online version (or https://rb.gy/5wuzm)   45

3.1 Peeter Neeffs (I), *The Interior of the Dominican Church, Antwerp, Looking East, with the Procession of the Holy Sacrament*, painted in 1636. Oil on panel, 67.7 × 105 cm. Amsterdam, Rijksmuseum   65

3.2 Theodoor van Thulden, *Locorum Insignium ac viae triumphalis qua ser.mus princeps, Ferdinandus Austriacus, Hispaniar, Infans. etc. Antverpiam est ingressus, designatio*, engraved in 1639–1641. Paper 45.8 × 76.2 cm. Amsterdam, Rijksmuseum   66

3.3 Anonymous, *La Citadelle d'Anvers batie par de Duc d'Albe l'an MDLVIII*, seventeenth century. Paper 13.7 × 16.9 cm. Leuven, Katholieke Universiteit   67

FIGURES, MUSIC EXAMPLES AND TABLES   XI

3.4   Theodoor Galle (attributed to), *Mirakel van de Slag bij Lepanto 1571*, engraved in 1610. Paper 15 × 8.9 cm. Amsterdam, Rijksmuseum   70
3.5   Conrad Lauwers, *Plattegrond van Scherpenheuvel*, printed in 1661–1669. Paper 44.4 × 46 cm. Amsterdam, Rijksmuseum   71
3.6   Frans Hogenberg, *Citadel van Antwerpen, ca. 1570*, engraved ca. 1580–ca. 1635. Paper 19 × 27.5 cm. Amsterdam, Rijksmuseum   73
3.7   Anthonis Vermeeren, *Missae et motetta I. II. III. IV. vocum cum instrumentis auctore Anton. Vermeren, phonasco & organista in Castro Antverpiano* (Antwerp, erfgenamen Phalesius: 1660), frontpage. Paris, Bibliothèque nationale de France   82
4.1   Panorama of Leuven around 1605, drawn by Joost van der Baren and published with annotations in Justus Lipsius, *Lovanium, sive opidi et academiae eius descriptio, libri tres* (Antwerp, Plantijn-Moretus: 1605). Universiteit Antwerpen, Ruusbroecgenootschap. RG 2036 A 5   94
4.2   Seventeenth-century plan of Sint-Pieterskerk and the organisations resident at its forty-four altars. Leuven. Stadsarchief. Cuvelier 4143   96–97
5.1   Cloister of the friary of Santa Caterina. Drawing by M. Redon (undated). Barcelona. Arxiu Històric de la Ciutat. Fons Gràfics, Rg. 19227   119
5.2   *Estatutos de la Academia bajo la invocación del Angelico Doctor S[an]to Thomàs erigida con autoridad ordinaria, y Apostolica en la Yglesia de Santa Catha[lina] V[i]r[gen] y M[a]r[tir] Orden de Pred[icadore]s en Barcelona por los años de 1584* (eighteenth-century copy). Barcelona. Arxiu Històric de la Ciutat. *Documentació personal de Marià Aguiló* caja 1   121
5.3   Francesc Camprubí et al., *Lumen domus o Annals del convent de Santa Caterina de Barcelona* (MS, 1603–1802), vol. 1, fol. 102v. Barcelona. Universitat de Barcelona, Ms. 1005   122
5.4   *Goigs de Sant Thomas de Aquino, Doctor Quint de la Iglesia* (Barcelona, Ioan Iolis: 1726). Barcelona. Biblioteca de Catalunya, 1 Go M 114   125
5.5   *Villancicos que se cantaron en el Real Convento de Santa Cathalina [...] en las Fiestas que tributan, y consagran los Academicos Discipulos á su Angelico Maestro Santo Thomas de Aquino [...] cantòlos la Capilla de la Iglesia Cathedral, siendo Maestro de ella el Licenciado Francisco Valls* (Barcelona, Bartholome Giralt: 1712). Madrid. Biblioteca Nacional de España, VE/1304   135
5.6   Francesc Valls (1665–1747), *Villancico a 15 con ministriles y violines al Smo. Sto.: Angelicos espiritus celestes* [1697], alto part of choir 1. Barcelona. Biblioteca de Catalunya, M 1483/10   136
5.7   Francesc Valls (1665–1747), *Villanco. a 12 con claris. y violis. a Sto. Thomas de Aquino: Sombras cobardes* [1708], tiple 1 part of choir 1. Barcelona. Biblioteca de Catalunya, M 1470/16   136

XII   FIGURES, MUSIC EXAMPLES AND TABLES

5.8 Francesc Valls (1665–1747), *Villancico a 16 a Sto. Thomás de Aquino: Oy q. al sol de las escuelas* [1698], tenor part of choir 1. 11.5 cm wide. Barcelona. Biblioteca de Catalunya, M 1481/20   137

6.1 The processional route for the celebration of the feast days of St. George and St. Denis. Author's drawing based on the coloured map of Tomás Vicente Tosca of ca. 1738   165

7.1 Icon of Christ known as the *Acheropita*, housed in the Cappella del Sancta Sanctorum near the Basilica of S. Giovanni in Laterano, Rome   178

7.2 Icon of the Virgin and Child known as the *Salus Populi Romani*, housed in the Cappella Paolina of the Basilica of S. Maria Maggiore, Rome   179

7.3 Doorway in the Palazzo dei Conservatori, Campidoglio, Rome, headed by the name of the Università dei Macellari   183

7.4 *Statuti, Ordini e Constitutioni della Venerabile Compagnia et Università delli Barbieri e Stufaroli dell'Alma Città di Roma* (Rome, Paolo Blado: 1593)   188

7.5 Bust with reliquary of St. Eligius of Noyon, Università e Nobil Collegio degli Orefici, S. Eligio degli Orefici, Rome   193

7.6 S. Maria di Loreto di Fornai and Trajan's Column from *Prospectus Locorum Urbis Romae Insign[ium]*. Etching by Lievin Cruyl, 1666   194

8.1 Robert Hall, *A Plan of the Borough & Port of Boston* (Boston: 1742), showing the medieval street layout, the market place near St. Botolph's church, and the River Withom (orientation: east at top)   206

8.2 Goods liable to poundage passing through Boston port, 1390–1548 (£)   206

8.3 St. Botolph, Boston, south aisle, site of the pre-Reformation Lady Chapel. The doors in the south wall mark the location of the screen and organ loft   209

8.4 Annual turnover, Boston Lady Guild, 1515–1538 (£) (rental data incomplete for the year 1526–1527)   209

8.5 Boston Lady Guild accounts, 1527–1533 (Lincoln, Lincolnshire Archives Office 6-CHAR/2/1, part 2), showing bailiff's account for Boston rents, for the year to Thursday of Whitsun week, 29 Henry VIII, 1528   216

10.1 Lucas Kilian after Hans von Aachen, *Michael Adolph von Althann* (Augsburg, Dominicus Custos: 1600–1604). Engraving   247

10.2 Carlo Abbate, *Regulae contrapuncti ex operibus Zerlini et aliorum* [...] (Oslavany, Caspar Haugenhoffer: 1629), title-page   251

10.3 Title-page of *Flores verni ex viridario Oslaviensi divi tutelaribus Communio* [...] (Vienna, Matthaeus Formica: 1628)   252

10.4 Wenzel Hollar, *Pons Pragensis* (Prague Bridge: 1635?)   255

10.5 Heinrich Hiesserle von Chodaw, *Raiss-buch und Leben*, fol. 101 r (detail)   258

11.1 Jakob Balde, S.J., *Ehrenpreiß Der Allerseeligisten Jungkfrawen vnd Mutter GOttes MARIÆ Auff einer schlechten Harpffen jhres vnwürdigen Dieners gestimbt/ vnd* gesungen. Zu Nutz/ Trost/ vnd wolgefallen aller SODALIVM in vnser lieben Frawen Bruderschafften (Munich, Lucas Straub: 1647), [i] v. Vienna. Österreichische Nationalbibliothek   290

13.1 Milan. Archivio Storico Civico e Biblioteca Trivulziana, Cod. Triv. 383 fols. 40v–41r, colophon and first page of the tabula   328

13.2 Milan, Archivio Storico Civico e Biblioteca Trivulziana. Cod. Triv. 383 fol. 31r, part of the common office, with directions regarding the discipline and 'in canto' rubric introducing the lauda *Quando Signore Iesù serò y may / grato e cognoscente*   335

13.3 Milan. Archivio Storico Civico e Biblioteca Trivulziana, Cod. Triv. 416 fols. 42v–43r, addition to the office for times of plague with rubric regarding the discipline and introducing the lauda *O alta regina con la Trinitade*   344

13.4 *Raccolta d'alcuni hinni, con i suoi versetti, et responsorii da dirsi al matutino, alle laudi & al vespro le domeniche, & feste di tutto l'anno. Per uso, & commodità delli Fratelli della Ven. Scola de Disciplini di Santa Marta in Porta Ticinese di Milano* (Milan, Nella Stampa Arcivescovale [sic]: 1695), title-page (exemplar: Milan, Archivio Storico Civico e Biblioteca Trivulziana, attachment to Cod. Triv. 521)   349

14.1 Miniature depicting a puy in process from *Receuil palinodique, comprenant principalement des chants royaux, des ballades, des rondeaux de la Conception, de la Passion et des Pauvres* […] (sixteenth century). Bibliothèque nationale de France. Français 19184 fol. 295r   366

15.1 *The Encounter of Prince Conan and St. Ursula* (ca. 1522). Altarpiece of Santa Auta, attributed to Cristóvão de Figueiredo and Garcia Fernandes. National Museum of Ancient Art, Lisbon   383

15.2 African couple in prayer to Our Lady of the Rosary. Altarpiece of Our Lady of the Rosary. Unknown author, late sixteenth century. Church of Santa Catarina, Lisbon   387

15.3 Statutes of the Brotherhood of Our Lady of the Rosary of Black Africans (1565). Biblioteca Nacional de Portugal: https://purl.pt/24087   396

16.1 Santa Fe de la Laguna hospital: chapel, presbytery and altar   417

16.2 Santa Fe de la Laguna: hospital chapel and high choir   418

16.3 Nurío hospital: chapel and low choir   419

16.4 Santa Fe de la Laguna hospital: chapel and atrium   420

16.5 Nurío hospital: chapel and painted ceiling   421

16.6 Nurío hospital: chapel and detail of painted ceiling (invocation of the Loretan litany)   422

17.1 Capilla de las Ánimas Benditas del Purgatorio. Granada, Iglesia del Sagrario   438

17.2 Platform of Ambrosio de Vico (ca. 1600)   439

17.3 *Gazetilla curiosa o Semanario granadino.* Papel XIII (Monday, 2 July 1764). Biblioteca Virtual de Andalucía   442
17.4 *Expediente* on brotherhoods in the city of Granada (1769). Archivo de la Parroquia del Sagrario leg. 28   443
17.5 Topographical map of the city of Granada by Francisco Dalmau (1796)   445
17.6 Nuestra Señora del Triunfo. Alonso de Mena (1631)   446
17.7 Statutes of the Confraternity of the Ánimas del Purgatorio based at the church of El Sagrario (1541). Biblioteca Nacional de España. MSS/18451   454
17.8 Itinerary of the Corpus Christi procession in Granada   455
17.9 The route of the burial procession held for the condemned to death organised by the Confraternity of Corpus Christi, de Misericordia y de Ánimas Benditas del Purgatorio   457
17.10 Sedan chairs (*sillas de mano*) used to carry the viaticum from the churches of Granada. Choir of the Royal Chapel of Granada   461
17.11 *Letras que cantó la música de la Capilla Real en* [...] *festividad de las Quarenta horas* (1692) Biblioteca Nacional de España. VE/129/41   462
18.1 City plan of Tarragona by Enrique Florez (1769), in "Antiguedades Tarraconenses" in *España Sagrada* 80   476
18.2 Enrique Florez's 1769 city plan georeferenced using QGIS   477
18.3 The statue of the Eccehomo (1545) in the the tympanum of the Church of Nazareth, headquarters of the Confraternity of the Sang de Jesucrist in the Plaça del Rei, Tarragona   480
18.4 Retable (1495–1504) in the monastery of Santa Magdalena del Belloch, headquarters of the Confraternity of Santa Magdalena of market gardeners in the church of Sant Llorenç in the Plaça de Sant Llorenç, Tarragona   481
18.5 The route of the early morning Candlemas procession charted on the historic map by Enrique Florez, with a transparency of 50% over an OpenStreetMap base. Software: ARGIS on line   485
18.6 Nodes of processional routes visualised on Florez's 1769 map, with 50% transparency over an OpenStreetMap base. Software: Instamaps   490
18.7 Via Triumphalis. From a model of the Roman Forum of the Citerior Province in Tarraco   491
18.8 Centrality graph showing the density of processional occupation of urban space in post-tridentine Tarragona. Source: Gephy   492
18.9 Tarragona: processional route 1 charted on the historic map by Enrique Florez, with a transparency of 50% over an OpenStreetMap base. Software: ARGIS on line   496
18.10 Tarragona: processional route 2 charted on the historic map by Enrique Florez, with a transparency of 50% over an OpenStreetMap base. Software: ARGIS on line   498

FIGURES, MUSIC EXAMPLES AND TABLES

18.11 Tarragona: processional route 3 charted on the historic map by Enrique Florez, with a transparency of 50% over an OpenStreetMap base. Software: ARGIS on line   500
18.12 Tarragona: processional route 4 charted on the historic map by Enrique Florez, with a transparency of 50% on an OpenStreetMap base. Software: ARGIS on line   501
19.1 Anonymous, Portait of Isabel de Josa (1490–1564). Located in the meeting room of the town hall of Vercelli. The inscription reads: VEN: ISABELLA LOSA DE CARDONA NAT: HISP: / COLLEG. FVNDATRIX OBIIT V: MARTIR: MDLCXIV / AETATIS SUAE LXXV   511
19.2 The stations where polyphonic responsories (R) were sung during the procession from the Portal de Sant Antoni to the church of Santa Maria del Pi and in the church cemetery according to the 1658 description   525
19.3 The 1526 route of the procession of the bones and the change to the itinerary as minuted in the *Deliberacions* of the meeting of the community of priests of Santa Maria del Pi in 1623   529
19.4 The route taken for the procession of the bones according to the description of 1630, including the Plaça San Jaume but returning along the carrer dels Boters   531
19.5 The route from the Portal de Sant Antoni to the Creu Cuberta   533
19.6 The remains of the *porxo* or portico of the church of Sant Antoni, Barcelona, where those participating in the procession gathered to take the boxes of bones to the parish church of Santa Maria del Pi for burial   535
19.7 View of the Portal and Plaça Nova, Barcelona. Coloured engraving by Jean Baptiste Reville – Louis-François Couché in Alexandre Laborde, *Voyage pittoresque et historique de l'Espagne* (Paris, L'Imprimerie de P. Didot l'Aîné: 1806–1802)   536

Music Examples

10.1 Ludovico Manfredi di Guastalla, *Jubila popule meus* (opening)   266
11.1 "O Jesu süß wer dein gedenckt". Text from *Bruderschafftbüchel Deß süssen Namen Jesus* (Munich, Melchior Segen: 1644) 73. Melody adapted from Bäumker, W., *Das katholische deutsche Kirchenlied in seinen Singweisen von den frühesten Zeiten bis gegen Ende des siebzehnten Jahrhunderts* (Freiburg – St. Louis: 1883) vol. 1, 386 no. 125   286
11.2 Johann Haym von Themar, Litany of the Saints (excerpt), from *Litaniae textus triplex* (Augsburg, Josias Wörli: 1582)   292

11.3   Gregor Aichinger, "Pange lingua gloriosi" (excerpt), from *Solennia augustissimi Corporis Christi* (Augsburg, Johannes Praetorius: 1606)   295
11.4   Rudolph di Lasso, "Ecce tu pulchra es" (excerpt), from *Alphabetum Marianum* (Munich, Nikolaus Heinrich: 1621)   298
16.1   *Uarhi iurhixe* ('Lady Virgin'). Oral tradition, Santa Fe de la Laguna, Michoacan   425
16.2a–b   Loretan litany. Oral tradition, Santa María Ostula, Michoacan   426–427

Tables

3.1   Singers of the Confraternity of Our Lady of the Rosary, 1610–1652   77
3.2   Minstrels at Antwerp Castle   79
3.3   Books acquired by the Confraternity of Our Lady of the Rosary, 1610–1652   81
6.1   The three general processions held in Valencia in connection with the Christian conquest of the city and the expulsion of the *moriscos*   164
9.1   The confraternity oratorio in Italy (1660–1830)   232
9.2   Musical oratorios and confraternities in Italy (1660–1830)   232
10.1   The contents of *Flores verni ex viridario Oslaviensi divis tutelaribus Communionis Hierarchicae sacri* […] (Oslavany, Caspar Haugerhoffer: 1628)   263–264
13.1   The metrical items in the Trivulziana manuscripts with an indication of those marked as to be performed 'in canto'   336–338
17.1   Classification labels for confraternities on the *Historical Soundscapes* digital platform   447
18.1   Digital cartography software used in the CONFRASOUND research project   474
18.2   The confraternal ecosystem of Tarragona in the early seventeenth century   483
18.3   General processions in early modern Tarragona   486–488
18.4   The distances of the five main processional routes of post-tridentine Tarragona   492

Note on the Editor

Tess Knighton took her Ph.D. in Cambridge in 1984, and is an ICREA Research Professor affiliated to the Universitat Autònoma de Barcelona. She has published widely on the culture and music of the Iberian world in the medieval and early modern periods, including the collective volumes *Companion to Music at the Courts of Ferdinand and Isabel* (2017) and *Hearing the City in Early Modern Europe* (2018). She has led several research projects and is currently principal investigator of the ERC research project 'How Processions Moved: Sound and Space in the Performance of Urban Ritual (c.1400–c.1700)'.

Notes on the Contributors

Henry Drummond
studied musicology at the University of Oxford and is currently a Senior Researcher at the KU Leuven and Alamire Foundation. His research covers early modern musical reform, devotional music, and music written within royal courts in Iberia and the Low Countries. He has published articles in a number of journals, and has completed a monograph entitled *The Cantigas de Santa María: Power and Persuasion at the Alfonsine Court* (2023).

Konrad Eisenbichler
is Professor Emeritus in Reformation and Renaissance Studies of the University of Toronto. The recipient of the Lifetime Achievement Award from the Canadian Society for Renaissance Studies, he is the author, editor, or translator of more than thirty books, including *A Companion to Medieval and Early Modern Confraternities* (Brill, 2019) and the prize-winning monograph *The Boys of the Archangel Raphael: A Youth Confraternity in Florence, 1411–1785* (1998).

Ferran Escrivà-Llorca
is Associate Professor of Musicology at the Universidad Internacional de Valencia. His research focuses on the cultural history of the Habsburgs in the Iberian world, and early modern historiography, with special interest in urban musicology and soundscapes as tools for a richer knowledge of music history. He works primarily on issues of material culture, especially music books and music libraries.

Daniele V. Filippi
studied musicology at the universities of Cremona and Heidelberg. He held research fellowships at Boston College and at the Schola Cantorum Basiliensis before becoming a tenure-track researcher at the Università degli Studi di Torino in 2022. A specialist in vocal music from the period 1450–1650, he has published critical editions, books, articles and book chapters on such composers as Compère, Palestrina, Victoria, Marenzio and Giovanni Francesco Anerio.

Alexander J. Fisher
took his doctorate in musicology at Harvard University and is Professor of Music at the University of British Colombia. A specialist in music, sound and religious culture in early modern Germany, he is the author of *Music and Religious Identity in Counter-Reformation Augsburg, 1580–1630* (2004), and

Music, Piety and Propaganda: The Soundscapes of Counter-Reformation Bavaria (2014).

Sergi González González

took his doctorate in musicology from the Universitat Autònoma de Barcelona, where he currently holds a postdoctoral position. His research focuses on the study of the soundscape within the framework of urban musicology, and on historical digital cartography through the lens of sound studies, with special attention to historical performative events and the connections established with urban spaces.

Erika Supria Honisch

is Associate Professor of Critical Music Studies at Stony Brook University, having previously served as Assistant Professor on Music History at the University of Missouri-Kansas City. With a doctorate in Music History and Theory from the University of Chicago, she specialises in sacred music in sixteenth- and seventeenth-century Central Europe, with particular interests in early modern music prints, and music and religious pluralism in Austria and the Czech lands under Habsburg rule.

Elisa Lessa

took her doctorate in Historical Musicology at the Universidade Nova in Lisbon. She is a researcher at the Centre for Humanistic Studies and Associate Professor at the Universidad do Minho in Braga. She has published widely on early Portuguese music history and co-edited the volume of essays *Ouvir y escrevir paisagens sonoras. Abordagens teóricas e multidisciplinares* (2020). Her recent research focuses on the musical life of female convents in Portugal.

Ana López Suero

studied Musicology at the Universidad de Valladolid, and took her doctorate there in 2021. Currently she is a Margarita Salas postdoctoral researcher at the Universidad de Valladolid and an associate researcher at KU Leuven. Her research focuses on the transmission of music between Spain and the Netherlands during the Spanish period.

Ascensión Mazuela-Anguita

took her doctorate in musicology at the Universitat de Barcelona in 2012 and is an associate professor of the Music Department, University of Granada. She is author of *Artes de canto en el mundo ibérico renacentista* (2014) and *Women in Convent Spaces and the Music Networks of Early Modern Barcelona* (2023), and has published essays on music in early modern urban ceremonial and traditional Spanish music. She is a member of the Real Academia de Bellas Artes de Granada.

Noel O'Regan

took his doctorate in musicology from the University of Oxford in 1988. He was Reader in music and is currently an honorary research fellow at the University of Edinburgh. He is the author of the book *Institutional Patronage in Post-Tridentine Rome* (1995) and numerous articles on Roman sacred music in the late sixteenth and early seventeenth centuries, and is currently studying the role of music in Roman confraternities in this period.

Dylan Reid

studied history at the University of Oxford, from where he graduated in 1995. Currently, he is a Fellow at the Centre for Renaissance and Reformation Studies at the University of Toronto. He has published about urban culture in early modern Rouen and, more broadly, about literary associations in Europe. He is the editor of *Spacing* magazine, a print quarterly about contemporary urban issues, and is the author of the *Toronto Public Etiquette Guide* (2017).

Antonio Ruiz Caballero

has doctorates in History from the National Autonomous University of Mexico and in Art History and Musicology from the Universitat Autònoma de Barcelona. He currently works as a research professor at the National School of Anthropology and History in Mexico. His main research interests are the history of colonial music in New Spain, devotional music and oral tradition polyphonies.

Juan Ruiz Jiménez

took his doctorate in musicology at the Universidad de Granada in 1995, and is currently a fellow of the Real Academia de Bellas Artes de Granada. His research and publications focus mainly on sacred and instrumental music in late medieval and early modern Spain, as well as in GIS technologies applied to urban music history. He is the founder and director of development of the academic content of the digital platform *Historical Soundscapes*.

Nicholas Terpstra

is Professor of History at the University of Toronto. He works at the intersection of politics, gender, religion and charity, with attention to space, sense and migration, and has published widely in these fields. Recent publications include *Senses of Space in the Early Modern World* (2023), *Mapping Space, Sense, and Movement in Florence: Historical GIS and the Early Modern City* (with Colin Rose, 2016), *Cultures of Charity: Women, Politics, and the Reform of Poor Relief in Renaissance Italy* (2013) and *Faith's Boundaries: Laity & Clergy in Early Modern Confraternities* (2012).

Xavier Torres

is Professor of Early Modern History at the Universitat de Girona. His research has focused on the social and political history of early modern Catalonia. He is currently working on the reception of the Italian musical oratorio in eighteenth-century Barcelona and his publications include *La Guerra dels Segadors* (2006), *Naciones sin nacionalismo. Cataluña en la Monarquía Hispánica (siglos XVI–XVII)* (2008), and *Música en sociedad. El oratorio musical en Italia (siglos XVII–XVIII)* (2023).

Emanuela Vai

is Head of the Bate Collection of Instruments, where she leads on all research, conservation and curatorial aspects. She is also Senior Fellow and Head of Research at Worcester College, Oxford, and founder of the 'Digital Humanities and Sensory Heritage Network' at The Oxford Research Centre in the Humanities (TORCH). Her publications focus on musical instruments, soundscapes, space and the senses in Renaissance social life.

Magnus Williamson

studied music at Magdalene College, Oxford, and took his doctorate in musicology from Royal Holloway, University of London, in 1999. He is currently Professor of Early Music at Newcastle University. He has published widely on the history and performance practice of sixteenth-century English music and has led research projects including *Tudor Partbooks* (AHRC, 2014–2017), *Aural Histories* (AHRC, ongoing), *Bee-ing Human* (Leverhulme Trust, ongoing) and *Henry VIII on tour* (AHRC, ongoing).

CHAPTER 1

Introduction: Sounds of Body and Spirit – Sense, Space, and Motion in Confraternities

Nicholas Terpstra

1   Introduction

Our earliest historical references to confraternities are references to *sound*. There have been many scholarly arguments about whether confraternities were primarily burial societies, or mutual assistance groups, or vehicles for male or female sociability, or administrative boards for hospitals or parishes, or spiritual co-operatives focused on buying indulgences, providing dowries, arranging funerals and offering Requiems. All very practical stuff, and by no means mutually exclusive. But when we turn to the records, what we find is sound.

At their most public, we hear the sound of whips on human flesh, the shuffling of hundreds and thousands of marchers, and their cries of 'Peace and mercy'. We see crowds jamming into huge newly built mendicant churches to hear sermons and to sing popular religious songs. We find public performance of devotional plays that give visual and aural form to the gospel message. At their most private, we hear the sound of softly spoken prayers in an oratory, or consoling words at a sickbed followed by the moaning in a funeral procession. We hear laude sung in Requiem Masses, and find dead members returned to memory and life when their names are spoken at the annual feast.

From the thirteenth to the sixteenth centuries, confraternities were born in popular movements. Those movements – and those confraternities – were defined by the *sounds* they made. They were distinguished by how they brought together sound, sense, and motion, both in public and in private. At their origin in the thirteenth and fourteenth centuries the most basic division was between those confraternities that emphasised penitence in their private and collective life, and those that emphasised praise and thanks to God. Their popular Italian names – *disciplinati* and *laudesi* – referred in the first place to the sounds they made. It is important to recall that these names did not arise from their charitable services, their geographical location, or their administrative organisation. These popular names originated in what their communities *heard* when they listened to these confraternities.

Disciplinati expressed penitence on behalf of their communities. They took the spontaneous flagellation of massive public devotional movements and regularised it. Chroniclers' accounts emphasise the sound of their public processions of penitence. The slashing sounds of whips on bare backs, the cries of 'misericordia', and the sounds of hundreds of men, women and children moving in procession while reciting prayers. By the sixteenth century, their processions may have been smaller, and almost entirely male, but the sounds of confraternal public devotion remained the sonic accent of feast days and galvanised larger crowds during plague or famine. In their closed and private company oratories, sound was again the critical marker of their devotions: they recited the Divine Office together, and listened to each other giving sermons. In fifteenth-century Florence, many discipline confraternities were called Companies of the Night because they performed their penitential exercises after the day's work. They accentuated the sensory deprivation of darkness by snuffing the lights before beginning to whip themselves. They would continue flagellating for the time it took to recite a particular penitential psalm or prayer. We are left with a compelling sensory image: a room in total darkness with only the sound of whips, moans and a prayer being recited by all the men together or perhaps one designated reader. Blocking or erasing sight accentuated sound. In public processions, and even in some private meetings, disciplinati wore the white or black robes and hoods that erased their individual profile. They might be able to identify each other only by the sound of their voice.

At the other end of the devotional spectrum, *laudesi* companies channelled the energy of public devotional movements into large participatory worship events which some structured and shared in handwritten and printed collections called *laudari*.[1] Once a week or once a month, Bolognese laudesi streamed into the mendicant churches of their quarter in order to hear sermons and to sing songs of praise to the Virgin, to Christ, or to the saints. Some of these evolved into hymns marking seasons like Advent. The tune and tempo might change during Lent and Holy Week, or when famine, plague, or drought hit.[2] Florentine laudesi gathered for processional, ferial, or festive services. Processions were often monthly, and some confraternities, like that of San

---

[1] See Marco Piano's guest-edited double issue of *Confraternitas* 30.1–2 (2019) on "Confraternity *Laudari*" for a series of articles and texts from central Italy.

[2] Terpstra N., *Lay Confraternities and Civic Religion in Renaissance Bologna* (Cambridge: 1995) 1–13, 49–68.

Zanobi, processed during the Offertory in the Mass, two by two with lit candles. The ferial and festive services were in the evenings, and those who did not attend regularly were disciplined. Fourteenth-century groups organised Sunday afternoon training and rehearsal sessions (like the later catechetical Schools of Christian Doctrine) so that members would learn the tunes and lyrics. This frequently involved responsive singing with two members at the head giving the strophes while the rest of the members responded with refrains.[3]

For laudesi, singing was not simply what they *did*; it was who they *were*. Singing was the realisation of their brotherhood. It was not an ornament in worship, but rather was considered to be efficacious in salvation. It guarded and protected the bodies of the living and the souls of the deceased, and bore both to paradise. What chroniclers wrote about was not the charitable hospitals these groups later opened or the help they gave to members' families when a mother or father died, but the sounds of men, women and children singing in public, either in mendicant churches or on streets during feast days.

The studies in this collection focus on the rituals and texts of these confraternities, and sometimes draw on the accounts of contemporaries who were struck by what they were hearing and seeing. Konrad Eisenbichler expands on the importance of laude singing as one of the devotional activities of the adolescents and young men gathered in Florence's youth confraternities, noting as well how the training and experience allowed them to expand their repertory from these spiritual songs employed in worship to songs used in public performances like plays and oratorios. Two *disciplinati* groups in Milan, Sant'Agata and Santa Marta, incorporated laude and rhythmic prayers into their celebration of the Divine Office. Daniele Filippi explores a series of Latin and vernacular texts marked for singing found in a set of late-fifteenth-century manuscripts. Some they sang in their oratory, and others while processing through the streets of Milan. Ana López Suero finds that musical performance and patronage was also a key activity of the Confraternity of Our Lady of the Rosary founded in Antwerp by the Duke of Alba when he was working to rebuild Catholic community and worship. The Rosary confraternity's payments for music books, instruments and hired performers point to its sense of how it was to rebuild Catholicism in the face of Protestant challenges by using music in worship and public performance. Choral music was also part of the Catholic sonic armature being assembled in Vienna to combat Ottoman incursions. Erika Honisch explores how youths trained in Piarist schools were being

---

3   Wilson B., "Music and Merchants: The *Laudesi* Companies in Early Renaissance Florence", *Renaissance & Reformation/Renaissance et Réforme* (new series) 13.1 (1989) 151–171, here 158–59.

fashioned as a 'musical militia' to consol Christians held captive, employing the musical theory of Gioseffo Zarlino (1517–1590) and motets in the *stile nuovo*. And in contemporary Mexico friars and clergy were using popular polyphony to build communities of faith. Antonio Ruiz Caballero shows how men and women were acculturated into the Catholic faith through song, learning to sing in two or more parts in their confraternities with the help of professional singers or liturgists. These were sometimes clerics and sometimes indigenous or mixed race 'interpreters' who were trained in liturgical, ritual and catechetical practices and who often built these sonic exercises around specific images or devotions. Sometimes the singing of confraternal choirs expanded to all members of the local communities as a popular spiritual practice.

These examples underscore the fact that confraternities do not fall into neat binaries of penitential and praising groups. Particularly by the sixteenth century, groups combined both emphases in their private, collective and public devotions, and they braided sound, sight and movement together in their actions and their identity. They formed acoustic communities, to take the term coined by the composer and musicologist Barry Truax. He described an acoustic community as 'any soundscape in which acoustic information plays a pervasive role in the lives of the inhabitants'. The significant role of sound lies in the perception that acoustic cues and signals are a key way that communities are able to keep in touch constantly with what is happing internally on a daily basis.[4] Listening to confraternities means finding that place where sense, space and motion meet: *sound* marks time, space and movement. It is the sense that first reaches those outside the groups – processions were heard before they were seen –, and it is the sound that often arrests them and that they comment on. Truax was building the notion of 'acoustic community' in part on R. Murray Schafer's concept of the 'soundscape', an ecology of sound distinguishing foreground and background sounds, sound signals and soundmarks in the creation of a sonic environment.[5] They created confraternal community through the many-layered, varied and interacting sounds that they made, heard and shared.

Confraternity members were lay liturgists in civic religious ceremonies that were public and vital, and they were evaluated on the sounds they made.

---

4 Truax B., *Acoustic Communication* 2nd ed. (Wesport CO – London: 2001) 66–92.
5 Schafer R.M., *The Soundscape. Our Sonic Environment and the Tuning of the World* (New York: 1994). See also two recent essay collections edited by Tess Knighton: *Hearing the City in Early Modern Europe* (co-edited with Ascensión Mazuela-Anguita) (Turnhout: 2018); and *Iberian Confraternities and Urban Soundscapes* Special Issue *Confraternitas* 31.2 (2020); cf. Knighton T., "Introduction: Listening to Confraternities" 3–13, here 8–9.

Some had this as their focus from the very beginning. Emanuela Vai describes as 'sensoryscape' how sense, space and motion came together in the events staged by Bergamo's Confraternity of the Misericordia, known locally as the MIA. Professional musicians gathered together with members of this elite civic group as they moved through the city connecting its sites, shrines, public squares and charitable institutions, often together with the beneficiaries of their charity. From out of the group's ledgers, diaries, inventories and legal records Vai draws the details of how the MIA mobilised sight, smell and sound in exceptional displays of civic religious piety. Leuven's confraternities, guilds and religious houses shared among themselves the responsibilities that Bergamo's MIA concentrated in its own hands, and again used sound above all in a series of processions by which they instantiated and animated the townspeople's devotion to the Virgin Mary. Henry Drummond also finds in contemporary documents such as a chronicle penned by the city's clerk, the details of chants, bells, musical instruments and angel choirs that members used to enact their devotion as they moved around the town bringing sacred images of patron saints with them on foot and on processional floats. The context of early modern globalisation pushed these public expressions of acoustic community beyond the kinds of traditional insiders or stakeholders found in Bergamo and Leuven. Both in Lisbon and the southern Algarve coast of Portugal – where up to a tenth of the population could be of African descent –, black brotherhoods preserved the languages, music and dances of the African communities from which their members had been seized, enslaved and transported. Elisa Lessa finds that Portuguese communities incorporated these acoustic communities into the soundscapes of both religious and secular ceremonies, though always with limitations based on race and status. So, for example, Rosary brotherhoods were favoured by black Africans as being relatively more open, but their statutes still prohibited office-holding by those who were enslaved and by "white moors", indigenous, or mixed race members.[6]

In other cases, the civic dimension expanded only over time, and might both reflect and push an evolution in the confraternity's membership and purpose in relation to both ecclesiastical and secular priorities. Music and sound bound

---

[6] A Nahuatl brotherhood's 1595 regulations excluded Spaniards, blacks and mixed race members; see: Dierksmeier L., *Charity For and By the Poor: Franciscan-Indigenous Confraternities in Mexico, 1527–1700* (Norman OK: 2020) 119. See also: Valerio M., "Black Dancers and Musicians Performing Afro-Christian Identity in Early Modern Spain and Portugal", Salucrù R. – Armenteros I. (eds.), *Slavery Dynamics in Medieval and Modern Mediterranean Markets: Circulations and Mobilities* (Naples: 2018); accessible on-line through PALARA: Publication of the African-American Research Association 24 (2020) 47–56: https://doi.org/10.32855/palara.2020.008.

together students, singers and confraternal members of Barcelona's Academy and Confraternity of St. Thomas Aquinas when they lifted the saint's image from its place in the city's Dominican friary and took it through the streets and squares of the city. Ascensión Mazuela-Anguita draws on both published contemporary accounts and detailed manuscript records as she recreates the spiritual soundscape that resulted when these participants opened their acoustic community to the broader city. In contemporary Valencia, a brotherhood of St. George that had originated in the military and political struggles of the mid-fourteenth century and had grown over the following century to become one of the city's largest (with 500 male and 600 female members) demonstrated how Iberia's confraternal civic religion was evolving from the late medieval into the Renaissance and early modern periods. Ferran Escrivà-Llorca shows how, from an early focus on mutual assistance in sickness and death, it steadily expanded its contributions to the public cult, above all in elaborate processions and performances around the feasts of St. George (23 April) and St. Denis (9 October). The feast of St. Denis also marked the *Reconquista* of Valencia in 1237, and became a multi-sensory celebration of militant Catholicism; as such it put the St. George brotherhood front and centre in the public celebrations of other military victories from the late fifteenth to the early seventeenth centuries. Noel O'Regan finds that Catholic reform movements helped push Rome's confraternities towards more public performances of a more overtly religious and devotional nature. Many of these confraternities had emerged out of or functioned in part as artisanal brotherhoods focused on mutual assistance and civic celebration, but from the mid-sixteenth century they turned their attention to competitive devotional consumption that took the form of expanding relic cults, ever more impressive churches, and public musical performances. Sergi González González traces the sonic dimension of a similar evolution in artisanal confraternities in the Catalonian coastal town of Tarragona, tracing their processional circuits, measuring how they marked and filled these routes with sound, and aligning these sensory and kinetic dimensions with the temporal rhythms of both workplace and church. Tess Knighton uses similar mapping technology to focus in on the processions organised by the Confraternity of Nostra Senyora dels Desamparats (Our Lady of the Unprotected), based at the parish church of Santa Maria del Pi in Barcelona, to collect the bones of the condemned from outside the city walls and give them Christian burial in a specially designated part of the church cemetery. Her study demonstrates how digital means allow a richer understanding of the process by which sense, space and motion came together, through the recreation and positioning of the distinctive sounds of the procession as it moved through the city.

INTRODUCTION: SOUNDS OF BODY AND SPIRIT　　　　　　　　　　　　　　7

These examples show how often confraternal acoustic community was central to the urban soundscape. But what about fraternities' communal life within their oratories and meeting halls? Sound set the pace for devotions, sometimes as a stopwatch, but more often as a metronome. The prayer of the brothers whipping themselves not only determined the length of time in minutes that they must flagellate, but set the pace for it and enacted the conviction that prayer is a groaning to God. Singing laude was another vocalisation of prayer, also efficacious for the souls of those singing, those listening, and those deceased. As Eisenbichler's discussion of youth confraternities shows, the sounds of these groups in particular could be devout or disruptive, music or noise. In the case of an elite group like Florence's San Raphael, it ranged from the sounds of public and private oratorios and plays to the shouts of boys playing on its ballcourts. These youths likely would not have remained in their community if sports were not as much a part of their emotional and sensory life together as laude and plays.

To speak then of a confraternity as an acoustic community is to recognise that laude and prayer were how confraternity members *enacted* both charity and community. Most of the spiritual works of charity were profoundly *sonic*: giving correction to sinners, instructing the ignorant, counselling the doubtful, comforting the sorrowful, praying for the living and the dead. Only two might be silent: bearing wrongs patiently, and forgiving all injuries. Even the works of corporal charity were marked by sound. It was fundamental to the help for the sick and dying. When brothers came to the house of a member who was sick or dying, they were to encourage him through the songs, prayers, psalms and stories that made up the *ars moriendi*. In his or her funeral procession, they were to be mourners who accompanied the body to the grave, again with song. At the annual confraternal feast, a good part of the time was taken up with a public reading of the names of those who had died. Even if confraternities were to be seen primarily as burial societies, focus could not only be on the physical charity of providing a grave or feeding a widow. Charity to the dying was built on orality as much as on physical actions. Some charitable institutions run by confraternities became such masters at this that they offered their services for a fee. This is particularly clear in cases of orphanages, whose young male wards were often the paid mourners in civic funeral processions, processing behind the body in robes while bearing candles or torches and singing. What began as a service for deceased members of the confraternities that operated these homes came to be offered to the public as a paid service that raised significant revenue to keep the homes running. The boys' ethereal and regulated funereal laments came in counterpoint to the emotional wails of the deceased's relatives. Orphanages in Bologna hired music masters to train the boys for this work, and then had the boys join their own worship and sing the Office and at Mass.[7] Barcelona's Confraternity of St. Thomas Aquinas also gave choral training to the boys in its academy and then had them sing in the confraternity's services and feasts.

The enactment through rituals around death underscores why confraternities can be approached from the perspective of acoustic community. As Tess Knighton has suggested, using Truax's idea of acoustic communities means

> looking at the ways in which sound signals, sonic markers, sound symbolism, acoustic profiles, boundaries and horizons might be discerned in [...] specific urban context[s], and how they are linked spatially to the topography and environment of the city as well as temporally to the cycles, rhythms and activities of everyday urban life.[8]

So here sense, space and motion come together in the private communal devotions and the public civic religious exercises of lay confraternities from the late medieval into the early modern period. And the soundscape reached beyond sung and played devotions. The black African confraternities in Portugal and Brazil described by Lessa danced both in private meetings and at public festivals. Rouen's Immaculate Conception of the Virgin organised an annual large poetry contest called a *puy* where all the poems submitted were read aloud by their authors to the judges and audience over the course of a highly scripted five-hour celebration in a local monastic hall. Audiences heard a wide range of accents and oratorical ability, starting with the sermon – specified as having to be brief – that launched the event. Dylan Reid expands on the contest, setting it in the context of many similar public recitations organised by confraternities in northern France and the Lowlands, underscoring that the acoustic dimension of these festivals was not only about aural and musical performance, but about reception on the part of the listening crowd. The experience of citizens hearing the same thing at the same time in the same space was critical to the puy as a convergence of Rouen's civic and acoustic community.

With the aim to capturing the full meaning of acoustic community, it has to be recognised that the concept of community is not limited to individual confraternities, but develops holistically across cities and towns. Some authors are using digital technology to capture both its acoustic range and its urban scale.

---

7 Terpstra N., *Abandoned Children of the Italian Renaissance: Orphan Care in Florence and Bologna* (Baltimore: 2005) 163, 169–73.
8 https://www.ub.edu/artsoundscapes/acoustic-communities-in-early-modern-barcelona/.

Juan Ruiz Jimenez applies digital cartography to mapping the soundscape of Granada as it undergoes post-conquest Christianisation. Pogroms and expulsions had disrupted the former geographical separation of Jews, Christians and Muslims, and it would be up to sound to create a new civic coherence. Sergi González González takes some of the same markers – processions, festivities – and with digital means recreates the broadest urban sound ecosystem of Tarragona, incorporating preaching, prayers, whips, bells and theatre.

2 Early Modern Evolutions

Many of the defining characteristics of confraternal acoustic community had deep medieval roots and continued to flourish into the early modern period. Was there anything that changed? I'd like to suggest four things: First, whether and how paid and professional performers changed acoustic community. Second, how sound may have functioned as a weapon in contemporary religious conflicts. Third, whether the idea of acoustic community gains resonance when we look at confraternities outside of Europe. Fourth, how acoustic community might have sounded outside of Catholicism.

2.1 *Paid Professional Performance*

Paid mourners at funerals were not the first or only trained professionals to take over what had been a participatory action, but they remained relatively rare outside the ranks of the most elite medieval and Renaissance groups. This changed through the course of the sixteenth century, when listening to confraternities increasingly meant listening not to what members sang, chanted, or spoke, but to performances that they paid others for. Paid singers certainly sang for fourteenth- and fifteenth-century groups in Florence, but they were largely gifted artisans, often quite poor, who were paid out of charity. By the later fifteenth century, the Sunday afternoon laudesi rehearsals had declined, and members' singing at Requiem Masses seems to have followed. In the sixteenth century, some brotherhoods began ceding this activity to mendicant orders, particularly those who no longer had either the members or money to maintain their obligations.[9] Jonathan Glixon has detailed the shift to professionals on a different level in early modern century Venice. There the six main *scuole grandi* competed for the honour of having the most impressive and progressive concerts and worship services. Few members were sufficiently skilled,

---

9 Wilson, "Music and Merchants" 166–167.

so confraternities paid professional singers. As costs mounted, the *scuole* deliberately recruited wealthy members to be their confraternal head, with the implicit or explicit requirement that these elite individuals would personally fund the confraternity's musical programme for the course of their term in office. Merging the devotional economy of competitive achievement with the social economies of political achievement produced impressive music but reduced confraternal members to audiences much like the crowds who listened to their processions.[10]

Venice was perhaps exceptional, given the importance of music to its cultural life, but it was by no means unique. The competition of conspicuous consumption among peers that drove the elite in the republic of Venice operated with similar results in absolutist polities. The Valencian Confraternity of Saint George employed professional singers and musicians to create the appropriate sonic impression in public festivities honouring royal and imperial crusading engagements. These were celebrations of both a dynasty and a faith, and the assertion that the two were fundamentally one could not be left to either amateurs or to upper class members who shied away from public musical performance. Members of the elite Rosary confraternity established by the Duke of Alba in contemporary Antwerp felt much the same way, and invested considerable sums in hiring professional musicians for their services and performances. The brotherhood became an important vehicle bringing together Flemish and Spanish musicians. Shifting musical modes and expectations meant that it was not only elite confraternities that hired professional singers and musicians; artisanal groups emulated them as they too tried to have an impact on the urban soundscape. The Roman confraternity of bakers (*Compagnia dei Fornari*) supported a small choir in its church dedicated to the Madonna of Loretto, and some of the popular confraternities which in Mexico gathered mixed populations and many new Christians also hired professional singers either to carry out the musical accompaniment to the divine Office and Mass, or to teach and lead members themselves in their choral expression.

The professionals these confraternities hired could be among the leading musicians of the age. Magnus Williamson notes that the confraternity responsible for music in the Lady Chapel of St. Botolph's church in the Lincolnshire port town of Boston sponsored one of the largest choirs in England, and was able to draw John Taverner from Oxford in the 1530s. This would change suddenly when confraternities were disbanded as part of ecclesiastical reforms in the 1540s, and when the English church began to push congregational singing

---

10 Glixon J., *Honoring God and the City: Music at the Venetian Confraternities* (Oxford: 2003) 89–161.

instead. Yet catholic laity did not cease to sing, particularly in confraternities, as Alexander Fisher shows. Responding perhaps to the vigorous embrace of hymns and psalms by their Lutheran counterparts, German Jesuits hired leading musicians like Georg Victorinus, Bernhard Klingenstein, Gregor Aichinger and Rudolph de Lasso to compose music for confraternal worship and even to direct choirs made up of confraternity members. Some of these musicians were confraternity members themselves.

Apart from music, the theatrical tradition of *sacre rappresentazione* or mystery plays where confraternity members performed for each other was common across Europe in the fourteenth and fifteenth centuries. It declined through the later fifteenth century, and in the sixteenth came to be overshadowed by other forms of vocal performance involving theatre.[11] The poetry recitals of Netherlandic Chambers of Rhetoric and Rouen's Confraternity of the Immaculate Conception were one example of this. Another was the emergence of the oratory as a new means of bringing together music, theatre and biblical narratives in a form meant both to teach and to entertain, just as the mystery plays had. Philip Neri was still a layman when in 1548 he founded the Confraternity of the Holy Trinity to oversee charity and care for pilgrims and hospital patients in Rome. In the communal context of that confraternity he began bringing together the voiced devotions – traditional hymns and laude, prayers, bible readings, and holy narratives – that gradually developed into the oratory as a musical form and then by extension as a form of communal life and activity that took music as a form of service; it was perhaps the ultimate form of acoustic community. Neri took holy orders in 1551, and his community developed into one of the many hybrids of confraternal and clerical devotional activity that multiplied through the later sixteenth century as reformers aimed to incorporate elements of Tridentine discipline without sacrificing the flexibility of lay confraternities. Neri's new communities of the Oratory gathered as a congregation rather than an order, with members bound by promises rather than vows. The oratorio as a musical form with operatic elements developed separately from the Oratory as an ecclesiastical form yet, as Xavier Torres shows, some local congregations developed the musical form more assiduously in imitation of Neri. Florence's Oratorians performed twenty to forty oratorios

---

11   Barr C., "From *Devozione* to *Rappresentazione*: Dramatic Elements in the Holy Week *Laude* of Assisi", in Eisenbichler K. (ed.), *Crossing the Boundaries: Christian Piety and the Arts in Italian Medieval and Renaissance Confraternities* (Kalamazoo: 1991) 11–32; Stewart P.A.V., "Staging the Passion in the Ritual City: Stational Crosses and Confraternal Spectacle in Late Renaissance Milan", in Presciutti D.B. (ed.), *Space, Place, and Motion: Locating Confraternities in the Late Medieval and Early Modern City* (Leiden: 2017) 217–243.

annually, while about half of all productions in the city were undertaken by confraternities. In cities like Bologna and Venice, confraternities undertook a quarter or a third of all productions, almost always featuring professional choirs singing for select and elite audiences, who might follow with a printed text that could be shared and saved.

It would be roughly a century before Protestant composers began writing oratorios as well. This might seem strange, given the fact that oratorio texts both Catholic and Protestant were frequently drawn directly from the Bible, and that Neri in particular saw them as having a didactic function. Music made the biblical stories more memorable and underscored the lessons emotionally. Yet there was deep unease on the part of Protestants about turning the Word of God into a form of entertainment performed by professionals for a fee. Asking whether recitation of that Word could be severed from worship and turned into a performance was a serious question about the appropriate acoustic community for the Bible to be read and heard. Yet the reason why there were so few Protestant oratorios before the mid-eighteenth century could be as much sociological as theological: Protestantism lacked the wealthy and elite lay religious corporations such as confraternities and Neri's quasi-confraternal Oratories that commissioned and staged oratorios. The Haarlem composer Cornelis Thymanszoon Padbrué seems to have been the first North European Protestant to write an oratorio with his 1647 composition *The Tears of Peter and Paul*, but without institutional support he did not repeat or extend the exercise. It would be another half century before the form took off in Protestant cultures with Johann Sebastian Bach (1685–1750) composing within ecclesiastical settings in Germany and Georg Frideric Handel (1685–1759) writing for charitable institutions, like the foundling homes of London and Dublin.

A second sonic performative exercise that expanded out from confraternities in this period was the Forty Hours' Devotion. It was being practised in Milan in the 1530s, but expanded quickly in Rome after Neri introduced it for the Confraternity of the Holy Trinity. It was less clearly an example of theatre, at least at the start. Yet it was sonic, kinetic and material, and as it expanded, the auditory and theatrical elements grew. Devotees had quietly though not silently prayed the *Ave Maria* and *Pater Noster* of the Rosary continually around a series of churches between the Mass of Exposition that launched it and the Mass of Deposition that concluded it. As the devotional practice grew, sonic regulations shaped it around an alternation of sound and silence, presence and absence. Clement VIII's 1593 orders for the Forty Hours Devotion emphasised silence: other Masses should be suspended, bells should be silenced, and women should not participate through the night. Carlo Borromeo and Ignatius

Loyola emphasised sound, putting the prayers of the Rosary in acoustic and spiritual competition with Carnival and also at other times in the liturgical year. The Forty Hours' Devotion soon gained more elaborate physical and material settings, with ever more complex musical and staged settings through the period of the Baroque. Confraternities and churches competed in the game of what Angelo Torre described as 'devotional consumption'.[12]

3 Sound as a Weapon and Boundary Marker

As religious disputes multiplied between confessional groups in the period of the Reformation, the sounds of confraternal processions were used more aggressively to mark territory and incite violent reactions from religious enemies. In late sixteenth- and seventeenth-century France, priests employed Holy Sacrament confraternities to expose Huguenots, deliberately sending these brotherhoods into Protestant areas to see who would not bow and remove their hat when the host passed by. In Livorno, processions of young Catholic males would move through the Jewish quarter in order to incite aggressive responses from young Jewish males. This was particularly a problem in the eighteenth century, when North African immigration brought in large numbers of Jews who were unaccustomed to living with Catholic microaggressions, and who responded more vigorously to these challenges.

Alexander Fisher shows how some of the new confraternities emerging across Germany in the mid-sixteenth century quite deliberately focused their devotion around those parts of Catholicism that conservative Lutherans found most objectionable: the transubstantiated Eucharist, the Immaculate Virgin Mary, the Rosary, the souls in Purgatory, and the hosts of local and universal intercessory saints who were either drawn from church tradition or were honoured members and martyrs of new missionary orders like the Jesuits. Many matched the Protestants in their enthusiasm for vernacular singing. They used it to confirm, reinforce and spread the faith, generating a phenomenal variety of music that was widely published and distributed. Juan Ruiz Jiménez extends this process of spiritual confrontation and conversion to Granada, where the mission work was essentially an extended and multisensory form of Christian acculturation launched after the conquest in 1492. Using the digital platform *Historical Soundscapes* and working across the twenty-three parishes

---

12   Torre A., *Il consume di devozioni. Religione e communità nelle campagne dell'ancien regime* (Venice: 1995).

of the city, he classifies confraternities into distinct types based on how they used sensorial forms and cultural activities to occupy and convert the city's spaces and people from Islam to Christianity. Erika Honisch notes a variant on this boundary setting when a noble convert from Lutheranism established a Catholic confraternity open to Christians of all confessions that also focused its energies on challenging Islam, using musical processions to attract donations to its cause of redeeming Christians captured by the Ottomans.

There was nothing new about using sound and motion to mark space, community and conflict in the Reformation period. These cases show sound being used as a weapon to draw the line between those inside and outside the faith: essentially the acoustic community as boundary marker and missionary tool. Whether it was Valencia's Brotherhood of St. George publicly commemorating religious victories over both Moors and Protestants, or Viennese Redemption confraternities using new musical forms and theories to comfort Christians held captive by the Ottomans, sound helped to make public who was inside and who was outside the community.

4   Confraternal Acoustic Community outside Europe

Outside Europe, the roles, activities and success of confraternities differed significantly in different settings, often depending on whether and how they mobilised sound, sense and motion. This in turn depended both on different priorities of mission orders and the different social requirements of host societies. When the different confraternities active in the Americas and Africa in particular are compared, it is clear that different forms of acoustic community emerged in part out of distinctions between missionary orders, and in part out of distinct cultural traditions.

A wide range of black African and indigenous confraternities set the parameters of Catholic worship for Iberian colonies in the Americas and Asia. Laura Dirksmeier has found for Mexico that Franciscans were far more active and effective in establishing and mobilising confraternities among indigenous Catholics than Dominicans were, in large part because they emphasised preserving African and indigenous American acoustic communities in these majority populations.[13] Franciscans saw confraternities as vehicles for preserving and building on the Nahuatl language as an indigenous *lingua franca* across Mexico. They gave confraternity members more agency in controlling

---

13   Dierksmeier, *Charity* 37–68.

and running the groups, and doing so in Nahuatl and with local cultural traditions. Brotherhoods sponsored by Franciscans were spaces where the Bible was read and sermons were preached in Nahuatl, and where indigenous Catholic believers could sing songs, watch spiritual plays, and learn Catholic Doctrine in the language. Indigenous singers and musicians were the principal performers in the Mass, and the confraternities were places where they trained and practised. Franciscan missionaries understood how language, song and literature were emotional carriers of meaning and identity, and built on this, so that Franciscan confraternities were sensory brotherhoods. Dominicans, by contrast, kept closer control over the confraternities they established and used them as vehicles for teaching and enforcing orthodoxy. Instead of a single *lingua franca*, they developed brotherhoods and texts around various local indigenous languages. They also emphasised training in worship and catechism more than song. This meant that each language had a narrower range of acoustic resources and fewer of them: fewer songs, fewer texts, fewer plays. And fewer members. Dominican confraternities were fewer in number and tended to be smaller in size, with the singular exception of the confraternities of the Rosary. Dominican confraternities in Mexico also tended to be more orthodox.[14]

Similarly, Nahuatl devotional theatre could be where tensions between traditional and Catholic views were worked out, with results not always purely orthodox. In these cases, the acoustic community formed a middle ground or bridge between indigenous and European culture, like the auditory dimension of what Cécile Fromont has described as a 'space of correlation' where distinct cultural and religious groups fashioned a common form not readily captured by the older language of syncretism or hybridity.[15]

In Brazil, confraternities were also where traditional African sounds, senses and movements were preserved in the brotherhoods that black enslaved peoples organised among themselves. John Thornton, Nicole von Germeten and Miguel Valerio have described how, across the Americas, confraternities were organised according to self-described nations and kingdoms. These functioned as acoustic communities that preserved the languages, stories, ritual and musical cultures, as well as the social norms of different African communities.[16] In

---

14 Dierksmeir, *Charity* 98–124.
15 Fromont C., *The Art of Conversion: Christian Visual Culture in the Kingdom of Kongo* (Chapel Hill NC: 2014); and Fromont C., "Penned by Encounter: Visibility and Invisibility of the Cross-Cultural in Images from Early Modern Franciscan Missions in Central Africa and Central Mexico", *Renaissance Quarterly* 75.4 (2022) 1244–1254.
16 Thornton J., *Africa and Africans in the Making of the Atlantic World, 1400–1800* (2nd edn.) (Cambridge: 1998) 323–324; Germeten N. von, *Black Blood Brothers: Confraternities*

some cases, they employed Kongolese and Kabundan catechisms and liturgical materials in their worship, so that African Catholics could worship using the resources of the oldest African Catholic church. Brazilian and some Mexican brotherhoods elected kings and queens and preserved African social forms. The Brotherhoods of Our Lady of the Rosary were among the most common confraternities among displaced African populations, in part because they had greater agency. In Brazil, they were the first to organise these elections among Kongolese populations, both enslaved and free.[17] Kinship was not the dominant organising principle in these groups, and the elections better reflected African social and corporate organisational modes, including those that organised armies and social and religious life, as found in examples in Kongo, Sierra-Leone and Guinea Bissau. Some focused around burial, some around peacemaking, and others aimed to preserve the solidarity and forms of particular nations, like the Akan-speaking Koromanti in Barbados.[18]

Music was a powerful form of cultural transmission in these groups and their organisation of social life and festivities that preserved African musical modes and instruments among both enslaved and free black populations. Elisa Lessa's discussion of various groups underscores a fundamental tension: while the confraternities were established and supported as vehicles of Christian assimilation, their distinct acoustic community preserved group identity as expressed in music and dance, and they were integrated into secular and religious processions and festivities both in Portugal and Brazil. Across the Atlantic, a mid-eighteenth century Brazilian lay brotherhood petitioned the crown for permission to continue its long practice of singing songs in 'the Angolan Idiom'.[19] Here again, Kongo and Kongolese Catholics led the way. From the time when its rulers first embraced Christianity in 1491, an Afro-European Christian musical tradition developed. Some European forms came through missionaries, but much came also through sailors and traders, both from Portugal and other European countries. The music transmitted was vocal as well as instrumental, and tunes and lyrics were often secular, resulting in the kinds of adaptation also seen in Germany and England, where secular tunes were turned to lay religious hymns. Catholic and Protestant missionaries of the seventeenth and eighteenth centuries noted the energy and engagement of the singing,

---

and *Social Mobility for Afro-Mexicans* (Gainesville FL: 2006); and Valerio M., "Black Confraternity Members Performing Afro-Christian Identity in a Renaissance Festival in Mexico City in 1539", *Confraternitas* 29.1 (2018) 31–54, here 33–34.
17 Thornton, *Africa and Africans* 202–204; Dierksmeir, *Charity* 120–121.
18 Thornton, *Africa and Africans* 219–20; Valerio, "Black Confraternity Members" 34; 39–46.
19 Thornton, *Africa and Africans* 217.

INTRODUCTION: SOUNDS OF BODY AND SPIRIT 17

and the use of African instruments and complex rhythms and syncopation in both religious and secular settings, often in the context of dance.[20] There were some string and wind instruments, and more use of bells, drums, and percussion generally, both in worship and at festive and funeral times. This carried over among the African enslaved in the Americas. Masters and authorities in English slave plantations found this threatening and attempted to ban it, while in Brazil it could be used more openly. It is not clear what role confraternities played in developing and preserving this music. Some eighteenth-century transcriptions from Jamaica survive, though this was in an English Protestant context where there were no confraternities to develop the forms, and where African music and instruments were sometimes seen as threatening.[21] It might be asked, then, whether in the context of colonial slave societies, the extent and vibrancy of acoustic community among the enslaved was different if the colonisers were Catholic or Protestant?

There is another area where this may have made a difference. The greater emphasis placed on both special revelation and on ancestors in African Christianity reduced the role of priests (for example, in Kongolese Catholicism) and made lay communal groups like brotherhoods more important to the practice of Christianity. Revelation might come through dreams and signs and was shared aurally within confraternal communities. In contexts of colonial dominance, as in the Americas and the Philippines, missionary priests and orders often fought this. In contexts of political subordination, as in China and Japan, they had to accommodate it. The situation in large parts of early modern Africa was more like that in China and Japan, at least until the eighteenth century, and so the highly developed musical and cultural forms of African Christianity both in and outside confraternities were better articulated, more robust, and more often challenged when brought over to the Americas. Taking the approach of acoustic community highlights dynamics around the role of confraternities in African Catholic acoustic communities; their role in the development and transmission of African Christianity in the Atlantic world remains to be explored more closely.

5 Confraternal Acoustic Community outside Catholicism

In order to explore this point about confessional difference further, a look at how confraternal acoustic community *may* have functioned outside

---

20 Thornton, *Africa and Africans* 228; Valerio, "Black Dancers and Musicians".
21 Thornton, *Africa and Africans* 226.

Catholicism proves useful. Jewish confraternities and Protestant lay worship offer two ways of testing this.

Jewish confraternities (*hevrot*) expanded from the sixteenth century, and focused more often on mutual aid, dowries and burials in communities that were often very poor. In a context where expulsion and diaspora shaped communal life, they served immediate social and communal needs. Jewish funeral processions were the only ones that might move through parts of many Christian communities. In larger centres such as Venice, Prague, Frankfurt and Amsterdam, this extended to socialisation of young males in particular, and while this largely involved study of Torah and Kabbalah, it could include some festivity and dancing.

Did ghetto restrictions on space and mobility restrict or accentuate the operation of confraternities as acoustic communities? Ghettoisation was certainly a factor that opened avenues for newer pious exercises, as clearly emerged around Venice in the 1570s. The *Shomrim la-Boker* (watchers of the dawn) and *Me'ire' Chachar* (those who awake the dawn) both performed pre-dawn prayers and penitential rituals adapted from Safed; the penitence here responded to exile and anticipated salvation and did not involve flagellation. From the mid-sixteenth century, Modena's *Hatzot Laila* had collective 'recitation of a midnight rite mourning the destruction of the temple and praying for its return'.[22] Groups for young men known as *Tikkun Hazot* performed midnight vigils, and the series of nocturnal rituals expanded with the availability of coffee: Jewish coffee house culture was to some extent confraternal culture, and sociability almost certainly increased as a result.[23] In 1681, the Shomrim la-Boker congregation, which was active in both Venice and Modena, commissioned a Christian composer Carlo Grossi to set a Hebrew text to music. In the 'Cantata ebraica in dialogo', a male soloist and a group of men engage in sung dialogue. The soloist asks why they are so joyful, and they respond that it is because they are a company gathered together to celebrate the anniversary of their brotherhood and to celebrate the joy of their messianic hope. They had gathered before dawn to 'unload bitter thoughts before God, and in this way bring redemption and the coming of the Messiah'.[24]

Midnight gatherings for prayers were not open to women. This gendering of Jewish confraternal piety limited opportunities for female participation

---

[22] Francesconi F., *Invisible Enlighteners: The Jewish Merchants of Modena from the Renaissance to Emancipation* (Philadelphia: 2021) 185.

[23] Horowitz E., "Coffee, Coffeehouses, and the Nocturnal rituals of Early Modern Jewry", *AJS Review* 14 (1989) 17–46.

[24] Francesconi, *Invisible Enlighteners* 125–126.

outside of charity, and so it seems that acoustic community in Jewish confraternities would have been less well developed too. The exception here was the late seventeenth-century Sabbatean movement, which recognised women's prophetic gift and allowed them to participate in oral rituals. They gravitated to it in turn, but when the Sabbatean movement collapsed after Sabbetai Tzevi's apostasy and death in 1676, they suffered further surveillance and restriction.

In the Protestant context, it is perhaps odd that just as the lay singing of vernacular hymns seemed to decline in some parts of Catholic Europe, it exploded among Protestants. Many of the innovations that supposedly distinguished Protestant from Catholic worship – vernacular sermons, public reading of scripture and vernacular congregational singing – had been commonplaces of lay confraternal acoustic community for centuries across Catholic Europe. In Germany, England and the Netherlands, Protestant church orders took long-standing confraternal practices and adopted them as the participatory foundation of new state church worship orders, above all in singing vernacular hymns and psalms. Protestants built their identity as devotional communities around this aspect of acoustic community, with distinct standards as to texts (psalms or adaptations), popular tunes, and plainsong or harmony, with printed psalters and hymnals to ensure that they would sing in unison.[25] The extraordinarily rich and well documented musical life of confraternities enjoyed by laity in the port town of Boston may have disappeared once Henry VIII's changes to church order put an end to the confraternities and parish guilds. Yet this musical devotion may also have been transferred, moving from the restricted acoustic community of the confraternity to the enlarged community of the parish under the patronage of the vestry, the new body which in many English parishes took over devotional duties previously handled by parish guilds.

The question remains: did Protestant appropriation of vernacular song as a defining feature of their worship make it anathema to Catholics? Or were there post-Tridentine ecclesiastical strictures at work among Catholics to restrict vernacular singing? New regulations had certainly curbed lay preaching and public reading of vernacular Bibles, two of the central staples of fifteenth-century confraternal worship and acoustic community.[26] It is certainly curious that as

---

25 Terpstra N., "De-institutionalizing Confraternity Studies: Fraternalism and Social Capital in Cross-Cultural Contexts", in Black C. – Gravestock P. (eds.), *Early Modern Confraternities in Europe and the Americas: International and Interdisciplinary Perspectives* (Aldershot: 2006) 274–283, here 273–276.
26 Corbellini S., "The Plea for Lay Bibles in Fourteenth and Fifteenth Century Tuscany: The Role of Confraternities", in Terpstra N. – Prosperi A. – Pastore S. (eds.) *Faith's Boundaries: Laity and Clergy in Early Modern Confraternities* (Turnhout: 2012) 98–106.

at least some Catholic confraternities seemed to move away from older modes of lay vernacular practices of acoustic community, these same modes were made central to Protestant parish worship, where confraternities themselves had been eliminated.

Confraternities gave many their most immediate experience of Christian worship in the later medieval and early modern periods. How they evolved through this period is still being assessed, and this often means skirting the clerical preoccupation that continues to shape much of the religious history of the period. Questioning the impact on confraternal acoustic community of paid and professional performance, the use of sound as a weapon in religious conflicts within Europe and as a form of community building outside of it, as well as the operation of confraternal acoustic community outside of Catholicism, allows some means of moderating that preoccupation. Focusing on sense, space and motion affords a better way to understand how confraternities as acoustic communities shaped medieval and early modern soundscapes. It builds on what is known of confraternal musical patronage and performance, and makes it possible to track how the brothers and sisters took that music – and much else – out into the public spaces of their cities and towns. With recitations, festive plays and oratories they used print to amplify voices and project them further. With processions, laude and funeral laments, they braided the kinetic, vocal and emotive elements of civic life into a bond connecting the temporal and spiritual. As confraternities became part of global cultural exchanges, this bond became one of the paradoxes of missionary outreach and the correlations generated in exchange. They could be intended by some as vehicles for acculturation, but in practice they helped reinforce some displaced communities and preserve their songs, stories and languages. There is no single story here, but many intersecting narratives and soundscapes.

Bibliography

Barr C., "From *Devozione* to *Rappresentazione*: Dramatic Elements in the Holy Week *Laude* of Assisi", in Eisenbichler K. (ed.), *Crossing the Boundaries: Christian Piety and the Arts in Italian Medieval and Renaissance Confraternities* (Kalamazoo: 1991) 11–32.

Corbellini S., "The Plea for Lay Bibles in Fourteenth and Fifteenth Century Tuscany: The Role of Confraternities", in Terpstra N. – Prosperi A. – Pastore S. (eds.), *Faith's Boundaries: Laity and Clergy in Early Modern Confraternities* (Turnhout: 2012) 87–112.

Dierksmeier L., *Charity For and By the Poor: Franciscan-Indigenous Confraternties in Mexico, 1527–1700* (Norman OK: 2020).

Francesconi F., *Invisible Enlighteners: The Jewish Merchants of Modena from the Renaissance to Emancipation* (Philadelphia: 2021).

Fromont C., *The Art of Conversion: Christian Visual Culture in the Kingdom of Kongo* (Chapel Hill NC: 2014).

Fromont C., "Penned by Encounter: Visibility and Invisibility of the Cross-Cultural in Images from Early Modern Franciscan Missions in Central Africa and Central Mexico", *Renaissance Quarterly* 75.4 (2022) 1221–1265.

Germeten N. von, *Black Blood Brothers: Confraternities and Social Mobility for Afro-Mexicans* (Gainesville FL: 2006).

Glixon J., *Honoring God and the City: Music at the Venetian Confraternities* (Oxford: 2003).

Horowitz E., "Coffee, Coffeehouses, and the Nocturnal rituals of Early Modern Jewry", *AJS Review* 14 (1989) 17–46.

Knighton T., "Introduction: Listening to Confraternities", in Knighton T. (ed.), *Iberian Confraternities and Urban Soundscapes*, Special Issue *Confraternitas* 31.2 (2020) 3–13.

Knighton T. – Mazuela-Anguita A. (eds.), *Hearing the City in Early Modern Europe* (Turnhout: 2018).

Piano M. (ed.), "Confaternity *Laudari*", Special issue of *Confraternitas* 30.1–2 (2019).

Schafer R. Murray, *The Soundscape. Our Sonic Environment and the Tuning of the World* (New York: 1994).

Stewart P.A.V., "Staging the Passion in the Ritual City: Stational Crosses and Confraternal Spectacle in Late Renaissance Milan", in Presciutti D.B. (ed.), *Space, Place, and Motion: Locating Confraternities in the Late Medieval and Early Modern City* (Leiden: 2017) 217–243.

Terpstra N., *Abandoned Children of the Italian Renaissance: Orphan Care in Florence and Bologna* (Baltimore: 2005).

Terpstra N., "De-institutionalizing Confraternity Studies: Fraternalism and Social Capital in Cross-Cultural Contexts", in Black C. – Gravestock P. (eds.), *Early Modern Confraternities in Europe and the Americas: International and Interdisciplinary Perspectives* (Aldershot: 2006) 273–276.

Terpstra N., *Lay Confraternities and Civic Religion in Renaissance Bologna* (Cambridge: 1995).

Thornton J., *Africa and Africans in the Making of the Atlantic World, 1400–1800* (2nd edn.) (Cambridge: 1998).

Torre A., *Il consume di devozioni. Religione e communità nelle campagne dell'ancien regime* (Venice: 1995).

Truax B., *Acoustic Communication* (2nd edn.) (Wesport CO – London: 2001).

Valerio M., "Black Confraternity Members Performing Afro-Christian Identity in a Renaissance Festival in Mexico City in 1539", *Confraternitas* 29.1 (2018) 31–54.

Valerio M., "Black Dancers and Musicians Performing Afro-Christian Identity in Early Modern Spain and Portugal", in Salucrù R. – Armenteros I. (eds.), *Slavery Dynamics in Medieval and Modern Mediterranean Markets: Circulations and Mobilities* (Naples: 2018).

Wilson B., "Music and Merchants: The Laudesi Companies in Early Renaissance Florence", *Renaissance & Reformation/Renaissance et Réforme* (new series) 13.1 (1989) 151–171.

PART 1

The Participation of Confraternities in Urban Ceremonial

∴

CHAPTER 2

The 'Sensoryscape' of the Good Friday Procession in Early Modern Venetian Bergamo

Emanuela Vai

Abstract

This chapter explores the multiple sensory registers through which urban events were encountered and experienced in early modern Bergamo, located on the westernmost boundaries of the Venetian *Terraferma*. It focuses specifically on the sensory politics of the Good Friday processions that were organised by the Confraternity of the Misericordia Maggiore, and considers how these events were encountered by embodied spectators. This confraternity was highly prestigious in the sixteenth and seventeenth centuries and the liturgical and secular processions they staged around the Venetian-ruled town were spectacles of multisensory experience where sight, scent, sound and space were entangled in celebration and worship. Examining the expansive sensorial field of the Confraternity of the Misericordia Maggiore, this chapter presents the concept of 'sensoryscapes' to capture the intra-active entanglements between material environments, objects and the human sensorium during processions in the early modern period. By bringing historical sources from the confraternity's archives into dialogue with the field of sensory studies, it is argued that these multisensory events were vital tools of civic self-fashioning through which the confraternity could demonstrate its power and wealth to an embodied public in Bergamo.

Keywords

confraternities – history of the senses – multisensory – soundscapes – processions – early modern Italy

This chapter explores the multiple sensory registers through which urban events and public rituals were encountered and experienced in early modern Bergamo, a small provincial town located at the foot of the Alps on the westernmost boundaries of the Venetian *Terraferma*.[1] It focuses specifically on the sensory politics of the urban processions that were organised by the Confraternity of the Misericordia Maggiore. Founded as a charitable institution in 1265, between the fifteenth and eighteenth centuries this pious independent lay confraternity became one of the most wealthy and powerful institutions in Bergamo.[2] The confraternity served many charitable purposes, like similar institutions in the Veneto and beyond: assisting the poor; developing youth education programmes; maintaining and decorating their church (the Basilica of Santa Maria Maggiore); organising church services; and enhancing the music performances within the basilica by teaching, hiring and paying musicians and singers for the liturgical offices. Beyond their activities in the basilica, they also organised processions around the town throughout the year. The liturgical and secular processions they staged were spectacles of multisensory experience where sight, scent and sound were entangled in celebration and worship. These events were also vital tools of civic self-fashioning with which the confraternity could demonstrate its power and wealth to an embodied public in Bergamo.

In this chapter, I examine the relationship between space, objects and the senses specifically in Good Friday processions, and consider how these events were encountered by embodied spectators. Bringing historical sources from the confraternity's archives into dialogue with the field of sensory studies and scholarship on early modern urban space and public spectacles, this chapter uses the concept of 'sensoryscapes' to capture the intra-active entanglements between material environments, objects and the human sensorium that

---

1 This project has received funding from the European Union's Horizon 2020 research and innovation programme (grant agreement no. 945361). The research was supported previously at various stages by the Royal Historical Society, the Caligara Foundation for Interdisciplinary Studies and the Ateneo di Scienze, Lettere e Arti di Bergamo. Versions of this chapter were presented in several fora at the University of St. Andrews and Cambridge (2018), at the Renaissance Society of America annual meeting (2019) and at the Art History Research Seminar at the University of Oxford (2019). I am very grateful to Deborah Howard, Iain Fenlon and Nick Terpstra for stimulating discussions on a number of occasions and for their comments; Elizabeth Eva Leach for valuable suggestions on the text; and Bonnie Blackburn and Leofranc Holford-Strevens for checking my translations from the original text.

2 See Little L., *Liberty, Charity, Fraternity: Lay Religious Confraternities in Bergamo in the Age of the Commune* (Bergamo-Northampton: 1988) 107–122; see also: Cossar R., *The Transformation of the Laity in Bergamo, 1265–c.1400* (Leiden – Boston: 2006) 17–59; Locatelli G., "L'istruzione in Bergamo e la Misericordia Maggiore", *Bergomum* 4 (1910) 57–169, here 111; and Carlsmith C., *A Renaissance Education: Schooling in Bergamo and the Venetian Republic, 1500–1650* (Toronto: 2010) 134–139.

unfolded during urban processions in the early modern period. In doing so, this chapter builds on recent work that has been carried out on early modern 'soundscapes', a rich area of research enquiry that focuses on historical constructions of sound and its social meanings in relation to the built environment. The concept of the 'soundscape' has provided a valuable analytical prism through which historians have begun to approach historical constructions of sound within urban space, as well as the meanings and identities that were produced through sound–space dynamics. A focus on soundscapes places an emphasis on the social and spatial dimensions of sound, directing attention to the interplay of the material environment and sonic phenomena within everyday life.

Expanding on this work, this chapter uses the concept of the 'sensoryscape' to make analytical elbow room for other modalities of early modern sensory experience, alongside sound. As the historian James M. Murray has suggested, an understanding of the politics of public rituals must necessarily account for 'their sights, smells, sounds [...] *and the role all parts played in the whole*'.[3] Approaching the Good Friday processions in Bergamo as part of the expansive sensorial field of the Confraternity of the Misericordia Maggiore, this chapter argues that the sensoryscape of Bergamo was a key political arena through which the confraternity consolidated and communicated its 'magnificenza'. This is a term frequently encountered in the confraternity's archives that might be understood as describing a sensory-political project aimed at ascertaining both divine proximity and earthly political power for the confraternity by expressively promoting its own self-image through public displays of wealth and status.[4] At a time when theatrics and performance were central to the experience of public worship and to the communication of political power, no task was more pressing than governing the urban sensoryscape. Perhaps nowhere is the interactivity between space and the human sensorium better captured than in the multisensory event of the early modern urban procession.

---

3   Murray J.M., "The Liturgy of the Count's Advent in Bruges, from Galbert to Van Eyck", in Hanawalt B.A. – Reyerson K.L. (eds.), *City and Spectacle in Medieval Europe*, Medieval Studies at Minnesota 6 (Minneapolis – London: 1994) 137–152, here 143 (emphasis added).

4   The terms 'magnificenza' and 'magnificenta' are recurrently encountered within the archival sources over a period of sixty years, depending on who is using the term and whether they are more inclined to the Italian or Latin, respectively. For consistency I use 'magnificenza' throughout this chapter.

1 Early Modern Sensoryscapes

There is now a growing cross-disciplinary interest in the political, historical and social significance of the senses and emotions.[5] This theoretical interest, which has been described by some commentators as constituting a 'sensory turn' (or return[6]), has occurred across the arts, social sciences and humanities, giving rise to new sub-fields of sensory scholarship such as sensory history, sensory ethnography and social studies of the senses.[7] Within the historical disciplines, in particular, sensory studies has emerged as a dynamic field of investigation, with the senses offering a valuable window onto the past. For the historian, archival records have proven to be a rich repository of sensory and emotional experience. Letters, diaries, travelogues and other historical sources provide a wealth of sensory descriptions and form what Holly Dugan has called an 'historical archive of sensation', through which much can be gleaned about how people in the past understood, engaged with and inhabited their worlds.[8] These sensory descriptions help to texture the past and allow investigation, at least partially, into the historical meanings attributed to the senses and the role that the senses played in shaping cultural values as well as meanings and conceptions of space, community, the production of identities, beliefs and social relations. This interest in the senses has demonstrated that embodied and affective experiences and subjectivities are produced and structured equally

---

5   Newhauser has termed this 'sensorial research'. See Newhauser R., "The Senses in Medieval and Renaissance Intellectual History", *Senses and Society* 5 (2010) 5–9 (5). On the history of the senses see also, amongst others: Halsall F., "One Sense is Never Enough", *Journal of Visual Arts Practice* 3 (2004) 103–122; Howes D. (ed.), *Empire of the Senses: The Sensual Culture Reader* (Oxford: 2005) 1–17; Jones C.A., "The Mediated Sensorium", in Jones C.A. (ed.), *Sensorium: Embodied Experience, Technology, and Contemporary Art* (Cambridge MA: 2006) 5–49; Di Bello P. – Koureas G., "Other than the Visual: Art, History and the Senses", in Idem (eds.), *Art, History and the Senses: 1830 to the Present* (Surrey: 2010) 1–18; Hamilakis Y., *Archaeology and the Senses: Human Experience, Memory, and Affect* (Cambridge: 2014) 111–128 (112–119). Other noteworthy scholarship in this direction includes the contributions to *Senses and Society*, an academic journal dedicated to the sensory turn and the *Sensory Formations* series published by Bloomsbury. On the history of emotions, see, among others: Hills H. – Gouk P., "Towards Histories of Emotions", in Hills H. – Gouk P. (eds.), *Representing Emotions: New Connections in the Histories of Art, Music and Medicine* (London: 2005) 15–34; Martín-Moruno D. – Pichel B. (eds.), *Emotional Bodies: The Historical Performativity of Emotions* (Chicago IL: 2019).
6   Lauwrens J., "Welcome to the Revolution: The Sensory Turn and Art History", *Journal of Art Historiography* 7 (2012), available at: https://arthistoriography.wordpress.com/7-dec2012/. (accessed 10 May 2019).
7   See, respectively, Smith M.M., *Sensory History* (Oxford: 2007); Pink S., *Doing Sensory Ethnography* (Los Angeles – London: 2009); Howes D. – Classen C., "The Social Life of the Senses", *Ars Vivendi Journal* 3 (2013) 4–23.
8   Dugan H., *The Ephemeral History of Perfume: Scent and Sense in Early Modern England* (Baltimore: 2011) 5.

by the material features of a specific environment and by the social and cultural contexts in which sensuous encounters took place. Sensory researchers acknowledge at the outset that attempts to understand historical sensorial and affective experiences are speculative and incomplete. The meanings of sensory experiences are necessarily 'hostage to the context' in which they were produced.[9] An epistemological and ontological gap separates interpretation of the sensory descriptions found in archival accounts from how they were understood and experienced by people in the past. That is to say, sensing is a cultural and social practice that changes over time.[10]

The sensory turn in early modern studies arose, in part, as a response to a long-standing scholarly preoccupation with early modern visual cultures of spectacle, display and representation, where the focus was predominantly centred around the sense of sight.[11] Sensory studies scholarship has attempted to expand visuo-centric analyses by directing critical attention to other sensory modalities, opening avenues for multisensory, proprioceptive and phenomenological engagements with the past.[12] From the smells of sixteenth-century Venice, to the role that touch played in structuring social relations in early modern Europe, senses other than the visual were important to how early modern subjects categorised, felt and interpreted their sociocultural experience.[13]

In the expanding literature on early modern sensoriality, much work has focused on the sense of sound, particularly in relation to the historic production of space and subjectivity.[14] Hearing and listening to sonic forms, from church bells to noisy machinery, has been shown to be deeply implicated in

---

9   Smith M.M., "Producing Sense, Consuming Sense, Making Sense: Perils and Prospects for Sensory History", *Journal of Social History* 40.4 (2007) 841–858 (841).
10 Given the increase in funding directed towards digital reconstructions of sensory spaces, these questions should be of paramount epistemological concern to sensory researchers.
11 As Crary has highlighted, an emphasis on spectatorship and 'visuality' can easily generate 'a model of perception and subjectivity that is cut off from richer and more historically determined notions of "embodiment"': Crary J., *Suspensions of Perception: Attention, Spectacle, and Modern Culture* (Cambridge MA: 2001) 3.
12 Steward J. – Cowan A. (eds.), *The City and the Senses: Urban Culture Since 1500* (Aldershot: 2007).
13 On touch, for example, see: Gowing L., *Common Bodies: Women, Touch and Power in Seventeenth-Century England* (New Haven: 2003); Rudy K.M., *Touching Parchment: How Medieval Users Rubbed, Handled and Kissed their Manuscripts* (Cambridge: 2023). On smell, see: Wheeler J., "Stench in Sixteenth Century Venice", in Cowan A. – Steward J. (eds.), *The City and the Senses: Urban Culture Since 1500* (Aldershot: 2007) 25–38.
14 Strohm R., *Music in Late Medieval Bruges* (Oxford: 1985); Corbin A., *Village Bells: Sound and Meaning in the Nineteenth Century French Countryside* (Paris: 1994); Smith B.R., *The Acoustic World of Early Modern England: Attending to the O-Factor* (Chicago IL: 1999); Kendrick R., *The Sounds of Milan, 1585–1650* (Oxford: 2002); and Harding V., "Introduction: Music and Urban History", *Urban History* 29 (2002) 5–7.

the daily experience of early modern subjects.[15] The concept of the soundscape, in particular, has been regularly deployed in an effort to describe or capture relations between space, meaning and identity in early modern sonic environments. A dynamic field of research activity has now formed around investigations of historic soundscapes and the acoustic communities these gave rise to. The term 'soundscape' can be traced back at least to the late 1960s and the coinage of this concept is often attributed to the Canadian composer R. Murray Schafer.[16] For Schafer, the soundscape refers to 'any acoustic field of study'.[17] Schafer suggested that 'We may speak of a musical composition as a soundscape, or a radio program as a soundscape or an acoustic environment as a soundscape'.[18] In the historical disciplines, it is the 'acoustic environment' as soundscape that has been most thoroughly pursued.[19] Here, the soundscape is often presented as the aural equivalent of landscape insofar as it refers to everything that the ear is exposed to 'in a given sonic setting'.[20] The concept of landscape has, of course, been thoroughly problematised. This problematisation has involved highlighting the socially constructed nature of the gaze that sees the land and the ways in which practices and process of producing landscapes structure relations with the land through specific ways of historically and culturally produced ways of looking. Theorists have also subjected the soundscape concept to similar critical unpacking.[21]

---

15   On church bells as part of the urban soundscape in early modern Florence, see: Atkinson N., "Seeing Sound: Mapping the Florentine soundscape", in Terpstra N. – Rose C. (eds.), *Mapping Space, Sense and Movement in Florence. Historical GIS and the Early Modern City* (Abingdon: 2016) 149–168. On noise, see: Atkinson N., *The Noisy Renaissance: Sound, Architecture, and Florentine Urban Life* (University Park, PA: 2016). On noisy machinery, see: Howard D., "Architecture and Invention in Venice and the Veneto in the Later Sixteenth Century", in Israëls M. – Waldman L.A. (eds.), *Renaissance Studies in Honour of Joseph Connors*, Villa i Tatti: The Harvard University Center for Italian Renaissance Studies 29, 2 vols. (Cambridge MA: 2013) vol. II, 363–372, here 368, in which Howard discusses the noise of flour-milling machines.

16   Murray Schafer R., *The New Soundscape: A Handbook for the Modern Music Teacher* (Scarborough ON: 1969). For a similar usage of the concept in the same year, see: Southworth M., "The Sonic Environment of Cities", in *Environment and Behaviour* 1.1 (1969) 49–70.

17   Murray Schafer R. *The Soundscape: Our Sonic Environment and the Tuning of the World* (Rochester VE: 1997) 7.

18   Ibidem.

19   Richard Leppert uses the phrase 'sonoric landscape'. See Leppert R., *The Sight of Sound: Music, Representation, and the History of the Body* (Berkeley: 1995).

20   Samuels D.W. – Meintjes L. – Ochoa A.M. – Porcello T., "Soundscape: Toward a Sounded Anthropology", *Annual Review of Anthropology* 39 (2010) 329–345.

21   Ingold T., "Against Soundscape", in Carlyle A. (ed.), *Autumn Leaves: Sound and the Environment in Artistic Practice* (Paris: 2007) 10–13. See also: Helmreich S., "Listening Against Soundscapes", *Anthropology News* (December 2010) 10.

Like landscapes, soundscapes are the produced effect of social practices, politics and ideologies.[22] Through the analytic of soundscapes, historians have sought to examine the perceptual situatedness of people in particular environments and the way in which individuals and communities were constituted through acts of listening and hearing (often filtered through the institutions of the state or church). As embodied experience, sound has been shown to be especially vital to the construction of early modern social identity and a central 'means by which people account[ed] for their version of reality'.[23] As Christopher M. Woolgar has simply put it, 'sound transmitted much more than the literal message of the text'.[24] Niall Atkinson has noted that 'a city's soundscape was as much an impression of its identity as it was a medium through which social relations were forged and negotiated by both ritual and transgressive practices'.[25]

At the same time, however, the sensory archive has shown that sound and other senses were by no means experienced in isolation. Rather, the lived experience of early modern environments cut across sensory categories, with archival accounts of events sometimes invoking touch, taste, sight, sound and smell in a single sensory description. While focusing on an isolated sense can greatly enhance understandings of a particular sensation, this also risks isolating the involvement and participation of the other senses in the historical production of meaning. Sensorial research often focuses on histories of particular sensations, but historians must also account for what Mark M. Smith has called the 'history of intersensoriality', by which he means the diverse ways in which 'the senses worked together and in concert, not in isolation'.[26] Expanding the concept of soundscape to account for other sensorial experiences, I use here the term 'sensoryscape', which offers one way to approach the multisensory

---

22 The soundscape concept also brings with it its own political and ideological baggage. Schafer's initial engagement with the concept was rooted in the cybernetic systems thinking of the 1970s ecology movement, and arose from a concern with the noise pollution of modern technologies of mediation. Through the soundscape concept, Schafer sought to address what he identified as the growing impoverishment of aural experience in the twentieth century. As such, underpinning his project is a somewhat romantic materialist environmentalism that very much roots the aural experience of late modernity within a narrative of sensory destitution wrought by machinic industrialisation.

23 Leppert R., *The Sight of Sound: Music, Representation, and the History of the Body* (Berkeley: 1995) 15. See also: Knighton T., "Orality and Aurality: Contexts for the Unwritten Musics of Sixteenth-Century Barcelona", in Knighton T. – Mazuela-Anguita A. (eds.), *Hearing the City in Early Modern Europe* (Turnhout: 2018) 295–308.

24 Woolgar C.M., *The Senses in Late Medieval England* (New Haven – London: 2006) 2.

25 Atkinson, "Seeing Sound" 149.

26 Smith M.M., "Looking Back: The Explosion of Sensory History", *The Psychologist* 23.10 (2010) 860–863 (860).

dynamics of early modern urban life and the moments of entangled sensoriality that historians encounter in the archive. The potential of the sensoryscape concept lies in the fact that it is not tied to any specific sensory register and, as such, it makes analytical room for the participation of the senses in each other and for the multiple sensuous and socialised meanings and affects that may arise from the inter- and intra-activity of the human body within specific material environments and socio-historical contexts.[27] The concept of the sensoryscape speaks not only to the material environments within which sacred and secular events unfolded, but also to the material and affective objects, substances and other 'things' (clothing, torches, relics, feelings, etc.) that were encountered within that environment and formed part of the sensory-material world.

2 The Confraternity of the Misericordia Maggiore

Bergamo sits on the main communication route from Milan to Venice [Fig. 2.1]. The town had been ruled by the Visconti of Milan in the fourteenth century.[28] Bergamo was home to many religious communities in the fifteenth and sixteenth centuries, including parish communities, flagellant companies (*disciplinati*) and companies for the relief of prisoners (*carcerati*), as well as more than twelve hospitals created between the twelfth and fourteenth centuries, to house and help the sick, the poor and pilgrims passing through the city.[29] In 1428, Bergamo passed under Venetian control. As the Venetian Republic established its *Terraferma* dominion in the fifteenth century, a key strategy of power was the creation of a sense of local autonomy within the towns it ruled [Fig. 2.2].[30] In Bergamo, this was partly achieved by granting the management

---

27 At the same time, it must be highlighted that this is an analytical tool rather than a historic term. Further critical reflection is needed on the current trend of theorising social experience in terms of 'scapes'. The scape suffix could run the risk of presenting social experience as a bounded, coherent and self-contained whole. Such an analysis is beyond the scope of the present chapter; see also: Roodenburg H. (ed.), *A Cultural History of the Senses* (London: 2014) 6–17.
28 Rota S., *Per una storia dei rapporti fra Bergamo e Venezia durante il periodo della dominazione: Secoli XV–XVIII* (Bergamo: 1987) 15–23.
29 Cossar, *Transformation* 8.
30 Campbell S., *The Endless Periphery* (Chicago: 2019) 25–43. Law J.E., *Venice and the Veneto in the Early Renaissance*, Variorum Collected Studies Series 672 (Aldershot: 2000) xiii; Knox G., "The Colleoni Chapel in Bergamo and the Politics of Urban Space", *Journal of the Society of Architectural Historians* 60.3 (2001) 290–309, here 298–299. See also: Muir E. – Weissman R.F.E., "Social and Symbolic Places in Renaissance Venice and Florence", in Agnew J.A. – Duncan J.S. (eds.), *The Power of Place: Bringing Together Geographical and Sociological Imaginations* (Boston: 1989) 81–103.

THE 'SENSORYSCAPE' OF THE GOOD FRIDAY PROCESSION IN BERGAMO

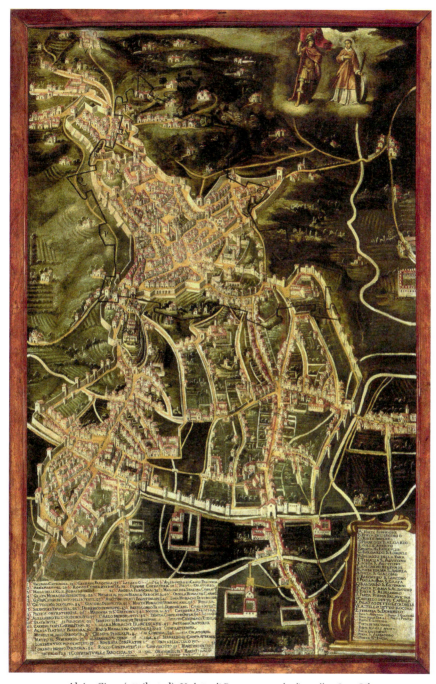

FIGURE 2.1   Alvise Cima (attributed), *Veduta di Bergamo a volo d'uccello*, 1693. Oil on canvas, 107.5 cm × 166.8 cm
COURTESY OF THE BIBLIOTECA CIVICA MAI, BERGAMO

FIGURE 2.2   Enea Salmeggia (Talpino), *Martirio di Sant'Alessandro*, painted 1623. Oil on canvas, 620 cm × 500 cm, Basilica di Sant'Alessandro in Colonna (detail of the City of Bergamo under Venetian dominion)
GALLERIA DELL'ACCADEMIA CARRARA, BERGAMO (CC BY-SA 3.0)

of the Basilica of Santa Maria Maggiore to the Confraternity of the Misericordia Maggiore [Figs. 2.3 and 2.4].[31]

In 1453, the Venetian rulers obtained a papal bull which exempted the basilica in perpetuity from episcopal interference.[32] This enabled the confraternity to operate the basilica in a virtually autonomous manner. Under the management of the confraternity, the basilica became a prestigious church within the town. Archival documents record the close connection between the Confraternity of the Misericordia Maggiore's basilica and the town as a whole in the fifteenth and sixteenth centuries. A 1632 account notes:

---

31   Knox G., "The Unified Church Interior in Baroque Italy: S. Maria Maggiore in Bergamo", *The Art Bulletin* 82 (2000) 679–701, here 682; Zizzo G., "S. Maria Maggiore di Bergamo Cappella della Città. La basilica bergamasca nei secoli XII e XIII", *Archivio Storico Bergamasco* 2 (1982) 207–229.

32   Bergamo. Biblioteca Civica Mai. Archivio della Misericordia Maggiore. 886: *Pro Immunitate ecclesiae*, fol. 13v; see also Cossar, *Transformation* 17–50.

FIGURE 2.3 Basilica of Santa Maria Maggiore, Confraternity of the Misericordia Maggiore, Bergamo (façade and main entrance)
PHOTO BY AUTHOR

FIGURE 2.4 Piazza Vecchia and Palazzo del Podestà, Bergamo
PHOTO BY AUTHOR

> Et con perpetuo concorso di tutti gli ordini della città, gli quali, allettati dalla ampiezza, bellezza, et ornamento di essa, et molto più dall'esquisitezza dell'officiatura, et pontualità delle ceremonie fatte secondo il rito di S.ta Romana Chiesa, frequentano piú questa (chiesa), che ogni altra Chiesa (in città).[33]

> And with the constant gathering of the citizens of all orders in the city, who, enticed by the size, beauty, and splendour [of this church] and even more by the exquisiteness of the divine offices and exactness of the ceremonies conducted according to the rite of the Holy Roman Church, attend this church more than any other (in the city).

Marcantonio Michiel (1484–1582) and Marin Sanuto (1466–1536), in their travels around the Venetian mainland, both describe how the basilica – in continuous competition with the cathedral and other churches in the town – had a much greater importance in the local ecclesiastical hierarchy than its rivals. Sanuto, who visited Bergamo in 1483, described the church as the 'city's chapel' ('cappella della città') and praised its decoration ('É bellissima, grande et bene adornata').[34] Marcantonio Michiel, writing in 1516, commented that Bergamo 'does not have a more famous church in the city' ('ut nulla sit in urbe aedes celebrior') than Santa Maria Maggiore.[35] By contrast, he describes the town's cathedral as poorly cared for and rarely frequented, ('negligentia et avaritia eorum, quorum est ea cura, absoluta adhuc non sit, infrequens incultaque habetur').[36]

The importance of the basilica in the urban environment is key for understanding the power of the confraternity in early modern Bergamo [Fig. 2.5]. The symbolic power of this church (and the political power of the confraternity) was deeply rooted in the production and performance of music.[37] With its vast

---

33 Bergamo. Biblioteca Civica Mai. Archivio della Misericordia Maggiore. 1116, *Processione del Venerdì Santo in città* (1632), fol. 1r.
34 'Cappella della città': Scalvini M.L – Calza G.P., *Bergamo 1516, città e territorio nella 'Descriptio' di Marcantonio Michiel* (Padua: 1984) 66; and Bergamo. Biblioteca Civica Mai. Archivio della Misericordia Maggiore. *Terminationes* (hereafter *T.*) 1280, fol. 131r–v; Sanuto Marin, *Itinerario di Marin Sanuto per la terraferma veneziana nell'anno 1483*, ed. R. Brown (Padua: 1847) 77.
35 Scalvini M.L. – Calza G.P., *Bergamo 1516, città e territorio nella 'Descriptio' di Marcantonio Michiel* (Padua: 1984) 66: 'Mariae aedes neque tam vetustae dicationis, utpote ducentesimo circiter ab hinc anno inchoata, neque sacerdotis dignitate par, ob operantium tamen sanctitatem et frequentiam ita a popolo visitur, ut nulla sit in urbe aedes celebrior'.
36 Ibidem.
37 Di Pasquale M., "Aspetti della pratica strumentale nelle chiese italiane fra tardo medioevo e prima età moderna", *Rivista italiana di musica sacra* 16.2 (1995) 263–268; Roche J., "Music at S. Maria Maggiore, Bergamo, 1614–1643", *Music and Letters* 47 (1966) 296–312, here 302.

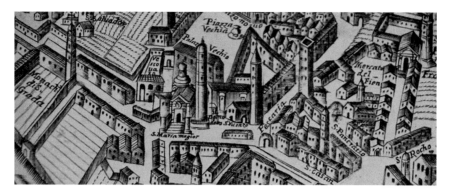

FIGURE 2.5   Stefano Scolari, *Perspective Plan of Bergamo*, 1680 (detail). Copper engraving, 77 cm × 104.2 cm
ISTITUTO ITALIANO DI ARTI GRAFICHE (CC BY-SA 3.0)

and diverse music repertory, the Basilica of Santa Maria Maggiore had long played an important role as a music chapel within the Venetian *Terraferma*. A large repertory of liturgical polyphony and early polychoral music has been documented at Santa Maria Maggiore through a variety of sources in the confraternity's archive.[38] Administrative documents provide valuable insights into the rich musical life of the basilica between the sixteenth and seventeenth centuries, and suggest an explicit interest in enhancing and enriching the musical repertory and activities of the church. Investment in music played a central role in fashioning and communicating the wealth and divine proximity of the confraternity to an embodied public. A number of statements specifically relate to the need to increase the quality and quantity of music on offer, with no expense spared.[39] With increased research into various sound effects and the polychoral style in the sixteenth century, new aesthetic concepts were taking shape in Northern Italy, and the innovative musical forces of the time found fertile ground in the Basilica of Santa Maria Maggiore.[40] The confraternity became highly prestigious in the sixteenth and seventeenth centuries and hired a succession of remarkable church composers and musicians for ceremonies, performances and other events.

---

38   Towne G., "Over the Hills and Far Away: The Place of Bergamo in the Development and Transmission of Polychoral Music", in Folegana L. – Ingesti A. (eds.), *Dal canto corale alla musica policorale. L'arte del "coro spezzato"* (Padua: 2014) 69–80.

39   Benaglio Marc'Antonio, *Institutione e Ordini della Misericordia Maggiore di Bergamo* (Bergamo, Valerio Ventura: 1620) 4–6; Bergamo. Biblioteca Civica Mai. Archivio della Misericordia Maggiore. *Spese*, 1392 fol. 591r.

40   Roche, "Music" 296–314. See also: Padoan M., *La musica in S. Maria Maggiore a Bergamo nel periodo di Giovanni Cavaccio (1598–1626)* (Como: 1983) 18–22. On Cavaccio, see also: Rosenholtz-Witt J., "Musica, crisi, e la politica della riforma a Bergamo nel primo seicento", *Archivio Storico Bergamasco* LXXXV (2023) 423–432.

Along with details of considerable investment in music, archival records often report discussions of whether it was appropriate to spend so much money on enhancing the musical and decorative aspects of the church. Yet willingness to enhance the confraternity's liturgical and musical performances is persistently justified by two interlinked and often overlapping expressions: 'for magnificence' ('pro magnificenza') and 'for devotion' ('pro devotione'), which formed the basis of many discussions and decisions within the meetings of the governing body. Musicologists have highlighted how, in other Venetian contexts, references to *magnificenza* often imply the performance of sumptuous *cori spezzati* and *prima pratica* music.[41] The pursuit of *magnificenza* was also intimately tied to political prestige and social pre-eminence. As Gerbino and Fenlon have suggested, in late sixteenth- and early seventeenth-century Italy, *magnificenza* 'acted as a mechanism for converting wealth into status and power'.[42] At the same time, these investments were also designed to please a higher audience, that is, to win divine mercy for the town of Bergamo by inspiring devotion among the faithful. The expenses allocated for music performances, from events staged inside the basilica to those that unfolded in urban space (such as processions), were also justified by the need to gather the majority of the population and the faithful under the wing of the confraternity.[43]

Processions were central to the performative production of the confraternity's power, prestige and status. Indeed, processions worked to 'amplify the liturgy outside, in the Piazza processing to other areas of the city [...] but also to knit together the social fabric of the city through communal ritual acts'.[44] The processions, parades, pageants, triumphal entries and other public ceremonies that marked the annual calendar were key occasions for urban communities. From the late medieval period onwards, an expansion of public interest and participation in urban events had been underway, culminating in the opulent spectacles associated with the early modern period.[45] The theatricality

---

41 Roche, "Music" 304. On *cori spezzati* see also, among others: Bryant D., "The 'cori spezzati' of St Mark's: Myth and Reality", *Early Music History* 1 (1981) 165–186 (170–175); Carver A.F., *Cori Spezzati: The Development of Sacred Polychoral Music to the Time of Schütz* (Cambridge: 1988) 1. On the *prima pratica*, see: Palisca C., "Prima pratica", *Grove Music Online* (2001) https://doi.org/10.1093/gmo/9781561592630.article.22350 (accessed 12 April 2022).
42 Gerbino G. – Fenlon I., "Early Opera: The Initial Phase", in Haar, J. (ed), *European Music, 1520–1640* (Woodbridge, UK: 2006) 472–486, here 485.
43 Bergamo. Biblioteca Civica Mai. Archivio della Misericordia Maggiore. 1280 *T*, 1612–1622 (1617) fol. 92v.
44 Fenlon I., "Urban Soundscapes", in Fenlon I. – Wistreich R. (ed.), *The Cambridge History of Sixteenth-Century Music* (Cambridge: 2019) 209–259, here 234.
45 Hanawalt B.A. – Reyerson K.L., *City and Spectacle in Medieval Europe* (Minneapolis – London: 1994) xv; Muir E., *Civic Ritual in Renaissance Venice* (Princeton: 1981) 185–211.

of processions and other staged public ceremonies in early modern Europe has been widely noted.[46] Analogies to theatre are often drawn to highlight the spectacular, performative and scenographic elements of these events and to draw attention to the close relationship between urban planning, ceremony and architectural design. However, the theatre metaphor does not only speak to the visually spectacular and performative nature of early modern processions and ceremonies but also to their multisensory dynamics. Just as theatres were dense sites of sensory richness, the choreographed processions and other public events that took place in early modern cities were multisensory and affective bodily experiences.[47]

Processions were moving performances charged with meaning. The kinetic experience dominated civic spaces, street after street, square after square, and transformed the urban area into a sacralised environment. They impressed residents and foreign spectators alike and often blended and blurred sacred and secular imperatives. In Venice, for example, processions were 'essentially a spectacular display of civic and religious belief (all of the clergy of the city walked in the procession together with civic dignitaries), local customs and traditions were allied to liturgical practice in a highly festive and theatrical ritual of instruction, indoctrination, and propaganda'.[48] Indeed, as was characteristic of early modern urban rituals, religious events invariably had a political dimension, which sometimes invaded the 'political field to become propaganda'.[49] Processions also established hierarchies between religious and secular institutions. In the context of ducal processions in sixteenth-century Venice, Edward Muir has shown that these events had symbolic, hierarchical and spatial aspects.[50] Alexandra F. Johnston has underlined that religious

---

46 See, for example: Muir. E., *Civic Ritual* 185–211; Fenlon I., *The Ceremonial City: History, Memory and Myth in Renaissance Venice* (New Haven: 2007) 85–127; Fisher A., "'Mit Singen und Klingen': Urban Processional Culture", in Filippi D. – Noone M. (eds.), *Listening to Early Modern Catholicism: Perspective from Musicology*, Intersections 49 (Leiden – Boston: 2017) 187–203.

47 On the multisensory aspects of early modern theatre, see: Arab R. – Dowd M.M. – Zucker A. (eds.), *Historical Affects and the Early Modern Theatre* (New York: 2015); Karim-Cooper F., "The Sensory Body in Shakespeare's Theatres", in Kern-Stähler A. – Busse B. – de Boer W. (eds.), *The Five Senses in Medieval and Early Modern England*, Intersections 44 (Leiden – Boston: 2016) 269–285.

48 Fenlon, "Urban Soundscapes" 238.

49 Fisher A., *Music, Piety, and Propaganda: The Soundscapes of Counter-Reformation Bavaria* (Oxford: 2014) 1–3; Rabaglio M., "Drammaturgia popolare e teatro sacro. Riti e rappresentazioni del Venerdì Santo nel Bergamasco", *Quaderni dell'archivio della cultura di base* 12 (1989) 11–24.

50 Muir E., *Civic Ritual* 185–211; see also Muir E. – Weissman R.F.E., "Social and Symbolic Places" 81–103.

institutions 'were constantly negotiating their relationship with other secular and religious authorities'.[51] Through processions, religious institutions sought to fashion and promote their own self-image in order to establish their power, influence and authority 'in relationship to the countervailing powers surrounding them'.[52] As such, Elsje van Kessel has observed that these events played a crucial role in the 'political power play' between rival institutions.[53] Susan Verdi Webster has described the processions associated with Holy Week in sixteenth century Seville as a 'contest among confraternities'.[54] Verdi Webster notes that during this period, processions 'were transformed from simple, humble homages into ornate spectacles that increasingly involved issues of material and political competition'.[55]

Confraternities sought to overawe spectators with the aim of creating an experience that 'provoked strong affective responses in the audience'.[56] The choreographed processions and other public events that took place in early modern cities were events of sensory richness and affective bodily experience.[57] This was certainly the case with the Good Friday procession in seventeenth-century Bergamo.

3 The Good Friday Procession in Bergamo

In Bergamo, the Confraternity of the Misericordia Maggiore organised grand processions and other public events around the streets of the town throughout the liturgical year. Financed by the confraternity, these processions were elaborate spectacles of sight, sound, and scent that enabled that institution to extend its political presence out into the space of the town, demonstrating its wealth and status.[58] The sensory impact of these processions was significant.

---

51   Johnston A.F., "Introduction", in Johnston A.F. – Hüsken W. (eds.), *Civic Ritual & Drama* (Amsterdam: 1997) 7–14, here 7.
52   Ibidem.
53   Van Kessel E., "The Making of a Hybrid Body: Corpus Christi in Lisbon, 1582", *Renaissance Studies* 34.4, Special Issue on Visual and Spatial Hybridity in the Early Modern Iberian World (2020) 572–592, here 577.
54   Verdi Webster S., *Art and Ritual in Golden-Age Spain: Sevillian Confraternities and the Processional Sculpture of Holy Week* (Princeton: 1998) 163.
55   Ibidem.
56   Ibidem.
57   Johnston G.A., "Embodying Devotion: Multisensory Encounters with Donatello's *Crucifix* in S. Croce", *Renaissance Quarterly* 73 (2020) 1179–1234, here 1207–1219.
58   Costa E., "Tra rito e teatro: l'azione rituale in prospettiva pedagogica", *Comunicazioni Sociali* 2.3 (1985) 75–81.

Diary accounts provide a glimpse of the sensory texture of these events, often evoking the colours and fragrances, the sounds of music and bells and the sights that accompanied ceremonial display. In seventeenth-century Bergamo, Good Friday processions were major events and were inseparably linked with the image and identity of the Confraternity of the Misericordia Maggiore. These processions were 'one of the greatest solemnities' ('una delle maggiori solennità'), as one diarist remarked, in which 'all the citizens, both the clergy and the laity, participate with the greatest devotion' ('concorrono tutti li cittadini Ecclesiastici e secolari con grandissima devotione').[59] The Good Friday procession was strictly staged and choreographed, from the positioning of the participants forming the parade, to the space and route of the ambulatory performance.

Vivid, if fragmented and fleeting, descriptions of the sensorial dynamics of Good Friday processions can be explored through eyewitness commentaries. Two historical accounts in particular make it possible to enter into the multisensory experience of the Good Friday procession in early modern Bergamo: a diary from 1632 and another from 1650, both written by anonymous diarists.[60] These two diaries loosely trace the route the procession followed, the major processional icons and actors, and describe its sensory aspects. The level of detail these documents provide would suggest the diarists were close to the Confraternity of the Misericordia Maggiore, and familiar with the conventions and rules of the institution. Drawing from these accounts, with their ellipses, biases, and blind spots, what follows is a partial interpretation of what this procession might have entailed.

The 1632 diary reports that 'one of the most important celebrations that occurs [...] is the Good Friday procession' ('una delle maggiori solennità [...] è la processione del Venerdì Santo').[61] This procession began and concluded at the confraternity's Basilica of Santa Maria Maggiore, rather than Bergamo Cathedral, as might typically be expected. This testifies to the status and power of the Confraternity of the Misericordia Maggiore. The 1632 diary reveals that participants from across the town gathered in the basilica before the procession, which was 'officiated by chaplains, clerics and salaried singers with great

---

59 Bergamo. Biblioteca Civica Mai. Archivio della Misericordia Maggiore. 1116 (1632) fol. 1r.
60 Bergamo. Biblioteca Civica Mai. Archivio della Misericordia Maggiore. 1116 *Processione del Venerdì Santo in città* (1632); Bergamo. Biblioteca Civica Mai. Archivio della Misericordia Maggiore. Sala 1, 10. 2/3 *Effemeridi* (1650). See: Meli A., "Bergamo 1650: da un prezioso diario inedito, la processione del Venerdì Santo", *L'Eco di Bergamo* 27 (March 1964); and Rabaglio, "Drammaturgia populare" 90–91, 98–99.
61 Bergamo. Biblioteca Civica Mai. Archivio della Misericordia Maggiore. *Processione*, fol. 1r.

magnificence and splendour, and with constant attendance of all the citizens and orders of the city' ('officiata da cappellani, chierici e cantori salariati con grandissima magnificenza e splendore e con perpetuo concorso di tutti li cittadini, et di tutti gli ordini della città').[62] The celebration began at night, with a series of solemn chants that took place within the precinct of the basilica:

> Si è cominciato il Mattutino, quale è stato cantato solennemente, et li musici hanno cantato le profezie di Geremia, et li responsorij delle lezioni di S. Agostino et S. Paolo, et il Miserere delle Laudi, il Benedictus, et l'altro miserere ultimo, et verso la fine di detto matutino si sono dispensati li candelotti di cera di gran peso.[63]

> The Matins was begun, which was sung solemnly, and the musicians sang the Prophecies of Jeremiah, and the responsories to the lessons of St. Augustine and St. Paul, and the *Miserere* of Lauds, the Benedictus, and the final *Miserere*, and towards the end of Matins the heavy wax candles were distributed.

The performance of a key penitential text such as the *Miserere* would have created an emotional intensity, setting the tone for the entire procession and conjuring feelings of penitence, guilt, compassion and sorrow. The 1632 account emphasises the emotional impact of the *Miserere* among the attendees and the wider community, highlighting that 'the whole city was moved' ('tutta la città si è commossa').[64]

The 1650 diary traces the Good Friday processional route and the music sung along the way. After the liturgical event inside the basilica, the event moved outside with a procession that circumnavigated the town, following demarcated routes within the Venetian-built town walls [Fig. 2.6]. Music, the beating of drums and the pealing of bells accompanied the procession as it wound through the town and these sounds continued throughout the entirety of the ritual [Fig. 2.6].

After beginning in the basilica, sources describe the processional route along the streets of Bergamo [Figs. 2.7 and 2.8]:

---

62   Ibidem.
63   Bergamo. Biblioteca Civica Mai. Archivio della Misericordia Maggiore. *Effemeridi*, fol. 62r.
64   Bergamo. Biblioteca Civica Mai. Archivio della Misericordia Maggiore. *Processione*, fol. 3v.

THE 'SENSORYSCAPE' OF THE GOOD FRIDAY PROCESSION IN BERGAMO 43

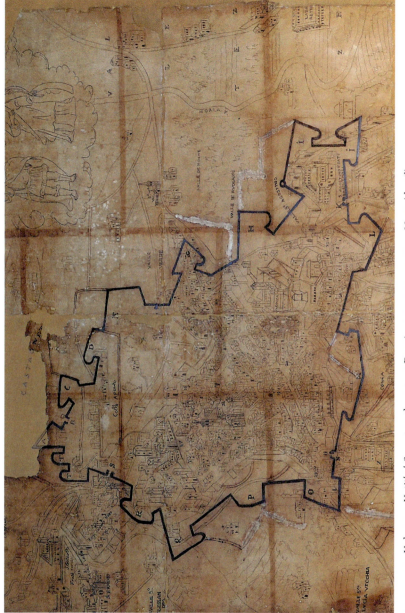

FIGURE 2.6 Unknown, *Untitled*. Seventeenth century. Drawing on paper. 107 cm × 166 cm (detail)
COURTESY OF THE BIBLIOTECA CIVICA MAI, BERGAMO

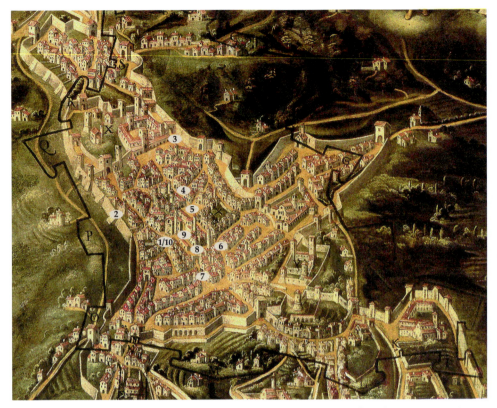

FIGURE 2.7 Alvise Cima (attributed), *Veduta di Bergamo a volo d'uccello* (detail of a bird's-eye view of Bergamo within the Venetian walls). Numbers on the map mark the locations of buildings, squares and streets along the route of the Good Friday Procession, as mentioned in the archival sources: 1./10. S. Maria Maggiore; 2. S. Grata e Salvecchio; 3. S. Agata; 4. Corsarola; 5. Piazza Vecchia; 6. Gombito Tower; 7. S. Cassiano; 8. Fish market; 9. Cathedral
SKETCH BY AUTHOR

> La processione [...] uscisse [= esce] per la porta che è appresso la fontana et di lì è instradata dalli ss. ministro et presidenti della Misericordia et va per la strada dritto per quanto dura il monastero delle monache di S. Grata in columnellis et di poi volta per la strada del Salvecchio sino alla fontana appresso sant'Agata et di la va per la Corsarola in piazza Vecchia et di poi per Gombito al mercato delle scarpe et di lì per la Contrada di S. Cassiano passa in pescaria e va a passare avanti la facciata del Domo et avanti il sotto palazzo et entra in S.M. per la porta grande et va a terminare al sepolcro sull'altare del quale viene esposto il ss. Sacramento.[65]

---

65 Bergamo. Biblioteca Civica Mai. Archivio della Misericordia Maggiore. *Effemeridi*, fols. 63r–64r.

THE 'SENSORYSCAPE' OF THE GOOD FRIDAY PROCESSION IN BERGAMO   45

FIGURE 2.8   Historical GIS (HGIS) analysis of the sixteenth-century map of Bergamo (Esri ArcGIS Education CC BY-SA 4.0). Numbers on the map mark the locations of buildings, squares and streets along the route of the Good Friday Procession: 1./10. S. Maria Maggiore; 2. S. Grata e Salvecchio; 3. S. Agata; 4. Corsarola; 5. Piazza Vecchia; 6. Gombito Tower; 7. S. Cassiano; 8. Fish market; 9. Cathedral. See the QR code on the top right corner of the image for the interactive digital online version (or https://rb.gy/5wuzm)

The procession […] left through the door near the fountain and from there it was routed by the Officers and Superiors of the Misericordia, and goes straight down the street as far as the convent of the nuns of Santa Grata in Columnellis [2] and from there it turns into Salvecchio street [2] as far as the fountain next to Sant'Agata [3] and from there it goes along Corsarola [4] to Piazza Vecchia [5] and then towards the Gombito tower [6] to the shoe market, and from there through the district of San Cassiano [7], passing through the fish market [8] and goes in front of the façade of the Cathedral [9] and in front of the lower palace it enters Santa Maria Maggiore [10] through the main door and ends at the sepulchre on whose altar the Most Holy Sacrament is displayed.

Music formed a fundamental component of this procession and both diarists note the aural richness of the ceremonial event.[66] As the procession advanced through the town's streets, with moments of pause and recollection at other churches, much music was heard along the route, with musicians performing the *Miserere* and the *Popule meus* throughout the procession and 'when the procession is finishing, the musicians sing the *Tantum ergo Sacramentum* as soon as all the people were gathering again [in the Church]' ('fratanto che si finisce la processione, li musici cantano subito, arrivata tutta la gente, e vien cantato il *Tantum ergo Sacramentum*').[67]

The event was also filled with chanting, litanies, drums, polyphony, bells and many other sounds. The noise of the procession would have permeated the town, with the built space modulating and shaping these sounds in turn. Alexander Fisher, among others, has observed that, in contrast to the visual media of processions, such as banners, vestments and monstrances, sound was a particularly 'powerful vehicle for communication' because it enabled the transmission of messages far beyond spectators' direct sightlines.[68] As in other urban contexts, 'voices and bells synched to a collective bodily motion'.[69] The churches along the route were ordered to ring their bells as the procession moved and approached each of them. In doing so, the confraternity was affirming and asserting its authority over the town.

In addition to these sonic elements, the procession was also a visual and kinetic event that generated meaning through movement. The procession made its way through the town, with musicians singing and members of the clergy and other religious institutions strategically moving in hierarchical order. Participants in the processional display were organised by status, as in other Venetian contexts, and positioning within the procession was fundamental to the perception of this performative event.[70] The procession involved a large number of participants from across social classes and religious and civic hierarchies, and it also included members from the basilica's choir and singers employed specifically for the occasion. Soldiers were hired by the confraternity

---

66   See also: Fisher A., "'Mit Singen Und Klingen'" 187–203; and Escrivà-Llorca F., "The Procession of the Relics of São Roque (Lisbon, 1588)", in Knighton T. – Mazuela-Anguita A. (eds.), *Hearing the City in Early Modern Europe* (Turnhout: 2018) 229–240, here 238.

67   Bergamo. Biblioteca Civica Mai. Archivio della Misericordia Maggiore. *Effemeridi*, fols. 63r–64r.

68   Fisher, "'Mit Singen und Klingen'" 189.

69   Atkinson, "Seeing Sound" 164.

70   Muir, *Civic Ritual* 189–211.

to manage the procession (and to emphasise its importance): 'those streets [where the procession passes] are armed with soldiers of the *presidio*, to whom the Misericordia gives a *brenta* of wine for their services' ('quali strade vengono tutte armate dei Soldati del presidio ai quali la Misericordia dona una brenta di vino per ricognitione').[71]

In the 1632 account the diarist describes how the procession involved all of the highest representatives of the civic and religious spheres of Bergamo, further suggesting the political power of the confraternity and the role of the procession as a means to consolidate this power and status. In this instance, the Good Friday procession appears as both a devotional and promotional event for the confraternity itself. However, the 1650 account suggests a decline in processional participants and speaks to tensions among competing religious institutions in the town arising from the positioning of confraternity members in the procession:

> Avanti che fosse istituita questa compagnia della carità (Misericordia Maggiore), a questa processione si univano tutte le altre scuole de' disciplini della città, che dovevano essere più di 300, ma perchè questi signori della carità (Misericordia Maggiore) che sono li principali gentihomini della città pretendono la precedenza da dette scuole, queste per non cedere non sempre vengono alla processione.[72]

> Before the foundation of this charitable confraternity (Misericordia Maggiore) this procession was also attended by all the other *scuole* of flagellants in town, which ought to have been more than 300, but because the members of this confraternity, who are the principal gentlemen of the city, claim precedence over those *scuole* (in the procession), some of the abovementioned *scuole*, so as not to give in, do not always attend the procession.

The different religious communities participating in the procession could be recognised visually by their dress and their position in the strict political structure of the event. In 1650, the procession was composed as follows:

> Processione qual fu cominciata dalli disciplini vestiti di verde che sono quelli di S. Rocco di città et ve ne furono alcuni puochi in fine vestiti di

---

71 Bergamo. Biblioteca Civica Mai. Archivio della Misericordia Maggiore. *Effemeridi*, fol. 64r.
72 Bergamo. Biblioteca Civica Mai. Archivio della Misericordia Maggiore. *Effemeridi*, fol. 63r.

bianco ma però senza croce et tre di loro fecero la disciplina per la processione a carne nuda, dietro a questi seguitavano li ss. Disciplini della Carità che sono vestiti di negro con un capello dietro le spalle et una fiamma sopra il mantelletto negro che portano.[73]

The procession started with the flagellants dressed in green, which are those from the church of San Rocco in the city, and there were also a few at the end dressed in white but without a cross, and three of them mortified their bare skin during the procession; behind them followed the flagellants of the *Carità* who were dressed in black with a hood on their shoulders and [the symbol of] a flame on the short black mantle that they wore.

The procession told the story of the last agonies of Christ, culminating in a dramatisation of the funeral of Christ.[74] Sacred dramaturgy took on heightened significance in early modernity. Religious practices were revisited with a diversity of new *apparati* embedded with religious symbolism and political propaganda. These processions communicated the Passion of Christ by way of sensation, allowing 'people to participate emotionally in the religious tradition's soteriological view of the world'.[75] Indeed, Donnalee Dox and Amber Dunai have observed that the 'Dramatisation of Christianity, whether written for performance in churches, religious houses, or public spaces, offered people the opportunity for an embodied, affective response to the abstraction of theology'.[76] As Verdi Webster has shown for similar practices in Spain, the clothes and the bare skin of flagellants 'offered a visceral spectacle of bodily suffering' that strongly involved the emotional participation of the public.[77] Public participation is highlighted in the 1632 account, which remarks that the Good Friday celebration was 'performed with great participation from the

---

73 Bergamo. Biblioteca Civica Mai. Archivio della Misericordia Maggiore. *Effemeridi*, fol. 62r.
74 On the affective dimensions of flagellation performed as part of public urban events, see Flynn M., "The Spectacle of Suffering in Spanish Streets", in Hanawalt B.A. – Reyerson K.L. (eds.), *City and Spectacle in Medieval Europe*, Medieval Studies at Minnesota 6 (Minneapolis – London: 1994) 153–168.
75 Dox D. – Dunai A., "Sacred Feeling: A Dramaturgy of Medieval Religious Emotion", *Performance Matters* 3.1 (2017) 7–18; see also: Johnson G., "Embodying Devotion: Multisensory Encounters with Donatello's Crucifix in S. Croce", *Renaissance Quarterly* 73.4 (2020) 7–18, here 12–13.
76 Dox, "Sacred Feeling" 9.
77 Verdi Webster, *Art and Ritual* 155.

citizens and with procession and music' ('fatta con grande ricorso di popolo et con processione e musica').[78]

The diarist emphasises the role that music, in particular, played in eliciting audience participation. In the context of sixteenth century Venice, Fenlon foregrounds music, as well as other sensory aspects, as central vehicles through which public participation in ceremonial events was enabled: 'as with so many of the civic and devotional rituals that took place in towns and cities, a form of dialogue between participants and spectators took place, articulated by shared texts underpinned by music'.[79] The music and liturgies performed during the Good Friday procession in Bergamo would have enabled the crowd to participate through singing, chanting, praying and sometimes crying.

The presence of a participatory audience was of political significance. As David Garrioch has shown 'participation in religious services and processions marked by bells and singing helped shape a spiritual community', as well as a sense of communal identity.[80] These religious events elicited the active participation of an audience in order to direct communal devotion not only towards the divine but also towards the religious order running the event. The music, noise, colour, smells and motion of the procession encouraged audience participation through the senses, giving rise to a sensory community established through a shared set of momentary stimuli, which aimed to channel participants and observers alike towards devotion. As Louise Deschryver has argued, 'outward sensory stimuli were believed to directly influence the inner state of devotion'.[81] The sensory experience and devotional impact of the procession would likely have affected many of those involved, from onlookers watching the event pass by, to those walking behind the procession, to the confraternity members and town representatives who were leading the procession. As such, the distinction between 'participants' and 'audience' would thus have been blurred.[82]

---

78   Bergamo. Biblioteca Civica Mai. Archivio della Misericordia Maggiore. *Processione*, fols. 1r–4r.
79   Fenlon, "Urban Soundscapes" 239.
80   Garrioch D., "Sounds of the City: The Soundscape of Early Modern European Towns", *Urban History* 30.1 (2005) 5–25, here 15.
81   Deschryver L., "You Only Die Once: Calvinist Dying and the Senses in Lille and Tournai During the Dutch Revolt", *Early Modern Low Countries* 4.1 (2020) 35–57, here 50.
82   Normore C., *A Feast for the Eyes: Art, Performance, and the Late Medieval Banquet* (Chicago: 2015) 73.

Following the flagellants, the archival sources suggest that an effigy of the deceased Christ was carried on a bier.[83] Verdi Webster highlights the participatory effect of processional sculptures like this, which are not static objects but move through ceremonial space and, as such, do not operate in 'an aesthetic or symbolic space distinct and separate from that of the viewer: instead, their intended effect depends upon a situation in which the observer is literally a participant in the event'.[84] In the 1650 account, this processional sculpture

> fu portata da due sacerdoti [...] vestiti con tonicelle di bianco dietro, essendo avanti a detta bara due chierici con torcette accese e due dietro, venne poi il clero di Santa Maria con la sua croce d'argento davanti essendo i primi li chierici con il loro candelotto per uno, et di poi li musici che cantavano in processione il *Miserere* et il *Popule meus* dietro a questi venivano li sacerdoti cappellani e li residenti con il loro candelotto acceso in mano et erano seguiti da quelli chierici che portavano dodici gran torcie di cera avanti il ss. Sacramento (che fu portato da detto Signor Priore Francesco Basso sotto il baldacchino tra il diacono et il sottodiacono) et detto baldacchino era qui portato da quattro sacerdoti residenti con le cotte et stole bianche [...] dietro al baldacchino vi erano li signori Rettori, signor Camerlengo, Governatore, abati della città curiali et tutti li genilhomini più conspicui della città.[85]

> was carried by two priests [...] wearing short tunics, white behind; in front of the sepulchre two clerics with little lighted torches and two others behind; then came the clergy of Santa Maria Maggiore with their silver cross in front, with first the clerics, each with his own candle, and then the musicians, who were singing the *Miserere* and *Popule meus* in procession, followed by the priests, chaplains, and the residents (chaplains) with their lighted candles in their hands [...] and they were followed by those clerics who were carrying twelve wax torches before the Holy Sacrament (which was carried by the said Prior Francesco Basso under the baldachin between the deacon and the subdeacon) and this baldachin was carried here by four resident priests with white stoles and surplices [...], behind the baldachin were the *Rettori*, the Chamberlain,

---

83 Bergamo. Biblioteca Civica Mai. Archivio della Misericordia Maggiore. *Processione*, fol. 3r; Bergamo. Biblioteca Civica Mai. Archivio della Misericordia Maggiore. *Effemeridi*, fol. 62r.
84 Verdi Webster, *Art and Ritual* 58.
85 Bergamo. Biblioteca Civica Mai. Archivio della Misericordia Maggiore. *Effemeridi*, fol. 63r.

the Governor, the curial abbots of the local parishes, and the most outstanding citizens of the town.

The 1632 document indicates that the bier supporting Christ was surrounded by 'a great quantity of wax torches' ('una grande quantità di torce di cera').[86] Following the effigy was the holy sacrament, displayed in an ostensorium and carried by the prior under a baldachin. This information is reported in both sources. Like the figure of Christ, the holy sacrament was also surrounded by 'a large number of torches' ('un gran numero di torce').[87] In particular, the 1650 account explains that clerics carried twelve large wax torches in front of the holy sacrament.[88] These twelve torches symbolised the twelve apostles who followed Christ in his earthly life. According to the 1650 diary, behind the ostensorium followed the city authorities, then marched all those who were engaged at various levels with the confraternity, priests, clerics, and students of the school run by the confraternity who each carried a lit candle and, finally, the faithful paraded, who, in turn, carried lit candles.[89]

The diarist describes this event as 'one of the noblest conducted in Lombardy for the large amount of music and wax that is used in this procession as well as almost all the windows, walls and doors of the houses through the streets where the procession passes' ('è stimata una delle più nobili che si fanno in Lombardia per la gran quantità di cera che si adopera in detta processione come anche per quasi tutte le fenetre, muri et porte delle case per le strade ove detta processione passa').[90] In addition to light, the candles and torches would have produced a specific smell and generated a sensation of warmth. The vast quantities of candlewax used for the Good Friday procession, combined with the music, created a powerful sensory impact, clearly worthy of commentary. Beyond its religious symbolism, the wax also played a central role in staging the wealth and opulence of the confraternity and, for the 1650 diarist, the confraternity's nobility. Such descriptions invite us to consider candles as material and sensorial objects and to further examine the wider values and associations that may have attached to the material properties of candlewax. Wax was not easily affordable. Private households and even early modern courts would use tallow lamps that burned animal fat rather than candlewax to illuminate their

---

86 Bergamo. Biblioteca Civica Mai. Archivio della Misericordia Maggiore. *Processione*, fol. 3r.
87 Bergamo. Biblioteca Civica Mai. Archivio della Misericordia Maggiore. *Effemeridi*, fol. 62r.
88 Bergamo. Biblioteca Civica Mai. Archivio della Misericordia Maggiore. *Effemeridi*, fol. 63r.
89 Ibidem.
90 Bergamo. Biblioteca Civica Mai. Archivio della Misericordia Maggiore. *Effemeridi*, fol. 64r; a similar description can also be found in Bergamo. Biblioteca Civica Mai. Archivio della Misericordia Maggiore. *Processione*, fol. 3r.

interiors. Wax was therefore often donated to churches, mainly in the form of candles, for special occasions, such as the annual feast days of civic patron saints.[91] The large amount of wax used by the Confraternity of the Misericordia Maggiore for the Good Friday processions in Bergamo thus suggests substantial financial investment in overawing the local populace with a display of wealth and power.

The objects, spaces and performances in and through which the procession occurred thus played a central role in shaping the sensory experience of the event. In the streets and *strettoie*, the acoustic properties of the built environment shaped the ways that sounds were heard, while the flickering lights of torches sensuously reflected on windows and walls. The movement of the procession was accompanied by shifting sound and light, creating an immersive multisensory spectacle.

After winding through the town, the procession ended in the Basilica of Santa Maria Maggiore. The *Tantum Ergo* was performed and the effigy of Christ was placed inside a *machina-sepolcro* that had been expressly constructed for the occasion and installed inside the basilica. It was a wooden temporary architecture of considerable proportions, inside which there were two levels: the *Santissimo* was placed on the top level and the figure of the deceased Christ was placed below. A description of this theatrical structure was recorded by the Augustinian monk Donato Calvi (1613–1678). He described this sepulchre as follows:

> Era della patria antico costume fabbricar in questi giorni, correndo la settimana maggiore in S. Maria Maggiore, superba, e vasta machina di legno, che tutto il sito teneva della Chiesa, verso la parte meridionale, e rappresentava glorioso palazzo, tutto ornato con varie statue d'Angeli, e Profeti al naturale, con pitture, e maestosi colonnati, e al di sopra altiera loggia, che scopriva di dentro il Monte Calvario toccante con le Croci alla sommità della Chiesa, arricchita la nobil mole d'innumerevoli lumi, fra i quali spiccava il lampadario di 365 lumi adorno, che nella sera del Venerdì santo rinovavano li splendori del sole. Nel mezzo poi una capella con maestosa pompa guernita, di cui sopra l'ara si riponeva il Santissimo Sagramento, dopo la processione di detto Venerdì notte, e sotto nell'apparente sepolcro, che si vedeva, la statua rappresentante Christo deposto dalla Croce, che pur in una bara, era stata in processione portata. Degno certo, e

---

91   See Marchand E., "Material Distinctions: Plaster, Terracotta, and Wax in the Renaissance Artist's Workshop", in Anderson C. – Dunlop A. – Smith P. (eds.), *The Matter of Art: Materials, Practices, Cultural Logics, c. 1250–1750* (Manchester: 2015) 160–179, here 167.

maestoso non meno che divoto edificio, che già ogni anno in tal tempo si rinnovava ma che l'anno 1652, per la fabrica della Chiesa tralasciato, hor non più s'ammira che per qualche occasione di quarant'hore.[92]

It was the ancient custom in those days, during Holy Week, to construct in Santa Maria Maggiore, a superb and vast wooden structure that occupied a large area of the Church towards the south, and represented a glorious palace, all adorned with various statues of angels and prophets, with paintings, and majestic colonnades, above which there was a lofty loggia, which displayed the Mount Calvary, [on the top of this structure] there were three crosses, so tall that they almost reached the top of the church. The whole structure was enriched with many lights all around, among them there stood out a chandelier adorned with 365 lights, which, on the evening of Good Friday, renewed the splendours of the sun. In the midst [there was] a chapel, pompously and lavishly decorated, on whose altar the Most Holy Sacrament was kept at night after the procession of the abovementioned Good Friday. Underneath, in the semblance of a sepulchre, there was a statue representing the body of the dead Christ taken down from the Holy Cross, which had been carried around in a coffin in the above-mentioned procession. A worthy structure for sure and no less majestic than devout, [the *machina*-sepulchre] was rebuilt in the church every year at that time, with great effort and diligence, until it was unfortunately no longer constructed after 1652 because of the works undertaken in the church itself, and now can only be admired on some occasions of the Forty Hours' devotion.

The *machina* is described by Calvi as a *palazzo*, a 'palace', articulated in three scenes: Sacrifice (the three crosses on the Calvario); Death (the body of Christ); and Resurrection (the Most Holy Sacrament). Calvi explains: '[…] and they enclosed the body of the dead Christ in the tomb and there, both in the evening and throughout the following day, the sacred tomb and above it the Most Holy Sacrament are continuously visited and adored with the greatest devotion' ('et si racchiude il corpo di Christo morto nel sepolcro et ivi cosí la sera come tutto il giorno seguente, vengono continuamente visitati et adorati la Sacra tomba et sopra di essa il Santissimo Sacramento con grandissima devotione').[93]

92　Calvi Donato, *Effemeride sagro profano di quanto memorabile sia successo in Bergamo*, vol. 1 (Milan, Francesco Vigone: 1676) 368.
93　Bergamo. Biblioteca Civica Mai. Archivio della Misericordia Maggiore. *Processione*, fol. 1r.

In other archival sources the sepulchre is described as a wooden structure in the shape of a colonnaded chapel decorated beautifully with a great number of lamps.[94] The 1650 diary provides more information:

> avanti a detto sepolcro li altri anni si poneva un gran lampadario di ferro pieno di lampadine accese quali illuminavano molto bene tutta la Chiesa perché stava levato in aria molto alto essendo sostenuto da una corda grossa ma perché quasi a ogni hora qualcheduna di quelle lampadine per il troppo calore si rompeva e cascava con l'oglio in terra onde molti veniva a macchiarsi, questi signori questo anno non l'hanno adoperato si che la chiesa usciva un puoco oscura per chè non sta bene perchè vi si ritrovano le donne.[95]

> in front of the sepulchre, in previous years they placed a large iron chandelier with numerous lighted lamps in front of this shrine which lit the whole church extremely well because it was raised high up, suspended by a thick cord. But because almost every hour one of these lamps broke and fell to the ground with its oil due to the intense heat, so that many people got oil on themselves, this year these lords have not used these lamps, so the church became somewhat dark (which is not good because women frequent the church).

The sepulchre encouraged a vertical perspective that was meant to drive the attention of the spectators upwards, in ascension to the Heavenly realm, while music would have echoed across the church. Throughout the seventeenth century, developments in scenic effects and theatrical machines were taking place in the theatre, with *machine* and *apparati* at the centre of artistic growth. Scenography plays a crucial part in this *maraviglia* in a variety of cultural contexts at the time, including Bergamo.[96] The event, with the *machina-sepolcro*, as the apex of the processional performance, had a dramatic emotional impact on the audience: 'and while it delights the sight, and flatters the ear, it steals the heart of the audience' ('e mentre diletta la vista, e lusinga l'udito, a riguardanti rapisce il cuore').[97] Temporary structures like the Good Friday

---

[94] Bergamo. Biblioteca Civica Mai. Archivio della Misericordia Maggiore. 1281 T (1623–1634), fol. 161v.
[95] Bergamo. Biblioteca Civica Mai. Archivio della Misericordia Maggiore. *Effemeride*, fol. 64r.
[96] Fantappiè F., *"Per teatri non è Bergamo sito". La società bergamasca e l'organizzazione dei teatri pubblici tra '600 e '700* (Bergamo: 2010) 41–58.
[97] Calvi, *Effemeride* 368.

machina-sepolcro, along with the candlewax and the investment in music and performance, when combined, were all important tools for participatory devotion, and powerful devices to showcase and promote the confraternity's *magnificenza* and prestige, communicating the appearance of wealth, abundance and divine blessing.

4 Conclusions

Processions organised by the Confraternity of the Misericordia Maggiore in seventeenth century Bergamo were elaborate, multisensory events combining spatial, kinetic, sonic, olfactory and visual dimensions. The sights, sounds and smells that made up the sensoryscape of the Good Friday procession were sure to have made lasting impressions on the citizenry. The first-hand accounts of the singing of music and sounds of liturgy, the pealing of bells, the blazing torch light and smell of melting candlewax, the sight of the flagellated flesh and the colours of the clothes and robes of the priests, priors and brothers, presents the procession as a dense site of sensory experience firmly rooted in urban space. The Good Friday procession was a sensorial entanglement of music, light and architecture that created a unique sensory arena for public devotion and for the expression of the confraternity's own *magnificenza*. Indeed, within the descriptions of the procession recounted here, this sensory experience is inseparably tied to the image and identity of the Confraternity of the Misericordia Maggiore as a wealthy and powerful institution. As Tess Knighton has observed, 'processions turned the whole city into a ceremonial theatre which linked its streets and monuments inextricably with the identity of those responsible for organising and funding the event, be it church, religious community or individual'.[98] In early modern Bergamo, the Good Friday procession becomes a form of sensory propaganda, demonstrating the opulence of the confraternity and reinforcing its political standing within the town. Verdi Webster has highlighted that 'The more intensely and completely the senses could be affected, the more emotionally compelling and successful was the procession'.[99] Sensory engagement was essential to the processional performance and its transformational impact on the spectators, creating a sensory community and enabling these events to function as powerful tools for political and social control.

---

[98] Knighton, *Hearing the City* 12.
[99] Verdi Webster, *Art and Ritual* 156.

While the scope of this chapter was necessarily limited to the Good Friday processions organised in Bergamo by the Confraternity of the Misericordia Maggiore in the seventeenth century, its relevance goes beyond those extraordinary processions, and encourages consideration of early modern sacred and secular rituals as multisensory events through which specific sensory communities were established. A focus on the sensoryscapes of urban processions foregrounds the intra-active relationship between the social, the sacred and the somatic. Such a focus makes room for theorising the embodied, experiential and multisensory dimensions of early modern urban ceremonies and can help to outline the contours of an early modern urban politics of the senses. Through the choreography of processions, the chanting of the liturgy, the performance of music and the orchestration of emotion, the various techniques through which confraternities shaped urban sensual space in order to solicit support for themselves, can be traced. The Good Friday processions in Bergamo, along with other ceremonial events, enveloped an embodied audience within the expansive sensorial field of the Confraternity of the Misericordia Maggiore. Sensory communities were established and brought together in affective and emotion-laden moments of spirituality, and these communities were encouraged to channel their religious and communal devotion towards and through the confraternity.

Bibliography

Primary Sources

Bergamo, Biblioteca Civica Mai, Archivio della Misericordia Maggiore:
  886 *Pro Immunitate ecclesiae.*
  928 *Ristauri.*
  1116 *Processione del Venerdì Santo in città* (1632).
  1, 10. 2/3 *Effemeridi* (1650).
  1280 *Terminationes.*
  1392 *Spese.*
  1677 *Registro delle Lettere.*
  2283 *Musica in S.M.M.*
  228 Capitoli, e oblighi dei Cantori di S.Maria.
Benaglio Marc'Antonio, *Institutione, e Ordini della Misericordia Maggiore di Bergamo* (Bergamo, Valerio Ventura: 1620).
Calvi Donato, *Effemeride sagro profano di quanto memorabile sia successo in Bergamo* vol. 1 (Milan, Francesco Vigone: 1676).

Secondary Sources

Arab R. – Dowd M.M. – Zucker A. (eds.), *Historical Affects and the Early Modern Theatre* (New York: 2015).

Atkinson N., "Seeing Sound: Mapping the Florentine soundscape", in Terpstra N. – Rose C. (eds), *Mapping Space, Sense and Movement in Florence. Historical GIS and the Early Modern City* (Abingdon: 2016) 149–168.

Atkinson N., *The Noisy Renaissance: Sound, Architecture, and Florentine Urban Life* (University Park PA: 2016).

Bryant. D., "The 'cori spezzati' of St Mark's: Myth and Reality", *Early Music History* 1 (1981) 165–186.

Campbell S., *The Endless Periphery: Toward a Geopolitics of Art in Lorenzo Lotto's Italy* (Chicago: 2019).

Carlsmith C., *A Renaissance Education: Schooling in Bergamo and the Venetian Republic, 1500–1650* (Toronto: 2010).

Carver A.F., *Cori Spezzati: The Development of Sacred Polychoral Music to the Time of Schütz* 2 vols. (Cambridge: 1988) vol.1.

Corbin A., *Village Bells: Sound and Meaning in the Nineteenth Century French Countryside* (Paris: 1994).

Cossar R., *The Transformation of the Laity in Bergamo, 1265–c.1400*, The Medieval Mediterranean 63 (Leiden – Boston: 2006).

Costa E., "Tra rito e teatro: l'azione rituale in prospettiva pedagogica", *Comunicazioni Sociali* 2.3 (1985) 75–81.

Crary J., *Suspensions of Perception: Attention, Spectacle, and Modern Culture* (Cambridge MA: 2001).

Deschryver L., "You Only Die Once: Calvinist Dying and the Senses in Lille and Tournai During the Dutch Revolt", *Early Modern Low Countries* 4.1 (2020) 35–57.

Di Bello P. – Koureas G., "Other than the Visual: Art, History and the Senses", in Di Bello P. – Koureas G. (eds.), *Art, History and the Senses: 1830 to the Present* (Surrey: 2010) 1–18.

Di Pasquale M., "Aspetti della pratica strumentale nelle chiese italiane fra tardo medioevo e prima età moderna", *Rivista italiana di musica sacra* 16.2 (1995) 239–268.

Dox D. – Dunai A., "Sacred Feeling: A Dramaturgy of Medieval Religious Emotion", *Performance Matter* 3.1 (2017) 7–18.

Dugan H., *The Ephemeral History of Perfume: Scent and Sense in Early Modern England* (Baltimore: 2011).

Escrivà-Llorca F., "The Procession of the Relics of São Roque (Lisbon, 1588)", in Knighton T. – Mazuela-Anguita A. (eds.), *Hearing the City in Early Modern Europe* (Turnhout: 2018) 229–240.

Fantappiè F., "*Per teatri non è Bergamo sito*". *La società bergamasca e l'organizzazione dei teatri pubblici tra '600 e '700* (Bergamo: 2010).

Fenlon I., *The Ceremonial City: History, Memory and Myth in Renaissance Venice* (New Haven: 2007).

Fenlon I., "Urban Soundscapes", in Fenlon I. – Wistreich R. (eds.), *The Cambridge History of Sixteenth-Century Music* (Cambridge: 2019) 209–259.

Fisher A., "'Mit Singen und Klingen': Urban Processional Culture", in Filippi D. – Noone M. (eds.), *Listening to Early Modern Catholicism: Perspective from Musicology*, Intersections 49 (Leiden – Boston: 2017) 187–203.

Fisher A., *Music, Piety, and Propaganda: The Soundscapes of Counter-Reformation Bavaria* (Oxford: 2014).

Flynn M., "The Spectacle of Suffering in Spanish Streets", in Hanawalt B.A. – Reyerson K.L. (eds.), *City and Spectacle in Medieval Europe*, Medieval Studies at Minnesota 6 (Minneapolis – London: 1994) 153–168.

Garrioch D., "Sounds of the City: The Soundscape of Early Modern European Towns", *Urban History* 30.1 (2005) 5–25.

Gerbino G. – Fenlon I., "Early Opera: The Initial Phase", in Haar J. (ed.), *European Music, 1520–1640* (Woodbridge: 2006) 472–486.

Gowing L., *Common Bodies: Women, Touch and Power in Seventeenth-Century England* (New Haven: 2003).

Halsall F., "One Sense is Never Enough", *Journal of Visual Arts Practice* 3 (2004) 103–122.

Hamilakis Y., "Senses, Materiality, Time. A New Ontology", in *Archaeology and the Senses: Human Experience, Memory, and Affect* (Cambridge: 2014) 111–128.

Hanawalt B.A. – Reyerson K.L, *City and Spectacle in Medieval Europe*, Medieval Studies at Minnesota 6 (Minneapolis – London: 1994).

Harding V., "Introduction: Music and Urban History", *Urban History* 29 (2002) 5–7.

Helmreich S., "Listening Against Soundscapes", *Anthropology News* (December 2010) 10.

Hills H. – Gouk P. (eds.), "Towards Histories of Emotions", in *Representing Emotions: New Connections in the Histories of Art, Music and Medicine* (Aldershot: 2005) 15–34.

Howard D., "Architecture and Invention in Venice and the Veneto in the Later Sixteenth Century", in Israëls M. – Waldman L.A. (eds.), *Renaissance Studies in Honour of Joseph Connors*, Villa i Tatti: The Harvard University Center for Italian Renaissance Studies 29, 2 vols. (Cambridge, MA: 2013) vol. II, 363–372.

Howes D. (ed), *Empire of the Senses: The Sensual Culture Reader* (Oxford: 2005).

Howes D. – Classen C., "The Social Life of the Senses", *Ars Vivendi Journal* 3 (2013) 4–23.

Ingold T., "Against Soundscape", in Carlyle A. (ed.), *Autumn Leaves: Sound and the Environment in Artistic Practice* (Paris: 2007) 10–13.

Johnson G.A., "Embodying Devotion: Multisensory Encounters with Donatello's Crucifix in S. Croce", *Renaissance Quarterly* 73 (2020) 1179–1234.

Johnston A.F., "Introduction", in Johnston A.F. – Hüsken W. (eds.), *Civic Ritual & Drama* (Amsterdam: 1997) 7–14.

Johnston G., "Embodying Devotion: Multisensory Encounters with Donatello's Crucifix in S. Croce", *Renaissance Quarterly* 73.4 (2020) 1179–1234.

Jones C.A., "The Mediated Sensorium", in Jones C.A. (ed.), *Sensorium: Embodied Experience, Technology, and Contemporary Art* (Cambridge MA: 2006) 5–49.

Karim-Cooper F., "The Sensory Body in Shakespeare's Theatres", in Kern-Stähler A. – Busse B. – de Boer W. (eds.), *The Five Senses in Medieval and Early Modern England*, Intersections 44 (Leiden – Boston: 2016) 269–285.

Kendrick R., *The Sounds of Milan, 1585–1650* (Oxford: 2002).

Knighton T., "Foreword", in Knighton T. – Mazuela-Anguita A. (eds.), *Hearing the City in Early Modern Europe* (Turnhout: 2018), 7–15.

Knighton T., "Orality and Aurality: Contexts for the Unwritten Musics of Sixteenth-Century Barcelona", in Knighton T. – Mazuela-Anguita A. (eds.), *Hearing the City in Early Modern Europe* (Turnhout: 2018), 295–308.

Knox G., "The Colleoni Chapel in Bergamo and the Politics of Urban Space", *Journal of the Society of Architectural Historians* 60.3 (2001) 290–309.

Knox G., "The Unified Church Interior in Baroque Italy: S. Maria Maggiore in Bergamo", *The Art Bulletin* 82 (2000) 679–701.

Lauwrens J., "Welcome to the Revolution: The Sensory Turn and Art History", *Journal of Art Historiography* 7 (2012), available at: https://arthistoriography.word press.com/7-dec2012/.

Law J.E., *Venice and the Veneto in the Early Renaissance*, Variorum Collected Studies Series 672 (Aldershot: 2000).

Leppert R., *The Sight of Sound: Music, Representation, and the History of the Body* (Berkeley: 1995).

Little L., *Liberty, Charity, Fraternity: Lay Religious Confraternities in Bergamo in the Age of the Commune* (Bergamo – Northampton: 1988).

Locatelli G., "L'istruzione in Bergamo e la Misericordia Maggiore", *Bergomum* 4 (1910) 57–169.

Marchand E., "Material Distinctions: Plaster, Terracotta, and Wax in the Renaissance Artist's Workshop", in Anderson C. – Dunlop A. – Smith P. (eds.), *The Matter of Art: Materials, Practices, Cultural Logics, c. 1250–1750* (Manchester: 2015) 160–179.

Martín-Moruno D. – Pichel B. (eds.), *Emotional Bodies: The Historical Performativity of Emotions* (IL: 2019).

Meli A., "Bergamo 1650: da un prezioso diario inedito, la processione del Venerdì Santo", *L'Eco di Bergamo* 27 (March 1964).

Muir E. – Weissman R.F.E. "Social and Symbolic Places in Renaissance Venice and Florence", in Agnew J.A. – Duncan J.S. (eds.), *The Power of Place: Bringing Together Geographical and Sociological Imaginations* (Boston: 1989) 81–103.

Muir E., *Civic Ritual in Renaissance Venice* (Princeton: 1981).

Murray J.M, "The Liturgy of the Count's Advent in Bruges, from Galbert to Van Eyck", in Hanawalt B.A – Reyerson K.L. (eds.), *City and Spectacle in Medieval Europe*, Medieval Studies at Minnesota 6 (Minneapolis – London: 1994) 137–152.

Newhauser R., "The Senses in Medieval and Renaissance Intellectual History", *Senses and Society* 5 (2010) 5–9.

Normore C., *A Feast for the Eyes: Art, Performance, and the Late Medieval Banquet* (Chicago: 2015).

Padoan M., *La musica in S. Maria Maggiore a Bergamo nel periodo di Giovanni Cavaccio (1598–1626)* (Como: 1983).

Palisca C., "Prima pratica", *Grove Music Online* (2001), available at: https://doi.org/10.1093/gmo/9781561592630.article.22350.

Pink S., *Doing Sensory Ethnography* (Los Angeles – London: 2009).

Rabaglio M., "Drammaturgia popolare e teatro sacro. Riti e rappresentazioni del Venerdì Santo nel Bergamasco", *Quaderni dell'archivio della cultura di base* 12 (1989) 11–24.

Roche J., "Music at S. Maria Maggiore, Bergamo, 1614–1643", *Music and Letters* 47 (1966) 296–312.

Roodenburg H. (ed.), *A Cultural History of the Senses in the Renaissance* (London: 2014).

Rosenholtz-Witt J., "Musica, crisi, e la politica della riforma a Bergamo nel primo seicento", *Archivio Storico Bergamasco* LXXXV (2023) 423–432.

Rota S., *Per una storia dei rapporti fra Bergamo e Venezia durante il periodo della dominazione: Secoli XV–XVIII* (Bergamo: 1987).

Rudy K.M., *Touching Parchment: How Medieval Users Rubbed, Handled and Kissed their Manuscripts* (Cambridge: 2023).

Samuels D.W. – Meintjes L. – Ochoa A.M. – Porcello T., "Soundscape: Toward a Sounded Anthropology", *Annual Review of Anthropology* 39 (2010) 329–345.

Sanuto Marin, *Itinerario di Marin Sanuto per la terraferma veneziana nell'anno 1483*, ed. R. Brown (Padua: 1847).

Scalvini M.L – Calza G.P., *Bergamo 1516, città e territorio nella 'Descriptio' di Marcantonio Michiel* (Padua: 1984).

Schafer R.M., *The New Soundscape: A Handbook for the Modern Music Teacher* (Scarborough, ON: 1969).

Schafer R.M., *The Soundscape: Our Sonic Environment and the Tuning of the World* (Rochester VE: 1997).

Smith B.R., *The Acoustic World of Early Modern England: Attending to the O-Factor* (Chicago: 1999).

Smith M.M., *Sensory History* (Oxford: 2007).

Smith M.M., "Looking Back: The Explosion of Sensory History", *The Psychologist* 23.10 (2010) 860–863.

Smith M.M., "Producing Sense, Consuming Sense, Making Sense: Perils and Prospects for Sensory History", *Journal of Social History* 40.4 (2007), 841–858.

Southworth M., "The Sonic Environment of Cities", *Environment and Behaviour* 1.1 (1969) 49–70.

Steward J. – Cowan A. (eds.), *The City and the Senses: Urban Culture Since 1500* (Aldershot: 2007).

Strohm R., *Music in Late Medieval Bruges* (Oxford: 1985).

Towne G., "Over the Hills and Far Away: The Place of Bergamo in the Development and Transmission of Polychoral Music", in Folegana L. – Ingesti A. (eds.), *Dal canto corale alla musica policorale* (Padua: 2014) 69–80.

Van Kessel E., "The Making of a Hybrid Body: Corpus Christi in Lisbon, 1582", *Renaissance Studies* 34.4, Special Issue on Visual and Spatial Hybridity in the Early Modern Iberian World (2020) 572–592.

Verdi Webster S., *Art and Ritual in Golden-Age Spain: Sevillian Confraternities and the Processional Sculpture of Holy Week* (Princeton: 1998).

Wheeler J., "Stench in Sixteenth-Century Venice", in Cowan A. – Steward J. (eds.), *The City and the Senses: Urban Culture Since 1500* (Aldershot: 2007) 25–38.

Woolgar C.M., *The Senses in Late Medieval England* (New Haven – London: 2006).

Zizzo G., "S. Maria Maggiore di Bergamo *Cappella della Città*. La basilica bergamasca nei secoli XII e XIII", *Archivio Storico Bergamasco* 2 (1982) 207–229.

CHAPTER 3

Musical Interactions at the Confraternity of Our Lady of the Rosary in Antwerp in the Seventeenth Century

Ana López Suero

Abstract

The Cofradía de Nuestra Señora del Rosario (Confraternity of Our Lady of the Rosary in Antwerp) was founded before 1570 under the aegis of the Duke of Alba. It was one of the many confraternities devoted to the cult of the Virgin of the Rosary that sprang up in Europe as a result of the Counter Reformation. One of its account books, preserved in the State Archive in Antwerp, contains many examples of payments to musicians and for musical works and instruments during the first half of the seventeenth century. However, it has not received due attention until now. Based on the detailed information found there, this paper discusses the instruments commissioned by the institution, the musicians who worked in its service and their ties with other local institutions, the celebrations in which they participated, and the music they performed. Analysis of these accounts placed in context shows that, in addition to being an important patron of music in Antwerp, the Confraternity of Our Lady of the Rosary fostered a fruitful cultural exchange between Flemish and Spanish musicians.

Keywords

Antwerp – cultural exchange – musical interactions – musicians – Rosary

1   Introduction

In St. Paul's Church in Antwerp, a sculpture of the Virgin holding a rosary is set into an ornate altar in one of the pillars. The church, which is known to be the remains of the old Dominican Monastery, is today the seat of the Broederschap van Onze-Lieve-Vrouw van de Heilige Rozenkrans (Confraternity of Our Lady of the Holy Rosary). Supposedly founded in 1571 'in gratitude for the victory' of John of Austria at the Battle of Lepanto,[1] this brotherhood became one of the most popular confraternities in the city in the following decades, although successive riots and fires over the years have erased most traces of its origins. Recent research shows that the Confraternity of Our Lady of the Rosary was closely linked to the Spanish community in Antwerp in the seventeenth century, and played a prominent role in the patronage of the arts in the city.[2] Several researchers have drawn attention to the musical activity associated with the church in which it was based. However, the interactions that took place between Spanish and Flemish musicians within the confraternity have been overlooked.[3]

The important role that brotherhoods played in the expansion of the Spanish empire, in promoting interaction between people of different cultures and in fusing their symbolic representations, has been brought to the fore by Manuel Apodaca Valdez.[4] Though Apodaca Valdes's research focuses on the Hispanic-American colonies, his approach is useful for studying the results of cultural interactions in The Netherlands during the 'Spanish period'

---

1 See the website of the Broederschap van Onze-Lieve-Vrouw van de Heilige Rozenkrans (in English and Dutch) https://www.sintpaulusantwerpen.be/en/parish-liturgy/chapels/holy-mary-of-the-rosary/ [accessed 9 March 2023].
2 Muller J.M., "Communication visuelle et confessionnalisation à Anvers au temps de la Contre-Réforme", *Dix-septième siècle* 240.3 (2008) 441–482, here 469–470.
3 Spiessens G., "Anthonis Vermeeren: Organist en zangmeester van de Antwerpse citadel in de 17e eeuw", *Orgelkunst* 7 (1984) 21–26; Rasch R., *De cantiones natalitiæ en het kerkelijke muziekleven in de Zuidelijke Nederlanden gedurende de zeventiende eeuw* (Utrecht: 1985) 236–238; Schreurs B., *Anthonis Vermeeren (1618–ca. 1685), zangmeester en organist aan de citadel te Antwerpen, en zijn bundel Missae et motetta: op. 3, Antwerpen, Phalesius, 1665* (Bachelor's dissertation, Catholic University of Leuven: 1989); Élissèche C.Y., "Les musiciens et la musique de l'église espagnole d'Anvers, 1568–1681", in Colin M.A. – Corswaren E. – Élissèche C.Y. – Morales J. (dirs.), *Marquer la ville, affirmer l'identité: Musique, dévotion et espaces nationaux (Italie et anciens Pays-Bas espagnols XVIe–XVIIe siècles)* (Brussels: 2022) 65–84.
4 Apodaca Valdez M., *Cofradías Afrohispánicas: Celebración, resistencia furtiva y transformación cultural* (Leiden – Boston: 2022) 2: 'Nos interesa también explorar las representaciones simbólicas de las culturas que interactúan entre sí y que son generadoras de identidades emergentes, de pensamiento y expresiones estéticas. En lo concerniente al discurso sobre las identidades, partimos de la noción antropológica y sociológica de que la identidad es un proceso, nunca una esencia fija. La identidad individual y colectiva es cambiante, producto de las relaciones entre el yo y el Otro, entre la unidad étnica y la diferencia cultural' ('We are also interested in exploring the symbolic representations of cultures that interact with each other and that are generators of emerging identities, thought, and aesthetic expressions. Regarding the discourse on identities, we start from the anthropological and sociological notion that identity is a process, never a fixed essence. Individual and collective identity is changing, as a result of relations between self and Other, between ethnic unit and cultural difference').

(1556–1713). In view of the fact that the city of Antwerp was home to a large Spanish population at the time, questions arise as to the musical relations that developed between Spaniards and Flemings in this context. By examining the festivities celebrated by the Confraternity of Our Lady of the Rosary, the relationships of the musicians who worked in its service, and the music performed in its celebrations, I will show in this chapter how this institution may have been key in the transmission of music between Spanish and Flemish musicians in Antwerp.

2   The Confraternity of Our Lady of the Rosary

Devotion to Our Lady of the Rosary dates back to the early thirteenth century, thanks to Domingo de Guzmán, founder of the Dominican Order. The first confraternity of Our Lady of the Rosary was founded in Cologne in 1475 by the friar Jacob Sprenger. This devotion spread rapidly throughout Europe and was embraced by many lay brothers and sisters from different social layers, from merchants to nobles and royalty. Members of the Habsburg family connected to Spain and the Low Countries, such as Margaret of Austria, Charles V, Mary of Hungary, Philip II and the Archdukes of Austria Albert and Isabel Clara Eugenia, were deeply devoted to the Virgin of the Rosary.

The confraternity became particularly popular in 1571, when Pope Pius V (who was also a Dominican) granted spiritual benefices to all believers who wished to take part in the second Holy League. Shortly afterwards the Battle of Lepanto took place and the Virgin of the Rosary was believed to have interceded for the victory of Christianity. From that time on, she was regarded as the protector of Catholics in their fight against the infidels, be they Turks or Protestants. This association had such an impact on the Spanish army that many confraternities with this advocacy were set up in the parishes of military bases.[5]

2.1   *The Confraternity of Our Lady of the Rosary in Antwerp*
In Antwerp, Our Lady of the Rosary became a powerful confraternity which in the early seventeenth century garnered no fewer than 22,000 members, almost

---

5   Mínguez Cornelles V.M., "'Auxilium Habsburgicum'. La Virgen del Rosario y Lepanto", in Mínguez Cornelles V.M. – Rodríguez Moya I. (dirs.), *La Piedad de la Casa de Austria: arte, dinastía y devoción* (Gijón: 2018) 39–62, here 43, 47; Romero Mensaque C.J., "La universalización de la devoción del Rosario y sus cofradías en España. De Trento a Lepanto", *Angelicum* 90.1 (2013) 217–246, here 242–243.

FIGURE 3.1   Peeter Neeffs (I), *The Interior of the Dominican Church, Antwerp, Looking East, with the Procession of the Holy Sacrament*, painted in 1636. Oil on panel, 67.7 × 105 cm.
Amsterdam, Rijksmuseum
IMAGE © RIJKSMUSEUM

half the inhabitants in the city.[6] It was presumably founded by the friars of the Dominican Monastery in Antwerp.[7] And not inadvertently, a collection of fifteen paintings representing the mysteries of the Rosary made by Peter Paul Rubens, Anton van Dyck, Jacob Jordaens and other Flemish leading painters hung on the walls of the monastery's church as Peter Neefs the younger depicted in 1636 [Fig. 3.1].[8] Some of them are still exhibited today in St. Paul's Church.

---

6   "Rapport adressé au Souverain Pontife, Paul V, par Malderus, évêque d'Anvers, sur l'état de son diocése en 1615", *Analectes pour servir à l'histoire ecclésiastique de la Belgique* 1 (1864) 98–122, here 105–106; Schollier E., "Un indice du loyer. Les loyers anversois de 1500 à 1873", in Fanfani A., *Studi in onore di Amintore Fanfani* I–VI (Milan: 1962), vol. V, 605–617, here 612. Chronologically, the closest reference that Schollier mentions in his study is that of 1612, when Antwerp had a population of 58,918 inhabitants.
7   Hubert J., *Op zoek naar een verdwenen kerk en haar inhoud. Onderzoek naar de kerk van de Antwerpse Citadel (1574–1832)* (Antwerp: 2008) 74–75. The details of the confraternity's foundation are unclear. According to Hubert, a papal bull was bestowed for this purpose on 5 October 1588 to father Nicolaus Neelsius, then provincial of the Dominicans in Low Germany. However, no sources confirming this assertion have been found.
8   Muller, "Communication visuelle" 469.

However, the confraternity's headquarters was placed elsewhere, namely at St. Philip and St. Jacob's Church, the parish of Antwerp Castle. The castle, as it was regularly known, was none other than the fortress ordered to be built in 1567 by the Duke of Alba to host the Spanish army and its retinue [Figs. 3.2 and 3.3]. In St. Philip and St. Jacob's Church there was a chapel named after its founder, Colonel Cristóbal de Mondragón – governor of the castle in 1585–1596 and himself a brother of the confraternity – with an altar dedicated to the Virgin of the Rosary.[9] The Castle's Church was dedicated to Catholic worship from its construction until the city was taken by French troops in the late eighteenth century, except for a period of Protestant rule (1577–1585). Unfortunately, the whole stronghold is disappeared today.

The surviving documentation relating to the confraternity is scarce, but two sources overlooked by previous scholars will form the basis of this study. One of these is the volume *Flor de las Rosas. Tratado de la Cofradía del Rosario*, written by Fernando de Pineda and published by Daniel Vervliet in Antwerp in 1571.

FIGURE 3.2 Theodoor van Thulden, *Locorum insignium ac viae triumphalis qua serenissimus princeps, Ferdinandus Austriacus, Hispaniarum Infans etc. Antverpiam est ingressus, designatio*, engraved in 1639–1641. Paper 45.8 × 76.2 cm. Amsterdam, Rijksmuseum
IMAGE © RIJKSMUSEUM

---

9   Hubert, *Op zoek* 52. The chapel was built to host the Captain's grave and that of his wife. Another altar dedicated to St. Barbara was placed in the same chapel.

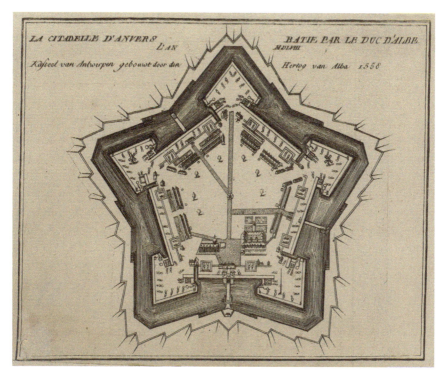

FIGURE 3.3   Anonymous, *La Citadelle d'Anvers batie par de Duc d'Albe l'an MDLVIII*, seventeenth century. Paper 13.7 × 16.9 cm. Leuven, Katholieke Universiteit
IMAGE © KATHOLIEKE UNIVERSITEIT

In his prologue, Pineda dedicated the work to the III Duke of Alba, Fernando Álvarez de Toledo, then governor of the Netherlands and the most distinguished brother of the confraternity.[10] The other source is the only surviving

---

10   Pineda Fernando de, *Flor de las Rosas. Tratado de la Cofradía del Rosario*, "Epístola dedicatoria" (Antwerp, Daniel Vervliet: 1571) without foliation: 'La mucha devoción que tiene a su Cofradía del Rosario se manifiesta en la mucha honra que Vuestra Excelencia le ha hecho escribiéndose por cofrade, en lo que es tan honrada como cuando el Emperador Federico se escribió' ('The great devotion that you have to your Confraternity of the Rosary is shown by the great honour that Your Excellency has done to it by inscribing yourself as a confrere, in which it is as honoured as when Emperor Frederick inscribed himself'). Through Pineda's dedication it is known that the Confraternity of Our Lady of the Rosary in Antwerp was founded long before the Battle of Lepanto, since the license to print and sell the treatise was supplied by the Consejo Real de Flandes on 24 December 1570 and by the Chancillería de Brabante on 13 July 1571. The battle took place in October 1571.

account book of the confraternity; it is written entirely in Spanish and records the expenses of the period 1610–1652.[11]

2.2 The Celebrations of the Confraternity

The Confraternity of Our Lady of the Rosary celebrated a series of feast days every year. The treatise *Flor de las Rosas* shows that the festivities devoted to the Virgin (Candlemas, Annunciation, Assumption and Nativity) were the most important,[12] although the expenses recorded in the account book reveal that large sums of money were also invested in Christmas Eve, Holy Week and Corpus Christi. The ceremonial relating to death was also a major duty for the brothers. A funeral was organised whenever a member died, and if the brother to be honoured was poor, the confraternity would pay for the funeral and, where specified, the musicians.[13] Furthermore, an anniversary for deceased brothers was celebrated after each of the feasts of the Virgin,[14] and a High Mass and a procession were held for the deceased on All Souls' Day and every

---

11　Antwerp. Rijksarchief. Sint-Philippus- en Sint-Jacobuskerk 419. This book is part of a set of six volumes of accounts. The other five books preserved in the same collection with call numbers 409–412 comprise the *gastos* (expenses) and *recibos* (incomes) of St. Philip and St. Jacob's Church in 1662–1718. The book with call number 420 contains expenses of the *Cofradía de las Ánimas del Purgatorio* (Confraternity of the Souls in Purgatory) in 1697–1719. Mistakenly, all the six books were considered by previous scholars to contain expenses of the church. The abbreviations used in this chapter are: *guilder (fl), stuiver (st), placa (pl)*, real (r). 'Placa' is the Spanish word for 'stuiver'. The correspondence is: 1 *guilder* = 20 *stuivers* = 4 *reales* = 136 *maravedís*; 1 *felipe* or *escudo* = 2 *guilders* and 10 *stuivers*; 1 *stuiver* = 6.8 *maravedís*.

12　Pineda, *Flor de las Rosas* 171. The obligation to celebrate these festivities is similar in the constitutions of Confraternities of the Rosary found in other places; see: Romero Mensaque C.J., "Los comienzos del fenómeno rosariano en la España Moderna. La etapa fundacional (siglos XV y XVI)", *Hispania Sacra* 66.2 (2014) 243–278.

13　Antwerp. Rijksarchief. Sint-Philippus- en Sint-Jacobuskerk 419, March 1616: 'Murió Fonseca, soldado de [capitán] Santander, y por no tener con qué enterrarse pagué el felipe que acostumbra a dar la cofradía para la misa y cantores, 10 [rs]'. Translation: 'Fonseca, a soldier of [Captain] Santander, died, and for not having anything for his burial I paid the *felipe* that the brotherhood usually gives for the mass and singers, 10 [rs]'.

14　Antwerp. Rijksarchief. Sint-Philippus- en Sint-Jacobuskerk 419, February 1644. A total amount of 2 *guilders* and 13 *stuivers* was paid for: 'El aniversario que se dijo por los fieles difuntos después de la festividad de la Purificación de Nuestra Señora: al señor capellán mayor por la misa cuatro reales, a cada diácono un real son dos reales, al sacristán un real, al maestro de capilla seis placas, a cada cantor tres placas, al organista cuatro, al alzafuelles dos' ('The anniversary that was said for the faithful deceased after the festivity of the Purification of Our Lady. To the senior chaplain for the mass four *reales*, to each deacon one *real* are two *reales*, to the sacristan one *real*, to the choirmaster six *stuivers*, to each singer three *stuivers*, to the organist four, to the assistant of the bellows two').

Sunday of the year. The feasts of St. Philip, St. Jacob, St. John, St. Cecilia and St. Barbara were also celebrated each year, and processions were held on special occasions, such as the prayers against the plagues that struck the city in 1618 and 1620,[15] and the Jubilee of 1634.[16]

The Virgin of the Rosary was venerated with a High Mass and a procession every 7 October to commemorate the victory at Lepanto. The first procession held in Antwerp for this purpose was immortalised decades later in an engraving in which the Virgin, holding a rosary surrounded by roses, is being carried through the city followed by the most important representatives of the council, the clergy and the guilds [Fig. 3.4]. The etching was made long after the battle, but the report written by the Antwerp merchant Godevaert van Haecht in his diary in November 1571 confirms that the triumph was celebrated with great joy as soon as the news reached the Netherlands:

> Ende op den 15 dach begonden sy, tot Antwerpen 3 daghen lanck alle dagen drymael de groote clocke te luyden ende daerenboven werdt by den magistraet beloven allen ambachten en guldenbroeders haer tegen den 18 dach te bereyden om triomphelyck te vieren en oock allen natiën; ende voer d'eerste deden de papen processie generale met den berrende keersen, daer de Poortugaloysers, Genevoysers en Italianen medegingen. En des avonts werdt generale vieringe gedaen, doer de gansche stat.

> And on 15 [November] in Antwerp they rang the big bell for three days, three times each day, and furthermore, the magistrate ordered all the craftsmen and guild members to prepare for the triumphant celebration on the 18th, and also all the nations. And for the first time the Catholics held a general procession with burning candles, in which Portuguese, Genoese and Italians joined. And in the evening a general celebration was held in the entire city.[17]

---

15 Antwerp. Rijksarchief. Sint-Philippus- en Sint-Jacobuskerk 419, June 1618: 'Viernes 22 de junio se trujeron cuatro cantores de la villa para la misa y procesión general que se hizo por la peste, 2 fl o8 [pl]' ('Friday, 22 June, four singers of the city were brought for the mass and general procession that took place due to the plague, 2 fl o8 [st]').

16 Antwerp. Rijksarchief. Sint-Philippus- en Sint-Jacobuskerk 419, May 1634: 'Pagose a los cantores por cantar la letanía mayor en el Santo Jubileo que se celebró desde 14 hasta 28 de mayo, 3 fl' ('Singers were paid for singing the major rogation on the Holy Jubilee which was celebrated on 14–28 May, 3 fl').

17 Van Roosbroeck R. (ed.), De kroniek van Godevaert van Haecht over de troebelen van 1565 tot 1574 te Antwerpen en elders (Antwerp: 1930) 154–155. I would like to thank Wilbert Hazelzet for kindly translating this text into English.

FIGURE 3.4　Theodoor Galle (attributed to), *Mirakel van de Slag bij Lepanto 1571*, engraved in 1610. Paper 15 × 8.9 cm. Amsterdam, Rijksmuseum
IMAGE © RIJKSMUSEUM

FIGURE 3.5 Conrad Lauwers, *Plattegrond van Scherpenheuvel*, printed in 1661–1669. Paper 44.4 × 46 cm. Amsterdam, Rijksmuseum
IMAGE © RIJKSMUSEUM

Although the scope of this procession in particular covered the entire city, most of the processions organised by the confraternity were probably carried out around the Castle Church, as was the case in other parishes in the city.[18] One of these smaller processions may have been the one taking place every Saturday and the first Sunday of the month in which the rosary was prayed. No record of their route has been found, but the report of a procession held in a similar place may give us an idea. The sanctuary of Our Lady of Scherpenheuvel, founded by Archdukes Albert and Isabel Clara Eugenia in the first decade of the 1600s in the region, was designed similarly to the Spanish Castle in Antwerp [Fig. 3.5].

18 Joukes V., *Processies en ommegangen in Antwerpen in de 17de eeuw* (Bachelor's dissertation, Catholic University of Leuven: 1990) 220.

A procession of the rosary carrying the miraculous image of the Virgin took place around the sanctuary every Sunday of the month.[19]

During one of the Archdukes' visits, the chaplain Philippe Chiflet, who was accompanying them, noted in his diary:

> Après les litanies se fit la procession du rosaire à cause du premier dimanche du mois, ainsy qu'on a accoustumé de le faire tous le premiers dimanches du mois. L'Infante accompagna la procession avec ses dames, en laquelle l'Image miraculeuse de la Vierge fut portée, mais non le Saint Sacrement. Et pendant que la procession se faisait, l'archiduc, pour ses incommodités, estait porté dans un chèse autour de l'église à mesure que la procession faisait un circuit plus grand autour de la ville, de manière qu'il rentrait dans l'église avec la procession.

> After the litanies, the procession of the rosary took place because it was the first Sunday of the month, in the way that it is customary on all the first Sundays of the month. The Infanta accompanied the procession with her ladies, in which was carried the miraculous image of the Virgin, but not the Holy Sacrament. And while the procession took place, the Archduke, because of his infirmities, was carried in a chair around the church at such a speed as to keep pace with the procession making a great circuit around the city, in such a way that he returned into the church with the procession.[20]

The procession described by Chiflet must have followed the path marked D (*platea circularis extra*) around the gardens of the sanctuary, where horse-drawn carriages and people strolling can be seen in the engraving in Figure 3.5. Similarly, the processions in Antwerp Castle must have started from St. Philip and St. Jacob's Church located at the left after the entrance of the fortress, been carried around the centre of the stronghold, and then returned to the church (Fig. 3.6). It is interesting to note that the accounts of the Confraternity show several payments for the maintenance of the trees placed in the path 'along which the procession passes'.[21]

---

19   Lantin A., *Scherpenheuvel: Oord van Vrede* (Retie: 1971) 230.
20   Lantin, *Scherpenheuvel* 237–238. The report is dated 5 May 1619. English translation of the text is extracted from Thøfner M., *A Common Art: Urban Ceremonial in Antwerp and Brussels during and after the Dutch Revolt* (Zwolle: 2007) 293.
21   Antwerp. Rijksarchief. Sint-Philippus- en Sint-Jacobuskerk 419, January 1612: 'Más di a Jacques artillero seis reales para unos árboles para plantar por donde anda la procesión 2

FIGURE 3.6 Frans Hogenberg, *Citadel van Antwerpen, ca. 1570*, engraved ca. 1580–ca. 1635.
Paper 19 × 27.5 cm. Amsterdam, Rijksmuseum
IMAGE © RIJKSMUSEUM

3   The Musicians

The ensemble of musicians that performed in the celebrations of the confraternity varied. A chapel master (*maestro de capilla*), an organist and two singers were paid on a regular basis, although more musicians were hired on particular occasions.

3.1   *The Chapel Masters*

The task of directing the music in the confraternity's celebrations fell to the chapel master. It is likely that the musicians leading the music at the confraternity's events were normally the *maestros de capilla* of the Castle Church, and previous scholars have suggested that this person may also have been

---

fl 13 [*pl*]' ('I gave Jacques the artilleryman six *reales* to plant some trees where the procession goes, 2 *fl* 13 [*pl*]').

responsible for playing the organ.[22] The chapel masters who appear in the records are the singers Bartolomé de Dueñas and Adolphe Lemire and the organist Anthonis Vermeeren, to whom I will refer in the following sections.

3.2 *The Organists*

The first organist of the Castle Church to whom reference is made is Anthoni Everaert. He participated in the events celebrated during the visit of the Duke of Mantua, Vincenzo Gonzaga, to Antwerp in 1599, and he was still holding that position when the organ maker Daniel Bader finished a new instrument for St. Philip and St. Jacob's Church in 1603.[23] Everaert apparently had strong ties to the Castle, since two other persons called by the same name, presumably his son and grandson, appear in the parish's baptismal records throughout the following decades. From 1610 on, the account book of the confraternity mentions an organist called Baldovín.[24] He may have held the position until August 1634, when the confraternity 'brought an organist from the city because the regular one was ill'.[25] In 1648 the organist and master of the singers in the Castle Church was Anthonis Vermeeren (1618–after 1667) of whom several printed works have been preserved. His son Francisco, who was also baptised in the Castle, succeeded him as both director of the musicians and organist between 1702 and 1719.[26]

Although the confraternity seems to have relied mostly on the musicians of the castle, organists working in the service of other institutions may also have taken part in its celebrations. Several payments made in 1610 indicate that a new organ was commissioned to be installed in the chapel where the confraternity had its headquarters. When the instrument was completed a year later, the cathedral organist was asked to examine it.[27] The organist of Antwerp Cathedral at the time was Raymundus Waelrant, the son of the editor,

---

22 Élissèche, "Les musiciens" 69–72.
23 Spiessens G., "*De hertog van Mantua* en de Antwerpse muziek in 1599", in Awouters M. – Ceulemans A.E. (eds.), *Orfeo son io: favola al suono de tutti gli stromenti* (Brussels: 2008) 76–91, here 80; Spiessens G., "Een orgel van Daniel Bader voor de Antwerpse Citadel in 1603", *Adem* 18.5 (1982) 263–264.
24 Antwerp. Rijksarchief. Sint-Philippus- en Sint-Jacobuskerk 419, August 1610.
25 Antwerp. Rijksarchief. Sint-Philippus- en Sint-Jacobuskerk 419, August 1634: 'Al organista que vino de la villa por estar el nuestro enfermo pagué 13 pl' ('To the organist who came from the city because ours was ill, I paid 13 *pl*').
26 Spiessens, "Anthonis Vermeeren" 22.
27 Antwerp. Rijksarchief. Sint-Philippus- en Sint-Jacobuskerk 419, March 1611: 'Al organista de la Iglesia mayor dos florines por la visita del órgano, 2 fl' ('To the organist of the Cathedral, two guilders for the appraisal of the organ, 2 *fl*').

printer and composer Hubert Waelrant (ca. 1517–1595).[28] As Raymundus was the organist of the most prestigious institution in the city, it is not surprising that the confraternity turned to him to assess the new organ. However, the weight of his prestige was not the only reason why the brotherhood sought his services. Indeed, Waelrant's relationship with the castle in Antwerp and the Spanish community in the Netherlands went beyond professional interests. In 1574 he had married Francisca de Aranda, the half-sister of the governor of the Spanish fortress in Ghent and the daughter of a wealthy Spanish merchant who had settled in Antwerp. In addition, his two brothers and one of his nephews had close links with the Spanish army.[29]

3.3 The Singers

The number of singers involved in events organised by the confraternity varied from two to ten, depending on the occasion. They were apparently employed by different institutions of the city, as shown by the payments made to the *cantores de la villa* (singers of the city) on the one hand, and to the *cantores del castillo* (singers of the castle) on the other. The instalments indicate that sometimes they performed together.[30]

The *cantores de la villa* were the so-called *stadsspeellieden* (musicians of the city). They belonged to the Confraternity of St. Job and St. Mary Magdalene, also known as the guild of musicians in Antwerp, which was based at the Collegiate Church of St. Jacob, the most important parish in the city after the cathedral. The *stadsspeellieden* were employed by the city council, but they also worked for a variety of other institutions in Antwerp, both civic and religious.[31] Lemire and Verplanquen were two such musicians (see Table 3.1). Adolphe Lemire was still *cantor de la villa* when he took part in the Tenebrae offices celebrated

---

28 Persoons G., *De orgels en de organisten van de Onze Lieve Vrouwkerk te Antwerpen van 1500 tot 1650* (Brussels: 1981) 82.
29 Weaver R.L., *A Descriptive Bibliographical Catalog of the Music Printed by Hubert Waelrant and Jan de Laet* (Warren MI: 1994) 338–341.
30 Antwerp. Rijksarchief. Sint-Philippus- en Sint-Jacobuskerk 419, December 1620: 'A los cantores de la villa esta noche tres florines para que se entretengan. Más a cuatro cantores cinco florines. A los cantores del castillo, sacristán, organista y su ayudante trece florines y cuatro placas' ('To the singers of the city tonight three *florins* for their entertainment. Plus four singers five *florins*. To the singers of the Castle, the sacristan, the organist and his assistant thirteen *guilders* and four *stuivers*').
31 Spiessens G., "Geschiedenis van de Gilde van de Antwerpse Speellieden, bijgenaamd Sint-Job en Sint-Maria-Magdalena. Inleiding en Deel I: XVIde eeuw", *Revue Belge de Musicologie* 22, 1.4 (1968) 5–50, here 5–8.

by the Confraternity of Our Lady of the Rosary in 1638,[32] and in 1639–1651 he was identified as *phonascus* (master of singing and declamation) in the parish registers of the Castle Church.[33] Likewise, Guilliam Verplancken was listed among the *stadsspeellieden* when he took part in the confraternity's celebrations in January 1649.[34] Later, he appears regularly as the singer Guillermo in the accounts of the Castle Church.[35]

The *cantores del castillo* were presumably the singers in the service of St. Philip and St. Jacob's Church. It is no coincidence that a significant number of Spaniards such as Pedro, Diego, Jerónimo and Bartolomé de Dueñas, Pedro and Diego Gómez, Juan de Lovera and Juan del Hoyo appear in the records of the confraternity in the 1620s. Because of their Spanish names, previous scholars assumed that these singers were in the service of St. Philip and St. Jacob's Church. However, the lack of account books for this parish prior to 1662 makes it impossible to confirm this hypothesis. Moreover, the absence of these names in the records of other parishes or institutions in the city raises the question of whether they were professional singers at all.[36]

The records of the confraternity confirm that soldiers took part in its celebrations.[37] Furthermore, the sacramental acts of the Castle Church show that many of the singers who participated in the celebrations of the confraternity in the first half of the seventeenth century had close links with the Spanish army. Table 3.1 presents a list of all the singers that appear in the confraternity's records. The singers Juan de Lovera and Juan del Hoyo seem to be clearly linked to Lucas de Lovera and Bartolomé del Hoyo, both *alféreces* (ensigns)

---

32 Antwerp. Rijksarchief. Sint-Philippus- en Sint-Jacobuskerk 419, March 1638: 'A dos tiples que asistieron a los misereres y tinieblas toda la cuaresma, 6 fl 10 [pl]. A Lemir cantor de la villa por lo mismo, 5 fl 10 [pl]' ('To two canti who attended the *Misereres* and Tenebrae all Lent, 6 *fl* 10 [*pl*]. To Lemir singer of the city for the same, 5 *fl* 10 [*pl*]').

33 Élissèche, "Les musiciens" 72.

34 Antwerp. Rijksarchief. Sint-Philippus- en Sint-Jacobuskerk 419, January 1649. Guilliam vander Plancken or Vanderplancken is listed among the *stadsspeellieden* in 1644–1651; see: Spiessens G., "Geschiedenis van de Gilde van de Antwerpse Speellieden bijgenaamd Sint-Job en Sint Maria-Magdalena: Deel II: 1600–1650", 28/30 (1974–1976) 24–111, here 56; Spiessens, G., "Geschiedenis van de Gilde van de Antwerpse Speellieden, bijgenaamd Sint-Job en Sint-Maria-Magdalena: Deel III: 1650–1700", *Revue Belge de Musicologie* 36/38 (1982–1984) 88–127, here 105.

35 Antwerp. Rijksarchief. Sint-Philippus- en Sint-Jacobuskerk 410, records from March 1665 on.

36 Rasch, *De cantiones natalitiæ* 238; Élissèche, "Les musiciens" 73. Both Rasch and Élissèche report the low numbers of Spanish musicians in other Antwerpian parishes.

37 Antwerp. Rijksarchief. Sint-Philippus- en Sint-Jacobuskerk 419, April–May 1642. On two occasions, soldier Valera was paid to sing by order of his superiors.

TABLE 3.1 Singers of the Confraternity of Our Lady of the Rosary, 1610–1652

Name	Function	First mention	Last mention
Adrián		March 1635	
Adrián (son of)		March 1643	June 1644
Baldovín (son of)		February 1633	March 1643
Bartolomé *el capón* (the castrato)		April 1612	
Cornelio	cantus	April 1648	January 1649
De Dueñas (Alonso)		April 1612	
De Dueñas, Bartolomé	cantus	December 1620	February 1623
De Dueñas, Diego		May 1610	April 1631
De Dueñas, Jerónimo		May 1623	April 1627
De Dueñas, Pedro		June 1620	April 1634
De Lovera, Juan		December 1627	April 1629
De Perpiñán, Juan	cantus	July 1644	March 1646
Del Hoyo, Juan	cantus	March 1625	June 1642
Escobar, Francisco		December 1630	January 1639
Gómez, Diego (son of Pedro Gómez)	cantus	April 1628	December 1632
Gómez, Pedro		December 1630	April 1637
Gómez, Pedro (son of Pedro Gómez)		April 1632	
Lemire	chapel master	March 1638	
Malagón		March 1625	
Marco Antonio		February 1639	April 1646
Martín	cantus	October 1651	
Navarro		March 1625	
Rueda		March 1625	April 1634
Varela (soldier)		April 1642	May 1642
Verplanquen	cantus	January 1649	

of the castle and majordomos at the confraternity. The brothers Bartolomé, Jerónimo, Diego and Pedro de Dueñas were the sons of Sergeant Alonso de Dueñas. Bartolomé and Jerónimo married in 1614 and 1634, respectively, to Maria van Eyck and Catharina Grison in the St. Philip and St. Jacob's Church.[38]

---

38 Antwerp. Rijksarchief. Parochieregisters San Felipe del Castillo, Huwelijken 17/04/1600–21/11/1637 fols. 117v, 139r, dated 16 September 1614 and 21 January 1634 respectively.

Their father witnessed Bartolomé's marriage, and Diego, the latter's brother, witnessed Jerónimo's when he was a *signifer* (banner bearer) at the castle. Pedro, fourth son of Sergeant Alonso de Dueñas, appears also as a witness at a wedding, and is identified as *sargento* (sergeant).[39]

3.4 Other Musicians

The confraternity's account book also records several payments to trumpeters, dancers, tabrets (players of the pipe and tabor) and minstrels. On Maundy Thursday one or two trumpeters were paid to play in the procession,[40] while a pipe and tabor player was wont to perform in the dances.[41] Dancers would take part in the processions held on the feasts of St. Jacob, the Assumption, the Nativity and Corpus Christi.[42] For the latter they received shoes, bells and clothes every year.[43]

Six minstrels, called *pifaroles* in the records, appear among the staff of the castle as early as 1587.[44] They also served at St. Philip and St. Jacob's Church and the confraternity apparently, and later records suggest that the group remained stable for much of the seventeenth century. Table 3.2 shows the minstrels that were listed in the castle in 1599 and 1664.[45] The information we have about these musicians comes mainly from the city records, as most of them

---

39 Antwerp. Rijksarchief. Parochieregisters San Felipe del Castillo, Huwelijken 17/04/1600–21/11/1637, fol. 136v, dated 29 August 1632.

40 Antwerp. Rijksarchief. Sint-Philippus- en Sint-Jacobuskerk 419, April 1618: 'A la trompeta un florín' ('To the trumpeter, one *guilder*').

41 Antwerp. Rijksarchief. Sint-Philippus- en Sint-Jacobuskerk 419, August 1623: 'Di dos florines para el tamboril y flauta en la danza que hubo el día de la fiesta de la Asunción de Nuestra Señora' ('I gave two *guilders* for the pipe and tabor at the dance on the feast of the Assumption of Our Lady').

42 Antwerp. Rijksarchief. Sint-Philippus- en Sint-Jacobuskerk 419: see the payments in July 1619; September 1619; August 1623; August 1636; and April 1644.

43 Antwerp. Rijksarchief. Sint-Philippus- en Sint-Jacobuskerk 419, May 1611: 'Más pagué catorce zapatos a quince placas el par, nueve a los danzantes, dos al pífano y tamborino, dos a los ángeles y uno al diablo' ('I paid fourteen shoes at fifteen *stuivers* each pair, nine [*stuivers*] to the dancers, two to the pipe and tabor, two to the angels and one to the devil').

44 Spiessens, "De hertog" 86; Élissèche, "Les musiciens" 77. A copy of the staff of the castle in 1587 is found in Antwerp. Felix Archief. Parochieregister 168, fol. 186r. In the list of menials, a salary for 6 unidentified *pifaroles* is considered: 'Para 6 pifaroles o músicos diez y ocho escudos. Seis a cada uno [sic]' ('For six pifaroles or musicians eighteen escudos. Six for each one [sic]').

45 Names in the right-hand column have been corrected according to the document 'Lista de los músicos y pifaroles que sirven en el Castillo de Amberes y capilla de San Felipe 1664' ('List of musicians and *pifaroles* who serve at Antwerp Castle and St. Philip's chapel 1664') (Antwerp. Felix Archief. Parochieregister 168, fol. 186v).

TABLE 3.2   Minstrels at Antwerp Castle

Minstrels 1599	Minstrels 1664
Bommaerts, Baltazar	Bommaert, Gerardo
Bommaerts, Bernaert	Collaert, Joannes
Cremers, Franchoys	Delft, Joannes van
Cremers, Steven	Goubaux, Francisco (substituted by Joannes van Delft)
Stockelmans, Frederick	Haes, Christianus
Verbraken, Gillibert	Halbos, Juan Baptista
	Michielssen, Ignatio

were registered at the Confraternity of Saint Job and Saint Mary Magdalene as well. Gillibert Verbraken is listed in the records of the musicians's guild in 1564–1593.[46] Verbraken's son, who bore the same name, became a protégé of the guild in 1609. Franchoys Creemers is inscribed from 1568 and his son Steven is found in the guild still in 1618.[47] Similarly, the brothers Bernaert and Baltazar Bommaerts and their descendants appear in the registers of the *stadsspeellieden* at least until 1641.[48] At the same time, the Bommaerts family seems to have held a continuous relationship with the Castle, as evidenced by the presence of Gerardo Bommaert among the minstrels registered there in 1664.

Juan Baptista Halbos (ca. 1620–1676) is first mentioned in the records of St. Philip and St. Jacob's Church in 1643, when he became the godfather to one of the daughters of Adolphe Lemire, then the *phonascus* of the Castle Church.[49] Apparently he was singer there between 1653 and 1663,[50] so it is not surprising that his eldest son Juan Bautista, born in 1645, entered the service of the Spanish fortress as a minstrel by 1664. Halbos the elder was also the compiler of *Vermaeckelycke Duytsche Liedekens met III. IV. V. stemmen*, a collection of songs in which there are some references to Spanish personalities

---

46   Spiessens G., "Gillis van Gewelde alias vander Locht: een Antwerps stadsspeelman en instrumentenbouwer (vòòr 1602–na 9 mei 1648)", *Celesta* 8.3 (1994) 120–128, here 121.
47   Spiessens, G., "Lenaert van Hove: Een Belhamel in een Antwerpse Dans- en Muziekschool bij het begin van de XVIIde eeuw", *Antwerpen* 14 (1968) 100–117, here 114.
48   Spiessens, "Geschiedenis [...] Deel II: 1600–1650" 110–111.
49   Antwerp. Rijksarchief. Parochieregisters San Felipe del Castillo, doopakten 01/01/1638–27/04/1658, fol. 179r, dated 27 February 1643.
50   Spiessens G., "Jan-Baptist Halbos en zijn bundel 'Duytsche Leidekens' (1663)", *Volkskunde* 103.2 (2002) 125–140, here 132.

and victories of the time.[51] The collection was dedicated to his friend Johannes Collaert (fl. 1628–1665), presumably the father of the minstrel known by the same name who worked at the castle in 1664. Collaert the elder may well have had a tight relationship with the Spanish community as well, since, at least in 1652, he was holding the position of *phonascus* at St. George's Church,[52] the parish where Spaniards in Antwerp were administered their sacraments before the Castle Church was built.

4   The Music

The confraternity often commissioned music books. Table 3.3 presents the entries in the account book relating to these commissions.[53] Unfortunately, the descriptions in the account book do not provide enough information to identify the works with certainty, although the surviving works of the musicians associated with St. Philip and St. Jacob's Church can provide some insight into the music that was performed in the confraternity's celebrations.

Although no music by Anthoni Everaerts, Bartolomé de Dueñas and Adolphe Lemire has survived, three collections of Masses and several motets by Anthonis Vermeeren have been preserved [Fig. 3.7].[54] His third book *Missae et motetta V. VI. VII. VIII. X. XI. XII. tam vocibus quam instr. Decantandae* (Antwerp, heirs of Phalesius: 1665) contains works for up to six voices and six instruments. His music was regularly performed in the other parishes of

---

51 *Vermaeckelycke Duytsche Liedekens met III. IV. V stemmen, van verscheyden vermaerde meesters van desen tijdt, by een vergadert door Ioannes Baptista Halbos* [...] (Antwerp, heirs of Petrus Phalesius: 1663); Spiessens, "Jan-Baptist Halbos" 125–140. See the songs 'Haes op van Valencijn' and 'Quevedo' by Philippus van Steelant (1611–1670).

52 Beghein S., *Kerkmuziek, consumptie en confessionalisering: het muziekleven aan Antwerpse parochiekerken c. 1585–1797* (Ph.D. dissertation, University of Antwerp: 2014) 206.

53 All records are extracted from Antwerp. Rijksarchief. Sint-Philippus- en Sint-Jacobuskerk 419.

54 *Missae et motetta I. II. III. IV. vocum cum instrumentis auctore Antonio Vermeren, phonasco et organista in Castro Antverpiano* (Antwerp, heirs of Petrus Phalesius, 1660); *Missae et motetta V. VI. VII. VIII. X. XI. XII. tam vocibus quam instrumentis decantandae, authore Anthonio Vermeeren, phonasco et organista in Castro Antverpiano*, liber tertius (Antwerp, heirs of Petrus Phalesius: 1665); *Missae et motetta I. II. III. IV. vocum cum instrumentis* [...] (Antwerp, heirs of Petrus Phalesius: 1668). Four more motets are included in *Florida verba; a celeberrimis musices auctoribus binis, ternis, quaternis, quinisque tam vocibus quam instrumentis; suavissimis modulis concinnata* (Antwerpen, heirs of Petrus Phalesius: 1661).

TABLE 3.3   Books acquired by the Confraternity of Our Lady of the Rosary, 1610–1652

Description		Date
De seis libros de canto para cantar las magníficats en la iglesia, un florín y cinco placas.	For six books of chant to sing the Magnificats in the church, 1 *guilder* and 5 *stuivers*.	May 1613
Por cuatro libros que se compraron para la iglesia, que fue un gradual y un antifonar y dos manuales pagué noventa y seis reales.	For four books that were bought for the church; they were one gradual and one antiphoner and two manuals, I paid 96 *reales*.	March 1617
De siete libros de música, siete florines.	For seven music books, 7 *guilders*.	January 1619
De unos libros de música cinco florines.	For some music books, 5 *guilders*.	January 1622
Compráronse unos libros de canto para el coro y se encuadernó otro viejo que estaba en el mismo coro. Pagué por todo dos florines [y] 6 placas.	Some books of chant for the choir were bought and another old [book] that was in the choir was bound. I paid for everything 2 *guilders* and 6 *stuivers*.	February 1627
Compráronse ocho libros de música para el coro 2 fl.	Eight music books were bought for the choir, 2 *guilders*.	June 1630
Compráronse nueve cuerpos de libros de canto para el servicio del coro. Pagose por ellos cinco florines.	Nine volumes of chant books for use of the choir were bought for five *guilders*.	April 1633
Por nueve cuerpos de libros de música y uno mayor para el órgano pagué, 2 fl 15 [placas].	For nine volumes of music books for the choir and a large one for the organ, I paid 2 *guilders* and 15 *stuivers*.	February 1634
De encuadernar trece libros de música quince placas.	For binding thirteen music books, fifteen *stuivers*.	September 1634
De seis libros de la magnífica, 1 fl 12 [placas].	For six books of Magnificats, 1 *fl* and 12 *stuivers*.	January 1635
De unos libros de música, 2 fl 2 [placas].	For some music books, 2 *gilders* and 2 *stuivers*.	January 1635
De unos libros de música para las misas cantadas, 1 fl.	For some music books for sung Masses, 1 *guilder*.	December 1640

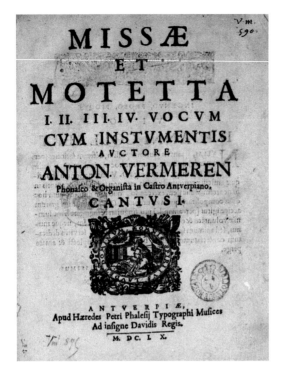

FIGURE 3.7
Anthonis Vermeeren, *Missae et motetta I. II. III. IV. vocum cum instrumentis auctore Antonio Vermeren, phonasco et organista in Castro Antverpiano* (Antwerp, heirs of Petrus Phalesius: 1660), front page. Paris, Bibliothèque nationale de France
IMAGE © BNF

Antwerp until well into the eighteenth century and was also widely distributed in the region and abroad.[55]

Furthemore, the confraternity often asked the *maestros de capilla* to compose villancicos for Christmas and Misereres for Lent.[56] The Spanish villancico was certainly well known in the city after the publication of Pedro Ruimonte's *Parnaso español de madrigales y villancicos* (Antwerp, Pierre Phalèse: 1614). At the same time, a genre comparable to the Spanish villancico, called the cantio natalitia, became extremely popular in the southern Netherlands during the seventeenth century, especially in Antwerp. Like the villancicos, the cantiones natalitiae were songs consisting of a series of stanzas with refrain, written

---

55 Spiessens, "Anthonis Vermeeren" 24. Spiessens reports having found exemplars of Vermeeren's works in the inventories of the following parishes: St. Jacob, St. Andrew (Antwerp), Our Lady (Huy), St. Walburga (Oudenaarde), St. Salvator (Ghent) and St. Mary (Lübeck).

56 Antwerp. Rijksarchief. Sint-Philippus- en Sint-Jacobuskerk 419, December 1615: 'Se dio al maestro de capilla dos florines por los villancicos que compuso' ('The choirmaster was given two *guilders* for the villancicos he composed'; March 1633): 'Al maestro de capilla por los misereres y Semana Santa cuatro florines' ('To the choirmaster for the Misereres and Holy Week four *guilders*').

in Latin or Dutch, and composed specifically for Christmas Eve. Anthonis Vermeeren composed at least two of these songs that have been preserved as loose sheets.[57] Given that the villancico and the cantio natalitia had many features in common, it is highly likely that the term villancico was used in the confraternity's ledger to refer to both the Spanish and Flemish styles of song.

The Misereres composed for the confraternity may also have been in line with local practices. Guido Persoons has argued that the motets at Antwerp Cathedral were regularly performed with one or two *canti* singing as one voice in unison while the organist embellished one of the remaining voices with an improvised canon. This hypothesis, he suggested, would explain the compilation of one hundred and twenty canons, all based on the cantus firmus 'Miserere mihi domine', preserved in Vienna 17771 as exercise material for such canonic improvisations.[58]

Indeed, this manuscript is attributed to the English virginalist John Bull who, after fleeing from England because of his Catholic faith, had first served the Archdukes Albert and Isabel Clara Eugenia in Brussels in the early 1610s, and then in Antwerp Cathedral in 1615–1628. Cathedral practices may have pervaded the Castle walls since, perhaps not by coincidence, one or two *canti* (who happened normally to be *cantores de la villa*) were hired each year by the Confraternity of Our Lady of the Rosary to sing a Miserere every Friday during Lent.[59] Indeed, a small harpsichord was acquired for these performances,[60] so it would not be surprising if the confraternity also used Bull's services.

5 Conclusions

The Confraternity of Our Lady of the Rosary was one of the most popular brotherhoods in Antwerp and a prominent music sponsor in the city. It had a rich activity within the castle walls, but it was also highly active in the city as revealed by the high number of brothers inscribed. It is likely that the citizens in Antwerp recognised the music performed in the numerous liturgical

---

57   Rasch, *De cantiones natalitiæ* 94.
58   Persoons, *De orgels* 264; Vienna, Österreichische Nationalbibliothek, Mus.Hs.17771; accessible online at https://digital.onb.ac.at/RepViewer/viewer.faces?doc=DTL_4667927 &order=1&view=SINGLE (accessed 26 March 2023).
59   Antwerp. Rijksarchief. Sint-Philippus- en Sint-Jacobuskerk 419, March 1616, March 1617, March 1618, March 1619, March 1622, March 1624, March 1639, March 1643.
60   Antwerp. Rijksarchief. Sint-Philippus- en Sint-Jacobuskerk 419, April 1620: 'Se ha traído una libra de incienso y un clavicordio que se hizo para los misereres, dos florines' ('A pound of incense was brought and a clavichord that was made for the *Misereres*, two *guilders*').

offices and processions celebrated by this institution, with which many of them presumably felt identified regardless of their origin. The musicians hired by the confraternity were strongly linked to the institutions of the city, but also to the Spanish community, including the army, with which they shared both professional and personal ties. The interactions of these musicians may have promoted the transmission of repertories between Spain and the Netherlands, although further research into their music is still needed to know more about the ramifications of their encounters.

Bibliography

Primary Sources

Florida verba; a celeberrimis musices auctoribus binis, ternis, quaternis quinisque tam vocibus quam instrumentis; suavissimis modulis concinnata (Antwerp, heirs of Petrus Phalesius: 1661).

Missae et motetta I. II. III. IV. vocum cum instrumentis auctore Antonio Vermeren, phonasco et organista in Castro Antverpiano (Antwerp, heirs of Petrus Phalesius: 1660).

Missae et motetta V. VI. VII. VIII. X. XI. XII. tam vocibus quam instrumentis decantandae, authore Anthonio Vermeeren, phonasco et organista in Castro Antverpiano, liber tertius (Antwerp, heirs of Petrus Phalesius: 1665).

Missae et motetta I. II. III. IV. vocum cum instrumentis auctore Antonio Vermeren, phonasco et organista in Castro Antverpiano (Antwerp, heirs of Petrus Phalesius: 1668).

Pineda F., *Flor de las Rosas. Tratado de la Cofradía del Rosario* (Antwerp, Daniel Vervliet: 1571).

Vermaeckelycke Duytsche Liedekens met III. IV. V stemmen, van verscheyden vermaerde meesters van desen tijdt, by een vergadert door Ioannes Baptista Halbos [...] (Antwerp, heirs of Petrus Phalesius: 1663).

Secondary Sources

[Anonymous], "Rapport adressé au Souverain Pontife, Paul V, par Malderus, évéque d'Anvers, sur l'état de son diocése en 1615", *Analectes pour servir à l'histoire ecclésiastique de la Belgique* 1 (1864) 98–122.

Apodaca Valdez M., *Cofradías Afrohispánicas: Celebración, resistencia furtiva y transformación cultural* (Leiden – Boston: 2022).

Awouters M. – Ceulemans A.E. (eds.), *Orfeo son io: favola al suono di tutti gli stromenti* (Brussels: 2008).

Beghein S., *Kerkmuziek, consumptie en confessionalisering: het muziekleven aan Antwerpse parochiekerken c. 1585–1797* (Ph.D. dissertation, University of Antwerp: 2014).

Colin M.A. – Corswaren E. – Élissèche C.Y. – Morales J. (dirs.), *Marquer la ville, affirmer l'identité: Musique, dévotion et espaces nationaux (Italie et anciens Pays-Bas espagnols XVIe–XVIIe siècles)* (Brussels: 2022).

Élissèche C.Y., "Les musiciens et la musique de l'église espagnole d'Anvers, 1568–1681", in Colin M.A. – Corswaren E. – Élissèche C.Y. – Morales J. (eds.), *Marquer la ville, affirmer l'identité: Musique, dévotion et espaces nationaux (Italie et anciens Pays-Bas espagnols XVIe–XVIIe siècles)* (Brussels: 2022) 65–84.

Hubert J., *Op zoek naar een verdwenen kerk en haar inhoud. Onderzoek naar de kerk van de Antwerpse Citadel (1574–1832)* (Antwerp: 2008).

Joukes V., *Processies en ommegangen in Antwerpen in de 17de eeuw* (Bachelor's dissertation, Catholic University of Leuven: 1990).

Lantin A., *Scherpenheuvel: Oord van Vrede* (Retie: 1971).

Mínguez Cornelles V.M., "'Auxilium Habsburgicum'. La Virgen del Rosario y Lepanto", in Mínguez Cornelles V.M. – Rodríguez Moya I. (eds.), *La Piedad de la Casa de Austria: arte, dinastía y devoción* (Gijón: 2018) 39–62.

Mínguez Cornelles V.M. – Rodríguez Moya I. (eds.), *La Piedad de la Casa de Austria: arte, dinastía y devoción* (Gijón: 2018).

Muller J.M., "Communication visuelle et confessionnalisation à Anvers au temps de la Contre-Réforme", *Dix-septième siècle* 240.3 (2008), 441–482.

Persoons G., *De orgels en de organisten van de Onze Lieve Vrouwkerk te Antwerpen van 1500 tot 1650* (Brussels: 1981).

Rasch R., *De cantiones natalitiæ en het kerkelijke muziekleven in de Zuidelijke Nederlanden gedurende de zeventiende eeuw* (Utrecht: 1985).

Romero Mensaque C.J., "La universalización de la devoción del Rosario y sus cofradías en España. De Trento a Lepanto", *Angelicum* 90.1 (2013) 217–246.

Romero Mensaque C.J., "Los comienzos del fenómeno rosariano en la España Moderna. La etapa fundacional (siglos XV y XVI)", *Hispania Sacra* 66.2 (2014) 243–278.

Schollier E., "Un indice du loyer. Les loyers anversois de 1500 à 1873", in Fanfani A., *Studi in onore di Amintore Fanfani*, vols. I–VI (Milan: 1962) V, 605–617.

Schreurs B., *Anthonis Vermeeren (1618-na 1685), zangmeester en organist aan de citadel te Antwerpen, en zijn bundel Missae et motetta: op. 3, Antwerpen, Phalesius, 1665* (Bachelor's dissertation, Catholic University of Leuven: 1989).

Spiessens G., "Geschiedenis van de Gilde van de Antwerpse Speellieden, bijgenaamd Sint-Job en Sint-Maria-Magdalena. Inleiding en Deel I: XVIde eeuw", *Revue Belge de Musicologie* 22, 1.4 (1968) 5–50.

Spiessens G., "Lenaert van Hove: Een Belhamel in een Antwerpse Dans- en Muziekschool bij het begin van de XVIIde eeuw", *Antwerpen* 14 (1968) 100–117.

Spiessens G., "Geschiedenis van de Gilde van de Antwerpse Speellieden bijgenaamd Sint-Job en Sint Maria-Magdalena: Deel II: 1600–1650", 28/30 (1974–1976) 24–111.

Spiessens G., "Een orgel van Daniel Bader voor de Antwerpse Citadel in 1603", *Adem* 18.5 (1982) 263–264.

Spiessens G., "Anthonis Vermeeren: Organist en zangmeester van de Antwerpse citadel in de 17e eeuw", *Orgelkunst* 7 (1984) 21–26.

Spiessens G., "Geschiedenis van de Gilde van de Antwerpse Speellieden, bijgenaamd Sint-Job en Sint-Maria-Magdalena: Deel III: 1650–1700", *Revue Belge de Musicologie* 36/38 (1982–1984) 88–127.

Spiessens G., "Gillis van Gewelde alias vander Locht: een Antwerps stadsspeelman en instrumentenbouwer (vòòr 1602–na 9 mei 1648)", *Celesta* 8.3 (1994) 120–128.

Spiessens G., "Jan-Baptist Halbos en zijn bundel 'Duytsche Liedekens' (1663)", *Volkskunde* 103.2 (2002) 125–140.

Spiessens G., "De hertog van Mantua en de Antwerpse muziek in 1599", in Awouters M. – Ceulemans A.E. (eds.), *Orfeo son io: favola al suono de tutti gli stromenti* (Brussels, 2008) 76–91.

Thøfner M., *A Common Art: Urban Ceremonial in Antwerp and Brussels during and after the Dutch Revolt* (Zwolle: 2007).

Van Roosbroeck R. (ed.), *De kroniek van Godevaert van Haecht over de troebelen van 1565 tot 1574 te Antwerpen en elders* (Antwerp: 1930).

Weaver R.L., *A Descriptive Bibliographical Catalog of the Music Printed by Hubert Waelrant and Jan de Laet* (Warren MI: 1994).

CHAPTER 4

Sound and Confraternal Piety in Early Modern Leuven

Henry Drummond

Abstract

Central to Leuven's religious life during the early modern era was the cult of the *Sedes sapientiae*, or the Virgin Mary embodied as the Seat of Wisdom. This chapter considers the *Sedes sapientiae*'s musical dimensions, focussing on the activities that took place at the cult's shrine in Leuven's main church, the Sint-Pieterskerk. Although most relevant archival sources were lost in the twentieth century, some early modern documents survive, including confraternal and ecclesiastical records that escaped the scrutiny of twentieth-century scholars. These sources describe the singing of liturgical chant at Mary's altar and offer rare perspectives on regulations that proscribed against specific types of confraternal sound within the Sint-Pieterskerk's shared sonic environment. These sources not only comment on sound's role as a tool to reinforce confraternal devotion; they also reflect upon other sensory stimuli – sight and scent – which, together with the sounds of confraternal activity, help demarcate social space. Sound comes to the fore as a social tool, navigating its way between prescribed liturgy and communal devotion, aiding early modern communities declaim both confraternal piety and civic autonomy.

Keywords

confraternity – sound – music – liturgy – urban studies – sensory history

Like most urban landscapes across early modern Europe, Leuven was one shaped by the societal force of the confraternity. Confraternities emerged as a key social component of late medieval and early modern cities. Founded to promote specific causes of piety – usually in favour of one or several saints – confraternities consisted of both lay and religious members, and often included powerful nobility, aristocracy, leaders of Europe's premier religious houses and the educated elite. Leuven's confraternal landscape was no exception, and the city boasted a significant number of organisations resident at its many churches. Confraternities' contributions to the social engines of northern French and Low Countries urban centres have been the recent focus of numerous ground-breaking studies. For the scope of this chapter, both Sarah A. Long's work (concerning Paris and Tournai) and Paul Trio's (for Ghent and the rest of Flanders) are particularly relevant.[1] Both have considered the complex features of confraternal life, and from a rich interdisciplinary perspective. Long's close study of musical book ownership has demonstrated the innovations in music production within urban confraternities.[2] Central to Long's argument is the function of musical books as material objects, the trade and dissemination of which played a central role in artistic activity in urban centres.

This chapter takes consideration of music and musical objects one step further, arguing that they can be viewed as an intrinsic part of a material culture. This material culture is particularly apparent when musical performance is tied up with transfers of goods and money, usually through confraternity members' legacies or bequests. The goals of these transfers were manifold. First, they were transactions of a religious nature. Money transferred for the purpose of musical performance functioned like any other material bequest within a confraternity. These bequests were enacted with the promise of a spiritual benefit, such as reduced time in purgatory. Second, and no less important, is their societal function. Music, just like more tangible objects, paid testament to a confraternity's wealth, generosity, and devotion. Music therefore showcased a confraternity and its members' social standing, influence, and prestige. In his studies of Flemish cities in the fifteenth century, Matthew Champion has questioned twentieth-century scholars' preoccupations with a 'disenchanted and secular modernity'.[3] Early modern religious attitudes did not necessarily make any distinction between the sacred and the secular.[4] Yet it is still worth

---

1 Long S.A., *Music, Liturgy, and Confraternity Devotions in Paris and Tournai, 1300–1550*, Eastman Studies in Music (Rochester NY: 2021); Trio P., "Confraternities as Such, and as a Template for Guilds in the Low Countries During the Medieval and the Early Modern Period", in Eisenbichler K. (ed.), *A Companion to Medieval and Early Modern Confraternities* (Leiden: 2019) 23–44 (Brill's Companions to the Christian Tradition); and idem, *Volksreligie als spiegel van een stedelijke samenleving: de broederschappen te Gent in de late middeleeuwen* (Leuven: 1993). For further studies of Low Countries confraternities, see Haggh B. – Trio P., "The Archives of Confraternities in Ghent and Music", in Haggh B. – Daelmans F. – Vanrie A. (eds.), *Musicology and Archival Research* (Brussels: 1994) 44–90.
2 Long, *Music, Liturgy, and Confraternity Devotions*, especially chapters 4–5 (46–208).
3 Champion M.S., *The Fullness of Time: Temporalities of the Fifteenth-Century Low Countries* (Chicago IL – London: 2017) 6.
4 Newman B., *Medieval Crossover: Reading the Secular against the Sacred* (Notre Dame IN: 2013).

noting that confraternity membership was often directed by non-religious factors, such as influence, prestige and the accumulation of material wealth.[5] In this chapter, I will consider how music works as a material good, bolstering a confraternity's and its members' prestige through its sensory effects on listeners within a devotional space, while also fulfilling religious functions as a gesture of civic piety.[6]

This chapter addresses the role of sound and music in confraternal worship at Leuven's most important religious building, the Sint-Pieterskerk.[7] While recent studies have examined the Sint-Pieterskerk's confraternities, music's function in their devotion has not been substantially addressed. What this chapter shows, however, is that music and sound formed a key component of confraternal activity, as both a manifestation of material culture and as a means through which organisational space, identity and influence were conveyed. Specific focus is given here to one of the Sint-Pieterskerk's most prestigious organisations, the Confraternity of Our Lady. Leuven was famous in the early modern era for its prominent cult of the Virgin Mary, which celebrated her associations with heavenly wisdom. While links between Mary and wisdom were by no means unique, Leuven's cult was particularly apposite given its importance as a university town from the fifteenth century onwards.[8]

The city's devotion towards the Virgin made the Confraternity of Our Lady a leading organisation, one that attracted a long list of ordinary townsfolk in its ranks. The confraternity was socially prestigious, too, including amongst its several hundred members a selection of society's most eminent figures from the early modern Low Countries. With this membership came bequests of

---

5 On the increasing importance of lay or secular priorities within confraternities, see Trio P., "Lay Persons in Power: The Crumbling of the Clerical Monopoly on Urban Devotion in Flanders, as a Result of the Rise of Lay Confraternities in the Late Middle Ages", in Black C. – Gravestock P. (eds.), *Early Modern Confraternities in Europe and the Americas* (London: 2006) 53–63; P. Trio, "Les confréries des Pays-Bas face au problème de la pauvreté, xvème–xvième siècle", in Lenoci L.B. (ed.), *Confraternite, chiesa e società* (Fassano: 1994) 277–288.
6 The research for this essay was undertaken while I was employed as a Senior Postdoctoral scholar funded by KU Leuven, the Alamire Foundation and the Fonds Wetenschappelijk Onderzoek – Vlaanderen (FWO).
7 For the most recent comprehensive study of the church building and its institutions throughout history, see Dewilde B. – Huybens G. – Mellaerts D. (eds.), *De Sint-Pieterskerk te Leuven: geschiedenis, architectuur en patrimonium* (Leuven: 2022).
8 Note that the university was suppressed in 1797 when Belgium was integrated into the French Republic; see: Roegiers J. – Lamberts E. (eds.), *Leuven University, 1425–1985* (Leuven: 1990) 31. For similar closures of the city's religious buildings, see Maesschalck E. de, *Overleven in revolutietijd: een ooggetuige over het Franse bewind, 1792–1815* (Leuven: 2003) 24–26. For a general overview of France's annexation of the region, see: Hasquin H., "Van Fleurus tot de annexatie: een gekneusd land", in Hasquin H. (ed.), *België onder het Frans Bewind* (Brussels: 1993) 41–71.

money, jewellery, fabrics and other luxury items, and evidence of such largesse is amply attested through extant archival sources. Music forms an additional yet often unrecognised part of this enumeration of material wealth. Despite its ephemerality in performance, this chapter argues that music functions like a material object, one that can be sensed, valued and deployed at key moments alongside more tangible items. In Champion's appraisal of devotion at the Sint-Pieterskerk, the sound of sacred music emerges as a public demonstration of influence and piety, just as other senses were stimulated through the lighting of candles or the scent of incense. Together, these sensory stimuli reminded congregations of a confraternity's devotion and prestige. Music when performed was not just a statement of communal devotion, but also an aural reminder of its members' pious generosity. Musical performance thereby held an ancillary function, reminding listeners through the power of sound of a confraternity's devotion, as well as its financial and social standing.

1   Introducing Low Countries Confraternities

Confraternities throughout the Low Countries are complex, and their heterogeneity is apparent through different naming conventions.[9] The linguistic plurality in the Low Countries means duplicate terms exist in both Dutch and French, such as 'fraterniteit', 'broederschap' and 'confraterniteit' alongside 'fraternité' and 'confrerie'. Terms that were more general often arose from Latin cognate terms, such as 'communitas', 'confraternitas', 'universitas', 'societas', 'sodalitas' and 'consortium'. Not all these organisations were the same: for instance, religious confraternities could differ from craft and mercantile guilds, which were associations of tradespeople that catered to professions.[10] Chambers of rhetoric sponsored the crafting of text through religious plays, while other organisations provided militia that catered to the security and wellness of the civic population.[11] It is difficult to separate these various strands of

---

9   Trio, *Volksreligie als spiegel* 42; Verheyden C., *De broederschappen in de plattelandsparochies van de decanaten Brussel-Oost en Leuven, 17de–18de eeuw* (Ph.D. dissertation, Katholieke Universiteit Leuven: 2006) 18. Both Trio and Verheyden note a further term that is commonly used: 'kaland'.
10 Trio, "Confraternities as Such" 23.
11 Trio, "Confraternities as Such" 39. See also: Bruaene A.L. van, *"Om beters wille": rederijkerskamers en de stedelijke cultuur in de Zuidelijke Nederlanden, 1400–1650* (Amsterdam: 2008) 261, where five Leuven rhetoric chambers are identified. On military guilds in the Sint-Pieterskerk, see: Dewilde B., "Gilden en broederschappen", in Dewilde – Huybens – Mellaerts, *De Sint-Pieterskerk* 136.

civic organisation, since even those that held a more practical function – mercantile guilds, for instance – overlapped in their practices of devotion. While confraternities tended to a population's religious needs, organisations such as guilds also incorporated practices of religious worship, particularly when their trades or specialisms could be related to saints.[12]

This chapter's focus is on religious confraternities, since surviving Flemish records that detail their musical practices are more accessible. These organisations served two roles. Their main function was devotional in nature, furthering worship towards God, Mary or one of several patron saints. Their emphasis was on prayer, conducted both privately and at communal services. Secondary obligations were more concerned with charity, consisting of duties that most members were obliged to perform. For instance, members often had to care for those in their number who had fallen sick. In his study of Leuven confraternities, Christophe Verheyden emphasises the importance of conveying the blessed sacrament to such individuals, as well as attending deceased members' funerals.[13] As such, the confraternity's role was social, bringing together its membership throughout major life events. Since most confraternities were open to any member, regardless of their social standing, nobility and poorer classes shared spaces at meetings and ceremonies.[14] While guilds, military organisations and chambers of rhetoric had similar obligations, confraternities distinguished themselves in their inclusion of members regardless of their class, employment and, as is often the case, their gender.

Leuven's cult of Mary as the seat of wisdom (also known as the *Sedes sapientiae*) has been the object of serious scholarship since the nineteenth and early twentieth centuries. One of the most comprehensive early studies is

---

12   The degree of similarity between confraternities, guilds, chambers of rhetoric and other organisations was also regional. Note, for instance, that certain trade or guild confraternities in Iberia had a pronounced emphasis on devotional activities, and in the statutes of those in the Crown of Aragon they appear variously as 'confraries' (or 'cofradías' in Castilian) as well as 'gremis' ('gremios') or 'col·legis' ('colegios'); see: Knighton T., "Introduction: Listening to Confraternities", *Confraternitas* 31.2 (2020) 3–13 (9–10 especially note 27).
13   Verheyden, *De broederschappen in de plattelandsparochies* 17–18, note 29; Trio, "Confraternities as Such" 37.
14   While many confraternities were limited to men, there is rich scholarship on the important roles played by women; see: Brolis M.T., "A Thousand and More Women: The Register of Women for the Confraternity of Misericordia Maggiore in Bergamo, 1265–1339", *Catholic Historical Review* 88.2 (2002) 230–246. For a Low-Countries perspective, see: Decraene E., "Sisters of Early Modern Confraternities in a Small Town in the Southern Netherlands (Aalst)", *Urban History* 40.2 (2013) 247–270.

Léon Van der Essen's, compiled after the First World War.[15] While Van der Essen's work offers rich detail, it comes with historiographical biases. Van der Essen's study was the product of extensive research in the city's libraries and archives, which barely a decade earlier had been ravaged by the German army. It offers an authoritative survey of sources relating to Leuven's Marian cult, yet the historical context is apparent. For instance, in the epilogue Van der Essen condemns the Germans for destroying the old university library in 1914, while expressing hope that the Marian cult of the city and university would never again be threatened.[16] Van der Essen's work is reminiscent, therefore, of an era where devotion towards the *Sedes sapientiae* and other Catholic cults was still very much in practice, intimately tied up with civic and national identity.[17] It is reasonable to exercise caution with this study, given the political and religious concerns that motivated Van der Essen as much as his demands for scholarly rigour.[18] His work nevertheless offers a window into the rich holdings that were held in the former Sint-Pieterskerk archives. Most of these works are now lost, following extensive damage to the church during both World Wars.[19]

Unknown to Van der Essen were several documents, of which the most significant was compiled by the humanist Justus Lipsius. His book, which includes a description of the Marian cult and a collection of associated miracles, survives only in an unpublished manuscript at Leiden University Library.[20] Lipsius's

---

15 Van der Essen, L., *Notre-Dame de St-Pierre (Louvain): "Siège de la Sagesse", 1129–1927* (Leuven: 1927).

16 'C'est une affirmation de confiance dans l'avenir: le culte de Marie à Louvain et dans son Université ne sera jamais éteint; le Siège de la Sagesse, l'*Alma Mater* louvaniste, ne sera jamais renversé!', Van der Essen, *Notre-Dame* 138.

17 See for instance the use of religious devotion to foster a Belgian identity: Gevers, L. "Voor God, Vaderland en moedertaal. Kerk en natievorming in België, 1830–1940", *Revue Belge de Philologie et d'Histoire/Belgisch Tijdschrift voor Philologie en Geschiedenis* 79.4 (2001) 1301–1307.

18 Van der Essen was a Belgian unionist; however, he was also a prominent voice in the Flemish and Greater-Netherlandish movements; see: Van der Essen L., "De historische gebondenheid der Nederlanden", *Nederlandsche Historiebladen* 2.1 (1938) 153–189. From 1935, he was also a general member of the Verbond van Dietsche Nationaal Solidaristen (Verdinaso), a far-right organisation that promoted Flemish and corporatist policies; see: de Schrijver R. De – Derksen S. – Reijnen B. (eds.), "Leon van der Essen", in *Nieuwe encyclopedie van de Vlaamse Beweging* (Tielt: 1998) 81–89, here 86–87.

19 Some sources survived and were redistributed, with most being sent to Leuven's Rijksarchief, and smaller collections sent to the Stadsarchief and the archives of the Royal Library of Belgium in Brussels. Unless otherwise indicated, any source cited by Van der Essen can be assumed to be lost.

20 The manuscript was owned by Constantijn Huygens before passing to the Museum Lipsianum and then the Universiteitsbibliotheek Leiden [NL-Lu], conserved as MS Lips. 3(4); see: Landtsheer J. de (ed.), *Justus Lipsius: Diva Virgo Lovaniensis* (Wilder: 1999)

account of the *Sedes sapientiae* became the subject of increased interest from the 1990s, which led to the publication of an edition and scholarly study, thereby revealing significant additions to Leuven's already extensive miracle literature.[21] This chapter will assess these sources alongside others that have until now escaped scrutiny. The methodology, derived from a musicological perspective, ties in records of confraternal music-making, while considering other sensory stimuli within the sacred space of Leuven's new Sint-Pieterskerk. Together, these stimuli signal a confraternity's devotion while negotiating its influence within the church building.

2 The Soundscape of Early Modern Leuven

As in any other early modern urban centre of the Christian West, Leuven was filled with sonic reminders of religion. Alongside the city's main church, Leuven played host to several religious houses, which stood alongside each other in high concentration. The Leuven of the early modern period was a small city, and its Flemish neighbours – Bruges, Ghent, Antwerp and Brussels – had much larger populations. Yet Leuven commanded respect as the nexus of power for successive Dukes of Brabant, and because of this important connection with Flemish nobility, the city attracted religious communities.[22] In his description of the city in 1605, Lipsius enumerates these various sites of worship, together with a map of the city [Fig. 4.1]. The map highlights the sheer density of religious houses within the boundaries of the earliest of the city's walls: communities of canons regular lived alongside powerful monasteries, convents and parish churches. Near to the city, outside the second, larger wall, were similarly important abbeys, like those of Park and Vlierbeek. While being beyond the territorial boundaries of the early modern city, these institutions still exerted a profound influence on religious, commercial and cultural life. The focus of Leuven's civic activity was its main square, the Grote Markt. It was

---

viii. For further writings on Lipsius's collection, see: eadem, "Justus Lipsius's Treatises on the Holy Virgin", in Gelderblom A.-J. – Jong J.L. de – Vaeck M. van (eds.), *The Low Countries as a Crossroads of Religious Beliefs*, Intersections. Yearbook for Early Modern Studies 3 (Leiden – Boston: 2004) 65–88; eadem, "Iusti Lipsi Diva Lovaniensis: An Unknown Treatise on Louvain's *Sedes Sapientiae*", *Revue d'Histoire Ecclésiastique* 92.1 (1997) 135–142 (137).

21 Van der Essen was aware of Lipsius's work on similar shrines at Halle and Scherpenheuvel. While he had read of Lipsius's work on the *Sedes sapientiae*, he had not located any manuscript; see: Van der Essen, *Notre-Dame* 134–135.

22 Leuven was the old capital of the Duchy of Brabant, superseded by Brussels in the late thirteenth century.

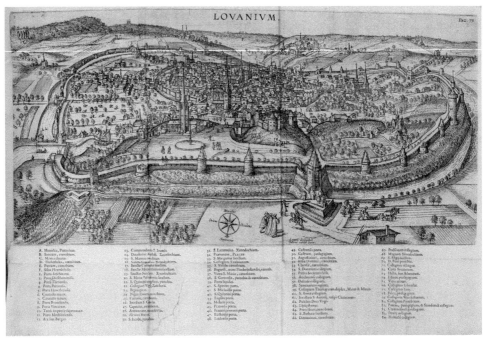

FIGURE 4.1 Panorama of Leuven around 1605, drawn by Joost van der Baren and published with annotations in Justus Lipsius, *Lovanium, sive opidi et academiae eius descriptio, libri tres* (Antwerp, Plantijn-Moretus: 1605). Universiteit Antwerpen, Ruusbroecgenootschap.
RG 2036 A 5
REPRODUCED WITH PERMISSION

the home of the Sint-Pieterskerk, the largest church within the walls. Located directly opposite were Leuven's most important buildings: the town hall, or Stadhuis, built between 1439 and 1469; the Tafelrond, built in the 1480s for the meetings of various city organisations; and headquarters for city guilds. Close by, on the Oude Markt, were the central administrative buildings for the burgeoning university.[23] Given its central location alongside buildings of civic and educational power, the Sint-Pieterskerk embodied Leuven's religious heart. The church's location, just a few paces from the university's headquarters, was emblematic. Its Marian cult, so intimately tied up with heavenly wisdom, offered a spiritual mirror to Leuven's prestige in terms of scholarship and scientific discovery. The growth of the university therefore went together with the prominence of the Sint-Pieterskerk's growing Marian devotion.

---

23 The central university buildings were originally located at the *Universiteitshal* from 1431, which was also home to the library from the seventeenth century until 1914.

The earliest Sint-Pieterskerk structure was a Romanesque edifice, about half the size of the present building. After this building was destroyed by fire, its ruins were razed to the ground, and work on the new building began from around 1425.[24] Construction continued for the next hundred years.[25] The building's larger dimensions, crafted in the newest style of the Brabantine Gothic, emphasised Leuven's wealth and influence as a former ducal town. Together with the newly renovated *Stadhuis*, the church commanded both regional and international renown. The new church's design also had practical ramifications in the way sound was experienced. Its new layout, with numerous side chapels, meant that the Sint-Pieterskerk could play host to multiple religious organisations, who used these spaces to erect their own private altars. Individuals from each organisation were held responsible for their chapel's upkeep, and certain altars were maintained by funds from specific guilds. Links between guilds and chapels were often maintained because of the associations between specific saints and trades. Thus, the new Sint-Pieterskerk building was occupied by both its canons regular, and a variety of civic organisations whose devotions occurred within the same physical space. Records survive of canons and other singers, associated with the church's collegiate chapter, who were responsible for sung music and organ playing from at least the 1440s; however, it is likely that other musicians were active in the church space, given the proliferation of confraternities, guilds and rhetoric chambers.[26] The various organisations known to have had connections with the Sint-Pieterskerk in the seventeenth century are depicted in a plan [Fig. 4.2].[27]

---

24 Financing was confirmed on 2 December 1425, but construction took place in phases after then; see: Doperé F. – Mellaerts D., "De romaanse en gotische Sint-Pieterskerk", in Dewilde – Huybens – Mellaerts, *De Sint-Pieterskerk* 1–39, here 15–38.

25 The final traces of the Romanesque building were only destroyed in 1499; Ibidem 28. For a visual representation of the building's evolution, see: Mellaerts D., *De Sint-Pieterskerk te Leuven: architectuur en kunstpatrimonium* (Leuven: 1998) 38–40.

26 See: Schreurs E., "De muziekbeoefening: ca. 1400–1797", in Dewilde – Huybens – Mellaerts, *De Sint-Pieterskerk* 226–243. On organs, see Huybens G., "Kapelmeesters, orgels en organisten, klokken, beiaarden en beiaardiers", in Dewilde – Huybens – Mellaerts, *De Sint-Pieterskerk* 244–263.

27 On this plan and the institutions mentioned, see Dewilde B. – Huybens G., "Een zestiende-eeuws altarenplan", in Dewilde – Huybens – Mellaerts, *De Sint-Pieterskerk* 142–147. Further information on the various confraternities can be found in Dewilde – Huybens – Mellaerts, *De Sint-Pieterskerk*, including Dewilde, "Gilden en broederschappen in de Sint-Pieterskerk, 15de–18de eeuw" 118–141; and Huybens, "Kapellen, altaren, epitafen en wandtapijten" 148–217. For the scholarship on musical practices of a single organisation, the Confraternity of the Holy Sacrament, see Champion, *Fullness of Time* (Chapter 2) 64–89. Musical sources that survive for this confraternity are described in Huybens, "Kapellen" 170–171.

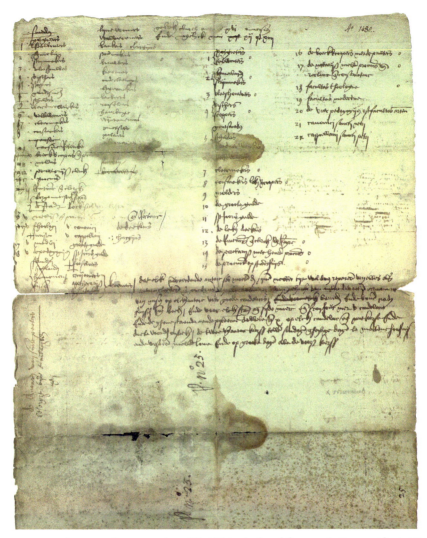

FIGURE 4.2 Seventeenth-century plan of Sint-Pieterskerk and the organisations resident at its forty-four altars. Leuven. Stadsarchief. Cuvelier 4143
REPRODUCED WITH PERMISSION

FIGURE 4.2 *cont.*

The number of organisations resident at the Sint-Pieterskerk varied over the years. This situation was by no means unusual. Records from other churches across Europe show a plurality of civic organisations that shifted as confraternities, guilds, and rhetorical chambers were founded, relocated and disbanded, often due to financial constraints.[28] As a nexus of political power, trade and learning, Leuven remained desirable in the eyes of the higher social classes throughout the early modern era. The Sint-Pieterskerk functioned as a place to unite these social strands, while also allowing them to give public demonstration of their piety. Amidst donations of jewellery, fabrics and money, music became a means to display devotion through cultural capital. The remainder of this chapter shows how music, despite its ephemeral nature, left lasting memories in the minds of its listeners, both for participants in the liturgy and bystanders who witnessed acts of piety within the church building.

3   Leuven's Cult of the Virgin Mary

To better understand Leuven's Marian confraternity, it is necessary to explore the Sint-Pieterskerk's Marian cult, when it began, and why the *Sedes sapientiae* was held in such high esteem. The special emphasis on the cult of the Virgin Mary within the city of Leuven has a long history that predates its earliest records. Its focus is a statue of the Virgin, made by Nicolas de Bruyn in 1442.[29] The Virgin appears seated on a throne resembling that of Solomon, with the Christ-Child in her lap. This statue was not the first to have appeared in the Sint-Pieterskerk. An earlier figure survives from the twelfth century, made in a Romanesque style, which is now preserved at the nearby Park Abbey.[30] This earlier statue was apparently held in high regard. Records survive of a precious mantle being made to dress it in September 1364, while there are further

---

[28]   Financial constraints for early modern confraternities often affected the availability of music; see: O'Regan N., "Music at Roman Confraternities to 1650. The Current State of Research", *Analecta Musicologica* 45 (2011) 132–158, here 145.

[29]   Numerous such statues exist elsewhere, particularly in the Low Countries. The statue still survives today, although it suffered serious damage during the bombing of May 1944, after which multiple fragments had to be reassembled; see: Mellaerts, *De Sint-Pieterskerk* 109; Van der Essen, *Notre-Dame* 14–21; Landtsheer, "De *Sedes sapientiae*", in Dewilde – Huybens – Mellaerts, *De Sint-Pieterskerk* 308–314, especially 310 on the 1944 damage and restoration.

[30]   See Van der Essen, *Notre-Dame* 22–25. Also mentioned by Lipsius: see Landtsheer (ed.), *Diva Virgo Lovaniensis* 9–10.

mentions of clothing being used from the fourteenth century.[31] While it is likely that this figure was important enough to have formed part of regular devotion within the church, surviving records of a Marian cult only emerge from when Nicolas de Bruyn was given the commission for his new statue.

Confraternity records from this time include a 'Register-boeck der mirakelen', which was once conserved in the church's sacristy.[32] This index of miracles was part of a body of literature on unusual events associated with the statue, most of which occurred throughout the early modern period. In his summary of the various sources Van der Essen details over one hundred events that took place until 1649.[33] They include a broad panoply of society, consisting of townspeople from or around Leuven itself. The most important collection Van der Essen identifies is Bernard Heymbach's *Diva Lovaniensis*.[34] A further source of interest is Lipsius's manuscript, bearing the similar title of *Diva Virgo Lovaniensis*. Lipsius's treatise offers a more international perspective, with a diverse range of figures who came to Leuven's shrine from locations beyond the Low Countries.[35] Lipsius's contributions to the *Sedes sapientiae* literature shows an expansion of the cult with a more cosmopolitan distribution of miracles that proved, in the minds of Leuven's citizens, the wider recognition of their patron.

The devotion towards the Virgin Mary involved individuals both within the Sint-Pieterskerk and further afield. Van der Essen indicates acts of Marian devotion that involved individuals at the church; these people were not necessarily attached to the confraternity, yet they still contributed towards the *Sedes sapientiae* cult. In a presumably lost source from 1445, an act calls for Salves and masses to be celebrated, accompanied by plainchant and organ in the main church building.[36] This act also specifies musical accompaniment at the lighting of candles. The association between illumination and specific plainchants was common: in the case of Leuven, Champion has written about the Sint-Pieterskerk's Confraternity of the Holy Sacrament, which sang the chant

---

31 See Van der Essen, *Notre-Dame* 23.
32 See Van der Essen, *Notre-Dame* 54.
33 See Van der Essen, *Notre-Dame* 53–69.
34 See Van der Essen, *Notre-Dame* 54–5.
35 Van der Essen, *Notre-Dame* 43–4 (which tells of four merchants coming from Sicily), 49–52 (concerning Daniel Wieseune, who travelled to the Rhineland), 57–59 (concerning Volcaart Jacobs van Enkhuizen, who sailed around the sea between Brittany and Great Britain). Lipsius also incorporated international figures such as Louis XI of France; see ibid. 8 and 81–89.
36 Van der Essen, *Notre-Dame* 41. Music was specified 'Au milieu de la lumière des cierges et d'autre luminaire'.

O nata lux de lumine during communion to mirror the luminosity of consecrated host wafers.[37] It is tempting, however tentatively, to ascribe Marian chants such as the *Ave Maris Stella* to this lost source. Mary's luminous quality brings forth, as the *Ave Maris Stella* proclaims, her ability to fill her followers with the wisdom of divine awareness.[38]

It was not just her wisdom that filled Leuven's citizens with hope. Mary was also upheld as protectress in times of war, disease and other disasters. Van der Essen notes that masses were sung at the altar of the *Sedes sapientiae*, possibly supported by the Confraternity of Our Lady, to commemorate several important battles that took place in Europe throughout the seventeenth century, including Vienna's deliverance from the Turks (1683), during which a *Te Deum* was sung; the Holy League's victory against the Ottomans during the Siege of Belgrade (1688); and a similar Imperial victory that took place at the Battle of Slankamen (1691).[39] Closer to home, the *Sedes sapientiae* was invoked through music to celebrate the Peace of Ryswick (1697). During the seventeenth and eighteenth centuries, there were also regular 'pestmisse' in the city, where the Virgin was summoned through sacred song to relieve the citizens from bouts of plague and other epidemics.[40]

There was a clear spiritual motive for such masses to be sung: they were believed to provide release from purgatory, not just for those who paid for them, but for anybody who attended. The cult of the *Sedes sapientiae* guaranteed indulgences to those who attended any Masses, Saturday lauds, or principal Marian feast days.[41] Champion demonstrates how indulgences specified a certain number of day's release from purgatory, and these days were granted at both papal and diocesan levels. For instance, relief from the fires of purgatory was guaranteed for ten days for anybody carrying a corpse and being present at a funeral Mass. Those who prayed for the bishop were spared twenty days, while those who rose respectfully for a priest received ten days' exemption.

---

37 Champion, *Fullness of Time* 80–82.
38 *Ave Maris Stella* had particular significance in the Low Countries, where Our Lady, Star of the Sea, enjoyed positions of patronage at important sites of pilgrimage such as the Basiliek van Onze-Lieve-Vrouw in Maastricht, which had both a prominent procession and a brotherhood of the Star of the Sea in the sixteenth century. The current brotherhood, founded in 1701 and temporarily suppressed during the French Revolution, is a later incarnation; see Ubachs P.J.H., *Handboek voor de geschiedenis van Limburg* (Hilversum: 2000) 141.
39 Van der Essen, *Notre-Dame* 42. The *Sedes sapientiae* was also believed to have protected the city from the Normans in 891, the military assault of Maarten van Rossem in 1542 and of Dutch troops in 1635; se Landtsheer, "*Sedes sapientiae*" 314.
40 Van der Essen, *Notre-Dame* 42.
41 Van der Essen, *Notre-Dame* 42–43.

These paled in comparison to the 20,014 years and 24 days' worth of indulgences one earned for reciting the *Adoro te in cruce pendentem* prayer.[42] Here, the importance of spoken or sung sound is paramount: devotion alongside or in accompaniment to the sound of prayer is associated with deliverance from sin.

Understanding the spiritual rewards Leuven's citizens hoped to obtain after death, the musical soundscape of the Sint-Pieterskerk can be revisited in a new light. Both commissioning and participating in sung services presented opportunities for faithful members to reduce publicly the amount of time required in purgatory as penance for their earthly sins. Musical commissions become comparable to the significant displays of charity and devotion from other, more tangible bequests. Together, these public statements of piety contributed both to the lustre of the confraternity's reputation, and to the promise of indulgences that its members would receive in the afterlife. Music can be viewed, therefore, as a further manifestation of material culture, directed ultimately towards the goal of spiritual fulfilment, with an additional function of displaying the social, financial and spiritual prestige of its members.

Records of such bequests are far older than the earliest surviving traces of the confraternity. Yet just as miracle records increased after the appearance of de Bruyn's statue, cases of member donations picked up after the 1440s. Van der Essen records bequests – many now lost – from both wills of deceased members, and from living donors.[43] These documents often specify the use of music to commemorate death anniversaries, either annually or more frequently. For example, Philippe Albert Sylvius's will requested an annual Mass with music, along with a lamp that should burn before Mary's statue.[44] A similar case survives from Marguert Colonere, who in 1446 requested two to three Masses at the altar of the Virgin Mary.[45] Sponsors varied greatly in how often repeated Masses were to be sung: Henri Hollandre and his wife made a

---

42   Champion, *Fullness of Time* 56. Champion also notes that indulgences were numerated for saying *Ave Maria* three times while a bell was rung, or for bowing when the Gloria was sung after the psalms, and at hearing the name of Jesus. Cited from the Leuven edition of Werner Rolewinck's *Fasciculus temporum* kept in Brussels; Brussels. Bibliothèque royale de Belgique/Koninklijke Bibliotheek van België. Inc.B.1463; see ibidem, note 183.

43   Given both the loss of many sources, and Van der Essen's own lack of clarity in describing them, the records in the remainder of this section must unfortunately come directly from Van der Essen, *Notre-Dame*. When possible, I have tried to identify where surviving sources might have been relocated.

44   Van der Essen, *Notre-Dame* 43; Brussels. Archives de l'État en Belgique/Het Rijksarchief in België. Archives ecclésiastiques. MS 1258 cap. 38.

45   Van der Essen, *Notre-Dame* 43; Archives capitulaires de Saint-Pierre à Louvain. Charter, listed as 'acte du 20 jan 1446'. Van der Essen also notes Jan Blanckaert and his wife

request in 1461 for eight Masses to be celebrated every eight years, while in 1471 Gauthier van den Timple and his wife asked for a Mass to be sung before the *Sedes sapientiae* statue every Friday at nine o' clock.[46] Often these bequests were made to accompany sales of property or transfer of other real estate. One such individual was Grégoire Cuypere Lathomus, who founded a Mass to be sung in 1474.[47] Others requested a hereditary tax to fund the singing of the hymn *Inviolata* on Sundays at the Virgin's altar.

Some of the claims sound optimistic: in 1487, Dominique de Baxadonis, a canon of the Sint-Pieterskerk, made a bequest for eternal Masses to be celebrated on Tuesdays and Saturdays immediately after the sung Mass in honour of the Virgin.[48] This service may have been a simple spoken service read by a single cleric, given the financial resources necessary to hire singers for repeat events. Yet bequests such as de Baxadonis's were by no means unusual. On the 8 September 1487, Elisabeth de Glymes, Countess of Salm, requested a Mass to be celebrated perpetually on Saturdays.[49] Such services presumably continued until the end of the *Ancien régime*, when this practice of devotion was almost unilaterally suppressed throughout Leuven and the rest of Flanders. The decline of such devotions is known from other records, such as a bequest of 1673 for Jean Cluts, vice-curate of Sint-Pieterskerk. In his will, Cluts asked for a weekly Mass to be celebrated every Sunday morning at a quarter past nine, which, records state, continued until 1761.[50]

Leuven's Confraternity of Our Lady was often the regulatory force behind such bequests. Founded on the 31 March 1445, the confraternity's main purpose was to promote the cult of the *Sedes sapientiae*, and to foster regular devotion towards her statue, both in the Sint-Pieterskerk and throughout the

---

Hedwige van Baussele, who request an annual Mass sung at the Virgin's altar; see ibid. 43 n. 5; Brussels. Archives de l'État en Belgique. Archives ecclésiastiques. MS 1282.

46 Van der Essen, *Notre-Dame* 43 note 4; Archives capitulaires de Saint-Pierre à Louvain. Testamenta fol. viii.

47 Van der Essen, *Notre-Dame* 47 note 5; Bibliothèque Université de Louvain. MS G.243 no. 725.

48 Van der Essen, *Notre-Dame* 43 note 6; Bibliothèque Université de Louvain. MS G.243 no. 712.

49 Van der Essen, *Notre-Dame* 43 note 7; Brussels. Archives de l'État en Belgique. Archives ecclésiastiques. MS 1283.

50 Van der Essen, *Notre-Dame* 44 note 1; Archives capitulaires de Saint-Pierre à Louvain. *Manuale officii distributionis sacrae communionis*, fols. 7r–9r; 27r–29r. See Van der Essen, *Notre-Dame* 44 note 2–3 for similar eighteenth-century bequests, some that mention sung prayers such as the *Dies irae*.

wider city.[51] From a handful of initiates at its founding, the Confraternity of Our Lady grew to include several hundred members. Their location for much of their early modern history was at the Virgin Mary's altar, located close to the rood screen in the nave of the Sint-Pieterskerk.[52] The duties of its members included numerous devotional acts, many of which would have included music. In the statute books of 1447, members were required to celebrate a Mass every Wednesday at the confraternity's altar.[53] In the same archival document, weekly Masses were held on Saturday mornings at seven o' clock; these required the attendance of a quorum of confraternity members. Each feast day of the Virgin included a large solemn Mass before the statue, during which the statue was relocated to prime position in the nave, in front of the rood screen.[54] Thus most of the responsibility for regular worship of the Virgin was held by the confraternity, with the canons of the collegiate church taking over on major Marian feast days.

One of the main responsibilities of confraternity members included celebration of the Office and Mass around All Souls' Day. Members were obliged to attend sung matins and a Requiem mass every October to commemorate those amongst its number who had died.[55] A further document notes that processions were organised by the confraternity in the months of June and October.[56] Whether such processions took place in the church building or the city's streets is uncertain, but what these records of sung services and processions show is that the Confraternity of Our Lady left regular reminders of its influence. Such reminders were visual, conveyed through the sight of services and processions; however, they were also sonic, through the reading of

---

51   Van der Essen notes that the confraternity was probably in existence from 1442 when the first miracles associated with the statue emerged. There is, however, no documentary evidence to support this claim; see Van der Essen, *Notre-Dame* 69.

52   The statue and its associated altar were located in the northern arm of the transept until the shrine was destroyed during bombing raids in May 1944; Mellaerts, *De Sint-Pieterskerk* 107–109. Prior to this, the statue was probably placed at the rood screen by (or underneath) the left of the three arches. The current rood screen is not the first, having been constructed in 1499–90. For more detailed debates on the placing of the statue, see Van der Essen, *Notre-Dame* 24–36.

53   Van der Essen, *Notre-Dame* 70 note 1; Bibliothèque Université de Louvain. MS G.242 no. 616.

54   Van der Essen, *Notre-Dame* 42 note 1; Archives capitulaires de Saint-Pierre à Louvain. Described as 'manuel du sacristain de l'autel'.

55   Ibidem.

56   Ibidem. Van der Essen argues that the mention of *Ons Lieve Vrouwebroeders* may refer to another Marian confraternity, although no trace of another one exists other than this specific confraternity of Our Lady.

text and performance of music. Thus, the confraternity's activities extended beyond influencing just its members, and reminded others of its presence both in the Sint-Pieterskerk and in the wider city.[57]

While Leuven's Marian confraternity was open to all, it profited from the membership of high-status figures. The register starting with the year 1447 introduces a cosmopolitan list of members by order of their rank.[58] Heading the register was Charles VII, King of France, and his son, the future Louis XI.[59] Upon his accession to the French throne, Louis XI bestowed 200 golden crowns on the confraternity. Such sums were substantial even by royal standards, amounting to approximately 3,333 days' work for a skilled tradesman.[60] Also on the list were Philippe III (Duke of Burgundy), his wife Isabelle of Portugal, Charles I (Duke of Burgundy), Margaret of York and Maximilian I.[61] The scribe describes these individuals as people who 'have richly endowed Our Lady', presumably bestowing similarly extravagant sums on the confraternity.[62] While royals featured prominently among its membership, the confraternity was also

---

[57] From at least the late fifteenth century, confraternity members also took part in the celebration of the office of the *Recollectio*. This service, conceived at Cambrai in 1457, combined – or recollected – the six most significant Marian feasts: the Immaculate Conception, Nativity, Annunciation, Visitation, Purification and Assumption. Its text, as Barbara Haggh Huglo has persuasively argued, was originally written by Gilles Carlier and its music by the celebrated composer Guillaume Dufay. During the Council of Trent the office was substantially revised, and the earliest edited version probably had its origins in Leuven; see: Haggh B., "The *Officium* of the *Recollectio festorum beate Marie virginis* by Gilles Carlier and Guillaume du Fay: Its Celebration and Reform in Leuven", in Delaere M. – P. Bergé P., *Recevez ce mien petit labeur: Studies in Renaissance Music in Honour of Ignace Bossuyt* (Leuven: 2013) 93–106, here 93; and Haggh-Huglo B., "Recollectio Festorum Beate Marie Virginis: Een liturgisch feest met gezangen van Guillaume Du Fay (1477–1797)", in Dewilde – Huybens – Mellaerts, *De Sint-Pieterskerk* 264–267. On the text of the office, see Van der Essen, *Notre-Dame* 85–91.

[58] NSCP 70: 'Ici commencent les princes, seigneurs territoriaux, rois, ducs, comtes, barons, chevaliers, écuyers, et leurs officiers, de France, Angleterre, Bourgogne, Brabant et de divers autres pays'; Archives capitulaires de Saint-Pierre à Louvain. Described as the 'registre de la confrérie', fol. 1r and following.

[59] Van der Essen, *Notre-Dame* 71; also recounted by Lipsius. See Landtsheer (ed.), *Diva Virgo Lovaniensis* 8 and 81–89.

[60] £62,440.49 in 2017, assuming a crown to be a quarter of a pound, and with 100 crowns being half this sum; National Archives, *Currency Converter: 1270–2017* (accessed 22 March 2023): https://www.nationalarchives.gov.uk/currency-converter/#currency-result.

[61] Isabel registered presumably after her 1447 pilgrimage to Leuven, and Charles after his 1468 visit. Margaret probably joined after her 1474 pilgrimage, and Maximilian possibly registered in 1505 after visiting with his son, Archduke Philip the Handsome; Van der Essen, *Notre-Dame* 75.

[62] Van der Essen, *Notre-Dame* 72: 'ont richement doté Notre-Dame'.

open to landed gentry, heads of powerful abbeys and churches and affluent commoners.[63] Listed are several prominent noble families from the environs of Leuven, Brussels, Mechelen and Antwerp. Of the religious members, no fewer than 49 beguines were included. There are leaders of important abbeys, including the abbots of Vlierbeek, Park, Grimbergen, St. Michael of Antwerp and Villers. High-ranking lay clerics also feature, hailing from important towns like Diest, Maastricht, Cambrai and St-Omer.

At least 250 commoners appear in the list of members beginning in 1447. They include residents of both Flanders and Wallonia, as well as various provinces throughout the Netherlands.[64] The commoners occupied a variety of jobs, with tradespeople featuring prominently. Yet while the confraternity was not an exclusive one, the impressive rollcall of names heading the membership list does suggest a certain aspiration towards prestige. Such aims would not have been unusual in an urban confraternity. In his survey of the Confraternity of the Immaculate Conception in sixteenth-century Rouen, Dylan Reid has shown how an impressive membership list presents a 'function of strengthening brotherhood between members of the civic elite'.[65] While Leuven's Marian confraternity was not exclusively composed of nobility and high-ranking clergy, its aspirational membership was integral to its social make-up. Such individuals played key roles in contributing towards lavish bequests that fashioned the sensory landscape of the Sint-Pieterskerk.

4   Regulating Confraternal Devotion in the Sint-Pieterskerk

To address the expansion of devotional practices, further roles were created within the Sint-Pieterskerk, designed to manage and maintain bequests. Some of the responsibilities of these individuals also included regulating musical life. These positions were held either by confraternity members, or by non-members with close links to the confraternity. A source that escaped Van der Essen's scrutiny is a bundle of contractual documents now kept in the Rijksarchief te Leuven MS 2021. These papers contain rich information on the reverence members were expected to show towards the *Sedes sapientiae* cult. Entitled the 'Conditiones pro custodibus sacristie B. Marie in D. Petri Lov.', they

---

[63] Van der Essen, *Notre-Dame* 73.
[64] Van der Essen, *Notre-Dame* 73–74.
[65] Reid D., "Piety, Poetry and Politics: Rouen's Confraternity of the Immaculate Conception and the French Wars of Religion", in Black C. – Gravestock P. (eds.), *Early Modern Confraternities in Europe and the Americas* (London: 2006) 151–170, here 154.

describe the responsibilities of custodians who cared for Mary's altar in the church over several centuries. Eleven copies of this contract exist in the manuscript bundle, dating from 1514 to 1720. Few of the custodians' responsibilities seem to have been altered over the course of two centuries, suggesting a sustained cult of devotion. Multiple hands wrote out the documents, copying from what was presumably a single, earlier common exemplar.[66] The responsibilities outlined in these documents emphasise devotion towards Mary at the Sint-Pieterskerk, particularly concerning the *Sedes sapientiae* statue and so show the influence that the confraternity had in the wider devotion of the church space.

These custodians had roles in the management of the altar in the confraternity's side chapel. Some of the tasks were menial, such as dusting and cleaning around the main altar and those of the side chapels on Sundays and on religious feast days.[67] Custodians also ensured that the statue of the *Sedes sapientiae* was placed in the correct location depending on the feast day and service.[68] More relevantly, some of the custodians' responsibilities also afford information on the regulation of sound in the church building. One of the main tasks was to ensure that the correct texts were read and sung at appropriate hours of the day in the church:

> It will also be required on other feast days to appear for the praise of the B. Virg. Mary, there to sing decently with a veil and robes before the altar, then to read the *Miserere* devoutly in the nave of the church, and the *De profundis* when gathered for the deceased, [and] to sprinkle the congregation with holy water.[69]

---

66 These copies are unnumbered; for the purposes of this article, they are categorised according to the order in which they appear in the archival bundle.

67 Leuven. Rijksarchief te Leuven. MS 2021 no. 1: 'Singulis diebus sabbathi tempestive imponet candelabra argentea pro missa solemni, curabitque ut sordes circumcirca Altare B.M.Virg. abstergantur, et per praedictam feminam verrantur, sicut et circa Altaria SS. Agathae et Aegidii'.

68 Leuven. Rijksarchief te Leuven. MS 2021 no. 9: 'Item sedero debebit in Dedicatione Lov. et per totam octavam a primo diluculo usque ad vesperam, vel alium in locum suum substituere pro oblationibus, etiam diebus illis, quando diva virgo ponetur in navi ecclesiae, similiter in die Parasceves, ante altare s. crucis, item in festo dedicationis ecclesie, exaltationis et inventionis s. Crucis sub salario consueto'.

69 Leuven. Rijksarchief te Leuven. MS 2021 no. 1: 'Tenebitur item alteriter diebus Feeriatis comparere in laudibus B. Maria Virg., ibidemque decenter cum superpelliceo et stola ante Altare cantare collectas, deinde in navi Ecclesie devote legere miserere et De profundis cum collectis pro defunctis, tandem populum aspergere acqua benedicta'.

This clause suggests that custodians were officials of relatively high influence within the church hierarchy, with an affiliation to the chapter, rather than the confraternities. They oversaw the activities within the main building, superseding whatever activities were taking place in the various side chapels. They ensured the confraternities' cohesion, coordinating their devotion throughout the Sint-Pieterskerk when it concerned prayers said to the Virgin Mary.

The custodians also interacted with those giving bequests to the Virgin Mary. Affluent individuals, both from Leuven and further afield, visited the shrine of the *Sedes sapientiae*, often leaving valuable items with which to endow the Virgin's cult. The guidelines laid out for the Sint-Pieterskerk custodians allude to this practice. One of their responsibilities includes receiving visitors who entered the church. The regulations state that the custodians must make themselves available from the beginning of the morning office until the middle of the eleventh hour. Custodians were held responsible for conveying worshippers and pilgrims to venerate the Virgin's shrine; however, as the guidelines also state, the custodians were to handle objects normally associated with acts of devotion:

> First and foremost, it will be so that every second or third day from the beginning of the morning service, until the middle of the eleventh hour, they will attend in the sacristy, in the service of those who come there to celebrate, administering to them ornaments, lamps and wine.[70]

> First of all, from matins until the eighth hour, they are to remain in the sacristy of Mary or on the bench before the sacristy to administer the ornaments of the pilgrims upon request, and from the ninth hour until the tenth hour. Those offerings that are made in the major festivals and dedication of Leuven, of which a separate chapter will be made.[71]

These guidelines bear witness to a strong tradition where material wealth formed a key part of spiritual devotion. Those who came to the Virgin's shrine at Leuven were involved in the exchange of material objects, through

---

[70] Leuven. Rijksarchief te Leuven. MS 2021 no. 1: 'Imprimis tenebitur alteriter singulis diebus ab initio officii matutini, usque ad medium xi.ᵃᵉ adesse sacristiae in obsequium eorum, qui illic ad celebrandum veniunt, administrando eis ornamenta, luminaria, et vinum'.

[71] Leuven. Rijksarchief te Leuven. MS 2021 no. 5: 'In primis tenebitur singulis diebus marie a matutinis usque ad octavam manere in sacristia vel in scamno ante sacristiam subministratinis ornamenta peregrinis petentibus celebrare, et ab hora nona usque ad decimam oblationes illas quae in maioribus solemnitatibus et dedicatione lovaniensi offeruntur, de quobis faciet capitula distincta'.

which their devotion might be recorded and displayed for onlookers to see. Gifts functioned as statements to a worshipper's piousness and generosity. To ensure that such statements were acknowledged, custodians were expected to keep reliable notes of any items they received. The guidelines state that any gifts intended as bequests or legacies were to be noted down, while a specific clause requests the itemisation of bequests funding musical activities:

> which, as in the more solemn festivals of the year, or in other ways collected, are bequeathed, and other secret gifts, [the custodian] shall annotate in a book intended for this purpose, from which he shall pay the musicians per head, and to those present, a sum according to what is ordinarily promised for the devotion of the B.V. Mary they are wont to [celebrate]. He is to return the above to master Fabrice, cleric, every month, if it is convenient, or at least at the end of each year around the feast day of St. John the Baptist.[72]

Material objects that feature prominently on such lists include items like jewellery. An illustrative case is a document from the same archive, Rijksarchief te Leuven, MS 2019. This source includes the will and testament of Barbara van der Eeckt, widow of Jacob de Beausart, dated 24 September 1578.[73] Van der Eeckt's inventory lists all her possessions, and the contents suggest that she was a woman of high social standing. Most of her bequests were intended to go to the Confraternity of St. Anne, also resident in the Sint-Pieterskerk. The inventory lists van der Eeckt's jewels in remarkable detail. These items, which would have been given to the confraternity after van der Eeckt's passing, might have been sold; however, they could also have been retained and displayed. Jewellery could have been used to adorn statues or presented elsewhere by the altar and would have served as a visual reminder of a patron's wealth and cultural influence.[74]

---

72 Leuven. Rijksarchief te Leuven. MS 2021 no. 1: 'Quae, sicut in solemnioribus anni festivitatibus, seu alias collecta, uti est legata, aliaque munera occulta, annotabit in libro ad hoc destinato, ex quibus solvet musicis per capita, et praesentibus tantam, juxta quod ordinarie pro Missis et laudibus B. Mariae v. antehac habere consuederunt, redditurus desuper statum Dno Clerico Fabrice singulis mensibus, si ita videatur, vel certo anno finiente circa festum Natale S. Joannis Baptiste'.

73 The inventory is dated 14 November 1578.

74 See also Elisabeth de Glymes, mentioned above: in 1487, she wrote a will where she bequeathed her best diadem to the *Sedes Sapientiae*. The piece of jewellery was adorned with pearls, diamonds and rubies. The bequest also came with three of her best dresses; Van der Essen, *Notre-Dame* 48 note 5; Brussels. Archives de l'État en Belgique. Archives

Many of these material bequests had more practical purposes. Light, in the form of candles, was often mentioned in confraternity members' bequests alongside musical performance. Candles offered practical assistance in the reading and singing of devotional texts for the office in periods of darkness. Yet even these items extended beyond mere functionality and could be deployed as a rich display of material wealth. Something as practical as a candle could be prized for its superior quality. The documents that list the responsibilities of the Sint-Pieterskerk custodians specifies that candelabras and candlesticks be resupplied on Sundays and feast days, and that they be carefully regulated to avoid wastage. High-grade tallow candles must be used by confraternities in their chapels, so as not to cause any smoke or unpleasant smell:

> He will ensure that the candles offered … are honestly consumed, nor will they cause smoke or stench, so that the candles of the altars may be changed to the height of the casket at the proper time, and that the musicians are supplied with tallow candles during the winter.[75]

> Likewise, on each Sabbath day [the custodians] will have to clean around the altar and used [candles] must be changed, and all silver candlesticks upon the altar [be supplied] with decent candles, and this shall be begun before sunrise.[76]

These sources of light held a practical function; however, due to the range of quality and through their associations with other objects of value, candles themselves came to signify material wealth. They supplied the light that was emblematic of divine help, as well as being associated with the luminous character embodied by the Virgin Mary, and members in their wills often requested these sources of light to be used at key points of confraternal devotion.[77] Calls for musical performance often accompanied such moments. Van der Essen

---

ecclésiastiques. MS 1379. Glymes was the second wife of Jacob, Count of Salm (d. 1475). His first wife died in 1487, so it is likely that he had married Glymes when these bequests were made. Glymes herself died in 1495.

[75] Leuven. Rijksarchief te Leuven. MS 2021 no. 1: 'Curabit item, ut candelae oblata sive cerei aut alia honeste consumantur, neque fumum aut faetorem causent, ut Cerei Altaris ad certam dumtaxat altitudinem mutentur debito tempore, et musicis in hÿeme candelas ex sero subministres'.

[76] Leuven. Rijksarchief te Leuven. MS 2021 no. 1: 'Item singulis diebus sabathinis tenebitur altare circum circa purgare et inferii vertere et omnia candelabra argentea in altari ponere cum honestis candelis et hoc antequam summum factum inchoabitur'.

[77] Champion, *Fullness of Time* 80–83.

notes that donations of material objects like candles appeared with specific instructions for their use to accompany the singing of liturgical chant. For instance, Gerard Fabri, Master of Arts at the University, made a bequest in 1470 for a hereditary rent to have 'a candle which should burn before the statue of the Holy Virgin Mary whenever they celebrate mass or sing lauds at her altar'.[78] Thus, light emerges as a visual reminder of a confraternity member's devotion, which is only amplified further by its presence alongside the sonic cue of spoken and sung devotional texts.

5   Conclusions

The archival sources that document Leuven's civic and religious life offer a reflection on the experiences that individuals underwent as they partook in their acts of devotion. In the early modern environment of Leuven's Sint-Pieterskerk, the main church building provided a very different sound world from that experienced today. Music held a function distinct from the reverence placed upon it in contemporary performance practice. Liturgical chant was sung throughout the ecclesiastical building, both in the main choir of the Sint-Pieterskerk and in the numerous side chapels that fringed the structure as confraternities held their own services. Voices in prayer therefore competed with the sound of liturgical music, while the sensory overload was increased by other stimuli, such as the smells of candles and incense.

The convergence of voices had such an effect that individuals were employed with the specific job of reinforcing the devotion of certain texts and chants over others. Devotion was often semi-private given its occurrence in side-chapels, yet was simultaneously also public. Sound was a witness to the devotion of confraternity members, whose lavish aural bequests for sung Masses sat alongside the visual adornments of jewels, robes and expensive vestments. The sonic jostling for attention was one that was integral to church life, even if it was met with opposition from those arguing that church devotion should be focussed, restrained and dignified.[79] Conflicts over sound mirrored similar debates concerning the sights and smells of confraternal worship

---

[78] Van der Essen, *Notre-Dame* 45 note 1; Brussels. Archives de l'État en Belgique. Archives ecclésiastiques. MS 1281, described as 'document du 19 mars 1470' [n. st.].

[79] For instance, the promotion of communal, unison singing of pious songs in the vernacular; see: Grootes E.K. – Schenkeveld-van der Dussen M.A., "The Dutch Revolt and the Golden Age", in Hermans T. (ed.), *A Literary History of the Low Countries* (Rochester NY: 2009) 153–292, here 245.

that extended beyond the boundaries of side chapels. These debates, and the rules that followed, were designed to restrain certain aspects of confraternal worship. These regulations prevented overall dominance of individual confraternities within the greater ecclesiastical space. While such rules were overtly practical, they also existed to reinforce the social hierarchy within the Sint-Pieterskerk, with St. Peter and the Virgin Mary at its helm.

As Leuven and the rest of the Low Countries entered the era of the Reformation, Calvinists and iconoclasts often sought to limit the influence of confraternities. Protestant worship was an altogether different kind of devotion, one that concerned itself less with visual and sonic displays.[80] Under the Catholic faith that remained in the Spanish Netherlands, music, light and scent continued to be attributes that denoted both devotion and social standing, intimately tied up with a collective, confraternal spirituality. This brotherly devotion also existed, however, alongside expressions of the individual's devotion and social standing within a religious and political landscape. The social milieu that prevailed and amplified itself under the Spanish Netherlands was therefore embodied by a devotion that celebrated noisy liturgical plurality. It was communal yet defined by individual statements of religious and social expression. Such devotion therefore countered the clinical and focussed celebration of the one liturgy that was to take hold elsewhere in the Low Countries throughout the rest of the Reformation.

Bibliography

Primary Sources
Manuscripts and Archival Documents

Brussels. Archives de l'État en Belgique/Het Rijksarchief in België:
   MS 1281.
   MS 1282.
   MS 1283.
   MS 1258.
   MS 1379.
Brussels. Bibliothèque royale de Belgique/Koninklijke Bibliotheek van België:
   MS Inc.B.1463 (a version of Werner Rolewinck's *Fasciculus temporum*).

---

[80] On the communal practice of devotion within Calvinism versus Catholic individualism, see the debates on social order laid out in Boer W. de, "Calvin and Borromeo: A Comparative Approach to Social Discipline", in Comerford K.M. – Pabel H.M. (eds.), *Early Modern Catholicism: Essays in Honour of John W. O'Malley, S.J.* (Toronto 2001) 84–96.

Leuven. Rijksarchief te Leuven:
 MS 2019.
 MS 2021, described as the 'Conditiones pro custodibus sacristicie B. Marie in D. Petri Lov'.
Leuven. Stadsarchief:
 MS Cuvelier 4143.
Leiden. Universiteitsbibliotheek:
 MS Lips. 3(4) (Justus Lipsius's *Diva Virgo Lovaniensis*).
Sources of the former Archives capitulaires de Saint-Pierre à Louvain, presumably lost or relocated (in which case the present location is unknown):
 Source described as the 'register-boeck der mirakelen'.
 Source described as a 'chartrier: acte du 20 jan 1446'.
 Source described as 'testamenta fol. viii'.
 Source described as the 'registre de la confrérie'.
 Source described as a 'manuale offitii distributionis sacrae communionis'.
 Source described as a 'manuel du sacristain de l'autel'.
Sources of the former Bibliothèque Université de Louvain, presumably lost or relocated (in which case the present location is unknown):
 MS G.242 no. 616.
 MS G.243 no. 712.
 MS G.243 no. 725.

Old Printed Books

Heymbach B., *Diva Lovaniensis*, seu mira beneficia a Dei Parente Lovanii ad aram sibi sacram in aede D. Petri, libri tres (Leuven, C. Coenestenius: 1665).

Lipsius J., *Lovanium, sive opidi et academiae eius descriptio, libri tres* (Antwerp, Plantijn-Moretus: 1605).

Secondary Sources

Boer W. de, "Calvin and Borromeo: A Comparative Approach to Social Discipline", in Comerford K.M. – Pabel H.M. (eds.), *Early Modern Catholicism: Essays in Honour of John W. O'Malley, S.J.* (Toronto: 2001) 84–96.

Bruaene A.L. van, *"Om beters wille": rederijkerskamers en de stedelijke cultuur in de Zuidelijke Nederlanden, 1400–1650* (Amsterdam: 2008).

Brolis M.T., "A Thousand and More Women: The Register of Women for the Confraternity of Misericordia Maggiore in Bergamo, 1265–1339", *Catholic Historical Review* 88.2 (2002) 230–246.

Champion M.S., *The Fullness of Time: Temporalities of the Fifteenth-Century Low Countries* (Chicago IL – London 2017).

Decraene E., "Sisters of Early Modern Confraternities in a Small Town in the Southern Netherlands (Aalst)", *Urban History* 40.2 (2013) 247–270.

Dewilde B. – Huybens G. – Mellaerts D. (eds.), *De Sint-Pieterskerk te Leuven: geschiedenis, architectuur en patrimonium* (Leuven: 2022).

Dewilde B. – Huybens G., "Een zestiende-eeuws altarenplan", in Dewilde B. – Huybens G. – Mellaerts D. (eds.), *De Sint-Pieterskerk te Leuven: geschiedenis, architectuur en patrimonium* (Leuven: 2022) 142–147.

Dewilde B, "Gilden en broederschappen in de Sint-Pieterskerk, 15de–18de eeuw", in Dewilde B. – Huybens G. – Mellaerts D. (eds.), *De Sint-Pieterskerk te Leuven: geschiedenis, architectuur en patrimonium* (Leuven: 2022) 118–141.

Doperé F. – Mellaerts D., "De romaanse en gotische Sint-Pieterskerk", in Dewilde B. – Huybens G. – Mellaerts D. (eds.), *De Sint-Pieterskerk te Leuven: geschiedenis, architectuur en patrimonium* (Leuven: 2022) 1–39.

Gevers L. "Voor God, Vaderland en moedertaal. Kerk en natievorming in België, 1830–1940", *Revue Belge de Philologie et d'Histoire/Belgisch Tijdschrift voor Philologie en Geschiedenis* 79.4 (2001) 1301–1307.

Grootes E.K. – Schenkeveld-van der Dussen M.A., "The Dutch Revolt and the Golden Age", in Hermans T. (ed.), *A Literary History of the Low Countries* (Rochester NY: 2009) 153–292.

Haggh-Huglo B., "Recollectio Festorum Beate Marie Virginis: Een liturgisch feest met gezangen van Guillaume Du Fay (1477–1797)", in Dewilde B. – Huybens G. – Mellaerts D. (eds.), *De Sint-Pieterskerk te Leuven: geschiedenis, architectuur en patrimonium* (Leuven: 2022) 264–267.

Haggh B. – Trio P., "The Archives of Confraternities in Ghent and Music", in Haggh B. – Daelmans F. – A. Vanrie A. (eds.), *Musicology and Archival Research* (Brussels: 1994) 44–90.

Haggh B., "The *Officium* of the *Recollectio festorum beate Marie virginis* by Gilles Carlier and Guillaume du Fay: Its Celebration and Reform in Leuven", in Delaere M. – P. Bergé P., *Recevez ce mien petit labeur: Studies in Renaissance Music in Honour of Ignace Bossuyt* (Leuven: 2013) 93–106.

Hasquin H., "Van Fleurus tot de annexatie: een gekneusd land", in Hasquin H. (ed.), *België onder het Frans Bewind* (Brussels: 1993) 41–71.

Huybens G., "Kapellen, altaren, epitafen en wandtapijten", in Dewilde B. – Huybens G. – Mellaerts D. (eds.), *De Sint-Pieterskerk te Leuven: geschiedenis, architectuur en patrimonium* (Leuven: 2022) 148–217.

Huybens G., "Kapelmeesters, orgels en organisten, klokken, beiaarden en beiaardiers", in Dewilde B. – Huybens G. – Mellaerts D. (eds.), *De Sint-Pieterskerk te Leuven: geschiedenis, architectuur en patrimonium* (Leuven: 2022) 244–263.

Knighton T., "Introduction: Listening to Confraternities", *Confraternitias* 31.2 (2020) 3–13.

Landtsheer J. de "De *Sedes sapientiae*", in Dewilde B. – Huybens G. – Mellaerts D. (eds.), *De Sint-Pieterskerk te Leuven: geschiedenis, architectuur en patrimonium* (Leuven: 2022) 308–314.

Landtsheer J. de, "Iusti Lipsi Diva Lovaniensis: An Unknown Treatise on Louvain's Sedes Sapientiae", *Revue d'Histoire Ecclésiastique* 92.1 (1997) 135–142.

Landtsheer J. de, "Justus Lipsius's Treatises on the Holy Virgin", in Gelderblom A.-J. – Jong J.L. de – Vaeck M. van (eds.), *The Low Countries as a Crossroads of Religious Beliefs* (Leiden: 2004), 65–88.

Landtsheer J. de (ed.), *Justus Lipsius: Diva Virgo Lovaniensis* (Wilder: 1999).

Long S.A., *Music, Liturgy, and Confraternity Devotions in Paris and Tournai, 1300–1550*, Eastman Studies in Music (Rochester NY: 2021).

Maesschalck E. de, *Overleven in revolutietijd: een ooggetuige over het Franse bewind, 1792–1815* (Leuven: 2003).

Mellaerts D., *De Sint-Pieterskerk te Leuven: architectuur en kunstpatrimonium* (Leuven: 1998).

National Archives, *Currency Converter: 1270–2017* (accessed 22 March 2023): https://www.nationalarchives.gov.uk/currency-converter/#currency-result.

Newman B., *Medieval Crossover: Reading the Secular against the Sacred* (Notre Dame IN: 2013).

O'Regan N., "Music at Roman Confraternities to 1650. The Current State of Research", *Analecta Musicologica* 45 (2011) 132–158.

Reid D., "Piety, Poetry and Politics: Rouen's Confraternity of the Immaculate Conception and the French Wars of Religion", in Black C. – Gravestock P. (eds.), *Early Modern Confraternities in Europe and the Americas* (London: 2006) 151–70.

Roegiers J. – Lamberts E. (eds.), *Leuven University, 1425–1985* (Leuven: 1990).

Schreurs E., "De muziekbeoefening: ca. 1400–1797", in Dewilde B. – Huybens G. – Mellaerts D. (eds.), *De Sint-Pieterskerk te Leuven: geschiedenis, architectuur en patrimonium* (Leuven: 2022) 226–243.

Schrijver R. De – Derksen S. – Reijnen B. (eds.), "Leon van der Essen", in *Nieuwe encyclopedie van de Vlaamse Beweging* (Tielt: 1998) 81–89.

Trio P., "Confraternities as Such, and as a Template for Guilds in the Low Countries During the Medieval and the Early Modern Period", in *A Companion to Medieval and Early Modern Confraternities*, Eisenbichler K. (ed.), Brill's Companions to the Christian Tradition (Leiden: 2019) 23–44.

Trio P., "Lay Persons in Power: The Crumbling of the Clerical Monopoly on Urban Devotion in Flanders, as a Result of the Rise of Lay Confraternities in the Late Middle Ages", in Black C. – Gravestock P. (eds.), *Early Modern Confraternities in Europe and the Americas* (London: 2006) 53–63.

Trio P., "Les confréries des Pays-Bas face au problème de la pauvreté, xvème–xvième siècle', in Lenoci L.B. (ed.), *Confraternite, chiesa e società*, (Fassano: 1994) 277–288.

Trio P., *Volksreligie als spiegel van een stedelijke samenleving: de broederschappen te Gent in de late middeleeuwen* (Leuven: 1993).

Ubachs P.J.H., *Handboek voor de geschiedenis van Limburg* (Hilversum: 2000).

Van der Essen L., "De historische gebondenheid der Nederlanden", *Nederlandsche Historiebladen* 2.1 (1938) 153–189.

Van der Essen L., *Notre-Dame de St-Pierre (Louvain): "Siège de la Sagesse", 1129–1927* (Leuven: 1927).

Verheyden C., *De broederschappen in de plattelandsparochies van de decanaten Brussel-Oost en Leuven, 17de–18de eeuw* (Ph.D. dissertation, Katholieke Universiteit Leuven: 2006).

CHAPTER 5

Music and Students in the Academy and Confraternity of St. Thomas Aquinas in Barcelona (1588)

Ascensión Mazuela-Anguita

Abstract

The Academy and Confraternity of St. Thomas Aquinas was founded in 1588 in the Dominican friary of Santa Caterina, Barcelona, by Salvador Pons (1547–1620) and Pere Joan Guasch (1553–1613), both friars and teachers of the community. (Six years earlier, an academy and confraternity of the same advocation had been founded among the members of Valencia University on the initiative of Diego Mas.) The *Annals del convent de Santa Caterina de Barcelona* (a three-volume manuscript held in the library of the Universitat de Barcelona) reflect the importance of music in the ceremonies mounted by the Barcelona confraternity, especially in those for the feast-day of St. Thomas, when liturgical services took place and the saint's image was carried in the procession that involved the students. This chapter, through analysis of documentation of the friary, assesses the role of music in confraternal ceremonial and analyses the ties established through the confraternity between institution, students and the soundscape of Barcelona at the beginning of the early modern period.

Keywords

academy and confraternity of St. Thomas Aquinas, Barcelona – friary of Santa Caterina, Barcelona – music and urban ceremony – processional music – students' music

According to the annals of the Dominican friary of Santa Caterina in Barcelona, an academy and confraternity in honour of St. Thomas Aquinas was founded there in 1588. It was made up of university students and Thomist professors who endorsed the Dominicans against the Jesuits. This institution, which is interchangeably referred to as academy and as confraternity, persisted to the eighteenth century. A variety of archival documents reflect the importance of music as part of ceremonies organised by this confraternity, in particular on the occasion of St. Thomas Aquinas's feast day, when liturgical celebrations, literary competitions, academic discourses, and a procession taking the image of the saint took place. This chapter assesses, through an analysis of archival documentation such as foundation statutes, handwritten music, printed villancico lyrics and chronicles, the role that music played in the ceremonial of this confraternity and the links that were established, through music, between the friary, the students and the soundscape of Barcelona in the early modern period.

An important source for this analysis is the *Lumen Domus* or annals of Santa Caterina friary, which is a type of diary or book of memoirs which was handwritten in three volumes and that is preserved in the library of the University of Barcelona.[1] Redacted by Dominican friars, this work comprises the story of the institution from its foundation in 1219 to 1802; the friary finally disappeared in 1835. The annals are structured into triennials coinciding with the three-yearly election of the prior. The first volume, initiated by Francesc Camprubí in 1603 at the request of the prior Rafael Rifós, includes the history of the friary from its foundation to 1634. The second, from 1635 to 1701, was written by Raimundo Forner at the request of Pere Màrtir Moxet in 1642, while the third volume, to 1802, was an assignment of Tomás Ripoll in 1743 and was redacted by Pere Màrtir Anglès, the friary librarian, who was also commissioned to complete the previous volumes. A transcription of the third volume, corresponding to the eighteenth century, has recently been published by the historian Alejandro López Ribao,[2] while the first two volumes remain unpublished. López Ribao has indicated that this is one of the most complete *Lumen Domus* among those preserved for the ecclesiastic province of Aragón and that the objective of this type of chronicle was 'to form and fuel a convent identity'.[3] The source for these annals is 'a series of preparatory chronicles and previous compilations of news which are gathered in different volumes'.[4] The manuscript of Santa Caterina consists of thousands of pages which reflect the imbrication of the friary in the political and ceremonial life of the city and which contain numerous musical references, for instance in relation to organ repair, the role of music in the ceremonial of particular festivities, and

---

1 Camprubí F. et al., *Lumen domus o Annals del convent de Santa Caterina de Barcelona* (MS, 1603–1802), 3 vols. Barcelona. Universitat de Barcelona. Ms. 1005–1007.
2 López Ribao A.J., *Transcripción y estudio del Lumen Domus o Anals del convent de Santa Caterina verge i màrtir de Barcelona. Orde de Predicadors* (Salamanca: 2021).
3 López Ribao, *Transcripción y estudio del Lumen Domus* XXI, XI ('fundar y alimentar una identidad conventual').
4 López Ribao, *Transcripción y estudio del Lumen Domus* XXI: 'una serie de crónicas preparatorias y anteriores recopilaciones de noticias agrupadas en diversos volúmenes'. He refers to MSS 946 and 986 preserved in the library of the University of Barcelona.

the musical component of the activities developed by the confraternities that were based at this friary space.

1 Students and the Dominican Friary of Santa Caterina in Urban Ceremonial

The friary of Santa Caterina played a fundamental role in the political life of Barcelona and in the ceremonial of important urban festivities in the early modern period, such as the Corpus Christi procession or St. George's feast day, as set out by the city chroniclers in the *Dietaris de la Generalitat* [Fig. 5.1].[5] The status of this friary was such that other religious institutions in Barcelona imitated it with regards to the solemnity with which festivities and processions were celebrated there, as the friary always enjoyed a great affluence of public, and music was considered by these friars as a primordial element in attracting people. For instance, according to the annals, on the occasion of the festivity of St. Raymond of Penyafort in 1612, the Mass was very solemnly sung in three choirs, as well as Second Vespers and the Office of Compline, so that music was listened to throughout the day, and the chronicler specifically indicates that music was a means of attracting many people.[6] Music was also an essential component of the ceremonial as it allowed the friary to enhance its status in the urban hierarchy: for example, according to the friary chroniclers, during Philip III's visit to Barcelona in 1599, when the king left the palace for the first time to listen to an Office it was to attend Vespers at Santa Caterina friary ('fonch la primera axida de palacio per anar a sentir officis que feu lo dit rey'). He explicitly stated that he did not want a choir from outside ('lo rey expressament no volgue capella de cantoria sino nostro cant'), but the singing of Santa Caterina friars; by implication, this was a sign of prestige for the friary.[7] Likewise, the annals remark that during a visit of Philip II to Barcelona in

---

5   Cases i Loscos L. et al. (eds.), *Dietaris de la Generalitat de Catalunya* (Barcelona: 1994), 10 vols.
6   Camprubí et al., *Lumen domus* vol. 1, fol. 267r: 'la missa del dia fonc solemnissima a tres choros de cantoria; las segonas vespres y completas similiter en fi que tot lo dia era oyr musica que jo crec que esta es un medi per a tenir molta gent'.
7   Camprubí et al., *Lumen domus* vol. 1, fols. 154v–156r: 'Item als 19 dia seguent fonch auisat lo pare prior com lo rey vindria a oyr vespras en nostra iglesia juntament ab las personas reals encontinent ampaliarem la iglesia adobantla lo millor que era posible tambe al sacrari y sacristia procurarem adornar lo mes be [...] fet asso los dos cantors entonaren lo te deum laudamus y la professo pressegui alternatim ab lo orga, que lo rey expressament no volgue capella de cantoria sino nostro cant; y dura aquest cantar fins lo rey sigue en son strado y assentat juntament ab les personas reals, y aqui matex començarem vespres que era vigilia

FIGURE 5.1   Cloister of the friary of Santa Caterina. Drawing by M. Redon (undated). Barcelona. Arxiu Històric de la Ciutat. Fons Gràfics, Rg. 19227

1584 to accompany his daughter Catherine – who had just married the duke of Savoy and was to board a ship in Barcelona –, the king's chaplain died and was buried in the friary.[8] The funeral rites included a procession in which the royal

---

de la assencio, y lo cantar era tirat un poch, al tercer y quint psalm sonaue lo orga alternatim, quant arribaren al magnificat lo p[ar]e prior ab la capa de brocat ana encensar al altar major ab acollits y assistents y turibol […]. Aqui se ha de notar que sta fonch la primera axida de palacio per anar a sentir officis que feu lo dit rey'.

8   Camprubí et al., *Lumen domus* vol. 1, fols. 95v–96r: 'Item en lo present any de 1584 vingue en Bar[celona] lo rey Philip segon ab lo princep y las dos infantes la menor de las dos ço es dona Catherina auia casat ab lo duch de Saboya y per acompanyarla a la embarcatio vingue dit rey a Barcelona y en sta ocasio estant assi lo duch de saboya en Barcelona vingue a visitar la nostra iglesia y conuent, ab grandissim acompanyament de grandes y del tuson, y en la iglesia molta musica mentres auia missa en lo altar major tenia per confessor vn frare nostre home molt celebre y gran religios amich de la comunitat a la qual nunca faltaua a instantia del qual vingue dit duch en nostra casa. // Item estant en Bar[celona] dit rey, mori lo prior major de calatrava capella del rey y dexa sepultura entre los religiosos nostres morts y axi se

chapel participated and performed a 'very solemn absolution' in the convent church. The following day, the royal chapel returned to the friary to perform the Divine Office. The chronicler emphasises that these ceremonies were 'of great honour for the convent'. Thus, the presence of the music of the royal chapel at Santa Caterina friary was another expression of prestige for the institution in 1584, just as it gained status when it was selected by Philip III as the first religious institution in which to hear the celebration of an Office during his 1599 stay in Barcelona.

Music also formed part of the ceremonies organised by the confraternities that were based in the friary over the centuries, such as the Confraternity of the Rosary, that of the Most Holy Name of Jesus – which were entities institutionally associated with the Dominican Order –, the Confraternity of St. Raymond of Penyafort, that of St. Catherine Virgin and Martyr, the Confraternity of the Most Holy Sacrament (also known as the Minerva), and the congregation of the Good Death (*Congregació de la Bona Mort*). There were also guilds related to the friary, such as those of weavers of veils or silk, hosiery makers and other needlework and weaving work, and ribbon makers (*perxers*).[9]

A special type of confraternity based at this friary was the academy and confraternity of St. Thomas Aquinas since its purpose was not only devotional but also academic: namely to promote the Thomistic philosophy and theology, mainly among youth people. The Confraternity of St. Thomas was formed by professors, 'honest people of any status' and, above all, by students. Students had an important agency in the life of Santa Caterina friary inasmuch as, from its foundation, the friary had been the seat of a Dominican *Estudio General*, where degrees in philosophy and theology could be obtained. The origin of the

---

feu solemnissimament acompañant la professo la propia cantoria y capella del rey y fonch asso a la tarda y anarem lo acercar a la plassa de la blanqueria en vna de aquellas cases en la qual mori staua amortallat ab son habit propri ab vn escapulari de sant domingo tambe per orde del rey vingueren molts cauallers principals al enterro y professo y al entrar a la nostra iglesia prengueren lo cos y feretio los cauallers y lo portaren fins al cor, que lo demes cami nosaltres lo portauem y ab prou treball. Ja en asso la capella dels cantors entonaren vna absolta principalissima y apres soterraren al dit prior a la nostra sepultura vella que sta en la capella santa Anna sempre cantant los de la capella fonch en asso tot gran lo concurs de la gent que entre atxes y gent nos offegauem en la iglesia. Item en lo dia seguent tornaren los cauallers ab la cantoria y feren lo offici ab grandissima solemnitat, en fi cosa de reys, com tal persona merexia y tocaua al honor del rey y corona fonch sta jornada de molta honra per al conuent'.

9   López Ribao A.J., "Las cofradías y asociaciones seglares del convento de Santa Catalina virgen y mártir de Barcelona en el siglo XVIII", *Teología Espiritual* 61.180 (2017) 365–390; and ibid., *El convento de Santa Catalina virgen y mártir, de Barcelona, en el siglo XVIII* (Salamanca: 2021) 221–238.

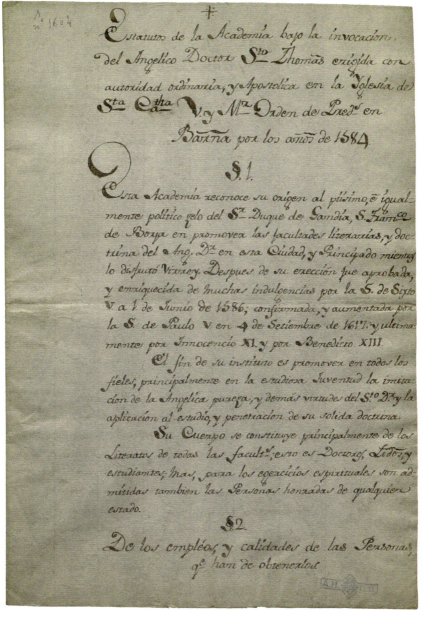

FIGURE 5.2 *Estatutos de la Academia bajo la invocación del Angelico Doctor S[an]to Thomàs erigida con autoridad ordinaria, y Apostolica en la Yglesia de Santa Catha[lina] V[i]r[gen] y M[a]r[tir] Orden de Pred[icadore]s en Barcelona por los años de 1584* (eighteenth-century copy). Barcelona. Arxiu Històric de la Ciutat. *Documentació personal de Marià Aguiló* caja I

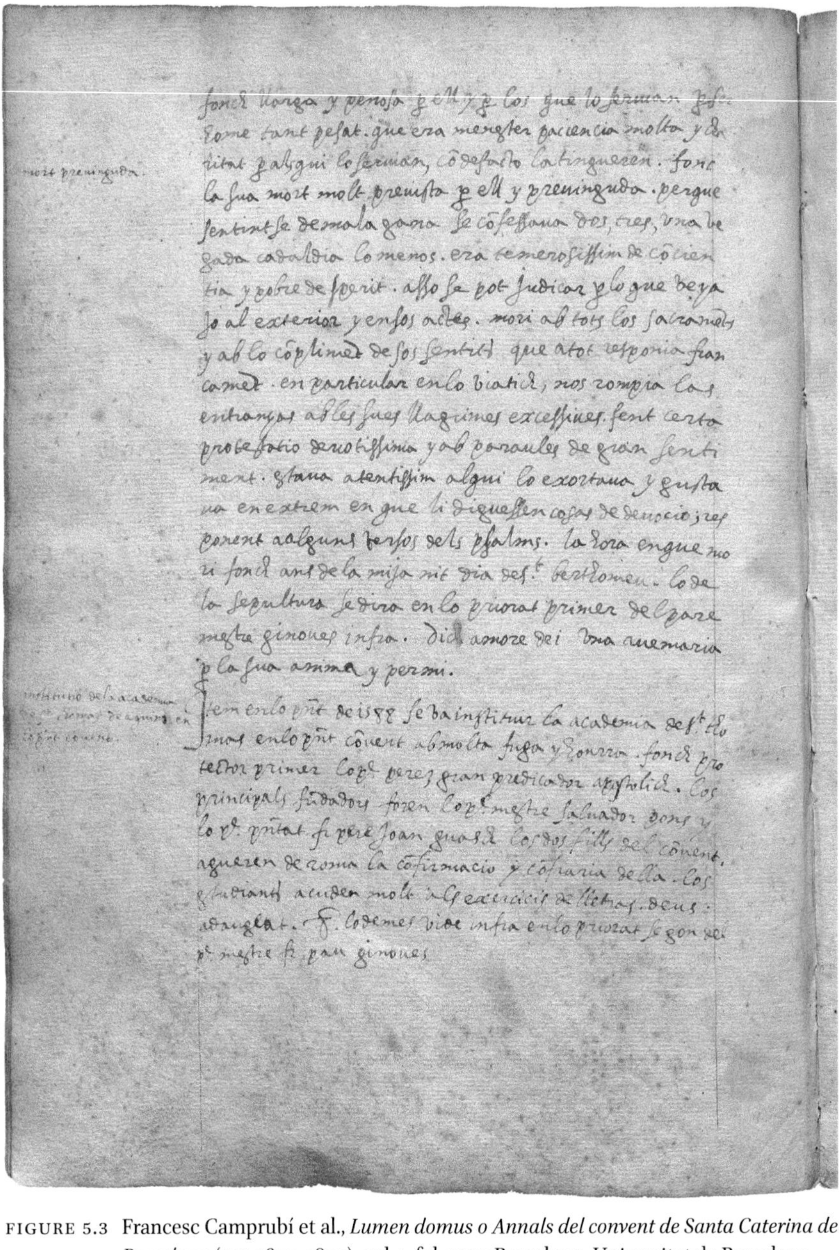

FIGURE 5.3 Francesc Camprubí et al., *Lumen domus o Annals del convent de Santa Caterina de Barcelona* (MS, 1603–1802), vol. 1, fol. 102v. Barcelona. Universitat de Barcelona, Ms. 1005

confraternity lies, according to its founding statutes of 1584,[10] in the promotion of St. Thomas Aquinas that Francisco de Borja, viceroy of Catalonia, had established in Barcelona in the first half of the sixteenth century [Fig. 5.2].[11] The confraternity was approved by a papal bull of Sixtus V in 1586 and confirmed by Paul V in 1617, and then by Innocent XI in 1681 and by Benedict XIII.[12] The annals of the friary indicate that this confraternity was established there in 1588 by Salvador Pons and Pere Joan Guasch, who were friars and masters of students at Santa Caterina [Fig. 5.3].[13]

Confraternities formed by students were also found in other places. In 1582, an academy and confraternity, also under the advocation of St. Thomas Aquinas, had been instituted among the university students in Valencia, where a confraternity of poor students also existed.[14] The current confraternity of

---

10 Several handwritten copies of these foundation statutes of 1584 are extant. The earliest is considered to be the *Estatutos de la Academia bajo la invocación del Angelico Doctor S[an]to Thomàs erigida con autoridad ordinaria, y Apostolica en la Yglesia de Santa Catha[lina] V[i]r[gen] y M[a]r[tir] Orden de Pred[icadore]s en Barcelona por los años de 1584* (eighteenth-century copy), Barcelona. Arxiu Històric de la Ciutat. *Documentació personal de Marià Aguiló* caja 1. New statutes were approved in 1711; see Voltes P.M., "Estatutos aprobados por la academia de Santo Tomás de Aquino de Barcelona, en 1711", *Analecta Sacra Tarraconensia* 34.2 (1961) 341–360.

11 Tusquets i Terrats J., "El Cardenal Joan-Tomàs de Boxadors i la seva influència en el Renaixement del Tomisme", *Anuari de la Societat de Filosofia* 1 (1923) 243–304 (250 n. 1).

12 López Ribao, *El convento de Santa Catalina* 297; Rossich Estragó A., "Segimon Comas i Vilar, acadèmic i preceptista", in Solervicens Bo J. – Miralles Jori E. (eds.), *El (Re)descobriment de l'edat moderna: estudis en homenatge a Eulàlia Duran* (Barcelona: 2007) 431–461, here 441.

13 Camprubí et al., *Lumen domus* vol. 1, fol. 102v: 'Item en lo present de 1588 se va instituir la academia de st. thomas en lo present conuent ab molta fuga y honrra. fonch protector primer lo p[ar]e perez gran predicador apostolich, los principals fundadors foren lo p[ar]e Mestre saluador pons y lo p[ar]e pr[esen]tat fr[a] pere joan guasch los dos fills del conuent, agueren de Roma la confirmacio y la confraria della, los studiants acuden molt als exercicis de lletras deus adaugeat […]'. On Salvador Pons, see, among other works: Fernández Luzón A., *La Universidad de Barcelona en el siglo XVI* (Ph.D. dissertation, Universitat Autònoma de Barcelona: 2003) 492–495: http://hdl.handle.net/10803/4791; and Ruiz Fargas M., *La biblioteca del Convent de Santa Caterina de Barcelona sota el mecenatge de fran Tomàs Ripoll, 1699–1747* (Ph.D. dissertation, Universitat de Barcelona: 2019) vol. 1, 33: http://hdl.handle.net/10803/669226.

14 See "Sobre la m[erce]d que supp[li]ca la confradria de los estudiantes pobres de la Ciudad de Valencia" (12 August 1593), Barcelona. Arxiu de la Corona d'Aragó [ACA]. Consejo de Aragón. Legajo 0651 nº118: 'El syndico de la cofadria [*sic*] de los pobres estudiantes de la ciudad de Valencia refiere en su memorial que esta cofadria es muy pobre porque no tiene renta y que los estudiantes que se socorren della son muchos y que asi no basta la limosna que se allega para sustentarlos ni para los reparos de la casa, y por esso es grande la necesidad que padescen, y para remedio della sup[li]ca por licencia para hechar joyas

students in Seville had its precedent in the Confraternity of the Denials and Tears of St. Peter, which was famous in the seventeenth century for its irreverency, and the archival documents include allusions to the students' mischief.[15] Also in Salamanca there was a confraternity formed by professors and students from the university in defence of the students who were prisoners in the university prison, with statutes approved by the university senate and confirmed by Philip II in 1568.[16] These students had the obligation of visiting the prisoners and making sure that they received fair treatment. If one of the confraternity members died, the others were obligated to attend the burial.

In the case of the Barcelona confraternity, the focus of the ceremonial was the festivity of St. Thomas Aquinas; as in the exercises in piety prescribed in the confraternity's foundation statutes, the confraternity members were required to attend the offices and spiritual exercises celebrated in the octave of the feast day, and would obtain many indulgences.[17] Eighteenth-century printed sheets containing *goigs* in honour of St. Thomas performed in Santa Caterina friary include a summary of the indulgences that would be granted to the confraternity members according to Sixtus V's 1586 bull as well as those of successive popes [Fig. 5.4].[18] Those confraternity members who, after confessing and taking communion on St. Thomas's feast day, visited the saint's chapel and asked God for peace among Christians, for the end of heresies and for the exaltation of the church, would obtain plenary indulgence and the remission of their sins.[19] The confraternity members would also obtain indulgences

---

en la dicha ciudad y reyno de Valencia en tanta cantidad que le queden francas quatro mil libras'. This request was accepted.

15   Matute y Gaviria J., *Anales eclesiásticos y seculares de la muy noble y leal ciudad de Sevilla, metrópoli de Andalucía que contienen las más principales memorias desde el año de 1701, en que empezó a reinar el rey D. Felipe V, hasta el de 1800, que concluyó con una horrorosa epidemia* (Seville: 1887), 3 vols., vol. 1, 132.

16   Alejo Montes F.J., *La cofradía en defensa de los estudiantes presos en la cárcel de la Universidad de Salamanca del siglo XVI* (Salamanca: 2016).

17   *Estatutos de la Academia*: 'Que en la festividad del S[anto] D[octo]r procuren los Academicos asistir a los Divinos oficios, y egercicios espirituales de su Octava, o sea Novenario, en q[u]e ganan muchas indulgen[cia]s'.

18   See, for example: *Goigs de Sant Thomas de Aquino, Doctor Quint de la Iglesia* (Barcelona, Ioan Iolis: 1726); and *Goigs de Sant Thomas de Aquino, Doctor Quint de la Iglesia* (Barcelona, Hereus de Joan Jolis: [1780?]).

19   'Sumari breu de las indulgencias concedidas als confrares de la confraria, y academia del angelich Doctor Sant Thomàs de Aquino [...]', printed in *Goigs de Sant Thomas de Aquino, Doctor Quint de la Iglesia* (Barcelona, Ioan Iolis: 1726): 'Item, tots los Confrares, que confessats, y combregats en lo dia de la Festa de Sant Thomàs (que es à 7 de Mars) desde las primeras Vespres, fins post lo Sol de aquel dia, visitaràn la Capella de dit Sant Doctor, y allí pregaràn à Deu per la pau entre los Princeps Christians, extirpaciò de las heretgias, y

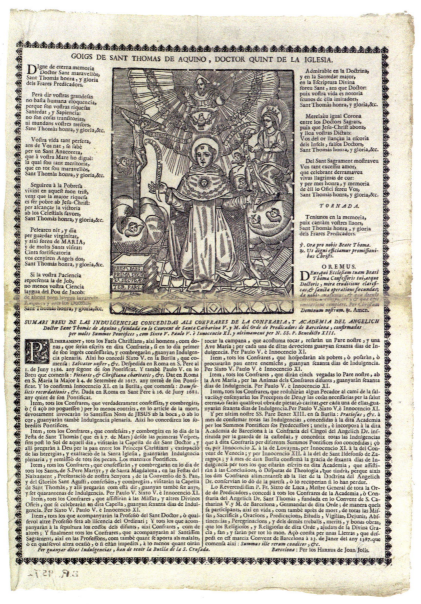

FIGURE 5.4 *Goigs de Sant Thomas de Aquino, Doctor Quint de la Iglesia* (Barcelona, Ioan Iolis: 1726). Barcelona. Biblioteca de Catalunya, 1 Go M 114

if they attended the celebrations at St. Thomas's chapel and accompanied the saint's procession, as well as the bodies of the deceased – members and non-members of the confraternity –, and the Most Holy Sacrament in processions or on other occasions.

According to the friary's annals, in 1588 the altar of St. Thomas was renewed as it was in a very poor state, and a new image of the saint was created with the purpose of increasing devotion to him. This was considered to be justified since the friary was the headquarters of the confraternity devoted to the saint, and numerous students and secular people visited St. Thomas's chapel on the saint's feast day.[20] The chapter of the annals corresponding to the triennial 1591–1594 includes a bequest of Tomás Sala, one of the friars, who had been the organist of the friary for thirty years, according to which a silver stand and a chasuble had to be made for the image of the saint.[21] The annals indicate that the academy had not been very active for a few years before 1598 and, consequently, in that year it was proposed that the usual academic and devotional practices should be resumed.[22] In order to do so, the confraternity elected

---

exaltacio de la Santa Iglesia, guanyaràn Indulgencia plenaria, y remissiò de tots sos pecats. Los mateixos Pontifices'.

20 Camprubí et al., *Lumen domus* vol. 1, fol. 106r: 'Item en lo altar de s[an]t thomas de aquino feren en agust del temps la imatge de bulto de dit sant que cert staua dit altar molt pobre; y les hores lo renouaren vn poch p[er] que se tingues mes deuocio en particular tenint en casa la academia, ab tanta frequentatio de studiants (co[m] dire en altra ocasio) que es contento veurer lo dia de la festa de dit sant y tambe per los seculars que visiten la sua capella'.

21 Camprubí et al., Lu*men domus*, vol. 1, fol. 115v: 'Item lo p[ar]e fra thomas sala predicador g[e]n[er]al y fill ja molt Vell del p[rese]nt conuent feu fer la peanya de plata a la figura de sant thomas de aquino questa a la sacristia que abans era de fusta y lo demes de plata, cosa impropria per cert y tambe vn calser y casulla feu fer per son regalo dit pare a sonat lo orga de casa alguns trenta anys'.

22 Camprubí et al., *Lumen domus* vol. 1, fol. 152r–v: 'Item com en lo vltim any del priorat del p[ar]e Mestre ramon Pasqual ço es 1588 fos instituida en lo present conuent la academia de sant thomas de aquino y apres de alguns anys se era lo negoci molt refredat tant en lo que tocaua al exercici dels studiants com tambe en lo acudir a ells y a la deuocio per la negligentia nostra perço ara la han tomada a refrescar y posarla de la forma y manera que staua lo costum era cada any per lo dia de sant thomas se tenian a la vigilia y al dia conclusions generals; aquel dia confessauen y combregauen los estudiants: y tambe acudien als dias de festa y diumenges a la tarda a tenir conclusions a la aula y alli se exercitauen y moltes altres coses, cert posades a bon punt que era contento veurerho y apres per la negligentia se refrendaren de manera que vuy als 8 de nohembre que es diumenge 1598 se juntaren en la aula de theologia del conuent los lectors del conuent y juntament ab molts doctors y studiants seculars y elegiren per protector de la academia al señor Onofre coll ardiaca major de la seu de Barcelona y per rector della al señor doctor tello cathedratich en ars de la vniuersitat y dos studiants collectors que tenen offici de aplegar los dines dels

Onofre Coll, head archdeacon at the cathedral, as protector, and Dr. Tello, an art professor at the university, as rector. Two students were also appointed to collect the students' dues each month. Thereafter, the annals reflect how the solemnity with which the festivity of St. Thomas organised by the students increased over the years. Moreover, the students acquired importance in other ceremonies of the friary, such as the cloister procession of the octave of the Corpus Christi, in which they participated by carrying their banners and an image of St. Thomas, or the yearly feast day of St. Raymond of Penyafort celebrated in January.

2 The Confraternity's Musical Arrangements for the Ceremonial on the Occasion of St. Thomas Aquinas's Feast Day

In other youth confraternities, such as that of the boys of the Archangel Raphael in Florence, which has been studied by Konrad Eisenbichler, music tended to be a fundamental component in the training of the confraternity members, and the Florentine confraternity, in particular, was connected to major figures in music history such as Jacopo Peri, Vincenzo Galilei, Girolamo Mei or Giulio Caccini.[23] In the case of the Barcelona confraternity, students were the 'promoters' and organisers of ceremonies with a strong musical component and were in charge of raising the money to cover the cost of music. Among the organisational issues with which the confraternity board members dealt, was the composition of villancicos for the festivity of St. Thomas or the preparation of the wooden platforms on which the musicians who participated in the celebration would be located.[24] In contrast, the students of Jesuit

---

studiants a cada mes y altres officials tambe per lo bon gouern de la academia y axi se es bellament concertada nostre señor done perseuerantia. Amen'.

[23] Eisenbichler K., *A Youth Confraternity in Florence, 1411–1785* (Toronto: 1998) 235: 'More than any of the other arts, music was probably Arcangelo Rafaello's most important contribution to cultural life in Florence. The membership as a whole, and the most musically gifted youths in particular, received musical training and were then given an opportunity to perform in public. Coupled with the presence within the membership of youths with talent in the visual arts and in theatre, this proved to be a powerful mixture that produced, especially in the late sixteenth and early seventeenth century, a critical mass of gifted young men who, without exaggeration, helped to change the course of European musical history'.

[24] Chapter 5 of the 1711 statutes is entitled 'Modo de disposar las festas de Sant Thomas': 'Que lo P. Prior junt ab los sis Majorals hagan y degan fer convidar als quatre Rectors per tractar lo major lluhiment de las quatre festas annuals determinant y publicant lo die se comensaran disposant tambe lo dels quatre Predicadors, los qui hauran de officiar lo de

colleges of the same period themselves performed music at urban ceremonies, and several chronicles refer to their *pandorgas*, consisting of parades in which the students participated dressed in burlesque costumes and playing musical instruments with the purpose of making 'noise' and express joy through the city streets.[25]

The structure of the celebration of St. Thomas's festivity revolved around the actual feast day (7 March), and began on the eve, with a duration that varied over the years. The festivity included solemn liturgical celebrations with music, usually performed by the cathedral choir, which was paid for singing in the friary.[26] The cathedral chapel master was responsible for composing villancicos for the occasion. The festivities also involved *conclusions*: discourses or discussions on a proposition that were advocated by members of the academic community. These discourses were usually attended by Franciscan friars, important members of the nobility, the city councillors (*consellers*) and their deputies. According to the chronicler, the festivities on 7 March 1602 were celebrated as was usual, with the difference that the students asked the friars to take charge of the *conclusiones* in alternate years, arguing that they paid for the festivity, and what that implied to cover the cost of the 'music, music chapel, and candles'.[27] The chronicler considered it to be positive, as it would increase secular professors and students' fondness for the academy

---

compondrer los villancicos y tot lo demes concernent a ellas, elegit per est effecte un dia de aula poca pres passada la festa del Reys a las deu horas del mati com y tambe per totas las demes dependencias se offeriran tant en lo tocant al pastor ara sia per adornos de la capella de Sant Thomas, o per tot y qualsevol altre cosa tocant a la Academia hagan y degan fer convidar als quatre Rectors y executar tot lo que a la major part de ells los seran mes ben vist y no altrament. Advertint que sempre y quant se convide per Academia o per junta privada sia sempre en nom del P. Prior y quatre Rectors'. Chapter 22 remarks that 'Al Fuster que la Academia tindra acelariat li toca limpiar lo retala [sic] y la demes fabrica de la capella; li toca fer y parar tots los catafalcs per la musica y per tots los conclusionistas'. See: Voltes, "Estatutos aprobados por la academia [...]" 347, 358.

25   Mazuela-Anguita A., "Las pandorgas a través de sus fuentes: Música estudiantil en el mundo hispánico a inicios de la Edad Moderna", *Cuadernos de Música Iberoamericana* 32 (2019) 347–370.

26   For instance, in 1652, the cathedral choir received four *lliures*. Camprubí et al., *Lumen domus* vol. 2, 134: 'en la festa de sant thomas se ha de aduertir que lo conuent y no los academichs feren la festa y fou que dit conuent lo dia del sant feu venir la cantoria de la seu y cantaren la missa major a cant de orga y los donaren del con[ven]t quatre lliures'.

27   Camprubí et al., *Lumen domus* vol. 1, fol. 195v: 'Item vuy als 7 de mars 1602 se es feta la festa del glorios pare sant thomas de Aquino (com se acostuma) sino que ara los estudiants han acordat ab lo conuent que ja que ells pagan la festa, ço es la musica y cantoria y cera que era cosa de raho tinguessens ells alguna honrra y participasen della en lo del tenir conclusions com any y altre lo conuent alternatim per al dit dia y axi com demanassen cosa posada en raho, han començat aquest any y desta manera sera de continuar y axi

and their attendance at the festivity ceremonies. The celebration also included literary competitions, and a solemn procession through the cloister in which the *Te Deum* was sung with the intervention of the organ, and villancicos were performed by the cathedral choir. The attendance of high-profile figures at the ceremonial organised by the confraternity is always noted by the chroniclers. Examples are Joan Moncada i Gralla (d. 1622), Archbishop of Tarragona, who attended the St. Thomas Aquinas festivities accompanied by his brother the Marquis of Aytona in 1616;[28] Philip V accompanied by the count of Zinzendorf in 1710, which involved the singing of the Mass by the royal chapel at Santa Caterina;[29] Luis Antonio Fernández Portocarrero y Mendoza, Count of Palma del Río and former viceroy of Catalonia, accompanied by his wife María Leonor de Moscoso Osorio; João Almeida Portugal (1663–1733), Count of Asumar and Portuguese ambassador in Catalonia; and Luisa Ana de Moncada y Benavides (d. 1716), Duchess of Híjar, in 1713;[30] or Juana Spínola de la Cerda (1683–1738), vicereine of Catalonia, in 1717.[31] Likewise, the huge attendance of the public at this celebration in particular was considered by the chroniclers in 1617 as only comparable to that on the occasion of the feast of canonisation of St. Raymond of Penyafort in 1601.[32]

---

      tindran mes afficio los doctors y studiants a la nostra academia y sta fonc la causa de que vingueren molts studiants y assistiren a dita festa'.

28 Camprubí et al., *Lumen domus* vol. 1, fol. 287v: 'La missa fonct noua de vn religios a ella foren conuidats los concellers y diputats lo señor archabisbe de tarragona don joan de Moncada y son jerma lo marques stos a la tribuna'.

29 López Ribao, *Transcripción y estudio del Lumen Domus* 183–184: 'Lo rey és vingut en casa y ha exit la comunitat a rèbrer-lo ab la forma acostumada. Ha cantat lo offici la capella real [...]. Lo comte Zinzendorf després de tornar de Alemaña ha tornat a exercir son offici al costat del rey'.

30 López Ribao, *Transcripción y estudio del Lumen Domus* 233: 'Vuy en las conclusions de philosofia, que ha tingut don Joseph Lapeyra, que éran impresas en Roma com las de ayr, assistiren en lo acte lo compte de Palma, virrey que fou de Cataluña, ab molts altres grandes y señors, però asentats en los banchs sens distinció. Lo comte de Asumar, embaxador de Portugal, estigué en la tribuna de la sagristia, en la altre la comtesa de Palma, duquesa de Íxar, ab altres señoras y mare del conclusionista. Lo nunci no vingué encara que estave convidat'.

31 López Ribao, *Transcripción y estudio del Lumen Domus* 308: 'Lo segon dia vingué a l'ofici la princessa Pio, virreina'.

32 Camprubí et al., *Lumen domus* vol. 1, fol. 290v: 'Item la festa del glorios pare sant thomas de aquino que comptam als 7 de mars del present any se es feta ab molt mes auentatge que los any passats axi ab musica com en lluminaria per que en la professo anauen 147 atxes blancas en lo del concurs de la gent no se que dir que puga ser mes pus tot lo dia estigue la iglesia tant plena que ab particular consideratio deyan los experimentats no podía ser mes, ni vn tal se auia vist sino ab les festas de la canonizacio de sant ramon y ara'.

Analysis of the friary's annals makes it possible to assess the transcendence of music in the ceremonial organised by the students. For example, in 1614 the chronicler considered the celebration of St. Thomas's feast day by the students to be highly innovative, so that he wanted to leave a written record of it. The students obtained a licence to carry out a parade along the city streets with trumpets and drums on the eve at 2pm. The *conclusiones* took place with the attendance of a great many students, and the Office of Compline was sung in polyphony with the participation of organ and wind-players. Afterwards, there were fireworks and music by wind-players, trumpets and drums on the friary church roof for more than two hours. After the Office of Compline, there was also lute music 'behind the curtain in front of St. Thomas's altar'. This music that was not 'seen' must have generated an extraordinary sensorial experience among the multitude who witnessed the celebration and is described by the chronicler as 'extremely sweet' and 'good for the faith'.[33]

---

33   Camprubí et al., *Lumen domus* vol. 1, fol. 279r–v: 'Item vuy als 7 de mars del present any dia de la festa del glorios pare sant thomas de Aquino han volgut los senyors academichs y studiants de la academia fundada alguns anys ha en lo present conuent celebrar la festa de dit sant y puch dir vna cosa que per a mi y per lo dietari es stada cosa molt noua y nunca desde son principi feta fins a la present jornada y per ser negoci de tanta gloria de deu y honra del ordre feria agrauiar la festa si no sen dexaue memoria en lo present dietari a de manera que moguts los dits Academichs del spirit sant vns quants diez abans prengueren resolutio de començar y empendrer ells la tal festa y elegiren per asso certs studiants que fossen los promotors y se encarregassen del faedor y axi ab les sues incansables diligentias han feta dita empresa demanant primer y cercant almoynes, que sens diner no si fan festas y procuraren llicentias del ordinari per fer vna crida per la ciutat ab atambors y trompetas per a la vigilia y dita crida se feu a las dos hores apres mig jorn ço es partint de nostra casa auent cercat y rodats los claustros de dins tocant primer los atambors y trompetas a les quals seguia lo standart al qual portaue vn doctor ab la borla y insignias de doctor y dos collaterals studiants vestits de llarch y tornats al pati axint per la portaria lo dit doctor y collaterals pujaren a cauall cada qual a la mula ab gualdropa alli aparellades y de aqui partiren per las semoleras ab gallart ayre y concert portant los collaterals cada qual son cordo de la bandera deuant dels quals las trompetas y tabals y segons digueren rodaren tota ciutat negoci fonc aquest que mogue gran brogit y aplauso a tota la gent si be los emulos (ut dicunt) arrugauen lo nas. Apres a la hora acostumada se tingueren les conclusions dins la iglesia ab gran concurs de studiants y acabades se cantaren les completas ab gran solemnitat a cant de orga y musica del orga y ministrils. Acabades completas que ja sera fosch, començaren les alimaries sobre la iglesia ço es fochs de teya y graellas, la musica dels ministrils, trompetas y atambors que va durar mes de dos hores. Tot asso ha causant gran brogit y alegria a la ciutat, la qual gozaue dels fochs, coets y tirs de arcabussos, molt a son pler per ser la nit molt acomodada sens perturbatio de temps. La lluminaria de la capella del sant fonc molta y ben concertada y tambe ben empaliada dita capella. Tambe dites les completas ague musica baix de cortina dauant lo

On the feast day itself, High Mass was solemnified by the cathedral singers in two choirs and by wind-players.[34] After the solemn Office of Compline, the procession began. For the first time, the procession left the convent premises and took place in the evening and not in the morning. The retinue included drum players on horseback, trumpets, wind-players, the students, Santa Caterina friars, and the music chapel, in addition to the tabernacle with the figure of St. Thomas Aquinas. The procession started in the main chapel, entered the cloister, went out through the porter's lodge and along Mossèn Jorba street, turned into Bòria street and Llana Square, and returned along Semoleres street, entering the patio and the church through St. Raymond's gate, and finishing at the main chapel.[35] The last day of the octave, the members of the confraternity commissioned the singing of a solemn anniversary in St. Thomas's chapel in

---

    altar de sant thomas sta musica era de llauts et a la fe bona y suauissima. Asso fonc lo que sera fet a la vigilia'.

34 Camprubí et al., *Lumen domus* vol. 1, fols. 279v–280r: 'Lo offici major digue lo pare prior y cantaren la missa los cantors de la seu a dos choros y benissimament no faltaren los ministrils combregaren a la fi de la missa moltissimos studiants y quatre dells a la comunio tenian senglas atches blancas. A la tarda apres de auer predicat lo pare predicador de la seu qui es vn pare biscay que es vingut per a dit effecte de predicar la 40ª a la seu al qual segueix tota ciutat ab gran aplauso'. Likewise, in 1623 the participation of wind-players in the Mass is noted; see Camprubí et al., *Lumen domus* vol. 1, fol. 324r: 'han tingut ministrils a la missa major y al tancar'.

35 Camprubí et al., *Lumen domus* vol. 1, fol. 280r: '[…] y apres dites completas solemnes saleu la professo del sant si be fins ara se feya al mati apres del offici y no fora del conuent com ara en esta. A la qual professo anauen los tabals de cauall trompetas ministrils, lo standart que portaue vn doctor ab dos assistents tras del qual los studiants ab cera blanca y apres la creu y lo conuent ab ciris tras dels religiosos anauen 38 studiants ab atches blancas cada qual la sua y apres la cantoria y lo tabernacle ab la figura de sant thomas y portauen lo talem sis doctors de la vniuersitat. Lo cami desta professo fonc entrar al claustro y axir per la portaria y per lo carrer dit de mo[ssen] Jorba y de aqui girar a la boria y la plassa de la llana y samoleras y entrar al pati y iglesia per lo portal de sant ramon y tingue fi a la capella major de la qual era partida. Es esta vna festa y jornada de molta consideratio per ser primera que los studiants han feta de sant thomas y verdaderament apar ser vn particular impulso del spirit sant per lo que veyem los animos tot moguts a la deuocio y doctrina del sant y a la veritat ques diga pobrement se feya entre nosaltres esta festa tenint tot lo orde tantes y tals obligations a deu per auernos donat tal subjecte, que tanta honra ha causat, causa y causara a tota la iglesia catolica. Resta ara continuar y posar la dita festa y jornada en tal modo que puga durar y aumentar y importa molt que nosaltres donem calor y animo a dits studiants que en asso striba lo total augment perdicio. Be se dir que ha agradat a totom que aboca plena no cessan de dirne mil alabanças nostre señor ho encamine a gloria sua y honra desta sagrada religio y casa los proposits y bons intents que per momentos se descubren son molts y molt sancts que tenen dits academics no faltara sino excecutio. Dominus qui incepit ipse perficiat. Amen'.

honour of the souls of deceased students and academicians, with many students in attendance.[36]

Entries in the annals corresponding to the following years consistently indicate that the ceremonial was more grandiose than the year before. The chroniclers refer to 'miracles' that took place during these festivities, and some of these involved musicians as protagonists. For instance, in 1618 a musket landed in the yard of the friary, which was very crowded, but 'miraculously' did not affect the people nor the musicians.[37] Again in 1643, the annals include a comprehensive report on the festivities, as the ceremonial had been more solemn than was customary for the occasion of the reception of a relic from Toulouse.[38] In this case, it is specified that the cathedral choir sang as much polyphony as *contrapunto* or semi-improvised polyphony,[39] and the magnificence of the ceremonial in the procession is explained in detail. The procession had broadened its route significantly, even reaching the nunnery of Santa Maria de Jonqueres, where the nuns were looking at the procession through the lattices and balustrade that they had built on the gate of the patio of their convent for the occasion. The procession also reached Santa Ana square, where the nuns of Santa Maria de Montsió had prepared an altar. Even the nuns of Santa Maria de Pedralbes, whose convent was located outside the walls of the city, were watching the procession from the palace of the Marquis of Aytona situated in Portaferrissa street.[40]

---

36 Camprubí et al., *Lumen domus* vol. 1, fol. 280r-v: 'Item vuy al dia del cap de la octaua de dit pare sant thomas los Academics sobredits han fet cantar a la capella de sant thomas vn aniuersari molt solemne per las animes dels studiants y academics defunts y armaren vn gran y alteros tumol al derredor del qual cremauen 12 atxes blancas al qual aniuersari assitien molts studiants asso fonc molt agradable a tots com tot lo demunt dit'.

37 Camprubí et al., *Lumen domus* vol. 1, fol. 295r: 'Y a vn studiant volent tirar vn arcabuz sobre de la iglesia a la part del pati se desfarra lo archabus de la caxa y se esclata y caygue dit cano al pati ple de gent y no toca a ningu ni al studiant ni ve dins dell que eran los musichs no feu dany algu. Miracle admirable'.

38 Camprubí et al., *Lumen domus* vol. 2, 50–63.

39 Camprubí et al., *Lumen domus* vol. 2, 62: '[...] foren couidats al offici los s[enyo]rs concellers al offici al qual cantaren a dos chors y lo Introyt ab contrapunt los cantors de la seu [...]'.

40 Camprubí et al., *Lumen domus* vol. 2, 54–56: 'Parti la professo ab aquest orde y concert de nra. iglesia a la qual anauen ordenant 4 cabiscols del conuent prenent dret al carrer dels mercaders exint per lo portal major y al cap del carrer girà a ma esquerra, y abans de arribar a la boria girà a ma dreta per la plassa del oli despres dret a la font de st. Juan y Riera amunt fins a Junqueras, ahont ysqueran las religiosas ab vnas celosias y belustrada que hauian guarnit sobre lo portal del pati de dit monestir a veurer dita proceso; per lo carrer condal y dret al Portal del Angel, ahont estaue la sta. reliquia guarnida y collocada sobre las andas que los ssrs. Inquisidors tenen en lo conuent per la professo fan de st. Pere

Drums, trumpets, wind players and muskets are described as 'waking up instruments' ('instrumentos despertadores'), which were heard inside and outside the city from the distance of a league, so that, according to the chronicler, those who were not able to attend the festivity visually would at least have heard it.[41] Among the musicians who are specified only in a particular year, there were the minstrels, trumpets and clarions of the galleys of Catalonia in 1616,[42] and the company of blind *oracionero* musicians singing and playing in St. Thomas's chapel in 1643.[43] These companies of blind musicians had a social welfare objective. According to Abel Iglesias, twelve companies of blind *oracionero* musicians were founded in Barcelona between 1668 and 1727 with an average of six members each.[44] Even the poetry competition in honour of the saint that formed part of the celebration had an indispensable musical component. For instance, in reference to the festivities in 1603, the annals point out that 'in order to accompany the feast and bring joy, there was a group of wind-players in the organ loft with the purpose of entertaining the people who

---

mar. en la qual estauen los 4 Angels de plata que la confraria del Roser ha fet fer [...] proseguint la professo per la plassa de sta. Anna auall, ahont deuant lo monestyr de Montesyon trobarem vn altar adornat per las religiosas de dit monestir ab vn quadro del Angelich dr. st. thomas per cap de altar [...] arriba fins al cap de la dita plassa y entrà en lo vltim del carrer dels boters dins lo carrer de la portaferrisa deuant casa lo marquez de Aytona ahont estauen las religiosas del Monestir de Pedralbes despres per la plassa noua passant deuant lo palacio del bisbe deuant la dipputacio per la llibreteria per la deuallada de la preso ahont ja comensaue a ser nit y ab tantas atxes y vnidas que anaren sempre que fou cosa de veurer; per la boria plassa de la llana y per lo carrer de las semoleras sen entrà en lo pati [...]'.

41 Regarding the ceremonial in 1622, see Camprubí et al., *Lumen domus* vol. 1, fol. 313r: 'Pero tambe son dies de 24 horas y ja que ells no vulgan veurer ocularment la festa; a lo menos la ouen [*sic*] y de lluny y de prop, pus que ab trompetas, tabals, ministrils, arcabussos que son instruments despertadors; axi per los carrers y sobre la iglesia se dexan oyr dins y fora de ciutat fins a vna llegua alderredor'.

42 Camprubí et al., *Lumen domus* vol. 1, fol. 287v: 'Primerament han fetes moltes preuentions de coses festiuals com son fedas [*sic*] per a tota la iglesia a dos barrades, musica a dos chors vigilia a vespres y dia offici y vespres completas. Musica de ministrils de les galeras de cathalunya y de la ciutat, trompetas y clarins de dites galeras per saludar a tots los que entrauen a la iglesia. Coets y arcabusos teya [*sic*] per alimaries sobre de la iglesia tambors y banderas flamulas y standarts de les galeras per dintre y fora de la iglesia que tot asso fere gran remor y struendo'.

43 Camprubí et al., *Lumen domus* vol. 2, 51–56: 'estauen la Comp[any]a dels cegos cantant en la capella y altar de sant thomas ahont estauen tots los ciris encesos'; 'los cegos ab los instruments cantaren alguna mitja hora en la capella del Ang. Dr.'; 'despres sonaren los cegos vna estona en la capella de sant thomas com acostuman y aqui dona fi la professo y festa de aquest dia'.

44 Iglesias Castellano A., *Entre la voz y el texto: Los ciegos oracioneros y papelistas en la España Moderna (1500–1836)* (Madrid: 2022) 131–136.

did not understand what was being read there'.[45] The prayers and panegyrics that the academicians devoted to St. Thomas in these convent festivities were usually printed,[46] as also were the lyrics of the villancicos composed by the cathedral chapel master. For instance, for the festivities of 1712, the prior of the friary commissioned 1,400 copies of the villancico lyrics from the printer Bartomeu Giralt.[47] The earliest extant printed villancico lyrics for the festivity of St. Thomas Aquinas in the friary of Santa Caterina are dated 1687, with music by Joan Barter; the latest were printed in 1712 – coinciding with the siege of Barcelona by Philip v's troops –, with music by Francesc Valls [Fig. 5.5; Appendix 1].

Numerous villancicos dedicated to St. Thomas Aquinas were composed by Francesc Valls and are preserved at the Biblioteca de Catalunya in Barcelona, as part of the musical collection from Barcelona Cathedral (see Appendix 2). In the library catalogue, all these villancicos are dated to the eighteenth century without indication of a specific year. However, the comparative study of these pieces makes it possible to establish that some of them correspond to the printed lyrics and, in this way, to date them to a precise year. For example, in 1697 the lyrics of the villancicos composed by Valls for St. Thomas's feast day were printed and it has been possible to locate their music in the Biblioteca de Catalunya. A fragment of the second villancico, *Angélicos espíritus celestes*, is presented in Figure 5.6. Thanks to analysis of the lyrics, it is also possible to establish that the villancico *Sombras cobardes* was the first of the villancicos composed for the festivities of St. Thomas in 1708 [Fig. 5.7]. Similarly, comparative analysis makes it possible to attribute both to Valls and to Barter villancicos that had been catalogued as anonymous. For instance, the 16-voice villancico to St. Thomas *Hoy que al sol de las escuelas*, which is catalogued as

---

45   Camprubí et al., *Lumen domus* vol. 1, fols. 218v–219r: 'Item als 16 del dit mes [March 1603] y any que era la dominica in passione apres vespras se tingue en lo cor debaix de la iglesia vn certamen poetich o justa literaria a honor del glorios pare sant thomas de aquino fonc vna vista principal y curiosa la qual redunda en gran gloria de dit sant y tras de asso auia premis per als qui millor compondrian y tambe tres jutges per premiar als qui mes destrament faria los versos y obras poeticas y per acompanyar la festa y regosijarla auia en lo orga vna copla de ministrils y per entretenir la gent que no entenia lo que alli se llegia'.

46   Examples are Carlos de la Concepción, *Oracion panegirica y evangelica en aplauso del angel entre los doctores y doctor entre los angeles, Santo Thomas de Aquino* [...] (Barcelona, Vicente Surià: 1689); Pablo Andrés, *El sol en el signo de Tauro, el angelico maestro y quinto doctor de la Iglesia Santo Thomas de Aquino* [...] (Barcelona, Juan Jolis: [1695?]); Felipe Estevan, *Oracion primera que en las maximas fiestas que en el real convento de Santa Catalina Martir de esta Excelentissima Ciudad de Barcelona, consagraron al angelico Doctor S. Thomas de Aquino* [...] (Barcelona, Juan Jolis: 1708).

47   Camprubí X., *La premsa a Catalunya durant la Guerra de Successió* (Valencia: 2016).

FIGURE 5.5   *Villancicos que se cantaron en el Real Convento de Santa Cathalina [...] en las Fiestas que tributan, y consagran los Academicos Discipulos á su Angelico Maestro Santo Thomas de Aquino [...] cantòlos la Capilla de la Iglesia Cathedral, siendo Maestro de ella el Licenciado Francisco Valls* (Barcelona, Bartholome Giralt: 1712). Madrid. Biblioteca Nacional de España, VE/1304
© CREATIVE COMMONS

anonymous, is included among those composed by Valls in 1698 [Fig. 5.8], and the 16-voice villancico *Oy de la fama volante*, also catalogued as anonymous, was composed by Barter for St. Thomas Aquinas's feast day in Santa Caterina in 1694. Other examples are presented in Appendix 2. The music of other anonymous villancicos devoted to the Immaculate Conception and the Nativity,

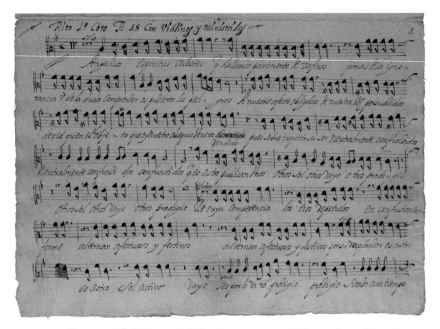

FIGURE 5.6 Francesc Valls (1665–1747), *Villancico a 15 con ministriles y violines al Smo. Sto.: Angelicos espiritus celestes* [1697], alto part of choir 1. Barcelona. Biblioteca de Catalunya, M 1483/10

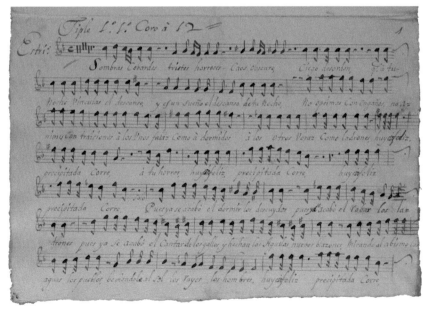

FIGURE 5.7 Francesc Valls (1665–1747), *Villanco. a 12 con claris. y violis. a Sto. Thomas de Aquino: Sombras cobardes* [1708], tiple 1 part of choir 1. 11.5 cm wide. Barcelona. Biblioteca de Catalunya, M 1470/16

FIGURE 5.8 Francesc Valls (1665–1747), *Villancico a 16 a Sto. Thomás de Aquino: Oy q. al sol de las escuelas* [1698], tenor part of choir 1. 11.5 cm wide. Barcelona. Biblioteca de Catalunya, M 1481/20

respectively, dating from the eighteenth century, contains annotations that refer to St. Thomas Aquinas's feast day and to the students' ceremonial.[48]

A villancico dedicated to St. Narcissus, bishop and martyr of Gerona, composed by Barter, is also preserved at the Biblioteca de Catalunya. With the incipit *Canten las aves*, this villancico includes some strophes dedicated to St. Thomas Aquinas.[49] Likewise, villancicos in honour of St. Thomas Aquinas, also preserved there, were composed by chapel masters of Gerona Cathedral, such as Francesc Soler (1625–1688), Josep Gas (1656–1713) and Manuel Gonima (c.1712–1792).

---

48   Barcelona. Biblioteca de Catalunya. M 699/11 fol. 10v: 'De acompañar St. Thomas, Monter, Joan, Gabriel Camps, Salvador. De la comunio dels estudiants lo die de la festa de St. Tomas, Joan, Gabriel Gallo, Gabriel Camps, Emanuel. De la Professo de St. Thomas, Monter, Joan, Gabriel Camps, Salvador. De la Professo del Carme, Monter, Joan, Gabriel Camps, Salvador'.

49   Barcelona, Biblioteca de Catalunya, M 748/8. The villancico has been published in Pavia i Simó J., *La Música a la Catedral de Barcelona durant el segle XVII* (Barcelona: 1986).

3 The Participation of the Confraternity and Students in Other Festivities

In addition to the feast day of St. Thomas Aquinas, the students also acquired a fundamental role in the ceremonial of the festivity of St. Raymond of Penyafort, the first inquisitor of the Kingdom of Aragon, which was celebrated in the friary with great solemnity. The festivities for the saint's canonisation in 1601 were organised by the friary, with dozens of processions that entered inside the friary church singing the *Te Deum*, which were described as most solemn.[50] In June 1618, according to the annals, the law students took charge of the confraternity of St. Raymond.[51] Thus, in January 1619 the students organised the festivities held for the saint.[52] In 1626, for instance, it is noted that the celebrations had proceeded as in previous years, although with regard to windplayer's music the festivities had fallen short, as the law students did not have much money and it was they who had the obligation to cover those expenses on behalf of the confraternity.[53] In 1643, the festivity counted on the participation of the *escolanets* from the cathedral, who sang villancicos to St. Raymond,

---

50 Rebullosa J., *Relacion de las grandes fiestas que en esta ciudad de Barcelona se han echo à la canonizacion de su hijo San Ramon de Peñafort, de la Orden de los Predicadores: Con vn sumario de su Vida, Muerte y Canonizacion, y siete Sermones que los Obispos han predicado en ellas* (Barcelona, En la Emprenta de Iayme Cendrat: 1601). See: Knighton T., "Relating History: Music and Meaning in the *relaciones* of the Canonization of St Raymond Penyafort", in Ferreira M.P. – Cascudo T. (eds.), *Música e História: Estudos em homenagem a Manuel Carlos de Brito* (Lisbon: 2017) 27–51.

51 Camprubí et al., *Lumen domus* vol. 1, fol. 297r: 'Item vuy dimars que comptam als 26 Juny lo conuent in pleno capitulo ha donada la confraria de sant ramon als señor studiants llegistas y canonistas y a baste de notari ab los pastes y condicions en ell contenguts del que ells ne son restats contentissims; asso es estat preuint primer dits studiants ab suplica y ab gran submissio donada per ells al pare prior y conuent'.

52 Camprubí et al., *Lumen domus* vol. 1, fol. 299v: 'La festa del glorios pare sant ramon que a son dia del present any se es celebrada, es estada com las passades ab grandissim concurs de gent, lluminaria en la iglesia y musica y altres coses adherents y festiuals totes son stades ab gran compliment, ab adjutori dels señor studiants de lleys que ells tenen la confraria de dit sanct y han començat ara y confiam que si no se cansan sera de gran importantia que ells sen poran molt honrrar'.

53 Camprubí et al., *Lumen domus* vol. 1, fol. 335r: 'la festa annyal del pare sant ramon es estada com las prop passadas si be en lo de la musica de ministrils es estada curta per lo que com los estudiants de lleys vajen curts de diners que ells tenem obligatio de fer aquex gasto pus es estat concertat axi en los anys prop passats y ells tenen la confraria: pero asso ha reparat lo honrarnos lo chor y altar lo nostre molt reverent pare prouincial que ab las suas canas reuerendas y sanctedad y exemple singular (a mon parer) ha suplit moltas faltas que per part nostra aura en lo demes se es fet com en los anys passats'.

Our Lady of the Rosary and the Most Holy Sacrament, hidden in the pulpit after dinner.[54]

The students also had an important role in the procession of Corpus Christi, in which they participated carrying torches, banners of the academy and the tabernacle of St. Thomas.[55] Still in 1745, the Corpus Christi procession counted on the participation of 570 students bearing torches.[56] The members of the Confraternity of St. Thomas also participated in other processions, such as those for pleading for rain (for example, on 15 June 1753) or against the plague (on 2 May 1775), or the procession held on Holy Friday, which processed through the convent premises with the participation of the cathedral choir.[57] On Holy Thursday the students already participated in the liturgical celebrations together with the friars of Santa Caterina and placed the academy banner on the organ so that it could be seen when the procession passed by the following day. The procession was preceded by a trumpet and counted on the participation of the cathedral choir singing the *Miserere* and, when the procession finished in the main chapel, the motet *O crux*. Other choirs participated in the procession as well as drum players.[58] In Valencia, the members of the confraternity of St. Thomas were likewise granted many indulgences and celebrated St. Thomas's feast day with great solemnity, including a procession accompanied by the students. From 1614 onwards, when the Valencian confraternity

---

54   Camprubí et al., *Lumen domus* vol. 2, 46: 'despres tot lo dinar los escolanets de la seu que estauen en la trona amagats cantaren villancicos de sant Ramon de nostra señora del Roser y del santisimo sacrament'.

55   López Ribao, *Transcripción y estudio del Lumen Domus* 365–366: 'No havent pogut fer la professó [Corpus Christi 1743] lo diumenge, com acostuma lo convent, per causa de haver plogut tota la tarde, se resolgué fer-se al cap de octava. Y com en la curta professó [*sic*] que tots anys en est dia se fa assitèscan los estudiants ab los pendons de l'Acadèmia, havent de altra part instant varias vegadas se portàs a la professó del diumenge de sant Thomàs, que ells lo acompañarían ab atxas, lo que may se havia posat en execució, per no saber com compòndrer los pendons de l'Acadèmia ab las banderas de la confraria del Roser, que indispensablement han de anar, se projectà un medi terme ab què tots estigueren contents'.

56   López Ribao, *Transcripción y estudio del Lumen Domus* 378.

57   Camprubí et al., *Lumen domus* vol. 1, fol. 296r: [April 1618] 'los dits studiants restaren molt satisfets y confortats y prengueren resolutio de venir al diuendres sanct a las sinc horas ab les atxes que porien y ab lo pendon y altres coses y aparells tenian y farian la professo de la santa spina per los claustros y dintre casa sens axir fora, esta professo se fa cada any en acabar lo sermo de la passio, y tambe que al dijous sanct vindrian a combregar los que porien ab los religiosos a la capella major; per adonar en tenent al poble, bisbe y pares teatinos, que ells no son minyons y que les sues empresas no son puerils sino de substantia y valor'.

58   See, for example, the ceremonial of Holy Thursday's procession in 1618; Camprubí et al., *Lumen domus* vol. 1, fols. 296v–297r.

ceased to exist, the students went in procession to carry St. Thomas's image on Holy Thursday.[59] Likewise, the youth confraternity of the Boys of the Archangel Raphael in Florence participated in numerous processions, in addition to the festivity in honour of its patron saint, the Archangel Raphael, on 31 December, which were as much public as private, such as the Corpus Christi, St. Maria Magdalene in July, St. Lawrence in August, All Saints, or, after the Council of Trent, the devotion of the Forty Hours. According to the annals, this devotion was also celebrated in Santa Caterina friary from 1608 onwards; it coincided with St. Thomas Aquinas's feast day, and resulted in arrangements by the Confraternity of the Rosary for 'great music and singing', imitating the 'singing at Montserrat chapel on Saturdays'.[60]

This preliminary survey indicates that the Barcelona Academy and Confraternity of St. Thomas Aquinas was extremely important over the centuries as promoter and financer of events in which music had a fundamental role. Moreover, through this ceremonial, the confraternity served as a link between the friary and the secular world of the university students. The analysis of the presence of music in the festivities organised by the students in Santa Caterina friary also reflects the socio-political situation of the city over time. For instance, in 1713 the procession proceeded through the cloister and did not leave the friary,[61] while in 1714, because of the siege of Barcelona, the festivities

---

59 Gallego Salvadores F.J., "El maestro Diego Mas y su tratado de Metafísica", *Analecta Sacra Tarraconensia* 43.1 (1970) 3–92, here 23–24; Falcó J.J., *Historia de las cosas más notables pertenecientes a este convento de Predicadores de Valencia* (MS) 149–150, Valencia. Biblioteca de la Universitat de València. BH Ms. 0204; Beltrán de Heredia V., "La Academia, la Cofradía y la fiesta de Santa Tomás en Valencia", *Ciencia Tomista* 35 (1927) 208–225, here 212.

60 Camprubí et al., *Lumen domus* vol. 1, fol. 243r: 'Item a la jornada del b. pare sant thomas de aquino y los dias seguents auem en aquest any començat de gozar en esta iglesia del jubileu de les 40 horas concedit per lo summo pontifice paulo v de bona memoria, al qual tenim grans obligations per ser tant affectat a nostra sagrada religio y axi lo concurs de la gent es estat com acostuma en sta iglesia tenint lo santisimo sacrament patent en lo altar major y lo diumenge que era lo 3 dia de dita indulgentia se començaren las completas tant solemnes que los confrares del roser han determinat ques digan a la capella de nostra señora certes jornades ab gran musica y cantoria que cert es cosa digne de oyr; a imitatio de les que als dissaptes se cantan a la capella de Monserrat de la present ciutat negoci es aquest que pot tenir raues y endret y tambe varietat per ocasions; jo me remet a la obra y experientia sols dire que crec se omplira la iglesia tant es cosa apazible y agradable y si en aquest concurs per ser tant gran no si segueixen inconuenients; be anira y sera cosa important la perseuerantia. deu ho encamine a gloria y honra sua y de la casa. Amen. [added:] Sols se son cantades dos vegades'.

61 López Ribao, *Transcripción y estudio del Lumen Domus* 234: 'Se entonà lo *Te Deum* que anaren cantant per lo claustro acompañats de l'orga tot lo que pogueren. Lo tabernacle de sant Thomàs anave en lo mateix puesto que en la professó general. Arribats en lo

in honour of St. Thomas Aquinas were not celebrated in the customary way, with the members of the confraternity organising the event; rather, it was the friars of Santa Caterina who paid the cathedral choir so that, at least, they sang the Mass.[62]

Appendix 1. Printed Lyrics of the Villancicos Composed for the Feast of St. Thomas Aquinas at Santa Caterina friary

Year	Printer	Chapel master	Location of copies	Incipits
1687	Rafael Figueró	Joan Barter	Arxiu Històric de la Ciutat de Barcelona	*Cantan las aves* *La Carroça de Ezequiel* *Ay como sube!* *De competencia gloriosa*
1688	Rafael Figueró	Joan Barter	Biblioteca de Catalunya; Biblioteca Balmes	*Victoria los Thomistas* *Viva España, digan* *Quien me la compra* *A de los Cielos*
1689	Rafael Figueró	Joan Barter	Biblioteca Nacional de España; Biblioteca Lambert Mata; Archivo Histórico Comarcal de Cervera	*A de las Letras* *Cortesanos Celestes* *De vn Angel las glorias*
1690	Rafael Figueró	Joan Barter	Arxiu Històric de la Ciutat de Barcelona	*Sale al campo del Oriente* *Qve sera Thomàs en el mundo?* *Al Sol, que nace cada año* *Si oy las Ciencias superiores*

presbiteri la comunitat dexà los ciris, los demés se quedaren mentres la cantoria cantà un villansico, acabat lo qual se digué la oració del sant y axí se acabà la festa'.

62 López Ribao, *Transcripción y estudio del Lumen Domus* 288: 'No obstant lo siti alguns religiosos han fet cantar un ofici a la capella de la Seu pegant-lo de sos diners sens que los cathedràtichs se sían mostrats en cosa'.

Appendix 1 (*cont.*)

Year	Printer	Chapel master	Location of copies	Incipits
1691	Rafael Figuerò	Joan Barter	Biblioteca de la Universitat de Barcelona	*Ha felizes esferas* *Atalayas Celestes* *Oy el emblema admiro* *Con Alegres acentos*
1692	Rafael Figuerò	Joan Barter	Biblioteca Nacional de España; Biblioteca de la Universitat de Barcelona	*Ha del Campo de Prodigios* *Al Clarin armonioso de la Fama* *Alados Paranimfos*
1694	Rafael Figuerò	Joan Barter	Biblioteca de la Universitat de Barcelona	*Oy de la fama volante* *La Republica del ayre* *Principio de la luz astro brillante* *Qvando al cielo dora*
1695	Rafael Figuerò; Thomas Loriente[a]	Joan Barter	Arxiu Històric de la Ciutat de Barcelona; Biblioteca Nacional de España; Biblioteca de la Universitat de Barcelona	*Què metrico acento* *Que confusion! que desgracia!* *Oy las Aves, los Astros, y Florès* *En diestra competencia*
1696	Rafael Figuerò	Joan Barter	Biblioteca Nacional de España; Biblioteca de la Universitat de Barcelona	*Del Angel Doctor los Timbres* *A de la luzida Tropa de los Astros* *Oy que à Thomas de Aquino* *En el Templo de la Fama*
1697	Rafael Figuerò	Francesc Valls	Biblioteca de Catalunya; Biblioteca Balmes; Biblioteca de la Universitat de Barcelona	*En los Imperios de Eòlo* *Angelicos espiritus celestes* *Pueble del ayre los vagos espacios* *Allà và una Xacarilla*
1698	Rafael Figuerò	Francesc Valls	Biblioteca Nacional de España; Biblioteca de la Universitat de Barcelona	*De trompa sonora, cisado metal* *Oy que al Sol de las Escuelas* *Para ilustrar la esfera* *Bvele veloz de la fama el acento*

Appendix 1 (cont.)

Year	Printer	Chapel master	Location of copies	Incipits
1699	Rafael Figueró	Francesc Valls	Arxiu Històric de la Ciutat de Barcelona; Biblioteca Nacional de España; Biblioteca de Catalunya; Biblioteca de la Universitat de Barcelona	*Dorada trompa que alagas* *Centinelas celestiales* *A de la Celeste Playa* *Enamorada de un Buey*
1700	Rafael Figueró	Francesc Valls	Arxiu Històric de la Ciutat de Barcelona; Biblioteca de Catalunya; Biblioteca Lambert Mata; Biblioteca de la Universitat de Barcelona	*Como en Thomas quatro partes* *Ha de las Angelicas esquadras del Zenid* *Qvestion dudosa examina* *A la novedad atienden*
1701	Rafael Figueró	Francesc Valls	Biblioteca Lambert Mata; Biblioteca de la Universitat de Barcelona	*Ya del Cielo la Esfera luminosa* *Rompen el viento las vagas Esferas* *Viendo, que al Angel Doctor* *Amante sagrado*
1702	Rafael Figueró	Francesc Valls	Biblioteca de Catalunya; Biblioteca Lambert Mata; Biblioteca de la Universitat de Barcelona	*Alados serafines, Celestes Gilgueros* *Oy Thomas Sacro Maestro* *Ha del Palacio del dia* *Discretos venid*
1703	Rafael Figueró	Francesc Valls	Biblioteca de Catalunya; Biblioteca Lambert Mata; Biblioteca de la Universitat de Barcelona	*En la infalible Eclyptica triunfante* *Ha de la Esquadra ardiente de las Luzes* *A Quien celebrar le toca* *Albricias Discretos*
1704	Rafael Figueró	Francesc Valls	Arxiu Històric de la Ciutat de Barcelona; Biblioteca de Catalunya; Biblioteca Lambert Mata; Biblioteca de la Universitat de Barcelona	*Invencibles Campeones* *Qve confusion sonora* *Grammaticos acudid* *Entre los festivos cultos*

Appendix 1 (*cont.*)

Year	Printer	Chapel master	Location of copies	Incipits
1705	Rafael Figueró	Francesc Valls	Arxiu Històric de la Ciutat de Barcelona; Biblioteca de Catalunya; Biblioteca Lambert Mata; Biblioteca de la Universitat de Barcelona	*A fin de enlaçàr primores* *Moradores felizes de Dèlos* *Esferas, Regiones* *Rompa del ayre la concava Esfera*
1706	Rafael Figueró	Francesc Valls	Biblioteca de la Universitat de Barcelona	*Pves de Thomas en el dia* *Ha de la Empirea Mansion* *Candores del Iazmin* *Respire sonòro*
1707	Rafael Figueró	Francesc Valls	Biblioteca de Catalunya	*Siendo tan sabia y valiente* *Inflamado el aliento* *Aves bolad, bolad* *Ha del Ilustre Templo*
1708	Rafael Figueró	Francesc Valls	Biblioteca de Catalunya; Biblioteca Lambert Mata	*Sombras covardes* *Plumas de mi Angel* *Rayo hermoso, si al Aguila ciegas* *Quien eres? Quien eres?*
1709	Rafael Figueró	Francesc Valls	Biblioteca de la Universitat de Barcelona	*En el Golfo de la Fe* *Ya claro el dia al Eco del Clarin* *Feudatarios de Minerva* *Angel Doctor*
1710	Rafael Figueró	Francesc Valls	Biblioteca Nacional de España; Biblioteca de Catalunya; Biblioteca de la Universitat de Barcelona	*Que busca entre las Ciencias su rumor* *Si Templo Soberano* *La Sabiduria, que a Thomas previò* *Pluma, que buelas velòz a la Esfera*
1712	Bartomeu Giralt	Francesc Valls	Biblioteca Nacional de España; Biblioteca de Catalunya; Biblioteca Lambert Mata	*Oy, Thomas, en essas Aras* *Angelicos Coros* *Llegad Ingeniosos*

a These lyrics were published by two printers.

Appendix 2. Villancicos by Francesc Valls Dedicated to St. Thomas Aquinas Preserved at the Biblioteca de Catalunya

Title given in the library catalogue and text incipit	Library call number	Date on which performed at Santa Caterina friary and order no.
Villancico a 12 con ministriles a Sto. Thom de Aquino: *Oy Thomas Santo maestro*	M 1480/3	
Villanco. a Sto. Thomas de Aquino con clarines y violines a 12: *Pues de Thomas en el dia*	M 1474/1	
[Villancico a 16]: *Publique el acento celebre la voz*	M 1689/2p	
Villancico a 12 con violines y clarin al Smo. Sacramento: *Rompa del ayre la diafana esfera*	M 1473/1	
Villancico a 16 con ministriles y violines a Sto. Tomas de Aquino: *Que confusion sonora*	M 1473/6	
Villanco. a 17 con violines y clarin a Sto. Tomas de Aquino: *Invencibles campiones*	M 1469/7	
Villancico a 16 a S. Franco. Xavier con clarines y violines: *En los Imperios de Eolo*	M 1479/12	1697/1
Villancico a 15 con ministriles y violines al Smo. Sto.: *Angelicos espiritus celestes*	M 1483/10	1697/2
Villancico a 14 a Sto. Thomás de Aquino: *Pueble del ayre los vagos espacios*	M 1471/4	1697/3
Villancico a 14 a Santo Thomas de Aquino: *Pueble del ayre los vagos espacios*	M 733/11	1697/3
A S. Raymundo villaco. a 14: *Pueble del ayre los vagos espacios*	M 1480/6	1697/3
Villancico a 16 a Sto. Thomas de Aquino: *Alla va una xacarilla*	M 1473/13	1697/4
Villancico a 16 a Sto. Thomas de Aquino: *Para illustrar la esfera del sol de Aquino*	M 1470/14	1698/3
Villancico a 12 a Sto. Thomas de Aquino con violines y clarin a S. Fraco. de Paula y S. Julian: *Buele veloz de la fama el acento*	M 1469/13	1698/4

Appendix 2 (*cont.*)

Title given in the library catalogue and text incipit	Library call number	Date on which performed at Santa Caterina friary and order no.
[Villancico 1] [a Sto. Thomás de Aquino]: *Dorada trompa que alagas*	M 1686/20	1699/1
Villancico a 8 con violines y clarin a Sto. Thomás de Aquino: *Centinelas celestiales*	M 1473/5	1699/2
Villancico a 12 con ministriles a Sto. Thomas de Aquino: *Ha de la celeste playa*	M 1470/17	1699/3
Villancico a 15 a Sto. Thomas de Aquino con ministriles: *Enamorada de un buey*	M 1473/4	1699/4
Villancico a 16 a Sto. Thomás de Aquino: *Como en Thomas quatro partes*	M 1479/19	1700/1
Villancico a 14 a Sto. Tomas de Aquino: *Ha de las angelicas esquadras*	M 1481/2	1700/2
Villancico a 11 con ministriles a Sto. Tomás de Aquino: *Question dudosa examina*	M 1482/10	1700/3
Villancico a 12 con ministriles A Sto. Thomás de Aquin: *Rompen del viento las vagas espheras*	M 1482/20	1701/2
Villancico a 14 con ministriles a Sto. Thomas de Aquino: *Alados serafines*	M 1479/11	1702/1
Villancico a 20 con ministr. y viols. a Sto. Thomás de Aquino: *Ha del palacio del dia*	M 1479/18	1702/3
Villancico a 16 con violines y clarin a Sto. Thomas de Aquino: *Discretos venid*	M 1482/5	1702/4
Villancico a 15 a Sto. Thomas de Aquino: *Ha de la esquadra ardiente*	M 1482/2	1703/2
Villancico a 13 a Sto. Thomás de Aquino y a S. Augustin: *A quien celebrar le toca*	M 1480/15	1703/2
Villancico a 18 a Sto. Thomás de Aquino viols. y ministrs.: *Albricias discretos*	M 1482/18	1703/4
Villanco. a 15 a Sto. Thomas de Aquino: *Grammaticos acudid*	M 1469/14	1704/3

Appendix 2 (*cont.*)

Title given in the library catalogue and text incipit	Library call number	Date on which performed at Santa Caterina friary and order no.
Villanco. a 16 con ministriles a Sto. Tomas de Aquino: *Entre los festivos cultos*	M 1473/20	1704/4
Villanco. a Na. Sra. a 15 con ministriles: *A fin de enlaçar primores*	M 1469/4	1705/1
Villancico [a 15]: *A fin de enlaçar primores*	M 1679/10	1705/1
Villancico a 14 con clarines y violines a Sto. Thomas de Aquino: *Respire sonoro*	M 1470/15	1706/4
Villanco. a 15 con miniss. a S. Thomas de Aquino: *Siendo tan sabia*	M 1480/12	1707/1
Villanco. a 13 a S. Thomas de Aquino con miniss.: *Aves bolad bolad*	M 1480/17	1707/3
Villanco. a 12 con claris. y violis. a Sto. Thomas de Aquino: *Sombras covardes*	M 1470/16	1708/1
Villanco. a 12 con vios. a S. Thomas de Aquio.: *Plumas de mi angel*	M 1470/18	1708/2
Villanco. a 15 con miniss. a S. Thomas de Aquino: *Rayo hermoso si al aguila ciegas*	M 1474/3	1708/3
Villanco. a 15 con miniss. a S. Thomas de Aquino: *Quien eres, quien eres*	M 1470/3	1708/4
Villanco. a 13 a Sto. Thomas de Aquino: *Pluma q. buelas veloz a la esfera*	M 1474/2	1710/4
Villancico a 9 con vv: *Oy Tomas en essas aras*	M 1480/16	1712/1

Appendix 3. Other Villancicos Dedicated to St. Thomas Aquinas That Are Catalogued as Anonymous at the Biblioteca de Catalunya Some of Which Can Be Identified through Concordances

Title given in the library catalogue and text incipit	Library call number	Date performed at Santa Caterina friary and order no.	Attribution
Villancico a 16 a Sto. Thomás de Aquino: *Oy de la fama volante*	M 1480/13	1694/1	Joan Barter
Villancico a 16 a Sto. Thomás de Aquino: *Oy que al sol de las escuelas*	M 1481/20	1698/2	Francesc Valls
Villancico a 16 a Sto. Thomás de Aquino: *A la novedad atiendan*	M 1482/17	1700/4	Francesc Valls
Villancico a 12 con ministriles a Sto. Thomás de Aquino: *Ya del cielo la esphera luminosa*	M 1482/11	1701/1	Francesc Valls
Villancico a 20 con ministr. y violis. a Sto. Thomas de Aquino: *Viendo que al angel doctor*	M 1482/4	1701/3	Francesc Valls
[Villancico a 16]: *En la infalible Ecliptica triumfante*	M 1482/17	1703/1	Francesc Valls
Villanco. a 13 con ministriles a S. Thomas de Aquino: *Candores del jazmin*	M 1479/16	1706/3	Francesc Valls
Villancico a 16 a Sto. Thomás de Aquino: *La republica del ayre*	M 1479/20	1694/2	
Villancico a 9 con vv a to. Thomas de Aquino: *Pues con el sol adorna*	M 1481/18		

Appendix 3 (cont.)

Title given in the library catalogue and text incipit	Library call number	Date performed at Santa Caterina friary and order no.	Attribution
Villancico segundo con violines y trompas A 40. Al Angelico Doctor Sto. Thomas de Aquino: *Cielos atiendan*	M 773/4		
Villancico à 11: *Ay que se abrassa*	M 745/16		
R[esponsio]n a 9: *Suspendase el ayre*	M 769/42		

Bibliography

Primary Sources

Andrés Pablo, *El sol en el signo de Tauro, el angelico maestro y quinto doctor de la Iglesia Santo Thomas de Aquino* [...] (Barcelona, Juan Jolis: [1695?]).

Camprubí Francesc et al., *Lumen domus o Annals del convent de Santa Caterina de Barcelona* (MS, 1603–1802), 3 vols. Barcelona. Universitat de Barcelona. Ms. 1005–1007.

Concepción Carlos de la, *Oracion panegirica y evangelica en aplauso del angel entre los doctores y doctor entre los angeles, Santo Thomas de Aquino* [...] (Barcelona, Vicente Surià: 1689).

Estatutos de la Academia bajo la invocación del Angelico Doctor S[an]to Thomàs erigida con autoridad ordinaria, y Apostolica en la Yglesia de Santa Catha[lina] V[i]r[gen] y M[a]r[tir] Orden de Pred[icadore]s en Barcelona por los años de 1584 (eighteenth-century copy), Barcelona, Arxiu Històric de la Ciutat, Documentació personal de Marià Aguiló, caja 1.

Estevan Felipe, *Oracion primera que en las maximas fiestas que en el real convento de Santa Catalina Martir de esta Excelentissima Ciudad de Barcelona, consagraron al angelico Doctor S. Thomas de Aquino* [...] (Barcelona, Juan Jolis: 1708).

Falcó Jaime Juan, *Historia de las cosas más notables pertenecientes a este convento de Predicadores de Valencia* (MS, 1720). Valencia. Biblioteca de la Universitat de València. BH Ms. 0204.

Goigs de Sant Thomas de Aquino, Doctor Quint de la Iglesia (Barcelona, Ioan Iolis: 1726).

Goigs de Sant Thomas de Aquino, Doctor Quint de la Iglesia (Barcelona, Hereus de Joan Jolis: [1780?]).

Rebullosa Jaume, *Relacion de las grandes fiestas que en esta ciudad de Barcelona se han echo à la canonizacion de su hijo San Ramon de Peñafort, de la Orden de los Predicadores: Con vn sumario de su Vida, Muerte y Canonizacion, y siete Sermones que los Obispos han predicado en ellas* (Barcelona, Iayme Cendrat: 1601).

"Sobre la m[erce]d que supp[li]ca la confradria de los estudiantes pobres de la Ciudad de Valencia" (12 August 1593), Barcelona, Arxiu de la Corona d'Aragó [ACA]. Consejo de Aragón. Legajos 0651 n°118.

Secondary Sources

Alejo Montes F.J., *La cofradía en defensa de los estudiantes presos en la cárcel de la Universidad de Salamanca del siglo XVI* (Salamanca: 2016).

Beltrán de Heredia V., "La Academia, la Cofradía y la fiesta de Santa Tomás en Valencia", *Ciencia Tomista* 35 (1927) 208–225.

Camprubí X., *La premsa a Catalunya durant la Guerra de Successió* (Valencia: 2016).

Cases i Loscos L. et al. (eds.), *Dietaris de la Generalitat de Catalunya* (Barcelona: 1994), 10 vols.

Eisenbichler K., *A Youth Confraternity in Florence, 1411–1785* (Toronto: 1998).

Fernández Luzón A., *La Universidad de Barcelona en el siglo XVI* (Ph.D. dissertation, Universitat Autònoma de Barcelona: 2003) http://hdl.handle.net/10803/4791.

Gallego Salvadores F.J., "El maestro Diego Mas y su tratado de Metafísica", *Analecta Sacra Tarraconensia* 43.1 (1970), 3–92.

Iglesias Castellano A., *Entre la voz y el texto: Los ciegos oracioneros y papelistas en la España Moderna (1500–1836)* (Madrid: 2022).

Knighton T., "Relating History: Music and Meaning in the *relaciones* of the Canonization of St Raymond Penyafort", in Ferreira M.P. – Cascudo T. (eds.), *Música e História: Estudos em homenagem a Manuel Carlos de Brito* (Lisbon: 2017) 27–51.

López Ribao A.J., "Las cofradías y asociaciones seglares del convento de Santa Catalina virgen y mártir de Barcelona en el siglo XVIII", *Teología Espiritual* 61.180 (2017) 365–390.

López Ribao A.J., *El convento de Santa Catalina virgin y mártir, de Barcelona, en el siglo XVIII* (Salamanca: 2021).

López Ribao A.J., *Transcripción y estudio del Lumen Domus o Anals del convent de Santa Caterina verge i màrtir de Barcelona. Orde de Predicadors* (Salamanca: 2021).

Matute y Gaviria J., *Anales eclesiásticos y seculares de la muy noble y leal ciudad de Sevilla, metrópoli de Andalucía que contienen las más principales memorias desde el año de 1701, en que empezó a reinar el rey D. Felipe V, hasta el de 1800, que concluyó con una horrorosa epidemia* (Seville: 1887), 3 vols.

Mazuela-Anguita A., "Las pandorgas a través de sus fuentes: Música estudiantil en el mundo hispánico a inicios de la Edad Moderna", *Cuadernos de Música Iberoamericana* 32 (2019) 347–370.

Pavia i Simó J., *La Música a la Catedral de Barcelona durant el segle XVII* (Barcelona: 1986).

Rossich A., "Segimon Comas i Vilar, acadèmic i preceptista", in Solervicens Bo J. – Miralles Jori E. (eds.), *El (Re)descobriment de l'edat moderna: estudis en homenatge a Eulàlia Duran* (Barcelona: 2007) 431–461.

Ruiz Fargas M., *La biblioteca del Convent de Santa Caterina de Barcelona sota el mecenatge de fran Tomàs Ripoll, 1699–1747* (Ph.D. dissertation, Universitat de Barcelona: 2019) http://hdl.handle.net/10803/669226.

Tusquets i Terrats J., "El Cardenal Joan-Tomàs de Boxadors i la seva influència en el Renaixement del Tomisme", *Anuari de la Societat de Filosofia* 1 (1923) 243–304.

Voltes P.M., "Estatutos aprobados por la academia de Santo Tomás de Aquino de Barcelona, en 1711", *Analecta Sacra Tarraconensia* 34.2 (1961) 341–360.

CHAPTER 6

The Sonic and Ceremonial Contribution of the Confraternity of Sant Jordi and the *Centenar de la Ploma* to Celebratory Processions in Valencia

Ferran Escrivà-Llorca

Abstract

The Valencia brotherhood of Sant Jordi was inextricably linked to the *Centenar del Gloriós Sant Jordi* (one hundred men of St. George), also known as the *Centenar de la Ploma*. This civic militia of crossbowman was created by Pere IV after the victory of 1365, during the siege of Morvedre in the war with Castile, and its main purpose was to guard and defend the royal flag of the city of Valencia, symbol of the king. The Confraria i Almoina de Sant Jordi (Brotherhood and Almshouse of Saint George) was founded only six years later (1371) and at first comprised 100 men and 150 women. At the end of the fifteenth century, Joan I was appointed a member of the brotherhood and increased the number to 500 men and 600 women. It was thus among the oldest and most celebrated in Valencia, together with that of Saint James and the Presbyters of the cathedral. Both the brotherhood and the militia were the protagonists of two of the most important annual festivities in the city from that time: Saint George and Sant Denis: 9 October, date of the Christian conquest of Valencia by Jaume I in 1237. Although the brotherhood was originally created to give aid, alms and burial to its members – who mostly belonged to the militia –, both confraternity members and the militia, as well as the buildings where they met, were remarkable agents in the changes in the urban soundscape of Valencia over the fifteenth and sixteenth centuries. They were prominent participants in the festive, large-scale celebrations for military victories – such as those of Ferdinand the Catholic in 1487, Emperor Charles V in 1547 or the Patriarch Juan de Ribera in 1610 (the expulsion of the Moors), or in the radical changes in the city and therefore in its acoustic spaces before and after the revolt of the Germania (1519–1523). Thus, the brotherhood of Saint George and the *Centenar de la Ploma* were direct protagonists and participants in the transformation of the medieval role of representation towards a more humanistic integration with the rise of the Habsburg dynasty during the sixteenth century.

Keywords

Valencia – *Centenar de la Ploma* – St. George – confraternity – processions

As is well known, St. George is patron saint of the chivalric orders.[1] His key appearance and intercession in many battles transformed the medieval paladin into the protector of kingdoms, kings and cities. Whether for the conquest of dragons or the Infidel, the saint was venerated in many European regions. In Valencia, his exalted intervention in the Battle of El Puig, on the feast of the Assumption of the Virgin, 15 August 1237, marked the triumph of the Aragonese King Jaume I against the Muslims. On 9 October that year, the king's victorious entry into the city was celebrated. Within a short period of time, devotion to the saint sprang up, and he was adopted as the patron saint of the Kingdom of Valencia. The Valencian chronicler Gaspar Juan Escolano (1560–1619) relates in his account of 1611 that 'the first [church] to be blessed after the main church [cathedral], was a mosque in honour of the patron saint St. George; and the king and his victorious army processed to [the church] with went an impressive display of crosses and clergy, on Saturday, the feast day of St. Denis' ('la primera que se bendijo después de la mayor, fue una mezquita a honrra del patrón San Jorge; y fueron a ella el Rey y su exercito vitorioso en concertada procession de cruzes y clerezia, el sábado día de San Dionysio').[2] The link between St. George and the city of Valencia, and its ceremonial and processions, was forged not only because he was the first royal patron saint in the Crown of Aragon, but also because of the quasi-mystical aura of the crusade against the Infidel that reached a key stage in Valencia.[3] Nevertheless, it was around the time of the centenary of the Christian conquest of the city in

---

1 I am grateful to Tess Knighton, Mª José Iglesias Pastén, Ana López Suero and Andrea Bombi for their comments and suggestions. This chapter forms part of the project 'The Contribution of Confraternities and Guilds to the Urban Soundscape, c. 1400–c. 1700', MINECO. CONFRASOUND (PID2019-109422GB-100). I+D+i – PGC TIPO B, 2020–2023.
2 Escolano Gaspar, *Segunda parte de la Década primera de la Historia de la insigne y coronada Ciudad y Reino de Valencia* (Valencia, Pedro Patricio Mey: 1611) 911–912.
3 The early contribution by the musicologist Higinio Anglés to the study of the musical elements of the military Order of St. George in the Crown of Aragon and devotion to him on the part of the Aragonese kings, is of considerable interest: Anglés H., "L'Ordre de Sant Jordi durant els segles XIII–XIV i la devoció dels reis d'Aragó al sant cavaller", in *Miscellània Fontserè* (Barcelona: 1961) 41–64.

1338 that devotion to St. George intensified and became an established part of the annual cycle of urban ceremonial there.[4]

This chapter focuses on the Valencian Confraternity of Sant Jordi and the closely related urban militia, the *Centenar de la Ploma*, and their sonic contribution to the ceremonial of the processions held on the saint's feast day (23 April) and that of St. Denis (9 October), as well as other similar urban rituals. The *Centenar de la Ploma* was the denomination used for the company of a hundred crossbowmen of the city of Valencia, which received this name because of the feather worn on their helmets. Their foundation dates to 1365 ('centum ballistarii vocati "de la Ploma"'),[5] in a similar manner to that of the Priorate of the Order of St. George of Alfama based in the saint's chapel in Valencia Cathedral. This chapel had been founded earlier in 1324 and complemented the other priorate held by the Order in Alfama in the diocese of Tortosa. That military order had been founded by Pere II of Aragon (1178–1213) in 1201, but had disappeared with that monarch's death; however, it was refounded by Pere IV of Aragon in 1324, and would finally be integrated into the powerful Order of Montesa.[6]

The company of the *Ploma* was formed as an urban militia of crossbowmen on foot, and consisted mainly of artisans and workers under the leadership of the Officer of Criminal Justice (*Justicia criminal*) of Valencia.[7] Their main role was to guard and have in its safe keeping the *Senyera* (the Valencian city flag), although previously the militia had been formed to help the king defend the city from the attacks mounted by King Pedro I of Castile. On 3 June 1365, by way of reward for their support, Pere II, at the instance of the judiciary and city councillors (*prohomes*), granted them a number of privileges and

---

4   For a summary of the legend of St. George and its impact on history and art in the Crown of Aragon, see: Sorolla-Romero T., "Dragones, sangre y campanas", in Mínguez Cornelles V. (ed.), *El linaje del Rey Monje. La configuración cultural e iconográfica de la Corona aragonensis (1164–1516)* (Castellón de la Plana: 2018) 27–52.
5   Martínez Vinat J., *Cofradías y oficios. Entre la acción confraternal y la organización corporativa en la Valencia medieval (1238–1516)* (Ph.D dissertation, Universidad de Valencia: 2018) 595.
6   On the *Centenar de la Ploma* and the Confraternity of St. George in Valencia, see the two classic studies: Querol y Roso L., *Las milicias valencianas desde el siglo XIII al XV. Contribución al estudio de la organización militar del antiguo Reino de Valencia* (Castellón de la Plana: 1935); and Sevillano Colom F., *El Centenar de la Ploma de la Ciutat de València 1365–1711* (Barcelona: 1966). On the Order of Montesa, see: Cerdà i Ballester J. et al. (eds.), *Santa María de Montesa la orden militar del Reino de Valencia (ss. XIV–XIX)* (Valencia: 2019).
7   The *Justicia criminal* was a municipal officer of justice in cities, towns and royal places who was elected every year to deal with judicial issues on behalf of the king. Furió A., *Història del País Valencià* (Valencia: 1995) 64; Valero de Bernabé L. – Eugenio M. de, "Instituciones nobiliarias del Reino de Valencia", *Hidalguía* 67.382 (2020) 91–126, here 104; Pérez García, P., *El justicia criminal de Valencia (1479–1707): una magistratura urbana valenciana ante la consolidación del absolutismo* (Valencia: 1991).

exemptions that greatly increased their prestige and standing, especially among the artisan classes and trade guilds.[8] In 1707 the *Centenar de la Ploma*, as a legally-recognised institution of the Valencian region, was abolished, as were the laws pertaining to regional Independence, as a result of the War of Spanish Succession (1701–1714).

1 The Confraternity of Sant Jordi

The Valencian Confraternity of Sant Jordi was founded on 10 July 1371 at the behest of the crossbowmen of the *Centenar*; it was modelled on the 'alms-based charity of St. Narcissus "whose holy body [is preserved] in Gerona", located in the city of Valencia' ('l'almoyna de St. Narcís, montsenyor Sent Narcís, cors sant de Gerona, ordonada en la Ciutat de València').[9] King Pere IV of Aragon approved the request for the foundation statutes in the name of the 'College of crossbowmen called "of the *Ploma*" [...] as members of the confraternity of the blessed knight and martyr, his lordship St. George' ('Col·legi dels ballesters apel·lats de la Ploma [...] com a confrares de la confraria del benaventurat cavaller e martre [*sic*] mossèn Sent Jordi').[10] In contrast to other major cities in the Kingdom of Aragon such as Barcelona, Palma de Mallorca or Gerona, in Valencia the confraternity did not consist of noble knights, although they shared their military roots.[11]

The confraternity's chapel was based in the church of Sant Jordi, which was not consecrated until 1401.[12] This church, the focal point of the urban

---

[8] Central to these privileges was that members could not be forced by royal officials to enlist in any troops nor to undertake guard duties, day or night; nor were they obliged to enter or sojourn in any castle against their will, nor be recruited by force to serve on battleships. They also held the privilege of being able to carry arms, by day and night, a perquisite that led to many conflicts on innumerable occasions.

[9] Martínez Vinat, "Cofradías y oficios" 598, based on the document preserved in the Arxiu de la Corona d'Aragó [ACA]. Real Cancillería reg. 921 fols. 87r–88v. See also: Sevillano Colom, *El Centenar de la Ploma de la Ciutat de València* 60.

[10] Sevillano Colom, *El Centenar de la Ploma de la Ciutat de València* 19.

[11] Ribot i Iglésias M., "La Confraria dels Cavallers de Sant Jordi de Barcelona en sus últimos tiempos", in *Primer Congrés d'Història Moderna de Catalunya* (Barcelona: 1984), vol. 1, 463–469; Ferrer Flórez M., "La cofradía de San Jorge y los orígenes de la R.S.E.M.A.P.", *Memòries de la Reial Acadèmia Mallorquina d'Estudis Genealògics, Heràldics i Històrics*, 10 (2000) 137–170, here 137–138; Negre i Pastell P., "La cofradía de san Jorge y la nobleza gerundense", *Annals de l'Institut d'Estudis Gironins* 6 (1951) 271–322, here 271–272.

[12] Before this date, the chapel of the knights of the Order of St. George was administered by the parish church of Sant Andreu.

celebration of festive processions, was located in the former square of Sant Jordi.[13] Inside the church, the confraternity's chapel was the first on the right-hand side, now with the figure of the Virgin of Victory presiding over the altar.[14] The confraternity also owned other buildings, such as the House of the Crossbows (*Casa de la Ballesteria*), where they held their meetings and the confreres and the members of the *Centenar* practised their arms and their ceremonial.[15] For many years, the main altar was presided over by the retable of St. George, a work considered by art historians to represent a magnificent example of international Gothic art of the Valencian school, dating from the first quarter of the fifteenth century. It belonged to the Confraternity of Sant Jordi and depicts the legend of the holy Christian warrior; in the second half of the nineteenth century, it was purchased in Paris for the South Kensington Museum, now known as the Victoria and Albert Museum.[16]

The feast of the patron saint of the church of Sant Jordi was commemorated annually on 23 April. Nearby, as can be read in the ordinations proposed by the members of the *Centenar* and approved by King Pere IV, the confraternity organised the mandatory yearly banquet so that the whole membership would gather together.[17] This feast involved rations for the poor to signal the brotherhood's charitable nature. General chapter meetings were held three times a year: on the last Sunday in August; the first Sunday of January; and the Sunday closest to St. George's day. Members of the confraternity paid 12 *diners* (1 *sou*) at each meeting.[18] It was led by an unspecified number of stewards (*mayorals*), and it employed a number of *andadors* or criers who called members together for meetings and on other occasions. The chapter had the king's permission to

---

13 The square formerly known as that of Sant Jordi almost coincides with the present-day square of Rodrigo Botet.

14 Gil Saura Y., "Memoria de un espacio montesiano desaparecido: La Iglesia y Colegio de San Jorge de la ciudad de Valencia", in Gil Saura Y. – Alba E. – Enric Guinot E. (eds.), *La Orden de Montesa y San Jorge de Alfama. Arquitecturas, imágenes y textos* (Valencia: 2019) 45–72, here 48–49.

15 This building is adjacent to the present-day Teatre Principal on the street named Poeta Querol.

16 Miquel Juan M., "El gótico internacional en la ciudad de Valencia: El retablo de san Jorge del Centenar de la Ploma", *Goya. Revista de arte* 336 (2011) 191–213. The retable can be seen at: https://collections.vam.ac.uk/item/O17807/altarpiece-of-st-george-altarpiece-master-of-the/.

17 Arxiu de la Corona d'Aragó [ACA]. Real Cancillería. reg. 3635 fols. 21v–23v. See also: Sevillano Colom, *El Centenar de la Ploma de la Ciutat de València* 59–65.

18 In Valencia, the Carolingian monetary system was used with the equivalence 1 *solido* = 12 *denarius*; see: Redish A., *Bimetallism: An Economic and Historical Analysis* (Cambridge: 2006) 5.

approve new statutes and provisions, on condition that the royal governor or his deputy was present. The earliest statutes prescribe the celebration of the patron saint's feast day:

> Annual gathering for St. George's Day.
> Item, that those of the said confraternity may gather every year, on the feast day of St. George, in the church that is built in his honour in the city of Valencia, to celebrate the solemnity of the feast there; and at Mass and Vespers, the candles must be lit, and the church must be the headquarters of the confraternity from now on. And whenever it is decreed, Masses may be sung for the souls of the benefactors of the confraternity. And that the officers of the said confraternity may establish, with the approval of the majority of the confraternity and each individual member, and pay to have the said Masses sung as necessary.[19]

As regards the 'Burial, Masses and prayers' ('Enterraments, misses i oracions') for confraternity members, the statutes specify:

> Item, that all those men and women who are members of the said confraternity are required to go to the burial of their confreres, and to say for their soul fifty times the Paternoster and fifty times the Ave Maria, when attending the burial or, at least, over the following eight days, or to say a Requiem Mass, or twice the penitential psalms with the litany.[20]

However, the increase in number of members and prestige of the confraternity obliged King Joan I of Aragon, at the behest of the members of the *Centenar*

---

19   Sevillano Colom, *El Centenar de la Ploma de la Ciutat de València* 62: 'Aplec anyal per sant Jordi. Item, que los de la dita almoyna se puxen aplegar cascún any, lo dia de la festa de Sent Jordi, a la església que a honor d'aquell és edificada en la Ciutat de València, e fer aquí solemnitat de la dita festa, e a la missa e a les vespres tenir sos ciris encesos, e la dita església sia lur cap d'aquí avant e de la dita almoyna. E cada vegada que'ls serà ben vist, puxen allí fer cantar misses per les ànimes dels dessús dits benfeytors de la dita almoyna. E, que'ls majorals de la dita almoyna puxen tatxar, ab consell de la major partida dels de la dita almoyna, e a cascún de la dita almoyna, a pagar en fer cantar les dites misses si necessari serà'.

20   Sevillano Colom, *El Centenar de la Ploma de la Ciutat de València* 64: 'Item, que tots aquells e aquelles qui seran de la dita almoyna, sien tenguts de anar a la sepultura de aquells qui seran de la dita almoyna, e dir per lur ànima cinquanta vegades lo pater noster e cinquanta vegades la Ave Maria, quan iran a la sepultura o, al tot menys, los deguen dir dins espay de vuit diez aprés següents, o fer dir una missa de Requiem, o dues vegades los Salms penitencials ab la letania'.

de la Ploma, to revise the statutes, and on 10 February 1393, the king and queen became members of the Valencian Confraternity of Sant Jordi. The most significant innovation of the new statutes was that 'all those who from now on want to have the privilege of belonging to the *Centenar de la Ploma*, must, whether they wish to or not, be a member of the said confraternity' ('que tots aquells que d'ací avant harán lo dit privilegi del *Centenar de la* Ploma, hajen a ésser, vullen o no, de la dita confraria'), indicating that from that moment the 'one hundred' were indivisible from the confraternity. As a result of this statute, a clause was inserted permitting an increase in the number of members of up to 500 men and 600 women, although women continued to be forbidden from holding office and attending the chapter meetings. This document also established the confraternity's possessions in the church of Sant Jordi: their chapel, ornaments, funerary materials and 'bells in the house of the church of Sant Jordi in Valencia, and which they can also use, enjoy and ring as they wish, now and in the future' ('campanes en la casa de l'esglesia de Sent Jordi de València, e de que aquelles aximateix usar, fruir e obrar, segons que'ls plaurà, ara e en l'esdevenidor').[21]

As Pablo Pérez has noted, during the fifteenth and sixteenth centuries, the *Centenar* had been transformed from a militia into a corporation dedicated to ceremonial enactment. The mandate to guard and defend the *Senyera* was representative of the longstanding legal independence of Valencia, and its presence in the major processions of the city thus held great symbolic significance.[22] However, one of the most important ways in which the Confraternity of Sant Jordi distinguished itself was that 'it was destined to become the epicentre of the "earthquake" caused by the brotherhoods' uprising' ('estaba llamada a convertirse en el epicentro del "terremoto" agermanado').[23] This was no trivial matter given that the Revolt of the Brotherhoods (*germanies*), which took place between 1519 and 1523, changed the political structure and resulted in profound social change in the kingdom of Valencia. This kind of protagonism on the part of the guild confraternities may well have been one of the main reasons that, following the Council of Trent, the Valencian clergy strove to reorganise the confraternities and bring them under greater control. For example, in the 1594 Valencian synod initiated by St. Juan de Ribera, at that

---

21 Sevillano Colom, *El Centenar de la Ploma de la Ciutat de València* 69.
22 Pérez García P., "En los márgenes de la Germanía: la cofradía de San Jorge y el regente Garcés de Jaunas", in González-Raymond, A. – Jiménez Monteserín M. – Quero F. (eds.), *Normes, marges et confins: hommage au professeur Raphaël Carrasco* (Montpellier: 2018), vol. 2, 227–241.
23 Pérez García, "En los márgenes de la Germanía" 235.

time Archbishop of Valencia, an attempt was made to correct the abuses that arose from confraternal feast-day celebrations which were considered to be scandalous and irreverent.[24] The majority of long-established confraternities with members who bore arms, such as those of Sant Jordi in Valencia, tended to lose popularity during this period and their activities to become limited to the arena of the communities' (*comuneros*) disputes.[25]

2   Processions

As in other Christian cities, the most important procession in Valencia was – and still is – that of Corpus Christi, with its representation of all the civic, military and ecclesiastical estates, as well as the parish and conventual churches. It was the ritual in which confraternities and guilds participated in a high-profile way. The Corpus procession also marked the main processional route and the itinerary followed by entries of royalty and other prestigious persons during the later Middle Ages and early modern period.[26] However, there were two other processions that stood out from dozens of others in the annual festive cycle and which shared a common denominator in the leading role played by the *Centenar de la Ploma*: the most important was that of St. Denis, followed by that of St. George.[27] The procession held on St. George's day, now little known, celebrated the patron saint of the Kingdom of Valencia until the eighteenth century when it gave way to deeply-rooted devotions, such as that of St. Vicent Ferrer which was enormously popular from the time of his canonisation by Pope Callixtus III in 1455.[28] It should be borne in mind that St. George represented the military branch of the Valencian Generalitat, or regional government, in the same way that the Virgen de la Antigua interceded for the ecclesiastical estate, and the Guardian Angel was the advocate of the cities

---

24   Benlloch Poveda A., "Sínodos valentinos y reforma a finales del siglo XVI", in *Corrientes espirituales en la Valencia del siglo XVI: (1550–1600). Actas del II Symposio de Teología Histórica (20–22 abril 1982)* (Valencia: 1983) 169–182, here 180.

25   Diago Hernando M., "El factor religioso en el conflicto de las Comunidades de Castilla (1520–1521): el papel del clero", *Hispania sacra* 5.119 (2007) 84–114.

26   Narbona Vizcaíno R., "Apreciaciones históricas e historiográficas en torno a la fiesta del Corpus Christi de Valencia", *Revista d'història medieval* 10 (1999) 371–382.

27   A good summary of the importance of these two procesiones is found in: Granell Sales F., "Commemorating a Providential Conquest in Valencia: The 9 October Feast", *Religions* 13.301 (2022) 1–22.

28   Valor Moncho P., "En torno a los orígenes de la devoción a san Vicente Ferrer en Valencia", in Callado Estela E. (ed.), *Tiempos de reforma. Pensamiento y religión en la época de Carlos V* (Madrid: 2022) 455–494.

of the kingdom, and this left its mark on iconography and music connected with Valencia. Good examples are found in the musical works dedicated to Valencian saints, held at the College of Corpus Christi, and the iconographical programme of the *Sala Nova* of the palace of the Generalitat.[29]

The various sources consulted for this study all point to the major role of the Confraternity of Sant Jordi and the *Centenar de la Ploma* in these two processions. The ceremonial relating to the symbolic representation of the military estate was established over the course of the century following the conquest of the city of Valencia (1338). The confraternity, together with the *Centenar de la Ploma*, quickly began to take a leading role in their corresponding annual festivities, which were similar in terms of ceremonial and participation. From 1610, a third procession, in commemoration of the expulsion of the Muslims, was added. The ceremonial or *consueta* of Valencia Cathedral, compiled in the sixteenth and seventeenth centuries, offers detailed information on these festivities, including the adornment of altars and chapels and the vestments worn by the clergy.[30] The altar boys (*escolans*) had to prepare and arrange the presbytery with the poles (*barrades*) needed to support the baldachin of red velvet. In the procession, the bishop rode on a donkey, carrying the relic of St. George (an arm with its hand). In addition, a ceremonial book created specifically for these processions was carried by a deacon and was used for the blessing of the flag. The *consueta* indicates that if the day of the procession fell on a Sunday, it should be held after Mass and the antiphons *Asperges me* or *Vidi aquam* ('los asperges') and *Signum salutis pone domine* should be sung during the blessing.[31] When the procession returned to the cathedral, a sermon – paid for by the city council – was preached, and then the bell was

---

29 Climent J., *Fondos Musicales de la Región Valenciana II. Real Colegio de Corpus Christi Patriarca* (Valencia: 1984) 20. Manuscript IV (Valencia. Archivo del Real Colegio-Seminario de Corpus Christi) is a nineteenth-century copy of musical settings by Juan Bautista Comes of *goigs* (sung praises) of Valencian patron saints instituted by the founder of the College of St. Juan de Ribera in accordance with Valencian tradition. There are settings dedicated to Nuestra Señora de la Antigua, St. Vicent Ferrer, the Guardian Angel and St. Maurus; see: Gil Saura Y., "De la sitiada de la Sala Nova a los retratos reales valencianos: Rostros de los diputados y la monarquía", in Furió A. – García Marsilla J.V. (eds.), *La veu del regne. 600 anys de la Generalitat Valenciana. La Generalitat Valenciana. Espais i imatges de la Generalitat*, 3 vols. (Valencia: 2020), vol. 3, 141–168.

30 Martí Mestre J. – Serra Estellés X., *La consueta de la Seu de València dels segles XVI–XVII. Estudi i edició del Ms. 405 de l'ACV* (Valencia: 2009) 239–242.

31 Martí Mestre – Serra Estellés, *La consueta de la Seu de València* 241.

rung for Mass.[32] The procession was held every year unless St. George's Day happened to fall on Easter Sunday.

The *consueta*, key to understanding Valencian liturgy and ceremonial of the time, makes no mention of the Confraternity of Sant Jordi, although it does refer to the brotherhoods of Sant James, Virgen Maria de la Seu and Sant Narcissus whose feast days were celebrated in the cathedral, while that of Sant Jordi took place in its homonymous church. These four confraternities were the oldest to be founded in Valencia. However, the ceremonial does afford insight into the different ways in which the bells were sounded to convey the death of a confraternity member and to signal confraternal participation in festivities, as well as the customary expenditure on, for example, the gratuities given by the stewards of the Confraternity of Sant Jaume to the altar boys on its feast day (25 July).[33] The *consueta* also provides information on the participation of these four confraternities in the liturgical life of the city, especially on the feast of the Assumption of the Virgin (15 August), which was the advocation of the cathedral since its consecration as well as that of almost all the churches of the Kingdom of Valencia following the Christian conquest.[34]

The feast day of St. Denis was celebrated slightly differently to that of St. George according to the ceremonial indicated in the *consueta* in that the sermon preached after the procession took the conquest of Valencia as its theme ('el de la Conquesta'); it also specifies: 'The subsacristan should not forget to give the bishop's assistant the book of the blessing of the flag, that is, for the blessing that is offered on St. George's Day' ('No s'oblide lo sotsagristà de donar a l'asistent del bisbe lo libre de la benedicció de la bandera, per la benedicció que·s fa en Sent Jordi').[35] Both this sermon, and that for St. George's Day, were preached in the cathedral square. On St. George's Day in 1413, the

---

[32] It is noteworthy that the adornments used for St. George's Day were retained for the following feasts of St. Mark (25 April) and St. Peter of Verona (29 April).

[33] Martínez Vinat J., "La cofradía de San Jaime", in Narbona Vizcaíno R. (ed.), *Ciudad y Reino: claves del siglo de oro valenciano* (Valencia: 2015) 266–271.

[34] Bayerri E., "El misterio de la Asunción de María en la liturgia hispana medieval", *Estudios Marianos* 6 (1947) 381–402. On the dramatic representations related to the feast of the Assumption in the Kingdom of Valencia, see: Quirante Santacruz L., *Teatro asuncionista valenciano de los siglos XV y XVI* (Valencia: 1987) 31; and on the music produced for the same occasion, see: Bombi A., "'Como vara de humo a su región'. Villancicos, oratorios y óperas asuncionistas en Valencia. (1679–1750)", in Lluís Sirera J. (ed.), *La mort com a personatge. L'assumpció com a tema. Actes del VI Seminari de Teatre i Música medievals. Elx, 29 al 31 d'octubre de 2000* (Elche: 2002) 53–91.

[35] The 1666 edition of the Sermon of the Conquest by Gaspar Blay Arbuxech is well known: *Sermo de la S. Conquista de la molt insigne noble, leal, e coronada ciutat de Valencia, predicat en la [...] esglesia metropolitana de dita ciutat a 9 de Octubre any 1666 [...] per*

sermon was given by fray Vicent Ferrer who was present in the city for Lent.[36] While the feast of St. Denis celebrated the Christian conquest of the city, the following Sunday the feast of the Dedication of Valencia Cathedral was also held. The procession mounted for the feast of St. Denis – the only one still to be celebrated today – became the quintessential representation for the celebration of the fight against the Infidel. From the Middle Ages, announcements by the town crier (*crides*) refer to this motivation: 'the said feast [should] be fully venerated and celebrated, and be the mercy and benign nature of Our Lord God Jesus Christ almighty, winner of battles that give victory to the Christians against the evil Saracens of the sect of the abominable Mahomet' ('que la dita festa sia complidament colta e celebrada e que sia mercé e benignitat del Nostre Senyor Déu Jesucrist tot poderós, lo qual és vencedor de les batalles que do victòria a cristians contra los malvats sarrahins seguents la secta del abominable Mahomet').[37] This celebration began in 1338 and the processional itinerary was established in tandem with that of the feast day of St. George. The visit to the church dedicated to the saint was obligatory, and, from a later date, the procession continued to the monastery of Sant Vicent Màrtir (de la Roqueta), extramuros, with all the customary paraphernalia, including the sound of trumpets, drums and crossbows of the *Centenar de la Ploma*. When the procession returned to the cathedral, the *Te Deum laudamus* was sung. The most important symbol of the St. Denis procession was the *Senyera*, which was consecrated during the ritual of St. George's Day.

The third procession, created in imitation of the other two in its ceremonial and symbolic significance, and in which both the Confraternity of Sant Jordi and the *Centenar de la Ploma* participated, was founded in 1610. Because of conflict with the *moriscos* (converted muslims) and the issuing of the decree of expulsion: 'the city and the council of Valencia, in order to perpetuate the memory of the expulsion of the *moriscos* [...] [ordain] that for ever there should be an obligation for future generations to make a general procession to the parish church of Sant Esteve' ('La ciudad y el consejo de Valencia para dexar eternizada la memoria de la expulsión de los Moriscos, [...] que para siempre quedasse obligación a los venideros de hacer procesión general a la parroquia

---

lo R. Docttor Gaspar Blay Arbuxech, prebere de la Real Congregacio del Oratori (Valencia, Geroni Vilagrasa: 1666).

36 Sanchis Sivera J., *Quaresma de sant Vicent Ferrer: predicada a València l'any 1413* (Barcelona: 1927) 319ff.

37 Valencia. Arxiu Històric Municipal [AHM], 3-IV-1341. *Manual de Consells*. A-4: fol. 40v. The document is reproduced and translated in Granell Sales F., "Commemorating a Providential Conquest in Valencia" 6.

de San Esteve').[38] This procession took place on Sunday 21 November 1610, coinciding with the feast of the Presentation of the Virgin, and went from the cathedral to the church of Sant Esteve, with a station at the College of Corpus Christi, and 'performed as on the feasts of St. George and St. Denis' ('fahedora com els dies de Sent Jordi i Sent Dionís').[39] According to Gaspar Escolano, the expense incurred by the procession was met by St. Juan de Ribera himself, who made 1000 ducats available for its foundation.[40] This third event thus formed part of a programme of processions that enacted the reaffirmation of the Christian faith and the fight against the Infidel. The expulsion of the *moriscos* from Spanish territories, beginning in 1609, shook the social and economic foundations of many places, especially in the Kingdom of Valencia where, although new Christians formed a minority, they held a key role in its economy and social hierarchy.

3   Processional routes

Table 6.1 outlines the processional routes followed by the three processions in which the Confraternity of Sant Jordi and the *Centenar de la Ploma* were the protagonists, and indicates the symbolic places through which they passed.[41] The most significant spaces were those of the cathedral, church of Sant Jordi, that of Sant Esteve, the city hall and the monastery of Sant Vicent de la Roqueta.[42] This monastery, built outside the city walls, was of great significance. Traditionally it is held to be the place where St. Vincent was martyred and buried, it being the church of the mozarabic community during the time of muslim rule.[43] With Jaume I's conquest, it was turned into a church, monastery and hospital and retained a highly significant role in the city's ceremonial calendar. From the first years after the conquest, it became a destination of

---

38   Escolano, *Segunda parte de la Década primera* 2001–2002.
39   Martí Mestre – Serra Estellés, *La consueta de la Seu de València* 357.
40   Escolano, *Segunda parte de la Década primera* 2004.
41   The documentary sources that provide information on these events include documentation of the city council (*Manual de Consells, Crides*), the *consueta* (or ceremonial) of the cathedral, chronicles and diaries.
42   Serra Desfilis A. – Soriano Gonzalvo F.J., *San Vicente de la Roqueta: historia de la Real Basílica y Monasterio de San Vicente Mártir, de Valencia* (Valencia: 1993).
43   Mozarabic was the term used to denote Christians who lived in regions under muslim rule; in general, they were arabicised in terms of culture but adhered to the Christian faith.

TABLE 6.1　The three general processions held in Valencia in connection with the Christian conquest of the city and the expulsion of the *moriscos*

Festivity	Dates	Places
St. Denis (9 October)	1338–present	cathedral church of Sant Jordi monastery of San Vicent streets of Valencia
St. George (23 April)	1238–ca. 1707 (?)	church of Sant Jordi cathedral monastery of San Vicent streets of Valencia
Expulsion of the *moriscos* (21 November/Presentation of the Virgin)	1610–1846	cathedral church of Sant Jordi church of Sant Esteve Corpus Christi College streets of Valencia

importance in processions and other events, with special rogative prayers to the martyr, all saints and the Virgin. The order of participants in the processions was strictly controlled, and is mentioned both in the municipal archival documentation and in several chronicles of the period. Leading the procession went all the clergy and friars, followed by the city guilds 'each with music and many representations' ('cascun ab sons y moltes invencions').[44] Then followed: 'Lo Centenar de Sant Gordi', with their banner; the viceroy and the bishop; and, after the governor and other royal officials, the *Justicia criminal*, who carried the city standard, together with many knights.

The standard itinerary for the processions of St. Denis and St. George was as follows [Fig. 6.1]: the procession left the cathedral through the door of the Almoina, past the archepiscopal palace, along the carrer de les Avellanes and to the church of Sant Jordi. Following the blessing of the flag, the procession continued in front of the convent church of Santa Tecla and turned right through the square of the church of Santa Catalina màrtir. It then continued past the main door of the church of Sant Martí, and passed in front of the convent of Sant Gregori. The procession stopped at that church to give thanks and say

---

[44]　Martí Mestre J. (ed.), *El Libre de Antiquitats de la Seu de València* (Valencia – Barcelona: 1994) vol. 1, 150.

THE CONFRATERNITY OF SANT JORDI AND THE *CENTENAR DE LA PLOMA* 165

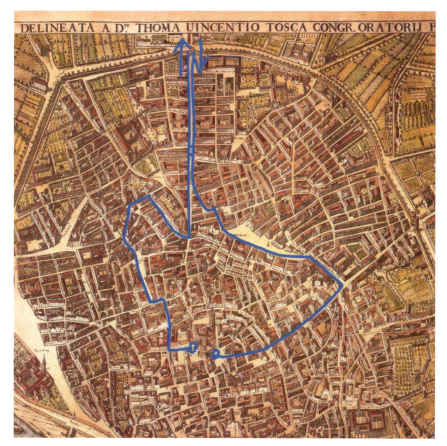

FIGURE 6.1 The processional route for the celebration of the feast days of St. George and St. Denis. Author's drawing based on the coloured map of Tomás Vicente Tosca of ca. 1738: *VALENTIA EDETANORUM, vulgo DEL CID, DELINEATA AD THOMA UICENTIO TOSCA CONGR. ORATORIJ PRESBYTERO*

prayers before the altar of Sant Jordi. Following this act of thanksgiving it continued along the carrer Sant Vicent to the Gate of Sant Vicent, and from there, straight ahead to the church and monastery of Sant Vicent de la Roqueta. On its return to the city centre, the procession passed by the church of Sant Agustí, where veneration was made to the Verge de Gracia. Finally, it passed by the convent of La Mercè, through the Mercat, Bolseria and Cavallers, re-entering the cathedral by the door of the Apòstols. The route of the November procession that commemorated the expulsion of the *moriscos* was markedly different. The processional entourage visited the College of Corpus Christi, in accordance with St. Juan de Ribera's foundation, and then went in the direction of the church of Sant Jordi [Fig. 6.1].

4 The Sonic Dimension of the Processions

Festive celebration and general procession were preceded by public announcements. In the case of the members of the confraternity of Sant Jordi, they were summoned by the municipal town crier and trumpeter: 'My lord and my lady: be present in the morning [...]' ('Mossenyer y vos madona / Siau demà per lo matí [...]'). Then followed the text of the corresponding edict. The Confraternity of Sant Jordi had its own text, preserved in the city council's official books of minutes (*Manuals de Consells*), as did the other three oldest Valencian confraternities (those of Sant Jaume, Nostra Señora de la Seu and Sant Narcís).[45] It is probable that the crier-trumpeter intoned or recited in the form of a distinctive sound signal for each of the different confraternities, with the result that it could be identified by the particular sound and text of its corresponding *crida*.[46]

The feast of St. Denis began with a proclamation by the civic authorities, with the municipal trumpets and drums hired by the Confraternity of Sant Jordi to accompany the publication of the corresponding edict:

> The said cry was arranged and ordered by the councillors to depart from the city hall in the following manner: that one hour before the public announcement, the trumpets, minstrels and drummers of the said city should go to the Confraternity of Sant Jordi, where the leaders of the *Desena* (the ten corporals of each section) of the company of the *Centenar* would be waiting for them; also there were many other soldiers of the said company, whom they had invited, together with the keyholder (*clavari*) bearing the white taffeta flag with the Cross of St. George, which the 'soldiers of the crossbow' [*Centenar*] are used to take in processions [...] all riding on horses that had been shod, with swords in their belt, [and] with the insignia of Saint George on their chests.[47]

---

45   Valencia. AHM. *Qüern de Provisions*. B-30: unfoliated.
46   Ferran Escrivà Llorca, "Soundscapes and Brotherhood in the Processions of the Redemption of Captives. The Case of Early-Modern Valencia", *Confraternitas* 31.2 (2020) 86–105, here 94–96.
47   *Crida de la processo y festes del glorios bisbe y martir Sent Dionis: del any Mil siscents trenta huit, fi de quart centenar de la Conquista de la present ciutat de Valencia / Manada fer y publicar per los Justicia y Jurats de la dita Ciutat* (Valencia, per Iuan Batiste Marçal Impressor: 1638): 'La desús dita Crida se dispongué, y ordenà per los senyors Jurats, que ixquen de la Casa de la Ciutat en esta forma. Que una hora abans de eixir a publicarse, anaren los trompetes, menestrils, y tabals de la dita Ciutat a la Confraria de Sent Jordi, hon estaven esperant los Caps de dehena de la Compañia del Centenar, ab molts altres soldats de dita Compañia, que aquells volgueren convidar, y lo Clavari ab lo pendó de tafetà blanc ab la Creu de sent Jordi, que acostumen a traure en les processons los soldats de la Ballesta;

The *Senyera* was lowered from the city hall accompanied by music and artillery salvoes, and was carried in the procession 'with great pomp and solemnity, music and rejoicing, and with the participation of the company of the *Centenar de la Ploma*, from the town hall to the cathedral church' ('ab molt acompanyament y solemnitat, música, e regosijo, e ab intervenció de la companyia del Centenar de la Ploma, des de la casa de la dita Ciutat a la Esglesia Cathedral de la Seu').[48] The divine office was celebrated with great solemnity in the cathedral, and included the Sermon of the Conquest. Little is known about the musical resources for these events, but the Mass celebrated on the commemorative feast in 1538 is known to have been performed by the singers of both the cathedral and the household of the Duke of Calabria ('los cantors del duch de Calàbria, y ab los de la Seu').[49] The 1538 description emphasises the solemnity of the ceremonial for the occasion, and refers to the *Centenar de la Ploma* participating in the procession 'with crossbowmen and harquebuses, and with the insignia of Sant Jordi, the flag of the *Centenar*, [and] with fifes and drums in war-like mode' ('anava lo Centenar de la ploma, ab ballestes y arcabuços y ab les insígnies de sent Jordi, ab la bandera del Centenar, ab pífanos y atambors a modo de guerra').[50]

The involvement of trumpets, bugles, drums and minstrels and the way in which they were used for creating sound and music in these processions has been studied in some detail by María José Iglesias Pastén.[51] The documents reveal that for the two celebrations of St. George and St. Denis, the distinctive sounds were performed in a specific way. The public display was largely characterised by three kinds of music: the dawn calls (*albadas*); the sounds that accompanied the flag; and those that surrounded the baldachin. All these moments were accompanied by the fifes and drums, as is demonstrated by repeated entries in the *Manuals de Consells*. Both the musical performers and the members of the *Centenar de la Ploma* were the protagonists in the soundscape of these processions. On the one hand, as Iglesias Pastén has pointed

---

[...], anant tots a cavall ab ferreguelos, y espases a la cinta, ab la Insignia de sent Jordi als pits [...]'.

48 *Crida de la processo y festes del glorios bisbe y martir Sent Dionis*.

49 Martí Mestre, *El Libre de Antiquitats de la Seu de València*, vol. 1, 148; Colella A., *Música y cultura renacentista entre Valencia y Nápoles: la corte valenciana de Fernando de Aragón, duque de Calabria (1526–1550)* (Madrid: 2019) 157–164; Villanueva Serrano F., "Mateo Flecha, el Viejo, en la Catedral de Valencia: sus dos períodos de magisterio de capilla (1526–1531? y 1539–1541) y su entorno musical", *Anuario Musical* 64 (2009) 57–108.

50 Carreres Zacarés S. (ed.), *Libre de memories de diversos sucesos y fets memorables e de cosas senyaladas de la ciutat e regne de Valencia (1308–1644)* (Valencia: 1930) 837–838.

51 Iglesias Pastén M.J., *Práctica y cultura musical en Valencia en el siglo XVII* (Valencia: 2022) 130–135.

out, these processions enjoyed a certain degree of exclusivity and prestige not found in other processions, and from the Middles Ages and through the sixteenth and, especially, the seventeenth centuries, the role of the members of the Confraternity of Sant Jordi became increasingly important until they had assumed a leading role.[52] On the other hand, the revitalisation of festive celebrations in the Baroque period endowed the *Centenar* with a symbolism that reached its height through the typical sounds of these feast days that themselves assumed a new symbolic dimension in modern festive apparatus.[53] The least complex, at least in terms of the number of performers of these sounds, were the dawn calls, usually played by *dolçaina* and *tabal* (traditional shawm and drums), and occasionally joined by a solo singer. An instrumental setting of an improvised text was sometimes gifted to the event by important figures of the city. Ruiz de Lihory, in his classic study *La Música en Valencia*, first published in 1903, refers to this kind of age-old traditional musical performance.[54]

Iglesias Pastén also singles out the 'sounds of the bandera' (*sones de bandera*), with reference to the instruments that played in front of the flag at certain moments.[55] These sounds were generally heard at the same time as the salvoes which took place from several points in the city, notably the tower at the Porta de Sant Vicent where 'some of the aforementioned *Centenar de Sant Jordi* [were] firing many cannons and harquebuses, giving the said flag a reception in accordance according with established tradition' ('alguns del dit Centenar de Sent Jordi tirant moltes bombardes y arcabuços rebent la dita Senyera seguint lo antiga costum').[56] The documents register the city council's payments for gunpowder for these festivities. For the procession of St. George's Day in 1611, the city authorities paid for 'trumpets, drums, lutes, bagpipes and other instruments that were played in front of the city's flag' ('trompetes, tabals, llaüts, cornamusses i altres instruments q[ue] sonaven davant la bandera de la

---

52 Iglesias Pastén, *Práctica y cultura musical en Valencia* 131.
53 Iglesias Pastén, *Práctica y cultura musical en Valencia* 131; Mínguez, V. et al., *Un planeta engalanado: la fiesta en los reinos hispánicos*. Triunfos barrocos. Serie Minor 1 (Castellón de la Plana: 2019) 59–60.
54 Ruiz de Lihory J., *La música en Valencia. Diccionario Biográfico y Crítico* (Valencia: 1903) 149–150; Iglesias Pastén, *Práctica y cultura musical en Valencia* 132. On the traditional aspect of these sounds, see Reig Bravo J., *La música tradicional valenciana: una aproximació etnomusicológica* (Valencia: 2011) 278–281.
55 Iglesias Pastén, *Práctica y cultura musical en Valencia* 132.
56 Valencia. Biblioteca Valenciana Nicolau Primitiu. Ms. 6. "Propostes y deliberacions del Consell General de la Insigne Ciutat de Valencia, celebrat en 28 de setembre del any de la Nativitat del Nostre Senyor Deu Jesu Christ 1538, per a la festa de Sent Dionís eo … Centenar de la Conquista" (Valencia: 1538).

dita ciutat').[57] This heterogeneous set of instruments, with wide differences in sonic volume, should be read as figurative and representative rather than sounding. The musicians who participated in these performances were contracted on a year-to-year basis, although the archival documents show that the same musicians were hired over a number of years for the processions of both St. George and St. Denis. This indicates that, despite there being no official record of a corps of musicians in the city, it did de facto exist until a city ensemble of instrumentalists was consolidated not long before 1524.[58] Clearly, these musicians became very familiar with the repertory played, very probably from memory, at these events.[59]

The third kind of sounds heard during these processions were those that accompanied the baldachin or palio (*sons de pali*). From time immemorial, the relic of St. George was carried beneath a palio; according to Iglesias Pastén, this tradition continued into the seventeenth century. The pomp and magnificence of these palioed events clearly mirrored those of royal entries and the Corpus Christi procession in which the king and the eucharist respectively processed under a palio.[60] Those instrumentalists who played close to the palio would have been the best players or those who held important positions. In seventeenth-century Valencia, the head minstrel played recorder, accompanied by other instrumentalists.[61] The playing of a recorder in the context of an ensemble of loud instruments would have had little impact in terms of sonority, and must be interpreted as an essentially symbolic act belonging to an old tradition.

5   Conclusions

The extant documentation affords a good overview of the involvement of the Confraternity of Sant Jordi and the *Centenar de la Ploma* in the processions

---

57   Valencia. AHM. *Claveria comuna. Manual d'Albarans*. J-124 (1610–1611), fol. 85r–v; cited by Iglesias Pastén, *Práctica y cultura musical en Valencia* 132.
58   Villanueva Serrano F., "Los ministriles de la ciudad de Valencia: de la contratación circunstancial a la institucionalización profesional (1524)", *Revista de Musicología* 62.1 (2019) 43–72.
59   Iglesias Pastén, *Práctica y cultura musical en Valencia* 133.
60   On the significance of the palio in Spanish ceremonial, see: Chamorro Esteban A., "El palio: un instrumento político en las ceremonias barcelonesas de los siglos XVI y XVII", in Pérez Álvarez M.J. – Rubio Pérez L.M. – Martín García A. (eds.), *Campo y campesinos en la España Moderna. Culturas políticas en el mundo hispano* (Leon: 2012) 1863–1873.
61   Iglesias Pastén, *Práctica y cultura musical en Valencia* 133.

held for the feasts of St. George and St. Denis in Valencia and of the soundscape they generated. It is clear that these two processions shared a wide range of elements in common from the time of the first centenary of the Christian conquest of the city. The highly symbolic profile of these processions, and their powerful impact, continued from the medieval period until the local laws [*forals*] of the Valencian region were dismantled. They were characterised by sound marks and a distinctive musical repertory, peculiar to the Confraternity of Sant Jordi; moreover, the sound of trumpets and drums of various kinds was inextricablay linked with the *Centenar de la Ploma* and with these festivities.

Fifteenth-century Valencia witnessed a period of economic prosperity and cultural growth that resulted in the consolidation of various urban rituals, including the procession of St. Denis. Nevertheless, the canonisation of St. Vicent Ferrer in 1455 initiated a sense of rivalry as regards the supremacy of certain festive events in the city that lasted for more than two centuries. In this context, civic institutions, religious communities, confraternities and guilds all competed for public recognition through apparel, placing, precedence, musics and other characteristics distinctive to each community. This rivalry often had to be resolved through lawsuits and, finally, by reaching some kind of mutual agreement.

In sum: over several centuries, these two processions (three, including that of St. Juan de Ribera) were celebrated annually in Valencia. However, from 1707, following the War of Spanish Succession and the introduction of the decree of the *Nueva Planta*, that marked the conclusion of the political status of the realms of the Crown of Aragon which were merged with the Crown of Castile, the celebration of St. George's Day, which had been losing popularity in comparison with other festivities, was abolished, while other festivities of profound significance for the city were transformed, as was the case of the procession of St Denis, following the suppression of the *Centenar de la Ploma*. In 1738 the centenary of the Christian conquest of the city of Valencia was commemorated with the incorporation of a company of crossbowmen in an attempt to keep alive its age-old symbolic nature, but without continuity. However, the triumph of absolutist over regional government spelt the end for the long-established ceremonial rituals, such as royal entries during which an oath was taken to uphold the laws of the region. These centuries-old rituals were replaced with other displays of power, such as royal proclamations, and reflected the military element that dominated the despotism of the Age of Enlightenment. Inevitably, these changes directly affected the participation of confraternities in urban festivities.

Bibliography

Primary Sources

Arbuxech Gaspar B., *Sermo de la S. Conquista de la molt insigne noble, leal, e coronada ciutat de Valencia, predicat en la [...] esglesia metropolitana de dita ciutat a 9 de Octubre any 1666 [...] per lo R. Docttor Gaspar Blay Arbuxech, prebere de la Real Congregacio del Oratori [...]* (Valencia, Geroni Vilagrasa: 1666).

Biblioteca Valenciana. Fondo Antiguo. "Propostes y deliberacions del Consell General de la Insigne Ciutat de Valencia, celebrat en 28 de setembre del any de la Nativitat del Nostre Senyor Deu Jesu Christ 1538, per a la festa de Sent Dionís eo [...] Centenar de la Conquista" (Valencia: 1538).

Crida de la processo y festes del glorios bisbe y martir Sent Dionis: del any Mil siscents trenta huit, fi de quart centenar de la Conquista de la present ciutat de Valencia. Manada fer y publicar per los Justicia y Jurats de la dita Ciutat (Valencia, Iuan Batiste Marçal: 1638).

Escolano Gaspar, *Segunda parte de la Década primera de la Historia de la insigne y coronada Ciudad y Reino de Valencia* (Valencia, Pedro Patricio Mey: 1611).

Secondary Sources

Anglés H., "L'Ordre de Sant Jordi durant els segles XIII–XIV i la devoció dels reis d'Aragó al sant cavaller", in *Miscel·lània Fontserè* (Barcelona: 1961) 41–64.

Bayerri E., "El misterio de la Asunción de María en la liturgia hispana medieval" *Estudios Marianos* 6 (1947) 381–402.

Benlloch Poveda A., "Sínodos valentinos y reforma a finales del siglo XVI", in *Corrientes espirituales en la Valencia del siglo XVI: (1550–1600). Actas del II Symposion de Teología Histórica (20–22 abril 1982)* (Valencia: 1983) 169–182.

Bernabé V. de – Martín de Eugenio L., "Instituciones nobiliarias del Reino de Valencia", *Hidalguía* 67.382 (2020) 91–126.

Bombi A., "'Como vara de humo a su región'. Villancicos, oratorios y óperas asuncionistas en Valencia. (1679–1750)", in Lluís Sirera J.L. (ed.), *La mort com a personatge. L'assumpció com a tema. Actes del VI Seminari de Teatre i Música medievals. Elx, 29 al 31 d'octubre de 2000* (Elche: 2002) 53–91.

Carreres Zacarés S. (ed.), *Libre de memories de diversos sucesos y fets memorables e de cosas senyaladas de la ciutat e regne de Valencia (1308–1644)* (Valencia: 1930).

Cerdà i Ballester J. – Pardo Molero J.F. – Guinot Rodríguez E. – Andrés Robres F. (eds.), *Santa María de Montesa la orden militar del Reino de Valencia (ss. XIV–XIX)* (Valencia: 2019).

Chamorro Esteban A., "El palio: un instrumento político en las ceremonias barcelonesas de los siglos XVI y XVII", in Pérez Álvarez M.J. – Rubio Pérez L.M. – Martín García A.

(eds.), *Campo y campesinos en la España Moderna. Culturas políticas en el mundo hispano* (Leon: 2012) 1863–1873.

Climent J., *Fondos Musicales de la Región Valenciana II. Real Colegio de Corpus Christi Patriarca* (Valencia: 1984).

Colella A., *Música y cultura renacentista entre Valencia y Nápoles: la corte valenciana de Fernando de Aragón, duque de Calabria (1526–1550)* (Madrid: 2019).

Diago Hernando M., "El factor religioso en el conflicto de las Comunidades de Castilla (1520–1521): el papel del clero", *Hispania sacra* 59.119 (2007) 84–114.

Escrivà Llorca F., "Soundscapes and Brotherhood in the Processions of the Redemption of Captives. The Case of Early-Modern Valencia", *Confraternitas* 31.2 (2020) 86–105.

Ferrer Flórez M., "La cofradía de San Jorge y los orígenes de la R.S.E.M.A.P.", *Memòries de la Reial Acadèmia Mallorquina d'Estudis Genealògics, Heràldics i Històrics* 10 (2000) 137–170.

Furió A., *Història del País Valencià* (Valencia: 1995).

Gil Saura Y., "De la sitiada de la Sala Nova a los retratos reales valencianos: Rostros de los diputados y la monarquía", in Furió A. – García Marsilla J.V. (eds.), *La veu del regne. 600 anys de la Generalitat Valenciana. La Generalitat Valenciana. Espais i imatges de la Generalitat* (Valencia: 2020) vol. 3, 141–168.

Gil Saura Y., "Memoria de un espacio montesiano desaparecido: La Iglesia y Colegio de San Jorge de la ciudad de Valencia", in Gil Saura Y. – Alba E. – Guinot E. (eds.), *La Orden de Montesa y San Jorge de Alfama. Arquitecturas, Imágenes y Textos* (Valencia: 2019) 54–72.

Granell Sales F., "Commemorating a Providential Conquest in Valencia: The 9 October Feast", *Religions* 13.301 (2022) 1–22. https://doi.org/10.3390/rel13040301.

Iglesias Pastén M.J., *Práctica y cultura musical en Valencia en el siglo XVII* (Valencia: 2022).

Martí Mestre J. (ed.), *El Libre de Antiquitats de la Seu de València* 2 vols. (Valencia – Barcelona: 1994).

Martí Mestre J. – Serra Estellés X., *La consueta de la Seu de València dels segles XVI–XVII. Estudi i edició del Ms. 405 de l'ACV* (Valencia: 2009).

Martínez Vinat J., *Cofradías y oficios. Entre la acción confraternal y la organización corporativa en la Valencia medieval (1238–1516)* (Ph.D. dissertation, Universitat de Valencia: 2018).

Martínez Vinat J., "La cofradía de San Jaime", in Narbona Vizcaíno R. (ed.), *Ciudad y Reino: claves del siglo de oro valenciano* (Valencia: 2015) 266–271.

Mínguez V. – Chiva Beltrán J. – Rodríguez Moya I. – González Tornel P., *Un planeta engalanado: la fiesta en los reinos hispánicos*. Triunfos barrocos. Serie Minor 1 (Castellón de la Plana: 2019).

Miquel Juan M., "El gótico internacional en la ciudad de Valencia: El retablo de san Jorge del Centenar de la Ploma", *Goya. Revista de arte* 336 (2011) 191–213.

Narbona Vizcaíno R., "Apreciaciones históricas e historiográficas en torno a la fiesta del Corpus Christi de Valencia", *Revista d'historia medieval* 10 (1999) 371–382.

Negre i Pastell P., "La cofradía de san Jorge y la nobleza gerundense", *Annals de l'Institut d'Estudis Gironins* 6 (1951) 271–322.

Pérez García P., *El justicia criminal de Valencia (1479–1707): una magistratura urbana valenciana ante la consolidación del absolutismo* (Valencia: 1991).

Pérez García P., "En los márgenes de la Germanía: la cofradía de San Jorge y el regente Garcés de Jaunas", in González-Raymond A. – Jiménez Monteserín M. – Quero F. (eds.), *Normes, marges et confins: hommage au professeur Raphaël Carrasco* 2 vols. (Montpellier: 2018), vol. 2, 227–241.

Querol y Roso L., *Las milicias valencianas desde el siglo XIII al XV. Contribución al estudio de la organización militar del antiguo Reino de Valencia* (Castellón de la Plana: 1935).

Quirante Santacruz L., *Teatro asuncionista valenciano de los siglos XV y XVI* (Valencia: 1987).

Redish A., *Bimetallism: An Economic and Historical Analysis* (Cambridge: 2006).

Reig Bravo J., *La música tradicional valenciana: una aproximació etnomusicológica.* (Valencia: 2011).

Ribot i Iglésias M., "La Confraria dels Cavallers de Sant Jordi de Barcelona en sus últimos tiempos", in *Primer Congrés d'Història Moderna de Catalunya* (Barcelona: 1984) vol. 1, 463–469.

Ruiz de Lihory J., *La música en Valencia. Diccionario Biográfico y Crítico* (Valencia: 1903).

Sanchis Sivera J., *Quaresma de sant Vicent Ferrer: predicada a València l'any 1413* (Barcelona: 1927).

Serra Desfilis A. – Soriano Gonzalvo F.J., *San Vicente de la Roqueta: historia de la Real Basílica y Monasterio de San Vicente Mártir, de Valencia* (Valencia: 1993).

Sevillano Colom F., *El Centenar de la Ploma de la Ciutat de València 1365–1711* (Barcelona: 1966).

Sorolla-Romero T., "Dragones, sangre y campanas", in Mínguez Cornelles V. (ed.), *El linaje del Rey Monje. La configuración cultural e iconográfica de la Corona aragonensis (1164–1516)* (Castellón de la Plana: 2018) 27–52.

Valor Moncho P., "En torno a los orígenes de la devoción a san Vicente Ferrer en Valencia", in Callado Estela E. (ed.), *Tiempos de reforma. Pensamiento y religión en la época de Carlos V* (Madrid: 2022) 455–494.

Villanueva Serrano F., "Mateo Flecha, el Viejo, en la Catedral de Valencia: sus dos períodos de magisterio de capilla (1526–1531? y 1539–1541) y su entorno musical", *Anuario Musical* 64 (2009) 57–108.

Villanueva Serrano F., "Los ministriles de la ciudad de Valencia: de la contratación circunstancial a la institucionalización profesional (1524)", *Revista de Musicología* 62.1 (2019) 43–72.

PART 2

Devotional Practice and Religious Reform

CHAPTER 7

Corporations or Confraternities? Strategies Adopted by Artisan Groups in Response to Pressures Arising from the Catholic Reformation

Noel O'Regan

Abstract

As in other European cities, Rome's artisans and professionals were organised into guilds from medieval times. While some doubled up as confraternities, or worked in parallel with such bodies, others remained as corporations while adopting practices associated with confraternities. From the 1540s, pressures from the incipient Catholic Reformation began to curtail these bodies' freedoms and nudge them towards a more outward show of religious observance in line with papal policies. This reached a climax after 1566 when Pope Pius V proscribed the long-established Assumption Day procession from S. Giovanni in Laterano to S. Maria Maggiore, hitherto the showpiece occasion for Roman artisan corporations. Thereafter, there was greater emphasis on performing individual cults, obtaining relics, rebuilding churches and concentrating attention on one or two patronal feasts. A noteworthy example was the comparatively rich Compagnia dei Fornai which encouraged a particularly strong cult, including supporting a small choir, in its church of S. Maria di Loreto near the Forum.

Keywords

confraternities – guilds – corporations – Catholic Reformation – procession – cult – patronal feast-day

From at least the twelfth to the mid-sixteenth century, Romans celebrated the feast of the Assumption with a great procession in which the icon of the *Santissimo Salvatore*, housed in the Sancta Sanctorum beside the basilica of S. Giovanni in Laterano [Fig. 7.1], was taken on the evening of 14 August to the basilica of S. Maria Maggiore to meet that basilica's icon of the Virgin, the

FIGURE 7.1 Icon of Christ known as the *Acheropita*, housed in the Cappella del Sancta Sanctorum near the Basilica of S. Giovanni in Laterano, Rome
PUBLIC DOMAIN. WIKIMEDIA COMMONS

Salus Populi Romani [Fig. 7.2].[1] In a symbolic re-enactment of the Assumption, the icons bowed to each other (called the 'Inchinata') and were placed side by side in the basilica overnight, and during solemn festal Mass the next morning,

---

1   For context and a full description of this procession, see Ingersoll R.J., *The Ritual Use of Public Spaces in Renaissance Rome* (Ph.D. dissertation, University of California at Berkeley: 1985) 224–258; Noreen K., "Serving Christ: The Assumption Procession in Sixteenth-Century Rome" in Pericolo L. – Richardson J.N. (eds.), *Remembering the Middle Ages in Early Modern Italy* (Turnhout: 2015) 231–245.

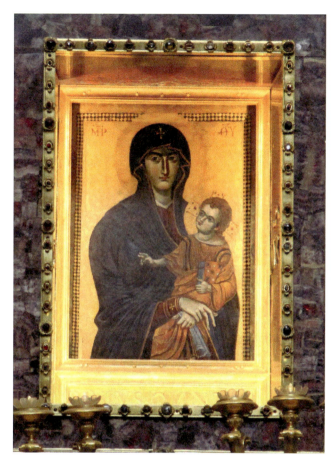

FIGURE 7.2 Icon of the Virgin and Child known as the *Salus Populi Romani*, housed in the Cappella Paolina of the Basilica of S. Maria Maggiore, Rome
PUBLIC DOMAIN. WIKIMEDIA COMMONS

after which the icon representing Christ was taken back to the Lateran.[2] The torchlight procession involved the city's civic government and all the corporations of the *arti e mestieri* – the professions and trades of the city – as well as

---

2 A similar procession still takes place in Tivoli near Rome on 14 August when an ancient image of Christ is paraded from the church of ss. Salvatore to that of S. Maria Maggiore where, after a threefold *inchinata*, it is placed next to an ancient image of the Virgin and remains there overnight. It is thought to have been modelled on the Roman Assumption procession. See Perry R., "The Medieval Inchinata Procession at Tivoli: Ritual Construction of Civic Identity in the Age of the Commune", *Journal of the Society of Architectural Historians* 76 (2017) 36–62. This article also gives some background information about the Roman procession.

two major devotional confraternities charged with the care of the two icons, ss. Salvatore ad Sancta Sanctorum and the Gonfalone. These were two of the city's oldest confraternities with origins going back to the late thirteenth century.[3]

The procession passed the Colosseum before following the ancient Via Sacra through the Roman Forum, symbolically reclaiming the city's most significant pagan spaces; it then proceeded through the Monti district to S. Maria Maggiore. At a series of stations outside churches along the way, the icon was symbolically washed. Each guild and artisan corporation carried a wooden float, adorned with the company's arms and attributes, and with candles. A tablet was set up on the Campidoglio in the fifteenth century, setting out the order in which the various corporations should process, in order to avoid disputes. This was the most important civic procession in medieval and early Renaissance Rome, a major occasion for public display of municipal identity, and of the city's guild structure in particular, led by the secular authority of the Senator and Conservators who had been based on the Campidoglio since medieval times. It was organised, not by the papal court, but by the new civic aristocracy (that is, not traditional baronial families like the Colonna and Orsini) which had come to dominate what became the Arciconfraternita del ss. Salvatore a Sancta Sanctorum.[4] The pope and the papal court did not normally take part in this procession.

While there is little specific record of involvement by musicians, they must have played a significant part.[5] The city's groups of *trombetti* and *piffari* based on the Campidoglio were certainly involved.[6] Observant Franciscan friars

---

3   For ss. Salvatore, see Pavan P., "La confraternita del Salvatore nella società romana fra Tre e Quattrocento", *Ricerche per la Storia Religiosa di Roma* 5 (1984) 81–90; idem, "Gli statuti della società dei Raccomandati del Salvatore ad Sancta Sanctorum (1331–1496)", *Archivio della Società Romana di Storia Patria*, 101 (1978) 35–96. For the Gonfalone, see Wisch B. – Newbigin N., *Acting on Faith: the Confraternity of the Gonfalone in Renaissance Rome* (Philadelphia: 2013).

4   Ingersoll, *The Ritual Use of Public Spaces* 227–229; Pavan, "La confraternita del Salvatore"; Noreen K., "Sacred Memory and Confraternal Space: The Insignia of the Confraternity of the Santissimo Salvatore (Rome)", in Ó Carragáin É. – Neuman de Veguar C. (eds.), *Roma Felix: Formation and Reflections of Medieval Rome* (Aldershot: 2007) 159–187.

5   The Tivoli procession was (and continues to be) led by musicians; see Perry, "The medieval Inchinata procession at Tivoli".

6   The most complete description of the procession is found in a 1462 document in Latin from the archive of the Arcionfraternita del ss. Salvatore (Rome. Archivio di Stato. Fondo Sancta Sanctorum 1009, non-foliated), first published in Millino B., *Dell'Oratorio di S. Lorenzo nel Laterano Hoggi detto Sancta Santorum* (Rome, Biagio Diversini – Felice Cesaretti: 1667) 143–158. It is quoted in Ingersoll, *The Ritual Use of Public Spaces* 245. Trumpets and drums joined the procession at the second ritual washing of the icon outside the church of S. Clemente.

from S. Maria in Ara Coeli, the city government's church on the Capitoline Hill, would most likely have taken part and chanted litanies and other items. The choirs of S. Maria Maggiore and S. Giovanni in Laterano may well have participated. The two devotional confraternities involved may also have hired some musicians.[7] It must have come as quite a shock, then, when Pope Pius V, within months of his election in January 1566, banned – or at least restricted – the procession.[8] Like other such bans, there was a convenient excuse: it had sometimes got out of hand, either in disputes over precedence, or through an over-enthusiastic populace crowding too closely, even trying to remove pieces of the icon as a relic. In the Holy or Jubilee Year of 1550 some of the *Macellari* (Corporation of Butchers), who had the privilege of guarding the image during the procession, had over-reacted to such a push and a Roman nobleman had been killed.

Beyond that, however, Pius V's action can be seen as part of a broader agenda in the wake of the Council of Trent to assert papal control over such popular displays of piety, and to redirect artisan corporations' energy into more official processions – such as those held during the octave of Corpus Christi, on Holy Thursday, and on patronal feastdays – all seen as more theologically legitimate. Pius's move against the August procession would have had some support among the city's patricians, keen to curb exercises of independent display on the part of organised artisans. Pius particularly wished to restrict the handling of sacred images to clerics and, by extension, to curb long-standing lay involvement with Rome's much venerated icons. A proper level of decorum in such celebrations was also becoming increasingly desirable: a report of the time described Pius's action as being directed at avoiding 'the many excesses of undisciplined youth and women of poor reputation'.[9] The curtailing of the procession coincided with an increasing number of *processiones triduanae* – series of processions held over three consecutive days – called by Popes to seek intercession for the Catholic cause in wars of religion, or other events, which

---

7   The same 1462 description mentions that the Compagnia de' Racommandati di Maria sempre Vergine (The Confraternity of the Gonfalone), accompanied by torches and musical instruments, made the procession seem like 'the ancient rite of triumphs of the Emperors [...] changed into the triumph of Christ'. See Wisch – Newbigin, *Acting on Faith* 161. The archive of the Gonfalone preserves the texts of two hymns, one in Latin and one in Italian, which seem to have been composed for use during the procession in 1499. No music for these survives. The texts, with translations, are given in Wisch – Newbigin, *Acting on Faith* 162–163.
8   No actual papal decree banning the procession has been discovered, but an *Avviso* of 7 August 1566 supports that supposition. See Ingersoll, *The Ritual Use of Public Spaces* 250, 258; Wisch – Newbigin, *Acting on Faith* 166.
9   See Noreen, "Serving Christ" 237.

were vying for support with more ancient rituals. In the short term, the pope also increased the money available for dowry presentations at the church of S. Maria sopra Minerva on 15 August, seeking to shift popular interest away from S. Maria Maggiore to that church instead.[10] As Richard Ingersoll has pointed out: 'the Assumption procession was a major expression of civic pride and independence; it was supplanted by a more dignified, papal-oriented ceremony that brought the feast back into the sphere of the Church both ideologically and topographically'.[11]

The oldest layer of Roman artisan corporation, known as *Nobil Collegio* or *Università*, was housed in the Palazzo dei Conservatori on the Campidoglio, the centre of Rome's civic government.[12] During the period of the papal absence in Avignon in the fourteenth century, power tended to be concentrated on the Campidoglio and in its civic structures. After its return, the papacy moved to reassert its authority and this process continued into the second half of the sixteenth century. When Michelangelo redesigned the hill from 1536, he incorporated the titles of the oldest of these *università* into the new façade of the Palazzo [Fig. 7.3]. Their main occupation was the regulation of their particular trade, or profession, and the relatively few surviving sets of guild statutes from before the 1560s reflect this. Those of the Bovattieri (cattle breeders) from 1526, for instance, go into great detail about the regulation of the cattle trade, but include just one short chapter on the cult; significantly, this refers only to the 15 August procession:

> De Festa fiendo in Assumptione Beatae Mariae de mense augusti. Item quod illi Consules qui fuerint in dicto festo […], teneantur et debeant facere et ordinare festum Beatae Mariae cum omni honore et veneratione, prout melius et honorabilius poterunt, ac fiere facere duo duppleria ac aliam ceram, confectiones et alia necessaria, prout hactebus extitit consuetum.[13]

> Of the celebration of the feast of the Assumption of the Blessed Mary in the month of August. Those consuls in office during the said feast […] are obliged to cause and organise the feast of the Blessed Mary with

---

10 Wisch – Newbiggin, *Acting on Faith* 167.
11 Ingersoll, *The Ritual Use of Public Spaces* 226.
12 Morelli G., *Le Corporazione di Arti e Mestieri a Roma dal XII al XIX secolo* (Rome: 1937); Giallombardo L., "Le Corporazioni d'arti e mestieri attive a Roma nel Seicento", in Santoni B.T. – Sagredo A. M. (eds.), *Luoghi della Cultura nella Roma di Borromini* (Rome: 2004) 457–481.
13 *Statuta nobilis artis Bobacteriorum Urbis* (Rome, Nucius Venacius: 1526) fol. 6r.

FIGURE 7.3 Doorway in the Palazzo dei Conservatori, Campidoglio, Rome, headed by the name of the Università dei Macellari
PHOTO BY THE AUTHOR

as much honour and veneration as they can, having two candelabra made, together with other wax candles, confections and whatever else is deemed necessary to continue the custom of these things.

Faced with pressure from an increasingly assertive papal curial administration in the wake of the Council of Trent, artisan corporations were forced to adopt new strategies in order to continue looking after their members' interests, both secular and spiritual. One such strategy was the founding of a confraternity to complement, or substitute for, the corporation. While many did indeed follow this path, some corporations decided to retain the status of *università* or *nobil collegio* and not found a confraternity, but they, too, adopted many of the religious trappings of such bodies. The process is complex to unravel, with Antonio Martini describing four different situations by the early seventeenth century: an *università* only, without a confraternity; both *università* and confraternity working in parallel, but without much contact; both again, but sharing the same statutes and working closely together; just a confraternity which also regulated the trade.[14] The situation is further complicated by three levels of membership: *maestri, lavoranti, garzoni* (masters, workers, apprentices); in some cases, each had a different organisation which might or might not share a location and a patron saint. In general terms, regulation of all aspects of the trade remained the primary concern of an *università*, where it continued to exist, whereas a *confraternita* was mainly concerned with the cult and with the spiritual welfare of members, although it might also undertake regulatory duties in the absence of an *università*.

The process of founding artisan confraternities (known as *Compagnia, Pia Unione, Confraternita,* or *Sodalizio*) had begun already in the fifteenth century.[15] Among the earliest were the Barbieri (barber surgeons) in 1440, followed by the Fornai Tedeschi (German bakers) in 1487; the Fornai Italiani followed suit in 1507. Others gradually followed, through the 1510s to 1540s, with a subsequent increase after the completion of the Council of Trent in 1563, particularly around the Holy (Jubilee) Year of 1575. Significantly, these bodies increasingly adopted the attitudes and customs of longer-established devotional confraternities. Taking a couple of examples, the Università dei Ferrari (metal workers) discussed setting up a confraternity from the 1550s onwards, but only succeeded in achieving recognition in 1575.[16] The corporation had been in the possession of its own church since 1453, subsequently rebuilt on a larger scale and dedicated to its patron San Eligio in 1561–1562. The new confraternity's foundation document allowed for the setting up of an oratory which was built adjoining the church in 1577, as well as the wearing of blue-grey habits, something which generally differentiated confraternity

---

14 Martini A., "Le confraternite e le università di arti e mestieri a Roma", in Crescentini C. – Martini A. (eds.), *Le Confraternite Romane: Arte, Storia, Committenza* (Rome: 2000) 13–23.
15 For details of individual artisan confraternities, see the individual entries in Fiorani L. et al., "Repertorio degli Archivi delle Confraternite Romane", *Ricerche per la storia religiosa di Roma* 6 (1985) 175–413; and in Lumbroso M.M. – Martini A., *Le Confraternite Romane nelle loro Chiese* (Rome: 1963).
16 Serra A., *Ferrari e vetturini a Roma dal Rinascimento all'Ottocento* (Rome: 1970).

members from others. The city's Marmorai (stonecutters) formed an *università* in 1406.[17] In 1570 they acquired the oratory of S. Silvestro, attached to the ancient church of ss. Quattro Coronati, as a base for spiritual reunions and liturgical celebrations. They remained in this intermediate position until 1596 when they obtained approval to set up a confraternity. It would be based in the church of S. Leonardo de Albis, but the *università* retained its oratory at ss. Quattro Coronati, whose four dedicatees acted as patron saints to both confraternity and *università*.

Oratories were crucial to the process of becoming more like devotional confraternities. They became the locus of spiritual formation of new members which was directed by two *maestri di novizii* chosen by the *confratelli* from their number, a common practice among devotional confraternities. Some artisan confraternities also began to use their oratories for the chanting of the Office of the Dead and/or the Office of the Blessed Virgin, usually on a monthly basis. This was done by a small number of *coristi*, chosen from among the membership on a rotating basis, who chanted in plainsong with perhaps some harmonisation in *falsobordone*. The 1636 Statutes of the Compagnia di S. Tomaso D'Aquino de'Librari di Roma (booksellers) based in the church of S. Barbara, for example, specify that ten *coristi* should be chosen on a three-monthly rotation; they were each given three ounces of pepper at the end of the period as recognition of their service.[18] Already in 1576, the statutes of another artisan confraternity, that of the Calzolari (shoemakers) instructed all its members to attend a sung Mass and the Office of the Dead on the first Tuesday of each month, with all the *maestri* (fully qualified practitioners of the trade) instructed to hold a lighted candle from the Elevation of the Mass to the end of the Office which followed it.[19] Absence was punished by the penalty of a pound of wax to be paid to the church. The same penalty was applied to those absent from the sung Mass, with a sermon, celebrated on the patronal feast of ss. Crispin and Crispiniano (25 October), as well as to those who missed First Vespers on that feast's vigil.

---

17   Kolega A., "L'Archivio dell'Università dei Marmorai di Roma (1406–1957)", *Rassegna degli Archivi di Stato* 52 (1992) 509–568; Leonardo M., "Gli Statuti dell'Universita de Marmorari a Roma: Scultori e Scalpellini (1406–1756)", *Studi Romani* 45 (1997) 269–300.

18   *Statuti della Venerabile Compagnia di S. Tomaso D'Aquino in S. Barbara de'Librari di Roma* (Rome, Stamperia della Reverenda Camera Apostolica: 1636) Book 3, Chapter 5. For more information on the confraternity see Misiti M.C., "Le confraternite dei librai e stampatori a Roma", *Rivista Storica del Lazio* 10 (1999) 29–55.

19   *Statuti, Ordini et Constituzioni dell'Arte de Calzolari dell'Alma Città di Roma* (Rome, Heredi di Antonio Blado: 1576) chapter 10.

Commemorating dead members and benefactors was another essential part of the cultic activity of all confraternities. The death of a *confratello* was announced as quickly as possible to members, who were obliged to pray for the repose of their soul; officials had to see that they obtained a proper burial, and that the corpse was accompanied to the grave by *confratelli* with candles and with the rites of the church, including chanted items of the liturgy. This guaranteed burial was one of the main attractions of confraternity membership, as was continuing remembrance in the annual *anniversarii* Masses held in November or immediately after the patronal feast. Artisan groups in possession of their own church supported a chaplain and undertook other expenses needed for regular liturgical obligations. Others made do with a side chapel in a host church, which might provide minimal services including a part-time chaplain. While women were not active members, those related to members and/or involved in the profession were welcomed as associates. The Compagnia di Fornai, for instance, had a *prioressa* for its female associates, as well as two female visitors of sick women, in 1567.[20]

This deepening of liturgical and devotional commitment by artisan confraternities is reflected in sets of statutes promulgated as the sixteenth century progressed. Those of the Fornai from 1567 provide a good example, one of the first to be approved in the wake of the Council of Trent. They lay out obligations to take confession and communion at least once a year, to fast on the vigil of their patronal feast-day, to say ten *Pater noster*s and *Ave Maria*s at least once a month for the souls of the dead, and to attend a communal Mass on the first Sunday of each month.[21] The statutes also direct that the income of the company should be spent in the following order: (i) the repair and maintainance of the church, its ornamentation and necessary fitting out: (ii) paying chaplains for Masses, as well as singers and others employed in celebrating the ordinary feasts of the church; (iii) the devotion undertaken with the goodwill of the company, including Masses and obsequies of dead brothers and sisters; (iv) matters concerning the divine offices and other solemnities which occur throughout the year and those ordered by the officials and men of the company; (v) the support of the poor and the sick; (vi) keeping the ordinary book-keeping registers up to date; (vii) paying procurators, notaries, solicitors and officials for their work for the company.[22] The order of priorities here

---

20 *Statuti della Venerabile Compagnia di S. Maria di Loreto de'Fornari Italiani di Roma* (Rome: 1567) chapter 2.
21 Ibidem chapter 7.
22 Ibidem chapter 17.

shows that the cult was by now centre stage, with the first four headings neatly summarising all that that entailed.

The same statutes prescribe a *maritaggio*, or granting of dowries to suitably qualified young girls, on the annual patronal feast-day celebration, the Nativity of the Blessed Virgin on 8 September.[23] They instruct that the Cardinal Protector should be invited for a symbolic presentation of purses containing the dowries (the actual dowries were not paid until some time after a successful marriage had been achieved). The girls went in procession, accompanied by 'honest matrons' – female associates of the confraternity – and preceded by *confratelli* dressed in their white habits, accompanied by polyphonic musicians ('con la musica'). Providing dowries to enable marriage was widely practised in this period, particularly by devotional confraternities, and was seen as a worthy charitable endeavour; the girls receiving dowries (referred to as *zitelle*) were always displayed in a procession, in which musicians invariably took part.[24]

The Statutes of the Confraternita dei Barbieri e Stufaroli (barbers and water-boilers) from 1593 are preceded by a preamble invoking scriptural authority in calling on the members to love God and their neighbour [Fig. 7.4]. It goes on to prescribe considerable fines for those caught misusing the names of God or Mary as swear-words:

> Ordiniamo, che qualunque biastemmasse il Nome dell'omnipotente Iddio, et del nostro Redentor Giesu Christo, et della pia et clementisima Madre sua Vergina Maria, cada in pena di dieci scudi, [...] et di due libre di cera bianca lavorata e de altri santi cinque scudi et un libra de cera [...] accioche vivendo noi laudabilmente et bene, possiamo in questo mondo, et poi nell'altro meritar la gratia dell'eterna salute dal nostro Signore et Redentor Giesu Christo.[25]

> We ordain that whoever blasphemes against the name of the omnipotent God, of our Saviour Jesus Christ, or his pious and clement Mother the Virgin Mary, should pay a fine of ten *scudi*, [...] and two pounds of worked white wax, and against the other saints, five *scudi* and one pound

---

23   Ibidem chapter 45.
24   Wisch – Newbigin, *Acting on Faith* 72–73, 89–90.
25   *Statuti, Ordini e Constitutioni della Venerabile Compagnia et Università delli Barbieri e Stufaroli dell'alma Città di Roma* (Rome, Paolo Blado: 1593), foreword.

FIGURE 7.4 *Statuti, Ordini e Constitutioni della Venerabile Compagnia et Università delli Barbieri e Stufaroli dell'Alma Città di Roma* (Rome, Paolo Blado: 1593)
OPEN ACCESS. GOOGLE BOOKS

of wax [...] so that living worthily and well, we may in this life, and afterwards in the next, merit the grace of eternal salvation by our Lord and Redeemer Jesus Christ.

This sets out the sort of Christian behaviour which was being encouraged of lay people at this time. The beginning of Part 2 of the statutes describes the cult in detail, summarising the obligations under which the members of this essentially ordinary artisan confraternity were placed:

In prima per honor et reverentia del culto divino statuimo, et dechiaramo che ogni persona dell'Università nostra [...] siano tenuti et obligati tutte le feste infrascritte insieme con li offitiali venire nella nostra Capella et stare dal principio della messa insino al fine, et ad ogn'altro offitio che in quella sarà celebrato; altrimenti per quante volte alcuno contrafacesse, sia tenuto alla pena di una libra di Cera bianca lavorata per Maestro, et mezza per lavorante, e garzone, eccetto quelli che haveranno licita scusa.[26]

Firstly, for the honour and reverence of the divine cult, we set down and declare that everyone who belongs to our *università* [...] is obliged to attend our chapel on all of the feasts listed below, together with the officials, and to stay from the beginning to the end of Mass, and to attend at all other offices celebrated in the same [chapel]; otherwise, for each offence, a penalty of a pound of worked wax for a master and half a pound for a worker and apprentice is imposed, except for those with a legitimate excuse.

The feasts included the first Sunday of each month, the third day of each of the three *pasque* (Easter, Pentecost and Christmas), the four principal feasts of the Madonna (Candlemas, Annunciation, Assumption, her Nativity), and the day of the universal obsequies of the dead (2 November). These obligations were not light, involving attendance on no fewer than twenty-one days in the year, as well as two further days for each of the three *pasque*. Similar lists can be found in other sets of artisan confraternity statutes, though not always as onerous. The 1593 Statutes of the Candelottari (candle makers) specify only the vigils of three feasts of the Madonna (Annunciation, Assumption, her Nativity) for attendance, but lay down that no work involving candles should be undertaken on any Sunday or major feast, including those of the Madonna and the Apostles.[27]

Statutes might provide detailed instructions about the celebration of the patronal feast. Those of the Barbieri e Stufaroli, for instance, indicate the following:

---

26   Ibidem part 2 fol. 7v.
27   *Statuti, Capitoli et Constitutioni del'Università de Candelottari di Roma* (Rome, Paolo Blado: 1593) chapter 2.

> Infra tutte le altre Feste ordiniamo et vogliamo che nella Festa et solennità di San Cosmo, et Damiano, secondo i tempi senza grandissima et licita caggione, sotto doppia pena, non manchino a giusta lor possanza venire: ove per i loro Sagrestani detta Cappella quanto sia possibile secondo l'anticha consuetudine, serà ornata di mortella, lauri, panni di razzi, tapeti, paramenti, argentaria, con soni, et qualunque altra cosa ad essa festività, et al culto divino opportuna; et faranno celebrare la Processione con offerta di Cera illuminata, et questo secondo li tempi occorrenti [...] et medesimamente siano tenuti far celebrar' ogni Festa comandata dalla S. Madre Chiesa, la Messa, et altre Orationi; et ogni Lunedì, et ogni Mercordì per l'anime delli passati di detta Università, et benefattori di quella et tutti li altri giorni, siano obligati far celebrare una Messa ordinaria.[28]

> Above all other feasts we ordain and wish that on the solemnity of ss. Cosmo and Damiano, no one should be missing, on double penalty, without a very good and legitimate reason; also that the said chapel should as far as possible be ornamented by the sacristans with myrtle and laurel, brocades, carpets, vestments, silver, with sounds and whatever else is appropriate for such a feast and for the divine cult; and they should organise a procession with lit candles, according to the season [...] and they should similarly be obliged to have Mass and other prayers celebrated on all feasts commanded by Holy Mother Church; and they are obliged to have an ordinary Mass celebrated every Monday and Wednesday for the souls of deceased members of the *università* and of deceased benefactors.

The word 'soni' here must refer to music in the broad sense, while a later chapter uses the more specific 'musica' (polyphony). As well as polyphony sung by hired-in singers, 'soni' could have included any or all of the following: organ music; plainchant sung by chaplains and friars; church bells; fanfares played by *trombetti* and more complex instrumental music played by *piffari*; all were commonly found in confraternity feast-day celebrations as attested to by archival evidence.[29]

---

28 *Statuti, Ordini e Constitutioni della Venerabile Compagnia et Università delli Barbieri e Stufaroli* (Rome, Paolo Blado: 1593) part 2, fols. 7ff.
29 See O'Regan N., *Institutional Patronage in Post-Tridentine Rome* (London: 1995); idem., "Music at the Roman Archconfraternity of San Rocco in the Late Sixteenth Century", in Antolini B.M. – Morelli A. – Spagnuolo V.V. (eds.), *La musica a Roma attraverso le fonti d'archivio, Atti del convegno internazionale, Roma 4–7 Giugno 1992* (Lucca: 1994) 521–552; Idem., "The performance of Roman Sacred Polychoral Music in the Late 16th

Another strategy to encourage devotion, while simultaneously attracting congregations to attend artisan churches, was the acquisition of relics. In 1613 the Confraternita di S. Omobono dei Sarti (tailors) obtained a relic, consisting of part of the hand of their patron saint, from his home city of Cremona. The Sarti had been recognised as a confraternity during the Holy Year of 1575. On 14 November 1613, the day following the saint's feast, the relic was consigned to the guardians of the confraternity in the presence of their cardinal protector, Carlo Conti.[30] Some motets were sung by a hired-in group of singers under the direction of the papal singer Orazio Crescentio, who was paid four *scudi* for the occasion, in addition to nine *scudi* paid for musicians who performed at the previous day's patronal feast.[31] Some days later – but still within the octave of the feast – on 17 November, the relic was brought in procession from the church of S. Giovanni dei Fiorentini, near the Tiber, to the church of S. Omobono near the Campidoglio. The chronicler Giacinto Gigli tells us that the streets along the way were decorated and that the relic was carried under a *baldacchino*, preceded by orphans from two of the city's orphanages, groups of friars and other religious from many of the city's male convents, and by a great number of the clothworkers, all with large lit candles in their hands.[32] Crescentio again organised external musicians, being paid the considerable sum of 35 *scudi* for the occasion, which must have involved a number of professional singing groups to complement the chanting friars.[33]

In 1620 the Confraternita dei Ferrari acquired a relic of part of the arm of its patron S. Eligio from that saint's bishopric of Noyon in France and organised a procession on the vigil of the patronal feast in 1620, with similar large-scale music. According to a chronicle in the confraternity's archive, the procession was 'intramezzata poi da cinque chori di musica delle prime voci di Roma che recavano graziosa melodia' ('interspersed with five choirs of music made up of the finest voices of Rome, bearing a graceful melody').[34] Unfortunately, the archive does not record the name of the organiser of these musicians, nor the

---

    and Early 17th Centuries: Evidence from Archival Sources", *Performance Practice Review* 8 (1995) 107–146.

30 Rome. Archivio del Vicariato, fondo S. Omobono dei Sarti 43 non-foliated.

31 Ibid. The breakdown in remuneration given to musicians for the feast-day, and for the consigning of the relic, is not specified in the recorded payment of 13 *scudi*, but the confraternity consistently spent 9 *scudi* on musicians for the patronal feast in other years close to this one.

32 Giacinto Gigli, *Diario romano (1608–1670)*, (ed.) G. Ricciotti (Rome: 1958) 28.

33 Rome. Archivio del Vicariato, fondo S. Omobono dei Sarti 43 non-foliated.

34 Rome. Archivio dell'Arciconfraternita dei Ferrari 173 (*Cronaca di Tommaso Ponzi archivista*) non-foliated.

sum expended. The Ferrari were not the only body with S. Eligio as their patron saint: the Università degli Orefici (goldsmiths) also celebrated his feast on 25 June. Unlike the Ferrari, the Orefici did not set up a confraternity, remaining to this day a *Nobil Collegio*; as a consequence, they did not build an oratory, nor did they wear a habit.[35] At the same time, they developed an active cult centred on their own church of S. Eligio, designed by Raphael and completed by the mid-1530s. Both bodies employed a chaplain, prayed for living and dead benefactors, organised funerals of members and distributed dowries to poor girls, prioritising those of their members. The richer Orefici seem generally to have spent more money on outside musicians, especially for the patronal feast, though the archives of the Ferrari provide rather less information on that score.[36] In 1628, the Orefici imitated the Ferrari by obtaining, in their turn, a relic taken from the head of S. Eligio; no information survives about the participation of musicians in a welcoming procession, but they would certainly have been present. Both relics were housed in richly decorated reliquaries in their respective churches, helping to increase both devotion and footfall [Fig. 7.5]. Also important in encouraging footfall was the acquisition of indulgences for those visiting their churches, especially on the patronal feast-day. Such indulgences were obtained from the Pope, through the help of the Cardinal Protector.

The most noteworthy example of an artisan confraternity mimicking devotional ones in promoting a strong cult, including the use of polyphonic music, is that of the already-mentioned Fornai. Shortly after recognition as a confraternity in 1507, they began to build a new church, to the design of Antonio Sangallo, near the Forum; it was dedicated to S. Maria di Loreto, whose image had adorned an earlier small church on the site [Fig. 7.6]. The Fornai's 1567 statutes specified that services in the church should be celebrated according to the rites of the Holy Roman Church, with a choir ('la musica'), an organ and an organist paid for that purpose.[37] By the 1570s the confraternity was employing the significant French musician and composer François Roussel to lead a few professional musicians based at the church, while a less experienced musician

---

35 The website of the Orefici provides a detailed history of the institution, including the acquisition of this relic www.universitadegliorefici.it (accessed 4 April 2023).

36 For further details of expenditure on musicians by the two bodies, see: O'Regan N., "Goldsmiths and Blacksmiths: Musical Patronage by Two Artisan Corporations in Early Modern Rome", in Rostirolla G. – Zomparelli E. (eds.), *Tra Musica e Storia. Saggi di varia umanità in ricordo di Saverio Franchi* (Rome: 2017) 61–73.

37 *Statuti della Venerabile Compagnia di S. Maria di Loreto de'Fornari Italiani di Roma* chapter 46.

FIGURE 7.5 Bust with reliquary of St. Eligius of Noyon, Università e Nobil Collegio degli Orefici, S. Eligio degli Orefici, Rome
PUBLIC DOMAIN. WIKIMEDIA COMMONS

was hired to lead the singing in the company's oratory.[38] Supporting even four proficient singers in the church proved difficult and the group was disbanded for a short while in 1594, only to be reinstated later that same year, with a collection taken up among the *confratelli* for the purchase of a larger organ which could supply any missing parts, as was becoming increasingly common for hard-pressed establishments.[39] By 1601, however, finances had improved

38   Rome. Archivio di Stato, fondo S. Maria di Loreto dei Fornai 60 *passim*.
39   Ibidem 135, fols. 141r–144v; see: O'Regan N., "Asprilio Pacelli, Ludovico da Viadana and the Origins of the Roman Concerto Ecclesiastico", *Journal of Seventeenth-Century Music* 6 (2000) http://www.sscm-jscm.org/jscm/v6/no1/Oregan.html.

FIGURE 7.6 S. Maria di Loreto di Fornai and Trajan's Column from *Prospectus Locorum Urbis Romae Insign[ium]*. Etching by Lievin Cruyl, 1666
ANDREW R. AND MARTHA HOLDEN JENNINGS FUND. OPEN ACCESS

and allowed for the employment of two boy sopranos, an alto, tenor and bass, a trombonist, an organist and a *maestro di cappella*. By 1613 there were two singers on each part, and this strength continued thereafter. Armando Serra has shown that, by at least 1624, the Fornai had the highest income of any of the artisan confraternities, higher indeed than many devotional confraternities; this can explain their success in funding regular musicians, the only artisan confraternity to do so.[40] They still brought in extra singers and players for their patronal feast on 8 September: in 1634, for example, there were three choirs of visiting musicians, as well as those in regular employment who may have made up a fourth choir.[41] The payment lists the services as Mass, both First and

---

40   Serra A., "Funzione e Finanze delle Confraternite Romane tra il 1624 e il 1797", *Ricerche per la Storia Religiosa di Roma* 5 (1984) 261–292.
41   See Morelli A., "Filippo Nicoletti (ca. 1555–1634) Compositore Ferrarese: Profilo biografico alla luce di nuovi documenti", in Alm I. – McLamore A. – Reardon C. (eds.), *Musica Franca: Essays in honor of Frank A. D'Accone* (Stuyvesant NY: 1996) 139–150.

Second Vespers, and the singing of the *Salve Regina* each evening during the octave. A separate payment of 4.80 *scudi* was made for musicians to accompany a procession with the *zitelle*. Such festal extravagance was increasingly employed by all confraternities, whether artisan, devotional, or those of foreign nationals in the city.

One artisan confraternity set up in the wake of the Council of Trent was the Confraternitas Musicorum de Urbe, better known under its Italian title of the Compagnia dei Musici di Roma. The forerunner of the Accademia Nazionale di Santa Cecilia, this body is of particular interest in the history of music. The papal bull *Rationi congruit* of May 1585 formally recognised the body with the grant of the usual indulgences; the bull indicates that the members had already been meeting for a few years.[42] It is described as a 'union of persons devoted to the art of music and to its study' whose main purpose was 'the praise, glory and honour of God, the carrying out of pious works and the salvation of the souls of the musicians themselves and those who support this union'.[43] The bull goes on to list the spiritual and charitable duties of the members: attendance at mass and other divine offices at their altar, chapel or church; giving dowries to poor girls; organising a hospice for poor or sick members; visiting any members who might be in prison and bringing them alms; making peace with their enemies; seeing to the burial of dead members and others; taking part in processions organised by the confraternity; accompanying the Blessed Sacrament to sick members; teaching boys music, grammar, writing and reading *gratis* for the love of God; and reciting the *Pater noster* and *Ave Maria* five times daily for the souls of deceased members.

Apart from teaching, these were standard requirements for confraternity members. What the bull omits to mention is, however, significant: there is no reference to controlling the profession or setting up an *università* or academy, though that possibility was presumably in the minds of the founders.[44] This

---

42 For the early history of this body, see: Giazotto R., *Quattro secoli di storia dell'Accademia Nazionale di Santa Cecilia* (Verona: 1970) vol. 1; Summers W. J., "The Compagnia dei Musici di Roma 1584–1604: A Preliminary Report", *Current Musicology* 34 (1982) 7–25; idem, "Music and Confraternal Life in Rome, 1584–1680: Some Observations on the Careers of Palestrina and the Roman School as Members of the Compagnia dei Musici di Roma", in Rostirolla G. – Soldati S. – Zomparelli E. (eds.), *Atti del III Convegno internazionale di studi palestriniani, Palestrina 1994* (Palestrina: 2006) 45–56.

43 The Latin text of the 1585 bull is given in Giazotto, *Quattro secoli* 9–11. An English translation is given in Hayburn R.F., *Papal Legislation on Sacred Music 95 AD to 1977 AD* (Collegeville MN: 1979) 70–72.

44 The Accademia dei Pittori e Scultori di Roma had been approved by Pope Gregory XIII in 1577, elevating the status of the existing Universitas Picturae ac Miniaturae, and this could have been in the minds of the founders of the Compagnia dei Musici. See Rossi S.,

new institution was initially set up as a confraternity, something not always recognised in the literature. A lack of archival documentation hampers knowledge of the first seventy-five or so years of the Compagnia's existence, but some evidence from the early 1620s suggests that it was effectively reactivated at that time.[45] It also attests to an agreement reached in 1622 with the Barnabite Fathers of the church of S. Paolo alla Colonna, that the Compagnia would now be based there, that its members would not wear habits, and that they would help out with the Barnabites' existing weekly Lenten devotional services.[46] The lack of archival documentation also means that we do not know anything about the musical activities of the Compagnia before the middle of the seventeenth century, but their main patronal feast of St. Cecilia must have been celebrated with elaborate music, as well as their other patronal feasts, that of the Visitation of the Blessed Virgin Mary and that of St. Gregory the Great.[47]

There were other musicians in the city, too: those who played in taverns and in the street, referred to as *sonatori ad'aria*. They also responded to the post-Tridentine spirit by forming, sometime before 1581, their own confraternity; it was based in the church of S. Rocco, one of a number of small artisan companies affiliated to that archconfraternity. In that year the Compagnia was given sixty candles of two ounces on the feast of Candlemas by the archconfraternity, together with candles of one pound and a half-pound for the guardian and the camerlengo respectively; that would imply a total membership of sixty-two.[48] Apart from that, nothing else is recorded about them in the S. Rocco archives. Nino Pirotta has published a set of statutes from c.1610–1611 which is the main surviving trace of the group.[49] Also dedicated to St. Cecilia, the Compagnia regulated the locations in which busking musicians played and prevented disagreements between them. Unfortunately, details of patronal or other feast-day celebrations are lacking.

These examples, taken from the archives of various artisan bodies, show some of the ways in which they responded to the changed climate in post-Tridentine

"La Compagnia di S. Luca nel cinquecento e la sua evoluzione in accademia", *Ricerche per la storia religiosa di Roma* 5 (1984) 367–394.

45 An entry in the *diario* of the papal singers for 14 November 1621 speaks of a 'compagnia nuova da erigersi de'cantori di Roma'. See Rome. Biblioteca Apostolica Vaticana. Fondo Cappella Sistina, Diario 40 fol. 61r.

46 See Giazotto, *Quattro secoli* 66–70.

47 A document from June 1622 indicates that members of the Compagnia were planning to have music for three choirs at the forthcoming feast of the Visitation (2 July). See ibidem 65.

48 Pirotta N., "Un'altra congregazione di Santa Cecilia", *Studi Musicali* 12 (1983) 221–238.

49 Ibidem.

Rome. Pius V died in 1572, but matters did not return to their previous state. His immediate successors, Gregory XIII and Sixtus V, continued the policy of centralised control of all Roman institutions, partly exercised through Cardinal Protectors who were elected by, or appointed to, all confraternities and religious orders. Celebrations by artisan and other corporations and confraternities were increasingly directed away from activities like communal meals and into more ordered, church-approved liturgies. Instead of one big central procession, artisan rituals were now parcelled up into separate zones of the city with greater emphasis placed on performing individual cults, petitioning for indulgences, obtaining relics and rebuilding churches. As with devotional confraternities and those for immigrants based in the city's national churches, artisan bodies turned increasingly to music of various kinds to add solemnity to feast-day celebrations, but also to reinforce allegiance to the ideals of the Catholic Reformation through communal chanting and processional singing. All such bodies increased the level of ceremonial surrounding activities such as processions with dowried girls, those with released prisoners (a privilege granted to many confraternities – including some artisan groups – to mark their patronal feast), those welcoming new Cardinal Protectors as they took up office,[50] and those taking members and visiting pilgrims around the city's four major basilicas or seven pilgrimage churches.[51] These invariably involved music in the broad sense of the term and, in particular, increasing amounts of elaborate polyphonic singing by hired-in professionals, who would be among the largest beneficiaries of these changes in strategy.

Bibliography

Black C., *Italian Confraternities in the Sixteenth Century* (Cambridge: 1989).
Fiorani L. et al., "Repertorio degli Archivi delle Confraternite Romane", *Ricerche per la storia religiosa di Roma* 6 (1985) 175–413.
Giallombardo L., "Le Corporazioni d'arti e mestieri attive a Roma nel Seicento", in Santoni B.T. – Sagredo A.M. (eds.), *Luoghi della Cultura nella Roma di Borromini* (Rome: 2004) 457–481.

---

50   For example, the Compagnia di S. Omobono dei Sarti employed the papal singer Vincenzo de Grandis to organise musicians for the installation of their new Cardinal Protector, Giulio Savelli, in 1616. Rome. Archivio del Vicariato, fondo S. Omobono dei Sarti 42 non-foliated.

51   S. Omobono paid two and a half *scudi* to one Jacomo Casio for singers of *falsobordone* who accompanied a procession to the seven pilgrimage churches in 1609 (ibidem).

Giacinto Gigli, *Diario romano (1608–1670)*, Ricciotti G. (ed.) (Rome: 1958).

Giazotto R., *Quattro secoli di storia dell'Accademia Nazionale di Santa Cecilia* (Verona: 1970).

Hayburn R.F., *Papal Legislation on Sacred Music 95 AD to 1977 AD* (Collegeville MN: 1979).

Ingersoll R.J., *The Ritual Use of Public Spaces in Renaissance Rome* (Ph.D. dissertation, University of California at Berkeley: 1985).

Kolega A., "L'Archivio dell'Università dei Marmorai di Roma (1406–1957)", *Rassegna degli Archivi di Stato* 52 (1992) 509–568.

Leonardo M., "Gli Statuti dell'Universita de Marmorari a Roma: Scultori e Scalpellini (1406–1756)", *Studi Romani* 45 (1997) 269–300.

Lumbroso M.M. – Martini A., *Le Confraternite romane nelle loro chiese* (Rome: 1963).

Martini A., "Le Confraternite e le Università di Arti e Mestieri a Roma", in Crescentini C. – Martini A. (eds.), *Le Confraternite Romane: Arte, Storia, Committenza* (Rome: 2000), 13–23.

Misiti M.C., "Le Confraternite dei Librai e Stampatori a Roma", *Rivista Storica del Lazio* 10 (1999) 29–55.

Morelli G., *Le Corporazione di Arti e Mestieri a Roma dal XII al XIX secolo* (Rome: 1937).

Noreen K., "Sacred Memory and Confraternal Space: The Insignia of the Confraternity of the Santissimo Salvatore (Rome)", in Ó Carragáin É. – Neuman de Veguar C. (eds.), *Roma Felix: Formation and Reflections of Medieval Rome* (Aldershot: 2007) 159–187.

Noreen K., "Serving Christ: the Assumption Procession in Sixteenth-Century Rome", in Pericolo L. – Richardson J.N. (eds.), *Remembering the Middle Ages in Early Modern Italy* (Turnhout: 2015) 231–245.

O'Regan N., *Institutional Patronage in Post-Tridentine Rome* (London: 1995).

O'Regan N., "Music at the Roman Archconfraternity of San Rocco in the Late Sixteenth Century", in Antolini B.M. – Morelli A. – Spagnuolo V.V. (eds.), *La musica a Roma attraverso le fonti d'archivio, Atti del convegno internazionale, Roma 4–7 Giugno 1992* (Lucca: 1994) 521–552.

O'Regan N., "The performance of Roman Sacred Polychoral Music in the Late 16th and Early 17th Centuries: Evidence from Archival Sources", *Performance Practice Review* 8 (1995) 107–146.

Pavan P., "Gli statuti della Società dei Raccomandati del Salvatore ad Sancta Sanctorum (1331–1496)", *Archivio della Società Romana di Storia Patria* 101 (1978) 35–96.

Pavan P., "La confraternita del Salvatore nella società romana fra Tre e Quattrocento", *Ricerche per la Storia Religiosa di Roma* 5 (1984) 81–90.

Perry R., "The Medieval Inchinata Procession at Tivoli: Ritual Construction of Civic Identity in the Age of the Commune", *Journal of the Society of Architectural Historians* 76 (2017) 36–62.

Pirotta N., "Un'altra congregazione di Santa Cecilia", *Studi Musicali* 12 (1983) 221–238.

Serra A., "Funzione e Finanze delle Confraternite Romane tra il 1624 e il 1797", *Ricerche per la Storia Religiosa di Roma* 5 (1984) 261–292.

Summers W.J., "The Compagnia dei Musici di Roma 1584–1604: A Preliminary Report", *Current Musicology* 34 (1982) 7–25.

Wisch B. – Newbigin N., *Acting on Faith: the Confraternity of the Gonzalone in Renaissance Rome* (Philadelphia: 2013).

CHAPTER 8

Confraternities and Music on the Eve of the Reformation: Early-Tudor Boston

Magnus Williamson

Abstract

No European country had more devotional confraternities than pre-Reformation England, and none of these insular confraternities was more spectacular than Boston's confraternity of the Virgin Mary. A thick volume of accounts (*GB-Lbl* Egerton 2886) records in detail the confraternity's musical patronage between 1514 and 1525; this is complemented by other stray documents at Lincolnshire Archives (covering the years 1525–6 and 1538–9). These records have informed the biography of the composer John Taverner and have been central to our understanding of confraternities and their patronage of music. The confraternity choir which sang in the Lady Chapel of St Botolph's, Boston, was one of the largest in England and reflected Boston's transmarine horizon – not least, the influence of the great Flemish confraternities. More recently, a further series of accounts have been identified in Lincolnshire Archives, from 1526 to the late-1530s. These show the confraternity at its financial peak and its steep decline. They prove that John Taverner migrated from Oxford to Boston in 1530, and they show how music was used to proclaim Boston's civic ambitions. More broadly they show the links between the important (if decaying) town and port of Boston, regional magnates, metropolitan and courtly interactions with guild and town, the shifting feudal alignment of the region during the troubled 1530s, and impact of doctrinal change on musical opportunities. As so often in Tudor England, professionalised musical traditions are most clearly and richly documented on the very eve of their extinction.

Keywords

England – guild – Boston – Taverner – Cromwell – reform – polyphony – organ

1 Introduction: English Confraternities as Musical Patrons

There is a broadly consistent pattern in the development of England's larger urban guilds, many of which were founded or formally incorporated in the later thirteenth century, grew in size, number and affluence during the fourteenth, became increasingly formalised during the fifteenth when many of them also cultivated polyphony. The guild of St. Nicholas, Bury St. Edmunds (Suffolk), for instance, was founded in 1282 to augment divine worship at St. Mary's parish church, in particular the feast of the Translation of St. Nicholas; it provided both spiritual and material succour to its members; it performed the Mass and Office of the Dead on its feast day and daily suffrages for dead members; it was buttressed by newer guilds during the fourteenth century, not least by the parish's Corpus Christi guild; by the 1460s it supported polyphony and organ playing.[1] A similar pattern of consolidation was followed somewhat later by the guild of the Holy Trinity at St. Peter's Church, Wisbech (Cambridgeshire). Founded before 1379 but not incorporated until 1453, the Wisbech Trinity Guild employed one chaplain by 1472, increasing to four by the 1540s; it maintained a grammar school like many other religious guilds, and in 1477 set up an almshouse. The guild's civic remit also included the repair of piers and wharfs, especially in the 1480s when John Morton, local diocesan bishop of Ely and future cardinal archbishop of Canterbury, instigated the Morton's Leam navigation, improving Wisbech's access to the sea.[2] In 1513, its clerk translated the guild's Latin statutes into English facilitating their recitation to, and comprehension by, guild members at their annual patronal feast – a reminder of the importance of commensality and collective governance.[3] When the guild's endowments and many of its responsibilities were transferred to the new secular corporation of Wisbech in the 1540s, the dissolution may not have been experienced as the complete rupture that it would seem to typify in hindsight.

---

1 Westlake H.F., *The Parish Gilds of Mediæval England* (London: 1919) 12–14; Tymms S. (ed.), *Wills and Inventories from the Registers of the Commissary of Bury St. Edmunds and the Archdeacon of Sudbury*, Camden Society, o.s. 49 (London: 1850) 17–18 (will of John Baret, 10 September 1463).

2 Westlake, *The Parish Gilds of Mediæval England* 107–108; London. The National Archives. E 301/110, m. 1r–v; Atkinson T.D. – Hampson E.M. – Long E.T. – Meekings C.A.F – Miller E. – Wells H.B. – Woodgate G.M.G, "Wisbech: Port, Nene Outfall, Canal", in Pugh R.B. (ed.), *A History of the County of Cambridge and the Isle of Ely* 4, *City of Ely; Ely, N. and S. Witchford and Wisbech Hundreds* (London: 2002) 263–265.

3 Atkinson T.D. – Hampson E.M. – Long E.T – Meekings C.A.F. – Miller E. – Wells H.B. – Woodgate G.M.G, "Wisbech: Guild of the Holy Trinity", in Pugh, *A History of the County of Cambridge* 255–256; Rosser G., "Going to the Fraternity Feast: Commensality and Social Relations in Late Medieval England", *Journal of British Studies* 33 (1994) 430–446.

Its Trinity Guild was one of nine confraternities that, combined, were able to sustain an *opus dei* disproportionate to Wisbech's population of 1,638 (ranked fiftieth in England at the time) or its taxable wealth.[4] As well as leveraging wealth from within and beyond the town, each guild enhanced specific feasts, altars, images or lights, while contributing to the cumulative provision within the parish as a whole. In particular, Wisbech's Corpus Christi Guild belonged to the first of two major waves of institutions prompted by the incursion of the *nova festa*.[5] The official promulgation of the feast of Corpus Christi in England during the 1310s spurred the establishment of fraternities to meet its distinctive ceremonial needs, not least the procession of the consecrated host: at Bury St. Edmunds (1317), Louth (1326), Lincoln (1328), Boston (1335), Grantham (1339), Coventry (1343), Leicester (1343), Lynn (ca. 1349), Northampton (1350) and Newark (1351).[6] The pattern was repeated a century later when fraternities of the Holy Name of Jesus fanned out across lowland England, in emulation of the famous Jesus Guild in the crypt of St. Paul's Cathedral (established by 1459),[7] and with active support from political and church leaders.[8] The number and dedications of parish fraternities in pre-Reformation England therefore serve as indices of the traffic of tastes and ideologies between

---

4 St. Peter (1327); Holy Trinity (1379); St. John Baptist (1384); St. Mary (1387); St. Thomas of Canterbury and Corpus Christi (both pre-1389), St. George, St. Lawrence and Holy Cross (all by 1462); Westlake, *The Parish Gilds of Mediæval England* 147–148; Sheail J., *The Regional Distribution of Wealth in England as Indicated in the Lay Subsidy Returns (1524/5)* (Ph.D. dissertation, University of London: 1968) 11; *Gazetteer*, citing London. The National Archives. E 179/81/131 and E 179/81/162a.
5 Pfaff R.W., *New Liturgical Feasts in Later Medieval England* (London: 1970); Rubin M., "Corpus Christi Fraternities and Late Medieval Piety", *Studies in Church History* 23 (1986) 97–109.
6 Rubin M., *Corpus Christi: The Eucharist in Late Medieval England* (Cambridge: 1991) 199–204 and 232–243. Westlake, *The Parish Gilds of Mediæval England* 49 and 138ff; one outlier, the Corpus Christi Guild of Norwich, claimed it had been established in 1278. The musical roles of the Coventry guilds are currently being researched by the project, *Aural Histories: Coventry 1451–1642* (UK Arts & Humanities Research Council, AH/W010186/1).
7 Cuthbert E.G. – Atchley F., "Jesus Mass and Anthem", *Transactions of St. Paul's Ecclesiological Society* 5 (1905) 163–169; New E., *The Cult of the Holy Name of Jesus in Late Medieval England, with Special Reference to the Fraternity in St. Paul's Cathedral, London, c.1450–1558* (Ph.D. dissertation, Royal Holloway: 1999) 78–80; Aveling J., *"In nomine Iesu omne genu flectatur" – The Late Medieval Mass and Office of the Holy Name of Jesus: Sources, Development and Practice* (Ph.D. dissertation, Bangor University: 2015) 88–101.
8 For instance, Thomas Heywood, who resourced the cult of Jesus in his cathedral; see: Cox J.C., "Benefactions of Thomas Heywood, Dean (1457–92), to the Cathedral Church of Lichfield", *Archaeologia* 52 (1890) 617–646, here 631–633. On Margaret Beaufort, mother of Henry VII, and her chaplain Henry Hornby; see: Jones M.K. – Underwood M.G., *The King's Mother: Lady Margaret Beaufort, Countess of Richmond and Derby* (Cambridge: 1992) 168–10 and 176–177.

metropole and provinces, reinforced by the close interoperation of parish guilds and more piecemeal chantry foundations.[9]

From the 1340s, confraternities and chantries led the way in equipping parish churches with the human and financial resources to sustain polyphonic traditions. In 1343, the parishioners of St. Magnus the Martyr, London Bridge, established a 'chauntry' (in fact, a guild, the two terms being often conflated) in honour of God and the Virgin Mary, whose chief purpose was to fund the singing of the *Salve Regina* every evening.[10] Outside the capital, similar enterprises were undertaken by parishioners in cities like Coventry as well as their regional trading partners. The parishioners of All Saints, Northampton, established their Guild of Our Lady in the thirteenth century for the recitation of Lady Mass. The church was centrally located at the main crossroads in this prosperous midlands town; the guild's revenues increased during the fourteenth century, and supported the singing of Marian antiphons each evening with polyphony, organ-playing and great solemnity ('cum voce organica, sufflatione organorum et magna solemnitate') and was attended by the laity in large numbers.[11] This was first recorded in the 1389 guild survey, but the practice had probably begun by 1347 when the priest Roger de Glenfeld was given episcopal mandate to maintain the town's only music school 'in the art of music as well as plainsong' ('arte musice [sic] quam cantu plano') on the enthusiastic testimony of burgesses and other 'honest men' of Northampton.[12] This is, I believe, the earliest evidence of a dedicated music school in England.

Some guilds were able to elevate parish worship to cathedral standards by 1500. At the magnificent church of St. Lawrence, Ludlow, in the borderlands

---

9   On metropolitan institutions being replicated in provincial parishes, see: Williamson M., "Revisiting the Soundscape of the Medieval Parish", in Harry D. – Steer C. (eds.), *The Urban Church in Late Medieval England: Essays in Honour of Clive Burgess*, Harlaxton Medieval Studies 29 (Donington: 2019) 17–35, here 23–24 (Blackburn); and idem, "Liturgical Polyphony in the Pre-Reformation Parish: a Provisional List and Commentary", RMA *Research Chronicle* 38 (2005) 1–43, here 36 (Macclesfield grammar school, Cheshire, founded by Sir John Percival, mayor of London, and replicated by his wife Thomasine neé Bonaventure at Week St. Mary, Cornwall, and then propagated to Malpas, Cheshire).

10 London. The National Archives. C 47/42/208. At its dissolution in 1548, the guild's annual income was £49 16s 8d; see: Kitching C.J. (ed.), *London and Middlesex Chantry Certificate, 1548*, London Record Society 16 (London: 1980) #25.

11 London. The National Archives. C 47/45/383.

12 Gynewell was present in Northampton 16–21 March 1347; see: Thompson A.H., "Register of John Gynewell, Bishop of Lincoln for the Years 1347–50", *Archaeological Journal* 68 (1911) 301–360, here 307n. Lincolnshire Archives. DIOC/REG/9 (Register of John Gynewell, Bishop of Lincoln) fol. 175v, dated 16 Calends April or 17 March 1347. I am most grateful to Dr Nicholas Bennett for bringing this to my attention.

between England and Wales, the Palmers' (Pilgrims') Guild drew up its statutes in 1284 when it employed three or four chaplains, increasing to seven by the 1340s. The guild's increase in membership from Wales and the English midlands,[13] and its growing portfolio of obit endowments from the 1390s, enabled it to invest heavily in the worship of St. Lawrence's church: the guild bought timber in 1446 for the making of choir stalls (which still survive), and it employed singing men and boy choristers by the 1480s;[14] by the 1540s, they included a warden and seven chaplains, two deacons, four singing men and six choristers.[15] The Lincolnshire town of Louth invested heavily in its musical provision, substantially aided by its guilds of St. Mary (which employed chaplains, lay clerks and, from 1478, a choir trainer) and of the Holy Trinity (which supported the school that educated the boy choristers).[16] One of the central functions of Louth's Mary Guild, since its foundation in 1329, was the singing of the *Salve regina* at sunset each evening before her image in the Lady Chapel of St. James's church.[17] However, in terms of its musical provision – indeed, by almost any measure: financial, geographical, political, cultural – the most magnificent of England's pre-Reformation religious confraternities was the Guild of St. Mary, Boston (Lincolnshire). In the words of the antiquarian John Leland, writing around 1540, St. Botolph's church was 'servid so with singging, and that of cunning men, as no paroche is in al England; the society and bretherhodde longging to this church hath caussid this, [and now] much lande longgith to this society'.[18]

---

13 Sparrow W.C., "A Register of the Palmers' Guild of Ludlow in the Reign of Henry VIII", *Transactions of the Shropshire Archaeological and Natural History Society* 7 (1883) 81–126.
14 Gaydon A.T. – Pugh R.B. (eds.), *A History of the County of Shropshire* II (London: 1973) 134–140.
15 Thompson A.H., "Certificates of the Shropshire Chantries", *Transactions of the Shropshire Archaeological and Natural History Society*, 3rd series 10 (1910) 69–392, here 327.
16 Discussed in detail in Williamson M., "The Role of Religious Guilds in the Cultivation of Ritual Polyphony in England: the Case of Louth, 1450–1550", in Kisby F. (ed.), *Music and Musicians in Renaissance Cities and Towns* (Cambridge: 2001) 82–93. An edition of the Louth guild *compotus* books for 1473–1504 (Lady Guild) and 1489–1528 (Trinity Guild) is in preparation for Lincolnshire Record Society.
17 London. The National Archives. C 47/41/190 (guild survey return, 1389, reporting on the foundation deed of 1329): 'Ad cantandam *Salve Regina* qualibet nocte in crepusculo coram Imaginem beate marie in capella predicta continue'.
18 Toulmin Smith L. (ed.), *The Itinerary of John Leland In or About the Years 1535–1543* (London: 1910) vol. v, 33: 'so well-served with singing, and of knowledgeable men at that, as no other English parish is; the society or fraternity belonging to this church is responsible and now has much land'.

2 Boston's Guild of Our Lady

Boston was still a village in 1086 when it was given by William I to Count Alan of Brittany. Alan, in turn, gave the church, mill and related lands to the Benedictine Abbey of St. Mary, York, whose monks established a summer fair at Boston in 1130 [Fig. 8.1]. Facilitated by its easy access to the North Sea, the port enjoyed a sustained boom during the thirteenth and fourteenth centuries: wool from across the English Midlands went via Boston to Flanders, while wine, timber and finished goods were imported from Gascony and northern Europe. Foreign merchants settled in the town and English traders established links with Boston's transmarine trading partners including, from 1369 to 1558, the Staple of Calais which acted as the exclusive entrepôt for insular wool exports to the continent.[19] By 1334, Boston was the fifth richest town in England, enabling the parishioners to rebuild St. Botolph's church on a monumental scale during the mid-fourteenth century.[20] However, their timing would prove to be unfortunate. Boston's officially recorded trade volumes fluctuated widely year-on-year [Fig. 8.2], but the trend is clear: the value of goods passing through Boston and subject to the poundage tax plummeted from nearly £14,000 (ten-year moving average) at the end of the 1390s to around £1,000 by the mid-1450s.[21] Although the main building works had been completed, the years of economic contraction coincided with the remodelling and furnishing of the quire (1380s–1420s) and the most ambitious element of all, the west tower or 'Boston Stump' which was begun around 1400 and reached its final 83-metre height after two further campaigns (1440s and ca. 1500–1515).[22] The

---

19 Thompson P., *The History and Antiquities of Boston* (Boston: 1856) 55; Haward W.I., "The Trade of Boston in the Fifteenth Century", *Associated Architectural Societies Reports and Papers* 41 (1932–1933) 169–178; Rigby S.H., *The Overseas Trade of Boston in the Reign of Richard II*, Lincolnshire Record Society 93 (Woodbridge: 2005); and idem., "Medieval Boston: Economy, Society and Administration", in Badham S. – Cockerham P. (eds.), *'The beste and fairest of al Lincolnshire': the Church of St. Botolph, Boston, Lincolnshire, and its Medieval Monuments* (Oxford: 2012) 8–28.

20 Monckton L., "'The beste and fairest of al Lincolnshire': the Parish Church of St Botolph, Boston", in Badham – Cockerham (eds.), *'The beste and fairest of al Lincolnshire'* 29–48, here 42–43. Monckton dates the main phase of work to the 1330s through to the 1370s.

21 Data from Rigby S.H., *Boston and Grimsby in the Middle Ages* (Ph.D. dissertation, University of London: 1982) 478–483. The peak year for poundage had been 1386–1387, with £20,804 of taxable goods passing through the port; the nadir was 1460–1461 with just £50. Poundage was usually charged at 1s per £ of goods, or 5%.

22 Monckton, "The Parish Church of St Botolph, Boston" 45.

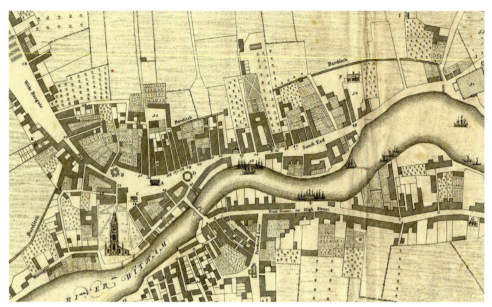

FIGURE 8.1 Robert Hall, *A Plan of the Borough & Port of Boston* (Boston, 1742), showing the medieval street layout, the market place near St. Botolph's church, and the River Withom (orientation: east at top)

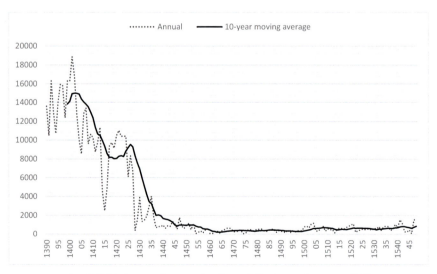

FIGURE 8.2 Goods liable to poundage passing through Boston port, 1390–1548 (£)

collapse in Boston's sea trade necessitated a diversification of funding sources in order for this *grand projet* to reach completion, and it can be no coincidence that Boston's Guild of Our Lady acquired papal indulgences from 1451.[23]

Boston's Guild of Our Mary (henceforth Lady Guild) had been founded in 1260 at the height of the town's mercantile boom; by 1389 it sustained two chaplains and two daily Masses, one held at dawn and the other at 9AM, so that wayfarers might hear Mass before or after they travelled.[24] It was the largest of nineteen religious guilds in St. Botolph's church, rivalled in national importance only by the socially exclusive Corpus Christi Guild and, as the beneficiary of local testamentary bequests, by the Guild of the Seven Martyrs [Fig. 8.3].[25] Only the final decades of the Lady Guild's financial records survive: a bound volume of annual *compoti* for 1514–1525 preserved in the British Library [Fig. 8.4];[26] a series of annual *compoti* for 1526–1538 kept at Lincolnshire Archives, which

---

23   Twemlow J. (ed.), *Calendar of Entries in the Papal Registers Relating to Great Britain and Ireland, 10: 1447–1455* (London: 1915) 86–87: (19 April 1451, Nicholas V): indult that current guild brethren and those joining within five years will receive plenary remission after confessing. An earlier grant by Pope Boniface IX of May 1401 had allowed 100 days' remission for guild brethren attending Lady Mass *cum nota* in St. Botolph's; Bliss W.H. – Twemlow J.A. (eds.), *Calendar of Papal Registers Relating To Great Britain and Ireland, 5: 1398–1404* (London: 1904) 391.

24   Westlake, *The Parish Gilds of Mediæval England* 157; Thompson, *History and Antiquities of Boston* 334. The BVM guild of Northampton made similar provision for the needs of wayfarers.

25   Badham S., "'He Loved the Guild': the Religious Guilds Associated with St. Botolph's church, Boston", in Badham – Cockerham (eds.), *'The beste and fairest of al Lincolnshire'* 49–73, here 51 and 58. The Boston guilds were: BVM (documented 1260–1548); Seven Martyrs (1450–1539); St. Peter & St. Paul (1396–1548); Corpus Christi (1335–1548); St. Katherine (1349–1537); Apostles (1450–1535); Trinity (1389–1548); St. James (1389–1535) St. George (1354–1548); St. John the Baptist (1389–1533); St. Simon & St. Jude (1368–1533); All Hallows (1478–1533); St. Thomas (1486–1533); Assumption (1508–1533); Ascension (1389–1537); Holy Rood (1450–1533); St. Anne (1509 only); St. Anthony (1519–1527); and Fellowship of Heaven (ca. 1446 only).

26   London. The British Library. Egerton 2886. This 303-folio volume was apparently bought for £2 from a curiosity shop in Boston and sold for £90 to Bernard Quaritch who sold it in turn to the British Library; see: Stokes J. (ed.), *Lincolnshire, 2: Editorial Apparatus*, Records of Early English Drama (Toronto: 2009) 471, citing research by the antiquarian William Cragg (1860–1950).

resurfaced only in 2014;[27] two Henrician inventories;[28] and the Lincolnshire certificates in the 1548 chantry survey.[29] These records show that by 1514, the guild employed between nine and ten chaplains, between seven and nine lay clerks and eight choristers.[30] This number broadly corresponds with the workforce described in the papal confirmation of the guild's privileges, issued by Pope Julius II in 1504, which mentions that the guild maintained seven priests and twelve clerks, a choir of nineteen, who sang the daily offices, as well as twelve almsfolk.[31] Further confirmations and extensions of the guild's grants were secured in 1511, 1518 (following a three-year lobbying campaign, masterminded by Thomas Cromwell) and 1526.[32] These grants state that the guild's basic joining fee was 6s 8d followed by annual subscriptions or 'soulscot' of 8d,[33] that the membership included men and women, that new members were recruited in far-flung places by itinerant chamberlains, and that brethren visiting Boston's Lady Chapel on designated feasts would gain merits equivalent to

27   Lincoln. Lincolnshire Archives Office. MISC DON 169 (1518–1519, bailiffs' accounts only, corresponding to a lacuna in London. The British Library. Egerton 2886), BB/4/C/1/1 (1525–1526). Lincoln. Lincolnshire Archives Office. 6-CHAR/2/1 (1526–1538, unfoliated and filed in five parts), and BB/4/C/1/2 (1538–1539, Boston bailiffs' account only). The accounts for 1526–1538 were believed lost for many decades, having been in the custody of the Charity Commission between 1901 and July 2014 when they were accessioned by Lincolnshire Archives.
28   Lincoln. Lincolnshire Archives Office. BB/4/A/2/1A (1523–1524 or 1529–1530) and BB/4/A/2/1B (2 July 1533), partially transcribed in Ramsay N. – Willoughby J.M.W. (eds.), *Hospitals, Towns and the Professions*, British Medieval Library Catalogues 14 (London: 2009) 10–14 and 14–19; the 1534 inventory is in Thompson, *History and Antiquities of Boston* 141–146.
29   London. The National Archives. E 301/33; Forster C.W. – Thompson A.H., "The Chantry Certificates for Lincoln and Lincolnshire, returned in 1548, under the Act of Parliament of 1 Edward VI", *Associated Architectural Societies Reports and Papers* 37.2 (1925) 247–275, here 255–260.
30   London. The British Library. Egerton 2886, fols. 16v, 117v (1518–1519). After 1527, the number of lay clerks increased to between eleven and twelve, before decreasing after 1535 to nine (1536–1537), seven (1537–1538), and finally six (by 1548) (Lincoln. Lincolnshire Archives Office. 6-CHAR/2/1 parts 2 and 5); see Forster – Thompson, "The Chantry Certificates" 258.
31   Haren M.J. (ed.), *Calendar of Entries in the Papal Registers Relating to Great Britain and Ireland* 18 (Dublin: 1989) 171–172 (7 September 1504). No mention is made of choristers in the 1504 grant.
32   Haren M.J. (ed.), *Calendar of Entries in the Papal Registers Relating to Great Britain and Ireland* 19 (Dublin: 1998) 290.
33   But fees may in fact have been as high as 13s 4d for the joining fee and 3s 4d for annual subscriptions; see: Swanson R.N., *Indulgences in Late Medieval England: Passports to Paradise?* (Cambridge: 2007) 375–376.

ON THE EVE OF THE REFORMATION: EARLY-TUDOR BOSTON 209

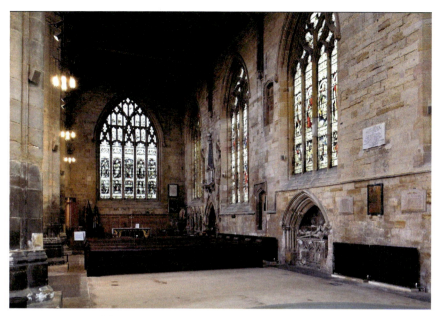

FIGURE 8.3 St. Botolph, Boston, south aisle, site of the pre-Reformation Lady Chapel. The doors in the south wall mark the location of the screen and organ loft
IMAGE © COLIN MURRAY, UNDER IWM NON-COMMERCIAL LICENCE

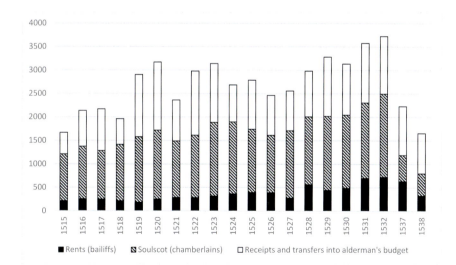

FIGURE 8.4 Annual turnover, Boston Lady Guild, 1515–1538 (£) (rental data incomplete for the year 1526–1527)

a pilgrimage to Rome.[34] Above all, the Lady Guild's prestige rested on its papal indulgences, chiefly, from around 1516 onwards, the *Scala Coeli* pardon.[35]

3   A Case-Study Year: 1529–1530

The Lady Guild's complicated cash-flow is recorded in a series of engrossed *compoti*. These accounts were rendered at the end of each accounting year in readiness for the fraternity feast at Corpus Christi and the handover of roles from one year's office-holders to the next. Each year's fascicle amounts to approximately 30 parchment folios, each measuring up to 30 × 22 cm, so the cumulative total for the years 1514–1538 is therefore around 600 folios of detailed financial records. The richness and complexity of the guild's operations are therefore best illustrated by focusing on a single case-study year, 1529–1530, from the rediscovered series of guild *compoti*. In this year, the guild's rents from cottages, tenements, arable land, meadows and pastures amounted to £487 18s 8½d (approximately £200,000 or €235,000 at current values).[36] This income was collected by three bailiffs, responsible for different locales around Boston, who each kept detailed accounts in their own draft book (or *quaternum*: all of these have now been lost). The bailiffs oversaw the upkeep of their properties but also subsidised a share of the guild's central operations direct from their own devolved budgets. In 1529–1530, for example, the bailiff of Boston contributed £6 3s 4d to the accommodation costs of nine lay clerks.[37] The bailiff for lands in Boston's rural hinterland included, among the costs for repairing sea dykes, 40s for the construction of a tabernacle for the church's patronal image of St. Botolph and for mending the organ.[38] This organ

---

34   Haren, *Calendar of Entries in the Papal Registers* 18: 172 (Easter, Corpus Christi, Whitsun, Nativity of the BVM and Assumption of the BVM).

35   Lunt W.E., *Financial Relations of the Papacy with England, 1327–1534* (Cambridge MA: 1961) 500–501; Morgan N., "The Scala Coeli Indulgence and the Royal Chapels", in Thompson B. (ed.), *The Reign of Henry VII*, Harlaxton Medieval Studies 5 (Stamford: 1995) 82–103; Swanson, *Indulgences in Late Medieval England* 54–56; MacCulloch D., *Thomas Cromwell: A Life* (London: 2018) 31–35.

36   Following the Bank of England's inflation calculator: https://www.bankofengland.co.uk /monetary-policy/inflation/inflation-calculator. Nearly all rents or farms were paid in cash, save for a few assize rents payable with root ginger or half a pound (225 g) of pepper.

37   Lincoln. Lincolnshire Archives Office. 6-CHAR/2/1 part 2, *compotus* of William Day, bailiff of Boston ('Allocatio pro cameris clericorum').

38   Lincoln. Lincolnshire Archives Office. CHAR/2/1 part 2, *compotus* of John Nele, bailiff of Kirton ('Custus reparacionum fossatorum marinalium cum aliis'). The bailiff of Boston also provided the stone carver with a rent-free cottage next to the grammar school near St. Botolph's church (Lincoln. Lincolnshire Archives Office. 6-CHAR/2/1 part 2, *compotus*

had been constructed ten years earlier by Anthony Duddington of London with support from the then bailiff of Boston (who contributed 22s 4d towards the total cost of £32 3s 4d).[39] The bailiff of lands bequeathed to the guild by its one-time alderman, John Robynson (d. 1526), paid the salaries of two chantry priests who sang in St. Botolph's church, who wore the same liveries as the Lady Guild's chaplains, and whose musical competences had been defined in Alderman Robynson's will.[40] The cumulative expenditure across the three bailiffs' accounts in 1529–1530 amounted to £282 ½d, from which the three officials transferred £85 into the alderman's budget, carrying over their remaining surpluses to the following year.

Meanwhile, the chamberlains gathered soulscot through their itinerant progresses, each keeping their own accounts from which they offset their running costs and, like the bailiffs, contributing to the guild's central operations. The two senior chamberlains and their clerks assumed general responsibility for southern and northern England respectively. They paid equal shares of the costs of the annual Corpus Christi feast,[41] the obit of Anne of Bohemia (queen of Richard II and 'prime benefactor' of the guild),[42] and the purchase

    of William Day (under 'Decasus et allocacio reddituum cum warrectagione terre videlicet in ... Wormegate')). The main cost, of £73 4d, was borne by the alderman (Lincoln. Lincolnshire Archives Office. 6-CHAR/2/1 part 2, *compotus* of Thomas Robertson (under 'Solucio super facturam tabernaculi sancti Botolphi')).

39 London. The British Library. Egerton 2886 fol. 135 (Reginald Duchefeld, bailiff of Boston: 'Custus organiste') and fol. 151v (John Robynson, alderman: 'Empcio nouorum organorum').

40 Lincoln. Lincolnshire Archives Office. 6-CHAR/2/1 part 2, *compotus* of Richard Clerc, bailiff of John Robynson's lands ('Salaria duorum capellanorum', £12 18s 8d; 'Anniversaria', 70s 8d); Lincoln. Lincolnshire Archives Office. Boston Borough 1/B/7 (will of John Robynson, 25 February 1525/6), fol. 6: 'two suche honest & well disposed prystes [...] of good conversacion which shall syng plainsong & faborden [...] [and shall receive] salarie cvj s. viij d., a gowne, clothe price of every yarde therof iij s. iiij d., of the colour of the other prystes of the ⟨said⟩ guilde'.

41 Lincoln. Lincolnshire Archives Office. 6-CHAR/2/1 part 2, *compotus* of William Wadeney, chamberlain for Boston South Rode, 'Expensi ad festum corporis Christi' (£12 16s 2½d on bread, wine, beer, beef, mutton, lamb, goose, chicken and other victuals, on carriage of banners, cross, torches and thuribles, and on actors and performers [*histriones* and *mimes*] and other entertainment costs); Lincoln. Lincolnshire Archives Office. 6-CHAR/2/1 part 2, *compotus* of Laurence Belman, chamberlain for Boston North Rode, 'Expensi ad festum corporis christi et in octavo eiusdem'. This replicates chamberlains' accounts going back to 1514; see: Stokes J. (ed.), *Lincolnshire, 1: The Records*, Records of Early English Drama (Toronto: 2009) 27–37.

42 Lincoln. Lincolnshire Archives Office. 6-CHAR/2/1 part 2, Wadeney and Belman *compoti*, under 'Anniversarii' (6s 8d). Anne died on 7 June 1394, a date propitiously coincident with the fraternity feast when Easter Sunday fell after 7 April.

of cloth for choir liveries.[43] In 1529–1530 the two chamberlains were assisted by six vice-chamberlains, each responsible for progresses far from Boston: one vice-chamberlain for the south-eastern counties of Kent, Sussex, Surrey and Calais; one for Devon and Cornwall; one for Wales and the Marches; one for north-western England; and one for Ireland and the Isle of Man. Each chamberlain, his clerk and servant, recruited new members and collected dues from existing ones at fairs and markets in population centres, and recorded members' names and contributions in their *quaterni* which were audited after their progresses;[44] the names were then copied fair into parchment registers back home in Boston.[45] These progresses incurred substantial costs in horse-hire and shoeing, saddles, boots and baggage.[46] Even after the deduction of these costs and the payment of clerks and auditors, however, the chamberlains generated large sums in 1529–1530: altogether, they raised £1,483 19s 9d in sales of pardons, spent £1,319 17s 10¼d (which included periodic cash transfers to the alderman's budget), and handed £164 16s 8¾d in surplus to their successors for the following year. The chamberlains' cash transfers formed the backbone of the alderman's budget: in 1529–1530, he received £622 18s 8d (modern equivalent £436,000 or €510,000) which was deposited in the guild's treasury

---

43   Lincoln. Lincolnshire Archives Office. 6-CHAR/2/1 part 2, Wadeney and Belman *compoti*, under 'Empcio liberaturae vesturae capellanorum, clericorum et pauperum bedarie' (Wadeney, £12 8s 3½d) and 'Liberatura vestura capellanorum, clericorum cum aliis plus Liberatura vestura officiariorum, pauperum bedarie et choristarum' (Belman, £12 8s 3¾d). The two chamberlains had also contributed 25% each to choir salaries until 1521: London. The British Library. Egerton 2886 fol. 142 and fols. 16v, 43, 72v–73, 97r–v, 100, 103, 104v, 119v, 144 and 169v ('Stipendia and Salaria') and fol. 144v ('Empio [sic] necessariorum pro choristis').

44   None of the chamberlains' *quaterni* survive, but a comparison can be made with the extant 'riding books' compiled by the sergeants of the Ludlow Palmers' Guild; see: Swanson, *Indulgences in Late Medieval England* 134.

45   Lincoln. Lincolnshire Archives Office. 6-CHAR/2/1 part 2, *compotus* of Thomas Robertson, alderman ('Soluciones necessarie pro choro'): in 1529–1530, 8s 8d was spent on twenty-six skins of parchment for the register of Devon and Cornwall.

46   For instance, Lincoln. Lincolnshire Archives Office. 6-CHAR/2/1 part 2, *compotus* of Nicholas Felde, vice-chamberlain for the south-east and Calais ('Expensi forinseci', £41 16s 1d on progress; 'Soluciones necessarie', 11s 4d on shoeing of horses, ink, paper, etc.). The king's printer Richard Pynson had printed the guild's letters of confraternity until his death in December 1529: London. The British Library. Egerton 2886 fol. 241 (*compotus* of John Robynson, alderman, 1522–1523, under 'Empcio litterarum et brevium cum pergameno'). In 1524–1525 Pynson printed 10,000 letters and associated items for the guild, see: Swanson, *Indulgences in Late Medieval England* 173.

in 'Tailors' Hall', a now-lost annexe between the Lady chapel and quire of St. Botolph's church.[47]

The guild's central officer was the alderman, elected to serve for a year from Thursday in Whitsun Week, and sometimes serving multiple terms of office.[48] The alderman for 1529–1530 was Thomas Robertson, merchant of the Staple of Calais.[49] His *recepta* for 1529–1530 comprised the bailiffs' and chamberlain's *denarii*, as well as offerings made at the offertory box of the BVM, testamentary legacies, cash withdrawals from the guild treasury, arrears and repaid loans: £1,090 3½d in all.[50] From these funds the alderman paid the stipends of eleven chaplains (£55) and eleven lay clerks, the master of the grammar school, the keeper of the Lady Chapel, and the guild's secretary, the London lawyer Geoffrey Chamber (£73 6s 8d).[51] The alderman also funded fringe benefits to the choir and to visiting singers throughout the year.[52] In 1529–1530, this included several payments to the lay clerks: 3s 4d for singing Christmas carols ('clericis huis gilde pro suis karralles in festo nativitatis domini'); 16d for wine on the first Sunday of Lent; 3s 4d as a goodwill payment in Easter week; 3s 4d at the time of the election of the alderman and chamberlains; and a further 3s 4d at the patronal feast of St. Botolph on 17 June, when the choir received their salaries (and when the king's waits were present). Visiting singers were also paid.[53] Some of these payments corroborate evidence of musical activity in their home institutions: for instance, the local collegiate church at Tattershall, workplace of William Munke, paid 2s reward and 8d accommodation by the

---

47   Lincoln. Lincolnshire Archives Office. 6-CHAR/2/1 part 2, *compotus* of Thomas Robertson, alderman, under 'Recepta denariorum de camerariorum et vice camerariorum huius gilde'; illustrated in Badham, "He Loved the Guild" 70.

48   Robertson was also alderman in 1523–1524 (London. The British Library. Egerton 2886 fol. 259v). John Robynson had been alderman sometime before 1514 and again, continuously, from 1518 to 1523 (ibid., fols. 24, 125, 149, 176v, 202 and 230v).

49   London. The National Archives. PROB 11/27/75 (will, 10 July 1534). He had joined Boston's Corpus Christi guild in 1532.

50   Lincoln. Lincolnshire Archives Office. 6-CHAR/2/1 part 2, *compotus* of Thomas Robertson, alderman ('Summa totalis receptorum cum arreragiis'). The repaid loans in 1529 were to John Wendon, *magister organorum* (ibid., 'Adhuc recepta denariorum extra thesauro gilde').

51   Lincoln. Lincolnshire Archives Office. 6-CHAR/2/1 part 2, *compotus* of Thomas Robertson, alderman ('Salaria capellanorum and Stipendia clericorum et aliorum').

52   All subsequent references from Lincoln. Lincolnshire Archives Office. 6-CHAR/2/1 part 2, *compotus* of Thomas Robertson, alderman ('Expensi confratrum et extraneorum ad tabernas' and 'Regarda').

53   Similar entries from 1519–1526 are transcribed in Stokes, *Lincolnshire* vol. 1, 33–37.

Lady Guild in 1529–1530;[54] and King's College, Cambridge, the most likely employer of 'Mr Fuller, singer' who was paid 5s.[55] In other cases, however, the guild's transactions cast light on poorly-documented institutions: for instance, a singer who came from Hull (5s),[56] another from Higham Ferrers (20d),[57] and a third from Wakefield (Yorks) who went to Boston for the feast of the Visitation on 2 July (3s 4d).[58] Two large and unusual payments were also made in 1529–1530. Richard Gouge, one of the guild's lay clerks,[59] was paid 20s for riding to the king's chapel for purpose unspecified, but probably to secure exemption of the guild's singers from forced recruitment.[60] The composer John Taverner was

---

54 Munke was present at the surrender of Trinity College, Tattershall, on 4 February 1544/5; he served as organist and master of the choristers at Lincoln Cathedral, 1552–1559 (London. The National Archives. E 322/234); Bowers R., "Lincoln Cathedral: Music and Worship to 1640", in Owen D. (ed.), *A History of Lincoln Minster* (Cambridge: 1994) 47–76, here 76. In the same year, singers from Boston, Tattershall and Lincoln were paid for performing at Bardney Abbey, OSB, near Lincoln; see: Stokes, *Lincolnshire* vol. 1, 345.

55 Probably John Fuller, born Bury (Suffolk) ca. 1510: chorister at Kings' College, Cambridge (1522), scholar of Eton College (ca. 1523–28), scholar of King's College (1528–1530), and gentleman of the Chapel Royal ca. 1535–1543; see: *Letters and Papers, Foreign and Domestic, of the reign of Henry VIII*, Addenda I/i (London: 1929) 105, citing London. The National Archives. SP 1/233; Sterry Sir W. (ed.), *The Eton College Register, 1440–1698* (Eton: 1943) 133; Ashbee A. – Lasocki D. (eds.), with Holman P. – Kisby F., *A Biographical Dictionary of English Court Musicians* (Aldershot: 1998) vol. 1, 450, and, with different dating, Ashbee A. (ed.), *Records of English Court Music* VII (Aldershot: 1993) 424.

56 Holy Trinity, Kingston upon Hull, 100 km north of Boston, was served by at least eight chantry priests including the grammar master who employed a parish clerk 'to teche children to sing'; see: Page W. (ed.), *The Certificates of the Commissioners Appointed to Survey the Chantries, Guilds, Hospitals, etc., of the County of York* II, Surtees Society 92 (1895) 340–346.

57 Higham Ferrers College (Northants), 90 km south-east of Boston, was founded in 1422 by Henry Chichele, Archbishop of Canterbury. In a visitation of 1520, the college housed a warden and five chaplains, four lay clerks and six choristers; see: Thompson A.H. (ed.), *Visitations in the Diocese of Lincoln 1517–1531* vol. II, Lincoln Record Society 35 (1944) 163–165.

58 Wakefield parish church, 145 km north-east of Boston, was well-staffed with clergy, hosting thirteen chantry priests by the 1540s; see: Page, *Certificates* (306–316).

59 Gouge joined the guild's choir in June 1529 and was still in post in 1548; see: Forster – Thompson, "Chantry Certificates" 258. He was also a skilled scrivener as, in the same year 1529–1530, he was also paid 20s for copying the guild register in duplicate (Lincoln. Lincolnshire Archives Office. 6-CHAR/2/1 part 2, *compotus* of Thomas Robertson, alderman, 1529–1530, under 'Expensi et soluciones necessarie').

60 Lincoln. Lincolnshire Archives Office. 6-CHAR/2/1 part 4, *compotus* of Nicholas Robertson, alderman, 1533–1534 ('Feoda Consiliarii auditorium cum aliis'): 'M[agistro] Crane, M. Choristarum < xl^s > domini Regis'. An exemption had already been secured from William Crane in 1524–1525 (London). The British Library. Egerton 2886 fol. 299v ('Expensi

also paid 20s, plus accommodation and, in a sign of things to come, seven yards of linen cloth costing 5s 7d for a surplice.[61] A native of Boston, Taverner had been unwillingly recruited to train the choristers at Cardinal Wolsey's lavish Oxford college in 1526. Taverner left Cardinal College at Easter 1530 as soon as Wolsey's political eclipse permitted, joining the Lady Guild's choir as a lay clerk at Whitsun – a role for which he was already being measured up before the guild's administrators prepared their 1529–1530 accounts for audit.[62]

The alderman was also responsible for funding the upkeep of the eight choristers. In 1529–1530 this entailed the expenditure of £7 5s 9¾d on their apparel: hoses, linen shirts, doublets, caps, orange tawney cloth, shoes (in four batches of eight pairs), ink horns, pen cases, bags and, of course, surplices.[63] The choristers received potations on Ember Thursday and later in Lent (2s in all), 8d at Easter, and another 8d at election time (on Thursday of Whitsun week).[64] The choristers' tonsuring (a mere 12d) was also paid from the alderman's account, along with the purchase of 62½ gallons (or 284 litres) of wine for the priests celebrating *Scala celi* and other Masses, of 5,200 communion wafers, of incense, lamp oil and other ritual equipment, along with fees for obits administered by the guild.[65] If the purchases of wafers and communion wine reflect the frequency of Masses supported by the guild's clergy, the alderman's purchase of a hogshead of table wine for the annual Corpus Christi feast in the guildhall gives some indication of the number (or thirst) of guild brethren and

    et soluciones necessarie'). The guild's choir received persistent and unwelcome attention from Cardinal Wolsey in the 1520s; see: Bowers R., "The Cultivation and Promotion of Music in the Household and Orbit of Thomas Wolsey", in Gunn S.J. – Lindley P.G. (eds.), *Cardinal Wolsey: Church, State and Art* (Cambridge: 1991) 178–218, here 190.

61 Lincoln. Lincolnshire Archives Office. 6-CHAR/2/1 part 2, *compotus* of Thomas Robertson, alderman ('Expensi confratrum et extraneorum ad tabernas' and 'Soluciones necessarie et expensi forinseci').

62 Taverner's family background, transfer to Boston and later career as a royal servant are examined in Williamson M., "Taverner at Boston" (forthcoming).

63 Lincoln. Lincolnshire Archives Office. 6-CHAR/2/1 part 2, *compotus* of Thomas Robertson, alderman ('Soluciones necessarie pro choristis').

64 Lincoln. Lincolnshire Archives Office. 6-CHAR/2/1 part 2, *compotus* of Thomas Robertson, alderman ('Regarda').

65 Lincoln. Lincolnshire Archives Office. 6-CHAR/2/1 part 2, *compotus* of Thomas Robertson, alderman ('Soluciones pro choro', £4 19s 4½d total; 'Custus obbituum sive Anniversariorum', £12 5s 11d).

FIGURE 8.5 Boston Lady Guild accounts, 1527–1533 (Lincoln. Lincolnshire Archives Office. 6-CHAR/2/1, part 2), showing bailiff's account for Boston rents, for the year to Thursday of Whitsun week, 29 Henry VIII, 1528
PHOTO: AUTHOR

sisters who attended the annual fraternity feast on 16 June 1530:[66] a hogshead, containing 63 gallons, equates to 382 standard 75 cl bottles [Fig. 8.5].[67]

4 Boston's Networks

The number of musicians hired temporarily or recruited permanently from far afield is but one indication of the Lady Guild's networks: regional, national

---

66 Lincoln. Lincolnshire Archives Office. 6-CHAR/2/1 part 2, *compotus* of Thomas Robertson, alderman ('Soluciones necessarie et expensi forinseci'); the wine cost 40s 6d, with 6d portage.

67 Associated costs for entertainments at the Corpus Christi feast are numerous. In 1530, 2d was paid to five boys from the city of Lincoln, for leaping [*saltantes*] before the festal procession, 3s 4d to four trumpeters, and 3s 4d to an instrumentalist [*sitharista*] playing on the feast and its eve (Lincoln. Lincolnshire Archives Office. 6-CHAR/2/1 part 2, *compotus* of Thomas Robertson, alderman, 1529–30, under 'Regarda').

and international.[68] In part this was an inevitable by-product of the guild's wealth. Referring once again to the case study year, 1529–1530, it is worth recalling that the disposable income allotted to Alderman Robertson amounted to nearly £1,100. This was comparable with the annual cost of maintaining a ducal household: for instance, of Edward Stafford, Duke of Buckingham (1478–1521).[69] Its purchasing power alone allowed the Lady Guild to exert a strong gravitational force as an employer, but the guild's method of revenue raising also enabled it to reach outwards. In 1521–1522, a decade after he had left Lincolnshire to become cantor of Durham Cathedral 250 km away, the composer Thomas Ashwell provided the guild with polyphony.[70] Leonard Matson, one of the guild's lay clerks from 1526 until 1537,[71] received payments for copying music on numerous occasions; indeed, between 1530 and 1534 Matson achieved the distinction of being the only Tudor parish musician to receive a regular *per annum* salary as a music copyist.[72] In 1530 he was paid 2s for copying polyphony sent by William Rocetour, vice-chamberlain for the

---

68   Other payments to visiting entertainers in 1529–1530, in addition to those discussed above: the king's players at the patronal feast (20s 8d) and on another unspecified occasion (6s 8d); the waits of Nottingham (20d); Cardinal Wolsey's players (6s 8d); a *sitharist* called Bland (4s) and the players of Lord Lumley ('lusoribus domini lumnay', 7s 6d) (all Lincoln. Lincolnshire Archives Office. 6-CHAR/2/1 part 2, *compotus* of Thomas Robertson, alderman, under 'Regarda').

69   Woolgar C.M., *The Great Household in Late Medieval England* (New Haven – London: 1999) 16, citing Stafford. Staffordshire Record Office [*GB-STA*] D641/1/3/8 (1503–1504: £1,168). By way of comparison, the guild's gross annual income of nearly £2,000 in 1529–1530, put it on a par with St Alban's and Reading Abbeys (£2,102 and £1,938 respectively in 1535), while the annual income of Cardinal College, Oxford, in 1529–1530 was £1,591 (London. The National Archives. E 36/104).

70   London. The British Library. Egerton 2886 fol. 204 ('Regarda diversis personis'): 'Et solutum Magistri < 25s > Watson (et) Thome < 10s > Assewell pro diversis cantibus pro eisdem emptis et punctuatis pro choro beate Marie'. Ashwell moved to Durham between 1511 and 1513; see: Harrison F.L, *Music in Medieval Britain* (London: 1958) 429–430.

71   Lincoln. Lincolnshire Archives Office. BB/4/C/1/1, fol. 5, *compotus* of John Litster alias Copley, bailiff of Boston, 1525–1526 ('Allocaciones'), and 6-CHAR/2/1 part 5, *compotus* of William Spynke, alderman, 1536–1537 ('Stipendia clericorum et aliorum ministrorum gilde').

72   Lincoln. Lincolnshire Archives Office. 6-CHAR/2/1 parts 2 and 4, *compoti* of John Copley alias Litster, Robert Tomlinson and Nicholas Robertson, alderman, 1530–1534 ('Stipendia clericorum'). On top of his already high termly salary of 60s per term, Matson was given 10s termly 'pro prykkyng canticorum' (£12 salary plus £2 copying per annum). Matson pre-empted by a decade the appointment of the court musician Robert Colson, 'pricker of books for the kings chapell' (1542–1553); see: Ashbee – Lasocki, *Biographical Dictionary* 279.

south-eastern counties at Calais for the upcoming year, 1530–1531.[73] A couple of years later, the purchase of a large book of polyphony would be recorded in the same breath as a business trip by Rocetour.[74] The chamberlains' necessary itinerancy clearly worked to the guild's advantage in sourcing new repertory from distant locations.

The most spectacular journey known to have been undertaken on the guild's behalf was the well documented and oft-narrated campaign by Thomas Cromwell to renew the guild's indulgences at Rome between 1517 and 1520.[75] This venture, coordinated by the guild's London lawyer Geoffrey Chamber, spearheaded by Thomas Cromwell, and later immortalised by the Boston-born Protestant hagiographer John Foxe, cost the guild £2,100.[76] Nevertheless, the return on this investment amply compensated for Boston's shrunken mercantile income, both for the community as a whole and for the guild's employees. In 1524–1525, for instance, some £242 13s 8d was disposed upon choir salaries alone.[77] The annual salaries for the guild's lay clerks, between £5 6s 8d and £10 (or £13 6s 8d for the organ player and the master of choristers), matched the best on offer elsewhere.[78] This enabled the guild to recruit and retain the best

---

73   Lincoln. Lincolnshire Archives Office. 6-CHAR/2/1 part 1, *compotus* of Thomas Robertson, alderman, 1529–1530 ('Regarda'): 'Leonardo Matson pro le prykkyng ij^{orum} canticorum missis [sic] per Wm Rocetour, ij^s'; and ibid., *compotus* of William Rocetour, chamberlain for Kent, Calais, Surrey, Sussex and other southern counties, 1530–1531.

74   Lincoln. Lincolnshire Archives Office. 6-CHAR/2/1 part 4, *compotus* of Nicholas Robertson, alderman, 1533–1534 ('Soluciones et expense necessarie'): 'denariis factis per dictum computante solutis et expendis ut in precio unius magni libri vocati *pryksongboke* cum aliis necessariis eidem aptis brevibus, litteris et aliis scriptis / Expensis forinsecis Willimi Rosetour equitanti usque Northampton cum una littera missa de Roberto Sawnders'.

75   London. The British Library. Egerton 2886 fol. 181r–v (*Compotus Galfridi Chambers Secretarii*); see: Swanson, *Indulgences in Late Medieval England* 122 and 449.

76   In 1526–1527, some £220 8s 5d was also spent on securing the lucrative Jubilee indulgence: Lincoln. Lincolnshire Archives Office. 6-CHAR/2/1 part 1, *compotus* of Geoffrey Wace, alderman, 1526–1527 ('Expensi et solutiones pro perquisitione et declaratione noue bulle apostolice').

77   London. The British Library. Egerton 2886, fols. 295–96.

78   For instance: Fotheringhay College, ranged from £1 10s to £3 11s 8d in 1527–8; St. Mary's College, Warwick, from £2 13s 4d to £7 in 1525–1527; Tattershall College, from £3 6s 8d to £5 6s 8d in 1558–1559 (post-dissolution pensions); Cardinal College, Oxford, £6 plus commons in 1527–1528; St George's Chapel, Windsor, £10 in 1541–1542; master of children, household chapel of Charles Brandon, Duke of Suffolk, £13 6s 8d on 18 June 1535 (Northampton, The Record Office [GB-NH] Westmorland Apethorpe 5.v.4/2; London). The National Archives. sc6/Henry VIII/3732 and E 101/518/14, fol. 8; London. The British Library. Harley Charter 47 A. 49; Windsor. Chapter Library xv.59.3; *Report on the Manuscripts of Lord De L'Isle & Dudley Preserved at Penshurst Place* 1, Historical Manuscripts Commission (London: 1925) 202.

singers: of the twelve clerks present in 1524–1525, nine remained in post for ten years or more: one of the three short-termers had been a chorister previously; another, the choir trainer Robert Testwood, was cherry-picked to run the choir at Cardinal Wolsey's flagship college in Ipswich.[79] The lay clerk Richard Hickes was already at Boston by Whitsun 1514, remaining in the Lady Guild's service until his death twenty years later.[80] He invested his £10 annual salary wisely, entering trade as a mercer, taking on a servant and an apprentice, building a property portfolio in town, sourcing fashionable clothes in London, and leaving his children cash legacies comfortably exceeding the expectations of most Tudor singers' children.[81] He left cash bequests to sixteen Boston guilds, his children married locally, he was deeply invested in Boston, but he was in fact a native of Gloucestershire.[82] Richard Hickes exemplifies the economic and cultural pull of the Lady Guild, whose revenues enabled it to recruit the best singers from across the kingdom who, in turn, re-invested their earnings in the local economy.

5   Conclusion: Endings, 1536–1545

Perhaps the most politically significant musicians to visit Boston in the 1530s were Thomas Alwey and Nicholas Cutler, respectively chaplain and master of the singing boys in the household chapel of Charles Brandon, Duke of Suffolk. Alwey appeared in Boston at Eastertide (early April) 1537, when he spent a week in St. Botolph's along with another singer (or singers) from the duke's chapel.[83] The following year, Cutler lodged with the duke's nine chapel boys in the house of the Lady Guild's singer John Reynold (who was deputed to take

---

79   Bowers, 'The cultivation and promotion of music' 198–199.
80   London. The British Library. Egerton 2886 fol. 16v; Lincoln. Lincolnshire Archives Office. 6-CHAR/2/1 part 4, *compotus* of William Spynke, alderman, 1533–1534 ('Stipendia clericorum').
81   Hickman D. (ed.), *Lincoln Wills 1532–1534*, Lincoln Record Society 89 (Woodbridge: 2001) 195–197 (will, dated 19 August 1533, proved 3 March 1533/4). He bequeathed 40 marks (£26 13s 4d) each to his sons Jasper, Christopher and Melchior, and £40 to his daughter Frideswide.
82   Hickman, *Lincoln Wills* 195–197, mentions his son-in-law John Reynold (lay clerk, Lady Guild, 1531–1538) and brothers Thomas Hickes of Tetbury, 230 km south-east of Boston, and William Hickes of Cromhall ('Crommell'), in the same part of Gloucestershire.
83   Lincoln. Lincolnshire Archives Office. 6-CHAR/2/1 part 5, *compotus* of William Spynke, alderman, 1536–1537 ('Regarda'): 'in regardo dato thome Allwey capellano Ducis Suffold [sic] cum al' cantator' ['cum alio cantatore' or 'cum aliis cantoribus'] servient 'in ecclesia per unam septimanam in festo pasche, x^s'.

a salmon to the duke by way of *Dankopfer*).[84] Nicholas Cutler of Eye (Suffolk) had been master of the children of the ducal chapel since June 1535, when Brandon was still based in East Anglia.[85] Cutler's presence in Boston in 1537 and 1538 was no accident: only a few months previously, in October 1536, the Lincolnshire rebellion and the ensuing Pilgrimage of Grace, had shaken the Henrician regime to its foundations.[86] The Duke of Suffolk played a central role in quashing the rebellion, and Henry VIII decided to move his reliable friend across the feudal chess-board of lowland England, from East Anglia to Lincolnshire, with the inducement of a fashionable brick-built residence: Tattershall Castle, 20 km north of Boston.[87] The castle was granted to Suffolk on 4 April 1537, the very week when the duke's chaplain was present at Boston taking the measure of his master's new feudal domains.[88]

Boston was the most important urban centre in the new ducal territory, but it had also distinguished itself as a loyalist stronghold in the autumn of 1536.[89] This put it in stark contrast to Louth, another town of rich guilds and heavy investment in its musical provision which was at the centre of the Lincolnshire rebellion.[90] Resentment had been aroused by early monastic dissolutions in the Louth area, by the abolition of feasts and by rumours of confiscation, but was ignited by careless remarks among the choirmen of St. James's church. The religious trajectory of St. Botolph's went in precisely the opposite direction. Just as the royal supremacy was extinguishing the spiritual commodities that had enabled Boston to weather the loss of its coastal trade in the fifteenth century, the parishioners of St. Botolph faced another economic and spiritual catastrophe: a brief glimpse of Figure 8.2 shows the Lady Guild's collapsing

---

84 Lincoln. Lincolnshire Archives Office. 6-CHAR/2/1 part 5 (1537–1538), under 'Regarda': 'in regardis datis Mr Cutlarr, M. puerorum cantancium ducis Suffold [sic] cum expensis eorum in domo Johannis Reynolde, xiiij^s viij^d'; and 'Expense infra ville de Boston': 'Expensi de georgii Wynsover in domo Johannis Reynoldes, iiij^s vj^d ... expensi dicti Johannis equitanti apud Ducem Suffold [sic] cum uno le Samonde, vij^d soluto pro le Samonde, v^s'. Cutler had been master of the duke's chapel children since June 1535. For a similar sojourn by the duke's chapel choir in 1535, see: Dickens A.G. (ed.), *The Register or Chronicle of Butley Priory, Suffolk, 1510–1535* (Winchester: 1951) 68.
85 London. The British Library. Harley Charter 47 A. 49. See: Gunn S.J., *Charles Brandon, Duke of Suffolk, c. 1484–1545* (Oxford: 1988), 170; and Bindoff S.T., *The House of Commons, 1509–1558*, I (London: 1982) 383–385 under 'Honyng, William' (Cutler's son-in-law).
86 Hoyle R.W., *The Pilgrimage of Grace and the Politics of the 1530s* (Oxford: 1985) 93–157; Gunn, *Charles Brandon* 144–152; MacCulloch, *Thomas Cromwell* 372–397.
87 Gunn, *Charles Brandon*, 152; MacCulloch, *Thomas Cromwell*, 430–431.
88 *Letters and Papers, Foreign and Domestic, of the reign of Henry VIII*, XII/i (1890) 511–512.
89 On 4 October 1536, two days after the first disturbances at Louth, John Foster of Boston warned the town to be ready to serve the King (London. The National Archives. SP 1/110 fol. 166).
90 Williamson, 'The role of religious guilds in the cultivation of ritual polyphony' 82–93.

revenues after the mid-1530s. Having staked all on the sale of expensively acquired indulgences in order to cultivate the richest possible *Opus Dei*, the parishioners of Boston voluntarily liquidated their confraternities in 1545 in favour of erecting a civic corporation. Later on, their religious enthusiasm would morph into the most fervent expressions of Protestantism, and to the founding of godly colonies in the New World.

Bibliography

Primary Sources

Letters and Papers, Foreign and Domestic, of the reign of Henry VIII, XII/i (London: 1890).
Letters and Papers, Foreign and Domestic, of the reign of Henry VIII, Addenda 1/i (London: 1929).

Secondary Sources

Ashbee A. (ed.), *Records of English Court Music* VII (Aldershot: 1993).
Ashbee A. – Lasocki D. (eds.), with Holman P. – Kisby F., *A Biographical Dictionary of English Court Musicians* (Aldershot: 1998).
Atkinson T.D. – Hampson E.M. – Long E.T – Meekings C.A.F. – Miller E. – Wells H.B. – Woodgate G.M.G, "Wisbech: Guild of the Holy Trinity", in Pugh R.B. (ed.), *A History of the County of Cambridge and the Isle of Ely* 4, *City of Ely; Ely, N. and S. Witchford and Wisbech Hundreds* (London: 2002) 255–256.
Atkinson T.D. – Hampson E.M. – Long E.T. – Meekings C.A.F – Miller E. – Wells H.B. – Woodgate G.M.G, "Wisbech: Port, Nene Outfall, Canal", in Pugh R.B. (ed.), *A History of the County of Cambridge and the Isle of Ely* 4, *City of Ely; Ely, N. and S. Witchford and Wisbech Hundreds* (London: 2002) 263–265.
Aveling J., *"In nomine Iesu omne genu flectatur" – The Late Medieval Mass and Office of the Holy Name of Jesus: Sources, Development and Practice* (Ph.D. dissertation, Bangor University: 2015).
Badham S., "'He Loved the Guild': the Religious Guilds Associated with St. Botolph's church, Boston", in Badham S. – Cockerham P. (eds.), *'The beste and fairest of al Lincolnshire': the Church of St Botolph, Boston, Lincolnshire, and its Medieval Monuments* (Oxford: 2012) 49–73.
Bindoff S.T., *The House of Commons, 1509–1558*, 1 (London: 1982).
Bliss W.H. – Twemlow J.A. (eds.), *Calendar of Papal Registers Relating To Great Britain and Ireland, 5: 1398–1404* (London: 1904).
Bowers R,, "The Cultivation and Promotion of Music in the Household and Orbit of Thomas Wolsey", in Gunn S.J. – Lindley P.G. (eds.), *Cardinal Wolsey: Church, State and Art* (Cambridge: 1991) 178–218.

Bowers R., "Lincoln Cathedral: Music and Worship to 1640", in Owen D. (ed.), *A History of Lincoln Minster* (Cambridge: 1994) 47–76.

Cox J.C., "Benefactions of Thomas Heywood, Dean (1457–92), to the Cathedral Church of Lichfield", *Archaeologia* 52 (1890) 617–646.

Cuthbert E.G. – Atchley F., "Jesus Mass and Anthem", *Transactions of St. Paul's Ecclesiological Society* 5 (1905) 163–169.

Dickens A.G. (ed.), *The Register or Chronicle of Butley Priory, Suffolk, 1510–1535* (Winchester: 1951).

Forster C.W. – Thompson A.H., "The Chantry Certificates for Lincoln and Lincolnshire, returned in 1548, under the Act of Parliament of 1 Edward VI", *Associated Architectural Societies Reports and Papers* 37.2 (1925) 247–275.

Gaydon A.T. – Pugh R.B. (eds.), *A History of the County of Shropshire* II (London: 1973).

Gunn S.J., *Charles Brandon, Duke of Suffolk, c. 1484–1545* (Oxford: 1988).

Haren M.J. (ed.), *Calendar of Entries in the Papal Registers Relating to Great Britain and Ireland* 18 (Dublin: 1989).

Haren M.J. (ed.), *Calendar of Entries in the Papal Registers Relating to Great Britain and Ireland* 19 (Dublin: 1998).

Harrison F.L, *Music in Medieval Britain* (London: 1958).

Haward W.I., "The Trade of Boston in the Fifteenth Century", *Associated Architectural Societies Reports and Papers* 41 (1932–1933) 169–178.

Hickman D. (ed.), *Lincoln Wills 1532–1534*, Lincoln Record Society 89 (Woodbridge: 2001).

Jones M.K. – Underwood M.G., *The King's Mother: Lady Margaret Beaufort, Countess of Richmond and Derby* (Cambridge: 1992).

Kitching C.J. (ed.), *London and Middlesex Chantry Certificate, 1548*, London Record Society 16 (London: 1980).

Lunt W.E., *Financial Relations of the Papacy with England, 1327–1534* (Cambridge MA: 1961).

MacCulloch D., *Thomas Cromwell: A Life* (London: 2018).

Monckton L, "'The beste and fairest of al Lincolnshire': the Parish Church of St Botolph, Boston", in Badham S. – Cockerham P. (eds.), *'The beste and fairest of al Lincolnshire': the Church of St Botolph, Boston, Lincolnshire, and its Medieval Monuments* (Oxford: 2012) 29–48.

Morgan N., "The Scala Coeli Indulgence and the Royal Chapels", in Thompson B. (ed.), *The Reign of Henry VII*, Harlaxton Medieval Studies 5 (Stamford: 1995) 82–103.

New E., *The Cult of the Holy Name of Jesus in Late Medieval England, with Special Reference to the Fraternity in St. Paul's Cathedral, London, c.1450–1558* (Ph.D. dissertation, Royal Holloway: 1999).

Page W. (ed.), *The Certificates of the Commissioners Appointed to Survey the Chantries, Guilds, Hospitals, etc., of the County of York* II, Surtees Society 92 (1895) 340–346.

Pfaff R.W., *New Liturgical Feasts in Later Medieval England* (London: 1970).
Ramsay N. – Willoughby J.M.W. (eds.), *Hospitals, Towns and the Professions*, British Medieval Library Catalogues 14 (London: 2009).
Report on the Manuscripts of Lord De L'Isle & Dudley Preserved at Penshurst Place 1, Historical Manuscripts Commission (London: 1925).
Rigby S.H., *Boston and Grimsby in the Middle Ages* (Ph.D. dissertation, University of London: 1982).
Rigby S.H, *The Overseas Trade of Boston in the Reign of Richard II*, Lincolnshire Record Society 93 (Woodbridge: 2005).
Rigby S.H., "Medieval Boston: Economy, Society and Administration", in Badham S. – Cockerham P. (eds.), *'The beste and fairest of al Lincolnshire': the Church of St Botolph, Boston, Lincolnshire, and its Medieval Monuments* (Oxford: 2012) 8–28.
Rosser G., "Going to the Fraternity Feast: Commensality and Social Relations in Late Medieval England", *Journal of British Studies* 33 (1994) 430–446.
Rubin M., "Corpus Christi Fraternities and Late Medieval Piety", *Studies in Church History* 23 (1986) 97–109.
Rubin M., *Corpus Christi: The Eucharist in Late Medieval England* (Cambridge: 1991).
Sheail J., *The Regional Distribution of Wealth in England as Indicated in the Lay Subsidy Returns (1524/5)* (Ph.D. dissertation, University of London: 1968).
Sparrow W.C., "A Register of the Palmers' Guild of Ludlow in the Reign of Henry VIII", *Transactions of the Shropshire Archaeological and Natural History Society* 7 (1883) 81–126.
Sterry Sir W. (ed.), *The Eton College Register, 1440–1698* (Eton: 1943).
Stokes J. (ed.), *Lincolnshire, 1: The Records*, Records of Early English Drama (Toronto: 2009).
Stokes J. (ed.), *Lincolnshire, 2: Editorial Apparatus*, Records of Early English Drama (Toronto: 2009).
Swanson R.N., *Indulgences in Late Medieval England: Passports to Paradise?* (Cambridge: 2007).
Thompson A.H., "Certificates of the Shropshire Chantries", *Transactions of the Shropshire Archaeological and Natural History Society*, 3rd series 10 (1910) 69–392.
Thompson A.H., "Register of John Gynewell, Bishop of Lincoln for the Years 1347–50", *Archaeological Journal* 68 (1911) 301–360.
Thompson A.H. (ed.), *Visitations in the Diocese of Lincoln 1517–1531* II, Lincoln Record Society 35 (1944) 163–165.
Thompson P., *The History and Antiquities of Boston* (Boston: 1856).
Toulmin Smith L. (ed.), *The Itinerary of John Leland In or About the Years 1535–1543* (London: 1910).
Twemlow J. (ed.), *Calendar of Entries in the Papal Registers Relating to Great Britain and Ireland, 10: 1447–1455* (London: 1915).

Tymms S. (ed.), *Wills and Inventories from the Registers of the Commissary of Bury St. Edmunds and the Archdeacon of Sudbury* (London: 1850).

Westlake H.F., *The Parish Gilds of Mediæval England* (London: 1919).

Williamson M., "The Role of Religious Guilds in the Cultivation of Ritual Polyphony in England: the Case of Louth, 1450–1550", in Kisby F. (ed.), *Music and Musicians in Renaissance Cities and Towns* (Cambridge: 2001) 82–93.

Williamson M., "Liturgical Polyphony in the Pre-Reformation Parish: a Provisional List and Commentary", *RMA Research Chronicle* 38 (2005) 1–43.

Williamson M., "Revisiting the Soundscape of the Medieval Parish", in Harry D. – Steer C. (eds.), *The Urban Church in Late Medieval England: Essays in Honour of Clive Burgess*, Harlaxton Medieval Studies 29 (Donington: 2019) 17–35.

Woolgar C.M., *The Great Household in Late Medieval England* (New Haven – London: 1999).

CHAPTER 9

Who was Listening to Oratorio? Lay Confraternities and Patrician Music in Early Modern Italy

Xavier Torres

Abstract

In its early stages, the Italian oratorio was a devotional, non-liturgical (and with some operatic elements) musical genre conceived for the entertainment of what was essentially a select or exclusive audience, as contemporary urban *avvisi* indicate. Nevertheless, many oratorios were financed by devotional confraternities formed by a mix of social classes, notably in cities such as Rome, Florence and Bologna. But even in those cases, it would appear to be the case that the corresponding musical audience was not very different nor less restrictive in terms of social class. This can partly be explained because of the way in which the devotional confraternities themselves developed as increasingly aristocratic institutions, as is illustrated by the case of the city of Bologna, the focus of this paper.

Keywords

music – oratorio – confraternities – Italy – early modern history

1 Introduction

The musical oratorio was a genre of non-liturgical religious music that began to take shape in Rome and in Church dominions in the second half of the seventeenth century.[1] Initially, it can be described as a musical composition of sacred character, in narrative or dialogical form, written for voices, choirs and instruments but rarely staged. The narrative type usually included a narrator, the character of *Testo* (Text), who exposed the course of the action, while the characters of the dialogued oratorios could be human, superhuman (God,

---

1 This contribution is part of the research project PID-2022-140935B-100, funded by the Ministry of Science and Innovation of the Government of Spain.

angels) or allegorical (the theological virtues, vanity or other inappropriate behaviours). Unlike *Testo*, who was always expressed as a recitative or through declamatory chant, the other characters gave free rein to the different emotions implicit in the argument (pain, joy, horror, etc.) through more or less conventional (operatic) arias. In general, oratorio plots and librettos were based on adaptations of writings of biblical or hagiographical origin, with a marked predilection for the Old Testament in the first case and for the martyrs of early Christianity in the second, although the source of inspiration for allegorical oratorios could be freer or more random. There were oratorios in Latin, sometimes sponsored by a particularly select lay confraternity, but most were in the vernacular. The oratorios, whatever their language or modality, consisted of two parts or sections, separated by an interval, which was filled by the preaching of a sermon that related more or less with its theme or by spiritual meditation. In short, this might be a not-too-inaccurate description of what a musical oratorio was in Italy in the second half of the seventeenth century.

However, some musicologists have pointed out the inadequacies of such a description, since almost all of the features indicated, or at least some of them, also easily characterise other related genres of the Baroque period, such as moral dialogues, sacred cantatas or even the so-called 'sacred actions', somewhat more theatrical, but at the same time quite similar to oratorios. Yet if, on the one hand, the oratory approaches or resembles certain kinds of sacred or spiritual music, as is argued, then on the other hand, the opposite also occurs: genres of religious music, such as the motet, with the passage of time become more sophisticated or *oratorised*. Thus, in view of these problems, some authors prefer to speak of oratorical forms or types rather than of oratorios strictly speaking or in particular.[2]

If a rigorous musicological definition of this genre of sacred music presents certain difficulties, in terms of listening or audience, the situation seems much clearer: a musical oratorio was a type of non-liturgical sacred music conceived for the enjoyment of a rather select or exclusive audience. Especially, it may be added, when other no less distinguished variants of musical entertainment (opera, *drammi in musica*) were vetoed for one reason or another, whether it was due to the religious calendar (Lent) or one of the periodic papal prohibitions against theatrical spectacles. At least, this can be inferred from the contemporary city news sheets, or *avvisi*, which were wont to give details of both the different oratorical events in the corresponding cities and the related attendance.

---

2   See a recent summary of these types of problems in Besutti P., "Echi di storia e di tradizioni d'Abruzzo nelle musiche devozionali", in Dell'Olio A. (ed.), *L'oratorio musicale nel Regno di Napoli al tempo di Gaetano Veneziano (ca. 1656–1716)* (Naples: 2016) 121–138, here 121–123.

According to the Roman *avvisi* at the end of the seventeenth century, among the most assiduous attendees at musical oratorios were, in the first place, the celebrated (former) Queen Christina of Sweden; some ambassadors, such as those of Spain or France, who could end up funding some of these concerts; and Cardinals Benedetto Pamphili and Pietro Ottoboni, well-known enthusiasts of the oratorio genre. But together with these and other highly-ranked personalities, a substantial representation of the local aristocracy was also mentioned: that is, 'all the most qualified individuals of the [papal] court'; 'all the prelature and nobility'; some 'princes' (a rank of status); many 'gentlemen'; and the 'principal ladies' of the city, who, in one of the frequent oratorios promoted by cardinals, would have been gifted with a 'libretto of the [...] performance stamped in white satin and with a velvet cover'.[3]

In Rome, some of these events did indeed take place at the dwellings of cardinals (especially in the palace of the Apostolic Chancery), but the public that regularly listened to oratorios in the so-called Chiesa Nuova (Santa Maria in Vallicella) of the Oratorian congregation does not seem to be very different. The corresponding local *avvisi* indicate that it was usually composed of a 'large number of prelates, nobility and *popolo*'; this latter term was a way of designating non-nobility, although they were people who were undoubtedly wealthy. Sometimes the concerts also attracted ambassadors (for example, the Caesarean or imperial ambassador, the Venetian ambassador) as well as 'many cardinals, prelates and gentlemen', and, a good number of *virtuosi* (probably musicians) and, occasionally, *gente civile* (perhaps an allusion to legal professionals or to citizens of a certain rank, even if they were not ennobled). There were no women in the crowd.[4] In the city's other Oratorian church, San Girolamo della Carità, oratorios were also performed 'with an infinite gathering of nobility'.[5] And sometimes they were dedicated to the Federico II Sforza, Duke of Segni, also known as Prince of Genzano.[6]

---

3 All quotes are from Staffieri G., *Colligite Fragmenta. La vita musicale romana negli "Avvisi Marescotti" (1683–1707)* (Lucca: 1990) sheets 74, 82, 93 and 94.

4 Staffieri, *Colligite* sheet 59; Morelli A., *Il tempio harmonico. Musica nell'oratorio dei Filippini in Roma (1575–1705)* (Laaber: 1991) 187–188, here 411–422. Female exclusion by papal order is mentioned in Johnson J.L., *Roman Oratorio, 1770–1800. The Repertory at Santa Maria in Vallicella* (Ann Arbor: 1987) 5.

5 Franchi S. "Il Principe Livio Odescalchi e l'oratorio 'politico'", in Besutti P. (ed.), *L'oratorio musicale italiano e i suoi contesti (secoli XVII–XVIII)* (Florence: 2002) 141–258, Appendix 1, sheet 37.

6 *S. Caterina da Siena, oratorio del sig. Angelo Donato Rossi, accademico Infecondo, posto in musica da Giuseppe Valentini. E [...] dedicato all'illustrissimi [...] duca Don Federico Sforza, e duquessa Donna Livia Cesarini, duchi di Segni [...] prencipi di Genzano* (Roma, Stamperia di Antonio de' Rossi: 1705).

Something similar happened elsewhere. In Milan, at the end of the seventeenth century, the feast of St. Anthony of Padua was celebrated with a solemn musical oratorio in the Franciscan monastery that housed the saint's chapel. The corresponding *avvisi* show that for such events the said church was adorned 'majestically'; the music heard in it was invariably 'exquisite'; and the attendance was composed 'of the most flourishing nobility', in addition to many 'ordinary people' ('quantità di Popolo'), this latter term being interpreted, rather than as plebeian people or similar, as synonymous with people of non-noble condition or perhaps, simply and plainly, as an indication of the crowd in attendance. One or more oratorios were also celebrated for the feast of St. Maurus, now in the church of San Pietro Celestino, no less 'rich and superbly ornamented' than that of the Franciscans. And as in the previous case, the event was striking both for the 'singular exquisiteness of the music' and for 'the attendance of the most reputable nobility'. This also happened in the church of Santa Maria Segreta, of the Somascans, when they celebrated, again with the corresponding oratorio, the feast of the Guardian Angels, since there were gathered 'the flower and cream of the musicians' and 'all the nobility' of the city.[7]

Venice, in turn, was no exception. As described in the *Pallade Veneta* gazette (a 'collection of flowery and bizarre gallantries', as the headline of its first issue stated), the usual audience for the musical oratorios that took place in the famous hospitals of the city was made up by 'princes and princesses' (the prince-electors of Bavaria were regulars); cardinals and bishops; and 'all the nobility of the ladies and gentlemen'. As for the rest of the Venetians, there are only a few indications and these somewhat contradictory. It seems that, from time to time, common people, from the street or stationed in a nearby window, attempted to capture something of the music that was being performed inside the *ospedali*. As the chronicler on duty wrote, they were attempting (sometimes in vain) 'to console themselves [...] with even an echo at least of those paradisiacal voices' that were heard inside. Thus, ordinary people, in principle, did not figure among the audience of the Venetian oratorios. The exception, if there was one, would have been an oratorio, *Santa Maria Egizziaca penitente*, performed in the church of the Pietà on St. Augustine's day in 1687,[8] and which,

---

7 Grella D., "L'oratorio francescano e gli oratori per Sant'Antonio a Milano dal 1680 al 1715", *Il Santo. Rivista francescana di storia, dottrina, arte* 39 (1999) 567–599, here 576; Magaudda A. – Costantini D., "Un periodico a stampa di antico regime: la 'Gazzetta di Milano' (secoli XVII–XVIII). Spoglio delle notizie musicali per gli anni 1686–1699", *Fonti Musicali Italiane*, 1 (1996) 41–74, Appendix B, 56 and 62.

8 *Santa Maria Egizziaca penitente. Oratorio di Bernardo Sandrinelli. Da recitarsi in musica nel Pio Ospitale della Pietà di Venezia* (Venice, Gio. Battista Chiarello: 1687).

it seems, aroused such a wave of enthusiasm among the 'popolo' (*sic*) that the chronicler of the event took it for granted that it should be programmed again, 'eager as the nobility and the plebs (*sic*) were to satisfy themselves with what they heard' ('sentendosi la nobiltà e la plebe vaga di satiarne l'udito').[9]

In addition to the gazettes of the time, some more recent musicological studies are also quite conclusive. In Modena, for example, the oratorio musical was promoted by the House of Este, the lords of the city, it being, first and foremost, a devoted courtly entertainment, as well as a form of political propaganda.[10] In Mantua, the oratorios, also supported by their lords, the Gonzagas, took place in two rooms of the ducal palace, the Troya room (because of its decorative programme) and the so-called Nuova or Refettorio room, whose maximum capacities were between 150 and 250 people, respectively. It can be deduced from their relatively small size that the audience for the oratorios was basically limited to court personnel, the local ecclesiastical hierarchy and the urban or patrician elite.[11] In Bologna, the class rank of the attendees of musical oratorios is not known with any accuracy, although, at first, this new genre of sacred music 'was sponsored mainly by the [city] nobility', and this is already quite a clear hint.[12]

However, lords, nobles and patricians were not alone in promoting the musical genre of oratorios. As is known, many of these works were sponsored by lay and inter-status confraternities, especially, as will be seen, in cities such as Rome, Florence and Bologna.

2 Confraternity Oratorios: How Many were There and Where?

In fact, lay confraternities were always quite musical in and of themselves, at least as far as the practice of simple devotional chanting (*laude*) was concerned: participatory by definition (they all sang) and essentially catechetical or aimed at reinforcing the teaching of Catholic doctrine.[13] Not surprisingly,

---

9   The citations come from Selfridge-Field E., *Pallade Veneta. Writings on Music in Venetian Society 1650–1750* (Venice: 1985) Appendix 6, 9, 45 (Masses), 48 and 51 (listening from nearby windows).
10 Crowther V., *The Oratorio in Modena* (Oxford: 1992).
11 Besutti P., "Oratori in corte a Mantova: tra Bologna, Modena e Venezia", in Besutti (ed.), *L'oratorio musicale* 391–398.
12 Crowther V., *The Oratorio in Bologna (1650–1730)* (Oxford: 1999) 140–141.
13 On *laude*, see: Rostirolla G. – Zardin D. – Mischiati O., *La lauda spirituale tra Cinque e Seicento. Poesia e canti devozionali nell'Italia della Controriforma* (Roma: 2001). On the importance of music in the activities of confraternities, see, for example, Glixon J.,

lay confraternities were one of the Tridentine devices conceived to 'shape consciences and Christianise society', as can be seen in Archbishop Carlo Borromeo's Milan, as well as in other parts of the Catholic world that experienced the so-called Catholic reformation or renewal.[14] However, lay confraternities also used music for their own ends or purposes, that is, to increase the number of members, explore new sources of patronage, promote themselves as a corporation and achieve a pre-eminent position in the sphere of civic religion and urban ceremonial; always in 'sound competition' with other similar confraternities that aspired to the same status.[15] In summary, whether for the promotion of individual religiosity or rivalry on the civic stage, in the second half of the seventeenth century some confraternities specialised in the cultivation of musical oratorio.

Table 9.1 shows the importance of the confraternities' oratorio production, as well as their different impacts according to place or capital. The figures are based on a census or count of about 2,000 printed librettos of Italian musical oratorios from the period 1660–1830, prepared from both digital and regional catalogues of the *Online Public Access Catalogue* of the Italian *Servizio Bibliotecario Nazionale* (OPAC SBN).[16] Such a census does not include – and cannot include – all the musical oratorios of that period; on the one hand, because not all the oratorios performed were necessarily accompanied by a corresponding libretto, either because of funding restrictions or for other

---

"Singing Praises to God: Confraternities and Music", in Eisenbichler K. (ed.), *A Companion to Medieval and Early Modern Confraternities* (Leiden – Boston: 2019) 329–344.

14 Zardin D., "Relaunching Confraternities in the Tridentine Era: Shaping Consciences and Christianizing society in Milan and Lombardia", in Terpstra N. (ed.), *The Politics of Ritual Kinship. Confraternities and social order in Early Modern Italy* (Cambridge: 2000) 190–209; O'Regan N., "Church Reform and Devotional Music in Sixteenth-Century Rome: The Influence of Lay Confraternities", in Brundin A. – Treherne M. (eds.), *Forms of Faith in Sixteenth-Century Italy* (Aldershot: 2009) 215–232; and, more broadly, Donnelly J.P. – Maher M.W. (eds.), *Confraternities and Catholic Reform in Italy, France and Spain* (Kirksville: 1999).

15 O'Regan N., "'Per cagion della musica tutte le strade erano piene': Roles Played by Music in Articulating the Place of Confraternities in Early Modern Roman Society", in Filippi D.V. – Noone M. (eds.), *Listening to Early Modern Catholicism. Perspectives from Musicology*, Intersections 49 (Leiden – Boston: 2017) 259–275. As regards Venice, see: Glixon J., *Honoring God and the City. Music at the Venetian Confraternities, 1260–1807* (New York: 2003) 7–8.

16 The catalogues used were those of OPAC SEBINA Venezia, OPAC SEBINA Roma and OPAC SEBINA Napoli, which contain, especially in the first two cases, many references to other places, that is, librettos printed and published outside that strict geographical area.

reasons.[17] However, it can be supposed that few were produced without the printed text, given that the libretto, in addition to facilitating the understanding of the work (its sung or recited parts) and its argument (sometimes somewhat convoluted), had a commemorative purpose, consistent with the solemnity of the event. On the other hand, the cataloguing itself may present considerable shortcomings. In Venice, for example, scholars of the local oratorio counted about 500 librettos between 1667 and 1809 while our survey resulted in only 99 copies, a fifth of the total.[18] In the case of the Roman region, a conventional cataloguing shows the figure of 600 librettos from the end of the seventeenth century to the end of the eighteenth century while those of our sample come to 400, a much higher proportion than the Venetian sample, but still deficient by a third.[19]

However, the results of such a survey provide significant information. Thus, for the period between 1660 and 1830, one out of every five Italian musical oratorios were sponsored by lay confraternities; although in some cases or places, such as in Florence or Bologna, this proportion was considerably higher: up to one out of every two and one out of every four, respectively [Table 9.1]. Certainly, the Archconfraternity of the Santissimo Crocifisso in Rome, that of the Arcangelo Raffaello in Florence and that of Santa Maria de la Morte in Bologna, to name a few well-known or well-studied cases, consistently displayed a very high degree of musical activity, but in this period they also stood out in the production of oratorios (as can also be deduced from Table 9.2).

The relatively high proportion of oratorios produced by confraternities calls into question whether the musical audience of the confraternity oratorio (or at least of certain confraternities) was somewhat or substantially different from the oratorios promoted by cardinals, courtiers, patricians or even the Oratorian congregation: that is, whether their audience was broader in terms of status. The peculiar nature of those kinds of corporations, 'mixed' in more ways than one, may suggest that this was the case.

---

17 According to Vitali C., "Giovanni Paolo Colonna, maestro di capella dell'oratorio filippino in Bologna. Contributi bio-bibliografici", *Rivista Italiana di Musicologia*, XIV.1 (1979) 128–154, here 137, the Bolognese Oratorians performed oratorios long before the date of the first printed librettos; and Fanelli J.G., "Aesthetic and Practical Influences on the Tuscan Oratorio of the Late Baroque", in Besutti (ed.), *L'oratorio musicale* 323, mentions the problems of cost or printing in smaller towns, such as Pistoia.
18 Arnold D. – Arnold E., *The Oratorio in Venice* (London: 1986) Appendix.
19 Franchi S., *Le impressioni sceniche. Dizionario bio-bibliografico degli editori e stampatori romani e laziali di testi drammatici e libretti per música dal 1759 al 1800* (Rome: 1994).

TABLE 9.1   The confraternity oratorio in Italy (1660–1830)

Place	Total oratorios	Confraternity oratorio	Proportion of confraternity oratorio
ITALY	1962	397	20%
Florence	225	130	58%
Ferrara	88	26	30%
Milan	87	25	29%
Bologna	245	66	27%
Trapani	15	4	26%
Messina	27	6	22%
Rome	361	63	17.5%
Naples	33	5	15%
Palermo	67	3	4.5%
Modena	57	2	3.5%
Venice	99	3	3%
Padua	36	0	0
Perugia	56	0	0

SOURCE: DIGITAL CATALOGUES OF OPAC SBN VENEZIA, OPAC SNB ROMA AND OPAC SBN NAPOLI

TABLE 9.2   Musical oratorios and confraternities in Italy (1660–1830)

Rome		Florence		Bologna	
Ss. Crocifisso	53	S. Marco	78	S.M. della Morte	32
Pietà Nazione Fiorentini	6	Arcangelo Raffaello	21	S.M. della Vita	17
others	4	S. Jacopo	12	ss. Sebastiano e Rocco	8
		S. Niccolò	5	others	9
		S. Sebastiano	4		
		Others	10		
Total	63	Total	130	Total	66

SOURCE: DIGITAL CATALOGUES OF OPAC SBN VENEZIA, OPAC SBN ROMA AND OPAC SBN NAPOLI

3   What Was a Lay Confraternity?

Confraternities can be described as voluntary associations of mainly lay individuals, often inspired by the clergy (of the religious orders, in particular) and whose stated aim was the promotion of the religious life, both among their respective members and in society as a whole.[20] As such, members of confraternities were subject to a certain number of obligations of a personal nature, in order to 'discipline the soul', such as the periodic realisation of spiritual exercises, regular confession, hearing Mass and not blaspheming, to which can also sometimes be added, at least on paper or in the corresponding statutes, rejection of wealth, the singing of lauds or chastity (to whatever degree that might have been).[21] In turn, all the confraternities carried out some social welfare work, such as helping those in need (whether they were members of the confraternity or not), visiting prisons and hospitals (a fairly common activity) or giving spiritual solace to those sentenced to death (in order to save their souls *in extremis*).[22] Finally, these corporations, at least the most important ones, were present to a very high degree in local civic life, especially through their participation in exemplary celebrations and in many urban processions; according to contemporaneous chronicles, some of these, held with great apparatus, gathered a crowd ('moltitudine del Popolo') that devoutly followed the event.[23]

A great variety of lay confraternities existed, whether distinguished by size, function or affiliation. But, in general, this kind of corporation, which proliferated throughout the Catholic world, in step with the Catholic reformation or renewal of the period, remained unique in the society of its time. This was partly because they constituted a rare point of contact between the religious

---

20   An excellent overview of the *confraternite*, *compagnie* or Italian confraternities, although limited in chronology, is to be found in Black, C.F., *Italian Confraternities in the Sixteenth Century* (Cambridge: 1989).
21   For the case of the Modena confraternity of the Annunziata, see: Al Kalak M., "La disciplina dell'anima. Motivi teologici, influssi bernardiniani ed evoluzione controriformistiche negli statuti della Santissima Annunziata", in Al Kalak M. – Lucchi M., *Le regole dello spirito: norme, statuti e liturgie della Confraternità della Santissima Annunziata di Modena* (Modena: [2006]) 15–94.
22   On this last aspect, see: Prosperi A. (ed.), *Misericordie. Conversione sotto il patibolo tra Medioevo ed età moderna* (Pisa: 2007); Terpstra N. (ed.), *The Art of Executing Well. Rituals of Execution in Renaissance Italy* (Kirksville: 2008).
23   *Descrizione di tutto il magnifico apparato, e di quanto si fece nella solennità di tutto l'Ottavario celebrato nella Chiesa di S. Maria sopra Minerva. Per la festa di S. Pio Quinto* (Rome, Stamperia di Gio. Francesco Chracas: 1712) 10.

and secular spheres, usually so divided, if not in confrontation. This was not only because of the (variable) degree of supervision exercised by the religious authorities over the confraternity and its activities, but also because the fraternal sphere offered opportunities for spiritual and civic cooperation between clergy and laity, as well as a certain capacity for negotiation by the laity in religious matters.[24] However, that was not the only notable peculiarity since the lay confraternity, besides housing clergy and laity in one space, was inter-status by definition, and this contrasted sharply with the general environment, where such a mixture of ranks was seldom seen, while the (social, but also moral) distance between nobles and commoners was considered as insurmountable as it was necessary.[25]

Certainly, more often than not this unique feature was something implied or simply deduced from the fact that no status restrictions of access were specified in the confraternity statutes. However, in practice, the brotherhood affiliation was not entirely free. In some cases, the amount of membership dues could be a decisive deterrent and close the doors to the poor and less wealthy. In addition, there was the right of veto or rejection, predictably no less selective. In the Milanese Jesuit congregation of Madonna di Loreto anyone who aspired to gain entry had to be endorsed by one of its members, who, according to the established protocol, had to provide the name, surname and place of residence of the interested party so that an official of the congregation could investigate their moral life secretly and conscientiously.[26] Naturally, this was not an unusual case.

Even so, at times, heterogeneity or coexistence of status turned out to be such a distinctive peculiarity of the confraternity that it was recorded in writing in its particular statutes. The Venetian Compagnia dell'Oratorio, which was dedicated to instructing children of 'all conditions' in Christian doctrine (teaching to read those who did not already know and teaching the catechism

---

24   As Nicholas Terpstra points out in his "Boundaries of Brotherhood: Laity and Clergy in the social spaces of Religion", in Terpstra N. – Prosperi A. – Pastore S. (eds.), *Faith's Boundaries. Laity and Clergy in Early Modern Confraternities* (Turnhout: 2012) XI–XXXII.

25   Thus, one of the greatest political mistakes would be to treat the nobility as if they were hardly so and the masses as if they were almost so. In the first case, demoralization would grow; in the second, the masses would became "insolent", according to Sansovino Francesco, *Concetti politici* (Venice, Giovanni Antonio Bertano: 1578), fol. 8ov. For the "immeasurable moral distance" between the various social strata, see Jouanna A., *L'idée de race en France au XVIe. siècle et au début du XVIIe* (revised edition, Montpellier: 1981), vol. I, 27.

26   *Statuti della venerabile congregatione della Madonna di Loreto di Milano* (Pavia, Pietro Bartoli: 1605) 7–8.

to everyone), defined itself as a 'spiritual brotherhood of devout people of all conditions (*ogni conditione*)', who met on feast days, 'all together' to pray, take communion, recite penitential psalms or perform spiritual exercises.[27] In short, in a society characterised by the persistent cultivation of social difference and distance, both legally and in ordinary life, some confraternities neglected the barriers of status to cultivate what one author has called 'ritual kinship', and to present themselves as a genre of associations founded on fraternity or 'spiritual consanguinity'.[28]

This was not mere rhetoric. It is not always possible to know precisely the social composition of the confraternities of the period, but some data, although sparse or imprecise, is quite revealing. The so-called penitential confraternities, also known as flagellants, *disciplinati* or *battuti*, were generally more elitist than those strictly devotional or consecrated to the Marian cult or the saints, but all the evidence seems to indicate that even those had their minimum quota (around 10% of the total number of members) of artisans and small merchants, as was the case, at least, in fifteenth-century Florence. In the second half of the sixteenth century, the Roman archconfraternity of La Pietà dei Carcerati, inspired by the Jesuits, brought together above all many 'middle class' (merchants, lawyers, notaries), but also many nobles and artisans, in addition to a good number of clerics. Even in the great Venetian confraternities or *scuole* of the period, nobles (many) coexisted with artisans (between 10% and 25%, according to some calculations) and the poor (who were helped by the former). In one of them, the Scuola Grande di San Rocco, the inter-status ratio, throughout the sixteenth century, seems to have been as follows: about 500 nobles, twice as many artisans and small merchants when added together, and just over 500 individuals considered to be in need. In the other great *scuole* of the city, the social mix could vary slightly. In the Scuola Grande della Carità there were many lawyers and notaries, while in the Scuola Grande di San Marco there were haberdashers, goldsmiths and important traders in the silk market. Finally, in the Scuola di San Fantin, which was not 'grande' but nor was it one of the 'piccole' or minor ones, there was a broad social mix: from clergymen and nobles to shopkeepers and wool weavers, although in unknown proportions.[29]

27 *Ordini et capitoli della Compagnia dell'Oratorio* (Venice, Gabriel Giolito di Ferrarii: 1568) 5.
28 Meersseman G.G. – Pacini G.P., *Ordo Fraternitatis. Confraternite e pietà dei laici nel medioevo* (Rome: 1977) vol. I, 6–7; Weissman R.F.E., *Ritual brotherhood in Renaissance Florence* (New York: 1982); Terpstra N., "Introduction", in Terpstra (ed.), *The Politics of Ritual Kinship* 7.
29 Data is drawn respectively from Weissman, *Ritual* 111; Paglia V., *La Pietà dei Carcerati. Confraternite e società a Roma nei secoli XVI–XVIII* (Rome: 1980) 107–108; Pullan B., *Rich and Poor in Renaissance Venice. The Social Institutions of a Catholic State, to 1620* (Oxford:

4   Aristocratic Confraternities

However, figures are not everything, as with the passage of time, if not from the start, many confraternities experienced a process of growing aristocratisation, both in substance and in form.[30] In other words, many brotherhoods witnessed an increase in the number of high-ranking (and often very high-ranking) members, as well as an increase in their influence within the corporation. The result, as will be seen, was a sharper or more institutionalised distinction even between rich members and poor members or, at least, between higher-ranked members and lower-ranked members. But the ennoblement of the confraternities was also related to the fact that local elites (the city nobility, the ecclesiastical hierarchy) turned this kind of corporation into one of their favourite sources of sociability, spiritual patronage and public display. This appears to have been precisely the case of those confraternities that sponsored oratorios.

Indeed, some of them were unequivocally aristocratic from their beginnings. In the second half of the seventeenth century the Roman Archconfraternity of the Santissimo Crocifisso was known both for its refined musical activity and for its chosen affiliation. At its headquarters were performed (especially, in Lent) oratorios in Latin (another form of distinction) composed by the great masters of the time (Giacomo Carissimi, Alessandro Stradella) and interpreted by the best soloists of the great Roman musical chapels (the Sistine and Santa Maria Maggiore); and always before a highly select crowd. Such exclusivity was nothing new. The previous brotherhood had been founded in 1522 by the cardinal of Spanish origin Raimundo de Vico and his circle of friends, nobles and prelates, in order to encourage Christological devotion and carry out works of charity. A confraternity of a penitential character, its banners bore a crucifix and a scourge. By then it was already emerging as one of the most distinguished in the city, and in the second half of the sixteenth century, a cardinal of the Farnese family (Alessandro Farnese) would help finance the construction of its new oratory. Before the end of the century, none of the great names

---

1971) 96–98; Tonon F., *La Scuola Grande di San Rocco nel Cinquecento*, [Venice: 1999] 34–35; Urban L., "La Scuola Grande di San Rocco nelle feste veneziane", in Glixon J. – Lorenzo C. – Urban L. (eds.), *La Scuola Grande di San Rocco nella musica e nelle feste veneziane* ([Venice]: 1996) 41–75, here 41; and Traverso C., *La scuola di San Fantin o dei Picai. Carità e giustizia a Venezia* (Venice: 2000) 19.

30   The phenomenon is confirmed in studies such as Terpstra N., *Lay Confraternities and Civic Religion in Renaissance Bologna* (Cambridge: 1995) 96–102.

of the Roman aristocracy of the time were missing from its membership: from the Farnese to the Colonna families, as well as the Piccolomini and others.[31]

By that time, the phenomenon of ennobling confraternities was also quite evident in other places. The so-called Compagnia dei Poveri of Bologna, according to the official account, had been founded in 1576 by 'seven poor men', under the auspices of Cardinal Gabriele Paleotti. It was an extension or renewal of a very popular medieval Franciscan brotherhood of *laudesi* (or singers of *laude*): the Compagnia di Santa Maria delle Laudi e di San Francesco. The new confraternity, which had its headquarters in the hospital of Nosadella, exceeded a thousand members by the end of the sixteenth century, the majority being artisans (as previously). Its aims included helping the sick and imprisoned, teaching Christian doctrine, and rejecting luxury or worldly vanities. Its members were obliged to pray the Rosary once a week, in memory of deceased members; to participate in a monthly penitential procession; to give weekly alms; to visit the sick (to whom *laude* were sung) and to help one another. However, this dedication to social welfare, as well as the original Franciscan spirituality, weakened throughout the seventeenth century and all but died out following the entry into the corporation of many members of the local nobility (counts, marquises) and the ruling elite (the *senatori*), in addition to a good number of prelates. It was precisely these *honorati cittadini* who, in 1627, instituted the separation of the confraternity into a *compagnia* or brotherhood known as *stretta* (restricted) and another known as *larga* (open). This was not a unique case: other Bolognese confraternities had similarly been divided into two branches, *stretta* and *larga*, well before this time, including those of Santa Maria della Morte (of Dominican influence) and Santa Maria della Vita (within the Franciscan orbit), two of the earliest, from the first half of the fifteenth century.[32] In Rome, the separation received the names of *congregazione particolare* and *congregazione generale*, respectively.[33]

It is assumed that in the *stretta* or restricted branch the more rigorous members or those more committed to the proper religious activities of the confraternity met, while those of the *larga* or open branch, considerably less strict, specialised in social welfare or secular tasks. However, in practice, the

---

31   Capuano G., "L'Oratorio del ss. Crocifisso presso San Marcello: storia di un luogo di culto e di un genere musicale", in Cessac C. (ed.), *Les Histoires sacrées de Marc-Antoine Charpentier. Origines, contextes, langage, interpretation* (Turnhout: 2016) 63–88; Bianchi L., *Carissimi, Stradella, Scarlatti e l'oratorio musicale* (Rome: 1969) 29–133; Henneberg J. von, *L'oratorio dell'Arciconfraternità del Santissimo Crocifisso di San Marcello* (Rome: 1974).

32   Terpstra, *Lay Confraternities* 28–30 and 139–143.

33   O'Regan N., *Institutional Patronage in Post-Tridentine Rome. Music at Santissima Trinità dei Pellegrini 1550–1650* (London: 1995) 5.

stretta brotherhood was taken over by the more prominent members of the corporation, while the *larga* or more popular part was increasingly relegated, even though the *larga* branch of some confraternities did include gentlemen together with members of lesser status.[34] Yet in the statutes of other confraternities it was specified without embarrassment that its *stretta* branch could only be made up of individuals of 'honourable condition and quality', and that only they had the right to assume posts in the corporation.[35] In this way the status barriers were reintroduced into the heart of the brotherhood. This was not all: in keeping with a similar sociological evolution, musical activities, if there were any, as was often the case, also became more sophisticated and professional. In the second half of the seventeenth century the Compagnia dei Poveri of Bologna already had its own chapel master, and towards the end of the century he premiered his first musical oratorios, which were performed in an annex of the church of Nosadella and probably only enjoyed by the members of the *stretta* confraternity.[36]

5   Who Was Listening to Oratorios?

Another of the few Bolognese confraternities that could afford a musical oratorio, the archconfraternity of Santa Maria della Morte, had a similar profile, since many of the great patrician or senatorial lineages of the city were members (from the Bentivoglio and Boncompagni families to the Orsi and Pepoli), as well as a good number of cardinals and prelates. Hence their annual Good Friday oratorio was a representative city event that was attended, in addition to the local nobility, by the city magistrates (the *Gonfaloniere di Giustizia* and his officers, and the so-called *Anziani*) and even the cardinal legate, who represented papal authority. It was performed in the oratory (which has not survived) of the complex of Santa Maria della Morte, which included both church and hospital. As far as its audience is concerned, it can be argued that, on occasion, at the beginning of the eighteenth century, up to four hundred copies of the corresponding libretto were printed, although this number seems to be well above the maximum capacity of the oratory so that it can be conjectured

---

34   [Orsi Angelo Michele], *Racconto istorico dell'origine e fundazione della Veneranda Confraternità di S. Maria degli Angioli di Bologna* (Bologna, Girolamo Cochi: 1690) 26.
35   *Costitutioni, capitoli e statuti della veneranda e divota Compagnia della Immaculata Concettione della gloriosa Vergine Maria posta nella chiesa delli RR. Padri dell'ordine de' Servi di S. Giorgio di Bologna* (Bologna, Giacomo Monti: 1688) 46.
36   Fanti M., *La Chiesa e la Compagnia dei Poveri in Bologna. Una istituzione di mutuo soccorso nella società bolognese fra il Cinquecento e il Seicento* (Bologna: [1977]).

that it was usually well below that figure.[37] As in other cases, there is no way to establish the exact or whole social make-up of this potential audience.

Nevertheless, a gap in the documentation may possibly shed light on the likely audience. In 1719, when the roof of its oratory threatened to collapse, the confraternity of Santa Maria della Morte obtained special permission to hold its customary musical oratorio inside the church. The request, as well as the necessary change of location, was repeated in successive years. It is known that, in these instances, the precinct of the church was adorned for the occasion, but it was also carefully delimited (in the form of benches) in terms of status, in order to separate the ranks (or the ladies from the men where appropriate) and to welcome in proper fashion the civic and ecclesiastical authorities. On the day of the concert, the main door of the church was kept closed, and the attendees, that is, according to some sources, many 'nobiltà, Signori Confratelli et altri' ('nobility, gentlemen brothers and others') had to enter through a side door, guarded by two ushers belonging to the confraternity, who were also in charge of distributing the librettos for the oratorio. It is difficult to specify the exact meaning of the words 'Signori Confratelli', but they would seem not to refer to just any members, given that this confraternity was also divided into *stretta* and *larga* branches. Meanwhile, outside, the crowd (possibly the confraternity *larga*) awaited the final blessing with which the act and the oratorio ended.[38] Thus, it cannot be assumed 'who was listening to oratorios' in early eighteenth-century Bologna (or before or later), but, in the light of the few facts available concerning the audience for Italian musical oratorios, it is likely that the confraternity oratorios were also as select or status-biased as the Vatican oratorios or those that took place in churches such as the Chiesa Nuova of the Roman Oratorian congregation.

Perhaps in Florence, another major centre for the production of oratorios in general and confraternity oratorios in particular, the situation may have been rather different. In the second half of the seventeenth century, the

---

37 A plan of the oratory, with its characteristic rectangular layout, can be seen in Riepe J., *Die Arciconfraternita di S. Maria della Morte in Bologna. Beiträge zur Geschichte des Italienischen Oratoriums im 17. und 18. Jahrhundert* (Paderborn: 1998) 559. With regards its size, it can be compared with the twin oratory or almost of the archconfraternity of Santa Maria della Vita, still intact; see, *Il complesso monumentale di Santa Maria della Vita. Santuario-Museo-Oratorio* (Bologna: 2014) 44.

38 Data is drawn from the documentary appendix of Riepe, *Die Arciconfraternita* 463 A13; 464–470 A14; 473 A16a; and 474 A16b. According to the corresponding libretto, the oratorio performed that year was *Morte de Cristo. Da cantarsi nell'Oratorio dell'Arciconfraternità di Santa Maria della Morte, la sera del Venerdì Santo* (Bologna, li Rossi e Compagni: 1719).

Oratorians, based in the church (and square) of San Firenze, programmed between twenty and forty oratorios per year. For their part, the confraternities of the city offered about a dozen more on an annual basis. It is possible that all these, given that they were performed in 'public' and 'free', may have been more accessible than elsewhere. Indeed, even those sponsored by the city confraternities were 'extremely popular', according to the leading scholar of the Florentine oratorio.[39] The unusual account of the performance of a 'noble oratorio', *Il figliuolo prodigo*, in the church of the confraternity of San Jacopo, called del Nicchio, during Holy Week in the year 1712, appears to confirm this. The doors of the church were kept closed from a few hours before the event, although many people slipped through the open door of the sacristy, which, apparently, was only for members of the confraternity. Later, when the doors of the church were opened, a crowd filled all the spaces in the building, including the musicians' stage, which was in the presbytery. Apparently, many nobles had to take their seats there, around the musicians. Unfortunately, there is no further indication about the identity or social condition of the other members of the audience.[40]

Nevertheless, some of these Florentine corporations, and especially those that sponsored oratorios at the time, had a long and unequivocal aristocratic tradition, as was the case, for example, of the confraternity of Arcangelo Raffaello. Also known as della Scala, it enjoyed the patronage of the Grand Dukes of Tuscany and was initially dedicated to the teaching of aristocratic or well-off youth. Later it attracted young artists and members (nobles) of the Camerata Fiorentina, a group that cultivated the monodic style or 'recitar cantando'. This was not just any confraternity.[41] Nor was it a unique case: among those invited to aforementioned oratorio of the confraternity of San Jacopo del Nicchio the bishop of Fiesole, the papal nuncio Orazio Maria Panciatichi and Prince Gian Gastone, future seventh grand duke of Tuscany were present, together with many nobles.

It may be concluded that in matters of music the same principles or criteria governed as in the field of preaching, essentially diglossic or status-based in

---

39 Hill, J.W., "Oratory Music in Florence (II): At San Firenze in the Seventeenth and Eighteenth Centuries", *Acta Musicologica* 51 (1979) 246–267, here 267; Hill J.W., "Oratory Music in Florence (III): The Confraternities from 1655 to 1785", *Acta Musicologica* 58 (1986) 129–179, here 141–142.

40 The full narrative, in English, is in Smither, H.E., *A History of the Oratorio* (Chapel Hill: 1977) vol. I, 286–287.

41 Eisenbichler, K., *The boys of the Archangel Raphael. A Youth Confraternity in Florence 1411–1785* (Toronto: 1998) 78–83; Hill, J.W., "Oratory Music in Florence (I): 'Recitar cantando', 1583–1655", *Acta Musicologica* 51 (1979) 110.

nature. The good preacher, as prescribed in many contemporary treatises on preaching, had always to take into account 'whatever was the greater part of [the] audience, whether of nobles or commoners, whether of the learned (*letterati*) or of simple folk [...] and accommodate it', so that when the preacher addressed the 'popolo' he should not become over-elaborate ('exquisite'), conceptually-speaking.[42] However, if one could not or should not speak in the same way to the different social strata, there was also no reason for those same strata to listen to the same music together, especially when 'spiritual' listening of certain genres of music began to be considered another exclusive attribute of the nobility. On the contrary, shoemakers and shopkeepers, as well as people of 'crude understanding', enjoyed much more (or so some writers supposed) the street music of blind singers and instrumentalists.[43] In the realm of sacred music, that meant *laude* (simple) for some, the Masses and oratorios (sumptuous) for others, the few.

Bibliography

Primary Sources

Aresi Paolo, *Arte di predicar bene* (Rome, Ignatio de Lazari: 1664 [1624]).

Costitutioni, capitoli e statuti della veneranda e divota Compagnia della Immaculata Concettione della gloriosa Vergine Maria posta nella chiesa delli RR. *Padri dell'ordine de' Servi di S. Giorgio di Bologna* (Bologna, Giacomo Monti: 1688).

Descrizione di tutto il magnifico apparato, e di quanto si fece nella solennità di tutto l'Ottavario celebrato nella Chiesa di S. Maria sopra Minerva. Per la festa di S. Pio Quinto (Rome, Stamperia di Gio. Francesco Chracas: 1712). *Morte de Cristo. Da cantarsi nell'Oratorio dell'Arciconfraternità* DI SANTA MARIA DELLA MORTE, LA SERA DEL VENERDÌ SANTO (Bologna, li Rossi e Compagni: 1719).

Ordini et capitoli della Compagnia dell'Oratorio (Venice, Gabriel Giolito di Ferrarii: 1568).

[Orsi Angelo Michele], *Racconto istorico dell'origine e fundazione della Veneranda Confraternità di S. Maria degli Angioli di Bologna* (Bologna, Girolamo Cochi: 1690).

S. Caterina da Siena, oratorio del sig. Angelo Donato Rossi, accademico Infecondo, posto in musica da Giuseppe Valentini. E [...] dedicato all'illustrissimi [...] duca Don Federico Sforza, e duquessa Donna Livia Cesarini, duchi di Segni [...] prencipi di Genzano (Roma, Stamperia di Antonio de' Rossi: 1705).

---

42 This was recommended, for example, by the Teatino Monsignor Aresi Paolo, in the *Arte di predicar bene* (Rome, Ignatio de Lazari: 1664 [1624]) 383.

43 Dell'Antonio A., *Listening as Spiritual Practice in Early Modern Italy* (Berkeley: 2011) 82.

Sansovino Francesco, *Concetti politici* (Venice, Giovanni Antonio Bertano: 1578).

Santa Maria Egizziaca penitente. Oratorio di Bernardo Sandrinelli. Da recitarsi in musica nel Pio Ospitale della Pietà di Venezia (Venice, Gio. Battista Chiarello: 1687).

Statuti della venerabile congregatione della Madonna di Loreto di Milano (Pavia, Pietro Bartoli: 1605).

Secondary Sources

Al Kalak M. – Lucchi M., *Le regole dello spirito: norme, statuti e liturgie della Confraternità della Santissima Annunziata di Modena* (Modena: [2006]).

Arnold D. – Arnold E., *The Oratorio in Venice* (London: 1986).

Besutti P., "Echi da storia e di tradizioni d'Abruzzo nelle musiche devozionali", in Dell'Olio A. (ed.), *L'oratorio musicale nel Regno di Napoli al tempo di Gaetano Veneziano (ca. 1656–1716)* (Naples: 2016) 121–138.

Besutti P. (ed.), *L'oratorio musicale italiano e i suoi contesti (secoli XVII–XVIII)* (Florence: 2002).

Bianchi L., *Carissimi, Stradella, Scarlatti e l'oratorio musicale* (Rome: 1969).

Black C.F., *Italian Confraternities in the Sixteenth Century* (Cambridge: 1989).

Brundin A. – Treherne M. (eds.), *Forms of Faith in Sixteenth-Century Italy* (Aldershot: 2009).

Cessac C. (dir.), *Les Histoires sacrées de Marc-Antoine Charpentier. Origines, contextes, langage, interpretation* (Turnhout: 2016).

Crowther V., *The Oratorio in Modena* (Oxford: 1992).

Crowther V., *The Oratorio in Bologna (1650–1730)* (Oxford: 1999).

Dell'Antonio A., *Listening as Spiritual Practice in Early Modern Italy* (Berkeley: 2011).

Dell'Olio A. (ed.), *L'oratorio musicale nel Regno di Napoli al tempo di Gaetano Veneziano (ca. 1656–1716)* (Naples: 2016).

Donnelly J.P. – Maher M.W. (eds.), *Confraternities and Catholic Reform in Italy, France and Spain* (Kirksville: 1999).

Eisenbichler K., *The Boys of the Archangel Raphael. A Youth Confraternity in Florence 1411–1785* (Toronto: 1998).

Eisenbichler K. (ed.), *A Companion to Medieval and Early Modern Confraternities* (Leiden – Boston: 2019).

Fanti M., *La Chiesa e la Compagnia dei Poveri in Bologna. Una istituzione di mutuo soccorso nella società bolognese fra il Cinquecento e il Seicento* (Bologna: [1977]).

Filippi D.V. – Noone M. (eds.), *Listening to Early Modern Catholicism. Perspectives from Musicology* (Leiden – Boston: 2017).

Franchi S., *Le impressioni sceniche. Dizionario bio-bibliografico degli editori e stampatori romani e laziali di testi drammatici e libretti per música dal 1759 al 1800* (Rome: 1994).

Glixon J. – Lorenzo C. – Urban L., *La Scuola Grande di San Rocco nella musica e nelle feste veneziane* ([Venice]: 1996).

Glixon J., *Honoring God and the City. Music at the Venetian Confraternities, 1260–1807* (New York: 2003).

Grella D., "L'oratorio francescano e gli oratori per Sant'Antonio a Milano dal 1680 al 1715", *Il Santo. Rivista francescana di storia, dottrina, arte*, 39 (1999) 567–599.

Henneberg J. von, *L'oratorio dell'Arciconfraternità del Santissimo Crocifisso di San Marcello* (Rome: 1974).

Hill J.W., "Oratory Music in Florence (I): 'Recitar cantando', 1583–1655", *Acta Musicologica* 51 (1979) 108–136.

Hill J.W., "Oratory Music in Florence (II): At San Firenze in the Seventeenth and Eighteenth Centuries", *Acta Musicologica* 51 (1979) 246–267.

Hill J.W., "Oratory Music in Florence (III): The Confraternities from 1655 to 1785", *Acta Musicologica* LVIII (1986) 129–179.

Il complesso monumentale di Santa Maria della Vita. Santuario-Museo-Oratorio (Bologna: 2014).

Johnson J.L., *Roman Oratorio, 1770–1800. The Repertory at Santa Maria in Vallicella* (Ann Arbor: 1987).

Jouanna A., *L'idée de race en France au XVIe. siècle et au début du XVIIe* (revised edition, Montpellier: 1981).

Magaudda A – Costantini D., "Un periodico a stampa di antico regime: la 'Gazzetta di Milano' (secoli XVII–XVIII). Spoglio delle notizie musicali per gli anni 1686–1699", *Fonti Musicali Italiane* 1 (1996) 41–74.

Meersseman G.G. – Pacini G.P., *Ordo Fraternitatis. Confraternite e pietà dei laici nel medioevo* (Rome: 1977).

Morelli A., *Il tempio harmonico. Musica nell'oratorio dei Filippini in Roma (1575–1705)* (Laaber: 1991).

O'Regan N., *Institutional Patronage in Post-Tridentine Rome. Music at Santissima Trinità dei Pellegrini 1550–1650* (London: 1995).

Paglia V., *La Pietà dei Carcerati. Confraternite e società a Roma nei secoli XVI–XVIII* (Rome: 1980).

Prosperi A. (ed.), *Misericordie. Conversione sotto il patibolo tra Medioevo ed età moderna* (Pisa: 2007).

Pullan B., *Rich and Poor in Renaissance Venice. The Social Institutions of a Catholic State, to 1620* (Oxford: 1971).

Riepe J., *Die Arciconfraternita di S. Maria della Morte in Bologna. Beiträge zur Geschichte des Italienischen Oratoriums im 17. und 18. Jahrhundert* (Paderborn: 1998).

Rostirolla G. – Zardin D. – Mischiati O., *La lauda spirituale tra Cinque e Seicento. Poesia e canti devozionali nell'Italia della Controriforma* (Roma: 2001).

Selfridge-Field E., *Pallade Veneta. Writings on Music in Venetian Society 1650–1750* (Venice: 1985).

Smither H.E., *A History of the Oratorio* 1 (Chapel Hill: 1977).

Staffieri G., *Colligite Fragmenta. La vita musicale romana negli "Avvisi Marescotti" (1683–1707)* (Lucca: 1990).

Terpstra N., *Lay Confraternities and Civic Religion in Renaissance Bologna* (Cambridge: 1995).

Terpstra N. (ed.), *The Politics of Ritual Kinship. Confraternities and social order in Early Modern Italy* (Cambridge: 2000).

Terpstra N. (ed.), *The Art of Executing Well. Rituals of Execution in Renaissance Italy* (Kirksville: 2008).

Terpstra N. – Prosperi A. – Pastore S. (eds.), *Faith's Boundaries. Laity and Clergy in Early Modern Confraternities* (Turnhout: 2012).

Tonon F., *La Scuola Grande di San Rocco nel Cinquecento*, [Venice: 1999].

Traverso C., *La scuola di San Fantin o dei Picai. Carità e giustizia a Venezia* (Venice: 2000).

Urban L., "La Scuola Grande di San Rocco nelle feste veneziane", in Glixon J. – Lorenzo C. – Urban L. (eds.), *La Scuola Grande di San Rocco nella musica e nelle feste veneziane* ([Venice]: 1996) 41–75.

Vitali C., "Giovanni Paolo Colonna, maestro di capella dell'oratorio filippino in Bologna. Contributi bio-bibliografici", *Rivista Italiana di Musicologia* XIV.1 (1979) 128–154.

Weissman R.F.E., *Ritual Brotherhood in Renaissance Florence* (New York: 1982).

CHAPTER 10

Mustering Troops and Teaching Counterpoint: The Musical Incursions of a Central European Redemption Confraternity

Erika Supria Honisch

Abstract

In 1624, a print was issued in Vienna to mark the formal institution of the *Communio hierarchiae plentitudinis Aetatis Jesu*, a confraternity charged with consoling Christians held captive by the Ottoman Turks. Noting the Redemption confraternities connected to the Trinitarian and Mercedarian Orders, the author claimed that in every corner of Spain, 'rivers of mercy' flowed to comfort those in Muslim captivity, while the inhabitants of the Holy Roman Empire closed their ears to the groans of Christians imprisoned by the Ottoman Turks. Having recently founded a pan-European military order in order to curb Turkish advances in the Mediterranean, the new confraternity's principal benefactor, Michael Adolph von Althann, set about recruiting and training a musical legion. This paper traces the sonic influences and repercussions of Althann's brotherhood, connecting his *centuria musica* to an ambitious 1628 anthology of *stile nuovo* motets, a 1629 digest of Zarlinian music theory by the Genoese Franciscan Carlo Abbate and, not least, the multitudes of musical youths educated in the Piarist schools instituted by the Madrid-born Archbishop of Olomouc, Franz Seraph of Dietrichstein. Equipped both to console and to redeem, Althann's musical militia opened up new fronts in the battle for Central European souls.

Keywords

redemption confraternities – Michael Adolph von Althann – Trinitarian Order – Mercedarian Order – Ottoman Turks – Vienna – music

1 Introduction

On Sunday, 12 August 1635, while visiting Vienna, the Calvinist Prince Christian II of Anhalt-Bernburg (1599–1656) attended High Mass at the Jesuit Church and found himself engrossed in conversation with the zealously Catholic Imperial Confessor Wilhelm Lamormaini (1570–1648).[1] As the unlikely pair discussed religion, Christian listened with half an ear to a fundraising pitch for a confraternity that was – to judge from the details of his diary entry – impossible to ignore. It began after the Mass had concluded, when a nobleman, Count Michael Adolph von Althann (1574–1636) [Fig. 10.1], arrived in procession with his wife and children, accompanied by an entourage of sorts dressed in green and carrying green banners.

The count positioned himself at an altar set up in the square in front of the church and spoke, holding forth with a degree of force and enthusiasm that Christian encapsulated with the word *peroriren* ('to perorate').[2] The subject of Althann's disquisition was a new publication to be issued by the Communion of the Hierarchy of the Fullness of the Age of Jesus (*Communio hierarchiae plenitudinis Aetatis Iesu*), a confraternity he had founded in the early 1620s with the aim of redeeming Christians held captive by the Ottomans.[3] His dramatic appearance with his *confratres* in Vienna that day was typical of his efforts to drum up support for his brotherhood in the form of donations and new members.

---

1 See the diary entry dated 2/12 August 1635, as transcribed in *Digitale Edition und Kommentierung der Tagebücher des Fürsten Christian II. von Anhalt-Bernburg (1599–1656)*, Asch R.G. – P. Burschel P. (eds.). The entries for August 1635 are accessible at http://diglib.hab.de/edoc/edoo0228/id/edoc_edoo0228_fg_1635_08_sm/start.htm (accessed 1 July 2023). Equivalent letters such as i/j and u/v, faithfully transcribed in the digital edition, have been normalised here; all other orthography remains as in the original.

2 "Nach der ersten meße, hat man auf dem platz, die publication der hierarchischen Gemeinschaft außgerufen, vor der kirche, undt Altar so davor aufgerichtett gewesen, undt der Graf von Althejmb, hat selber darzu perorirt". See http://diglib.hab.de/edoc/edoo0228/id/edoc_edoo0228_fg_1635_08_sm/start.htm (accessed 1 July 2023).

3 Of the confraternity, Christian would already have been familiar with the confraternity, having conversed at some length with Althann about it in 1629. See his entry for 8/18 December 1629: http://diglan.hab.de/edoc/edoco00228/id/edoc_edoo0228_fg_1629_12_sm/start.htm (accessed 17 July 2024).

FIGURE 10.1   Lucas Kilian after Hans von Aachen, *Michael Adolph von Althann* (Augsburg, Dominicus Custos: 1600–1604). Engraving. https://www.nationalgalleries.org/art-and-artists/23067
HOLDINGS OF THE NATIONAL GALLERIES OF SCOTLAND

By his own account, Christian was so deeply immersed (*vertiefft*) in conversation with Lamormaini that he missed some of Althann's oration.[4] Still, the

---

4 'Ich habe es aber, in etwas versaümet zu sehen, weil ich mitt dem Patre Lemmermanno [Lamormaini], zu sehr im dißcurß mich vertiefft'. See http://diglib.hab.de/edoc/ed000228 /id/edoc_ed000228_fg_1635_08_sm/start.htm (accessed 1 July 2023).

militaristic gestures and sounds that followed did not escape him. He watched the 61-year-old count go inside the church and, as the Gospel was read, don vambraces (forearm guards) and pull his sword halfway out of its sheath. The Count held this position until the Gospel reading was finished, at which point the church filled with sound.[5] What he heard struck Christian for its variety: 'once more: Masses, ringing and dinging [*klingeley*], instrumental music [*Musicken*], and trumpets and drums, delivered intermittently, until it all came to an end'.[6] Christian's verbal profusion, redolent of contemporary Calvinist critiques of sonic excess, captures well the diversity of sounds available for deployment in central Europe by the third decade of the seventeenth century: not only sacred polyphony (*Messen*), punctuated by pealing bells and the unmistakably bellicose sounds of trumpet blasts and drums (*trompeten, heerpaucken*), but also *Musicken*, suggestive in this context of concerted music.[7]

The varied and up-to-date musical sounds that caught Christian's ear had been central to the confraternity's activities since its establishment in 1622 as an affiliate to the Order of Knights of the Militia Christiana (*Ordo Equitum Militiae Christianae*), formally constituted in 1618.[8] Althann founded that institution too, in partnership with Charles III Gonzaga (1580–1637), Duke of Nevers and Rethel, and Giovanni Battista Petrignani of Sforza (d. 1621), minor

---

5 Drawing the sword partially or entirely out of its sheath during the Gospel reading was widespread in equestrian orders, symbolizing the knight's readiness as *miles Christi* to fight for his faith; see: Warmington F., "The Ceremony of the Armed Man: The Sword, the Altar, and the *L'homme armé* Mass", in Higgins P. (ed.), *Antoine Busnoys: Method, Meaning, and Context in Late Medieval Music* (Oxford: 1999) 89–139, here 104.

6 'Darnach hats wieder, Meßen, klingeley, Musicken, vndt heerpaucken, vndt Trommeten, per intervalla gegeben, biß alles ein ende gehabtt, vndt scheinet, daß diß wergk einen guten vorsatz habe'. See: http://diglib.hab.de/edoc/ed000228/id/edoc_ed000228_fg_1635_08_sm/start.htm (accessed 1 July 2023).

7 For a representative example, see the advisedly specific complaint of Calvinist preacher Hawel Phaëton Zalensky in 1615 that 'the din of music, trumpets, violins, trombones, organs, drums, and other noises' was an incomprehensible and unnecessary addition to worship: 'Negsau ozdoba Cyrkwe a Chrámu nesrozumitedlná ta hřmotná Muzyka, Traub, hauslj, Pozaunů, Warhanů, bubnů a giných hluků'; see: Žalanský H., *O Posluchačjch Swatého Ewangelium* [...] (Prague, Jonata Bohutský: 1615) 184.

8 Confusingly, the confraternity and military order are often conflated, both in the secondary literature and in seventeenth-century references. For his part, Christian II described the Order as a 'Nebenorden' of the Militia Christiana following his December 1629 conversation with Althann. See http://diglib.hab.de/edoc/ed000228/id/edoc_ed000228_fg_1629_12_sm/start.htm (accessed 1 July 2023).

members of powerful families who shared Althann's lofty goals of establishing peace among Christian princes and curbing Ottoman activity in the Mediterranean and the eastern edges of the Holy Roman Empire.[9] The trio envisioned a chivalric order that would span Europe, with the Austrian Althann overseeing the eastern branch (the Empire, Bohemia, Poland, Hungary), the French-born Gonzaga the western branch, and the Italian Petrignani the southern branch. In practice, Althann's confraternity supplanted what was to have been the eastern branch of the Militia Christiana, and membership overlapped from the start.[10] The confraternity and military order were nonetheless distinct institutions with distinct organizational structures, distinct aims and distinct requirements for membership.[11] What they shared was an enterprising founder – Althann – and his vision of a musical legion of Christian soldiers, trained in music as they were in arms, and prepared to fight for Christian souls not only in the lands under Ottoman control, but also on the contested confessional terrain of the Holy Roman Empire itself.

---

9   Charles Gonzaga's goals were more ambitious still: a distant descendant of the Paleologus dynasty, the final ruling dynasty of the Byzantine Empire, he hoped to drive the Ottomans out of Constantinople and claim the throne for himself. See Parrott D., "A *prince souverain* and the French Crown: Charles de Nevers, 1580–1637)", in Oresko R. – Gibbs G.C. – Scott H.M. (eds.), *Royal and Republican Sovereignty in Early Modern Europe* (Cambridge: 1997) 149–187, here 161–162.
10 See the entry for "Althan(n), Michael Adolph, Graf von", and Magnus Ressel as cited in the entry for "Communio Hierarchica Plenitudinis Aetatis Jesu (pro Redemptione Captivorum) [...]" in the "Körperschaftsregister" of the edition of Christian II's diaries at http://diglib.hab.de/edoc/ed000228/start.htm (accessed 1 July 2023). In the "Epistola Pastoralis" that opens the publication issued to launch the confraternity, the papal nuncio Carlo Carafa implies in passing that the Knights of the Militia were also members of the confraternity (if not vice versa): "Meminerint illi personas Communionis, praesertim Equites de Ordine Militiae Christianae [...]"; see: Althann Michael A., *Institutio, confirmatio, et statuta Communionis hierarchicae plenitudinis aetatis IESU pro solatio afflictorum et in primis captivorum Turcicorum* (Vienna, Matthaeus Formica: 1624) 7.
11 Tomáš Parma's recent work on the Militia Christiana, rooted in archives in the Vatican, Vienna and Moravia, is indispensable; see especially Parma, T., "Řád Křesťanského rytířstva: mezi řeholní společností a konfraternitou", *Folia Historica Bohemica* 26 (2011) 247–265. A useful early overview of Althann's vision, for all that it conflates the military order and confraternity, is d'Elvert C., "Der Althan'sche Christus-Orden: Der christliche Vertheidigungsbund", *Notizen-Blatt der Historisch-Statistischen Section der Kais.-Königl. Mährisch-Schlesischen Gesellschaft zur Beförderung des Ackerbaues, der Natur- und Landeskunde* (1883 n°. 2) 12–13.

The musical incursions of Althann's confraternity reached deep into central Europe. They laid claim periodically to the streets and squares of Vienna and Prague, and transformed musical life first in Oslavany, a small Moravian town under Althann's jurisdiction, and subsequently in Mikulov (Nikolsburg), which became an important centre for the cultivation of the *stile moderno* in part because of personnel drawn north to support Althann's confraternity.[12] The Communio's battle plans and forays survive in the form of printed statutes and firsthand recollections of Althann's private conversations and public displays by such would-be recruits as Christian II, the Bohemian noble Heinrich Hiesserle von Chodaw (1575–1665), and the Prague Archbishop and Cardinal Ernst Adalbert von Harrach (1598–1667). Especially remarkable, however, are two music prints which, taken together, hint at the scale of Althann's plans for the musical armaments of his new confraternity, and the musical training to take place at the affiliated seminaries he supported in Vienna and Oslavany.

The more modest of the two prints, *Regulae contrapuncti excerptae ex operibus Zerline et aliorum* [...] (Oslavany, Caspar Haugenhoffer: 1629) [Fig. 10.2], is a counterpoint manual by the Franciscan friar and composer Carlo Abbate (ca. 1600–before 1640).[13] The second, *Flores verni ex viridario Oslaviensi divis tutelaribus Communionis Hierarchicae sacri* [...] (Oslavany, Caspar Haugenhoffer: 1628) [Fig. 10.3], is an anthology of stylistically diverse compositions, primarily by Italian composers – the bouquet of 'spring flowers' in the title – for which no editor or compiler is named. Issued a year earlier, it was the first volume of a planned, but ultimately unrealized, series of nine.[14]

---

12   On the significance of Mikulov in seventeenth-century music history, see: Sehnal J., *Adam Michna of Otradovice-Composer: Perspectives on Seventeenth-Century Sacred Music in the Czech Lands*, trans. J. Fiehler (Olomouc: 2016) 13–14; Sehnal cites foundational work by Trolda E., "Účast Moravy a Slezska na církevní hudbě v XVIII. Století", *Česká hudba* 24 (1920) 33–42, here 33.

13   Just a single copy of the *Regulae contrapuncti*, held in the Städtische Bibliotheken, Leipzig, is known, and was used as the basis of the facsimile edition issued in 1977 in Leipzig by the Zentralantiquariat der Deutschen Demokratischen Republik. That edition is viewable in its entirety via Google Books at https://www.google.com/books/edition/Regulae_contrapuncti/X6sYAQAAIAAJ (accessed 1 July 2023).

14   The phrase "MANIPULUS EX NOVEM PRIMUS" is given following the title on the title-page; see also fn. 16 below. On the use of floral titles for music prints in Italy, and in particular the use of floral metaphors as a way of signaling variety, see: Cypess R., "Girolamo Frescobaldi's *Fiori musicali*: Music and Flowery Metaphors in Early Modern Europe", *Journal of the Society for Seventeenth-Century Music* 2.1 (2022) https://sscm-jscm.org/jscm-issues/volume-28-no-1/.

FIGURE 10.2   Carlo Abbate, *Regulae contrapuncti ex operibus Zerlini et aliorum* [...] (Oslavany, Caspar Haugenhoffer: 1629), title-page

The title-pages of the music prints cast the contents and the users as weapons and warriors in a holy war: the counterpoint manual – a digest of Zarlinian contrapuntal theory – is adapted for the instruction of 'new recruits' ('tyrones'),[15] while the anthology of 'Masses, psalms, hymns, canticles, odes, motets, concertos, cantilenas, arias, and sacred madrigals by the leading

---

15   The full title of the counterpoint manual is *Regulae contrapuncti excerptae ex operibus Zerlini et aliorum ad breviorem Tyronum instructionem accommodate* [sic, lege accommodatae] *per Fratrem Carolum Abbate* [sic, lege Abbatem] *Genuensem, Ord. Min. Conv. Illustris. Rev. et Exc. Principis. Card. à Dietrichstain etc. Sacellanum et Musicum.*

FIGURE 10.3 Title-page of *Flores verni ex viridario Oslaviensi divi tutelaribus Communio* [...] (Vienna, Matthaeus Formica: 1628)
HOLDINGS OF THE DEPARTMENT OF MUSIC OF THE AUSTRIAN NATIONAL LIBRARY

musicians of the world and our age' is described as a maniple ('manipulus'), or unit, of the 'musical troops' ('centuria musica') of the Militia Christiana.[16]

---

16 The full title of the anthology is: *Flores verni ex viridario Oslaviensi divis tutelaribus Communionis Hierarchicae sacri; Id est, De Centuria Musica exercitus litterarii Militiae Christianae, continente Missas, Psalmos, Hymnos, Cantica, Odas, Motetas, Concertos, Cantilenas, Arias, et Madrigalia sacra praestantissimorum Orbis et saeculi nostri Musicorum. Manipulus ex novem primus*. The enigmatic phrase 'centuria musica exercitus litterarii Militiae Christianae' translates roughly as 'the musical troops of the army of letters of the Militia Christiana'.

'Centuria' was the term for a unit of the Roman army numbering 60–100 men; given the use of 'manipulus' (a 'handful of soldiers' in the Roman army) to describe this first volume, the phrase seems to refer metaphorically to the compositions themselves, which are positioned as a wing of the Militia Christiana, capable of waging war in their own

Known to music scholars since the early twentieth century, the *Regulae contrapuncti* and *Flores verni* are less curios of regional significance – although they are that, too – than they are artifacts of the vast, supranational devotional and musical networks in which redemption confraternities and their champions inevitably participated.[17] Taken together, they reflect Althann's hopes that music might be useful for the prayer and pious recreation of his Christian soldiers, and that it might be deployed strategically to draw attention to the redemptionist cause at home. His certainty that music for voices and instruments would be useful for both redeemer and redeemed reflects the influence of the Flemish historian Jean-Baptiste Gramaye (1579–1635) and expands the networks of influence still further. Gramaye was moved to tears and prayer by the music of Spanish redemptorists while being held for ransom in Ottoman-controlled North Africa for five months in 1619. By 1623, he was in central Europe, appointed by Althann – with the approbation of the papal nuncio Carlo Carafa – as religious superintendent for the Militia Christiana and the Communio Hierarchica Plenitudinis Aetatis Jesu, and as Administrator of Althann's Oslavany properties.[18]

2 Althann and the Militia Christiana

Born in 1576, Michael Adolph von Althann spent his early career in the Imperial army, battling Ottoman forces in Hungary during the Thirteen Years' War (1593–1606). He acquitted himself well in a conflict that saw many Imperial defeats, participating in the fleeting Habsburg victory at Stuhlweissenburg (Székesfehérvár) in 1601 and the defense of the fortress town

---

right. I am grateful to Adrian Horsewood and Jaya Lakshminarayanan for suggesting these interpretations.

17 Robert Eitner included a brief entry for the *Flores verni* in his *Biographisch-Bibliographisches Quellenlexikon* 4 (Leipzig: 1901) 3–4; he provides the full title, lists the named composers, working from the surviving *pars infima* held in the Austrian National Library in Vienna, but does not speculate about its music-historical significance. The prints are given rich local contextualisation in the meticulous, decades-long work of historian Jiří Sehnal in, for example, Sehnal, *Adam Michna*; and, especially, in Sehnal J., "Die adeligen Musikkapellen im 17. und 18. Jahrhundert in Mähren", in Biba O. – Jones D.W. (eds.), *Studies in Music History presented to H. C. Robbins Landon on his Seventieth Birthday* (London: 1996) 195–217 and 265–270; see in particular the discussion of Oslavany on 211.

18 Parma T., "Jean-Baptiste Gramay, primas Afriky, titulární arcibiskup upsalský a administrátor oslavanský", *Časopis Matice moravské* 131 (2012) 285–310, here 294–295; a German abstract is given on page 310. The appointments were not without their complications: a 1625 trip to Rome to confirm his new titles occasioned severe criticism; and it was only with difficulty that he was granted the powers that had been approved by Carafa; see Parma, "Jean-Baptiste Gramay" 295–296.

of Gran (Esztergom) in 1604. In 1608, in recognition of Althann's bravery on the battlefield, Emperor Rudolf II elevated him to the rank of Imperial count (*Reichsgraf*).[19] This was a hereditary office, unlike the title of Count Palatine (*Pfalzgraf*), and it gave Althann access to income, status and power on a scale to match his ambitions.[20]

Althann's aspirations were informed by his time in the army, his diplomatic experience as a Habsburg representative to the Sublime Porte in 1615, and his faith, which tended towards a zealous, if doctrinally flexible, Catholicism. Raised a Lutheran, he had converted in 1599, when it became expedient to do so if one wished to advance at the Rudolfine court. In a story that Jesuits at the Church of St. Anna in Vienna took up enthusiastically, his embrace of Catholicism was motivated by a near-death experience by the crucifix on Prague's Charles Bridge [Fig. 10.4]. When he failed to show sufficient respect by doffing his hat and kneeling as he passed by – this sort of refusal was one of the more public ways a Lutheran might signal his beliefs – he fell from his horse, the bridge split in two, and the earth opened precipitously before him.[21]

Convinced, he made his way to the nearby Jesuit college and embraced the Catholic faith. Because his conversion took place on the feast of St. Michael the Archangel, he vowed to name all his sons Michael, and all his daughters Maria, after the Virgin Mary. He kept his word: for all eight of his sons and all nine of his daughters.[22] It was probably at his behest that both the confraternity he founded and the military order that preceded and complemented it, the Militia Christiana, honoured St. Michael and the Virgin Mary as patron saints.

---

19   The Letter Patent for Althann's elevation to the Reichsgrafenstand specifically cites his bravery; see: Pecho C., *Fürstbischof, Putschist, Landesherr: Erzherzog Leopold und sein alternativer Habsburger Herrschaftsentwürfe im Zeitalter des Dreissigjährigen Kriegs* (Berlin: 2017) 130.

20   *Pfalzgraf* (Count Palatine), the other title used to show favour to courtiers or employees, was non-hereditary and thus less lucrative; recipients of this lesser, but still desirable, award during Rudolf II's reign include the painter Giuseppe Arcimboldo and the physician and composer of alchemical canons Michael Maier.

21   Louthan H., "Religious Art and the Formation of a Catholic Identity in Baroque Prague", in Cohen G.B. – Szabo F.A.J. (eds.), *Embodiments of Power: Building Baroque Cities in Europe* (New York: 2008) 53–79, here 68; the original source, evidently a print by the Jesuits of Vienna, is not specified, but Louthan cites the text given in Winkelbauer T., *Fürst und Fürstendiener: Gundaker von Liechtenstein, ein österreichischer Aristokrat des konfessionellen Zeitalters* (Vienna: 1999) 135. The story was known to d'Elvert, too, although he gives the year as 1598; see d'Elvert, "Der Althan'sche Christus-Orden" 12.

22   Althann's seventeen children were the products of two marriages: the first was to Elisabeth von Stotzingen (d. 1624), and the second, in 1627, was to Maria Eva Elisabeth von Sternberg (1605–1668), a member of one of Bohemia's oldest noble families. Her father, Adam II von Sternberg (1553–1623), was one of Ferdinand II's Catholic regents in Bohemia and as such narrowly escaped being defenestrated in 1618.

MUSTERING TROOPS AND TEACHING COUNTERPOINT 255

FIGURE 10.4 Wenzel Hollar, *Pons Pragensis* (Prague Bridge: 1635?)
HOLDINGS OF THE MUSEUM OF CZECH LITERATURE

Althann remained preoccupied with the Ottoman presence long after the 1606 Peace of Zsitvatorok brought the Thirteen Years' War to an inconclusive close. He was particularly distressed by the Ottoman practice of kidnapping Christians from border territories and holding them for ransom. He was troubled, as well, by the increasing fractiousness among Christian princes: not just the simmering confessional disputes that led to the outbreak of the Thirty Years' War in 1618, but also the Uskok War (1615–1617) between the Austrian Habsburgs, backed by Spain, and the Republic of Venice. The Uskok conflict, triggered by Habsburg support of Croatian pirates who attacked Ottoman vessels and Venetian merchant ships with equal enthusiasm, proved fortuitous for Althann: the possibility of securing a lucrative post as a commander in Austrian or Spanish service drew many ambitious military men to Prague in 1617, and it is in this context that Althann partnered with Gonzaga and Petrignani to form the Militia Christiana.[23]

The first gathering of those interested in joining the new military order took place in March 1618 in Olomouc, and by November of that year the Order had been officially constituted under the protection of the Virgin and St. Michael, and following the rule of St. Francis (the Third or Secular Order). Membership required proof of noble blood to the fourth generation. Commoners could be admitted, however, if their father had been a soldier. Crucially, given the emphasis on achieving Christian unity, confession was not a barrier to entry.

Initial interest in the Militia Christiana was such that in March of 1619, twenty-nine members were formally inducted into the Order in Vienna in the presence of Emperor Matthias (r. 1612–1619). The international roster of inductees included Count Giovanni Vincenzo d'Arco (d. 1621), who created, choreographed and directed a danced spectacle staged at the Imperial court in 1617 (the so-called *Phasma dionysiacum*); Henri Duval, Count of Dampierre (1580–1620), a veteran of both the Thirteen Years' War and the Uskok War; and Prince Nicolae Pătrașcu (1580–1627), in exile from Wallachia and also a veteran of the Thirteen Years' War.[24] The elaborate ceremony warranted a lengthy

---

23 Mat'a P., "Giovanni Vincenzo Conte d'Arco: Un Cavaglier Christiano tra armi e lettere", in Tongoni G. – Turrini R. (eds.), *La fabbrica della Collegiata* (Arco: 2013) 65–110, here 89–90; the article is also available in Czech, as Mat'a P., "Giovanni Vincenzo d'Arco: Křesťanský rytíř s múzou a mečem", in Tongoni G. – Turrini R. (eds.), *La fabbrica della Collegiata* (Arco: 2013) 199–225.

24 Khevenhüller Franz von, *Annales Ferdinandei* 9 (Vienna, Matthaeus Cosmerovius: 1646) 522–523. Significantly, Khevenhüller (521) emphasises the presence of 'a great many distinguished Roman Catholic princes, counts, and lords' ('viele vornehme Römische Catholische Fürsten, Graffen und Herren'). On the *Phasma dionysiacum*, which was of great importance politically, see especially Mat'a P., "Das *Phasma Dionysiacum Pragense*

description in that year's *Mercure François*, where it was reported that part of the ceremony unfolded in the open air at some distance from the city. Dressed in the Order's white mantles, inductees knelt on a Turkish carpet to pray.[25] Standing up, they lifted their swords and made the sign of the Cross three times; kneeling again, they placed two fingers on the Gospel and took oaths to defend the faith and

> repulse the audacious Turks, who have overrun the Mediterranean, and who snatch a great number of Christians, whom they kill or enslave, to the shame and disgrace of all Christianity.[26]

They then moved back inside the cathedral to be received into the Order and don its distinctive gold cross, enameled in blue – the color of the Virgin's robes [Fig. 10.5].[27]

Some days after the Vienna ceremony, Ferdinand Gonzaga, Duke of Mantua, also joined the Order.[28] Despite this promising start, the timing was inauspicious: within a few months of its founding, the Thirty Years' War broke out, and

---

und die Anfänge des Faschings am Kaiserhof", in Marschall B. (ed.), *Theater am Hof und für das Volk: Festschrift für Otto G. Schindler zum 60. Geburtstag* (Vienna: 2002) 67–80; Štědroň M., "Hudba v pražské slavnosti 'Phasma Dionysiacum' z roku 1617 (Konfrontace a posuny)", in Kroupa J. (ed.), *Ars Naturum Adjuvans: Sborník k poctě profesora PhDr. Miloše Stehlíka* (Brno: 2003) 10–14; and Seifert H., "Italian Musical Dramatic Genres at the Courts of the Austrian Habsburgs", in Weaver A. (ed.), *A Companion to Music at the Habsburg Courts in the Sixteenth and Seventeenth Centuries* (Leiden – Boston: 2021) 255–272, here 256–258.

25 *Cinquiesme Tome du Mercure François ou, Suitte de l'Histoire de nostre temps, sous le regne du Tres-Chrestien Roy de France & de Navarre, Louys XIII* (Paris, Estienne Richer: 1619) 225. The swearing-in ceremony is also described in Khevenhüller, *Annales Ferdinandi*, vol. 9, 521–524; some details differ.

26 *Mercure François* 225: 'Il se voit qu'il estoit erigé […] particulierement pour reprimer l'audace des Turcs, lesquels courent la Mer Mediterranee, et prenent grand nombre de Chrestiens, qu'ils font mourir, ou qu'ils rendent Esclaves, au dommage, et à la honte de toute la Chrestienté'. The *Mercure François* reproduces the articles of foundation as given in an available French translation, which I have not been able to identify.

27 The cross is briefly described in *Mercure François* 226. One inductee, the Bohemian nobleman Heinrich Hiesserle von Chodaw, included an image of the insignia in his manuscript *Reisebuch*, which is part travelogue, part autobiography; see Heinrich Hiesserle von Chodaw, *Raiss-Buch und Leben*, Knihovna Národního muzea v Praze, shelf no. VI A 12, fol. 101r; digitized at https://www.manuscriptorium.com/apps/index.php?direct=record&pid=AIPDIG-NMP_VI_A_12_1XHFIVF-cs. Hiesserle's depiction probably reflects what he saw. A more schematic depiction is given in Márquez José Micheli y, *Tesoro militar de Cavalleria* (Madrid, Diego Diaz de la Carrera: 1642) 71.

28 Khevenhüller, *Annales Ferdinandei* 523.

FIGURE 10.5   Heinrich Hiesserle von Chodaw, *Raiss-buch und Leben*, fol. 101 r (detail)
HOLDINGS OF THE NATIONAL MUSEUM OF THE CZECH REPUBLIC

outside observers caught wind of internal discord.[29] Additionally, the desire, widely shared, to honor the terms of the 1606 Peace between the Holy Roman Empire and the Ottomans prevented the Militia Christiana from undertaking the crusade longed for by its founders.

In October of 1622, worried about the souls of Ottoman captives, Althann formed a redemption confraternity modeled on those administered by the Trinitarians and Mercedarians in Spain, and sharing their twofold understanding of redemption as liberation from captivity and salvation through Jesus Christ.[30] The confraternity's name – the Communion of the Hierarchy of the Fullness of the Age of Jesus – invokes Ephesians 4:13, in which Paul calls for

---

29   Mennens Franz, *Militarium Ordinum origines, statuta, symbola, insignia, Iconibus additis genuinis* (Cologne, Petrus Salvinus: 1623) 90: 'At zizanniae ille superseminator hostis nescio quo titulo discordias gravis inter fundatores, sive Institutores interposuit, quo factum fuit, ut tanti incoepti cursus retardatus sit, vel maxima ex parte' ('But what sower of noxious seeds, the enemy, I know not under what title, interspersed serious discords among the founders or *Institutores*, which made it so that the course, as much as it had begun, was delayed for the most part').

30   The two orders are held up as models in Caraffa's preface (3) to the *Institutio, confirmatio, et statuta*. On the understanding of 'redemption' in this context, see: Escrivà-Llorca F., "Soundscapes and Brotherhood in Processions of the Redemption of Captives: The Case of Early Modern Valencia (Spain)", *Confraternitas* 31.1 (2020) 86–107, here 87.

the faithful to be led so that they might 'all come together in the unity of faith and in recognition of the Son of God, unto a perfect man, *in the measure of the age of the fullness of Christ*' (emphasis added). The new brotherhood honoured St. Francis and the recently canonised St. Ignatius Loyola, in addition to St. Michael and the Virgin Mary.[31]

The confraternity's Jesuit and Franciscan fidelities are captured in the image that occupies most of the *Flores verni* title-page (see Figure 10.3) and the entirety of the verso of the *Regulae contrapuncti* title-page. It depicts a Latin cross with the letters 'ihs' in the centre and the four words 'In hoc signo vinces' inscribed on each arm of the cross, girded by the corded belt characteristic of Secular Order of Franciscans, with five knots symbolizing the five wounds of Christ. The numbers thirty-three – the age of Christ – and nine for the nine choirs of angels, figured prominently in the confraternity's rites, induction fees and organisation.[32]

Membership was open to both clergy and laity.[33] Astonishingly, it was also open to all Christians, regardless of confession, as the Militia Christiana itself was. Christian II of Anhalt-Bernburg discovered in 1629 that his Calvinist faith would be no barrier to entry when Althann tried unsuccessfully to recruit him during a visit to Prague: ten years into the Thirty Years' War, Althann remained personally committed to uniting Christendom. While the papal nuncio Carlo Carafa publicly stressed the brotherhood's potential 'to preserve and conserve orthodoxy, and reduce schismatics and heretics' in Germany as in Turkey, in private Althann expressed more flexibility.[34] Lutherans, Calvinists and other Christians could join the brotherhood '[b]ecause the Count of Althann takes all those who are baptized in Christ's name to be Christians and good people', Christian wrote in his diary on 8/18 December 1629, 'and all those who are baptized in Christ's name are worthy of the Order – with the Pope's approval, moreover'.[35]

---

31 *Institutio, confirmatio, et statuta* 103.
32 *Institutio, confirmatio, et statuta* 5 and throughout; the Gloria was to be recited thirty-three times daily, for example.
33 A passage in the printed statutes addressing the division of the membership begins 'Cum autem ab hac Communiore [*sic*] nemo excludatur [...]'; see *Institutio, confirmatio, et statuta* 31. That members are to follow the rule of the Third Order of Francsicans is indicated in the statutes; see *Institutio, confirmatio, et statuta* 84.
34 Carafa, preface to *Institutio, confirmatio, et statuta* 4.
35 'Er hat zwar noch einen nebenorden, den er communionem hierarchiae Ecclesiasticae nennet, denselben können lutrische, reformirte, vndt andere Christen auch bekommen. Denn er der graf von Altheimb helt alle vor Christen vndt gute leütte, die auf Christi nahmen getaufft sein, welche tauffe der Mahometh allein verbotten hatt, sonst keine secte, vndt alle die auf Christi nahmen, getauft seindt, seyen des ordens würdig, auch mitt des pabsts bewilligung'. See http://diglib.hab.de/edoc/ed000228/id/edoc_ed000228_fg_1629 _12_sm/start.htm (accessed 1 July 2023).

The confraternity's primary purpose, however, was to redeem Christians held captive in Ottoman-controlled lands. Specifically, it was to provide them with spiritual consolation in captivity and arrange for their release through ransom payments. Althann ultimately devoted over 300,000 *fl.* of his own money to this cause, and worked assiduously to raise further funds. His appeals, which often involved musical performance, could be quite dramatic. On the Feast of the Apparition of St. Michael (8 May) in 1631, for instance, the confraternity held a service at Prague Cathedral at which new members were inducted, each paying a 33 *fl.* fee. At Communion, in the presence of an illustrious gathering of courtiers and diplomats, Althann and his wife Maria Eva signed a vow of chastity. Althann then took a piece of paper and placed it at the foot of the altar; it contained a pledge to donate 5000 *fl.* annually to support thirty-three priests or soldiers in converting the Turks and liberating their slaves, and 9 × 33 *florins* each for processions beginning at Prague's Franciscan Church of St. James and the Jesuit Church in Vienna.[36] Music for the service was furnished by hired musicians – local trumpeters and students from the Jesuit College – a point that did not go unnoticed by the Archbishop of Prague, Ernst Adalbert von Harrach, an amateur musician, and a careful and informed listener whose relationship with the local Jesuits was often strained.

A crucial figure in the confraternity's establishment was Althann's Oslavany Administrator, Jean-Baptiste Gramaye. Gramaye's assertions that thousands of Christians held captive in North Africa had converted to Islam alerted readers across Europe to the risk of apostasy.[37] It may have been at Gramaye's suggestion that page after page of the confraternity's statutes, printed in Vienna in 1624, is given over to listing Christians held captive in Buda, along with the status of efforts to redeem them; his printed account of his own captivity concludes with a similar listing. It was probably also thanks to Gramaye, who knew the power of print, that the Brno printer Caspar Haugenhoffer was brought to Oslavany to serve as the official printer of the Communio Hierarchiae, a

---

36 Von Harrach Ernst Adalbert, entry for 8 May 1631, transcribed in Keller K. – Catalano A. (eds.), *Die Diarien und Tagszettel des Kardinals Ernst Adalbert von Harrach (1598–1667)* 2: Diarium 1629–1646 (Vienna – Cologne – Weimar: 2010) 41–42: '[...] et mettendo una scrittura al piede dell'altare, che conteneva in sostanza, che egli hipothecava tutto il suo, che importa più di 300.000, per una fondatione cioè di 5.000 fiorini annui, da mantenere 33 persone che servissero, o con esser preti, o con esser soldati, alla conversione de' turchi, et per liberare i schiavi di quel paese'.

37 Parma T., "Jean-Baptiste Gramay, primas Afriky, titulární arcibiskup upsalský a administrátor oslavanský", *Časopis Matice moravské* 131.2 (2012) 285–310.

designation that shows up on the title-page of both the *Flores verni* and *Regulae contrapuncti*.³⁸

In most respects, Althann's confraternity resembled other Redemption confraternities. Like the Trinitarians and Mercederians, it used musical processions to attract donations. Its provisions for musical training were unusual, however, and the publication of music and music theory specifically intended for the confraternity's use was without precedent in the Austrian and Czech lands. Even the most prestigious and musical of confraternities at the court of Rudolf II, the Confraternitas Corporis Christi in Aula Caesarea, issued no such prints, for all that it counted several Imperial composers among its members, and motets by the Imperial chapel master, Philippe de Monte (1521–1603), set texts used in the brotherhood's devotions. That music was given pride of place in the activities of the Communio Hierarchica may be partly due to Gramaye, whose experience in captivity had attuned him to its power to provide solace and renew faith. In his published diary entry for the feast of St. John the Baptist in 1619, Gramaye reports that eight priests celebrated Mass with voices and instruments; their singing and playing moved the listeners, who responded with sincere prayers intermingled with tears.³⁹ But the emphasis on music likely also responds to regional apathy towards the plight of the Germans, Czechs, Moravians, Poles and Hungarians in Ottoman captivity. As Carafa wrote in his preface to the confraternity's statutes, '[I]n Spain, Italy, France, rivers of mercy flow [...] to console the unhappy captives; only in the Empire

---

38   In the *Regulae contrapuncti* this appears as 'Typis Comm⟨unionis⟩ Hier⟨archiae⟩ Ca sparus Haugenhofferus', and for the *Flores verni* it reads 'Typis Comm⟨unionis⟩. supr. Casparus Haugenhofferus'. Significantly, when Cardinal Franz Seraph von Dietrichstein had two confessionally charged sermons printed by Haugenhoffer in 1628, the cross image is included (at the end of the print) but Haugenhoffer is not identified as the Communio's printer; see Dietrichstein Franz Seraph von, *Zwo Predigten deren Eine am Hochheyligen Fest unser lieben Frawen Verkündigung uber gleich damahls in den Marggraffthumb Mähren wegen der Religions Reformation Herrn- und Ritterstands publicierte Patenten* [...] *Die Ander am Sontag Laetare von der Communion under Einerley gestalt* (Oslavany, Caspar Haugenhoffer: 1628).

39   Gramaye Jean-Baptiste, *Diarium rerum Argelae gestarum ab anno MDCXIX. In quo Argelae descriptio, vita, Religio, et mores Barbarorum, miseria captivorum statusque Ecclesiae Africanae describuntur* (Cologne, Albinus Dusseldorpff: 1623) 29: 'Illucscente festo S. Ioannis, [...] assistente 8. Sacerdotum fere habituatorum numero, cum instrumentis Musicis, et mentito avium cantu, et Musica, Missa celebravi, incredibili cum applausu fidelium, quorum plures lachrymis preces assiduas miscebant [...]'. See also: Gramaye Jean-Baptiste, *Africae illustratae libri decem, in quibus Barbaria, gentesque eius ut olim, et nunc describuntur* [...] (Tournai, Adrianus Quinque: 1622), which is quoted in *Institutio, confirmatio, et statuta* 91.

are [...] ears hardened to the groans of the prisoners'.[40] As part of his campaign to open up the ears of his compatriots, Althann committed his own funds to Oslavany supporting thirty-three music students in Vienna – again reflecting the age of Christ – and nine in Oslavany.[41] They were to be provided with a suitable music library and diverse musical instruments and trained in both vocal and instrumental performance in order to provide music in church services, particularly at the celebrations of patronal feast days.[42]

The *Regulae contrapuncti* gives a good sense of the basis for instruction. An efficient and occasionally opinionated digest of counterpoint theory largely based on Zarlino, it was prepared by the Franciscan composer Carlo Abbate, whom Althann had hired to teach at the Oslavany seminary. By 1629, when the print was issued, Abbate had departed Oslavany for another Moravian town, Mikulov, where he entered into the service of Cardinal Franz Seraph of Dietrichstein, whose own musical enthusiasms were considerable. Although he used his new titles ('sacellanus et musicus') on the title-page, he dedicated the print to Althann: for how could there be a more suitable dedicatee than the one who had furnished the Oslavany seminary with a printer capable of printing the 'spiritual songs' that were the first fruits of his labor?[43] From this, it can be surmised that Abbate was probably the compiler of the *Flores verni* anthology, which had appeared the previous year.

Abbate begins with a definition of counterpoint and moves systematically through the various intervals, before laying out the rules for dissonance treatment and other contrapuntal fundamentals. Complex matters, and those without practical application, are avoided, save for a brief discussion of the genera

---

40   Carafa, preface to *Institutio, confirmatio, et statuta* 3: 'Vident uberem messem, quam faciunt Patres Ordinum B. Mariae de Mercede, et ss. Trinitatis de redemptione Captivorum in consolandis, confirmandis, liberandis, quovis anno Hispanis, Italis, Gallis; perennesque de fontibus misericordiae rivulos fluere per ista regna et Provincias, ad solatia infelicium captivorum, se autem solos pene hominum pro derelictis haberi, in Imperio solo clausas misericordiae fores, obturatas ad *audiendum gemitus compeditorum*' [italics original].

41   On the Vienna foundation, see *Institutio, confirmatio, et statuta* 40: 'Quod S. Pancratii titulo Viennae Fundator in suam et Communionis accepit protectionem, notabili dote consignata pro sustentatione 33 Studiosorum musica, tam vocali, quam instrumentali, officium divinum in templo peragentium'. And a little later on, '[...] et quotidie bis in musica se exercere, habentes ad eum finem et Bibliothecam musicam insignem, et omnia instrumentorum musicorum genera'. On the Oslavany foundation, see: Sehnal, "Die adelige Musikkappellen" 211.

42   See *Istitutio, Confirmatio, et Statuta* 75–76 ("De Officio Musicorum") and 80 ("De Festis et Supplicationibus Communionis").

43   '[...] meis spiritualibus cantiunculis in ea locum dedit', in Abbate, *Regulae contrapuncti* fol. A 2r.

in which he dismisses the chromatic and enharmonic genera as impossible to sing. The book is well-suited, in other words, to the 'new recruits' ('tyrones') mentioned on the title-page, whether at Althann's Oslavany and Vienna seminaries, or at the seminary that Dietrichstein was working on establishing in Mikulov. That the Piarists who ran that seminary ordered a Palestrina Mass from Rome in 1633 is suggestive of its continuing relevance.[44]

Just a single low-voice (*pars infima*) partbook survives of the *Flores verni* anthology. It is clear from this fragment, however, that the anthology responds to Althann's hopes that music could be of educational and spiritual use to his Christian legionaries when they were not occupied with matters of war. Its brief dedication, signed by the Oslavany choristers ('Chorus Musicorum Oslaviensium'), is addressed to Althann's son Michael Ferdinand (ca. 1610–1658), who was a member of the seminary and certainly the most ideal of candidates for both the confraternity and the military order.[45]

The anthology contains twelve compositions setting texts that honour the Virgin and St. Michael, along with the Jesuits St. Ignatius Loyola and St. Francis Xavier (see Table 10.1 for a transcription of the index).

TABLE 10.1 The contents of *Flores verni ex viridario Oslaviensi divis tutelaribus Communionis Hierarchicae sacri* [...] (Oslavany, Caspar Haugenhoffer: 1628)

	Entries as given in the Ordo et Index Cantionum	*Honoree*
1	*Ave Maria*. Motetum cum symphonia, a 2. Ten. 2. Cant. & 2. Violini. *Ad. Banchieri.*	Virgin Mary
2	*Iubila popule meus*. Cantilena, a 6. Bas. Alt. 2 Ten. & 2. Cant. *M. Oslaviensis, notis Stephani Bernardi.*	Virgin Mary
3	*Stabat mater dolorosa*. Hymnus, a 2. Cant. & Ten. *F. Anerij.*	Virgin Mary
4	*O quam pulchra es*. Concertus, a 2. Ten. & Cant. *del Milleuille.*	Virgin Mary
5	*Quando praeliabatur*. Aria, a 2. Cant. & Alt. ò Bas. *M. Oslaviensis, symphonia Galiazzi de Sabbatinis.*	St. Michael the Archangel
6	*Magne Dux paradisi*. Madrigale, a 2. Cant. 2. Ten. Bas. & Alt. *M. Oslaviensis symphonia Stephani Bernardi.*	[St. Michael the Archangel]

---

44 Sehnal, *Adam Michna* 12.
45 See *Flores verni*, verso of title-page: 'Candidato ordinis Militiae Christianae, et Communionis Hierachicae [sic], Principi juuentutis in seminario paterno [...]'.

TABLE 10.1 The contents of *Flores verni ex viridario Oslaviensi* [...] (*cont.*)

	Entries as given in the Ordo et Index Cantionum	Honoree
7	*Princeps gloriosissime.* Cantio, a 2. Cant. & Bas. *Rud. Lassi.*	St. Michael the Archangel
8	*Gaudeamus omnes.* Introitus Missae, a 3. Ten. *Rug. Giouanelli.*	St. Ignatius Loyola
9	*Sancte Confessor.* Madrigale, a 2. Cant. 2. Ten. Bas. & Alt. *M. Oslaviensis symphonia Stephani Bernardi.*	St. Ignatius Loyola
10	*Quasi stella Matutina.* Concertus, a 2. Cant. & Bas. *F. Pij.*	St. Francis
11	*Sancte Francisce.* Motetum, a 2. Ten. & Bas. *Agiuti Cornettae.*	Francis Xavier
12	*Exaltate Deo.* Psalmus, Cant. Solo. *Nicolai Corradini.*	? [not present in source]

The pieces are composed for one to six voices, and at least some required a basso continuo. What the index omits can be filled in from other sources for the compositions. Francesco Milleville's *O quam pulchra es*, for example, is known to have been written for three voices and continuo, from its appearance a few years earlier in Lorenzo Calvi's *Seconda raccolta di sacri canti* (Venice, Alessanro Vincenti: 1624). One item, the *Ave Maria* setting by Adriano Banchieri which opens the print, calls for additional instruments: the 'Ordo et Index Cantionum' specifies two violins in addition to the four singers (two cantus and two tenors), a scoring reinforced by the genre designation 'motetum cum symphonia'.

The compiler's insistence on categorising the pieces by genre echoes the generic plenitude broadcast on the print's title-page, but is also suggestive of his sensitivity to style: Milleville's *O quam pulchra es* is aptly described as a 'concerto', for instance. For all its detail, however, the index raises questions about genre, authorship, and the relationship of the contents to music previously printed elsewhere. Moreover, while it is clear enough that the Banchieri rubric '*cum* symphonia' (emphasis mine), refers to the presence of instrumental sinfonias, it is harder to determine what 'symphonia' means when it appears without the prefatory *cum*, as it does in the index entries for three pieces attributed to an otherwise anonymous 'Magister Oslaveniensis'. For all three – *Quando praeliabatur* and *Magne Dux*, both for St. Michael, and *Sancte confessor*, for St. Ignatius – an additional composer is named. A similar double attribution is given for *Iubila popule meus*, although in this case the word 'notis' is used instead of 'symphonia' ('Magister Oslaviensis, notis Stephani Bernardi'). The proliferation of genre designations – motet, cantilena, aria, concerto, madrigal – is also puzzling, and the rationale for their use is not immediately evident.

Symptomatic of Haugenhoffer's inexperience in printing music, the *Flores verni* has typographic errors more serious than the odd misplaced letter: metre signatures are sometimes inconsistent (as in *Jubila popule meus*, which gives both C and ₵) and pitches are occasionally misplaced. Also, in *Jubila popule meus*, B-flat signatures which signal the *cantus mollis* system are not always indicated and where they are missing, accidentals were not added within the system to compensate. Still, the multitude of handwritten corrections in the surviving partbook indicate that the music was singable and that, where it was not, care was taken to make it so.

It is tempting to brush away these odd designations as the eccentricities of a compiler seeking in the first place to impress, the opaque terminology as symptoms of a struggle to organise stylistically diverse pieces, and the unusual double attributions as misattributions. Yet the compiler was an accomplished Italian composer, well-versed in the old and new styles, and it is unlikely he did not have something specific in mind when compiling the index. Imagining the logistical challenges he faced in putting together even a single volume of repertory suitable for the very specific devotional needs of Althann's confraternity and the Vienna and Oslavany seminaries is suggestive, inviting a closer look at both the texts and the underlying musical fabric. Scrutiny of *Quando praeliabatur* in this way helps explain both the double attribution – to Galiazzo Sabbatini (1597–1662) and the 'Magister Oslaviensis – and the curious use of the word *symphonia* in a composition without obbligato instruments. That the text is otherwise unknown opens up the possibility that it is a contrafact. Searching Sabbatini's *Il primo libro de madrigali concertati a due, tre e quattro voci* (Venice, Alessandro Vincenti: 1625) for two cantus and alto or bass reveals that this aria for St. Michael is in fact a Latin re-texting of Sabbatini's setting of an Alessandro Striggio text ('Eran ninfe e Pastori') from *Il Trionfo di Dori*. 'Symphonia' is thus meant here in the venerable sense of sonic concord and is the term Abbate used to signal the composer of the music. 'Magister Oslaviensis', probably Abbate, devised a new text that would both fit the pre-existing music and be useful for the feast days which the confraternity was obligated to celebrate with music. Based on this, it is probable that both *Magne Dux* and *Sancte confessor* are also contrafacts, in this case of compositions by Stefano Bernardi (1580–1637). Indeed, it is impossible not to note that the text for *Magne Dux* hails 'the leader of our Militia, invincible on the seas and on earth' ('Caput nostrae Militiae invictum in mari et in terra').

Accounting for the six-voice *Jubila popule meus* setting 'notated' ('notis') by Stefano Bernardi is less straightforward, but puzzling through the problem hints at circulation networks that otherwise leave few traces. None of

EX. 10.1   Ludovico Manfredi di Guastalla, *Jubila popule meus* (opening)

Bernardi's pre-1628 music prints calls for more than five voices, much less the unusual scoring of two cantus, alto, two tenors and bass. Significantly, the text *Jubilate popule meus* is rare but not unique, and thus unlikely to be a contrafact. It appears in two other prints: the *concerti ecclesiastici* for two, three, four, and six voices by the Franciscan friar Lodovico Manfredi di Guastalla (d. 1632), first printed in 1620 and its 1623 reprint.[46] Combining the two cantus parts that are preserved in the sole surviving *Flores verni* partbook with the three voices (Altus, Basso, Quintus) that survive from Manfredi's 1620 print creates a harmonious and up-to-date invitation to jubilate [Ex. 10.1].

The designation 'notis Stephani Bernardi' may simply mean, then, exactly what it says: that it was 'notated by Bernardi', and that Abbate obtained his copy of the piece from Bernardi. Bernardi was active in central Europe at this time, first in Neisse (Nysa, Lower Silesia) in 1623–1624 while in the service of Archduke and Prince-Bishop of Breslau Karl Joseph von Österreich, and by 1627 in Salzburg, where he served Archbishop Paris Lodron.

---

46   Manfredi di Guastalla Lodovico, *Il primo libro di concerti ecclesiastici a due, tre, quattro, e sei voci* [...] *con il Basso Continuo per sonar nell'Organo* (Venice, Alessandro Vincenti: 1620); reprinted in 1623.

3 Conclusions

The final references in Christian of Anhalt-Bernburg's diary to Althann's redemption projects are dated January 1642, in the grim final decade of the Thirty Years' War. The prince records a conversation with Emperor Ferdinand III's brother, Archduke Leopold Wilhelm, which turned to recollections of Althann who had died six years earlier, and whose hopes, in their judgment, had fallen victim to terrible circumstance. The archduke commented that the old count had meant well with his Turkish campaigns, but was too frail to take on such a burden alone.[47] He added that if the princes of Christendom had taken up the struggle against the Ottomans together, rather than quarreling amongst themselves, they would already be in Constantinople. Instead, he lamented, there was war everywhere – Germany, Spain, Italy, the Netherlands, England, Scotland and Ireland – 'spreading internally, like a wildfire'.[48]

Founded on the eve of the Thirty Years' War to establish peace among Christian princes and drive the Ottomans out of Europe and the Holy Land, the Militia Christiana was a failure by its own measure: Christian princes fought each other viciously and Ottomans pushed even further into the Empire. The Order itself, which had only ever established footholds in Greece, Wallachia and Bosnia, disappeared by the middle of the seventeenth century. As the French Jesuit historian Philippe Briet put it, the Militia was "a work of splendid appearance […], started with greater pomp than wisdom allowed, [which] […] vanished, to the laughter of the Christians and the contempt of the Muslims".[49] A few decades later, the English antiquarian Elias Ashmole mused picturesquely that it seemed as though 'that notable Comet, which appeared […] four days after [the Order] was instituted, showed its sudden splendor and

---

47 See the diary entry dated 21 January 1642, as transcribed in *Digitale Edition und Kommentierung der Tagebücher des Fürsten Christian II. von Anhalt-Bernburg (1599–1656)*, Asch R.G. – Burschel P. (eds.); see http://diglib.hab.de/edoc/ed000228/id/edoc_ed000228_fg_1642_01_sm/start.htm (accessed 1 July 2023).

48 See the diary entry dated 21 January 1642, as transcribed in *Digitale Edition und Kommentierung der Tagebücher des Fürsten Christian II. von Anhalt-Bernburg (1599–1656)*, Asch R.G. – Burschel P.; see http://diglib.hab.de/edoc/ed000228/id/edoc_ed000228_fg_1642_01_sm/start.htm (accessed 1 July 2023): 'Itzt wehre krieg überall, in Deutzschlandt, Spannien, Italien, Niederlandt, Engellandt, Schottlandt, Irrlandt, undt kröch[e] der krieg umb sich, wie ein lauffendes Fewer'.

49 Briet Philippe, *Pars Quarta Tomi Secundi a Capta Constantinopoli per Turcas ad praesentem annum seu Ab anno Christi 1453. ad 1663* (Paris, F. Muguet: 1663) 429: 'magnum in speciem opus, et majori inchoatum pompa quam prudentia propagatum, quod tandem etiam cum Christianorum risu evanuit, cum Mahumetanorum contemptu […]'.

decay', and concluded, somewhat disdainfully, that 'the Mahumetans, for whose destruction it was instituted, heard only the name and report of it'.[50]

Briet and Ashmole were right: the Militia Christiana and the Communio Hierarchica pro Redemptione Captivorum fell far short of their founders' promises. The Militia's footholds were limited to Greece, Wallachia and Bosnia. The confraternity spread at least to Poland, where it was championed by the Polish Franciscan friar and composer Wojciech Dembołęcki, and it is suggestive that a copy of the confraternity's 1624 statutes survives today in Slovenia, even though it made little headway elsewhere.[51] What Briet and Ashmole could not discern from their distant vantage points, however, was that Althann's musical aspirations for his Christian soldiers left an enduring mark on the region, laying the groundwork for musical institutions that were ultimately more successful. His devotional and musical priorities – commitment to the Immaculate Conception, cultivation of the *stile moderno*, instruction in both vocal and instrumental music – were absorbed into these other institutions. By 1630, the personnel connected to the Oslavany seminary (including, not least, Gramaye) had relocated to Mikulov. Cardinal Dietrichstein had recently founded his own musical seminary there, led by the Piarist teaching order, which Althann had in 1625 proposed might be spiritually united with his military order and confraternity.[52] Two years later, Dietrichstein reissued the confraternity's statutes in Vienna, updating them with reference to his own projects in Moravia, but dedicating the print to Althann, the brotherhood's elderly founder.[53]

Bibliography

Primary Sources

Abbate Carlo, *Regulae contrapuncti excerptae ex operibus Zerlini et aliorum ad breviorem Tyronum instructionem accommodate* [sic, lege accomodatae] *per Fratrem Carolum Abbate* [sic, lege abbatem] *Genuensem, Ord. Min. Conv. Illustris. Rev. et Exc. Principis. Card. à Dietrichstain etc. Sacellanum et Musicum* (Oslavany, Caspar Haugenhoffer: 1629).

---

50   Ashmole Elias, *The Institution, Laws & Ceremonies of the Most Noble Order of the Garter* (London, J. Macock: 1672) 94.
51   Dembołęcki Wojiech, *Summula Statutorum communionis hierarchiae plenitudinis aetatis Jesu pro redemptione captivorum* [...] (Warsaw, Joannes Rosowski: 1626).
52   Parma, "Jean-Baptiste Gramay" 296.
53   Dietrichstein Franz Seraph von, *Vocatio, Institutum, et Confirmatio Communionis Hierarchiae Plenitudinis Aetatis Jesu vel Descriptionis Militiae Aetatis Jesu* (Vienna, Gregorius Gelbhaar: 1632).

[Abbate Carlo (ed.)?], *Flores verni ex viridario Oslaviensi divis tutelaribus Communionis Hierarchicae sacri; Id est, De Centuria Musica exercitus litterarii Militiae Christianae, continente Missas, Psalmos, Hymnos, Cantica, Odas, Motetas, Concertos, Cantilenas, Arias, et Madrigalia sacra praestantissimorum Orbis et saeculi nostri Musicorum. Manipulus ex novem primus* (Oslavany, Caspar Haugenhoffer: 1628).

[Althann Michael Adolph von (ed.)?], *Institutio, confirmatio, et statuta Communionis hierarchiae [sic] plenitudinis aetatis IESU pro solatio afflictorum et in primis captivorum Turcicorum* (Vienna, Matthaeus Formica: 1624).

Anhalt-Bernburg Christian II von, *Digitale Edition und Kommentierung der Tagebücher des Fürsten Christian II. von Anhalt-Bernburg (1599–1656)*, ed. Asch R.G. and P. Burschel P. (Wolfenbüttel: 2013).

Ashmole Elias, *The Institution, Laws & Ceremonies of the Most Noble Order of the Garter* (London, J. Macock: 1672).

Briet Philippe, *Pars Quarta Tomi Secundi a Capta Constantinopoli per Turcas ad praesentem annum seu Ab anno Christi 1453. ad 1663* (Paris, F. Muguet: 1663).

Dembołęcki Wojiech, *Summula Statutorum communionis hierarchiae plenitudinis aetatis Jesu pro redemptione captivorum [...]* (Warsaw, Joannes Rosowski: 1626).

Dietrichstein Franz Seraph von, *Zwo Predigten deren Eine am Hochheyligen Fest unser lieben Frawen Verkündigung uber gleich damahls in den Marggraffthumb Mähren wegen der Religions Reformation Herrn- und Ritterstands publicierte Patenten [...] Die Ander am Sontag Laetare von der Com[m]union under Einerley gestalt* (Oslavany, Caspar Haugenhoffer: 1628).

Gramaye Jean-Baptiste, *Africae illustratae libri decem, in quibus Barbaria, gentesque eius ut olim, et nunc describuntur [...]* (Tournai, Adrianus Quinque: 1622).

Gramaye Jean-Baptiste, *Diarium rerum Argelae gestarum Ab Anno MDCXIX. In quo Argelae descriptio, vita, Religio, et mores Barbarorum, miseria Captivorum statusque Ecclesiae Africanae describuntur* (Cologne, Albinus Dusseldorpff: 1623).

Harrach Ernst Adalbert von, *Die Diarien und Tagszettel des Kardinals Ernst Adalbert von Harrach (1598–1667)* 2: Diarium 1629–1646, ed. Keller K. – Catalano A. (Vienna – Cologne – Weimar: 2010).

Khevenhüller Franz von, *Annales Ferdinandei* vol. 9 (Vienna, Matthaeus Cosmerovius: 1646).

Márquez, José Micheli y, *Tesoro militar de Cavalleria* (Madrid, Diego Diaz de la Carrera: 1642).

Mennens Franz, *Militiarium Ordinum origines, statuta, symbola, insignia, Iconibus additis genuinis* (Cologne, Petrus Salvinus: 1623).

Mercure francois 5 (Paris, Estienne Richer: 1619).

Žalanský Hawel, *O Posluchačjch Swatého Ewangelium* (Prague, Jonata Bohutský: 1615).

Secondary Sources

Cypess R., "Girolamo Frescobaldi's *Fiori musicali*: Music and Flowery Metaphors in Early Modern Europe", *Journal of the Society for Seventeenth-Century Music* 2.1 (2022); https://sscm-jscm.org/jscm-issues/volume-28-no-1/.

d'Elvert C., "Der Althan'sche Christus-Orden: Der christliche Vertheidigungsbund", *Notizen-Blatt der Historisch-Statistischen Section der Kaiserlich-Königliche Mährisch-Schlesische Gesellschaft zur Beförderung des Ackerbaues, der Natur- und Landeskunde* (1883) 12–13.

Escrivà-Llorca F., "Soundscapes and Brotherhood in Processions of the Redemption of Captives: The Case of Early Modern Valencia (Spain)", *Confraternitas* 31.1 (2020) 86–107.

Louthan H., "Religious Art and the Formation of a Catholic Identity in Baroque Prague", in Cohen G.B. – Szabo F.A.J. (eds.), *Embodiments of Power: Building Baroque Cities in Europe*, (New York: 2008) 53–79.

Maťa P., "Giovanni Vincenzo d'Arco: Křesťanský rytíř s múzou a mečem", in Tongoni G. – Turrini R. (eds.), *La fabbrica della Collegiata* (Arco: 2013) 199–225.

Maťa P., "Giovanni Vincenzo Conte d'Arco: Un Cavaglier Christiano tra armi e lettere", in Tongoni G. – Turrini R. (eds.), *La fabbrica della Collegiata* (Arco, 2013) 65–110.

Maťa P., "Das *Phasma Dionysiacum Pragense* und die Anfänge des Faschings am Kaiserhof", in Marschall B. (ed.), *Theater am Hof und für das Volk: Festschrift für Otto G. Schindler zum 60. Geburtstag* (Vienna: 2002) 67–80.

Parma T., "Řád Křesťanského rytířstva: mezi řeholní společností a konfraternitou", *Folia Historica Bohemica* 26 (2011) 247–265.

Parma T., "Jean-Baptiste Gramay, primas Afriky, titulární arcibiskup upsalský a administrátor oslavanský", *Časopis Matice Moravské* 131 (2012) 285–310.

Parrott D., "A *prince souverain* and the French Crown: Charles de Nevers, 1580–1637", in Oresko R. – Gibbs G.C. – Scott H.M. (eds.), *Royal and Republic Sovereignty in Early Modern Europe* (Cambridge: 1997) 149–187.

Pecho C., *Fürstbischof, Putschist, Landesherr: Erzherzog Leopold und sein alternativer Habsburger Herrschaftsentwürfe im Zeitalter des Dreissigjährigen Kriegs* (Berlin: 2017).

Seifert H., "Italian Musical Dramatic Genres at the Courts of the Austrian Habsburgs", in Weaver A. (ed.), *A Companion to Music at the Habsburg Courts in the Sixteenth and Seventeenth Centuries* (Leiden – Boston: 2021) 255–272.

Sehnal J., *Adam Michna of Otradovice-Composer: Perspectives on Seventeenth-Century Sacred Music in the Czech Lands*, Fiehler J. trans. (Olomouc: 2016).

Sehnal J., "Die adeligen Musikkapellen im 17. und 18. Jahrhundert in Mähren", in Biba O. – Jones D.W. (eds.) *Studies in Music History presented to H.C. Robbins Landon on his Seventieth Birthday* (London: 1996) 195–217.

Štědroň M., "Hudba v pražské slavnosti 'Phasma Dionysiacum' z roku 1617 (Konfrontace a posuny)", in Kroupa J. (ed.), *Ars Naturum Adjuvans: Sborník k poctě profesora PhDr. Miloše Stehlíka* (Brno: 2003) 10–14.

Trolda E., "Účast Moravy a Slezska na církevní hudbě v XVIII. Století", *Česká hudba* 24 (1920) 33–42.

Warmington F., "The Ceremony of the Armed Man: The Sword, the Altar, and the *L'homme armé* Mass", in Higgins P. (ed.), *Antoine Busnoys: Method, Meaning, and Context in Late Medieval Music* (Oxford: 1999) 89–139.

Winkelbauer T., *Fürst und Fürstendiener: Gundaker von Liechtenstein, ein österreichischer Aristokrat des konfessionellen Zeitalters* (Vienna: 1999).

CHAPTER 11

Confraternities, Congregations and Aural Culture in Counter-Reformation Germany

Alexander Fisher

Abstract

The fate of confraternities in post-Reformation Germany was profoundly shaped by the history of religious division. On the eve of the Reformation, major cities like Cologne and Augsburg enjoyed a vibrant confraternal tradition balancing spiritual devotion and public charity, but the advancement of Lutheranism would undermine confraternities alongside traditional clerical, monastic and devotional culture. The Council of Trent would lay the groundwork for a revival in confraternities in the German-speaking lands (as elsewhere), but a crucial question would be the degree to which they would be instrumentalised in the service of Catholic reform and renewal. If some late-medieval confraternities managed to persist, many new confraternities emerging in the late sixteenth and early seventeenth centuries devoted themselves to potentially divisive spiritual objects – the Virgin Mary, the Eucharist, the Rosary, and the communion of Saints – and explicitly embraced a Tridentine agenda. The most striking development was the Jesuit establishment of Marian Congregations whose membership cut across lines of social class and, eventually, gender as well. The marked increase in confraternities and Jesuit-led congregations in German cities was accompanied by a soundscape that embraced songs, litanies, polyphony and a variety of other acoustic phenomena. The periodic meetings of confraternities were a locus for music of varying sophistication, while the processions that increasingly shaped urban space featured sounds ranging from songs, litanies and polyphony to bell-ringing and even gunfire. Songs were prescribed in confraternal statutes and handbooks, and some confraternities (such as the Andernach Confraternity of St. Cecilia and the Ingolstadt Congregation of Mary Victorious) even enjoyed bespoke songbooks printed for their use. Collections of litanies were published with the devotions and processions of confreres in mind, most notably the great *Thesaurus litaniarum* (1594) by the music director of the Munich Jesuits, Georg Victorinus. Some confraternities enjoyed rather sophisticated musical cultures and formed ready audiences for the burgeoning amount of distinctly Catholic polyphony issued by German presses after 1600. Specific collections issued by composers like Bernhard Klingenstein, Gregor Aichinger, and Rudolph di Lasso – some of them confreres themselves – offered music suited to a range of abilities, thus situating confraternities as a nexus where varied Catholic acoustic cultures might blend and interact.

Keywords

confraternities – Germany – Counter-Reformation – music – sound

The caesura of the Protestant Reformation profoundly changed the fundamental nature and sonic expressions of German confraternities. By the late fifteenth century, many German cities enjoyed a vibrant tradition of lay confraternities, brotherhoods that balanced spiritual devotion with a wide range of charitable functions, and that operated with some independence from ecclesiastical oversight.[1] But in the sixteenth century the foundations of confraternal life began to crumble in areas receptive to Reformation thought, as the intercessory cult of the saints and the Virgin Mary came under sustained attack and civic magistrates began to assume responsibility for public charity. In this environment many lay brotherhoods faltered, paralleling a broader crisis in monastic institutions and in church discipline more generally.[2] The Council of Trent made gestures toward the regulation and supervision of confraternities, but clerical oversight was first strictly prescribed in Clement VIII's bull *Quaecumque* of 1604, which insisted that bishops supervise the founding and regulation of confraternities, and personally approve their statutes.[3]

By this time there was a remarkable expansion in German lay confraternities, soon to be joined by an increasing number of Marian sodalities or congregations (*sodalitas, congregatio*) founded by the Society of Jesus for a variety of ages and social groups. Established during a time of increasing confessional tensions across the German-speaking lands, post-Tridentine confraternities tended toward demonstrative, and even militant, expressions of Catholic identity that deepened religious fissures: confraternal devotions and

---

1   On the background of late medieval and early modern German confraternities, see: Becker T.P., *Konfessionalisierung in Kurköln: Untersuchungen zur Durchsetzung der katholischen Reform in den Dekanaten Ahrgau und Bonn anhand von Visitationsprotokollen 1583–1761* (Bonn: 1989) 181–96; and Schneider W. "Wandel und Beharrung. Bruderschaften und Frömmigkeit in Spätmittelalter und früher Neuzeit", in Molitor H. – Smolinsky H. (eds.), *Volksfrömmigkeit in der frühen Neuzeit* (Münster: 1994) 65–84.
2   Schneider, "Wandel und Beharrung" 67.
3   Ibidem 67–68.

processions were sites in which both visual and aural media reshaped confessional space in sometimes provocative ways.[4]

Aural culture responded in distinctive ways to the demonstrative confessionalisation of post-Tridentine confraternities. Evidence for the musical culture of confraternities is mainly evident along two axes that will comprise the first part of this chapter: their regular meetings and devotions, generally conducted in consecrated worship spaces; and secondly, in the context of their increasingly vibrant and demonstrative culture of processions and pilgrimages to holy places. It will be seen that confraternities with substantial means and aspirations could routinely engage professional musicians, obtain music and instruments, and even hire musical directors to lead ensembles and performances. The second part of this chapter explores the substantial, yet little studied, repertory of published music that can be connected with German confraternities and congregations in the post-Tridentine period through the era of the Thirty Years War. Confraternities were ideal audiences for Catholic hymnody: particular songbooks were sometimes prescribed for their use, and a number of confraternities even enjoyed bespoke printed collections designed for their devotions and processions. The prominent sonic role of the recited or sung litany in both services and processions, moreover, encouraged the publication of polyphonic litanies in a variety of styles suited to both mobile and fixed ensembles. Finally, a number of polyphonic musical collections – some composed by confreres themselves – can directly be connected to confraternities and congregations in Würzburg, Speyer, Augsburg and Munich. Consideration of these repertories, representing a range of sophistication from vernacular song to elaborate polyphony, encourages a more holistic understanding of Catholic soundscapes in an age of post-Tridentine reform and heightening confessional tensions.

---

4   Ibidem 67–68; see also: Remling L., *Bruderschaften in Franken. Kirchen- und sozialgeschichtliche Untersuchungen zum spätmittelalterlichen und frühneuzeitlichen Bruderschaftswesen* (Münster: 1986) 30–32. In this chapter, the terms 'congregation' or 'sodality' will specifically denote the Marian Congregations established by the Jesuits, while the term 'confraternity' will be used for other lay brotherhoods, some of which predated the arrival of the Society of Jesus in Germany. By the seventeenth century, confraternities routinely admitted women; independent female 'consororities' were far more rare (but note the Consorority of St. Ursula at Cologne, discussed below).

1   German Confraternities and Aural Culture

The musical legacy of pre-Reformation confraternities is difficult to trace in detail, but it is known that a variety of liturgical plainchant was sung during their regular services and processions. Sacramental (Corpus Christi) confraternities, for example, typically celebrated a weekly *Engelamt* or *Engelmesse* (a devotional Mass honouring the Virgin Mary) that was attached to a theophoric procession; among the favoured liturgical antiphons were those associated with the feast of Corpus Christi like *O quam suavis, O sacrum convivium,* or *Homo quidam fecit*.[5] Confreres conceivably participated in the singing, but more generally they engaged the parish schoolmaster and choirboys who were compensated with money, food, or drink.[6] Some confraternities endowed special services featuring the singing of the Marian antiphon *Salve Regina*, such as the St. Sebastian confraternity at Römhild, which in 1483 donated a *Salve* service 'for the aid and comfort' of their members that would be performed by the schoolmaster in the church every evening between the feasts of the Assumption and the Nativity of the Virgin Mary.[7] Given that confraternities conceived of themselves as corporations of both the living and the dead, the commemoration of those who had recently died was a central task: they celebrated regular vigils and Masses for the dead (*Totenvigil, Seelamt*) with the musical assistance of the schoolmaster and his students.[8]

The post-Tridentine church laid the groundwork for a revival in confraternal culture generally, including in the German-speaking lands. A crucial difference, though, was the extent to which lay devotion would be instrumentalised in the service of Tridentine reform and renewal. While some confraternities maintained the looser corporate model of the late Middle Ages – the example of Cologne, an imperial city whose magistracy never embraced the Reformation, is especially striking here[9] – many new or refounded confraternities devoted themselves to distinctive and potentially divisive objects, including the Virgin Mary, the Eucharist, the Rosary, the saints or departed souls in purgatory. Male elites such as local bishops, nobility, patricians and the religious orders urged the foundation of confraternities and regulated their activities through

---

5   Remling, *Bruderschaften in Franken* 222–236, citing Franconian examples from Schleusingen, Hildburghausen, Schmalkalden and Mergentheim. See also: Brückner W., *Frommes Franken. Kult und Kirchenvolk in der Diözese Würzburg seit dem Mittelalter* (Würzburg: 2008) 28.
6   Remling, *Bruderschaften in Franken* 223–228.
7   Ibidem 245.
8   For Schmalkalden, see ibidem 223–224; see also: Schneider, "Wandel und Beharrung" 77–79.
9   Mallinckrodt R. von, *Struktur und kollektiver Eigensinn: Kölner Laienbruderschaften im Zeitalter der Konfessionalisierung* (Göttingen: 2005) 88–90.

published statutes, but their membership extended to broad sectors of the urban populace and increasingly included women as well, who sometimes outnumbered men.[10] The most significant development was the emergence of the Jesuit-founded Marian Congregations, organisations that fully embraced the ideals of post-Tridentine devotion and became large and conspicuous presences in many German cities of Catholic and mixed confession.[11] Devotional meetings and processions, featuring a variety of visual and aural media, were accordingly designed to reinforce Catholic identity from within and to impress – or provoke – Protestant bystanders.[12]

Reconstructing the musical culture of German confraternities is a challenging enterprise given the scattered nature of archival sources, but it can be concluded that music played an important role for many of them; in some cities otherwise lacking prominent and well-resourced musical ensembles (for example, Cologne) confraternities may have been leading sites for urban musical practice.[13] Regular confraternal meetings and devotions traditionally featured a limited repertory of liturgical plainsong: most commonly, the Trinitarian hymns *Veni Creator Spiritus* or *Veni Sancte Spiritus* opened their devotional gatherings, which otherwise featured varied complexes of prayer, sermons and exhortations. Confraternities routinely paid singers and musicians for the regular commemorations (*Besingnisse*) of recently deceased members, whose communion with the living persisted after death; these practices were especially important for the so-called *Totenbruderschaften* dedicated to prayer for souls in purgatory.[14] Special observances might be conducted for the

---

10 On male domination in post-Tridentine Marian piety, see: Heal B., *The Cult of The Virgin Mary in Early Modern Germany. Protestant and Catholic Piety, 1500–1648* (Cambridge: 2007) 279–281. On the considerable female confraternal membership in the Münster diocese, for instance, see: Laqua-O'Donnell S., *Women and the Counter-Reformation in Early Modern Münster* (Oxford: 2014) 68–70.

11 Duhr B., *Geschichte der Jesuiten in den Ländern deutscher Zunge in der ersten Hälfte des XVII. Jahrhunderts* (Freiburg im Breisgau – St. Louis: 1913), vol. II/2, 81–122.

12 Remling, *Bruderschaften in Franken* 31; see also Chatellier L., *The Europe of the Devout: The Catholic Reformation and the Formation of a New Society*, trans. J. Birrell (Cambridge – New York – Paris: 1989) 19–25.

13 Körndle F., "Die Musikpflege bei den Kölner Bruderschaften im Vergleich zu anderen Städten", in Pietschmann K. (ed.), *Das Erzbistum Köln in der Musikgeschichte des 15. und 16. Jahrhunderts* (Kassel: 2008) 157–169.

14 On the *Totenbruderschaften*, see: Mann H.J., "Die barocken Totenbruderschaften. Entstehung, Entwicklung, Aufgabe, Struktur, Verwaltung und Frömmigkeitspraxis. Ein kultur-, gesellschafts- und frömmigkeitsgeschichtliche Untersuchung", *Zeitschrift für bayerische Landesgeschichte* 39 (1976) 127–151. A 'Seelampt mit der Music', for example, was performed monthly by the Augsburg Confraternity of Departed Souls; see *Reglen vnd Ablas Sambt etlichen gebet der andechtigen Todten Brueserschafft bey den P. P. Dominicanern*

passing of noble princes and patrons. Following the death of Duke Wilhelm V of Bavaria in 1626, for instance, the Holy Cross Confraternity 'for a good death' met once per month in the Jesuit church of St. Michael to hear a sermon and to 'sing edifying German songs with the accompaniment of the organ'.[15] Times of celebration and renewal also compelled confraternities to provide suitable music, such as a performance of the festal Ambrosian hymn *Te Deum laudamus* for the election of new prefects and officers. For instance, the 1645 statutes of the Corpus Christi Confraternity at St. Peter's, Munich, prescribe that the election of a new prefect demanded the group's assembly before the exposed Sacrament in its monstrance, 'then first shall be sung a motet about the Venerable Sacrament, then a short sermon by the archconfraternity's priest should be heard, and then the *Te Deum laudamus* is to be begun, or a litany in its place'.[16] Extant statutes are generally vague on whether prescribed texts should be spoken or sung, but for the feast days of a confraternity's principal patron more specific directions are sometimes encountered. The statutes for the Munich Congregation of the Nativity of the Virgin Mary, for instance, prescribe that at the conclusion of second Vespers on that feast day, 'a figural [polyphonic] litany is sung at 5PM after Compline, and after this a procession is held with the most holy Sacrament'.[17]

Music and sound took on a distinctly political valence when confraternities reacted to reports of military victories or threats during the course of the Thirty Years War. Founded at Ingolstadt in 1612, the Congregation of Mary Victorious responded to the course of the war with particular vigour. The death of the Swedish king Gustavus Adolphus at the Battle of Lützen in November 1632 led the congregation in December to hear an exhortation, after which 'the hymn *Te Deum* was sung by five choirs of musicians in thanksgiving for various favours received, and especially for [our] victory and the death of the king of Sweden'.[18] The *Te Deum* was heard again in the congregation's oratorio in March 1634, when the allegedly treasonous Catholic general Albrecht von Wallenstein was assassinated in Bohemia, and once again in September four

---

      in Augspurg (Augsburg, Veronica Aperger: 1659) 7. For similar examples from Augsburg, see: Fisher A.J., *Music and Religious Identity in Counter-Reformation Augsburg, 1580–1630* (Aldershot: 2004), 165–166.

15   Sattler M.V., *Geschichte der Marianischen Kongregationen in Bayern* (Munich: 1869) 83.

16   Stadtarchiv München. Kirchen- und Kultusstiftungen 959 fol. 8r–v.

17   *Statuta. Regel, Ablas, vnd Gebett, der Hochlobl: vralten Bruderschafft* […] *der Seeligsten Jungfraw Mariæ Ihrer geburdt* (Munich, Nikolaus Heinrich: 1645) fol. [A8]r.

18   Stadtarchiv Ingolstadt. A v 19 fol. 9r. Note that this observance overlooks the fact of the Swedish victory despite the king's death in battle.

days after the Catholic victory at Nördlingen (6 September 1634).[19] Protestant military threats compelled the congregation to respond with penitential services including supplicatory litanies, such as in June of 1648:

> On 24 June at noon the sermon was attended by many, and the Rosary was recited in turns with our singing of the litanies of the holiest Name of Jesus in German, with two boys leading [the singing]. At noon on 29 June the same devotion was held in the company of much of the populace, with the exhortation, Rosary, and the singing of the litanies in the aforementioned manner. On 13 July, Tuesday in the Octave of the Dedication, and on Thursday and Saturday as well, at four o'clock in the afternoon, a [bell] signal having been given, the litanies of the holiest Name of Jesus were recited in German, led by the [congregation's] president, as well as the Rosary for the needs of those present and for the aversion of war.[20]

For their devotions many confraternities engaged external musicians, who were sometimes drawn from elite ensembles. The passing in 1578 of Count Bartholomäus von Portia, one of the early patrons of the Munich Marian Congregation, led this group to hold a memorial service with a Requiem Mass sung by the Bavarian ducal chapel under the direction of the famed Orlando di Lasso.[21] Two years later, the Congregation conducted a service on Maundy Thursday at the Jesuit college featuring darkened windows, a representation of Christ on the Mount of Olives, and a performance by the ducal chapel of Lasso's Penitential Psalms, music that heretofore had been reserved for the ears of the ducal family alone, but now sounded in a conspicuous public ritual.[22] Information about particular repertories performed during confraternal gatherings is very rare, but indications of payments for musicians are liberally scattered through archival sources. Processions or pilgrimages to remote locations sometimes required negotiations to secure musicians along the route or at the destination. The Landshut confraternities of the Holy Sepulchre, of Our Lady of Altötting and of the Rosary prominently featured in a September 1603

---

19 Hofmann, S., "Maria de Victoria – Nachruf auf die einstige Kirche der Kongregation Maria vom Sieg", *Sammelblatt des Historischen Vereins Ingolstadt* 85 (1976) 81–137, here 94.
20 Stadtarchiv Ingolstadt. A V 19, fol. 10r.
21 Sattler, *Geschichte der Marianischen Kongregationen in Bayern* 38, relying on the account of Lipowsky F. J., *Geschichte der Jesuiten in Baiern* (Munich: 1816) 190.
22 Crook D., "A Performance of Lasso's Penitential Psalms on Maundy Thursday 1580", in Schmid B. (ed.), *Orlando di Lasso in der Musikgeschichte* (Munich: 1996) 69–77; see also Sattler, *Geschichte der Marianischen Kongregationen in Bayern* 40–41; and Lipowsky, *Geschichte der Jesuiten in Baiern* 199.

pilgrimage to the parish church of Unsere Liebe Frau in Munich, where the relics of St. Benno, recently translated to this church, attracted an expanding following of devotees. The collegiate chapter of St. Martin and Castulus in Landshut fielded a musical ensemble for the pilgrimage, but also made requests to the bishop of Freising, the Munich Jesuits, and indeed the ducal court of Maximilian I of Bavaria, to provide musicians at various stages of the journey. As a result of these negotiations the sounds accompanying this pilgrimage would likely have included litanies and vernacular pilgrimage songs – indeed a new 'Andächtiger Rueff' for St. Benno had been published that year and may have been available to the pilgrims[23] – but also bell ringing upon departure, transit and arrival in the towns along the route, as well as polyphonic music in the churches where the pilgrimage made a station.[24]

Larger and well-endowed confraternities sometimes organised their own musical ensembles and directors and maintained inventories of music and instruments. The Cologne burghers' congregation, which had formally introduced singing for their devotions by 1612, formed a choir of singers that soon became an independent body within the group: those wishing to join had first to serve as assistants (*succentores*) before being admitted to the ensemble. Vernacular folksongs, psalms and litanies formed their repertory.[25] The 1616 statutes of the Confraternity of the Transfiguration of the Saviour at Würzburg make provision for both a prefect and vice-prefect for music, who were charged with organising and leading the musicians, and caring for the music books.[26] A 1653 inventory for the Congregation of the Purification of the Virgin Mary, also at Würzburg, enumerates twenty-seven diocesan songbooks, the *Catholische Sonn- und Feyertägliche Evangelia* with music by Philipp Friedrich Buchner, and a Franconian pilgrimage manual; the confraternity also possessed a regal with tin pipes and two violins.[27] At Ingolstadt, the Congregation of Mary Victorious had access to regals in its church by 1639, and received a new organ built by

---

23 *Ein Andächtiger Rueff für die Pilgram. Vom H. Bischoff Bennone: Darinn sein Leben gueten Theils, vnd etliche Wunderwerck begriffen* (Munich, Adam Berg: 1603) [lost].
24 Fisher A. J., *Music, Piety, and Propaganda: The Soundscapes of Counter-Reformation Bavaria* (New York: 2014) 326–329.
25 Müller A., *Die Kölner Bürger-Sodalität. 1608–1908* (Paderborn: 1909) 10, 40, 57.
26 *S. Salvatoris Transfigurati apud Wirceburgenses erectae Fraternitatis Ordinationes et Statuta* ([Würzburg]: 1616) fols. D3v–[D4]r.
27 Bayerisches Staatsarchiv Würzburg. Historischer Verein für Unterfranken und Aschaffenburg MS fol. 1103 67–68. The songs of the *Catholische Sonn- und Feyertägliche Evangelia* were published in two volumes at Würzburg in 1653 and 1656; their texts, consisting of rhymed paraphrases of the Gospels and Epistles, have been attributed to Archbishop Johann Philipp Schönborn of Mainz; see: Kirsch D. – Meierott L., "Geistliche und weltliche Musik in den mainfränkischen Territorien: Würzburg, freie Reichsstadt

Augustin Freund and Hans Georg Rumpf in 1646; a 1667 inventory indicates that the church's choir held 'nine sleeveless garments for musicians [...] a songbook for the musicians; 2 bass viols; 1 spinet; 1 alto viol; and 1 discant viol'.[28] In Munich, the Lesser Marian Congregation for Gymnasium students and laity is known to have a musical director by 1629, and in some later years engaged two men at once to hold this post, a move that speaks to a musical programme of some sophistication.[29] The precise repertory assembled by these directors is difficult to reconstruct, but a 1678 inventory of the music library of St. Peter's in Munich records a separate collection for the Corpus Christi Archconfraternity of music by 'autores novi': it includes concertato Masses and psalms by Georg Arnold, Masses by Jakob Banwart, motets by Maurizio Cazzati and Giovanni Legrenzi, and an anonymous concertato *Te Deum* for voices and instruments.[30] Though modest in size, the inventory confirms the archconfraternity's interest in modern concertato church music with a variety of vocal and instrumental timbres; it is conceivable, moreover, that the group was able to access the parish's much larger music library that this source indexes in detail.

To a degree the Marian Congregations in German towns participated in the vibrant tradition of Jesuit religious theatre, in which music could play a prominent role: even if, in most cases, the music itself is no longer extant.[31] For the canonisation of St. Ignatius and St. Xavier in 1622, the Congregation of the Annunciation of the Virgin Mary at Ingolstadt produced its own drama celebrating the lives of the two saints, in which a fifteen-voice choir of angels likely sang at the opening and conclusion.[32] In 1631 the same congregation mounted a 'teutschen Comoedi' on the life of St. Paul that probably featured

---

Schweinfurt und Aschaffenburg", in P. Kolb – E. Krenig (eds.), *Unterfränkische Geschichte* (Würzburg: 1999) vol. IV/2, 575.

28 Hofmann, "Maria de Victoria" 104–105, 136.
29 Bayerische Staatsbibliothek München. Clm 2323 fol. 91v and *passim*.
30 Pfarrarchiv St. Peter. 2 Ms. arch. 8 [no. 450-II] fols. 194v–195r. These prints can tentatively be identified as Arnold Georg, *Operis secundi liber I. missarum: psalmorum: et Magnificat a quinque vocibus* (Innsbruck, Michael Wagner: 1656; Répertoire International des Sources Musicales [RISM] A/I, A2162); Jakob Banwart, *Pars prima missarum brevium* (Konstanz, Johann Geng: 1649; no RISM siglum); Mauricio Cazzati, *Le concertate lodi della chiesa militante* (Milan, Giorgio Rolla: 1647; RISM A/I, C1580); and Giovanni Legrenzi, *Harmonia d'affetti devoti* (Venice, Alessandro Vincenti: 1655; RISM A/I, L1611).
31 On various examples of congregational plays from Eichstätt, Ingolstadt and Innsbruck see Scheitler I., *Schauspielmusik. Funktion und Ästhetik im deutschsprachigen Drama der Frühen Neuzeit* (Tutzing – Beeskow: 2015) vol. 2, 71–81. See also Duhr, *Geschichte der Jesuiten* vol. II/2, 115–116.
32 *Summarischer Jnhalt der Comœdien vnnd Triumph, von den Heyligen, IGNATIO DE LOYOLA Stiffter deß Ordens der Societet IESV; vnd FRANCISCO XAVERIO* (Ingolstadt, Gregor Hänlin: 1622) fol. D 3r.

instrumental as well as vocal music; at the conclusion the confraternity's 'Guardian Angel [...] invites the spectators again to [hear] a fine music'.[33] The title of the play *Maria* [...] *Dramate Paraenetico-Musico invocanda* presented in 1644 by the Cologne Marian Congregation tantalisingly suggests a substantial musical component, but the details are sadly lost.[34] The lack of surviving musical sources prevents a good understanding of the style of music performed by (or for) the sodalists in these productions, but the melodies may have resembled the accessible thoroughbass songs of composers like Johannes Khuen or the Jesuit Albrecht Graf Curtz.[35]

If polyphonic and instrumental music was demanded on festal occasions, everyday devotion probably featured a regular diet of vernacular song. Singing in German was a mode of reinforcing religious orthodoxy and of linking liturgical observance with lay devotion;[36] without question it was also a symbolic riposte to the now well-established repertory of Protestant chorales. The sodalists of the Jesuit Marian Congregations are known to have favoured vernacular translations of the Psalter, available with accessible melodies in Kaspar Ulenberg's *Die Psalmen Davids in allerlei Teutsche gesangreimen bracht* (1582).[37] For instance, the Cologne congregation for unmarried men [*Junggesellen*], which identified specific 'cantores' and 'succentores' among its members, regulated singing in a special 'Ratio cantus' (ca. 1650) that prescribed the regular performance of vernacular psalms; moreover, a dedicated index of the psalms from the years 1691 and 1694, arranged according to the sequence of the Sunday Gospels, is bound with a copy of Ulenberg's psalter owned by the Cologne burghers' sodality.[38] Exhortations to singing were frequently accompanied by admonishments to reject secular songs and those of the 'heretics'. Notable in this regard is the *Catholische Geistliche Gesänge* (Cologne: 1608) published by the Confraternity of St. Cecilia at Andernach, whose preface to the reader

---

33 Scheitler, *Schauspielmusik* vol. 2, 72–73.
34 Niemöller K.W., "Gottestracht und Ioculatores: die Anfänge des Musiktheaters in Köln", in Schwandt C. (ed.), *Oper in Köln. Von den Anfängen bis zur Gegenwart* (Berlin: 2007) 20–21.
35 See, for example, Curtz's *Harpffen Davids mit Teutschen Saiten bespannet* (Augsburg, Veronica Aperger: 1659). For discussion see Scheitler, *Schauspielmusik* vol. 2, 77.
36 Mallinckrodt, *Struktur und kollektiver Eigensinn* 185–187, 269–273, 397–408.
37 Ulenberg Kaspar, *Die Psalmen Dauids in allerlei Teutsche gesangreimen bracht* (Cologne, G. Calenius – J. Quentels Erben: 1582; RISM B/VIII, 1582⁰⁹).
38 The 'Ratio cantus' appears in Historisches Archiv der Stadt Köln. Jesuiten A 56 fols. 158v–160v. See also: Schmitz, A., "Archivstudien über die musikalischen Bestrebungen der Kölner Jesuiten im 17. Jahrhundert", *Archiv für Musikwissenschaft* 3 (1921) 421–446, here 442–443. On the 1691 and 1694 indices, see: Solzbacher J., "Die Psalmen Davids, in allerlei deutsche Gesangreime gebracht durch Kaspar Ulenberg, Köln 1582", *Kirchenmusikalisches Jahrbuch* 34 (1950) 41–55, here 54–55.

decries the Protestants for having driven out many 'holy and Godly songs' for the Virgin Mary and the saints:

> And in the place of the same [they introduced] a German Psalm and songbook (entitled the 'Bonn' Psalm or songbook), printed at Bonn, and planted it here and there in the minds of all; this [book] was used and loved so much (perhaps because no other German Catholic [book] was available at the time) that due to the lack of exemplars it was printed a second time, offered for sale, and through it some part of Lutheranism (which is now difficult to extirpate) is conserved and maintained.[39]

Indeed it was the success of this *Gsangbüchlein Geistlicher Psalmen* (Bonn: 1550), emphasising psalm paraphrases above all, that urged on the St. Cecilia confraternity to offer its own book as an alternative.[40] As will be seen, this was one of a number of printed songbooks that testify to the vibrancy of vernacular song as a devotional vehicle for confreres themselves and for the broader communities they hoped to influence.

For post-Tridentine confraternities demonstrative processions inculcated collective identity and shaped and projected a distinctly Catholic notion of urban space. After a long period of decline and neglect in the sixteenth century,[41] processions experienced a remarkable revival by the turn of the seventeenth, particularly at the hands of the Jesuits who prized open displays of confessional allegiance. Most confraternities mounted a procession on or around their titular feast day, but they also participated actively in processions with a stronger confessional valence, such as those for the feast of Corpus Christi, on the evening of Good Friday – often conducted by torchlight and featuring displays of self-flagellation – and for the translation of

---

39   *Catholische Geistliche Gesänge, Vom süssen Namen Jesu, vnd der Hochgelobten Mutter Gottes Mariae &c. Von der Fraternitet S. Ceciliae Zu Andernach in Lateinisch vnd Teutsche verß Componirt vnnd Collegirt* (Cologne, Gerhart Grevenbruch: 1608; RISM B/VIII, 1608⁰²), preface "An den Christlichen Leser".

40   *Gsangbüchlein Geistlicher Psalmen, hymnen, leider, vnd gebet, Durch etliche Diener der Kirchen zuo Bonn, fleissig zuosamen getragen, mercklich gemeret, vnd in geschickte Ordnung zusamen gestelt, zuo übung vnd brauch der Christlichen gemeine* (Bonn, Laurentius von der Mülen: 1550; RISM B/VIII, 1550⁰⁵). An earlier, 1544 edition is lost. See: Heidrich J., "Reformatorisches 'Strohfeuer' im Rheinland. Das *Bönnische Gesangbuch* von 1544", in Pietschmann (ed.), *Das Erzbistum Köln* 149–156, here 149–156. Another example of a warning against "Ketzerische Psalmen und gesäng" may be found in a 1610 manual for the Cologne burghers' sodality, the *Handbuchlein Der Bruderschafft unser L. Frawen und H. drei Koningen* (Cologne, Bernard Wolters: 1610) 193.

41   See, for instance, Becker, *Konfessionalisierung in Kurköln* 196–199.

relics to designated churches. In cities of mixed faith or in those close to the confessional frontier, these spectacles had the potential visually and aurally to provoke Protestant bystanders. In the biconfessional city of Augsburg, for instance, the Trinity Confraternity – whose principal devotional object was the nearby Eucharistic shrine of Andechs – made a request for papal indulgences that championed singing as provocation:

> Here in Augsburg, and in the countryside, this praiseworthy brotherhood has carried out many devotions and divine services (and still does); thus pious, Catholic, and ardent Christians have held public processions with banners into and out of all of the [city] gates, and organised several choirs in great numbers which sang German and Latin Litanies of All Saints, and many Protestants walking by saw this and stood there with terrified hearts, and many of them showed reverence to the clergy.[42]

Indeed a Protestant attack on such a procession in the city of Donauwörth in 1606 led to the loss of that city's free imperial status and its absorption by the Catholic duchy of Bavaria, an episode that helped to trigger the formation of the rival Protestant Union and Catholic League in the years leading up to the Thirty Years War.[43]

The sounds heard in confraternal processions are not often specified precisely, but the surviving evidence suggests a range of musical and non-musical sounds including vernacular songs, litanies, instrumental music, bell ringing, and sometimes the militaristic accompaniment of trumpets, drums and gunfire. To take the example of Würzburg, Bishop Philipp Adolf von Ehrenberg confirmed a new Corpus Christi Confraternity in 1630 whose opening service and procession on 12 May of that year has been carefully described.[44] Following a festal service at the cathedral featuring the bishop's court musicians, a lengthy procession of students, clergy, religious orders and confreres and consoeures set out, many bearing torches, candles, staves and banners; the focal point was the sacramental monstrance carried beneath a canopy, followed immediately by Bishop Ehrenberg himself. In the course of the

---

[42] *Concept der Bruderschafftt zum Heÿ: Berg Andex Suplication an die Bäbst: hey: zu Rom vmb zuerlanngen ettliche Indulgentias Anno Christi 1586*. Stadtarchiv Augsburg. Katholisches Wesensarchiv E458.

[43] Stieve F., *Der Kampf um Donauwörth im Zusammenhange der Reichsgeschichte* (Munich: 1875).

[44] Gropp I., *Wirtzburgische Chronick Deren letzeren Zeiten [...] Erster Theil von dem Jahr 1500. biß 1642* (Würzburg: 1748) 406–407.

procession were placed musicians from the linen bleachers' guild ('Plaicher Music') singing of the Venerable Sacrament; a group of student musicians ('Musica Studiosorum'); a group of 'clerical' musicians ('Musica Clericorum'); four trumpeters and the court musicians; instrumental musicians (likely the civic *Stadtpfeifer*) immediately preceding the monstrance; and musicians from the *Juliusspital* following behind, separating the men from the women. The rich aural tapestry of this founding procession suffused the city during a period of waxing fortunes for the imperial/Catholic forces in the Empire, coming in the wake of Emperor Ferdinand II's Edict of Restitution (1629) and shortly before the intervention of Gustavus Adolphus in Germany later that summer. In Ingolstadt, the Catholic victory at Nördlingen in September 1634 and the abatement of pestilence led the Congregation of Mary Victorious to join together with the Confraternity of St. Sebastian to mount a procession to the city's principal churches. It was claimed that 'over a thousand persons were counted in this procession. As it ended in our [the congregation's] oratorio, the Ambrosian hymn [*Te Deum laudamus*] was sung, during which festal explosions were heard three times from muskets and cannons, both large and small'.[45]

Confraternities and congregations directly organised the aforementioned processions, but on many other occasions they participated in civic processions involving a wider swathe of clergy, laity, religious orders and city magistrates. In many cities – Munich and Augsburg are notable in this regard – the annual Corpus Christi procession was a site of demonstrative and increasingly militaristic sounds, in which singing, litanies and musical performances were subsumed within a more militaristic soundscape punctuated by trumpet calls, drumming and the firing of muskets and cannon, all of which dramatised the Eucharist as a symbol of the church militant.[46] Moreover, the Marian Congregations formed the core of a series of conspicious processions organised in Cologne around the centennial of the founding of the Society of Jesus in 1640. In 1639 we read of a grand procession involving the ten catechism schools run by the Jesuits, the female Consorority of St. Ursula, the Burghers' Congregation, the Congregation of the Annunciation of the Virgin Mary, and other civic groups and musicians, who proceeded through the streets 'with pious songs and prayers'; at several stations the musicians performed, and were met with the 'clangor of trumpets mingled with drums'.[47] The centennial

---

45   Stadtarchiv Ingolstadt. A V 19 fol. 11r.
46   Fisher, *Music and Religious Identity* 245–256.
47   Schmitz, "Archivstudien" 439–440.

celebration on the feast of St. Ignatius the following year saw lavish processions and services: 'from here the clangor of trumpets and horns, from there the musicians' varied and sweet sounds of both voices and instruments, charmed not only the common people in the city, but also illustrious persons well into the night'.[48]

2   Musical Repertories Connected with Confraternities and Congregations

Compared with their counterparts south of the Alps, current understanding of the musical culture of German confraternities remains in its infancy, but the aforementioned evidence points to these groups as ready audiences for newly-published polyphonic music and vernacular songbooks.[49] The Marian Congregations, whose Jesuit patrons enjoyed active networks of musical transmission and deployed a wide range of music in their own services and devotional activities, can in fact be connected with a number of published collections that help to illustrate the range of music that might have been performed in both individual and corporate devotions.

An initial observation is that the published devotional books and statutes of confraternities – often issued by printers who did not routinely use the specialised technology of music typesetting – are frequently provided with texts that could have been sung, even in the absence of musical notation. A 1644 devotional book for the Confraternity of the Name of Jesus at the Benedictine cloister of Au am Inn, for instance, provides a quasi-liturgical sequence of texts (including litanies, psalms, collects, lections and hymns) for Rosary devotions and for canonical hours [*Tagzeiten*] of the feast of the Name of Jesus: the hymns or 'Lobgesänge' are individual strophes of 'O Jesu wie süß wer dein gedenckt', a widely-circulated German paraphrase of the medieval hymn 'Jesu dulcis memoria' attributed to Bernard of Clairvaux. At least two melodies connected to this text were in circulation by the time the confraternity's

---

48   Ibidem 440.
49   For Italy see, for instance: O'Regan N., *Institutional Patronage in Post-Tridentine Rome: Music at Santissima Trinità dei Pellegrini, 1550–1650* (London: 1995); idem, "Music at the Roman Archconfraternity of San Rocco in the Late Sixteenth Century", in Antolini B.M. et al. (eds.), *La musica a Roma attraverso le fonti d'archivio: Atti del Convengo internazionale, Roma 4–7 giugno 1992* (Lucca: 1994) 521–552; and Glixon J., *Honoring God and the City: Music at the Venetian Confraternities, 1260–1807* (Oxford: 2003). For Iberia, see the essays in Knighton T. (ed.), *Iberian Confraternities and Urban Soundscapes, Confraternitas* 31.2 (special issue) (2020).

Bruderschafftbüchel was published, most common being the following tune [Ex. 11.1].⁵⁰

EX. 11.1   "O Jesu süß wer dein gedenckt". Text from *Bruderschafftbüchel Deß süssen Namen Jesus* (Munich, Melchior Segen: 1644) 73

Examples of confraternal manuals providing singable texts without the aid of notation can easily be multiplied, but more striking is the publication of songs and songbooks explicitly for the use of confraternities and congregations. Large-scale songbooks connected directly to confraternities are rare; a notable exception is the aforementioned *Catholische Geistliche Gesänge* issued by the Confraternity of St. Cecilia at Andernach in 1608, a book of over 600 pages that rivals other comprehensive Catholic hymnals in scope.⁵¹ Far more common are shorter, pamphlet-sized collections. The complex of modest publications for the Trinity (Andechs) Confraternity at Augsburg issued in the 1580s by the cathedral vicar-choral Johann Haym von Themar suggests a range of devotional activities and languages: the series begins with a pair of German 'Creutzgesänge' on Christ's Passion and on the joys of paradise according to the writings of St. Augustine (1581); and continues with a trio of rudimentary polyphonic litanies designed for use during pilgrimages, the *Litaniae textus triplex* (1582). The *Christenliche Catholische Creutzgesang* (1584) offers songs on the Lord's Prayer, Hail Mary and Apostles' Creed, the recitation of

---

50   Text from *Bruderschafftbüchel Deß süssen Namen Jesus* (Munich, Melchior Segen: 1644) 73. Melody adapted from Bäumker, W., *Das katholische deutsche Kirchenlied in seinen Singweisen von den frühesten Zeiten bis gegen Ende des siebzehnten Jahrhunderts* (Freiburg – St. Louis: 1883) vol. 1, 386 no. 125. The melody had first appeared in *Catholische Kirchen Gesäng, auff die Fürnemste Fest deß gantzen Jahrs wie mann dieselb zu Cölln, vnnd anderstwo, bey allen Christlichen Catholischen Lehren pflegt zu singen* (Cologne, Peter von Brachel: 1619; RISM B/VIII, 1619⁰³). The less widely-circulated melody is also given by Bäumker in ibidem, vol. 1, 385 no. 124.

51   Of comparable size is the *Heylsamer Hertzentrost Das ist, Außerlesene Lobgeseng, vnnd Gedicht [...] Zu sondern Ehren der G[ott-] geliebten Bruderschafft vnserer [lie-] ben Frawen zu Würtzburg* (Würzburg, Conrad Schwindtlauff: 1615), a book of 560 pages for the Burghers' Congregation at Würzburg.

which gained the indulgences granted to the confraternity by Pope Sixtus V in 1587. The same year saw the publication of the *Drey Gaystliche und Catholische Lobgesang*, including Eucharistic songs to be sung in processions and after the Elevation in the Mass. Finally, Haym published the *Schöne Christenliche Catholisch Weinnächt oder Kindtleß wiegen Gesang* (1590), containing songs that customarily were sung during the Christmastide popular devotion of rocking the Christ child's cradle in the church; the book also contains a series of 'litanies' that are in fact monophonic songs (apparently newly composed) designed for processional and devotional use.[52]

The Marian Congregations of the Jesuits were also commonly the dedicatees of printed songs that might be used in their devotions and processions. The Congregation of Mary Victorious at Ingolstadt, for instance, received a set of Christmas songs in 1614 and, in 1616, a collection of songs on the virtues of penitence and humility, entitled *Hertzenmuth Der andächtigen Seel*. The songs in both prints had already been in circulation for some time, but were of relatively recent vintage and necessitated the addition of notated melodies by the printer.[53] Mirroring contemporary developments in secular song, Catholic songs increasingly added simple thoroughbass accompaniments that could easily be used or discarded according to circumstance. The major academic Congregation of the Annunciation at Würzburg received as a New Year's Gift in 1647 the *Sirenes Marianae*, a set of twenty-four thoroughbass songs in Latin on Marian and Christological themes; a revision, entitled *Sirenes Partheniae*, and a German version called *Keusche Meerfräwlein* for a broader

---

52   Haym von Themar Johann, *Ein Schön Lob oder Catholisch Creutzgesang, von der grosse frewd, zier, vnnd vnaussprechlichen Herrligkeit, deß Paradeyß* (Augsburg, Josias Wörli: 1581; RISM B/VIII, 1581[10]); ibidem, *Passion, oder Das aller heyligist bitter leiden vnd sterben Jhesu Christi* (Augsburg, Josias Wörli: 1581; RISM B/VIII, 1581[11]); ibidem, *Litaniae, textus triplex* (Augsburg, Josias Wörli: 1582; RISM A/I, H4905); ibidem, *Drey Gaystliche vnd Catholische Lobgesang, Christo vnserm einigen Seligmacher, vnd Mariæ allgemainer Christenhait fürbitten* (Augsburg, Josias Wörli: 1584; RISM B/VIII, 1584[13]); ibidem, *Christenliche Catholische Creutz gesang, vom Vatter vnser vnnd Aue Maria, von denn zwölff stucken deß Apostolischen Glaubens* (Augsburg, Josias Wörli: 1584; RISM B/VIII, 1584[12]); and ibidem, *Schöne Christenliche Catholisch Weinnächt oder Kindtleß wiegen Gesang* (Augsburg, Josias Wörli: 1590; RISM B/VIII, 1590[05]). See the discussion in Fisher, *Music and Religious Identity* 167–168, 259–261.

53   *Drey Andächtige Außerlesne WeyhnächtGesäng, darinn häilsame Lehrpuncten von der Geburt Christi begriffen* (Ingolstadt, Elisabeth Angermeyer: 1614; RISM B/VIII, 1614[08]); *Hertzenmuth Der andächtigen Seel. Das ist: Außerleßne, Andächtige, Lehr-vnd Geistreiche Gesänger* (Ingolstadt, Elisabeth Angermeyer: 1616; RISM B/VIII, 1616[11]). For further discussion, see: Fisher, *Music, Piety, and Propaganda* 147.

range of Marian Congregations would follow in 1649. The titles of these publications invoke the Homeric Sirens, vessels of temptation and seduction that are now turned to pious ends.[54] One of the most personal dedications to the Marian Congregations came in the form of the *Ehrenpreiß der allerseeligisten Jungkfrawen und Mutter Gottes Mariae* by Jakob Balde (1604–1668), a Jesuit poet, dramatist and preacher whose religious career is said to have begun during his law studies at Ingolstadt in 1624, when his nighttime serenade of a beloved was interrupted by the chaste sounds of Franciscan nuns chanting the liturgy from a nearby convent; he immediately smashed his lute and resolved upon a religious path.[55] The *Ehrenpreiß* may first have been published in 1638,[56] but the earliest extant edition of 1640 provides two slightly different versions of the same melody (one in the Dorian, the other in the Lydian mode), each with a thoroughbass accompaniment. The 1647 edition makes it clear that the Marian Congregations were the principal audience, as the title-page indicates that it was published 'for the benefit, comfort, and pleasure of the sodalists in the brotherhoods of our beloved Lady'.[57] Balde's poetry projects ecstatic devotion to the Virgin Mary, invoking the Marian sodalists directly in its thirty-third strophe:

---

54   *Sirenes Marianae, sive hymni in honorem B. Mariae V. et usum Partheniorum Sodalium concinnati* (Würzburg, Elias Michael Zinck: 1647); *Sirenes Partheniae, sive hymni, filio virginis, Christo Jesu, matri virgini Mariae sacri* (Würzburg, Elias Michael Zinck: 1649); *Keusche Meerfräwlein, Oder Geistliche Gesäng, CHRISTO IESV Vnserm Seligmacher: MARIÆ Seiner Gebenedeyten Mutter zu Ehren, auß Latein in Teutsch vbersetzt* (Würzburg, Elias Michael Zinck: 1649; RISM B/VIII, 1649[03]). On these publications see Hamacher T., "Sirenes Partheniae. Ein lateinisch-deutsches Gesangbuch des Barock", *Kirchenmusikalisches Jahrbuch* 52 (1968) 71–85; and Diergarten F., "Himmlische Sirenen und keusche Meerfräulein. Musik und katholische Reform in zwei Quellengruppen aus Würzburg und München", in F. Kleinehagenbrock, et al. (eds.), *Reformation und katholische Reform zwischen Kontinuität und Innovation* (Würzburg: 2019) 385–422. The invocation of the mythological sirens is echoed as well in another anthology of sacred concertos from Munich, the *Siren coelestis duarum, trium et quatuor vocum*, Georg Victorinus (ed.) (Munich, Adam Berg: 1616; RISM B/I, 1616[2]).

55   Westermayer G., *Jacobus Balde, sein Leben und seine Werke* (Munich: 1868) 16–17.

56   Duhr, *Geschichte der Jesuiten* vol. II/2, 121.

57   Balde Jakob, *Ehrenpreiß Der Allerseeligisten Jungkfrawen vnd Mutter GOttes MARAE Auff einer schlechten Harpffen jhres vnwürdigen Dieners gestimbt, und gesungen. Zu Nutz, Trost, und wolgefallen aller SODALIUM in vnser lieben Frawen Bruderschafften* (Munich, Lucas Straub: 1647; RISM B/VIII, 1647[12]).

Diß sey/ MARIA/ dir vertrawt
Von Tag zu Tag der Jahren:
Der dir vertrawt/ hat wol gebawt/
SODALES diß erfahren.
Jn letster Noth vnd bittern Todt/
Bitt/ thue mich nit verwerffen.
Erzaig dein Macht/ vertreib die Nacht:
Wirds jeder wol bedörffen.

Let this be entrusted to you, MARIA,
On each day of the year:
They who trust in you have raised themselves,
SODALISTS know this well.
In final need and bitter death,
Pray, cast me not away.
Show your power, dispel the night:
All shall well require it.

Balde's youthful tale is encoded here in the form of two notated monophonic melodies framed by the image of a shattered harp [Fig. 11.1]; above and below the harp appear the Latin captions 'Istos frangatur in usus […] Poterunt et frustra renasci' ('let them [i.e., the strings] be broken in use […] they can be remade, but in vain'), while the subtitle 'Sic quo[que] dulce sonat' ('This too sounds sweetly') is printed below the second melody. The restringing of the shattered harp, in other words, can serve no purpose compared with these sweet melodies.[58] The absence of the bass part illustrates how devotional thoroughbass songs could pivot between monophony and polyphony, depending on circumstance.

Even if published collections of Catholic song had multiple audiences – religious orders, students, catechists and lay devotees more generally – confraternities and congregations may have been the most immediate targets for compilers and printers. Erika Heitmeyer, for instance, has argued strongly that the expanded selection of Marian songs in the 1628 edition of the Paderborn *Gesangbuch* testifies to the active Jesuit role in Catholic reform in that diocese and to the rising prominence of their Marian Congregations.[59] The Jesuit

---

[58] Here the second melody is incomplete and truncated by one phrase, perhaps as a concession to its being fitted into the frame of the harp.

[59] *Christlich Catholisch Gesangbuch* (Paderborn, Heinrich Pontanus: 1628; RISM B/VIII, 1628[06]). On the connections to the Marian Congregations, see: Heitmeyer E. – Kohle M.

FIGURE 11.1　Jakob Balde, S.J., *Ehrenpreiß Der Allerseeligisten Jungkfrawen vnd Mutter GOttes* MARIÆ *Auff einer schlechten Harpffen jhres vnwürdigen Dieners gestimbt/ vnd gesungen. Zu Nutz/ Trost/ vnd wolgefallen aller* SODALIVM *in vnser lieben Frawen Bruderschafften* (Munich, Lucas Straub: 1647) fol. [i] v
VIENNA. ÖSTERREICHISCHE NATIONALBIBLIOTHEK. 507250-A MUS MAG

Psälterlein that first appeared at Cologne in 1637, eventually running to ten editions and 30,000 exemplars sold between then and 1653, may have owed its considerable success to the Marian Congregations.[60] Indeed it seems that the congregations were a principal audience for Jakob Gippenbusch's four-part polyphonic harmonisations of selected songs from the *Psälterlein* (1642), intended 'particularly for the use of sodalities, catechists and gymnasium [students]'; in his preface to the reader Gippenbusch writes that he has augmented the *Psälterlein* with additional 'Musicalische Cantiones' and psalms, 'for these have been requested and sought after partly by the sodalities, and partly from young students'.[61] The song 'O ihr Heiligen Gottesfreund' by the celebrated Jesuit poet Friedrich von Spee was sung in the procession and candle-offering ritual of the female Congregation of St. Ursula in Cologne, a consorority whose delivery of catechism instruction for girls led to their monikers *Jesuitinnen* or *Devotessen*. In fact, Spee's *Güldenes Tugendbuch*, printed posthumously in 1645, was dedicated to the St. Ursula Society, and some of its poems would appear with melodies in his famed *Trutz-Nachtigall* (1649).[62]

Litanies to the Virgin Mary (normally the Litany of Loreto), to the saints, or to the Name of Jesus were a distinctive and common sonic expression in Counter-Reformation confraternities, heard particularly in processions – where the regular ebb and flow of invocations and responses mirrored the footfall of devotees – but also in a range of other devotions. Performance practice is rarely indicated in confraternal manuals and statutes, suggesting a range of possible expressions from spoken recitation to plainsong, *falsobordone* and polyphony. Settings in quasi-*falsobordone* suited to processions may be seen in Johann Haym von Themar's aforementioned *Litaniae textus triplex* (1582), offered 'for use of

---

(eds.), *Das Paderborner Gesangbuch 1628: Reprint mit Kommentar* (Paderborn: 2007) 17–21, 29–33, 45, 72–76.

60   Bergerhausen H.-W., *Köln in einem eisernen Zeitalter, 1610–1686*, Geschichte der Stadt Köln 6 (Cologne: 2010) 193–195; Mallinckrodt, *Struktur und kollektiver Eigensinn* 185.

61   Gippenbusch J., *Psalteriolum Harmonicum Sacrarum Cantilenarum* (Cologne, Peter von Grevenbruch: 1642; RISM B/VIII, 1642[01]) fols. iii v–iv. On the Marian Congregations as an audience, see: Schmitz A., "Psalteriolum Harmonicum (1642). Ein Kölner Jesuiten-Gesangbuch", *Zeitschrift für Musikwissenschaft* 4 (1921) 18–26, here 18–20.

62   Spee F., *Güldenes Tugend-Buch. Historisch-kritische Ausgabe*, ed. T.G.M. van Oorschot – F. Spee, Sämtliche Schriften 2 (Munich: 1968), 693–694; see also: Conrad A., "Die Kölner Ursulagesellschaft und ihr 'weltgeistlicher Stand' – eine weibliche Lebensform im Katholizismus der Frühen Neuzeit", in Reinhard, W. – Schilling, H. (eds.), *Die katholische Konfessionalisierung. Wissenschaftliches Symposion der Gesellschaft zur Herausgabe des Corpus Catholicorum und des Vereins für Reformationsgeschichte 1993* (Gütersloh: 1995) 271–295, here 289–293; and Oorschot T.G.M. van, "Neue Frömmigkeit in den Kirchenliedern Friedrich Spees", in Breuer, D. (ed.), *Frömmigkeit in der frühen Neuzeit: Studien zur religiösen Literatur des 17. Jahrhunderts in Deutschland und Spanien* (Amsterdam: 1984) 169.

sodalities and confraternities going on pilgrimage to holy places'.[63] Containing twelve litanies to Jesus, the Virgin Mary and the saints, the consistent polyphonic formulas would have allowed confreres to easily memorise their respective parts and perform the responses while the procession was underway [Ex. 11.2].

EX. 11.2   Johann Haym von Themar, Litany of the Saints (excerpt), from *Litaniae textus triplex* (Augsburg, Josias Wörli: 1582)

The singing of litanies became closely associated with the Jesuit Marian Congregations in particular, which deployed them in processional, devotional and penitential contexts.[64] Indeed the founder of the first of these groups in Germany, Jakob Rem, S.J. (1546–1618), reported an apparition of the Virgin during the singing of this litany by a group of devotees before an image of her at Ingolstadt in 1604.[65] The threefold invocation 'Mater admirabilis' that triggered her apparition led to the establishment of a regular litany devotion there (the so-called *Mater ter admirabilis*) and surely inspired the development of others. By this time the Marian Congregation at Munich had already proven itself an audience for polyphonic litanies: an elaborately composed example is the *Litaniae Deiparae Virginis Mariae* of Costanzo Porta, a large-scale work running to an impressive length of nearly 300 breves for double choir first printed in Venice in 1575, but now offered (with a false attribution to Costanzo Festa) by the Munich printer Adam Berg in 1583. The work is said to be 'habitually sung in the chapel of the Marian sodality in the ducal Gymnasium of the Society of Jesus', a group that, as already mentioned, was an audience for Lasso's Penitential Psalms a few years previously.[66] Munich

---

63   Haym von Themar Johann, *Litaniae textus triplex* (Augsburg, Josias Wörli: 1582; RISM A/I, H4905). For discussion, see: Fisher, *Music and Religious Identity* 167–168, 259–61.
64   The devotional services of the Ingolstadt Congregation of Mary Victorious, for instance, often featured sung litanies on major feasts and as supplications during the threatening atmosphere of the Thirty Years War; see: Fisher, *Music, Piety, and Propaganda* 145–146.
65   Sattler, *Geschichte der Marianischen Kongregationen in Bayern* 60.
66   Festa Costanzo [actually Porta Costanzo], *Litaniae Deiparae Virginis Mariae, ex sacra scriptura collectae* (Munich, Adam Berg: 1584; RISM F643). On this litany see Fisher, *Music,*

also saw the largest collection of polyphonic litanies printed in early modern Europe, the *Thesaurus litaniarum* (1596) compiled by the Marian sodalist and music director of the Munich Jesuits, Georg Victorinus. Dedicating the print to the Marian Congregations of the Jesuits' Upper German Province, Victorinus expresses surprise that such a volume had not already appeared, for these litanies 'would be of the greatest use for pilgrimages undertaken to holy places; and now because it is in the nature of these times, more than ever, that it seems fitting to flee to such arms', probably a reference to the ongoing Thirteen Years War between the Austrian Habsburgs and Ottoman Turks. The sixty-seven polyphonic litanies to the Name of Christ, the Virgin Mary and the saints, composed by a range of local, regional and international musicians, spans a remarkable range of sophistication, from rudimentary *falsobordone*-like litanies in the manner of Haym von Themar to impressive polychoral examples in up to twelve parts that would likely have been performed only by professional choirs in fixed positions. Victorinus' *Thesaurus* testifies to the remarkable flexibility of the litany, which could be adapted for the widest range of congregational devotions.[67]

After the turn of the seventeenth century, German confraternities and congregations can also be connected to a series of liturgical, paraliturgical and devotional collections of polyphony, most of which have attracted little notice in the scholarly literature. The second of four books of posthumous motets for four to twenty-four voices (1605) by Alexius Neander, the music prefect of the St. Kilian seminar attached to the University of Würzburg, is dedicated by his student Wolfgang Getzmann to Archbishop Johann Schweickard of Mainz. Getzmann indicates, however, that it was published at the encouragement of the Marian Congregation at Würzburg and its principal patron, the Cistercian

---

Piety, and Propaganda 145–146; and Kendrick R.L., "'Honore a Dio, e allegrezza alli santi, e consolazioni alli putti': The Musical Projection of Litanies in Sixteenth-Century Italy", in Ditchfield, S. (ed.), *Plasmare il suono: Il culto dei santi e la musica (secc. XV–XVIII)* (Rome: 2009) 40.

67 Victorinus Georg (ed.), *Thesaurus litaniarum, quae a praecipuis hoc aevo musicis, tam in laudem sanctiss. nominis Iesu, quam in honorem Deiparae coelitumque omnium, quatuor, quinque, sex, plurium vocum compositae* (Munich, Adam Berg: 1596; RISM B/I, 1596²). For discussion, see: Fisher A.J., "*Thesaurus Litaniarum*: The Symbolism and Practice of Musical Litanies in Counter-Reformation Germany", *Early Music History* 34 (2015) 45–95. Much later, in 1680, the great Marian column or *Mariensäule* in Munich's market square (originally erected in 1638 in celebration of the withdrawal of Swedish forces) became the site of a weekly devotion by a newly-formed 'Marianische Compagnie' of laypersons, who would sing the Litany of Loreto with the accompaniment of paid singers and instrumentalists; see: Schattenhofer M., *Die Mariensäule in München* (Munich: 1970) 33–34; and Fisher, *Music, Piety, and Propaganda* 238.

abbot of Ebrach, suggesting that the Congregation may have performed or heard these motets.[68] A few years later a book of *Sacrarum cantionum* appeared at Venice from the Speyer cathedral organist Johann Münnich, bearing a dedication to the Corpus Christi Confraternity at the same church, recently founded under the auspices of the dedicated reformer Bishop Eberhard von Dienheim (r. 1581–1610). Scored for ensembles of four to eight voices, the volume contains motets with a Eucharistic emphasis, a Mass in imitation of one of Münnich's motets, and several psalm settings.[69]

More concentrated efforts to publish polyphonic music connected to confraternities are apparent in the imperial city of Augsburg and in the Bavarian residential capital of Munich. In Augsburg many of the leading Catholic musicians of the city – among them chapelmaster Bernhard Klingenstein, the organists Erasmus Mayr and Christian Erbach, instrumentalist Jakob Baumann, and the vicars-choral Gregor Aichinger and Johann Haym von Themar – belonged to the Confraternity of St. Sebastian and St. Barbara, a long-standing brotherhood for the cathedral personnel.[70] But groups more closely associated with Counter-Reformation ideals tended to generate published music. Haym von Themar's litanies and songs for the Trinity Confraternity has already been mentioned, but a more elaborate collection would appear in 1606 from Gregor Aichinger, who dedicated his *Solennia augustissimi Corporis Christi* to the Corpus Christi Confraternity at the Church of the Holy Cross, a brotherhood in which he counted himself a member.[71] Dedicated to the leadership of this group and its principal patron, Marcus Fugger (1564–1614), the print provides polyphonic settings in four to five voices of items for Second Vespers on the feast of Corpus Christi, Mass Propers for the same feast, and a set of processional hymns, consistent with the title-page's wording that the contents 'are customarily sung in the most holy sacrifice of the Mass and in the Offices of the same feast, and in public supplications and processions'. The stylistic range of the collection reflects a diversity of performance circumstances and abilities. While the Mass and Office music adheres to a traditional Netherlandish style, often featuring Gregorian *cantus firmi* in extended note values decorated

---

68 Neander Alexius, *Liber secundus R. D. Alexii Neandri Symphoniarchi* [...] *sacrarum cantionum* (Frankfurt am Main, Wolfgang Richter – Nikolaus Stein: 1605; RISM A/I, N309).

69 Münnich Johann, *Sacrarum cantionum 4. 5. 6. 8. vocum; sacrae* [...] *Confraternitati Venerabilis Sacramenti* [...] *in cathedrali ecclesia Spirensi* [...] *dedicatarum, liber primus* (Venice, Jacopo Cercagli: 1611; RISM A/I, M8111).

70 Fisher, *Music and Religious Identity* 165.

71 Aichinger Gregor, *Solennia Augustissimi Corporis Christi, in sanctissimo sacrificio missae et in euisdem festi officiis, ac publicis supplicationibus seu processionibus cantari solita* (Augsburg, Johann Praetorius: 1606; RISM A/I, A533). For discussion, see: Fisher, *Music and Religious Identity* 144–149.

EX. 11.3   Gregor Aichinger, "Pange lingua gloriosi" (excerpt), from *Solennia augustissimi Corporis Christi* (Augsburg, Johannes Praetorius: 1606)

by imitative counterpoint, a number of the processional hymns feature strict homophonic declamation and project a regular simplicity that would have suited the confraternity's public processions [Ex. 11.3]. It is tempting to imagine that some of this music would have resounded in streets during Augsburg's Corpus Christi procession, which by this time was assuming a monumental, theatrical character and was extending itself into Protestant neighbourhoods as a confessional provocation.[72]

Confraternities and congregations may also have been a suitable destination for Aichinger's other sacred music publications, over two dozen of which were printed between 1590 and 1626, largely in Augsburg and in the Jesuit strongholds of Dillingen and Ingolstadt. From 1607 onward (beginning with his *Cantiones ecclesiasticae*), Aichinger would frequently provide organ thoroughbass parts, making him one of the first German composers to essay the Italianate vocal concerto for small vocal ensembles. Concertos like those of the *Encomium verbo incarnato, eiusdemque matri augustissimae reginae coelorum musicis numeris decantatum* (Ingolstadt: 1617), setting Marian and Christological hymns and Marian antiphons for four voices and *bassus generalis*, may have been heard in confraternal gatherings; the lightly imitative texture with occasional – but restrained – vocal coloratura would probably have suited musicians with a range of abilities.[73] Indeed, the *Encomium verbo incarnato* had a connection with the Jesuit Marian Congregations, for the hymn texts for the seven Marian feast days (attributed to the Franciscan bishop and orator Cornelio Musso (1511–1574)) had already appeared as the conclusion of the Jesuit Jakobus Pontanus's *Parthenomētrika, id est, meditationes, preces, laudes in virginem matrem* (Augsburg: 1606), a set of Latin meditations on the

---

72   Fisher, *Music and Religious Identity* 249–256.
73   Aichinger Gregor, *Encomium verbo incarnato, eiusdemque matri augustissimae reginae coelorum musicis numeris decantatum* (Ingolstadt, Gregor Hänlin: 1617; RISM A/I, A546). For discussion, see: Fisher, *Music and Religious Identity* 183–184.

Marian feasts dedicated to the Augsburg Marian Congregation.[74] Plausibly this group would have appreciated hearing these hymns in Aichinger's fashionable settings.

The confraternities and congregations of Munich were also active sites for confraternal musical culture after the turn of the seventeenth century.[75] Musicians are commonly found as members and even leaders or founders of such groups: numerous members of the ducal cantorate, for instance, belonged to the lay confraternity of the Franciscan Cordeliers (1606ff); the two sons of Orlando di Lasso, Ferdinand and Rudolph, were apparently among its earliest members.[76] In 1617 the Archconfraternity of Corpus Christi at St. Peter's parish (1609ff), the focus of Eucharistic devotion in the Bavarian capital, received the dedication of Rudolph di Lasso's *Ad sacrum convivium*, a collection of sacred concertos for two to six voices and *bassus ad organum*, setting a variety of devotional texts. Identifying himself as the 'least client of your venerable sodality', Lasso pours effusive praise on the miracle of the transubstantiated host and offers his concertos for use during the octave of Corpus Christi, and, indeed, for any other Eucharistic observance. Compared to Aichinger's *Solennia* or *Encomium verbo*, Lasso's vocal writing is technically more demanding and implies the participation of professional singers, who may have been drawn from the ducal chapel for the devotions of this confraternity.[77]

The Marian Congregations and their pilgrimages have already been mentioned as a context for the polyphonic litanies of Victorinus's *Thesaurus litaniarum*.[78] Victorinus, along with several other court musicians, is known to have been a member of the Jesuit Congregation of the Annunciation of the Virgin Mary, and Rudolph di Lasso, in fact, served as a prefect of the Greater Latin Marian Congregation on three separate occasions between 1613 and 1620.[79] It is plausible that Lasso's large body of music published during

---

74 Pontanus Jakob, *Parthenomētrika, id est, meditationes, preces, lavdes in virginem matrem, potissimum ex Ecclesiasticis Græcorum monumentis. Ad usum Parthenianae Sodalitatis Augustanae* (Augsburg, David Frank: 1606).

75 Fisher, *Music, Piety, and Propaganda* 140–156.

76 As listed in the *Catalogus confratrum chordigerorum* (1606). Bayerisches Hauptstaatsarchiv München. Klosterliteralien, Bayerische Franziskanerprovinz 329. See also: Fisher, *Music, Piety, and Propaganda* 153–154; and Börner E., *Dritter Orden und Bruderschaften der Franziskaner in Kurbayern*, Franziskanische Forschungen 33 (Werl in Westfalen: 1988) 286.

77 Lasso Rudolph di, *Ad sacrum convivium modi sacri, novi et selecti, primum senis, mox binis, ternis, quaternis, quinis ac demum iterum senis vocibus* (Munich, Nikolaus Heinrich: 1617; RISM A/I, L1041). See also: Fisher, *Music, Piety, and Propaganda* 153.

78 On music in Munich's Marian Congregations, see: Fisher, *Music, Piety, and Propaganda* 141–147.

79 Sattler, *Geschichte der Marianischen Kongregationen in Bayern* 72–73, 248–249.

these years honouring the Virgin Mary – venerated as the patron saint of the Wittelsbach ruling house – would have been welcomed in these congregations. The forty-three sacred concertos for one to eight voices and *bassus ad organum* of Lasso's *Virginalia Eucharistica* (1615), setting a variety of liturgical and devotional texts honouring the Virgin, Christ and the Eucharist, may have appealed to the Marian Congregations in the same way that his *Ad sacrum convivium* addressed Munich's leading Eucharistic confraternity. The dedication of the *Virginalia* not to an earthly patron, but rather to the Virgin Mary of Loreto, would have deepened the print's association with the congregations' practice of Marian pilgrimage.[80] A richer network of connections between Lasso, the Jesuits and the Marian Congregations is suggested by his *Alphabetum Marianum* (1621), a set of fifty-seven sacred concertos for two to four voices and *basso ad organum*. Here Lasso identifies himself prominently as a sodalist of the Virgin Mary, and he praises his dedicatee, Bishop Veit Adam of Freising, as a member and illustrious patron of the Marian Congregation. In this connection Lasso explicitly mentions the *Sodalis Parthenius* (1621) by Kaspar Lechner, S.J., a lengthy Latin history and encomium to the Marian Congregations.[81] But more inspiration may have come from two Jesuit-authored manuals that had appeared in recent years, the *Alphabetum Sodalitatis B. Virginis* (Munich: 1616), a book outlining the virtues of the Marian Congregations;[82] and the *Alphabetum Christi* with its pendant, the *Alphabetum Diaboli* (Munich, 1618) by Johann Niess S.J., listing the respective virtues and vices for Christian youth.[83] In both the titles, the respective virtues and vices are arranged in alphabetical order, each followed by lengthy exegesis. This echoes the arrangement of the *Alphabetum Marianum*, where Lasso organises the concertos in alphabetical order by textual incipit, assigning three pieces to each of the nineteen letters (A through V). The format and paratexts of this collection, then, bring it into close association with the didactic aims of the Jesuits and the congregations

---

80 Lasso Rudolph di, *Virginalia Eucharistica. quae magnae Virgini, Virginisque filio vocibus singulis II. III. IV. V. VI. VII. octonis, cum basi continua memor gratusque concinuit* (Munich, Nikolaus Heinrich: 1615; RISM A/I, L1040). See the edition in Lasso, R. di, *Virginalia Eucharistica (1615)*, Fisher A.J. (ed.), Recent Researches in the Music of the Baroque 114 (Madison WI: 2002); and discussion in Fisher, *Music, Piety, and Propaganda* 113–126.
81 Lechner Kaspar, *Sodalis Parthenius. Sive libri tres quibus mores sodalium exemplis informantur. Opera maiorum sodalium academicorum B. Mariæ Virginis Annunciae in lucem dati* (Ingolstadt, Caspar Sutorius: 1621).
82 *Alphabetum Sodalitatis B. Virginis, Quod sanctissima, antiquissima, sapientissima SS. PP. schola composuit, exposuit, proposuit* (Munich, Nikolaus Heinrich: 1616).
83 Niess Johann, *Alphabetum Christi seu virtutes praecipuae quae adolescentes ornant* (Munich, Raphael Sadeler: 1618). On this manual, see: Duhr, *Geschichte der Jesuiten*, vol. II 2/2, 112–113.

they so passionately promoted. Like the *Virginalia* or the *Ad sacrum convivium*, Lasso's concertos present an imitative textural foundation decorated with virtuoso, melismatic flights suited to trained singers [Ex. 11.4].

EX. 11.4   Rudolph di Lasso, "Ecce tu pulchra es" (excerpt), from *Alphabetum Marianum* (Munich, Nikolaus Heinrich: 1621)

The aforementioned publications exhibit direct connections with post-Tridentine confraternities in the German orbit, but they represent only a small fraction of a much larger repertory of Catholic hymnody and polyphony for which confraternities and congregations would have made a ready audience. The distinct shift in the texts and paratexts of early seventeenth-century Catholic publications toward the explicit embrace of Marian, Eucharistic and sanctoral imagery paralleled an intensification of confessional identity and public demonstration among these groups, especially those founded under Jesuit auspices. As religious tensions heightened in the lands of the Holy Roman Empire and finally exploded in open warfare after 1618, the openly confessionalist character of Catholic confraternities and the media they cultivated – music and song, but also devotional literature, visual art and theatre – played no small part in the reinforcement of Catholic identity and the inscription of confessional boundaries against their Protestant antagonists. At the same time, the remarkable range of musical expression found in the extant repertory highlights confraternities and congregations as contexts where popular and more cultivated forms of music could intermingle. Vernacular monophony, Latin plainsong, *falsobordone* and rudimentary polyphonic litanies, simple homophonic hymns, thoroughbass songs and more virtuoso sacred concerti were performed and experienced by confreres drawn from the widest circles of society; as such this music sonically represents the mediating function of these groups, where the elite promotion of post-Tridentine reform and renewal interacted fruitfully with more organic expressions of traditional religiosity.

Bibliography

Primary Sources

RISM – Répertoire International des Sources Musicales.

Aichinger Gregor, *Solennia Augustissimi Corporis Christi, in sanctissimo sacrificio missae et in euisdem festi officiis, ac publicis supplicationibus seu processionibus cantari solita* (Augsburg, Johannes Praetorius: 1606; RISM A/I, A533).

Aichinger Gregor, *Encomium verbo incarnato, eiusdemque matri augustissimae reginae coelorum musicis numeris decantatum* (Ingolstadt, Gregor Hänlin: 1617; RISM A/I, A546).

Alphabetum Sodalitatis B. Virginis, Quod sanctissima, antiquissima, sapientissima ss. pp. schola composuit, exposuit, proposuit (Munich, Anna Berg: 1616).

Balde Jakob, *Ehrenpreiß Der Allerseeligisten Jungkfrawen vnd Mutter GOttes MARIÆ Auff einer schlechten Harpffen jhres vnwürdigen Dieners gestimbt, vnd gesungen. Zu Nutz, Trost, vnd wolgefallen aller SODALIVM in vnser lieben Frawen Bruderschafften* (Munich, Lucas Straub: 1647; RISM B/VIII, 1647[12]).

Bruderschafftbüchel Deß süssen Namen Jesus. Darinnen nit allein die Regul und Satzungen, sondern auch die Gnaden, Ablaß, unnd Freyheiten diser gnadenreichen Bruderschafft, sambt außerleßnen Gebettlein, Letaney und Psalmen zufinden (Munich, Melchior Segen: 1644).

Catholische Geistliche Gesänge, Vom süssen Namen Jesu, vnd der Hochgelobten Mutter Gottes Mariæ, &c. Von der Fraternitet S. Ceciliæ Zu Andernach in Lateinisch vnd Teutsche verß Componirt vnnd Collegirt (Cologne, Gerhart Grevenbruch: 1608; RISM B/VIII, 1608[02]).

Catholische Kirchen Gesäng, auff die Fürnemste Fest deß gantzen Jahrs wie mann dieselb zu Cölln, vnnd anderstwo, bey allen Christlichen Catholischen Lehren pflegt zu singen (Cologne, Peter von Brachel: 1619; RISM B/VIII, 1619[03]).

Christlich Catholisch Gesangbuch (Paderborn, Heinrich Pontanus: 1628; RISM B/VIII, 1628[06]).

Curtz Albrecht Graf, *Harpffen Davids mit Teutschen Saiten bespannet* (Augsburg, Veronica Aperger: 1659).

Drey Andächtige Außerlesne WeyhnächtGesäng, darinn häilsame Lehrpuncten von der Geburt Christi begriffen (Ingolstadt, Elisabeth Angermeyer: 1614; RISM B/VIII, 1614[08]).

Ein Andächtiger Rueff für die Pilgram. Vom H. Bischoff Bennone: Darinn sein Leben gueten Theils, vnd etliche Wunderwerck begriffen (Munich, Adam Berg: 1603).

Festa Costanzo [actually Porta Costanzo], *Litaniae Deiparae Virginis Mariae, ex sacra scriptura collectae* (Munich, Adam Berg: 1584; RISM F643).

Gippenbusch Jakob, *Psalteriolum Harmonicum Sacrarum Cantilenarum* (Cologne, Peter Grevenbruch: 1642; RISM B/VIII, 1642[01]).

Gsangbüchlein Geistlicher Psalmen, hymnen, leider, vnd gebet, Durch etliche Diener der Kirchen zuo Bonn, fleissig zuosamen getragen, mercklich gemeret, vnd in geschickte Ordnung zusamen gestelt, zuo übung vnd brauch der Christlichen gemeine (Bonn, Laurentius von der Mülen: 1550; RISM B/VIII, 1550[05]).

Handbuchlein Der Bruderschafft unser L. Frawen und H. drei Koningen (Cologne, Bernard Wolters: 1610).

Haym von Themar Johann, *Ein Schön Lob oder Catholisch Creutzgesang, von der grosse frewd, zier, vnnd vnaussprechlichen Herrligkeit, deß Paradeyß* (Augsburg, Josias Wörli: 1581; RISM B/VIII, 1581[10]).

Haym von Themar Johann, *Passion, oder Das aller heyligist bitter leiden vnd sterben Jhesu Christi* (Augsburg, Josias Wörli: 1581; RISM B/VIII, 1581[11]).

Haym von Themar Johann, *Litaniae, textus triplex* (Augsburg, Josias Wörli: 1582; RISM A/I, H4905).

Haym von Themar Johann, *Drey Gaystliche vnd Catholische Lobgesang, Christo vnserm einigen Seligmacher, vnd Mariæ allgemainer Christenhait fürbitten* (Augsburg, Josias Wörli: 1584; RISM B/VIII, 1584[13]).

Haym von Themar Johann, *Christenliche Catholische Creutz gesang, vom Vatter vnser vnnd Aue Maria, von denn zwölff stucken deß Apostolischen Glaubens* (Augsburg, Josias Wörli: 1584; RISM B/VIII, 1584[12]).

Haym von Themar Johann, *Schöne Christenliche Catholisch Weinnächt oder Kindtleß wiegen Gesang* (Augsburg, Josias Wörli: 1590; RISM B/VIII, 1590[05]).

Hertzenmuth Der andächtigen Seel. Das ist: Außerleßne, Andächtige, Lehr- vnnd Geistreiche Gesänger (Ingolstadt, Elisabeth Angermeyer: 1616; RISM B/VIII, 1616[11]).

Heylsamer Hertzentrost Das ist, Außerlesene Lobgeseng, vnnd Gedicht [...] Zu sondern Ehren der G[ott-] geliebten Bruderschafft vnserer [lie-] ben Frawen zu Würtzburg (Würzburg, Conrad Schwindtlauff: 1615).

Keusche Meerfräwlein, Oder Geistliche Gesäng, CHRISTO IESV *Vnserm Seligmacher:* MARIÆ *Seiner Gebenedeyten Mutter zu Ehren, auß Latein in Teutsch vbersetzt* (Würzburg, Elias Michael Zinck: 1649; RISM B/VIII, 1649[03]).

Lasso Rudolph di, *Virginalia Eucharistica. quae magnae Virgini, Virginisque filio vocibus singulis II. III. IV. V. VI. VII. octonis, cum basi continua memor gratusque concinuit* (Munich, Nikolaus Heinrich: 1615; RISM A/I, L1040).

Lasso Rudolph di, *Ad sacrum convivium modi sacri, novi et selecti, primum senis, mox binis, ternis, quaternis, quinis ac demum iterum senis vocibus* (Munich, Nikolaus Heinrich: 1617; RISM A/I, L1041).

Lechner Kaspar, *Sodalis Parthenius. Sive libri tres quibus mores sodalium exemplis informantur. Opera maiorvm sodalium academicorum B. Mariae Virginis Annunciatae in lucem dati* (Ingolstadt, Caspar Sutorius: 1621).

Münnich Johann, *Sacrarum cantionum 4. 5. 6. 8. vocum; sacrae [...] Confraternitati Venerabilis Sacramenti [...] in cathedrali ecclesia Spirensi [...] dedicatarum, liber primus* (Venice, Jacopo Cercagli: 1611; RISM A/I, M8111).

Neander Alexius, *Liber secundus R.D. Alexii Neandri Symphoniarchi [...] sacrarum cantionum* (Frankfurt am Main, Wolfgang Richter – Nikolaus Stein: 1605; RISM A/I, N309).

Niess Johann, *Alphabetum Christi seu virtutes praecipuae quae adolescentes ornant* (Munich, Raphael Sadeler: 1618).

Pontanus, Jakob, *Parthenometrika, id est, meditationes, preces, laudes in virginem matrem, potissimum ex Ecclesiasticis Graecorum monumentis. Ad usum Parthenianae Sodalitatis Augustanae* (Augsburg, David Frank: 1606).

Reglen vnd Ablas Sambt etlichen gebet der andechtigen Todten Bruederschafft bey den P.P. Dominicanern in Augspurg (Augsburg, Veronica Aperger: 1659).

S. Salvatoris Transfigurati apud Wirceburgenses erectae Fraternitatis Ordinationes et Statuta ([Würzburg]: 1616).

Sirenes Marianae, sive hymni in honorem B. Mariae V. et usum Partheniorum Sodalium concinnati (Würzburg, Elias Michael Zinck: 1647).

Sirenes Partheniae, sive hymni, filio virginis, Christo Jesu, matri virgini Mariae sacri (Würzburg, Elias Michael Zinck: 1649).

Statuta. Regel, Ablas, vnd Gebett, der Hochlobl: vralten Bruderschafft [...] der Seeligsten Jungfraw Mariæ Ihrer geburdt (Munich, Nikolaus Heinrich: 1645).

Summarischer Jnhalt der Comœdien vnnd Triumph, von den Heyligen, IGNATIO DE LOYOLA *Stiffter deß Ordens der Societet* IESV; *vnd* FRANCISCO XAVERIO (Ingolstadt, Gregor Hänlin: 1622).

Ulenberg Kaspar, *Die Psalmen Dauids in allerlei Teutsche gesangreimen bracht* (Cologne, G. Calenius & J. Quentels Erben: 1582; RISM B/VIII, 1582[09]).

Victorinus Georg (ed.), *Thesaurus litaniarum, quae a praecipuis hoc aevo musicis, tam in laudem sanctiss. nominis Iesu, quam in honorem Deiparae coelitumque omnium, quatuor, quinque, sex, plurium vocum compositae* (Munich, Adam Berg: 1596; RISM B/I, 1596[02]).

Victorinus Georg (ed.), *Siren coelestis duarum, trium et quatuor vocum* (Munich, Adam Berg: 1616; RISM B/I, 1616[2]).

Secondary Sources

Bäumker W., *Das katholische deutsche Kirchenlied in seinen Singweisen von den frühesten Zeiten bis gegen Ende des siebzehnten Jahrhunderts*, 4 vols. (Freiburg – St. Louis: 1883–1911).

Becker T.P., *Konfessionalisierung in Kurköln: Untersuchungen zur Durchsetzung der katholischen Reform in den Dekanaten Ahrgau und Bonn anhand von Visitationsprotokollen 1583–1761* (Bonn: 1989).

Bergerhausen H.-W., *Köln in einem eisernen Zeitalter, 1610–1686*, Geschichte der Stadt Köln 6 (Cologne: 2010).

Börner E., *Dritter Orden und Bruderschaften der Franziskaner in Kurbayern*, Franziskanische Forschungen 33 (Werl in Westfalen: 1988).

Brückner W., *Frommes Franken. Kult und Kirchenvolk in der Diözese Würzburg seit dem Mittelalter* (Würzburg: 2008).

Chatellier L., *The Europe of the Devout: The Catholic Reformation and the Formation of a New Society*, Birrell J. (trans.) (Cambridge – New York – Paris: 1989).

Conrad A., "Die Kölner Ursulagesellschaft und ihr 'weltgeistlicher Stand' – eine weibliche Lebensform im Katholizismus der Frühen Neuzeit" in Reinhard W. – Schilling H. (eds.), *Die katholische Konfessionalisierung. Wissenschaftliches Symposion der Gesellschaft zur Herausgabe des Corpus Catholicorum und des Vereins für Reformationsgeschichte 1993* (Gütersloh: 1995) 271–295.

Crook D., "A Performance of Lasso's Penitential Psalms on Maundy Thursday 1580", in Schmid B. (ed.), *Orlando di Lasso in der Musikgeschichte* (Munich: 1996) 69–77.

Diergarten F., "Himmlische Sirenen und keusche Meerfräulein. Musik und katholische Reform in zwei Quellengruppen aus Würzburg und München", in Kleinehagenbrock F. et al. (eds.), *Reformation und katholische Reform zwischen Kontinuität und Innovation* (Würzburg: 2019) 385–422.

Duhr B., *Geschichte der Jesuiten in den Ländern deutscher Zunge in der ersten Hälfte des* XVII. *Jahrhunderts* (Freiburg im Breisgau – St. Louis: 1913).

Fisher A.J., *Music and Religious Identity in Counter-Reformation Augsburg, 1580–1630* (Aldershot: 2004).

Fisher A.J., *Music, Piety, and Propaganda: The Soundscapes of Counter-Reformation Bavaria* (New York: 2014).

Fisher A.J., "*Thesaurus Litaniarum*: The Symbolism and Practice of Musical Litanies in Counter-Reformation Germany", *Early Music History* 34 (2015) 45–95.

Glixon J., *Honoring God and the City: Music at the Venetian Confraternities, 1260–1807* (Oxford: 2003).

Gropp I., *Wirtzburgische Chronick Deren letzeren Zeiten [...] Erster Theil von dem Jahr 1500. biß 1642* (Würzburg: 1748).

Hamacher T., "Sirenes Partheniae. Ein lateinisch-deutsches Gesangbuch des Barock", *Kirchenmusikalisches Jahrbuch* 52 (1968) 71–85.

Heal B., *The Cult of The Virgin Mary in Early Modern Germany. Protestant and Catholic Piety, 1500–1648* (Cambridge: 2007).

Heidrich J., "Reformatorisches 'Strohfeuer' im Rheinland. Das *Bönnische Gesangbuch* von 1544", in Pietschmann K. (ed.), *Das Erzbistum Köln in der Musikgeschichte des 15. und 16. Jahrhunderts* (Kassel: 2008) 149–156.

Heitmeyer E. – Kohle M. (eds.), *Das Paderborner Gesangbuch 1628: Reprint mit Kommentar* (Paderborn: 2007).

Hofmann S., "Maria de Victoria – Nachruf auf die einstige Kirche der Kongregation Maria vom Sieg", *Sammelblatt des Historischen Vereins Ingolstadt* 85 (1976) 81–137.

Kendrick R.L., "'Honore a Dio, e allegrezza alli santi, e consolazioni alli putti': The Musical Projection of Litanies in Sixteenth-Century Italy", in Ditchfield S. (ed.), *Plasmare il suono: Il culto dei santi e la musica (secc. XVI–XVIII)* (Rome: 2009) 15–46.

Kirsch D. – Meierott L., "Geistliche und weltliche Musik in den mainfränkischen Territorien: Würzburg, freie Reichsstadt Schweinfurt und Aschaffenburg", in Kolb P. – Krenig E. (eds.), *Unterfränkische Geschichte* (Würzburg: 1999) IV/2: 561–622.

Knighton T. (ed.), *Iberian Confraternities and Urban Soundscapes*, Confraternitas 31.2 (special issue) (2020).

Körndle F., "Die Musikpflege bei den Kölner Bruderschaften im Vergleich zu anderen Städte", in Pietschmann K. (ed.), *Das Erzbistum Köln in der Musikgeschichte des 15. und 16. Jahrhunderts* (Kassel: 2008) 157–169.

Laqua-O'Donnell S., *Women and the Counter-Reformation in Early Modern Münster* (Oxford: 2014).

Lasso R. di, *Virginalia Eucharistica (1615)*, Fisher A.J. (ed.), Recent Researches in the Music of the Baroque 114 (Madison WI: 2002).

Lipowsky F.J., *Geschichte der Jesuiten in Baiern* (Munich: 1816).

Mallinckrodt R. von, *Struktur und kollektiver Eigensinn: Kölner Laienbruderschaften im Zeitalter der Konfessionalisierung* (Göttingen: 2005).

Mann H.J., "Die barocken Totenbruderschaften. Entstehung, Entwicklung, Aufgabe, Struktur, Verwaltung und Frömmigkeitspraxis. Ein kultur-, gesellschafts- und frömmigkeitsgeschichtliche Untersuchung", *Zeitschrift für bayerische Landesgeschichte* 39 (1976) 127–151.

Müller A., *Die Kölner Bürger-Sodalität. 1608–1908* (Paderborn: 1909).

Niemöller K.W., "Gottestracht und Ioculatores: die Anfänge des Musiktheaters in Köln", in Schwandt C. (ed.), *Oper in Köln. Von den Anfängen bis zur Gegenwart* (Berlin: 2007) 11–26.

O'Regan N., *Institutional Patronage in Post-Tridentine Rome: Music at Santissima Trinità dei Pellegrini, 1550–1650* (London: 1995).

O'Regan N., "Music at the Roman Archconfraternity of San Rocco in the Late Sixteenth Century", in Antolini B.M. et al. (eds.), *La musica a Roma attraverso le fonti d'archivio: Atti del Convegno internazionale, Roma 4–7 giugno 1992* (Lucca: 1994) 521–552.

Oorschot T.G.M. van, "Neue Frömmigkeit in den Kirchenliedern Friedrich Spees", in Breuer D. (ed.), *Frömmigkeit in der frühen Neuzeit: Studien zur religiösen Literatur des 17. Jahrhunderts in Deutschland und Spanien* (Amsterdam: 1984) 156–171.

Remling L., *Bruderschaften in Franken. Kirchen- und sozialgeschichtliche Untersuchungen zum spätmittelalterlichen und frühneuzeitlichen Bruderschaftswesen* (Münster: 1986).

Sattler M.V., *Geschichte der Marianischen Kongregationen in Bayern* (Munich: 1869).

Schattenhofer M., *Die Mariensäule in München* (Munich: 1970).

Scheitler I., *Schauspielmusik. Funktion und Ästhetik im deutschsprachigen Drama der Frühen Neuzeit* (Tutzing – Beeskow: 2013–2015).

Schmitz A., "Archivstudien über die musikalischen Bestrebungen der Kölner Jesuiten im 17. Jahrhundert", *Archiv für Musikwissenschaft* 3 (1921) 421–446.

Schmitz A., "Psalteriolum Harmonicum (1642). Ein Kölner Jesuiten-Gesangbuch", *Zeitschrift für Musikwissenschaft* 4 (1921) 18–26.

Schneider W. "Wandel und Beharrung. Bruderschaften und Frömmigkeit in Spätmittelalter und früher Neuzeit", in Molitor H. – Smolinsky H. (eds.), *Volksfrömmigkeit in der frühen Neuzeit* (Münster: 1994) 65–84.

Solzbacher J., "Die Psalmen Davids, in allerlei deutsche Gesangreime gebracht durch Kaspar Ulenberg, Köln 1582", *Kirchenmusikalisches Jahrbuch* 34 (1950) 41–55.

Spee F., *Güldenes Tugend-Buch. Historisch-kritische Ausgabe*, ed. T.G.M. van Oorschot – F. Spee, Sämtliche Schriften 2 (Munich: 1968).

Stieve F., *Der Kampf um Donauwörth im Zusammenhange der Reichsgeschichte* (Munich: 1875).

Westermayer G., *Jacobus Balde, sein Leben und seine Werke* (Munich: 1868).

PART 3

Confraternities as Acoustic Communities

∵

CHAPTER 12

Music and Noise: The Sounds of a Youth Confraternity in Renaissance Florence

Konrad Eisenbichler

Abstract

This paper will examine the sounds associated with confraternities for young men (13 to 24 years old) in early modern Florence. From the *laude* that characterized *laudese* (singing) confraternities to the church hymns that were sung during services, there were plenty of occasions where music, both spiritual and religious, both vocal and instrumental, was performed by the youths and heard by their fellow members, guests, neighbours or passers-by. The youths also performed musically in non-religious events, such as when they mounted plays or, later in the seventeenth century, sung oratorios. And there were times when the youths were heard in non-musical fashion, such as when they played (much to the annoyance of their neighbours) in their *pallottolaio*, the ball-courts that were sometime part of their confraternity spaces. The variety of sounds produced by, and emanating from youth confraternities in early modern Florence attests to the range of activities that were part of the young men's spiritual, social, and communal growth and to the lively vitality of these institutions.

Keywords

music – singing – *laude* – oratorios – instruments – noise – youths – confraternities – liturgy – processions – theatre – plays – ball games

There is a saying that 'Children should be seen and not heard'. The fact, however, is that children are definitely heard. My research on the confraternities of young males aged thirteen to twenty-four in early modern Florence shows that these young males were very much heard, in many ways, by many people.[1] The most obvious way was during their prayer rituals in the confraternity

---

1 For a detailed and extensive examination of youth confraternities in Florence, see Eisenbichler K., *The Boys of the Archangel Raphael. A Youth Confraternity in Florence, 1411–1785*

when they recited their devotions or sang during their services, or when they engaged in discussion during their business meetings. Their audience, on these occasions, were their own fellow confraternity members; so the sounds they created were heard by a restricted and carefully selected group that both listened and contributed to them. But others heard them, too. Occasionally the confraternity would mount a special event, such as a more elaborate liturgical devotion or a theatrical performance, within the walls of their confraternity and open their doors to external visitors. Their audience in this case were the youths themselves, most or many of whom contributed to the sounds they made, and the spectators who had come to hear them, but not to contribute to the sounds (except with their own personal chatter during the event, a sound that was present but not programmed). The youths were also heard by people on the streets and piazzas of Florence when they left their confraternity building and processed, wearing their confraternity robes, carrying their *gonfalone* (confraternity banner) and singing hymns, through the city on their way to or from a specific location that varied depending on the occasion (the cathedral, a church, or another confraternity). Lastly, they were heard by their neighbours when the sounds they made in their confraternity travelled outside their windows and reached the people living nearby. This article will highlight some of these moments when youth confraternities became part of the private and/or public soundscape of the city and the manner in which they did so focusing, in particular, on the youths of the Confraternity of the Archangel Raphael, also known as *la Scala* or *della Natività*.[2]

1 Singing

What is interesting about the musical moments in the confraternity is that the music that was heard was not what might have been expected. Normally youth confraternities are categorised as *laudese* confraternities because they supposedly sang *laude*, that is, secular songs in the vernacular in praise of God, Jesus, the Blessed Virgin Mary, or the saints; and this they did. The 1427 statutes of

---

(Toronto: 1998); Polizzotto L., *Children of the Promise: The Confraternity of the Purification and the Socialization of Youths in Florence, 1427–1785* (New York: 2004); and, more generally, Taddei I., *Fanciulli e giovani. Crescere a Firenze nel Rinascimento* (Florence: 2001).

2 The name *della Natività* was given to the confraternity by Pope Eugenius IV because of a Nativity play they performed for him and the Florentine Signoria in 1430 at the church of San Pancrazio; the moniker *la Scala* came instead from the Ospedale della Scala where the same pope had granted the confraternity space for its oratory and rooms. For more on the confraternity's names, see Eisenbichler, *The Boys of the Archangel Raphael* 30, 47–48.

the youth Confraternity of St. John the Evangelist in Florence, for example, stipulate that at each *tornata* (prayer and business meeting) the youths were first to sing one or two *laude*, then recite the versicle *Adjutorium nostrum in nomine domini* with its responses, the *Confiteor*, the prayer to the Archangel Raphael, the seven penitential psalms, and the litanies; at the end of the meeting, they were to sing the *Magnificat* or the *Credo*.[3] The 1468 statutes of the youth Confraternity of the Archangel Raphael refer surprisingly little to the singing of *laude*; they mention only that, in lieu of reciting prayers, one or two *laude* could be sung by members present while waiting for others to arrive before starting a meeting so as not to induce idleness (*otio*) or idle chatter (*mormoratione*),[4] or that when they take part in a public procession in the city the youths should walk in an orderly fashion and sing hymns, psalms, and *laude*.[5] Archival records and surviving play scripts indicate that *lauda* singing also took place during short theatrical performances mounted at Christmas time that focused on the Nativity story: for example, Giovan Maria Cecchi's *Atto recitabile per alla Cappannuccia* (1573; One-Act Play Suitable for Recitation in Front of the Nativity Scene), composed for and performed by the youths of the Arcangelo Raffaello, has the performers sing two *laude* and a madrigal – clearly an indication of the more popular and less devotional aspect of the celebrations.[6] Aside from these few occasions, the records rarely mention the singing of *laude*, possibly because *lauda* singing was so common that the scribes did not think it worth their ink to record it, or because the youths simply did not regularly sing *laude*. If they did not normally sing *laude*, what did they sing?

---

3   Florence. Biblioteca Nazionale Centrale. Magl. XXXI, cod. 11 fols. 3r–v: 'Et l'uficio che abbino a dire alle nostre tornate sia questo. In prima si dichi una lauda o due come parrà al nostro guardiano. Et poi Aiutorium nostrum ecc. E.lla confessione et l'oraçione di Raphael archangelo. E poi i sette salmi penetençiali colle tanie e l'oraçioni con certe commemoraçioni de santi et una generale racomandigia. Et poi si ponghino a sedere et ordinare se v'è a fare nulla. E la Magnificat e 'l Credo cantando come parrà al nostro guardiano'.
4   Florence. Archivio di Stato. Capitoli, Compagnie religiose soppresse 752, chapter 8 fol. 4r: 'Et quando sei o più fussino nel nostro oratorio raunati uno incominci a llegere cose di sacra scrittura, et legga tanto che li sia fatto cenno dal Guardiano del restare o vero si canti qualche lauda o salmo per non dar luogho all'otio, né alla mormoratione'.
5   Florence. Archivio di Stato. Capitoli, Compagnie religiose soppresse 752, chapter 16 fol. 15r: 'Nello andare a processione osservino i fratelli ogni ordine, et gravità, et modestia, et pace delle menti loro per dare buono exemplo al populo, et cantisi hymni et salmi et laude, come sia ordinato et inposto'.
6   Giovan Maria Cecchi, *Five Plays for the Archangel Raphael*, trans. K. Eisenbichler (Toronto: 2020) 90, 94.

The records of the Arcangelo Raffaello show that, most of the time, the youths sang hymns and psalms. They mention in particular the *Te Deum, Laudate pueri Dominum, Magnificat, Laudate Dominum omnes gentes, Benedictus Dominus deus Israel* and 'il Credo maggiore'. Those of other youth confraternities echo this list. What is worth noting, aside from the fact that these are all standard hymns and psalms, is that they all, including the Credo, were in Latin. The youths were thus taught to perform in Latin. Though this seems to contradict the received wisdom that has *laudesi* confraternities singing mostly, if not solely, vernacular *laude*, it should be borne in mind that youth confraternities, with a strong mission to educate the young, would have sought to teach and foster a more elevated or learned singing among their members than the popular vernacular *laude* that were sung by *laudese* confraternities for adults, and this meant hymns, psalms and canticles in Latin.

The records also suggest that the quality of singing within the youth confraternity was high. The youths were actually trained to sing. Although the fifteenth-century statutes do not list the position of choir leaders, by the mid-sixteenth century a set of *ordinatori de' cori* (literally organizers of the choirs, plural) is listed in the regular slate of officers elected in the quarterly elections held every January, May and September. With the revisions to and updating of the statutes carried out in 1636 what had been a non-statutory position was made statutory. The formalisation brought a name change: the new officers in charge of music were no longer called *ordinatori de' cori*, but *cerimonieri*, a term that implied a much more prestigious role in the confraternity's administrative structure. According to the statutes, the *cerimonieri* were

> expected to prepare the choir for the celebration of the Divine Office according to the Roman rite, appoint the more practised brothers as leaders (*imponitori*), singers of the antiphonary (*antifonari*), and to other posts. For this reason they must arrive for prayer meetings at the confraternity early and teach them the ceremonies and rehearse the singing with them.[7]

The presence of *imponitori* (leaders) does not negate the participation of hired instructors. The first regular paid instructor to appear in the records

---

7   Florence. Archivio di Stato. Capitoli. Compagnie religiose soppresse 627 chapter 8, 17: 'A questi s'aspetta ordinare il coro per la celebrazione del divino uffizio secondo l'uso Romano, assegnando dei fratelli più esercitati per imponitori, antifonari, e altre cariche. Però nelle tornate devino anticipare la venuta alla Compagnia per ammaestrargli nelle cirimonie e esercitarli nel canto'.

is a semi-professional musician, the furrier (*vaiaio*) Michelangelo di Jacopo Mollazzi, hired on 1 July 1563 to teach music to ten of the confraternity younger members (*giovanetti*, probably aged thirteen to fifteen) for a fee of 2.5 *scudi* per month (30 *scudi* per year).[8] Mollazzi was still active twenty years later in June 1583, when he appears in the records as 'maestro di nostra Cappella della Musicha', a title that was subsequently applied to all music teachers at the Arcangelo Raffaello and clearly suggests an elevation in rank and professionalism.[9] By the seventeenth century, the confraternity was hiring professional musicians to train their members, often the incumbent chapel master at either the cathedral or the grand-ducal court, an indication of just how important singing had become at the confraternity and how much it was willing to spend to acquire professional music teachers. Among the professional musicians who served the Arcangelo Raffaello there were, among others; the composer, instrumentalist and singer Marco da Gagliano (1582–1643), a key figure in the birth and development of opera; his equally talented and proficient brother Giovan Battista da Gagliano (1594–1651); the composer Baccio Baglioni (15??–1649), later chapel master at the cathedral of Livorno; and the composer and organist Niccolò Sapiti (ca. 1610–1678), *maestro di cappella* at the cathedral.[10]

In the confraternity there were also some talented members whose musical talents were very much appreciated by their fellow confraternity brothers. One of these was Raffaello Gucci (ca. 1542/3–1609/10), who had joined the confraternity in 1573 at age thirty.[11] Although the confraternity statutes stipulated that members were to be between thirteen and twenty-four years of age, and

---

[8] Florence. Archivio di Stato. Compagnie religiose soppresse 160.7/8 Eisenbichler fol. 4v dated 1 July 1563: 'Ricordo questo di 1º di luglio 1563 come Michelangelo di Jacopo Mollazzi vaiaio comincio a insegnare di musicha ai giovanetti della nostra Compagnia, et con patto sempre dovessi havere a insegnare a 30 di detti giovanetti, et Girolamo di M⟨aest⟩ro Luca guardiano fussi obligato dargli et pagarli per sua provisione ogni mese scudi dua e 1/2'.

[9] Florence. Archivio di Stato. Compagnie religiose soppresse 162.21/22 fol. 44v, dated 26 June 1583: 'havendo dato ordine dell'imporre et letione per il nostro Michelagniolo Mollazzi maestro della nostra Cappella della Musicha'. Guido Burchi notes that there is no other information on Mollazzi as a musician except what is to be found in the records of the Arcangelo Raffaello; Burchi G., *Musica e musicisti nella Compagnia della 'Scala' di Firenze (1556–1785)* (Laura thesis, Università degli Studi di Firenze: 1971–1972) 1: 50 footnote 5bis.

[10] For further information on their contributions to the confraternity and a fuller list of music teachers, see: Eisenbichler, *The Boys of the Archangel Raphael*, 323–329 and *passim*.

[11] Florence. Archivio di Stato. Compagnie religiose soppresse 7/8 fol. 28r, dated 1 March 1572/3: 'Raffaello di Ser Francesco Gucci d'età d'anni 30' completes his novitiate and is elected a brother.

that they had to leave the confraternity at age twenty-four, an exception had clearly been made in Gucci's case. The records do not indicate or even hint at the reason for the exception, but Gucci's musical talents, amply documented in the confraternity records, may offer a clue: he was a talented singer, instrumentalist and music teacher, all of which were very useful qualities for the confraternity. Given Gucci's adult age at entry into the sodality and the fact that the records for the 1570s are very scanty, it might safely be assumed that he would not have been 'learning' music in the confraternity, but already performing it from as early as his noviciate and perhaps even teaching music to his *confratelli*; an entry from November 1585, for example, says that because the confraternity was temporarily without a chapel master, Gucci and the court musician Giulio Caccini (1551–1618) had stepped in to fill the void.[12]

The much more detailed records from the 1580s reveal that Gucci performed, both vocally and instrumentally, quite often, much to the admiration of his fellow confraternity members and occasional visitors to the oratory. The earliest record of one of his performances is dated 20 February 1582/3, when, together with Migliorotto Migliorotti, he sang an Office of the Dead while the confraternity was celebrating the Forty Hours devotion. This clearly was a special and public event attended not only by his *confratelli*, but also by a large number of external visitors, 'both men and women', who had come to the oratory for the occasion.[13] In the years that followed, Gucci performed both vocally and instrumentally. On 4 Novembber 1584, for example, he was part of a polychoral rendition of the *Miserere* (Psalm 50/51) and the *Benedictus* (Luke 1: 68–79) in which he sang in alternation with the choir while also accompanying himself on a *buonaccordo* (spinet or harpsichord). A month later, on 8 December 1584, he brought his own keyboard instrument to the confraternity and sang the *Te Deum*, the *Gloriosa*,[14] and the *Benedictus*. The following year, for All Souls 1585 (1 November) he again brought his instrument and sang, this time from inside a catafalque that had been erected in the oratory; a spooky performance, but

---

12   Florence. Archivio di Stato. Compagnie religiose soppresse 160.8/9 fol. 24r, dated 1 November 1583/4: 'Giovedì primo novembre [1584], giorno di tutti i santi. La sera si disse l'offzio con bellissima musica, e per non aver più maestro di cappella servì la Compagnia Ms. Raffaello Gucci nostro fratello, Ms Giulio Caccini musico di S.A.S.'.

13   Florence. Archivio di Stato. Compagnie religiose soppresse 162.21/22 fol. 23r: 'per dire l'ufitio de' morti si come è l'hordinario nostro per l'anima di tutti i fratelli et benefatori della casa [...] havendo parato di nero con morte si disse un bel ufitio de' morti inponendolo Migliorotto Migliorotti et Rafaello Ghucci, et si concorse di molto populo sì di huomini come di donne'.

14   'O gloriosa domina', the second part of the hymn 'Quem terra, pontus, aethera' composed by Venantius Fortunatus (530–609).

not an unprecedented one since the previous year the same effect had been achieved either by Giulio Caccini or by a young *castrato* that Caccini had brought along with him that day.[15] On 2 April, Holy Wednesday 1586, Gucci again sang in a polychoral setting of the *Benedictus* and the *Miserere* and accompanied himself on his instrument, this time, however, in alternation with a mixed choir of voices and five viols, something the scribe says 'satisfied very much'. Gucci repeated that performance each of the following evenings of Holy Week.[16] For All Souls' 1587 he joined together with Giulio Romano, Lelio Lenzoni and Niccoli *castrato* to sing not hymns, but madrigals. Gucci continued to sing and play at the confraternity on many occasions until 1600, when he stopped performing (perhaps because of age, seeing that by then he was close to sixty years old).[17]

2 Instrumental Music

The archival references to Gucci and Caccini demonstrate that in the second half of the sixteenth century music at the confraternity was often enriched by instrumental accompaniment. One of the earliest references to instruments in the confraternity records comes from Corpus Domini 1561, when the scribe recalled that Vespers that day were celebrated very solemnly, 'with many organs [...] and many lauds were also sung on the organs'.[18] The 'many organs' were probably small portable keyboard instruments that members had brought from home; there is no indication in the records that at this time

---

15   Florence. Archivio di Stato. Compagnie religiose soppresse 162.21/22 fol. 54r, dated 1 November 1584, All Souls' Day. Giulio Caccini is described in the records as 'musico di Sua Altezza Serenissima e nostro fratello', and the *castrato* he brought along as 'un suo putto castrato che a requisitione di Sua Altezza Serenissima tiene in casa, et l'insegna'. The records for all these occasions have been transcribed in Burchi, *Musica e musicisti*, vol. 2, docs. 25, 26, 40 and published in Hill J.W., "Oratory Music in Florence, I: 'Recitar Cantando' 1583–1655", *Acta Musicologica* 51.1 (1979) 133, docs. 4, 5, 7.
16   Florence. Archivio di Stato. Compagnie religiose soppresse 162.21/22 fol. 75v, dated 2 April 1586: 'al Benedictus et Miserere si fece dua cori, uno di 5 viole et voci, e l'altro Rafaello Ghucci col suo strumento quale soddisfeciono assai così si seghuirà le seghuenti sere'; transcribed in Burchi, *Musica e musicisti* vol. 2, doc. 43.
17   Florence. Archivio di Stato. Compagnie religiose soppresse 162.21/22 *passim*; transcribed in Burchi, *Musica e musicisti* vol. 2, docs. 43, 51 and published in Hill, "Oratory Music in Florence, I" 134: docs. 8, 9. I take the date of Gucci's 'retirement' from Burchi, *Musica e musicisti* vol. 1, 50 who says that Gucci performed 'fino ai primi del 1600' (until the early 1600s).
18   Florence. Archivio di Stato. Compagnie religiose soppresse 160.6/7 fol. 32v: 'si celebrò il S.mo vespro con gli organi molto solennemente; si cantò ancora molte lalde su gli organi'.

the confraternity owned an organ. A similar concert of organs formed part of the celebrations on 31 December 1563 for the feast of the Archangel Raphael; on that day, the scribe noted that Vespers were sung and 'many organs were played, just like in the morning'.[19]

Sometime around 1596 the confraternity acquired its own keyboard instrument: a *graviorgano*.[20] The instrument was a gift from the wealthy silk merchant Baccio Comi, one of the confraternity's most generous members.[21] Comi had purchased the instrument from the scientist and astronomer Galileo Galilei (1564–1642) who, when he was in Padua at the university, had bought it from the renowned instrument-maker Domenico da Pesaro, based in Venice, and had then brought it with him back to Florence. Galileo subsequently gave the organ on consignment to Giulio Caccini,[22] who then sold it to Baccio Comi. In an affidavit, Caccini declared that he himself had played that instrument on several occasions, both in the Confraternity of the Archangel Raphael and at Comi's house when the latter had the organ temporarily moved there for

---

19   Florence. Archivio di Stato. Compagnie religiose soppresse 160.7/8 fols. 8v–9r, dated 31 December 1563: 'S. Silvestro [...] et mentre si cantava Lauda Hyerusalem d.num pervenit musichalmente in versetto, et Salmo poi e Cori rispondevano [...] si cantò musichalmente da nostri Giovanetti [...] Si cantava Te Deum Laudamus musichalmente da nostri giovanetti, e Cori rispondevano [...] si disse musichalmente el nostro Vespro et sonoronsi gli organi come la mattina'.

20   A *graviorgano*, known in other cities as a *claviorgano*, was a very popular instrument that combined a small organ with an equally small harpsichord. For a fine study of this instrument at the Medici grand-ducal court in the seventeenth century, see Montanari G., "Organi e claviorgani del Granprincipe Ferdinando de' Medici", *Informazione Organistica* (2008) 281–368.

21   On 30 December 1643 a plaque was placed in the oratory to commemorate the generosity of Baccio Comi (d. 18 March 1604/5) and his brother Domenico (d. 13 Dec. 1605); the death dates of the two Comi brothers are taken from Florence. Archivio di Stato. Compagnie religiose soppresse 160.9/10 fol. 22 sin. Baccio supported other confraternities as well, especially the Compagnia dei Vanchetoni, in particular by contributing to the construction of its oratory; see Florence. Biblioteca Nazionale Centrale. MS Magliab. XXV, cod. 418 fol. 126. The artist Baccio del Bianco recalls that when his father lost his shop in Calimara in a fire, Baccio and Domenico Comi, 'generously and spontaneously' ('di lor carità e sponte') had the shop rebuilt and put him back in business as good as before; Baldinucci Filippo, *Notizie de' professori di disegno da Cimabue in qua* (Florence, Tartini e Franchi: 1728) 314.

22   Galileo's affidavit is in Florence. Archivio di Stato. Compagnie religiose soppresse 156.2/4, fasc. C; published in Burchi G., "Vita musicale e spettacoli alla Compagnia della Scala di Firenze fra il 1560 e il 1675", *Note d'Archivio per la Storia Musicale* n.s. 1 (1983) 9–50 (43 footnote 23).

special concerts by Caccini and the composer and violinist Giovan Battista Giacomelli, also known as Giovan Battista del Violino.[23]

There was also string music at the confraternity. As mentioned above, on 2 April 1586 Raffaello Gucci performed in alternation with a mixed choir of voices and five viols, a performance that was repeated on the following evenings. On 1 January 1588/89, there was music by viols, *buonaccordi* (small spinets), *traverso* flutes and voices. In short, a small ensemble of strings, keyboard instruments and woodwinds was beginning to accompany the confraternity's voices and enrich the sodality's devotional and musical life. Its sounds were enjoyed both by members and visitors present in the oratory and, it can be assumed, by neighbours and passers-by who heard the music as it wafted out the confraternity's windows. There is no indication in the confraternity records that brass or percussion instruments were ever played in the confraternity.

The quality of musical performances at the Confraternity of the Archangel Raphael was so high that it attracted the attention of the grand-ducal family. On 31 December 1589, for example, the Grand Duchess of Tuscany, Christine of Lorraine, visited the confraternity for the feast of the Archangel Raphael and heard Raffaello Gucci play his keyboard instrument and sing verses in alternation with a choir. Gucci was accompanied by the virtuoso violinist Giovan Battista Giacomelli.[24] The Grand-Duchess returned a few months later for Easter 1590, and then again for Vespers on 31 December 1591, the feast day of the confraternity's patron the Archangel Raphael. On these occasions the confraternity sang Vespers with musical accompaniment by Raffaello Gucci. The devotions were enhanced by a costumed choir consisting of three angels, one of which was the Archangel Raphael, interpreted by Bernardo di Raffaello Carraresi, who, holding a silver vase in his hand, sang the 'life' of the archangel in a most delicate and angelic voice.[25]

---

23 Florence. Archivio di Stato. Compagnie religiose soppresse 156.2/4, fasc. C; transcribed in Burchi, 'Vita musicale' 42 footnote 23. There are two 'Giovanni Battista del Violino', both born in Brescia; one is Giovani Battista Jacomelli (ca. 1550–1608), the other Giovanni Battista Fontana (1589–1630). Given the dates of the sale of the *graviorgano* to the confraternity, it seems safe to assume that Caccini's reference is to Jacomelli, the older of the two men.

24 Florence. Archivio di Stato. Compagnie religiose soppresse 162.21/22 fols. 114v–115r, dated 31 December 1589: 'si dette subito principio cantando uno verso rosso tolto l'altro del salmo Ms Raffaello Gucci con uno strumento che Giovan Battista del Violioni rispondendo l'altro verso et coro e così finì'.

25 Florence. Archivio di Stato. Compagnie religiose soppresse 162.21/22 fol. 144r, dated 31 December 1591: 'con una voce e modo tanto delicato piutosto angelico che humano'.

On this last occasion the Grand Duchess was so visibly moved by the youths' singing and devotions that the acting Guardian Father, Niccolò Antifassi, took advantage of the situation and asked a favour of her: he asked if she would enrol her new-born son Cosimo II in the confraternity. The Grand Duchess was at first surprised by such a request, but then agreed with pleasure.[26] The future Grand Duke Cosimo II thus became a member of the Arcangelo Raffaello at the tender age of seven months thanks, to a large extent, to the high quality of musical performances at the confraternity.

3   Oratorios

In the second half of the seventeenth century the confraternity's involvement with music grew considerably when a new musical genre entered its repertory: the oratorio. Not only was this a much more musically complex genre, but also much more demanding on the physical and human resources of the confraternity. That is because oratorios were always performed on a specially constructed temporary platform at the altar and this required much more labour, expense and commitment on the part of the confraternity. Oratorios also attracted (and, it might be added, depended on) a much larger audience, sometimes numbering in the hundreds, that was accommodated not only in the oratory itself, but also in the musicians' loft, in rooms with windows looking into the oratory, and even on temporary scaffolding erected for the occasion.[27]

Because of the disruption such a major undertaking could create in the confraternity's devotional practices, at the Arcangelo Raffaello oratorios were performed after the evening service. They were normally divided into two parts

---

26   Florence. Archivio di Stato. Capitoli, Compagnie religiose soppresse 162.21/22 fol. 144r–v, dated 31 December 1591; see also the entry fee payment for Cosimo II recorded in ASF. Crs 165.40/48 fol. 36r, dated 6 January 1591/2.

27   Hill J.W., "Oratory Music in Florence, III: The Confraternities from 1655 to 1785", *Acta Musicologica* 58.1 (1986) 129–170, here 133. Hill's description is drawn mostly from the records of the youth Confraternity of the Purificazione, or of San Marco, which became the foremost confraternity for the performance of oratorios in Florence. For the slightly different manner used by the Oratorians at their church of San Felice, see Hill J.W., "Oratory Music in Florence, II: At San Firenze in the Seventeenth and Eighteenth Centuries", *Acta Musicologica* 51.2 (1979) 247–167, here 251–254, and, for the musical aspects, 256–259. For a fascinating and detailed description of the performance of an oratorio at the Confraternity of San Jacopo detta del Nicchio, see Florence. Archivio di Stato. Compagnie religiose soppresse 1246.10 fols. 299v–300r, translated in Smither H.E. *A History of the Oratorio*. Vol. 1 *The Oratorio in the Baroque Era. Italy. Vienna. Paris* (Chapel Hill: 1977) 286–288.

of thirty to forty-five minutes, each separated by an intermission during which one of the youngest members of the confraternity recited an oration praising the feast day's saint in what was clearly seen as a virtuoso performance. On the evening of 31 December 1692, for example, the scribe records that:

> La sera [...] si disse l'offizio della B.ma Vergine cantato con solennità, ma senza musica, a cui datosi compimento cominciarono i musici l'Oratorio composto di nuovo da Antonio Fineschi da Radda; intitolato le Nozze di Tobbia; terminata la prima parte del quale, celebrò le lodi del S.o Protettore un figliuolo del Panciatichi, che sta di casa in via de Servi, uno de nostri fratelli, quale per suo vivace spirito, diede grandissima sodisfazione all'udienza; l'opera ancora era eccellente; onde molto più piacque; indi si riprese la seconda parte dell'Oratorio, quale ancor questo piacque in estremo non solo per le parole, quanto per la musica; si fecero poi le preci, si resero le grazie.[28]

> In the evening [...] we recited the Office of the Most Blessed Virgin, solemnly sung, but without instrumental accompaniment. When it was finished, the musicians began the Oratorio newly composed by Antonio Fineschi da Radda entitled *Tobias's Wedding*. When the first part was finished, a son of the Panciatichi, who lives in via de' Servi, one of our brothers, recited the praises of our Protector Saint [Raphael]; because of his lively spirit, the audience was most satisfied. The work [that is, the text of the praises] was also excellent, so people liked it all the more. Then the second part of the Oratorio started, and this also was extremely well received not only because of the words, but also for the music. We then said the prayers and gave thanks.

By separating the oratorio from the devotional components of their celebrations, by associating it with a public oration delivered by a talented young member of the sodality, and by hiring professional and semi-professional musicians to perform the music, confraternities clearly intended oratorios to provide delight rather than supplement devotion or offer instruction. The delight, however, came with its own set of problems. The mayhem of a crowded hall filled with expectant visitors and its effect on the evening's devotions is described in a 1712 journal entry from the Confraternity of San Jacopo detta del Nicchio: visitors lined up outside for hours waiting for the doors to open; when

---

28   Florence. Archivio di Stato. Compagnie religiose soppresse 163.26/27 fol. 83r, dated 31 December 1692.

they entered they filled the oratory and overflowed into the cloak room, the outer corridor, and were eventually accommodated 'right up to the musicians' stage'; although the confraternity had decided earlier to forego Vespers that day and proceed directly to Compline, when the time came to start the service it was obliged to forego Compline as well because of the crowd in the hall; and, lastly, during the performance cries of 'viva!' erupted from the audience 'in loud voices' at particularly well-performed passages. As a devotional event, the oratorio was an abysmal failure, but as public entertainment it succeeded, and so the scribe recorded with unconcealed pleasure that 'everything was greeted by general applause'.[29]

4 Music in Theatre

The theatrical aspects seen in seventeenth- and eighteenth-century oratorios were long anticipated by the confraternities' engagement with live theatre. Indeed, it was the practice in youth confraternities occasionally to mount a short play or skit either to illustrate or enrich a religious celebration such as Christmas, Easter or a feast day, or to distract members from more secular, and possibly sinful activities taking place elsewhere, especially at Carnival time. At first a song or a dance was inserted into the action of the religious plays (*sacre rappresentazioni*) that confraternities mounted in the fifteenth and sixteenth centuries. By the late sixteenth century, the amount of music performed in conjunction with theatrical performances expanded significantly, especially by way of the *intermedi* that were inserted as entr'actes into the comedies the youths were then performing. At the same time, ever more music was included in the moral interludes and one-act moralities the confraternity was mounting, to the point that some of these plays were eventually sung from beginning to end, and this long before the actual 'birth' of opera in the early 1600s.

While many theatrical presentations included music, the first one to be set all to music is Giovan Maria Cecchi's lost play *La presentazione di Gesù al Tempio* (the Presentation of Jesus at the Temple), performed by the youths in the Arcangelo Raffaello on 2 February 1584/5.[30] As a completely sung play,

---

29 Florence. Archivio di Stato. Compagnie religiose soppresse 1246.10 fols. 299v–300r, dated 27 March 1712; translated, with comment at the end, in Smither, *A History of the Oratorio*, vol. 1, 286–287.

30 Florence. Archivio di Stato. Compaganie religiose soppresse 160.8/9 fol. 6r: 'Alcuni nostri giovanetti rappresentano in musica quando la Vergine nostra insieme con S. Giuseppe vanno al tempio a offerire Giesù a Simeone, opera del sudetto Cecchi'.

this performance predates by more than a decade Jacopo Peri's 1598 staging of *Dafne*, normally considered to be the very first opera. In the seventeenth century, sung plays became more frequent at the Arcangelo Raffaello, but not the norm. The more usual practice remained that of incorporating song into theatrical performances or the singing of madrigals in costume. Some members clearly had a good voice and a strong thespian inclination; one of these was Camillo di Giovanni Rondinelli, who joined the confraternity as a novice on 30 November 1582.[31] After reciting a few sermons in the confraternity in January 1583, December 1584, and March 1585, on Sunday 28 April 1585 Rondinelli was the central figure in an allegorical triumph that had him costumed as a Victory riding a triumphal cart, accompanied by many angels, with Death and a Devil at his feet, and reciting yet another sermon.[32] Three months later, on Sunday 28 July, for the feast day of St. Mary Magdalene, once the Office of the Blessed Virgin had been sung by some members of the confraternity accompanied by Raffaello Gucci on his instrument, and once Mass had been celebrated, Rondinelli dressed up as the saint and, in the company of four angels, both sang and recited some verses in her voice.[33]

In the seventeenth century, the music incorporated into the performance of spoken theatre was often the work of talented composers and performers. In September 1622 Giovan Maria Cecchi's *Commedia della Benedizion di Giacob* (Play on the Blessing of Jacob), revised by Jacopo Cicognini, was staged five times: on 11 and 21 September 'for the women'; on the 18 and 26 September 'for the men'; and on 23 September for the Grand Duke and Grand Duchess.

It included music especially composed by two leading musicians of the time: Jacopo Peri (1561–1633), who was then chapel master at the Grand-Ducal court, and Giovanni Battista da Gagliano, at that time chapel master at the cathedral.

---

31   Florence. Archivio di Stato. Compagnie religiose soppresse 162.19/20 fol. 18v. His brothers Giulio and Orazio also joined as novices on that date.

32   Florence. Archivio di Stato. Compagnie religiose soppresse 162.21/22 fol. 64r, dated 28 April 1585: 'et il giorno il santo vespro, et finito Camillo Rondinelli recitò alcuni versi in abito d'una vittoria quale comparse in compagnia in sur uno trionfo appiè la Morte et il Diavolo acompagniata da di molti angioli et finito di recitare quello [che] doveva dire dua angioli distribuirno a tutti i fratelli che si trovorno presenti uno santo per ciaschuno di poi ciaschuno fu licentiato'. For the sermons recited in previous years, see Florence. Archivio di Stato. Compagnie religiose soppresse 162.21/22 fols. 21v, 55r, 59r, 62r, dated 6 January 1582/3, 25 December 1584, 10 March 1584/5 and 7 April 1585 respectively.

33   Florence. Archivio di Stato. Compagnie religiose soppresse 162.21/22 fol. 66v, dated 28 July: 'essendo l'ora si cominciò l'ufitio della madonna, et si fece una buonissima musicha tutta di giovani di Compagnia et il Ghucci sonava il suo strumento et finito si disse la santa Messa di poi Camillo Rondinelli recitò alcuni versi rapresentando Santa Maria Maddalena venendo imezo di quattro angioli'.

Peri composed the parts for God the Father and the Archangel Raphael, while Giovanni Battista da Gagliano wrote those for the choir of angels, shepherds and the instrumental parts.[34]

5 Noise

But not all the sounds coming from the confraternity were musical, impressive, or even pleasant. Some of them were unwelcome noise that disturbed the confraternity's neighbours. That is because several youth confraternities owned a ball court (*pallottolaio*) where members could play ball, in particular the game of 'il Pallone col bracciale', a precursor version of hand-ball. The purpose of such a ball court was to provide members with an acceptable physical outlet for their youthful energies and to keep them from wandering away into situations or locations that might lead them into trouble. In 1619, for example, the scribe of the Confraternity of Sant'Antonio da Padova noted 'that already a month ago we all agreed by common consent that, in order to flee some worse scandal or trouble, we would have a ball court built in our meadow so that, on feast days, after divine offices, our youths may linger/entertain themselves'.[35]

The confraternity then set up a committee to establish some basic rules for the use of the ball court so that things should proceed in an orderly way. Trouble, however, was not easily avoided, especially when neighbours complained about the noise emanating from these ball courts. The youth Confraternity of Sant'Alberto Bianco, for example, ran into difficulties with its neighbour, *cavaliere* Pesciolini, who brought a lawsuit against them for the excessive noise the ball players were making. The confraternity responded by gathering affidavits

---

[34] Florence. Archivio di Stato. Compagnie religiose soppresse 162.22/23 fols. 94r–95v at dates indicated: 'La revisione della Commedia con tutte le aggiunte di versi et prose, che di sopra si fa mentione se ne diede la cura et fu opera del Dottore Jacopo Cicognini uno de nostri fratelli, che mai non mancò così nell'insegnare, come nel rammentare in detta opera. Le musiche dell'Angelo Raffaello, ed Iddio Padre furno del S. Jacopo Peri, e tanto basti per commendarlo. Le musiche degl'Angeli, Pastori, e sinfonie furono di Ms. Gio.batta da Gagliano nostro Maestro di Cappella, e ne riportò lode universale; et in specie da Ser.mi Padroni'. See also: Burchi, 'Vita musicale' 15–17.

[35] Florence. Archivio di Stato. Compagnie religiose soppresse 134.2/3 fol. 35v, dated December 1619: 'Ricordo come sino dal mese passato ci risolvemo tutti di comun consegno per fuggire qualche scandalo o disordine maggiore di fare in sul nostro prato un pallottolaio, acciò i nostri giovani il giorno delle feste, dopo i divini ufizi si possino trattenere'.

attesting to the presence of *pallottolai* in other confraternities.[36] In its affidavit, the Confraternity of the Arcangelo Raffaello pointed out that it had not one but two *pallottolai* and that they were located right under some windows of the Mazzinghi house next door, allegedly with no bother to the family living there. In their defence plea the youths of Sant'Alberto Bianco referred specifically to the affidavit from the Arcangelo Raffaello and noted that the Pesciolini, who were renters, did not need be concerned about noise since the Mazzinghi, who actually owned their house, had no complaints at all about the presence of two *pallottolai* under their windows.[37] In spite of this rationale, the archbishop ruled against them and ordered them not to play 'pallottole' or 'piastrelle' or any other game, nor to make any inappropriate noise under pain of an interdict for the confraternity and a fine of twenty-five *scudi* (175 *lire*) for each of the individuals involved. The judgement was severe, but perhaps merited. The game of *pallottole* does not seem to have been a quiet sport.

Eventually, even the Arcangelo Raffaello was obliged to move its ball courts to another location. By 1656 they had moved their *pallottolaio* to the garden of their Guardian Father's house. The records note that it had been built there because the Arcangelo Raffaello 'knew how necessary it was for the youths in the confraternity always to have a place where they could go for recreation and where they could gather on festive days after the usual meetings (*tornate*) and also on half-feast days in order to gather honestly and thus spend the free time that is so dangerous for youth'.[38] It is evident that although the confraternity was quick to defend the usefulness of a ball court for the moral well-being of its members, it still needed to take into consideration its peaceful co-existence with its neighbours and avoid disturbing them with excessive noise.

That peaceful co-existence applied to the brothers' relationship with each other, as well. Confraternity statutes and archival records indicate that a lot of emphasis was placed on mutual respect and peaceful coexistence, and this

---

36   Florence. Archivio di Stato. Compagnie Soppresse incamerate nel Bigallo, Compagnia della dottrina dell'Assunta e S. Alberto dei Fanciulli detta del ss Crocifisso e S. Alberto Bianco, fasc. 13 'Filza di documenti', contains the 'Attestationi che fanno le Compagnie nelle quali è Pallottolaio', dated 18 July 1624. I wish to thank Ludovica Sebregondi for having brought this document to my attention.

37   Florence. Archivio di Stato. Compagnie Soppresse incamerate nel Bigallo, Compagnia della dottrina dell'Assunta e S. Alberto dei Fanciulli detta del ss. Crocifisso e S. Alberto Bianco, fasc. 13 'Filza di documenti', unnumbered folio.

38   Florence. Archivio di Stato. Compagnie religiose soppresse 155.1/3 fasc. F unnumbered folio, dated 1 May 1656: 'conoscendo quanto sia necessario, che li Giovani della Compagnia habbino continuamente qualche luogo per passatempo ove possino adunarsi ne' Giorni festivi doppo le solite Tornate, et ancora nelle mezze festi per trattenersi in esso virtuosamente e passare l'Ozio tanto pericoloso alla Gioventù'.

seems to have worked. The Arcangelo Raffaello scribe, for example, records a fight in the hall only once in the confraternity's history (a difficult thing to believe), noting that

> During the festivities for our Patron the Archangel Raphael, two of our brothers had an argument, or came to blows, in our oratory. For this reason this morning the 11th [of January 1562] they were reprimanded by our Father Corrector, and warned in front of the entire confraternity, and he had them ask forgiveness of each other, and gave them a small penance to do.[39]

The entry points to the emotional volatility of some teenaged males, but also to the confraternity's efforts to keep such raucous behaviour in check.

Members were required to behave well not only in the confraternity, but also outside it. Confraternity statutes normally devote an entire chapter to the 'Life and Good Habits' of their members stipulating, for example, that members should be obedient to the Church and to their parents, keep chaste, recite certain prayers at different times in the day, attend Mass daily, avoid places of ill repute (such as taverns) and morally dangerous pastimes (such as card playing, jousts, or skirmishes), nor were they to gossip or tell lies.[40]

The temptation to indulge in raucous behaviour, however, was there. Ottavio Pollini, a member of the Arcangelo Raffaello, was

> erased from the confraternity rolls and excluded [...] for having caused arguments on several occasions, and for having played cards several times after having been reprimanded for this, and for having broken the gilded garland on the confraternity door, and for many other things that are better left unsaid.[41]

---

39   Florence. Archivio di Stato. Compagnie religiose soppresse 160.8/9, dated 11 January 1561/2: 'Per la Festività del nostro Protettore l'Arcangelo Raffaello due de' nostri fratelli fecero questione insieme, o alle pugna in nostra Compagnia, per questo in detta mattina del dì 11 del sudetto mese furono dal nostro P. Correttore ripresi, et ammoniti nel mezzo di Compagnia, e fece chieder perdonanza l'uno all'altro, e data loro un poca di penitenza'.

40   Florence. Archivio di Stato. Capitoli, Compagnie religiose soppresse 752 fol. 9r: 'Item che non si giuochi ad alchun giuocho, né si stia a vedere giucare et maximamente a giuochi vietati dalla Santa Madre Chiesa. Et non sia giucatore né bestemiatore, né mormoratore, né dichino bugie. Et non usino i nostri fratelli in luoghi dove si tengha taverne, né usino di nocte in alchun luogho o ridotti di balli o suoni o canti disonesti. Né dove si faccino giostre schermaglie o altri expectaculi populari'.

41   Florence. Archivio di Stato. Compagnie religiose soppresse 160.6/7, dated 25 May 1562.

Half a century later, another member, Tommaso di Stefano Chiari, was expelled for having punched a brother at the confraternity door.[42] The confraternity did not look kindly on this sort of behaviour and censured the offender; fortunately, however, such behaviour was extremely rare and confraternity youths, on the whole, contributed much more pleasant sounds to Florence's private and urban landscape.[43]

6 Conclusion

From creating beautiful music to making unwanted noise, youth confraternities in early modern Florence were very much part of the local urban soundscape. Their devotional activities were enriched by a variety of musical forms, some old, some new; these ranged from Latin hymns to vernacular *laude*, from psalms to madrigals, from vocal to instrumental music, from string to keyboard instruments, with performances by gifted amateurs and professional musicians that attracted the attention and interest, not to mention the participation, of even the highest echelons of Florentine society. At the same time, these young men were very much young men, ready to play ball games and make so much noise that neighbours complained and filed suits against them. Briefly put, in Florence confraternity youths were seen, but also very much heard.

Bibliography

Primary Sources
Florence, Archivio di Stato
Capitoli, Compagnie religiose soppresse 627.
Capitoli, Compagnie religiose soppresse 752.

---

[42] Florence. Archivio di Stato. Compagnie religiose soppresse 160.8/9, dated 2 June 1609. For a chart and study of expulsions from the adult confraternity of Gesù Pellegrino in 1334–1369, see Henderson J., *Piety and Charity in Late Medieval Florence* (Oxford: 1994), 135–140.

[43] For a more extensive discussion of raucous behaviour in confraternities, see Eisenbichler K., 'Adolescence and Damnation: Sin and Youth in Florentine Confraternities', in Arnade P. – Rocke M. (eds.), *Power and Public Behaviours. Essays in Honour of Richard C. Trexler*, CRRS Essays and Studies 17 (Toronto: 2008), 77–94; and Eisenbichler K., 'Mauvais Enfants et Confréries: Les péchés des jeunes à Florence à la fin du XVe siècle', in Cazes H. (ed.), *Histoires d'enfants: représentations et discours de l'enfance sous l'Ancien Régime* (Quebec: 2008) 261–274. For a more general discussion about youths and misbehaviour, see Ottavia N., *Il seme della violenza: Putti, fanciulli e mammoli nell'Italia tra Cinque e Seicento* (Rome – Bari: 1995).

Compagnie religiose soppresse 134.2/3.
Compagnie religiose soppresse 155.1/3, fasc. F.
Compagnie religiose soppresse 156.2/4, fasc. C.
Compagnie religiose soppresse 160.6/7.
Compagnie religiose soppresse 160.7/8.
Compagnie religiose soppresse 160.8/9.
Compagnie religiose soppresse 162.21/22.
Compagnie religiose soppresse 162.22/23.
Compagnie religiose soppresse 163.26/27.
Compagnie religiose soppresse 165.40/48.
Compagnie religiose soppresse 1246.10.
Compagnie Soppresse incamerate nel Bigallo, Compagnia della dottrina dell'Assunta e S. Alberto dei Fanciulli detta del ss. Crocifisso e S. Alberto Bianco, fasc. 13 'Filza di documenti'.

Florence, Biblioteca Nazionale Centrale di Firenze

Magliab. xxv, cod. 418 Del Migliore Ferdinando Leopoldo. 'Zibaldone Istorico, 28. Compagnie' and 'Registro delle compagnie di Firenze'.

Magliab. xxxi, cod. 11 fols. 2r–9r 'Capitoli, 1427' [Compagnia di San Giovanni Evangelista].

Baldinucci Filippo, *Notizie de' professori di disegno da Cimabue in qua* (Florence, Tartini e Franchi: 1728).

Secondary Sources

Burchi G., *Musica e musicisti nella Compagnia della 'Scala' di Firenze (1556–1785)* (Laura thesis, Università degli Studi di Firenze: 1971–1972).

Burchi G., "Vita musicale e spettacoli alla Compagnia della Scala di Firenze fra il 1560 e il 1675", *Note d'Archivio per la Storia Musicale* n.s. 1 (1983) 9–50.

Cecchi G.M., *Five Plays for the Archangel Raphael*, trans. K. Eisenbichler. Renaissance and Reformation Texts in Translation 14 (Toronto: 2020).

Eisenbichler K., "Adolescence and Damnation: Sin and Youth in Florentine Confraternities", in Arnade P. – Rocke M. (eds.), *Power and Public Behaviours. Essays in Honour of Richard C. Trexler*, CRRS Essays and Studies 17 (Toronto: 2008) 77–94.

Eisenbichler K., "Mauvais Enfants et Confréries: Les pêchés des jeunes à Florence à la fin du xve siècle", in Cazes H. (ed.), *Histoires d'enfants: représentations et discours de l'enfance sous l'Ancien Régime* (Quebec: 2008) 261–274.

Eisenbichler K., *The Boys of the Archangel Raphael. A Youth Confraternity in Florence, 1411–1785* (Toronto: 1998).

Henderson J., *Piety and Charity in Late Medieval Florence* (Oxford: 1994).

Hill J.W., "Florentine *Intermedi sacri e morali*, 1549–1622", in *La musique et le rite sacré et profane. Actes du XIIIe Congrès de la Société Internationale de Musicologie*, 2 vols. (Strasbourg: 1986) vol. 2, 265–301.

Hill J.W., "Oratory Music in Florence, I: 'Recitar Cantando' 1583–1655", *Acta Musicologica* 51.1 (1979) 108–136.

Hill J.W., "Oratory Music in Florence, II: At San Firenze in the Seventeenth and Eighteenth Centuries", *Acta Musicologica* 51.2 (1979) 247–267.

Hill J.W., "Oratory Music in Florence, III: The Confraternities from 1655 to 1785", *Acta Musicologica* 58.1 (1986) 129–179.

Montanari G., "Organi e claviorgani del Granprincipe Ferdinando de' Medici", *Informazione Organistica* (2008) 281–368.

Niccoli O., *Il seme della violenza: Putti, fanciulli e mammoli nell'Italia tra Cinque e Seicento* (Rome: 1995).

Polizzotto L., *Children of the Promise: The Confraternity of the Purification and the Socialization of Youths in Florence, 1427–1785* (New York: 2004).

Smither H.E. *A History of the Oratorio*. Vol. 1 *The Oratorio in the Baroque Era. Italy. Vienna. Paris* (Chapel Hill: 1977).

Taddei I. *Fanciulli e giovani. Crescere a Firenze nel Rinascimento* (Florence: 2001).

CHAPTER 13

'In parole' and 'in canto': The Songs and Prayers of the Disciplinati in Early Modern Milan

Daniele V. Filippi

Abstract

Studies of the Italian lauda, and more generally of communal singing in the fifteenth and sixteenth century, have mostly focused on Central and North-Eastern Italy, leaving Milan in a grey area. A scarcely known set of late-fifteenth-century manuscripts currently held at the Biblioteca Trivulziana contains, however, several offices for the confraternities of Disciplinati (or Battuti) of Sant'Agata and of Santa Marta. The offices include various kinds of rhythmic prayers, both in the vernacular (*laude*) and in Latin, some of which are explicitly labelled for singing. Based on the study of these manuscripts and other contextual evidence, the present chapter explores the role of such confraternities in the soundscape of early modern Milan, also highlighting their remarkable contribution to public processions.

Keywords

Milan – communal singing – lauda – flagellant confraternities – Carlo Borromeo

1   Four Manuscripts for Two Confraternities

The Biblioteca Trivulziana in Milan holds four remarkable confraternal manuscripts from the late fifteenth century.[1] They were written for two different Milanese confraternities of flagellants (the *disciplini* or *disciplinati* or *battuti*): Cod. Triv. 383 for the confraternity of Sant'Agata; and Cod. Triv. 416, 417, 418 and

---

[1]   I wish to thank the staff of the Archivio Storico Civico e Biblioteca Trivulziana, Milan, in particular Dr. Loredana Minenna, for their kind assistance during my research. I am also grateful to codicologist Martina Pantarotto for her advice.

419 for the confraternity of Santa Marta in Porta Ticinese.[2] They all contain offices and prayers, including some for processions, in Italian and Latin. As will be seen, they explicitly attest that Milanese disciplini sang during such offices, and offer interesting examples of how Italian laude were used alongside other prayers and songs.[3]

Ms. 383 is a small paper manuscript (202 × 144 mm) of 52 folios, mainly written by a single professional scribe in Gothic rotunda (with a few additions by different, less skilled hands), with red rubrics, red and blue *litterae notabiliores*, as well as some pen-flourished initials and decorations.[4] The detailed colophon at fol. 40v [Fig. 13.1] provides information on the name of the scribe (the otherwise unknown Bernardus Martignonus), the names of the Sant'Agata confraternity officials (the prior Imolus de Crispis and the subprior Christoforus de Cataniis), and the dating of the manuscript: 17 September 1476, 'under the reign of Galeazzo Maria "Anguigero" [belonging to the Visconti-Sforza dynasty], fifth Duke of Milan'. The manuscript contains an office for the Assumption of the Blessed Virgin, an office for Advent, and a common office; it is also provided with a table of the contents at fols. 41r–42v. Additions include further prayers

---

2   From hence forward I will indicate the manuscripts simply as Ms. 383, Ms. 416, etc. Briefly described in the Trivulziana catalogues by Porro and Santoro (see below), these manuscripts have been mentioned by several scholars from various disciplines, including Alberigo G., "Contributi alla storia delle confraternite dei disciplinati e della spiritualità laicale nei secc. XV e XVI", in *Il Movimento dei Disciplinati nel Settimo Centenario dal suo inizio* (*Perugia 1260*) (Perugia: 1962; repr. 1986) 156–252, here 169–170n4; Banfi L., "Review of R. Bettarini, *Jacopone e il Laudario Urbinate*", *Giornale storico della letteratura italiana* 150 (1973) 393–411, here 407–408n21; and Longo P.G., *Letteratura e pietà a Novara tra XV e XVI secolo* (Novara – Borgomanero: 1986), *passim*. Ironically, both Alberigo and Banfi announced forthcoming studies of the manuscripts that however, to the best of my knowledge, have never seen the light. The first musicological mention of the manuscripts is in Prizer W.F., "Popular Piety in Renaissance Mantua: The Lauda and Flagellant Confraternities", in Zayaruznaya A. – Boorman S. – Blackburn B.J. (eds.), *Qui musicam in se habet: Studies in Honor of Alejandro Enrique Planchart* (Middleton WI: 2015) 183–221 *passim*.

3   The standard reference for the laude of the disciplinati is Barr C., *The Monophonic Lauda and the Lay Religious Confraternities of Tuscany and Umbria in the Late Middle Ages* (Kalamazoo: 1988), which focuses on the early period of the flagellant movement in Central Italy. Further useful considerations and references are found in Prizer, "Popular Piety in Renaissance Mantua".

4   See Porro G., *Catalogo dei codici manoscritti della Trivulziana* (Turin: 1884) 222; Santoro C., *I codici medioevali della Biblioteca Trivulziana: catalogo* (Milan: 1965) 57; Pontone M., *I manoscritti datati dell'Archivio storico civico e della Biblioteca Trivulziana di Milano*, Manoscritti datati d'Italia (Florence: 2011) 31; and MANUS ONLINE, https://manus.iccu.sbn .it/cnmd/0000196889. A full digitisation is available at https://graficheincomune.comune .milano.it/GraficheInComune/immagine/Cod.+Triv.+383,+c.+Iv+-+c.+1r.

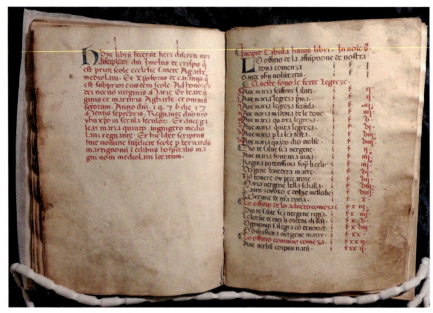

FIGURE 13.1 Milan. Archivio Storico Civico e Biblioteca Trivulziana, Cod. Triv. 383 fols. 40v–41r, colophon and first page of the tabula
© COMUNE DI MILANO – ALL RIGHTS RESERVED

about several saints (Martin, Andrew, Lawrence, and Roch) and a Marian hymn.[5]

Unfortunately, the four Mss. 416–419 do not have any colophons. Based on the watermarks of the first three codices, Caterina Santoro assigned them to the late fifteenth century,[6] which, pending more accurate palaeographical investigations of the various (prevailingly Gothic) scripts, seems perfectly plausible. At least one detail in Ms. 416 indicates that it was penned under Sforza rule but was also used during the successive French occupation, after the fall of Ludovico il Moro in 1499–1500: the text of a prayer for the reigning duke at fol. 34v was changed from 'al nostro [*illegible*] ducha de Milano' to 'al nostro *Re et* ducha de Milano'.[7]

Ms. 416 (203 × 145 mm) has 74 folios, written by at least five different hands. It contains an office for Lent including the Seven Penitential Psalms, litanies and other prayers; an evening office for Fridays ('ofizio da dire li venerdì de pasione

---

5 All the descriptions mentioned above erroneously state that the manuscript contains only the Assumption office, the *tabula* and the additions.

6 See Porro, *Catalogo dei codici manoscritti della Trivulziana* 222, and especially Santoro, *I codici medioevali* 71–72 for more thorough descriptions of this and the subsequent manuscripts.

7 A similar correction occurs at fol. 37r: 'ti degne de conservare la nostra citade' was changed to 'ti degne conservare *il re et* la nostra citade'.

da sera'), with specially added prayers for the time of plague; an office for the day of the Holy Cross; and the so-called Short Office of the Cross (largely based on the hymn *Patris sapientia*).

Ms. 417 (200 × 145 mm) has 75 folios, written by several hands: basically, each office was written by a different scribe, often on paper of a different kind. As in its sister manuscripts, later corrections and additions, as well as the darkening of page corners, attest to prolonged use. The manuscript contains offices for a specific portion of the liturgical year: an Advent office, a Christmas office, one for St. Stephen, another one for Christmastide (with additional prayers related to the feasts of St. John the Apostle and of the Holy Innocents), an office for the Circumcision of Jesus, and finally one for Epiphany.

Ms. 418 is smaller than the previous ones (160 × 115 mm) but thicker (128 folios). Written by several hands, it includes the Seven Penitential Psalms with further prayers; an office for an unspecified period or feast; an office which, according to a rubric added at fol. 33v, was intended for the period between Epiphany and the Ambrosian Carnival, but whose prayers seem more appropriate for Eastertide; an office for the feast of the Holy Cross and for Good Friday ('Questo offitio sie da dire el die de sancta croce et in die de passione'); the Short Office of the Cross (as in Ms. 416, but without explanations in the vernacular); and an Easter office ('Ofitio de la resurectione'). The contents of Ms. 418 seem therefore to complement liturgically those of Ms. 417 and partially overlap with those of Ms. 416.

Ms. 419 is similar in size to Ms. 418 (165 × 120 mm) and has 73 folios (with a modern flyleaf added at the beginning). Differently from the previously described manuscripts, it is entirely dedicated to prayers and songs for processions. What seems to be a basic scheme for a procession is complemented by specific prayers for liturgical periods (for example, from Easter to Ascension) or host/destination churches (such as Santa Maria della Scala).

Before I turn to the structure and the texts of the offices, I will consider the institutions for which these manuscripts were prepared. First of all, whereas the colophon of Ms. 383 explicitly connects it with the confraternity of Sant'Agata, how is it possible to know that Mss. 416–419 belonged to Santa Marta? On the one hand, the information provided by Giulio Porro in his catalogue of the library then belonging to the Trivulzio family (1884) must be relied on.[8] On

---

8   Porro, *Catalogo dei codici manoscritti della Trivulziana*; Porro had access to previous inventories and materials regarding the collection (see his preface to the catalogue on page xiv). The rich Trivulzio collection was acquired by the city of Milan in 1935 and merged with the Historic Civic Archive and further collections, to form the institution now known as Archivio Storico Civico e Biblioteca Trivulziana, hosted in the Castello Sforzesco (https://trivulziana.milanocastello.it).

the other hand, the texts of rubrics and prayers provide a few clues: St. Martha is the only saint, apart from the patron of Milan, St. Ambrose, to be invoked three times in a litany included in Ms. 416 (fol. 13v) and in its appended prayers (fol. 16r), as well as in Ms. 418 (fol. 13v);[9] and a rubric in Ms. 419 refers to a prayer to be pronounced 'behind [the church of] Santa Marta' ('dreto de sancta Marta', fol. 9r), apparently at the beginning of the processions that started inside the oratory ('in front of our home altar', 'denanze a l'altà de caxa', fol. 2r).

The confraternity of the Disciplini di Santa Marta in Porta Ticinese[10] was considered the earliest company of flagellants in the city: as such it obtained pride of place in the general processions after Archbishop Carlo Borromeo's reform of 1572.[11] According to the eighteenth-century erudite Serviliano Lattuada, the confraternity moved from its previous oratory to a newly built one, close to San Giorgio in Palazzo, in 1497: the new church contained remarkable artworks, including an altarpiece by Bernardino Luini (1481/1482–1532) with the Blessed Virgin among St. Martha and St. Mary Magdalene, an ancient processional crucifix, and frescoes representing St. Domenico Loricato – an eleventh-century Camaldolese, disciple of St. Pier Damiani and precursor of the flagellants' penitential practices – and Raniero Fasani (*fl.* 1260–82), the acknowledged initiator of the *battuti* movement, both 'dressed in the habit of the disciplini'.[12] In its early phase, during the fourteenth century, the confraternity ministered to convicts sentenced to death, but later the task passed to the Scuola of San Giovanni alle Case Rotte. The Disciplini of Santa Marta gathered for praying and processing, and performed charitable duties, supported by bequests.[13] Membership was open to men and women.

---

9   The same happens with St. Agatha (and again St. Ambrose) in a litany included in Ms. 383 (fols. 24v–28r).

10 Not to be confused with the homonymous confraternity of Porta Orientale. Milan was divided into districts named after the various gates (*porte*) in the city walls.

11 Castiglione Giovanni Antonio, *Gli honori de gli antichi disciplinati* [...] *Decuria prima* (Milan, Giovanni Battista Bidelli: 1622) 81: 'Segue in ultimo col primo grado di precedenza tra tutte le Compagnie de' Disciplini la Scuola di S. Marta, vicina alla Collegiata di S. Georgio al Palazzo in Porta Ticinese'.

12 Lattuada Serviliano, *Descrizione di Milano*, 5 vols. (Milan: Giuseppe Cairoli, 1737–1738) III: 142–145. The church was destroyed in 1787 after the suppression of the confraternity the previous year.

13 Archivio di Stato di Milano. *Archivio generale del Fondo di Religione* 696 contains a seventeenth-century document that summarises the various goods distributed to the poor by the confraternity (food, wine, salt and vestments) based on various bequests from 1513 to 1656. Interestingly, among the testators the name of the printer Pacifico Ponzio, or

The confraternity of Sant'Agata in Porta Romana too was among the most ancient companies of disciplini in Milan, apparently second only to Santa Marta.[14] Their church, provided with relics, was close to the Basilica of San Nazaro Maggiore. A detail in the text of Ms. 383 suggests that their prayer book might have been partly derived from other manuscripts in use at Santa Marta: at the bottom of fol. 28v, a prayer invokes God 'whose Son deigned to be a guest in the house of the blessed Agatha' ('cuius filius in ede beate Agathe hospitari dignatus est').[15] A different hand wrote 'Marte' above 'Agathe', thus restoring the proper sense of the sentence: it was clearly St. Martha of Bethany who hosted Jesus in her house, as mentioned in the Gospel (Luke 10:38–42), not the third-century Sicilian martyr St. Agatha. Likely, the scribe of the manuscript was ordered to copy these prayers from a book belonging to the sister confraternity of Santa Marta (or possibly to another confraternity dedicated to that saint), with the proviso that the name of Martha was substituted by that of Agatha, in order to appropriate the book. An excess of zeal led him to change the name in this case too, although the modified prayer no longer made much sense. To amend the situation, different hands added a note in the margin, probably 'non dicitur' ('not to be said'), and another one at the top-right margin of the facing folio (29r), where the prayer ends: 'de sancta Agatha', possibly requiring the insertion of an appropriate prayer for the confraternity patroness.

Occasionally, the two confraternities performed joint offices: for instance, according to an eighteenth-century document, a will of 1499 required the *scuole* of Santa Marta in Porta Ticinese, Sant'Agata in Porta Romana, Santa Marta in Porta Orientale and San Giovanni Battista in Porta Comasina to pray an office together every year for the soul of the testator.[16] A comparison of the Advent offices in Mss. 383 and 417, however, shows a similarity of construction and many shared texts, but also substantial textual and structural variants.

---

       da Ponte appears (bequest of 1594). Most of the Santa Marta papers preserved at the State Archive deal with seventeenth- and eighteenth-century administrative issues.

14   Lattuada, *Descrizione di Milano* II: 314–320. See also Castiglione, *Gli honori de gli antichi disciplinati* 80–81.

15   On the circulation of texts among earlier confraternities, see: Mascherpa G., "Percorsi confraternali nel medioevo lombardo. Sulle laude in volgare di un codice laurenziano (ms. Ashburnham 1179)", *Filologia italiana* 13 (2016) 23–45.

16   Archivio di Stato di Milano. *Archivio generale del Fondo di Religione* 696, unnumbered fols., will of Francesco del Conte and related papers.

2 The Lauda in Its Habitat

A few traits emerging from an examination of the Trivulziana manuscripts seem especially noteworthy. First of all, the mix of Italian and Latin, both in the rubrics and in the prayers; both languages appear in a highly irregular textual format, with shaky spellings, inconsistencies and alterations of metrical forms. This bilingual character (found in other Milanese religious books of the period)[17] attests to the social and cultural mix of lay confraternities. A second notable aspect is the performative nature of these books and of their texts: not only do the manuscripts contain rubrics, as liturgical books do, but they also include explanations and directions, normally in the vernacular, to be pronounced by the prayer leader in order to introduce an office or one of its parts. Furthermore, these books amalgamate to the distinctive penitential exercise of the discipline (recurrently enacted during the recitation of standard prayers) sung and recited elements of different origins and apparently disparate 'genres', ranging from liturgical, to paraliturgical, to devotional (insofar as such labels are useful as reference points in an often seamless continuum of religious textuality and practice).

A good example is the brief Christmas office included in Ms. 417 (fols. 17r–23v). After the initial standard versicle and response ('Domine exaudi orationem meam. / Et clamor meus ad te veniat') and a Latin oration ('Oremus. Grata tibi sit quesumus domine hodierne nativitatis domini nostri Iesu Christi hec oblatio [...]'), is found a remarkable Italian rubric:

> Chossì como havemo laudato lo nostro Signore in parole, anchora lo laudaremo con alchune verssy in canto.
>
> As we have praised our Lord in words, we will praise him again with some sung verses.

Similar instructions, that vary the phrasing but retain the clear performative opposition between *in parole* and *in canto* (or *in canti*), recur over and over again in these manuscripts: they are especially important because they give

---

17   See Cattaneo E., "Istituzioni ecclesiastiche milanesi", in *Storia di Milano* IX (Milan: 1961) 509–722, here 667, 695. The booklet of the *Litanie triduane* edited by Pietro Casola in 1494 had Italian rubrics, and collections of Sunday Gospel and Epistle readings in Italian were printed in the 1470s.

a clear indication of which items were actually sung during the offices.[18] The sung verse thus introduced is the Latin carol *Verbum caro factum est*, with refrain and seven stanzas. The subsequent instruction prescribes the recitation of a lauda:

> Anchora diremo una altra lauda in parole, dicendo:
>
> Again we will recite another lauda in words, saying:

Note that the phrase 'another lauda' implies that the same term was also used for *Verbum caro factum est*. The lauda *In la degna stalla del dolze mamolino* follows, with ripresa and fourteen stanzas. After the lauda, an instruction prescribes the taking of the discipline while praying the *Pater noster* and *Ave Maria*. There follows another Christmas-themed oration encircled by versicles and responses. Then a new instruction introduces a sung lauda:

> Anchora diremo alchuni versi in canti laudando e magnificando lo nostro Salvatore, dicendo:
>
> Again, we will say some verses in song, praising and magnifying our Savior, saying:

The lauda is *Laudemo l'amore divino*, here presented with ripresa and six stanzas. The subsequent instruction calls for 'un'altra lauda in parole', which, rather surprisingly, is the same *Laudemo l'amore divino*, but in a much longer version (eighteen stanzas). This happens in other cases too: within one office or across offices, a shorter version of the same piece is introduced by an 'in canto' rubric, whereas a longer one is accompanied by an 'in parole' rubric.

There follows a new instruction prescribing the *Pater-Ave* 'fazando la disiplina', with versicles and oration, followed by another 'in canti' rubric: the sung verse is *Ave Iesu Christe verbum Patris*. Interestingly, this prayer, most commonly beginning with *Ave Domine Iesu Christe* and often found in books of hours and other prayer books, was set in a cycle of polyphonic *motetti missales* copied in the choirbook Librone 1 prepared for Milan's Duomo under Franchinus Gaffurius ca. 1490.[19] As is often the case in these offices, the next rubric moves

---

[18] Here, as in several other cases in these manuscripts, a later hand expunged the rubric and the sung verses with pen strokes (see below for further comments).

[19] See Ferro E., "'Old Texts for New Music'? Textual and Philological Observations on the Cycles 'Salve Mater Salvatoris' and 'Ave Domine Iesu Christe' from Librone 1", in

the prayer focus from Christ to the Virgin Mary, and introduces 'another prayer' ('una altra pregera'), namely the lauda *Ave Maria fontana viva / ferma speranza de la vita activa*, in which the first words of each stanza, taken together, form the Latin *Ave Maria* prayer. After a new session of self-flagellation and an oration with its versicles and responses, the office ends with an Italian valediction and the singing of the *Te deum* ('Te deum laudamus, te dominum confitemur in canto').

Another example is afforded by the common office included in Ms. 383 (fols. 22v–35v). The preliminary part of the office starts *ex abrupto* with the Eucharistic short hymn *Ave verum corpus natum* (here spelled *Ave verbum corpus natum*), without any instruction. There follows an introduction in Italian, asking God for peace 'especially in this city of ours of Milan and in all Lombardy' ('spetialmente in questa nostra citade de Milano e in tuta Lonbardia'). In the continuation, the prior, speaking in the first person, exhorts his 'brothers and companions' ('fratelli mey e compagnony') to fight against all temptation and to arm themselves with the sign of the cross. After which the office proper starts with a further long introduction in Italian, a series of prayers, and the customary direction to take the discipline while praying three Hail Marys. There then follow the litany of saints – with, as already mentioned, the names of Ambrose and Agatha in relief – and a sort of general prayer in Latin (for the confraternity leaders and all the congregation, for benefactors and others), and a lengthy prayer addressed to Christ in Italian, preceded and concluded by a *Pater noster* and *Ave Maria* with discipline. After an oration, the now familiar 'in parole'/'in canto' rubric is found, introducing the lauda *Quando Signore Iesù serò y may / grato e cognoscente*, with ripresa and eight stanzas [Fig. 13.2].[20] The subsequent rubric prescribes a prayer to the 'glorious Virgin Mary': *O stella matutina / dolze vergene Maria*, with ripresa and a long series of irregular stanzas, most starting with 'Prega per [...]' ('Pray for [...]') and encompassing a wide range of intentions. After further prayers, and seven Hail Marys with discipline, there follows another 'in parole'/'in canto' rubric, this time introducing the

---

Filippi D.V. – Pavanello A. (eds.), *Motet Cycles between Devotion and Liturgy*, Schola Cantorum Basiliensis Scripta 7 (Basel: 2019) 189–218; Filippi D.V., "Where Devotion and Liturgy Meet: Re-Assessing the Milanese Roots of the 'Motetti Missales'", in Filippi – Pavanello (eds.), *Motet Cycles between Devotion and Liturgy* 53–91, here 83–86 (where I erroneously referred to an Advent, instead of a Christmas, office); Filippi D.V. (ed.), *"Ave, Domine Jesu Christi": A Motetti Missales Cycle from the Milanese Libroni, attributed to Loyset Compère*, Motetti Missales Edition / Recent Researches in the Music of the Renaissance 182 (Middleton WI: 2024).

20 Here, too (fol. 31v), a later hand wrote an instruction in the internal margin ('el canto non dir' [or possibly: 'non dicitur']), and drew a vertical stroke to the left of the ripresa and the first two stanzas.

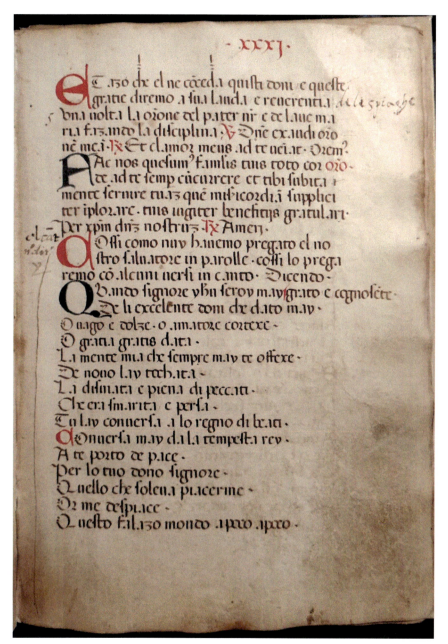

FIGURE 13.2 Milan, Archivio Storico Civico e Biblioteca Trivulziana. Cod. Triv. 383 fol. 31r, part of the common office, with directions regarding the discipline and 'in canto' rubric introducing the lauda *Quando Signore Iesù serò y may / grato e cognoscente*
© COMUNE DI MILANO – ALL RIGHTS RESERVED

lauda *Non temere oy pecatore*, with ripresa and sixteen stanzas. Then, an Italian exhortation initiates the prayers for the souls in purgatory, which include the psalms *Miserere* and *De profundis* 'fazando la disciplina'. One of the following prayers recommends to God, in garbled Latin, the 'souls of your male and female flagellant servants' ('animas famulis et famulabus tuis disciplinatis'). After further versicles and responses, a rubric prescribes the intonation of the *Te deum* ('se leva el Te deum laudamus'), if appropriate to the liturgical season, probably while moving from the church to the (upstairs) oratory,[21] and then the recitation of a final prayer in the oratory itself.

With this brief overview of the disciplini offices as attested in the five Trivulziana manuscripts, I can now focus on the sung repertory they contain. The following table lists all the metrical items included in the manuscripts, distinguishing those explicitly marked for singing by 'in canto' rubrics [Table 13.1].[22] (A preliminary table of external concordances for the Italian laude is given in the Appendix.)

TABLE 13.1 The metrical items in the Trivulziana manuscripts with an indication of those marked as to be performed 'in canto'

Incipit	Ms(s)	'in canto'
Anima benedeta / Dell'alto creatore	418	×
Anima innamorata / Di Yhesu vero sposo	417	
Ave dulcis, ave pia	417	
Ave fuit prima salus	383, 417	
Ave Maria fontana viva / Ferma speranza de la vita activa	383, 417, 419	× (417 [short version]; 419 [incipit only])
Ave stella matutina / Peccatorum medicina	416	
Ave verbum [*sic*] corpus natum	383	
Ave virgo sanctissima	418	

21 As suggested by a more explicit instruction at the beginning of the Advent office in Ms. 417: 'da poy se leva andando suxo in horatorio el Te deum laudamus' (fol. 13v). The premises of the disciplinati confraternities often had a ground-floor church (open to the faithful) and a meeting room or oratory on the first floor, used for confraternity meetings but also provided with an altar; see: Cecchini G., "Flagellanti (o Disciplinati o Battuti)", in Pelliccia G. – Rocca G. (eds.), *Dizionario degli Istituti di Perfezione* IV (Rome: 1977) cols. 60–72, here 70; and Rubini G., "La spiritualità del movimento dei Disciplinati", in Ghisini C. – Rubini G. (eds.), *I Disciplini: Ricerche sulle confraternite del Mantovano* (Mantua: 1989) 35–83, here 40–48.

22 The incipits have not been normalised (except for the capitalisation of proper names and *nomina sacra*); in case of multiple occurrences, I have privileged the 'less corrupt' form.

TABLE 13.1 The metrical items in the Trivulziana manuscripts (*cont.*)

Incipit	Ms(s)	'in canto'
Ave virgo virginum	417	
Ave Yhesu Christe verbum Patris	417	×
Canto zoioxo e dolze mellodie	383, 419	× (419)
Christi confessor / Presul adque pastor	419	
Dio te salve sancta vergene regina incoronata	383, 417	
Dulcis Yhesu memoria	418	× (short version)
Gaude sponsa Deo electa	417	×
Gaude virgo mater Christi	417, 418	× (both mss.)
Gaude Yhesu voluntatis	383	
Iesu fazo lamento	417, 418	× (417, 418 [short version])
In la degna stalla del dolze mamolino	417	
L'amore Yhesu venendo	417	×
Laudemo l'amore divino	417	× (short versions)
Maria diana stella	418, 419	× (both mss. [incipit only])
Maria vergene bella / Schala che ascende e guida a l'alto celo	383, 418, 419	× (419 in two occurrences)
Non temere oy peccatore	383, 418, 419	× (all mss.)
O alta regina con la Trinitade	416	
O croce sancta gloriosa et degna	416	
O croxe triumfante e gloriosa	416	×
O gloriosa vergene Maria / Perpetua vergene de le vere madre	416, 418, 419	
O imperatrixe de lo eterno regno	416	
O Spirito Sancto paraclito amoroso	419	× (incipit only)
O stella matutina / Dolce vergene Maria	383, 419	
O voy che amati lo creatore Dio	418, 419	× (both mss.)
Ogni omo s'alegra con devotione / In questo sancto Advento	383, 417	
Patris sapientia	416, 418	
Quando i' guardo lo mio Signore / Che pende in croxe cossì impiegato	416	× (one of two occurrences)
Quando Signore Yhesu serò y may	383	×

TABLE 13.1 The metrical items in the Trivulziana manuscripts (*cont.*)

Incipit	Ms(s)	'in canto'
Quando te guardemo in croce Signor nostro	416	
Regina potentissima / Sopra li cieli tu sey exaltata	383, 419	
Salve mater misericordie	418, 419	× (418 [short version])
Salve virgo que orbi presides	417	
Spiritu Sancto che inluminasto	419	×
Verbum caro factum est	417	×
Vergene benedeta / Madre del Salvatore	383, 418, 419	× (418 and 419, but not in all occurrences)

All in all, forty-four items bear an explicit 'in canto' rubric in the manuscripts.[23] Discounting the repetitions, a corpus of twenty-one single items (those marked in Table 13.1) emerge as destined for singing: six in Latin and fifteen in Italian. Additionally, Mss. 416, 417 and 418 have a total of eleven 'in canto' rubrics followed by blank spaces. The richest in 'in canto' rubrics is Ms. 417 (twenty-one rubrics), the poorest is Ms. 383 (only two; some pieces marked for singing in the concordances have different instructions). As already mentioned, the same piece can be labelled differently in different manuscripts, or even within the same manuscript when a shorter version is labelled 'in canto' and a longer one 'in parole'.

A glance at the second column in Table 13.1 is sufficient to grasp the interconnectedness of the repertory in the five manuscripts: about 60% of the metrical pieces have internal, often multiple, concordances in the corpus. A mapping of the internal concordances shows that Ms. 416 is the most 'isolated' (with only three concordances), whereas Mss. 418 and 419 share at least one piece, and up to seven or eight, with each of the other ones.[24] What is more, the fact that Ms. 383 has numerous concordances with Mss. 417, 418 and 419 is

---

23 The statistics in this paragraph do not take into account the *Te deum* and other similar items of liturgical origin (*Benedicamus domino*, *Benedicite*) marked for singing in the manuscripts.
24 Clearly, the fact that each manuscript covers partially or completely different liturgical seasons contributes to explain the relative lack, or abundance, of concordances.

an additional indicator that the offices of Sant'Agata shared common ground with those of Santa Marta.

3 The Manuscripts

The study of the manuscripts, their contents and their rubrics opens up many promising research avenues, but a number of questions remain to be considered, especially those regarding the concrete details of performance: first of all (at least from a musicological perspective), who sang? There are no clear indications comparable to those present in some later printed confraternity books, such as the *Libro da compagnie con i tre uffici della Madonna, e della Settimana santa* (Florence, heirs of Bernardo Giunta: 1565), whose rubrics often require two specially chosen brethren to start the songs, and the choir to answer or continue. The lack of administrative documents regarding the Sant'Agata and Santa Marta confraternities in this period make it impossible to know whether the two companies hired singers or made any other expenses connected with music, on a regular basis or for special occasions.[25] The tone and wording of the instructions, however, supports the idea that communal singing was normally practised by the confreres, possibly with the help of one or two cantors chosen from among the members. A further question relates to how long texts, such as those of some laude and Latin songs or prayers, were performed (whether recited or sung): did other written supports exist to prop up shared performance, or did soloists read from the booklet, while the choir answered with the easily memorisable refrains? Or did repetition of stanzas (first sung by one or two soloists and then repeated by the rest) enter into play? The fact that several 'in canto' rubrics in Mss. 416, 417 and 418 are followed by blank spaces or by no indication of the song in question, together with an instruction in Ms. 419 specifying that the song must be chosen according to the liturgical season ('Nota che lo canto però andarà sempre segondo li tempe', fol. 27r) suggests that at least in certain cases the choice of songs was made by drawing *ad libitum* from an established repertory. It is not clear how the later crossings and deletions of songs already mentioned and found in several sections of the manuscripts (notably in Ms. 416), should be understood. Did the confraternities reduce their singing practice at a certain point? If so, was it for lack of singers, for a deliberate change in their rituals, or for any other reason?

---

[25] Similar questions, in a broader perspective, are addressed in Prizer, "Popular Piety in Renaissance Mantua" 206–207.

Did it happen when the booklets were still in use, or during the preparation of (no longer extant) new copies, or of new and different books?

It is probably appropriate to mention, in this connection, the existence of two further books at the Trivulziana that Porro's catalogue associates with the Confraternity of Santa Marta. The acephalous Ms. 520 contains the Office of the Blessed Virgin, the Seven Penitential Psalms with their antiphons and orations, an Office of the Passion, an Office of the Dead, the Short Office of the Cross, an Office of the Holy Spirit, and an end-of-the-day office.[26] Some textual details and additions to the penultimate office betray an Augustinian character and indicate that the book was destined for a female community. It is a calligraphic parchment manuscript, with alternating blue and red *litterae notabiliores* and minor decorated initials; it has no mixture of languages and no signs of flagellant spirituality: in sum, compared to Mss. 416–419 it is a completely different kind of book. It might have belonged to the Augustinian nuns of Santa Marta to whom the confraternity sold its premises in 1497.[27] Ms. 521, in contrast, is a larger parchment manuscript containing liturgical hymns with notation;[28] it is not clear how Porro traced it back to the confraternity: both in the case of Ms. 520 and of Ms. 521, he might have been inspired by the respective attachments, two printed booklets for Santa Marta from around 1700 to which I will return at the end of this chapter. In its present form, Ms. 521 bears no distinctive signs or texts (not even a hymn for St. Martha), and, since it covers various liturgical hours, it seems more suitable to the needs of a monastic community than to those of a lay confraternity.

4   The Flagellant Confraternities

Scholarship on Italian flagellant confraternities has mainly focused on the period 1260–1400.[29] Moreover, whereas statutes, *regole*, and other documents have raised a certain interest in scholars from various disciplines, the

---

26   Porro, *Catalogo dei codici manoscritti della Trivulziana* 335; Santoro, *I codici medioevali* 116–117; MANUS ONLINE, https://manus.iccu.sbn.it/cnmd/0000182515.
27   Lattuada, *Descrizione di Milano* vol. 3, 143.
28   Porro, *Catalogo dei codici manoscritti della Trivulziana* 184; Santoro, *I codici medioevali* 117.
29   The classic reference is *Il Movimento dei Disciplinati nel Settimo Centenario dal suo inizio*; see also Alberigo G., "Flagellants", in Aubert R. (ed.), *Dictionnaire d'histoire et de géographie ecclésiastiques* XVII (Paris: 1971) cols. 327–337, and the various publications of the Centro di ricerca e studio sul Movimento dei Disciplinati. For a recent account of disciplinati ritual and art, see Chen A.H., *Flagellant Confraternities and Italian Art, 1260–1610: Ritual and Experience* (Amsterdam: 2018).

disciplinati prayer books have received marginal attention, or have been mined according to specific liturgical, theological, linguistic or philological interests. This is in line with a certain scholarly disregard for the devotional aspects of confraternity life.[30] A comprehensive list of the surviving prayer books, a comparative mapping of their contents and a contextualisation in the history of Christian spirituality is notably lacking. As early as 1962, the Italian Church historian Giuseppe Alberigo lamented in a seminal essay the lack of serious historical consideration of the disciplinati prayer books and the exclusively 'literary' approach to the laude in existing studies: under these specific perspectives, the situation seems hardly to have improved in the intervening sixty years.[31] Historian Augustine Thompson, for instance, has summarily described earlier *flagellanti* offices which seem comparable to those of the Trivulziana manuscripts, and listed some examples.[32] He has also underscored the mix of Latin and Italian, and the 'nobilitating' incorporation of Latin prayers derived from the liturgy, in order to add 'hieratic solemnity to a service in which the prayer intentions were pronounced in Italian so they might be understood by all'.[33] A few fifteenth-century manuscripts containing flagellant offices have been brought to the attention of scholars: among those that are relatively close to those under consideration here, both geographically and chronologically, are: the one for San Defendente in Lodi (ca. 1454);[34] that for the disciplinati-raccomandati of San Giuliano in Novara (second half of the fifteenth century);[35] and that for the disciplinati of Saluzzo (Piedmont,

---

[30]   Eisenbichler K. (ed.), *A Companion to Medieval and Early Modern Confraternities* (Leiden: 2019) Introduction 10.

[31]   See Alberigo, "Contributi alla storia delle confraternite" 170–171. In the same essay, he mentioned the 'exceptional group of manuscript books of prayers' (my translation) at the Trivulziana, and announced a forthcoming study: possibly because in subsequent years the Second Vatican Council became his main and long-lasting research theme, he does not seem ever to have published such a study (at least according to Spaccamonti L. – Faggioli M., "Bibliografia di Giuseppe Alberigo 1956–2008", *Cristianesimo nella storia* 29 (2008) 921–961).

[32]   Thompson A., *Cities of God: The Religion of the Italian Communes, 1125–1325* (University Park PA: 2005) 92–93.

[33]   Thompson, *Cities of God* 92.

[34]   Edited in Agnelli G., "Il libro dei Battuti di San Defendente di Lodi: Saggio di dialetto lodigiano del secolo decimoquarto", *Archivio storico per la città e comuni del circondario di Lodi* 21 (1902) 1–108. The dating is from Mascherpa, "Percorsi confraternali nel medioevo lombardo".

[35]   Edited and studied in Longo, *Letteratura e pietà*. In addition to some concordances with the Trivulziana manuscripts, noted by Longo, the manuscript also has 'in parole'/'in canto' rubrics.

mid fifteenth century).[36] William Prizer has collected other relevant materials and proposed a connection between the simple lauda settings in Ms. Paris. Bibliothèque Nationale, Rés. Vm.[7] 676 to Mantuan flagellant confraternities (three songs in the Trivulziana corpus have concordances with that manuscript: *In la degna stalla, Gaude virgo mater Christi* and *Verbum caro factum est*).[37] A systematic, comparative, and interdisciplinary study of these and other sources (including early printed *Libri da compagnie*) is among the obvious desiderata for the development of this research field:[38] the scope of such endeavour, however, goes well beyond the possibilities of the present chapter.

With regard to the Trivulziana manuscripts, and irrespective of the open questions listed above, a few significant data emerge from their study. First of all, the abundant presence of laude, which, given the lack of evidence in the musicological literature about the incidence of the genre in late medieval and early Renaissance Milan, is surely worthy of note. Furthermore, the laude are not merely 'attested', but presented in a rich and specific context. It is worth comparing these booklets with an earlier Milanese manuscript of laude, Ms. Z 94 sup. of the Biblioteca Ambrosiana, dated to the last quarter of the fourteenth century in a recent thesis by Masseo Purgato, and possibly made for the other confraternity of Santa Marta, that of Porta Orientale.[39] The Ambrosiana laudario confirms that laude were cultivated from much earlier among the Milanese disciplini, but the absence in it of performative instructions and of ritual context, while not surprising given the different character of the

---

36   Piccat M., *Il Laudario di Saluzzo* (Saluzzo: 2015).
37   Prizer, "Popular Piety in Renaissance Mantua".
38   For an office from the area between Cremona and Mantua, see: Grandi O., "Gli statuti quattrocenteschi dei Disciplini di Canneto sull'Oglio", in Ghisini – Rubini (eds.), *I Disciplini* 87–135; and Prizer, "Popular Piety in Renaissance Mantua" 198. For an early sixteenth-century office from Breno (Val Camonica, Brescia), see: Bino C. – Tagliani R., *Con le braccia in croce: la Regola e l'Officio della Quaresima dei disciplini di Breno* (Milan: 2012²). Further potentially interesting materials are listed in Landotti G., "La preghiera dei fedeli in lingua italiana dal secolo XIII al secolo XX", *Ephemerides Liturgicae* 91 (1977) 97–131, here 110–115. *Libri da compagnie* are listed and discussed in Alberigo, "Contributi alla storia delle confraternite" 209–213, and in Rusconi R., "Pratica cultuale ed istruzione religiosa nelle confraternite italiane del tardo medio evo: 'libri da compagnia' e libri di pietà", in *Le mouvement confraternel au Moyen Âge. France, Italie, Suisse. Actes de la table ronde de Lausanne (9–11 mai 1985)* (Rome: 1987) 133–153.
39   I am grateful to Masseo Purgato for generously sharing with me his knowledge about the manuscript in conversation as well as a copy of his Master's thesis: *Il Laudario dei Battuti di Santa Marta di Milano: studio e saggio di edizione* (Università degli Studi di Trento: 2021). Purgato is currently preparing an expanded study and critical edition of the manuscript as a doctoral project at the same university. There are only two concordances between the Ambrosiana laudario and the present corpus: no. 15, *Vuy che amasi lo creatore* (roughly corresponding to *O voy che amati lo creatore Dio*) and no. 31, *Gaude virgo mater Christi*.

manuscript, affords no precise clues about how and when the laude were intoned. The Trivulziana manuscripts, by contrast, illuminate the role of laude as part of complex collective rituals involving the inner and outer senses of the participants. For example, an instruction in Ms. 416 mentions that the discipline was taken in front of a crucifix, which, as in the case of the devotional artworks present in the church of Santa Marta in 1497, was typical of the decoration found in a disciplini oratorio:[40]

> Amantissimi e devotissimi padri e fradelli e sorelle spirituali in Christo Yesù, nuy siamo per la gratia de Dio qui gionti e congregati in questo locho ala operatione de la dissiplina denanze ala ymagine del nostro dillectissimo e begninissimo [sic] e misericordijssimo Signore Yesu Christo. (Ms. 416, fols. 1v–2v)

> Most affectionate and devout spiritual fathers, brothers and sisters in Christ Jesus, we are gathered together here in this place, for the grace of God, in order to perform the discipline in front of the image of our most beloved, benign and compassionate Lord Jesus Christ.

The songs were performed 'in praise and reverence' of the Lord or the Blessed Virgin ('a sua laude e reverentia') and 'a nostro amaystramento' (Ms. 383 fol. 18v), which can be translated as 'for the spiritual education' of the confreres. It is already important to know that the lauda *Quando i' guardo lo mio Signore / che pende in croxe cossì impiegato* was part of the disciplini repertory: but its meaning comes to life when, from Ms. 416 fol. 7v, it becomes clear that it was part of a Lenten office – the very office introduced by the rubric just mentioned about taking the discipline in front of the image of Jesus –, and that it was recited after the confreres had prayed the Seven Penitential Psalms, each followed by a self-flagellation session, asking for God's forgiveness. Within this devotional setting of contemplating gaze and self-identification, the lyrical consideration of the 'bono Yhesù', the 'good Jesus […] all covered in sores for our love', takes on a different tone and a much more vivid meaning. Examples could be multiplied. The lauda *O alta regina con la Trinitade* appears within a specially designed addition to the office for times of plague ('per tempo de morìa') (Ms. 416 fols. 42v–43v) [Fig. 13.3]. A long rubric explains that, after praying five Our Fathers and Hail Marys while taking the discipline in praise of the Five Wounds of Jesus and in order to ask God for the usual graces, the prayer will now focus on the Blessed Virgin, with the said lauda. After the lauda, which

---

40 It is interesting to compare this with the settings described and analysed in Chen, *Flagellant Confraternities and Italian Art* 47–57 ("Contemplation of images").

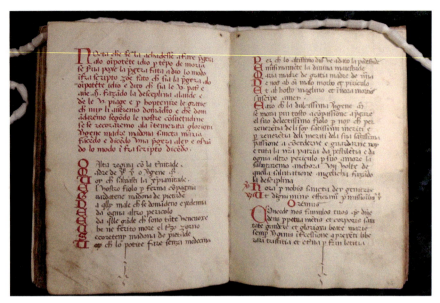

FIGURE 13.3   Milan. Archivio Storico Civico e Biblioteca Trivulziana, Cod. Triv. 416 fols. 42v–43r, addition to the office for times of plague with rubric regarding the discipline and introducing the lauda *O alta regina con la Trinitade*
© COMUNE DI MILANO – ALL RIGHTS RESERVED

demands the Virgin's miraculous assistance against 'quelli male che se domandeno epedemia' and 'quelle gande che sono tante venenoxe / che n'è ferito more el terzo zorno' ('those diseases called epidemic' and 'such malignant buboes that kill within three days'), a new session of Hail Marys *cum discipline* is introduced, as well as further prayers, including the *Regina coeli*. Another example is Ms. 419, with its variants of the processional prayers tailored to the various destination or host churches, which affords glimpses into the local resonances of certain lauda texts: according to a rubric at fol. 14v, *Maria vergene bella / **Schala** che asende e guida a l'alto celo* is good for any liturgical season, especially from Easter to Ascension Day, but it is also recommended for processions to the Milanese church of Santa Maria **della Scala**, instead of *O stella matutina*. As Prizer has already suggested, these manuscripts also demonstrate the relevance for the spirituality of Milanese disciplinati of laude praising the Seven Joys of Mary (most conspicuously in the Assumption office of Ms. 383) or variously glossing the *Ave Maria* (as with *Ave Maria fontana viva*, mentioned above).[41]

41   Prizer, "Popular Piety in Renaissance Mantua" 207–219.

As these examples show, these sources and comparable ones not only register the occurrence of certain laude and, in some cases, enable the mapping of their geographical and chronological distribution with the tools of philology and of the history of language, but also allow study of them in one of their actual habitats. Interestingly, that same bilingual habitat was populated by other species of texts too, which a rigidly taxonomic approach to literary and musical genres might tend to relegate to mutually separate compartments: for instance, extracts from Marian sequences or rhythmic prayers (whose circulation in the Milanese environment, probably fostered by religious orders of Roman observance, has long been obscured by the marginality of sequences in the official Ambrosian liturgy and in its books), and other Latin texts which were occasionally set as polyphonic motets. An excellent example is the already mentioned *Ave [domine] Iesu Christe*, found in Ms. 417 and used in the first four motets of the homonymous *motetti missales* cycle attributable to Loyset Compère:[42] the cycle was in all likelihood composed in the 1470s for Galeazzo Maria Sforza's chapel and was later included by Gaffurius in the Duomo Librone 1 (dated 1490). Another example is the hymn *Patris sapientia*, whose stanzas are distributed in, and form the core of, the various hours of the Short Office of the Cross: as I have contended elsewhere, the rubrics of Ms. 416 (fols. 60v–66v) seem to imply a consecutive collective performance of the entire office, thus indirectly helping to explain the transformation of the hymn into a cycle of polyphonic motets (*Natus sapientia*, in Munich. Bayerische Staatsbibliothek, Mus. MS 3154), and providing a reference-scenario for its performance.[43]

In sum, the laude are treated in the Trivulziana manuscripts as part of a shared and manifold corpus of texts and practices, together with structures and elements of liturgical origin (for example, antiphons and collects, or the *Te deum*), prayers that circulated in books of hours and devotional miscellanies (such as the Seven Penitential Psalms, various types of litany, or the Short Office of the Cross), as well as Latin songs and rhythmic prayers, in turn occasionally set by contemporary composers as polyphonic motets. Research is uncovering growing evidence that this culture of lauda was more widely rooted in fifteenth- to sixteenth-century Milan than standard accounts of the genre

---

42 See above. For the debated attribution, see the introduction to the forthcoming Motetti Missales Edition referenced above.

43 Filippi, "Where Devotion and Liturgy Meet" 86–88. The most up-to-date contribution about the anonymous motet cycle is: Cassia C. (ed.), *"Natus sapientia": A Motetti Missales Cycle from Munich, Bayerische Staatsbibliothek, Mus. Ms. 3154*, Motetti Missales Edition, Recent Researches in the Music of the Renaissance 184 (Middleton WI: 2023).

seem to suggest: repeated references in sermons by Milan-based Franciscans, the inclusion of two laude in Gaffurius's fourth codex, and the presence of a book of laude purchased in Venice in the library of the ducal secretary Cicco Simonetta are, together with the Trivulziana manuscripts, among the most intriguing clues.[44]

5 The Disciplini in the Soundscape of Milan

As Alberigo stated, starting from the second half of the fifteenth century the flagellant confraternities became less dependent on the waves of penitential fervour, and were increasingly engrained in the ordinary structure of Italian dioceses: they were present in many parishes and contributed to make up for the lack of cure of souls, to gather together lay Christians, and to give them a certain agency in an otherwise largely clerical Church.[45] In Milan too, the confraternities of disciplini were numerous:[46] probably more than thirty, according to various sixteenth-century lists.[47] Assuming, with due caution, that at least the main other confraternities held offices and processions similar to those of Sant'Agata and Santa Marta, it can be surmised that the disciplini movement was among the main agents for religious communal singing in the city. Its role was especially prominent during processions: scattered testimonies attest to this throughout the sixteenth century. For instance, the chronicler Giovan Marco Burigozzo reports on an imposing city procession in April 1529,

---

44   See Filippi D.V., "The Culture of Lauda in Early Modern Milan", *Music & Letters*, forthcoming.
45   Alberigo, "Contributi alla storia delle confraternite" 191 and 199–200. Giuliani M., "Assetti istituzionali delle confraternite disciplinate nella Milano di Carlo Borromeo", in Prosperi A. – Pastore S. – Terpstra N. (eds.), *Brotherhood and Boundaries: Fraternità e barriere* (Pisa: 2011) 323–349, here 334–340, discusses how the reform of the confraternities carried out by Carlo Borromeo in late sixteenth-century Milan followed these same principles.
46   On the history of the disciplini in Milan, see: Cattaneo, "Istituzioni ecclesiastiche milanesi" 687–691; Zardin D., "La riforma delle confraternite di disciplinati ed una sconosciuta *Regola della compagnia della Penitenza*", in idem, *San Carlo Borromeo ed il rinnovamento della vita religiosa dei laici: Due contributi per la storia delle confraternite nella diocesi di Milano* (Legnano: 1982) 7–54; idem, "Le confraternite in processione", in Cascetta A. – Zanlonghi G. (eds.), *Il teatro a Milano nel Settecento: 1. I contesti* (Milan: 2008) 161–191, here 178–184; Giuliani, "Assetti istituzionali"; and Chen, *Flagellant Confraternities and Italian Art* 191–197.
47   Giuliani, "Assetti istituzionali" 325–326.

in which the disciplini ('battudi') sang their litanies and prayers ('loro litanie et preghere [sic]').[48] Decades later, already under archbishop Carlo Borromeo, Giambattista Casale (a teacher and official in the Schools of Christian doctrine) records in his journal that, during a procession to the Duomo organised by the different *porte* of the city, 'The children sang the litanies and the disciplini sang beautiful psalms: surely it was a great joy to hear them' ('Li fanciulli cantavano le lettanie: et li disciplini cantavano de belli salmi, che certo era una iubilatione granda da sentire').[49]

Borromeo, however, must not have been entirely satisfied with the disciplini confraternities, as with so many other aspects of his diocese, and he acted with his characteristic energy.[50] In 1569 the second provincial council approved, under Borromeo's presidentship, a new rule requiring bishops to visit the confraternities and examine their constitutions and prayer books.[51] In 1572 the archbishop issued a new model rule for the confraternities, approved and enriched with indulgences by Pope Gregory XIII.[52] Beginning in 1573, it was printed as *Regola delle confraternita de i disciplinati* [...] *Riformata d'ordine di Monsignor Illustriss. & Reverendiss. il Cardinale Borromeo Arcivescovo* (Milan, Pacifico da Ponte).[53] The rule prescribes that all the companies of disciplini should participate in general processions on the three Sundays after the Octave of Easter, and intone the Seven Penitential Psalms (p. 8). In other ordinary processions, the disciplini should recite their morning office, or the litany, or sing some appropriate hymns, according to the feast or the occasion (p. 9). The master of the novices should instruct the new members 'in the Christian doctrine, in the way to say the office, in singing, and in the ritual' ('nella dottrina christiana, nel dir l'officio, nel canto et cerimonie'; p. 10). The *regolatore dell'officio* should assign, every month, the various parts of the office to be

---

48   Burigozzo Giovan Marco, *Cronica milanese* [...] *dal 1500 al 1544*, edited in *Archivio Storico Italiano* 3 (1842) 421–552, here 487.
49   I quote the text as published by Marcora C., "Il diario di Giambattista Casale", *Memorie storiche della diocesi di Milano* 12 (1965) 209–437, here 215.
50   Alberigo, "Contributi alla storia delle confraternite" 206.
51   See the acts of the council in *Acta Ecclesiae Mediolanensis* (Milan, heirs of Pacifico da Ponte: 1599) 74 (Titulus III, Decretum XXII).
52   In the words of Castiglione, 'una compiuta e perfetta regola, la qual volse che fosse commune a tutte le Schuole fatte all'hora e da farsi per l'avvenire col titolo de' disciplini' ('a complete and perfect rule, which he wanted to apply to all the existing and future confraternities of disciplini'): Castiglione, *Honori* 73.
53   As mentioned above, da Ponte was personally involved with the Confraternity of Santa Marta. I have consulted the exemplar at the Biblioteca Nazionale Braidense, Milan (shelfmark H-02-158). The *Regola* was also included in the *Acta Ecclesiae Mediolanensis* 899–910.

'intoned, sung, or recited' ('da intonare, cantare o dire', ibidem). The orders regarding the Washing of the Feet on Maundy Thursday explain that the hymn *Iesu dulcis memoria* should be sung during the ritual by specially chosen brethren: 'si canti da quelli fratelli alli quali sarà stato imposto l'hinno infrascritto' (p. 22). The communal prayer described in the chapter 'Modo di fare oratione in commune', though shorter and simpler, recalls the Trivulziana offices in its mix of Latin and vernacular, as well as in the inclusion of multiple intentions of prayer alternating with Our Fathers and Hail Marys (pp. 28–29). Specific instructions regarding the three general processions jointly held by the confraternities were repeatedly printed as booklets: in a version of 1625, the recommended songs include the hymn *Veni creator spiritus*, the Seven Penitential Psalms, the litany, as well as further hymns and psalms.[54]

It is not known whether the disciplini of Santa Marta adopted the new rules *ad litteram* for their own offices. According to recent research, Borromeo's intervention surely achieved a 'disciplining of the disciplini', but without levelling away the autonomy and the distinctive character of the oldest confraternities.[55] A final snapshot of their communal prayer, however, is offered by two booklets printed at the turn of the eighteenth century, and currently preserved at the Trivulziana as attachments to Mss. 520 and 521, respectively (see above). The *Officium proprium S. Marthae, quod, ut ab omnibus eius congregationis confratribus commodius recitaretur, haec formam* [sic] *in lucem prodiit* (Milan, B. Sirtori and bros.: 1705) is a complete Latin office of the patroness saint, encompassing all the canonical hours, from First Vespers to Compline, with no devotional paraphernalia. Judging by this booklet alone, it might be concluded that the prayer of the Santa Marta brethren had been 'normalized' during the post-Tridentine period and pruned of most of its characteristic elements. The other booklet, however, printed just ten years before, shows that this was not necessarily the case. The *Raccolta d'alcuni hinni, con i suoi versetti, et responsorii da dirsi al matutino, alle laudi & al vespro le domeniche, & feste di tutto l'anno. Per uso, & commodità delli Fratelli della Ven. Scola de Disciplini di Santa Marta in Porta Ticinese di Milano* (Milan, Nella Stampa Arcivescovale [sic]: 1695) [Fig. 13.4], though similar in format to the *Officium* of 1705 and displaying

---

54 *Ordini da osservarsi per le tre processioni generali che si fanno la 4. 5. & 6. dominica dopo Pasca di Resurrettione di N.S. da li scolari penitenti della città di Milano, & sua diocesi, con le preci et orationi da farsi in dette processioni* (Milan, G.B. Malatesta ad istanza di Ercole Vezolo: 1625). I have consulted the exemplar at the Biblioteca Ambrosiana, shelfmark S.N#.E.III.18; on this booklet, see Zardin, "Le confraternite in processione" 178–181.

55 Giuliani, "Assetti istituzionali" 328–329.

FIGURE 13.4   *Raccolta d'alcuni hinni, con i suoi versetti, et responsorii da dirsi al matutino, alle laudi* (Milan, Stampa Arcivescovale [sic]: 1695), title-page (exemplar: Milan, Archivio Storico Civico e Biblioteca Trivulziana, attachment to Cod. Triv. 521)
© COMUNE DI MILANO – ALL RIGHTS RESERVED

the same woodcut on the title page, has completely different contents:[56] Latin and Italian prayers and rubrics, numerous hymns, a Marian contrafactum of the *Te deum* ('Te matrem laudamus […]'), prayers to St. Martha, and, inter alia, rituals for accepting one or more new brethren. In tone and character, in the

---

56 Only this second booklet has the explicit association with Santa Marta *in Porta Ticinese*: the 1705 booklet might have been intended for either of the confraternities dedicated to the saint, or even for both of them.

combination of different languages and registers, as well as in the alternation of recited and sung items, it clearly shows a continuity with the longue-durée confraternal tradition to which the Trivulziana manuscripts belonged.

Appendix

The following table collects information regarding the concordances of the Italian lauda texts included in the offices of the Sant'Agata and Santa Marta confraternities; with no aim at completeness, it is provided here as a first orientation in view of a more thorough investigation of this repertory.

The five columns respectively contain:
- the incipit (not normalised);
- the shelfmark of the Trivulziana manuscripts that include the text;
- the page number (if any) of the corresponding entry or entries in the first two volumes of IUPI (where the reader will find references to the main historical listings and editions of laude);
- the concordances in sample contemporary sources, mostly belonging to other confraternities (normally indicated by the name of the city and a bibliographical reference; some of the referenced publications in turn point to further concordances);
- a reference to extant notated settings.

Abbreviations

IUPI   Santagata M. (ed.), *IUPI – Incipitario unificato della poesia italiana*, vols. 1–2 (Modena: 1988).

AL KALAK   Al Kalak M. – Lucchi M., *Il laudario dei disciplinati: Preghiere, invocazioni e laude dei confratelli modenesi nei secoli XV–XVI* (Modena: 2005).

Compendio   da Busto Albertino, *Compendio devotissimo de varie cose sancte e spirituale* ([Milan], [Giovanni Antonio d'Onate]: [1483?]).

FILOCAMO   Filocamo G. *"Orationi al cepo overo a la scala": le laude della Confraternita bolognese di S. Maria della Morte* (Università degli Studi di Bologna: 2015).

GABOTTO – ORSI   Gabotto F. – Orsi D. (eds.), *Le laudi del Piemonte* (Bologna: 1891).

GRANDI   Grandi O., "Gli statuti quattrocenteschi dei Disciplini di Canneto sull'Oglio", in Ghisini C. – Rubini G. (eds.), *I Disciplini: Ricerche sulle confraternite del Mantovano* (Mantua: 1989) 87–135.

LONGO   Longo P.G., *Letteratura e pietà a Novara tra XV e XVI secolo* (Novara – Borgomanero: 1986).

Luisi   Luisi F. (ed.), *Laudario Giustinianeo*, 2 vols. (Venice: 1983).
Piccat   Piccat M., *Il Laudario di Saluzzo* (Saluzzo: 2015).
Purgato   Purgato M., *Il Laudario dei Battuti di Santa Marta di Milano: studio e saggio di edizione* (Master's thesis, Università degli Studi di Trento: 2021).
Prizer   Prizer W.F., "Popular Piety in Renaissance Mantua: The Lauda and Flagellant Confraternities", in Zayaruznaya A. – Boorman S. – Blackburn B.J. (eds.), *Qui musicam in se habet: Studies in Honor of Alejandro Enrique Planchart* (Middleton WI: 2015) 183–221.

Incipit	Trivulziana Ms(s).	IUPI	Concordances in sample disciplinati sources	Extant notated settings
Anima benedeta / Dell'alto creatore	418	104–105	Bologna (Filocamo #13); Canneto sull'Oglio (Grandi 99; Prizer 198); Modena (Al Kalak 160); Novara (Longo 399 and 423)	Luisi II: 6–7
Anima innamorata / Di Yhesu vero sposo	417	106	*Compendio* 135v	
Ave Maria fontana viva / Ferma speranza de la vita activa	383, 417, 419	144	Novara (Longo 375 and 423)	
Canto zoioxo e dolze mellodie	383, 419	196	Novara (Longo 391 and 423); *Compendio* 139r	Luisi II: 23–24
Dio te salve sancta vergene regina incoronata	383, 417	(cfr. 434)		
Iesu fazo lamento	417, 418	641	Novara (Longo 356 and 425); *Compendio* 125r	
In la degna stalla del dolze mamolino	417	1013; 1017	Novara (Longo 387 and 425)	Luisi II: 78; Prizer 187
L'amore Yhesu venendo	417	843	*Compendio* 113r	Luisi II: 54–57

Appendix (*cont.*)

Incipit	Trivulziana Ms(s).	IUPI	Concordances in sample disciplinati sources	Extant notated settings
Laudemo l'amore divino	417	872	Novara (LONGO 396 and 424); *Compendio* 102v	LUISI II: 58
Maria diana stella	418, 419	1164		LUISI II: 94–95
Maria vergene bella / Schala che ascende e guida a l'alto celo	383, 418, 419	940	Bologna (FILOCAMO #109)	LUISI II: 73
Non temere oy peccatore	383, 418, 419	–	Novara (LONGO 362 and 425)	
O alta regina con la Trinitade	416	–		
O croce sancta gloriosa et degna	416	335; (cfr. 1115)		
O croxe triumfante e gloriosa	416	–		
O gloriosa vergene Maria / Perpetua vergene de le vere madre	416, 418, 419	1140		
O imperatrixe de lo eterno regno	416	739; 1158	Novara (LONGO 378 and 425)	
O Spirito Sancto paraclito amoroso	419	–		
O stella matutina / Dolce vergene Maria	383, 419	1205	Carmagnola (GABOTTO – ORSI 17); Saluzzo (PICCAT 86)	
O voy che amati lo creatore Dio	418, 419	(cfr. 1863)	Milan/Ms. Ambrosiana Z 94 sup (PURGATO #15)	

Appendix (*cont.*)

Incipit	Trivulziana Ms(s).	IUPI	Concordances in sample disciplinati sources	Extant notated settings
Ogni omo s'alegra con devotione / In questo sancto Advento	383, 417	1143; 1144	Carmagnola (Gabotto – Orsi 3); Saluzzo (Piccat 59)	
Quando i' guardo lo mio Signore / Che pende in croxe cossì impiegato	416	1376	Novara (Longo 359 and 425); cfr. Carmagnola (Gabotto – Orsi 93)	
Quando Signore Yhesu serò y may	383	1386		Luisi II: 117–118
Quando te guardemo in croce Signor nostro	416	1388		
Regina potentissima / Sopra li cieli tu sey exaltata	383, 419	1466; 1468	Modena (Al Kalak 65)	
Spiritu Sancto che inluminasto	419	–		
Vergene benedeta / Madre del Salvatore	383, 418, 419	1831	Canneto sull'Oglio (Grandi 99; Prizer 198); Novara (Longo 389 and 426)	Luisi II: 142

Bibliography

Primary Sources

Acta Ecclesiae Mediolanensis (Milan, heirs of Pacifico Da Ponte: 1599).

Burigozzo Giovan Marco, *Cronica milanese [...] dal 1500 al 1544*, edited in *Archivio Storico Italiano* 3 (1842) 421–552.

Castiglione Giovanni Antonio, *Gli honori de gli antichi disciplinati [...] Decuria prima* (Milan, Giovanni Battista Bidelli: 1622).

Lattuada Serviliano, *Descrizione di Milano*, 5 vols. (Milan, Giuseppe Cairoli: 1737–1738).

Officium proprium S. Marthae, quod, ut ab omnibus eius congregationis confratribus commodius recitaretur, haec formam [sic] *in lucem prodiit* (Milan, Giovanni Battista Sirtori and bros.: 1705).

Ordini da osservarsi per le tre processioni generali che si fanno la 4. 5. & 6. Dominica dopo Pasca di Resurrettione di N.S. da li scolari penitenti della città di Milano, et sua diocesi, con le preci et orationi da farsi in dette processioni (Milan, Giovanni Battista Malatesta ad istanza di Ercole Vezolo: 1625).

Raccolta d'alcuni hinni, con i suoi versetti, et responsorii da dirsi al matutino, alle laudi & al vespro le domeniche, & feste di tutto l'anno. Per uso, et commodità delli Fratelli della Ven. Scola de Disciplini di Santa Marta in Porta Ticinese di Milano (Milan, Stampa Arcivescovale [sic]: 1695).

Secondary Sources

Agnelli G., "Il libro dei Battuti di San Defendente di Lodi: Saggio di dialetto lodigiano del secolo decimoquarto", *Archivio storico per la città e comuni del circondario di Lodi* 21 (1902) 1–108.

Alberigo G., "Contributi alla storia delle confraternite dei disciplinati e della spiritualità laicale nei secc. XV e XVI", in *Il Movimento dei Disciplinati nel Settimo Centenario dal suo inizio (Perugia 1260)* (Perugia: 1962; repr. 1986) 156–252.

Alberigo G., "Flagellants", in Aubert R. (ed.), *Dictionnaire d'histoire et de géographie ecclésiastiques* XVII (Paris: 1971) cols. 327–337.

Barr C., *The Monophonic Lauda and the Lay Religious Confraternities of Tuscany and Umbria in the Late Middle Ages* (Kalamazoo: 1988).

Bino C. – Tagliani R., *Con le braccia in croce: la Regola e l'Officio della Quaresima dei disciplini di Breno* (Milan: 2012²).

Cattaneo E., "Istituzioni ecclesiastiche milanesi", in *Storia di Milano* IX (Milan: 1961) 509–722.

Cecchini G., "Flagellanti (o Disciplinati o Battuti)", in Pelliccia G. – Rocca G. (eds.), *Dizionario degli Istituti di Perfezione* IV (Rome: 1977) cols. 60–72.

Chen A.H., *Flagellant Confraternities and Italian Art, 1260–1610: Ritual and Experience* (Amsterdam: 2018).

Filippi D.V., "Where Devotion and Liturgy Meet: Re-Assessing the Milanese Roots of the 'Motetti Missales'", in Filippi D.V. – Pavanello A. (eds.), *Motet Cycles between Devotion and Liturgy*, Schola Cantorum Basiliensis Scripta 7 (Basel: 2019) 53–91.

Ghisini C. – Rubini G. (eds.), *I Disciplini: Ricerche sulle confraternite del Mantovano* (Mantua: 1989).

Giuliani M., "Assetti istituzionali delle confraternite disciplinate nella Milano di Carlo Borromeo", in Prosperi A. – Pastore S. – Terpstra N. (eds.), *Brotherhood and Boundaries: Fraternità e barriere* (Pisa: 2011) 323–349.

Grandi O., "Gli statuti quattrocenteschi dei Disciplini di Canneto sull'Oglio", in Ghisini C. – Rubini G. (eds.), *I Disciplini: Ricerche sulle confraternite del Mantovano* (Mantua: 1989) 87–135.
Il Movimento dei Disciplinati nel Settimo Centenario dal suo inizio (Perugia 1260) (Perugia: 1962; repr. 1986).
Landotti G., "La preghiera dei fedeli in lingua italiana dal secolo XIII al secolo XX", *Ephemerides Liturgicae* 91 (1977) 97–131.
Longo P.G., *Letteratura e pietà a Novara tra XV e XVI secolo* (Novara – Borgomanero: 1986).
Marcora C., "Il diario di Giambattista Casale", *Memorie storiche della diocesi di Milano* 12 (1965) 209–437.
Mascherpa G., "Percorsi confraternali nel medioevo lombardo. Sulle laude in volgare di un codice laurenziano (ms. Ashburnham 1179)", *Filologia italiana* 13 (2016) 23–45.
Piccat M., *Il Laudario di Saluzzo* (Saluzzo: 2015).
Pontone M., *I manoscritti datati dell'Archivio storico civico e della Biblioteca Trivulziana di Milano*, Manoscritti datati d'Italia (Florence: 2011).
Porro G., *Catalogo dei codici manoscritti della Trivulziana* (Turin: 1884).
Prizer W.F., "Popular Piety in Renaissance Mantua: The Lauda and Flagellant Confraternities", in Zayaruznaya A. – Boorman S. – Blackburn B.J. (eds.), *Qui musicam in se habet: Studies in Honor of Alejandro Enrique Planchart* (Middleton WI: 2015) 183–221.
Purgato M., *Il Laudario dei Battuti di Santa Marta di Milano: studio e saggio di edizione* (Master's thesis, Università degli Studi di Trento: 2021).
Rubini G., "La spiritualità del movimento dei Disciplinati", in Ghisini C. – Rubini G. (eds.), *I Disciplini: Ricerche sulle confraternite del Mantovano* (Mantua: 1989) 35–83.
Rusconi R., "Pratica cultuale ed istruzione religiosa nelle confraternite italiane del tardo medio evo: 'libri da compagnia' e libri di pietà", in *Le mouvement confraternel au Moyen Âge. France, Italie, Suisse. Actes de la table ronde de Lausanne (9–11 mai 1985)* (Rome: 1987) 133–153.
Santoro C., *I codici medioevali della Biblioteca Trivulziana: catalogo* (Milan: 1965).
Thompson A., *Cities of God: The Religion of the Italian Communes, 1125–1325* (University Park PA: 2005).
Zardin D., "La riforma delle confraternite di disciplinati ed una sconosciuta *Regola della compagnia della Penitenza*", in Zardin D., *San Carlo Borromeo ed il rinnovamento della vita religiosa dei laici: Due contributi per la storia delle confraternite nella diocesi di Milano* (Legnano: 1982) 7–54.
Zardin D., "Le confraternite in processione", in Cascetta A. – Zanlonghi G. (eds.), *Il teatro a Milano nel Settecento: 1. I contesti* (Milan: 2008) 161–191.

CHAPTER 14

Performing Poetry at Rouen's Puy of the Immaculate Conception

Dylan Reid

Abstract

The Puy of the Immaculate Conception of the Virgin – an annual poetry contest in Rouen hosted by the eponymous confraternity, founded in the late fifteenth century – was foremost an aural event. On the day of the contest, the poems were read out loud to the audience and judges. This oral presentation fundamentally shaped the poetry, ceremony and devotional impact of the event. It was also important for the creation of a sense of communal pride and identity in an event intended to boost the city's prestige and consolidate its sense of community. The contest in turn inspired other contests of poetry and music in the city that were also grounded in the primacy of listening.

Keywords

Rouen – Puy of the Immaculate Conception – poetry – music – urban ceremony – confraternities

On an early December Sunday in the first half of the seventeenth century in the French city of Rouen, a large, mixed audience of townspeople would have crammed into the hall of the Carmelite house in the heart of the city for the annual Puy of the Immaculate Conception of Our Lady. On a stage at the front, one of Rouen's most important citizens sat in a chair, the 'prince' for the day who would preside over the proceedings, flanked by a table with distinguished theologians and other worthies who would serve as judges. The excited buzz of the audience would have died down as a fanfare of trumpets announced the beginning of the event they had come to see, a contest of poetry in praise of the Immaculate Conception of the Virgin Mary. First, the winners of the previous year's contest went up on the stage. They recited their winning poem, followed by a gracious short poem of thanks to the prince, and then handed in the small, symbolic trophy they had won in exchange for a cash prize. After these preliminaries, thirty or more of their fellow townsmen, along with perhaps some visitors, read aloud the vernacular poems they had composed, elaborating on metaphors for the Virgin Mary's purity or developing eloquent expressions of devotion. They began with the long *chant royal* format, followed by shorter forms. Finally, some poets delivered additional poems 'to the prince' that were not in the competition, sometimes of a more secular or humorous nature. After five hours or so, all the poets had read their poems and the audience dispersed, perhaps speculating about who would be judged the winner when the judges deliberated the next day. Meanwhile, the brothers of the Confraternity of the Immaculate Conception of Our Lady that sponsored the contest, along with the poets, retired to a spectacular banquet hosted (and paid for) by the prince. The feast was accompanied by a contest of improvised comic verse, while the short piece of devotional theatre that once often capped it off was by then likely a thing of the past.[1]

The puy was primarily an aural event, with the poems read aloud by the poets to the audience and judges. These poems are known through surviving written documents, so it is inevitable that they have generally been approached as written, rather than spoken, texts. But, even though it is impossible to recreate the ephemeral soundscape of the puy, it is worth looking at – or rather, listening to – the event from the point of view of sound to consider some of the questions it raises and how those might have shaped the poetry, ceremony and devotional impact of the event.

The soundscape of the puy was unusual among confraternal events in that it was dominated by vernacular spoken verse (along with some Latin verse), rather than music or the words of religious ritual and sermons. It was also unusual in that its public activity, where the confraternity shared its visual and aural presence with the broader society, took place indoors rather than in public spaces in the manner of a typical confraternal procession. It was not unique – there were other puys in north-western France, and some other confraternities elsewhere sponsored poetry contests occasionally. Somewhat more frequently, some confraternities sponsored theatre, also in spoken verse,

---

1 Based on the revised seventeenth-century statutes, *Le Puy de la Conception de Nostre Dame Fondé au Convent des Carmes à Rouen Son Origine, Erection, Statuts & Confirmation* ([n.l., 1615]), supplemented by other sources noted in this chapter. The procedure in the sixteenth century was similar, but with some variations – see *Approbation et confirmation par le Pape Léon X des statuts et priviléges de la Confrérie de l'Immaculée Conception*, Frère E. (ed.) (Rouen, n.p.: 1520; facsimile edition, Rouen: 1864) fols. B iii–v. I am grateful to the Centre for Renaissance and Reformation Studies at the University of Toronto for its support for the preparation of this chapter.

in many parts of Europe, generally in public spaces. Of the rare confraternities that sponsored vernacular poetry, however, Rouen's was the largest, most famous and best documented, so it makes a useful case study.[2]

Music contributed to the puy's soundscape as well. Trumpet fanfares highlighted key points in the day. Music initiated the celebration for the confraternal brothers through a sung Mass before the public event, and could be integrated into the post-contest banquet and the theatre that sometimes accompanied it. And the idea of music was always present: as the basis and inspiration for the poetry, and sometimes as a metaphor in the poetry for the perfection of the Virgin Mary and the goal of harmony that was an essential mission of the confraternity.

1   Background

The Puy of the Immaculate Conception was founded in 1486 by some of the leading members of Rouen's elite. Rouen was, at the time, the second-largest city in France. It had been capital of the Duchy of Normandy, and after the abolition of that jurisdiction earlier in the fifteenth century it became home to the Parlement of Normandy – a royal high court of appeal – and other administrative bodies, as well as continuing as the seat of the Archbishopric of Normandy. As the transition point between sea-going ships sailing up the Seine river and river ships heading further east to Paris, it was an important commercial and manufacturing centre, with close trading and cultural ties to England and the Low Countries. The puy itself was an example of those ties: the puy movement had begun in the French-speaking Low Countries and worked its way south to Rouen.

Rouen's puy began as a fairly intimate event, but in the 1510s it expanded considerably. It moved from a smaller church to a larger location in the Carmelite house, expanded the number of formats and prizes, established

---

2   For an overview of the history of puys, see: Reid D., "Confraternities and Poetry: The Francophone Puys", in Eisenbichler K. (ed.), *A Companion to Medieval and Early Modern Confraternities*, Companions to the Christian Tradition 83 (Leiden: 2019) 385–405; Gros G., *Le poète, la vierge et le prince du Puy: étude sur les Puys marials de la France du Nord du XIVe siècle à la Renaissance* (Paris: 1992). On Rouen's Puy of the Immaculate Conception, see: Hüe D., *La poésie palinodique à Rouen, 1486–1550* (Paris: 2002); Reid D., "Patrons of Poetry: Rouen's Confraternity of the Immaculate Conception of Our Lady", in van Dixhoorn A. – Speakman Sutch S. (eds.), *The Reach of the Republic of Letters: Literary and Learned Societies in Late Medieval and Early Modern Europe*, 2 vols (Leiden: 2008) vol. 1, 33–78. The background overview that follows is based on these sources.

formal confraternal statutes, and persuaded nationally-known poets based at the royal court, such as André de la Vigne and Jean Marot, to participate. By the 1530s, as literary tastes changed, its profile became more local, but it remained one of the most notable events of the city. With the outbreak of the Wars of Religion in 1562, the puy began to suffer and became an outpost of the most radically Catholic faction of the city. It came close to collapse after the end of the wars with the victory of Henry IV, but was rescued by the president of the Parlement, who had supported Henry IV. It entered a new period of prosperity, with new statutes in 1614, until an interruption in 1654. A decade and a half later, it was revived and continued until the French Revolution.

The confraternity's membership was fairly small – rarely more than fifty – but very prestigious. Its members were a cross-section of Rouen's judicial, mercantile, landowning and clerical elite, with an emphasis on long-standing local families rather than those who had come from elsewhere. The prince who headed the confraternity was chosen every year based on seniority of membership. The annual poetry contest was held on the first Sunday after the feast of the Immaculate Conception (8 December). The day was presided over by the prince, with a panel of distinguished judges for the poetry and a large audience of townspeople of all stripes. The poets themselves were not usually members of the confraternity, but rather from the next rung of society: professionals such as lawyers, clerics, teachers and minor office holders, along with occasional merchants and artisans. The vernacular poetry was based on long-standing verse forms that included a refrain (sometimes called a 'palinod', which became a nickname for the event itself). The flagship format was the chant royal, which consisted of five stanzas of ten verses, plus the refrain at the end, concluded by a short *envoi* usually addressed to someone, often the prince, that explained the moral of the poem and rounded off with the refrain again. The ballad was a shorter three-stanza form similar to the chant royal, while the rondeau was an intricate short poem. Frequently, the poetry took the form of a metaphor for purity that was inevitably revealed to refer to the Virgin.[3] A prize for the Latin epigram was also introduced early on, while prizes for additional vernacular and Latin poetry formats were added in the seventeenth century.

---

3   For examples of the poetry, see: *Petite anthologie palinodique, 1486–1550*, Hüe D. (ed.) (Paris: 2002); and *Palinods présentés au Puy de Rouen: recueil de Pierre Vidoue, 1525*, Robillard de Beaurepaire E. de (ed.) (Rouen: 1897), available online via rotomagus.fr.

2 Voices

That the poems presented at the puy were spoken aloud is, to some extent, self-evident. The spectators did not cram into the hall to watch judges read poems silently. Listening to poetry was the central attraction, and this may explain why the first statutes, written in 1515, do not specify how the poems were read. However, plenty of circumstantial evidence points to the spoken nature of the event, and the statutes of 1614 are much more explicit. The other question is whether the poets read their own pieces, or had them read by a designated reader. The evidence suggests that most poems were read out by their authors, although in some circumstances another reader read them out.

The 1515 statutes do specify that the previous year's winners will 'luyre' ('read') their winning poems to open the event,[4] which can only mean reading them aloud (since they would not silently read their own poems in front of an audience), and also suggests that usually poets read out their own works. The posters advertising the puy also often refer to the poets as 'orateurs' ('orators'), as well as 'facteurs' ('authors') and 'poetes' ('poets'), suggesting that they were seen as speakers as well as writers.[5] One early poem (1522) calls on poets to gather to 'paroler et dire en motz parfouetz' ('voice and say in perfect words') the virtue of the Virgin Mary. Another early poem (1516) inviting people to attend the puy specifically asks the audience to 'ouyr' (hear) and 'escoutez' (listen) to the poetry. Similarly, a poem from 1654 that describes the puy refers to audience members who would 'entendray' (listen) and 'ouïr' (hear) the verses of the poets.[6]

The 1614 statutes are perhaps more explicit simply because they are more detailed, but it could also be that by the next century, the expansion of printing and literacy meant that the spoken nature of the contest was less obvious. It is not possible to be sure that what was specified in 1614 was already in place a century earlier, but it is suggestive of a tradition. After last year's winners had read out their poems, the statutes specify that the current year's poets in competition will then 'lire ou faire lire indifferemment' ('read or have

---

4 *Approbation*, fol. B iiir.
5 Bibliothèque nationale de France. Français 1715 (collection of the puy of 1533) fol. 1r; Bibliothèque municipale de Rouen. Ms. MM 19 (1522) fol. 1r; Bibliothèque municipale de Rouen. Ms. Y17 (1544), fol. 1r; Bodleian Library, Oxford, Douce 379 (1511), fol. 1r. Woolf D.R., "Hearing Renaissance England", in Smith M.M., *Hearing History: A Reader* (Athens – London: 2004) 112, discusses how the use of specific hearing words can be indicative of texts being conveyed orally.
6 *Petite anthologie* 338–339; ibidem 242; Ferrand David, *La Muse normande de David Ferrand*, Héron A. (ed.) 4 vols. (Rouen: 1891), vol. 4, 9–10.

read, indifferently') their compositions. So it appears that the poets themselves could read their poems, or someone else could read them out. It is possible that another person was the designated 'Lecteur' (Reader) that the prince was required to hire 'pour assister ceux qui presenteront et liront des compositions' ('to assist those who will present and read compositions'). Later, after the winners were chosen, the statutes indicate that the poets 'liront publiquement' ('will read publicly') their winning work.[7]

It is also worth noting the general atmosphere of the spoken word at and around the event, in addition to the formal poetry competition. Before the event, the prince, members of the confraternity and previous year's winners gathered to listen to a talk by a theologian (in the 1614 statutes this became the opening of the public event, and the statutes amusingly added that the talk 'will last no more than a quarter hour', suggesting some prior experience with long-winded preachers). The previous year's winners also recited a 'grace' – a thank-you in verse – to the prince when they exchanged their trophy for a monetary award (in private in 1515, but in public in front of the full audience in 1614). In the seventeenth century at least, the winners were summoned to do so by verbal announcement ('haute voix') as well as trumpets.[8] The soundscape was pervaded by speech.

3 Mixed Vocals

The puy presented a multiplicity of voices, but speaking one at a time. In this, it was unusual among confraternities, and even among urban soundscapes. Confraternal Masses and processions might feature one or two clerics chanting and preaching, or voices singing in unison. Confraternal theatrical productions would include several voices, but interacting with each other and speaking rehearsed roles written by someone else. City streets would feature a cacophony of voices all at once, with perhaps one voice such as a town crier occasionally standing out. It is not possible to recreate what it sounded like when that series of thirty or more townsmen got up on the stage at the front of the Carmelite hall to read their poetry. Even the poems that talk about the audience listening do not describe the voices speaking the poetry. But it

---

7 The statutes agreed in 1614 were published the next year in 1615: *Le Puy de la Conception* 44–45, 59. I am grateful to Sandra Cureau for sharing her transcription of part of these statutes.
8 *Approbation*, fols. B ii–iii; *Le Puy de la Conception* 42–43.

is possible to ask some questions that can at least encourage thinking about what the experience was like and how it affected the event.

For one thing, were there different levels of vocal skill: both in terms of projection, and in terms of expression? Many of the poets would have been in professions where vocal expression was important: churchmen who had to preach, lawyers who had to argue, teachers who had to hold student attention. In general, vocal expression was a valuable skill in a largely oral society. In the context of declaiming solemn verse in front of what was likely, for most of them, their largest audience, they would have channelled all their skills to present a performance at the highest register of which they were capable.[9] Nonetheless, even professionals' skills tend to vary, and there may also have been poets from the world of commerce who had not had formal or informal training in oral presentation. Even those with experience, meanwhile, might have varied in how well they gave expression to their verses.

A hint that the confraternity was aware that variation in vocal skills might influence who was judged the winner appears in the 1614 statutes. These indicated that the judging took place on the Monday after the public puy. On the Sunday, poems were read either by the poets or a designated reader. When it came to the judging, however, the statutes specify that 'le Lecteur choisi par ledit Prince, lira distinctement et intelligiblement trois divers Chants royaux' ('the Reader chosen by the Prince will read out distinctly and intelligibly three various Chants royaux') to the judges to start things off, and then continue with the rest of the poems.[10] In other words, for the judging, it is the same reader who reads out each poem, and in a more intimate setting. The explicit direction to read distinctly and intelligibly reveals the importance of that consistent oral presentation for fair judging, while suggesting these qualities were not always present during the public event. This procedure seems to recognise that the judging could be affected both by variations in expressiveness, and by difficulty in hearing in a larger setting.

Equally interesting is the procedure for judging. After those first three poems, the reader would read out another poem, and the judges would either discard one of the previous ones, or the new one.[11] It was a system created for judging oral presentation, rather than using written texts where all the poems could be sorted and reviewed together. Although all of the poems were

---

9   Hüe D., "Le poète du Puy et ses auditoires", in Wagner M.-F. – Le Brun-Gouanvic C. (eds.), *Les arts du spectacle dans la ville (1404–1721)* (Paris: 2001) 99.
10 *Le Puy de la Conception* 52.
11 Ibidem.

originally submitted in writing, they were still judged, even in this more intimate setting, on how they sounded. Listening had priority over reading.

4 Accents

Another question worth asking is about accents. Almost all of the poems were read by locals, and there was a distinctive Norman accent, as there would have been in any region at the time. In writing, as far as can be seen, all of the poems (with a few deliberate exceptions discussed below) appear in standard French; a close study would be needed to see if the local accent ever crept into the spelling, as it sometimes did in the written versions of local plays.[12] However, it seems likely that a variety of accents would have been present in the oral presentation. Clerics and lawyers who had studied in universities outside Normandy might have softened their accents. In addition, some of the poets were likely to have been immigrants from other regions and had accents of their own, and there were occasional guest poets from other regions and even the royal court. But other, less travelled poets probably recited their verse in their local Norman accent.

A more dramatic variation in the sound of the vernacular poems presented at the Puy took the form of surviving poems written in specific dialects. At least two poems, in 1516 and 1522, were presented in the dialect of Picardy, Normandy's neighbouring region to the north, presumably by migrants from that region.[13] More interesting are two early instances of verse in Norman dialect (or accent: the boundary between accent and dialect is porous, especially when being reproduced by the educated). In a morality play celebrating the Immaculate Conception presented after the puy of 1499, the character of the 'Peuple Commun de Normandie' ('Common People of Normandy') expresses his devotion to the Virgin in Norman dialect. The use of dialect in this instance symbolises a simple, pure faith in the devotion, by contrast to the theological arguments of the more sophisticated characters. A few years later, the musician Florent Coppin presented a ballad in Norman dialect, reproducing the

---

12 For a discussion of the Norman accent appearing in a text, see *Le vendeur de livres, farce anonyme du XVIᵉ siècle*, Abd-elrazak L. – Longtin M. (eds.) (Gatineau: 2022) 34–39. See also Lechanteur F., "La langue de Rouen au XVIIᵉ siècle", *Annales de Normandie* 2.3 (1952) 229–242, especially 237 for characteristics of the Norman accent.

13 *Petite anthologie* 335–337; Hüe, *Poésie palinodique* 420–421.

accent and distinctive vocabulary in an otherwise serious poem calling on poets to celebrate the Immaculate Conception.[14]

The most remarkable use of Norman dialect lay in the poems by the Rouen printer David Ferrand presented between the 1620s and 1640s. These were generally either comic, presenting incidents in the lives of everyday workers and students, or commentaries on current events. They were presumably mostly presented 'to the Prince' rather than in competition. Ferrand was a master of what would now be called code-switching; although he referred to the dialect as 'ma langue' ('my language'), he also regularly wrote for the puy and elsewhere in pure, well-educated French.[15]

The Norman dialect had existed as a purely oral language for centuries, and Ferrand's poetic technique reflected this oral nature. Most of his dialect poems are written as if spoken, either as a first-person narrator telling a story, or as a dialogue between friends. He effectively reproduced the buzz and rumour of the street conversations where the dialect thrived, enabling him to give effective expression to a language that had been developed purely through oral use.

Although, as well-educated members of the elite, the confraternal brothers and other poets may not have spoken the dialect themselves, they would have recognised and understood it from overhearing it in the streets and talking with servants, workers and artisans. Understanding Ferrand's dialect poems would have felt like a kind of insider knowledge, one that bound them together as a community and in their corporate identity as a regional elite. Ferrand reinforced this identity by tying the language to a Norman founding myth, the Scandinavian origins of the Duchy. He claimed direct descent for his language from the Viking speech of the first Dukes: '… ainchy pâlaient autrefois / Nos prumiers Ducs et prumiers reis / Qui des mots et des tours gothiques / Ont fait la langue purinique' ('thus in the past spoke / our first dukes and kings / who from gothic words and turns of phrase / created the purin language').[16]

The range of Norman accents – from simple variations in pronunciation to the full dialect – would be what was normally heard in Rouen's streets, part of its urban soundscape. The puy brought this local spoken soundscape into a more formal setting. In doing so, it brought a measure of prestige to this distinctive Norman vocal expression, whether in accented French or in dialect,

---

14   Tasserie Guillaume, *Le triomphe des Normands suivi de La Dame a l'agneau par G. Thibault*, Le Verdier P. (ed.) (Rouen: 1898) 46–51; *Petite anthologie* 338–339.
15   Ferrand, *Muse normande* vol. 1, 11. For French, see for example Ferrand David, *Inventaire generale de la Muse normande* (Rouen, David Ferrand: 1660) 241–244.
16   Lechanteur, *La langue de Rouen* 235–236. The 'langue purinique' was the name Ferrand used for the Rouen dialect.

elevating it to something worthy of conveying literature and thus enhancing a sense of local pride and community.

5 Listening

There are some hints about the audience's experience of listening to the puy, but again most of what is possible is to ask questions. Could everyone hear everything that was said? The sources indicate that the hall was often full: the puy had to move to a bigger hall in 1515 to accommodate the number of people who wanted to attend, and Ferrand often mentions that the audience was crowded. The Carmelite house was demolished in the French Revolution, so it is not known how many people were able to crowd in, but it was certainly in the hundreds. The hall's acoustics are likewise unknown, but presumably they were good, as they were in most churches where a preacher had to reach a large audience. The poets spoke from a stage at the front – as can be seen in one illumination – and the word 'puy' was likely derived from a word for a raised platform, which would have helped with projecting their voice [Fig. 14.1].[17]

The audience itself contributed to the puy's soundscape. Ferrand refers to the buzz of voices in the room in anticipation of the event, which had to be silenced by trumpets before the readings could proceed.[18] There is no indication as to whether audience members applauded or made approving noises after poems, but Ferrand comments that they did laugh at the comic poems read out after those in competition.[19] Noises of the city outside might have interfered too, although probably less so on a Sunday except for the regular ringing of bells.[20] But even with decent acoustics and relative silence, it seems possible that those at the back of the room might not have heard everything, especially if some poets were not as good at projecting their voices.

There is also the question of whether the audience understood everything. The audience was mixed, and deliberately so. The confraternity's first statutes referenced as a model Roman festivities that were celebrated 'tant par les senateurs et autres magistratz que par le vulgaire' ('as much by the senators and other magistrates as by the common people'). Ferrand depicts an audience

---

17   *Approbation*, fols. Av, Aviii; Smith M.M., *Sensing the Past: Seeing, Hearing, Smelling, Tasting, and Touching in History* (Berkeley: 2007) 43, 46 for church acoustics; for 'puy', Gros, *Le poète* 25–30, and Hüe, *Poésie palinodique* 19–20.
18   Ferrand, *Muse normande*, vol. 2, 110; 48.
19   Idem, vol. 4, 9–10.
20   Smith B., "The Soundscapes of Early Modern England", in Smith, *Hearing History* 90.

FIGURE 14.1   Miniature depicting a puy in process from *Receuil palinodique, comprenant principalement des chants royaux, des ballades, des rondeaux de la Conception, de la Passion et des Pauvres* [...] (sixteenth century). Bibliothèque nationale de France. Français 19184 fol. 295r
IMAGE © BIBLIOTHÈQUE NATIONALE DE FRANCE

that encompassed many levels of local society, including everyone from the distinguished confraternal brothers to bourgeois, artisans, cloth-workers and students.[21] The latter groups were likely at the back of the hall, with the more prestigious audience members up front. Between not hearing everything clearly and not understanding some of the more learned references, it seems likely some of the audience would not have caught the full effect of every piece of poetry. And, unlike reading, they could not puzzle out or go back over the text to figure it out.

On the other hand, this was an extraordinary event: when else would anyone get to hear hours of well-structured verse declaimed by different writers, all exploring one subject in a creative variety of ways? And there was plenty to recognise; Denis Hüe points out that many of the poets used metaphors based on familiar artisanal and agricultural work, evoking and elevating Rouen's everyday life back to the audience.[22] Missing some bits was unlikely to bother the listeners; and for some of the less educated auditors who might be only semi- or non-literate, hearing the poetry was likely a better way to receive it than trying to read the texts, even if not all of it was fully understood. As for the Latin poetry, it appears to have been part of the main event at first, but by the seventeenth century it was held separately on the Monday. It would have been aimed at a more limited audience of well-educated lawyers and clerics, along with advanced students.[23]

6 The Poetry

The poetry of the puy was strongly shaped by its oral presentation. Some poems even integrated voice in one way or another, as in the case of Ferrand framing his poems in spoken situations. Other poets also sometimes incorporated dialogue in their poems, framed them as call-outs to a community, or even spoke to the audience in the voice of Mary.[24] But two elements common to the vernacular poems at the puy stand out in particular: the refrain and the envoi. In the flagship chant royal format, the refrain was repeated six times, once at the end of each stanza and again at the end of the envoi, while it was repeated four times in the ballad and three times in the short rondeau. It functioned as

---

21 *Approbation*, fol. A vi; Ferrand, *Muse normande*, vol. 4, 8–10.
22 Hüe, "Le poète du Puy" 88, 96–97.
23 *Approbation*, fols. B iii–v; *Le Puy de la Conception* 51; Lavéant K., *Project d'édition de l'ensemble de l'oeuvre poétique de Guillaume Thibault (XVIe siècle) et édition des épigrammes latines* (DEA thesis, Université Rennes II – Haute Bretagne: 2002) 53–55.
24 For the voice of Mary, see: Hüe, "Le poète du puy" 106–107.

punctuation, structuring the listening experience, and it drew the listener in: by the end of the poem, the listener would be able to anticipate and possibly even repeat it when it came around.[25] That also meant that, even if listeners could not remember most of the verses, they might well remember the refrains of their favourite poems. Perhaps even, when telling friends and family about the event afterwards, they might have repeated a few of their favourite refrains, furthering the oral dissemination of that theme.

The envoi ('sending off') at the end of the chant royal and ballad was usually an address to someone: it could be to the Virgin, or a particular community, but most often it was to the prince. When reading the envoi as a text, it is easy to forget that the prince was actually there, present on stage, and it is possible to imagine some poets directly addressing him. The envoi was a specifically oral element of the poetry, one that only fully made sense in an oral presentation. Even when not addressed to the prince, it was a vocal call-out to a higher authority or audience that culminated the poem in the ears of the listeners.

7 Sound as Publication

Reciting the puy poems to the audience was a form of publication: literally, making the poem public. With an audience of several hundred, the poem probably reached as wide a public as many printed editions, and certainly a broader public, including some who would not be able to afford or perhaps even be able to read a printed book of poems. The puy, in fact, only ever printed one collection of its works in the sixteenth century; almost all surviving collections are manuscripts, either records of a particular year or private collections.[26] Reciting the poem at the puy was the most effective, rapid and affordable way to publish these works.

While the primary method of dissemination was vocal, however, it existed in symbiosis with a written text. The poets registered for the puy by submitting their poem in a written manuscript, one, the statutes specified, perhaps from experience, that was 'bien et lysiblement escriptz' ('well and legibly written') and could be disqualified for 'difficulte de lire et faulte de orthographier' ('being hard to read and spelling mistakes').[27] The submitted poems could

---

25   I am grateful to Mario Longtin for his helpful discussion of the effect of the refrain (personal communication).
26   *Palinods présentés au Puy de Rouen* is the only sixteenth-century printed text. For Hüe's discussion about the various surviving texts, see *Petite anthologie* 373–414.
27   Biblothèque national de France. Français 1715, fol. 2r.

also be disqualified in advance, based on the written text, if they did not meet the poetry format rules specified by the competition. The poems were read to the audience from that written manuscript, as well. In later years, theologians reviewed the manuscripts for any problematic content, even as the judging was done orally.[28]

What is more, the puy used written text to address some of the weaknesses of oral dissemination. The brothers were concerned that the same work might be submitted in multiple years, which could not be proved without a written record. The solution was the yearly collections of the poems, of which a few survive.[29] Writing was very much part of the world of the puy, which was founded almost simultaneously with the first printing press in Rouen.[30] The puy was advertised by written posters, and many of the confraternity's members, such as clerics and lawyers, were among the first adopters of print in the city. In the seventeenth century, David Ferrand printed his puy poems annually after the event (in booklets that were likely read aloud to others, further disseminating his work through the symbiosis of written and oral). The puy's emphasis on aurality, despite this written context, reflected the specific goals of the confraternity and the puy.

8   Community and Performance

One of these core goals was to reinforce the city's sense of community. The devotion of the Immaculate Conception was particularly strong in Normandy and connected to local legend, while still being somewhat controversial in the Church at large, and it was thus a key point of identity. Celebrating that devotion helped to reinforce a sense of community within the city. The confraternity was what can be considered a 'civic confraternity': one that lay claim to representing the whole city rather than a particular group within it. The brothers themselves came from a range of elite families across the entire city, and the puy gathered a range of poets and spectators from across the city's geographic and social groups.[31] To that end, the use of the spoken word in the Carmelite hall to exalt a specifically local devotion created an 'acoustic community', one consolidated by listening together to the same words at the same time, 'a shared system of sonic communication and identity recognition' in

---

28   *Approbation*, fol. B ii; *Le Puy de la Conception* 51.
29   *Approbation*, fols. B vii–B viii.
30   Reid, *Patrons of Poetry* 40.
31   Reid, *Patrons of Poetry* 39–40, 43–47, 58–60.

Tess Knighton's words.[32] Thierry Mantovani argues that collectively composing, presenting and listening to poems about the Immaculate Conception acted as a communion in celebration of that devotion.[33] This communal effect could only be accomplished through sound, and specifically in elaborating the imagery and symbolism of the Immaculate Conception, through the spoken word.

As well as the broader civic community, the confraternity also had an explicit goal of reinforcing the sense of brotherhood between its members. This goal was not mere rhetoric: civic elites were often riven by factions and needed to reinforce community. This more internal goal of community was also supported by sound; first, by attending a Mass together before the contest; and then, by a banquet afterwards for the brothers and poets, perhaps a louder affair lubricated by liquor and rich food, accompanied sometimes by a contest of improvised comic poetry, by musical entertainers and by a piece of devotional theatre.[34]

9   Representing

The declaimed poetry of the puy was part of what Mark M. Smith describes as a city's 'distinctive aural signature'.[35] It is notable that the puy expressed this signature somewhat differently from most confraternities. Rather than going out into the city streets to assert the confraternity's presence and role through sound, whether through processional music or, in some cases, theatre, the confraternity invited the city indoors to be enveloped within its acoustic community. And it was especially distinctive in that this acoustic community was primarily declaimed verse. There were other instances of public declaimed verse in Rouen, for example in royal entries and in carnival celebrations, but these were generally outdoors, in public, as part of processions.

The puy's uniqueness made it a notable element of Rouen's identity and brought the city prestige. A charming poem from the early sixteenth century, "Description et louenge des excellences de la noble cite de Rouen" ("Description

---

32 Knighton T., "Introduction: Listening to Confraternities", special issue "Iberian Confraternities and Urban Soundscapes", *Confraternitas* 31.2 (2020) 8. The concept of 'acoustic communities' is credited to Barry Truax.

33 Mantovani T., "Le manuscrit BNF ms. fr. 1538", in Arnould J.-C. – Mantovani T. (eds.), *Première poésie française de la Renaissance: autour des puys poétiques normands* (Paris: 2003) 96.

34 *Approbation*, fol. C i; Reid, *Patrons of Poetry* 49–51, 55–58.

35 Smith, *Sensing the Past* 44.

and praise of the excellences of the noble city of Rouen") cites the puy as one of the city's adornments. The writer Bonaventure des Périers said 'Vous savez qu'à Rouen on ne parle autrement qu'en rime' ('You know, in Rouen they speak only in rhyme'), while the poet Jean Bouchet wrote that 'les Normans ont des Muses l'octroy / De poesie' ('the Normans received the monopoly on poetry from the muses').[36] In a sense, by sponsoring a competition in which poets recited verse that praised a cause closely identified with the city, the confraternal brothers were recreating the experience of a royal court where court poets might write and recite verse in praise of the monarch or the causes the monarch championed. The way that the confraternity brought in court poets to participate in the puy in the 1510s is suggestive of this desire to emulate court prestige.

10 Performance

Speaking the poems to an audience also fulfilled another civic goal, that of training townsmen in eloquence. Carol Symes argues that all public life in medieval cities was in part performative, so the elements of public performance – 'persuasive speech, arresting behavior, demonstrative noise, eloquent gesture, commanding appearance' – were basic skills for city-dwellers.[37] Even for lawyers and clerics trained in oral presentation and argument, the kind of gracious speech required for negotiating and persuading in civic life, rather than arguing from authority, was a separate skill. The churchman Pierre Fabri was the second prince of the puy, and later wrote a manual of rhetoric whose poetry section draws heavily on the puy's works. In explaining his manual's goals, he wrote that 'Tout homme donc amy de bien publique doibt estudier a bien et prudentement parler, pour lequel il acquerra louenge, honneur et dignité; il sera certain refuge de sage conseil' ('Therefore every man who is a friend of the public good must study to speak well and prudently, for which he will acquire praise, honour and dignity; he will be a sure repository of wise counsel').[38] By providing an opportunity for townsmen to write gracious verse and perform it in front of an audience, the puy helped to train Rouen's citizens for civic life.

---

36 *Petite anthologie* 367. Herval R., *Histoire de Rouen* (Rouen: 1947–1949) 50; Bouchet Jean, *Epistres morales et familières du Traverseur*, ed. J.J. Beard (Paris: 1969) lxxiii.
37 Symes C., *A Common Stage: Theatre and Public Life in Medieval Arras* (Ithaca: 2007) 278.
38 Fabri Pierre, *Le grant et vray art de pleine rhétorique*, quoted in Szeliga D., "L'experience de navigateur source d'inspiration poétique à travers quelques chants royaux présentés par Jean Parmentier aux puys de Rouen et Dieppe", in Arnould, J.-C. – Mantovani T. (eds.), *Première poésie française de la Renaissance: autour des puys poétiques normands* (Paris: 2003) 268.

Even for those who did not compete, the opportunity to hear and see these performances of gracious speech provided an example to follow.[39]

11   Music

While spoken verse was the primary element in the puy's soundscape, music was also ever-present, integrated into and supporting the spoken word. In the first instance, verse itself was understood as closely related to music. The earliest puys had sometimes set the poetry to music, although that had long passed by the time Rouen's puy was founded. But these origins were reflected in the way all of the original vernacular poetry forms had names related to music: the chant royal literally translating as 'royal song', the ballad being a song form, and the rondeau originating in a dance song. The poem praising Rouen describes the puy's reciting of verse as 'chanterie' ('singing'). A puy poem by Des Maisons called on the poets, in the voice of the Virgin, to 'Solennisez en chantz melodieus / [...] Le mien concept' ('Solemnize in melodious songs / [...] my conception').[40] Like music, verse is structured, formal, rhythmic sound, and perhaps most notably, like music, it has heightened powers for catching the ear, engaging the emotions and moving an audience.

Music was also sometimes evoked in the poetry itself through musical metaphors for the perfection of the Immaculate Conception. Several poems over the years, for example, used the imagery of an organ. One of the goals of confraternities in general was brotherhood, or social harmony. As noted above, this goal was explicit in the puy's statutes, but it is harder to identify specifically in the poetry. However, music provided an ideal metaphor for expressing the goal of harmony – between men, and between mankind and God – more explicitly. Nicole Lescarre's winning chant royal of 1513 used the metaphor of a lute, with the refrain 'Le lucz rendant souveraine armonie' ('the lute that renders sovereign harmony'). The third stanza describes the instrument's manufacture, building the lute in words on the stage. In 1520, Nicole Le Vestu evoked a perfect motet, 'En ung subject quatre pars concordantes' ('Four parts in concord about one subject'). He returned to this symbol in 1523, celebrating a 36-part

---

[39]   This argument is developed in more detail in Reid D., "'To speak well and prudently': Literary Associations and Civic Corporate Culture", in van Dixhoorn, A. – Speakman Sutch S. (eds.), *Communication by Performance. Performative Literary Culture and the World of Learning (1200–1700)* (Leiden: 2023) 65–104.

[40]   Reid, "Confraternities and Poetry" 400; *Petite anthologie* 212, 369; Hüe, *Poésie palinodique* 887.

motet by the composer Johannes Okeghem. Hüe argues that Le Vestu attempts in this poem to recreate the effect of the entry of different voices that would be heard in a motet, thus reinforcing the evocation of music.[41]

Equally interesting are the poems that evoke the musical life of Rouen. One of David Ferrand's poems names some of the trumpeters who were regularly hired for the puy.[42] Most remarkable is a poem from towards 1540 by Mommain, a well-known local musician. In it, he calls on the city's instrumental musicians to celebrate through music, in the words of the refrain, 'En grand honneur le concept sans offense' ('With great honour the conception without sin'). It is an example of the vocative genre of puy poems, one tailored for an oral presentation, which generally address the Virgin or another figure, or a group such as the poets of the puy. In this one, Mommain addresses the musicians of Rouen by name and sometimes cites the instrument they are known for. He opens with himself,

> Sonne, Mommain, de ta flute argentine,
> Pour flageolleurs en ce Puy esmouvoir
>
> Play, Mommain, on your silvery flute,
> To move the performers at this Puy.[43]

Hüe notes that the instruments called on are festive ones, used in dance, including woodwinds, rebecs, and drums.[44] The effect is to create a kind of virtual instrumental ensemble to celebrate the Virgin joyously. It affords a contrast with the usual references to sacred music (through motets and organs) in puy poetry. The poem fits with the pattern Hüe notes of puy poems elevating everyday crafts to the level of the sacred, here asserting the status of festive musicians as worthy of joining the rhetorical professions of the usual puy poets, or the church choirs and organs of religious rituals, in praising the Virgin. It is a message reinforced by the last stanza and envoi, which evoke

---

41 Bibliothèque municipale de Rouen. Fonds de l'Academie 87p 14; *Petite anthologie* 179–184, 191–197, 198–200. Hüe, *Poésie palinodique* 746, and in general 727–760 for a discussion of musical imagery in puy poetry.
42 Ferrand, *Muse normande*, vol. 2, 121–122.
43 *Petite anthologie* 204–208. The *flageolet* was a small recorder-like instrument, but in local usage *flageol* could also refer to chatter or talk, and thus this could be a pun that refers both to musicians and to poets who speak their verse (see, for example, Ferrand, *La Muse normande*, vol. 2, 123; for Héron's note about this usage in his glossary, see vol. 5, 93).
44 Hüe, *Poésie palinodique* 752–754.

musicians who have died and can now play in paradise to 'resjouyr' ('rejoice') in the Immaculate Conception.

12 Trumpets

Poems that used musical imagery did not necessarily appear every year. But music itself was a regular presence at the puy. The music most integral to the puy was that of trumpets. Their use is specified explicitly in the statutes of 1614. It is not as clear whether they were used in the early years of the puy, although the illustration of the puy from an earlier period shows someone who may be holding a trumpet. The 1614 statutes required a trumpet fanfare to announce the previous year's winners when they went up to recite their winning poems at the beginning of the event, and for the announcement of the current year's winners. They may well have played at other significant intervals too. When Jacqueline Pascal, sister of the philosopher Blaise, won a prize at the tender age of 15 in 1540 (the first woman to win a prize), she declined to attend in person, and so the prize was taken to her 'en grande cérémonie, avec accompagnement de trompettes et de tambours' ('with great ceremony, accompanied by trumpets and drums').[45]

The trumpets supported the spoken text by punctuating key moments and, as Ferrand mentions in several poems, by silencing the buzzing of the spectators so that the poets could begin reciting their verse to an attentive audience. Ferrand was outraged when, in 1636, the prince decided not to hire trumpeters, allegedly due to miserliness. He wrote an entire chant royal with the refrain 'Les Palinots delogez sans Trompettes' ('The palinods departing without trumpets'), in which he recalled the sense of occasion created by their fanfares.[46] Musical accompaniment was an important element in many festive occasions, including confraternal processions, for these same reasons: to draw attention, to define an acoustic space, to punctuate events and to give a sense of occasion. Tess Knighton describes an example from Barcelona where a confraternity cancelled its procession because it could not include music. In 1540, the carnival society of Rouen, the Abbey of the Conards, launched a successful lawsuit ahead of carnival to overturn a ban on playing music in public. Indeed, Ferrand explicitly connects the lack of trumpets in 1636 to the loss of other musical festive occasions, such as village dances and the carnival celebrations

---

45   *Le Puy de la Conception* 43, 58; Bibliothèque nationale de France. Français 19184 fol. 295r; Frère E., *Une Séance de l'Académie des Palinods en 1640* (Rouen: 1867) 10.
46   Ferrand, *Muse normande*, vol. 2, 120–123; vol. 3, 110; vol. 4, 8.

of the Conards.[47] Even though the puy was an interior space without the same need to assert a role in public space, trumpets still held significant value in supporting the spoken word of the poems.

13 Other Music

While trumpets were the only music that was part of the puy itself, the event took place in a context of music, particularly vocal music. The day began with a solemn sung Mass for the confraternal brothers. The statutes of 1614 specify that the Mass be sung 'par les Religieux dudict ordre, Musiciens et Organiste' ('by the religious of the order [Carmelites], musicians and organist'). Sung Masses were also held on the feast day itself, 8 December, and on the Monday after the event. While the earlier statutes do not specify whether the Mass was sung, numerous references in the cathedral chapter records note that choirboys were frequently lent to the confraternity to sing at their Mass.[48] Music was also part of the banquet after the puy. The prince might hire musicians to accompany the banquet, as was done in 1546, where flute-players introduced the first course, joined by trumpets for the second course, and the third was opened by singers accompanied by violins.[49] The devotional plays that followed the banquet also often included music. In the 1499 *Triomphe des Normands*, Duke William of Normandy directs his chapel master to have his choir sing, followed by an instrumental piece by his minstrels. It is this music that prompts the Immaculate Conception-denying heretic villain, Sarquis, to enter on stage, complaining of the noise.

> Et paix, de par le diable! paix!
> Chantres, flusteurs, bailleurs de vent!

---

47 Knighton, T. "The Contribution of Confraternities to the Urban Soundscape of Barcelona in the Early Modern Period", special issue "Iberian Confraternities and Urban Soundscapes", *Confraternitas* 31:2 (2020) 108–135, here 113–114; Reid D., "Chevauchees, mascarades et jeux acoustumez: Jurisdiction over Carnival in Sixteenth-Century Rouen", in Bouhaïk-Gironès M. – Koopmans J. – Lavéant K. (eds.), *La Permission et la sanction : Théories légales et pratiques du théâtre (xive–xviie siècle)* (Paris: 2017) 165–199, here 177–178; Ferrand, *Muse normande*, vol. 3, 57–60.
48 *Le Puy de la Conception* 36, 50; Archives Départementales de la Seine-Maritime. Série G (Cathedral chapter deliberations), G 2155 (9 December 1536), G 2159 (10 December 1546), G 2171 (7 December 1576), G 2176 (5 December 1586).
49 Le Chandelier Baptiste, *La parthénie, ou banquet des Palinods de Rouen en 1546*, (ed.) F. Bouquet (Rouen: 1883), introduction by F. Bouquet cx, cxvii, cxxi.

> Hee! quelz gendarmaulx! quel convent!
> Mais ne cesserez vous jamais?
>
> Peace, by the devil! Peace!
> Choristers, flautists, purveyors of wind!
> Hey! What clankings! What a chatter!
> Will you never stop?[50]

So not only is harmonious music associated with the Virgin, but a dislike of music is associated with her enemies. After Sarquis is vanquished, the play ends with another song by the Duke's chapel choir.[51] In 1544, the play after the banquet was described as a 'chorale' and alternated spoken sections with sung quatrains. The seven arts, arriving to praise the Virgin, entered in two groups of three and four, singing, and then all sang at the end, their harmonious voices encapsulating the harmony brought to humanity by the Virgin.[52]

14 Patronage

Music was expensive. The 1614 statutes specify the amount the prince was required to pay for the singers and musicians for the Mass, as well as for the trumpets. The music for the banquet was at the prince's discretion, but for most princes, it was an occasion to show off their wealth and patronage, and at least some hired additional musicians. The puy was an opportunity for the princes to emulate landed aristocrats by being patrons of the arts, both of poetry and music. As Knighton says, 'sound signalled status, especially when the sounds and musics involved echoed those of the ceremonial generated by the highest echelons of society: princely, noble, ecclesiastical, and civic'. But Knighton

---

50   Tasserie, *Triomphe des Normands* 9. 'Flusters' was a generally derogatory term for bad flautists (*Le Dictionnaire de l'Académie française*, 1694, consulted online at https://artfl-project.uchicago.edu/content/dictionnaires-dautrefois). It has been translated as 'flautists' but may refer to a recorder rather than a transverse flute. 'Gendarmaulx' perhaps evokes the clanking of soldiers ('gendarmes') in their armour. 'Convent' at the time meant convent (*Dictionnaire de l'Académie française*), but perhaps is intended to evoke the chattering of a gathering of people, as well as punning in a sense of 'blowing together'.

51   Ibidem 70.

52   Bibliothèque municipale de Rouen. Ms. Y17, *Chorale qui fut sone*[?] *en la feste de la conception aud*[ict] *Rouen* […] *Ou sont introduicts dix personnages cest assavoir cssSapience divine Ignorance La Vierge et les sept arts liberaulx*, fol. 188.

also points out that, by the same token, hiring musicians could be a financial burden.[53] The fact that the statutes of 1614 specified minimum amounts the princes had to spend on music suggests an awareness that some might skimp, as the prince did in 1636 by not hiring trumpeters. Indeed, throughout the confraternity's existence, a constant tension between the desire for display and status and concern that the expenses of the event would discourage potential princes from volunteering played out, eventually contributing to the confraternity's temporary demise in 1654.[54] Music enhanced the confraternity's annual event, but it could also be a source of tension and contribute to its fall.

15   Conclusion

David Garrioch describes the early modern urban soundscape as 'complex enough to constitute a "system", with its own grammar and syntax'.[55] The puy indeed had its own syntax, one that in a sense echoed the cyclical structure of poems themselves. It had an expected chronological rhythm: coming around annually at the same time; structured by the same order of aural events; punctuated by trumpet fanfares. It was introduced by the Mass, the theologian's speech, and the graces of the past winners, warming up the brothers and the audience. For the main event, each poem was punctuated internally by the refrain, and wrapped up by the envoi that signalled the end of the poem and prepared the way for the next. The public event was concluded with lighter fare, the poems to the prince. And finally, the brothers and poets said farewell to the event with a banquet sometimes augmented by music, the reciting of improvised facetious poetry, or theatrical performance.

Garrioch also notes that sound 'was never divorced from the other senses',[56] and that was true of the puy as well. Its soundscape was supported by the visual: by texts, but also by splendour and ceremony. The stage was a visual spectacle, with the prince in his best finery at the centre, the panel of distinguished judges, and the poet declaiming on stage. In the seventeenth century, the stage had been repurposed from the decorations for the royal entry of Henry IV and must have presented a fine sight, while the statutes required that

---

[53] *Le Puy de la Conception* 36, 58; Knighton, "The Contribution of Confraternities" 110.
[54] Reid, *Patrons of Poetry* 57–58, 75.
[55] Garrioch D. "Sounds of the City: The Soundscape of Early Modern European towns", *Urban History* 30.1 (2003) 5–25, here 20.
[56] Ibidem.

the prince adorn it with tapestries.[57] The aural rhythm was supplemented by the visual rhythm of poets climbing the stage to speak, and trumpeters getting up for their fanfares. For the brothers and poets, the banquet added the other senses of taste, smell and touch as they enjoyed the delicacies laid on by the prince (in 1546 consisting of thirty-two appetizers, forty-three main dishes and forty desserts).[58] But for the most part, these other senses were deployed in support of the primary one, that of sound.

The soundscape of the puy was fairly distinctive to Rouen, and it propagated within the city. In the mid-century, other poetry competitions also emerged there. The Confraternity of the Passion, which had once produced mystery plays, briefly tried to pivot to poetry when that theatre was no longer popular. A secular puy of love poetry, the Puy of Sovereign Love, flourished in the 1540s. In the next decade, a Puy of the Poor, more official but also secular, was established through the city government to support poor relief. All of these efforts were relatively short-lived, however.[59]

The more long-lasting influence was actually in music. Sometime before 1529, the poet Charles de Saint Germain wrote a chant royal for the puy in which he imagined a puy for music: a singing contest before God, with the winning composition performed by the three elements of the Trinity as different voices (the Holy Spirit as soprano, God the Father as alto, Jesus Christ as bass) and with the Virgin as tenor.[60] Later in the century, the vision of a signing contest of sacred music came to pass. Rouen's Confraternity of St. Cecilia, which gathered together musicians (especially those involved with the cathedral choir) and music-lovers, began to organise a Puy of Saint Cecilia sometime before 1565 in which composers submitted devotional French *chansons* and Latin motets in competition for a prize. As with the concept of a puy, the idea of St. Cecilia as a patron of music had originated in the Low Countries, but migrated along trade routes to find this elaborate expression in Rouen. It was the first and one of the only such competitions known so far, and it continued until the eighteenth century.[61] In a sense, it was the puy concept coming full circle: from a competition of poetry that was inspired by music, to a competition of music inspired by poetry. Combining its cultural influences from the

---

57 Reid, *Patrons of Poetry* 69; *Le Puy de la Conception* 42.
58 Le Chandelier, *Parthénie*.
59 Reid, *Patrons of Poetry* 61–62.
60 *Petite anthologie* 185–187.
61 Reid D., "The Virgin and Saint Cecilia: Music in the Confraternal Puys of Rouen", *Confraternitas* 8.2 (1997) 3–7; Rice J.A., *Saint Cecilia in the Renaissance: The Emergence of a Musical Icon* (Chicago: 2022) 53–57, 65 for Low Country origins, 71–75 for another puy of Sainte Cecile in Evreux (also in Normandy) starting in 1570, and possibly one in Paris. Rice does not identify any others.

Low Countries with its wealth and prestige, Rouen developed a distinctive confraternal soundscape of aural performance, competition and celebration in both spoken verse and music.

Bibliography

Primary Sources

Approbation et confirmation par le Pape Léon X des statuts et priviléges de la Confrérie de l'Immaculée Conception, É. Frère (ed.) (Rouen, n.p.: 1520; facsimile edition, Rouen: 1864).

Ferrand David, *Inventaire generale de la Muse normande* (Rouen, David Ferrand: 1660).

Le Puy de la Conception de Nostre Dame Fondé au Convent des Carmes à Rouen Son Origine, Erection, Statuts & Confirmation ([n.l.: 1615]).

Secondary Sources

Bouchet Jean, *Epistres morales et familières du Traverseur*, Beard J.J. (ed.) (Paris – La Haye: 1969).

Ferrand David, *La Muse normande de David Ferrand* Héron A. (ed.), 4 vols. (Rouen: 1891).

Frère É, *Une séance de l'Académie des Palinods en 1640* (Rouen: 1867).

Garrioch D. "Sounds of the City: The Soundscape of Early Modern European Towns", *Urban History* 30.1 (2003) 5–25.

Gros G., *Le poète, la vierge et le prince du Puy: étude sur les Puys marials de la France du Nord du XIVe siècle à la Renaissance* (Paris: 1992).

Herval R., *Histoire de Rouen* (Rouen: 1947–1949).

Hüe D., *La poésie palinodique à Rouen, 1486–1550* (Paris: 2002).

Hüe D., "Le poète du Puy et ses auditoires", in Wagner M.-F. – Le Brun-Gouanvic C. (eds.), *Les arts du spectacle dans la ville (1404–1721)* (Paris: 2001) 80–109.

Knighton T., "Introduction: Listening to Confraternities", special issue "Iberian Confraternities and Urban Soundscapes", *Confraternitas* 31:2 (2020) 3–13.

Knighton T. "The Contribution of Confraternities to the Urban Soundscape of Barcelona in the Early Modern Period", special issue "Iberian Confraternities and Urban Soundscapes", *Confraternitas* 31:2 (2020) 108–135.

Lavéant K., *Project d'édition de l'ensemble de l'oeuvre poétique de Guillaume Thibault (XVIe siècle) et édition des épigrammes latines* (DEA thesis, Université Rennes II – Haute Bretagne: 2002).

Le Chandelier Baptiste, *La parthénie, ou banquet des Palinods de Rouen en 1546*, F. Bouquet (ed.) (Rouen, 1883).

Lechanteur F., "La langue de Rouen au XVIIe siècle", *Annales de Normandie* 2.3 (1952) 229–242.

Mantovani T., "Le manuscrit BNF ms. fr. 1538", in Arnould J.-C. – Mantovani T. (eds.), *Première poésie française de la Renaissance: autour des puys poétiques normands* (Paris: 2003) 75–104.

Palinods présentés au Puy de Rouen: recueil de Pierre Vidoue, 1525, Robillard de Beaurepaire E. de (ed.) (Rouen: 1897).

Petite anthologie palinodique, 1486–1550, Hüe D. (ed.) (Paris: 2002).

Reid D., "Chevauchees, mascarades et jeux acoustumez: Jurisdiction over Carnival in Sixteenth-Century Rouen", in Bouhaïk-Gironès M. – Koopmans J. – Lavéant K. (eds.), *La Permission et la sanction: Théories légales et pratiques du théâtre (xive–xviie siècle)* (Paris: 2017) 165–199.

Reid D., "Confraternities and Poetry: The Francophone Puys", in Eisenbichler K. (ed.), *A Companion to Medieval and Early Modern Confraternities*, Companions to the Christian Tradition 83 (Leiden: 2019) 385–405.

Reid D., "Patrons of Poetry: Rouen's Confraternity of the Immaculate Conception of Our Lady", in van Dixhoorn A. – Speakman Sutch S. (eds.), *The Reach of the Republic of Letters: Literary and Learned Societies in Late Medieval and Early Modern Europe*, 2 vols. (Leiden: 2008), 1: 33–78.

Reid D., "'To speak well and prudently': Literary Associations and Civic Corporate Culture", in van Dixhoorn A. – Speakman Sutch S. (eds.), *Communication by Performance. Performative Literary Culture and the World of Learning (1200–1700)* (Leiden: 2023).

Reid D., "The Virgin and Saint Cecilia: Music in the Confraternal Puys of Rouen", *Confraternitas* 8.2 (1997) 3–7.

Rice J.A., *Saint Cecilia in the Renaissance: The Emergence of a Musical Icon* (Chicago: 2022).

Smith B., "The Soundscapes of Early Modern England", in Smith M.M., *Hearing History: A Reader* (Athens – London: 2004), 85–111.

Smith M.M., *Sensing the Past: Seeing, Hearing, Smelling, Tasting, and Touching in History* (Berkeley: 2007).

Symes C., *A Common Stage: Theatre and Public Life in Medieval Arras* (Ithaca: 2007).

Szeliga D., "L'experience de navigateur source d'inspiration poétique à travers quelques chants royaux présentés par Jean Parmentier aux puys de Rouen et Dieppe", in Arnould J.-C. – Mantovani T. (eds.), *Première poésie française de la Renaissance: autour des puys poétiques normands* (Paris: 2003) 265–279.

Tasserie Guillaume, *Le triomphe des Normands suivi de La Dame a l'agneau par G. Thibault*, Le Verdier P. (ed.) (Rouen: 1898).

Le vendeur de livres, farce anonyme du XVIe siècle, Abd-elrazak L. – Longtin M. (eds.) (Gatineau: 2022).

Woolf D.R., "Hearing Renaissance England", in Smith M.M., *Hearing History: A Reader* (Athens – London: 2004) 112–135.

CHAPTER 15

Black Dancers and Musicians Performing Afro-Christian Identity in Early Modern Sources

Elisa Lessa

Abstract

The presence in Portugal of many Africans, extended over time, but notably in the sixteenth and seventeenth centuries in the regions of Lisbon and the Algarve, traces a perhaps surprising image of the importance of the musical practices of black brotherhoods. And, if the slaves tried to maintain and defend their identity and cultural heritage, Portuguese society apparently did not oppose such practices; rather, it seems that ethnic displays were appreciated, whether in religious manifestations or in secular processions and festivities. Through different historical sources, the role of black confraternities will be highlighted as spaces of cultural preservation in which music and dance constituted identity elements.

Keywords

Portugal – musical practices – black confraternities – identity – cultural heritage

1   Introduction

The presence in Portugal of many black Africans over several centuries, and particularly, in the sixteenth century in the regions of Lisbon and the Algarve, paints a perhaps surprising picture of musical practice in which black brotherhoods and confraternities were protagonists. From the second half of the fifteenth century onwards, hundreds of slaves were brought to Portugal; the majority of them entered through the port of Lisbon. By 1533, according to Jorge Fonseca's study in the collection of essays *Black Africans in Renaissance Europe*, 'There are slaves everywhere [...] Portugal is full of this kind of person'.[1]

---

1   Fonseca J., "Black Africans in Portugal during Cleynaerts's Visit (1533–1538)", in Earle T.F. – Lowe K.J.P (eds.), *Black Africans in Renaissance Europe* (Cambridge: 2005) 113–121, here 114.

Black African slaves were found in especially large numbers in the cities of Lisbon and Evora.[2] It would seem that black slaves tried to maintain and defend their identity and cultural heritage, and that their practices were not generally opposed by Portuguese society. Indeed, ethnic displays, whether in religious spectacle or secular processions and festivities appear to have been enjoyed in their new context. Based on analysis of different historical sources, the role of confraternities will be highlighted as offering spaces for cultural preservation in which music and dance constituted elements in the preservation of identity. The black Africans who were brought to Spain and Portugal as slaves endeavoured, as is often the case with immigrant populations, to maintain their identity by joining together and preserving their musical heritage. Spain accumulated perhaps the largest black population in Renaissance Europe. Before the end of the fifteenth century, black freemen founded their own confraternities in Valencia, Barcelona and Seville.[3] In Portugal, some of them had been baptised and broadly assumed local uses and customs. They also took part in civic and religious ceremonies in which they introduced their own songs and dances, but they were also officially permitted to celebrate their own culture, mainly on public holidays, during what became known as *festas de negros*. This occurred with the compliance of Portuguese society, which appears to have appreciated the vivacity and sensual character of the immigrants' artistic expressive forms.

During the sixteenth and seventeenth centuries, the upper echelons of the nobility and those who held high position in society, together with the ecclesiastical authorities, employed slaves as musicians, especially instrumentalists, in their service. A good example is illustrated in a detail from the Retable of St. Auta, which refers to the transfer from Cologne to Lisbon of the relics of that saint, in 1517. In the painting, six black musicians are represented, adding, by implication, a sonic backdrop to the meeting of Saint Ursula (Saint Auta's companion in martyrdom) with Prince Conan [Fig. 15.1]. The presence of these musicians emphasises the importance of music in a range of ceremonies as well as the participation of black Africans, who were widely recognised for their musical talent and skills that would have been necessary to participate in solemn urban ritual in Portugal.

---

2 In Portugal, during the reign of King Manuel I, new laws were legislated as a result of the new influx and population of slaves. The royal legislation on slavery between 1481 and 1514 is contained in the Manueline Ordinances, published for the first time in 1514, with a definitive edition in 1521; see: Lowe K.J.P, "Introduction: The black African Presence in Renaissance Europe", in Earle T.F. – Lowe K.J.P. (eds.), *Black Africans in Renaissance Europe* (Cambridge: 2005) 1–16.

3 Lawrence J., "Black Africans in Renaissance Spanish Literature", in Earle T.F. – Lowe K.J.P (eds.), *Black Africans in Renaissance Europe* (Cambridge: 2005) 70–93.

FIGURE 15.1   *The Encounter of Prince Conan and St. Ursula* (ca. 1522). Altarpiece of Santa Auta, attributed to Cristóvão de Figueiredo and Garcia Fernandes. National Museum of Ancient Art, Lisbon
IMAGE © DDF-IMC PHOTOGRAPHY. HTTPS://WWW.PINTEREST.CO.UK/PIN/14003448825932749/

Conversely, Portuguese culture was present in its African colonies, transmitted and practised largely by the Jesuits, who formed a major presence in the Portuguese colonial world, with missionaries in Africa, Asia and South America. The first Portuguese mission reached Angola in 1560 under the leadership of Captain Paulo Dias de Novais (ca. 1510–1589). The mission included four Jesuits: Fathers Francisco de Gouveia (d. 1575), who was their superior; Agostinho de Lacerda; and the brothers António Mendes and Manuel Pinto.[4] In 1593, reference is found to the existence of a Jesuit college of priests established in Angola.[5] Some years earlier, in 1584, Dias de Novais, the first Captain General of Angola from 1585 to 1589, had donated a piece of land in the city of Luanda to the Society of Jesus, and construction of the college began in 1605

---

4   On the Jesuits in Africa, see: Mkenda F. (S.J.), *Jesuits in Africa: A Historical Narrative from Ignatius of Loyola to Pedro Arrupe* (Leiden – New York: 2022); on-line at https://brill.com/display/title/60118?language=en (accessed 8/9/2023).
5   Brásio A., *Monumenta Missionaria Africana*, vol. 5: África Ocidental (1600–1610) (Lisbon: 1955).

and of the church in 1607. The work on the church was completed in 1636 and, according to contemporary witness, it was the largest and most sumptuous in Luanda and formed part of a grandiose complex of buildings consisting of the college and seminary as well as the church building. For over a century and a half, the Jesuit College, dedicated to the Holy Name of Jesus, was the main centre of teaching in Luanda, where not only Angolans studied to be ordained into the priesthood, but also students from Portugal and Brazil.[6]

In 1582, Dias de Novais sent a letter to Lisbon that bears witness to the role of music in evangelisation in Angola:

> Na ilha de Luanda, habitada por mais de três mil pessoas, os mais dêles gentios, e nas terras de Corimba e Caçanze, onde haveria ao todo uns oito mil gentios, empregaram os primeiros esforços do seu zêlo. O superior Garcia Simões deu-se a aprender a língua da região e dentro em pouco já os indígenas se confessavam com ele pela própria língua da terra, coisa nunca vista nestas partes, e todos o tinham por milagre [...]. Em 1578, contava o P. Baltasar Afonso que já tinham feito perto de duzentos cristãos, e outros vinham pedir a graça do baptismo [...]. Na segunda oitava da Páscoa daquêle ano de 1578, antes da morte de Garcia Simões, que faleceu a 12 de Maio, fizemos, conta Baltazar Afonso, um baptismo de setenta pessoas. Fomo-los buscar em procissão, com charamelas e suas candeias nas mãos, e palmas e capelas, coisa nunca vista nesta terra.[7]

> On the island of Luanda, [...] inhabited by more than three thousand people, most of them gentiles, and in the lands of Corimba and Caçanze, where there was a total of eight thousand gentiles, they [the Jesuits] exerted their first zealous efforts. The Superior, Garcia Simões, began to learn the language of the region and soon the natives confessed to him in the proper language of the land, something never before seen in these parts, and everyone considered him a miracle [...]. In 1578, Fray Baltasar Afonso recounted that there were already close to two hundred Christians, and that others came to ask for the grace of baptism [...]. In the second octave of Easter in the same year, 1578, before the death of Garcia Simões, who died on 12 May, we had, says Baltasar Afonso, a baptism of seventy people. We went to fetch them in procession, with

---

6 Martins I., "Igreja e colégio dos Jesuítas, Luanda, Angola", in *Heritage of Portuguese Influence/ Património de Influência Portuguesa* (HPIP) at https://hpip.org/pt/heritage/details/56.

7 Letter included in the Jesuit on-line library, *História da Companhia de Jesus na Assistência de Portugal* vol. 02b https://jesuitonlinelibrary.bc.edu.

shawms, and their candles in the hands, and palms and small shoulder capes: something unprecedented in this land.

That black African slaves from Luanda were musically literate and familiar with Spanish sacred polyphony is clear from a letter of 1592 sent by Father Francisco de Gouveia to the General of the Society of Jesus, in which he mentioned how they sang works by Cristóbal de Morales (ca. 1500–1553) and Francisco Guerrero (1528–1599) or performed them on flute or recorders:

> Cõ as frautas folguey em estremo. Vieraõ a muyto bom tempo. Os negros cantaõ toda a missa pequena de Morales e o motete de Saõto André a simco e huã Pamge limgua de Guerreyro e a tangem nas frautas cõ outras cousas ordinárias [co]m braua abilidade e muyto afynados; meu pay me lembra a cadapaso que os vejo [...]. Se lá poder aver Joam Castanho hum par de sacabuchas e alguãs charamelas velhas a bom preço, venhaõ que saõ muyto necessárias pera apréderem, porque saõ doze ou treze e tendo todos os estromentos aprendem muyto mais. O mestre hé o mais pintado homem pera os emsinar que pode ser.[8]

> I enjoyed the flutes greatly. They came in very good time. The blacks sing the whole of the small Mass of Morales and the motet of Saint Andrew in five [voices] and Guerrero's *Pange lingua*, and play [these pieces] on flutes with other common [instruments] [with] great skill and very well in tune; my father reminds me every time I see them [...]. If João Castanho can find a couple of sackbuts and some old shawms at a good price, bring them as they are sorely needed for them to learn, because there are twelve or thirteen of them and with all the instruments they learn a lot more. The master is the best qualified man to teach them.

Works by Morales and Guerrero were widely distributed along trade routes and in colonial territories.[9]

It is not altogether surprising, therefore, that when black Africans slaves reached Lisbon, at least some would have been trained as musicians and able

---

8 Brásio A. (ed.), *Monumenta Missionaria Africana*, vol. 4: África Ocidental (1469–1599): Suplemento aos séculos XV e XVI (Lisbon: 1954) 302.
9 On the transmission and reception of Morales's music in Spain, Northern Europe and the New World, see: Rees O. – Nelson B. (eds.), *Cristobal de Morales Sources, Influences, Reception* (Woodbridge: 2007). On the presence of works by Guerrero, Palestrina and Victoria in Goa in 1588, see: https://www.historicalsoundscapes.com/evento/986/goa.

to participate in major religious services. Indeed, Gouveia describes how he brought eight black free servants, who played shawms and flutes, from Angola to Portugal, and claimed that, if they had stayed in their home country, they could not have developed musically, perfecting their skills and participating in divine worship, in the same way. He asks that if he is to go to Rome, whether they should go with him:

> Carta do Padre Francisco Gouveia ao Geral da Companhia. SUMÁRIO – *Vinda de Barreira para tratar da missão de Angola. – Se convém retirar-se ou permanecer a Companhia em Angola – Traz consigo oito moços tangedores de charamelas e flautas e pergunta se os levará consigo a Roma* [...] Troixe oito moços naturais da terra, os mais delles nossos, mas criados como liures; são tangedores de charamelas e frautas e pareçeo aos padres que os troixesse, pera que se laa se acabasse de perder aquelle estado, como se tinha por prouauel, ao menos escapasse estes moços, e jütamente pera que se acabasse de aperfeiçoar no tanger, que pera autorizar as cousas de Deos naquellas partes mõta muito, e tãbê pera aprenderê algüs offiçios que laa nos faltaõ; se Vossa Paternidade ordenar que eu uaa desejo saber se yraõ tãbem estes moços, pera que laa se uejã as abilidades e bõas inclinaçoês daquella gente. Na bêçaõ de Vossa Paternidade muito me encomendo. // De Lisboa, 15. de Mayo de 93.[10]

> Letter from Father Francisco Gouveia to the General of the Society. SUMMARY – *Coming from Barreira to deal with the mission in Angola. – Whether it is convenient for the Company to leave or remain in Angola – He brings with him eight young men who play shawms and recorders and asks if he will take them with him to Rome* [...]. He [Father Francisco de Gouveia] brought eight young men from the land [of Angola], most of them ours, but brought up as freemen, who play shawms and flutes, and it seemed to the priests who brought them that if they lost their status there, as was deemed to be likely, at least these young men would escape, and all together so that they could perfect their playing, so by enhancing greatly the authority of Godly matters in those parts, and also to learn some skills that are lacking there; if you, Father, order me to go, I want to know if these young men will go too, so that the skills and good intentions of those people can be seen there. I commend myself greatly to your blessing, Father. // From Lisbon, 15 May 1593.

---

10   Brásio A., *Monumenta Missionaria Africana*, vol. 15: África Ocidental (1469–1599): Suplemento aos séculos XV e XVI (Lisbon: 1954) 331–332.

FIGURE 15.2 African couple in prayer to Our Lady of the Rosary. Altarpiece of Our Lady of the Rosary. Unknown author, late sixteenth century. Church of Santa Catarina, Lisbon
PHOTOGRAPHY BY JÚLIO MARQUES. IN HTTPS://WWW.ACM
.GOV.PT/DOCUMENTS/10181/27754/PRESENCA_AFRICANA_PT
.PDF/F330D2D0-5F61-40BE-93F2-D38D9FB35359

The church of the Jesuit College in Luanda hosted several brotherhoods, namely the Confraternity of Corpus Christi (*Corpo de Deus*), whose members were respected Portuguese citizens and the Confraternity of the Rosary (*Rosário*), which brought together free blacks as well as black slaves [Fig. 15.2]. In addition to owning a private chapel, they celebrated those feast days, and accompanied white confraternities with their banners, sermon, sung Mass and their traditional dances. In 1628, Bishop Dom Frei Francisco do Soveral established in Luanda a second Confraternity of the Rosary, with its own church, for black members. This served as their parish church, and its chaplain was obliged to teach the catechism to members in their own language, take their confession and accompany them to their graves.[11] Their feast day took place on the second Sunday of October, while the celebration held by the white population was celebrated on the first Sunday of that month. According to contemporaneous accounts, the feast in honour of Nossa Senhora do Rosário was very popular, attended by over 20,000 people.[12] The Church of Nossa Senhora do Rosário dos Pretos in Luanda was completed during the time of Governor Francisco de Távora (1669–1676).

On this church, the historian António Oliveira de Cadornega wrote:

> E porque se não queixem os pretos que se passe por eles em silêncio, têm a sua igreja particular muito linda e bem acabada, da invocação da Senhora do Rosário, muito bem ornada com bons frontais púlpito, coro e sacristia, tudo feito com perfeição, que o juiz que era então da Irmandade dos pretos, o Reverendo padre Diogo Rodrigues da Silva, que assistiu enquanto durou sua fábrica com seu dispêndio [...] tendo além da imagem da Senhora do Rosário de vulto, como as de S. Bento, São Domingos, nos altares colaterais; e no da mão esquerda o Santo, que ainda que foi preto nas cores, foi muito branco nas obras – São Benedito de Palermo [...] a quem festeja a gente preta, e particularmente a Senhora do Rosário, a segunda dominga de Outubro [...] que também era bom que os pretinhos, como naturais da terra, tivessem sua igreja, e o seu dia, o que em toda a parte lhe é dado, em que concorre inumerável gentio que se pode avaliar em mais de vinte mil almas, todos assistentes nesta cidade, os mais deles casados, e de comunhão, a maior parte escravaria, e alguns forros, que estão acostados nos moradores desta opulenta e nobre cidade.[13]

> And so that black people do not complain that they are passed over in silence, they have their private church, [which is] very beautiful and well built, under the invocation of the Lady of the Rosary, [and] very well decorated with good pulpits, choir and sacristy, all done perfectly, that the Reverend Father Diogo Rodrigues da Silva, who was then head of

---

11 Reginaldo L., *Os Rosários dos Angolas: Irmandades Negras, Experiências Escravas e Identidades Africanas na Bahia Setencentista* (Ph.D. dissertation, Universidade Estadual de Campinas: 2005) 35; Gabriel M. Nunes, *As Igrejas Antigas de Angola* (Luanda: 1981) 123; António Oliveira de Cadornega, *História Geral das Guerras Angolanas* (Lisbon: 1940–1942), vol. III, 28 note 42.
12 Fonseca J., *Religião e Liberdade. Os Negros nas Irmandades e Confrarias Portuguesas (séculos XV a XIX)* (Lisbon: 2016) 70.
13 Idem, vol. II, 26–28; cited in Gabriel, *As Igrejas Antigas de Angola* 123.

the Brotherhood of the Blacks, maintained the building financially [...] with the image of the Lady of the Rosary and those of St. Benedict [of Palermo] and St. Dominic at the side altars; and in the left-hand altar, the saint, who although he was black in colour, was very white in his works: Saint Benedict of Palermo [...] whom black people celebrate, and particularly, the [feast of the] Lady of the Rosary, on the second Sunday in October [...] that it would also be good for black people, as natives of the land, to have their own church, and their own feast-day, which has been granted them everywhere, in which countless gentiles – estimated at more than twenty thousand souls – attend, all present in this city, most of them married, and communicants, most of them slaves, and some freemen, who live alongside to the residents of this opulent and noble city.

According to Lucilene Reginaldo, devotion to the Rosary in Luanda was especially associated with captive and freed blacks.[14] The earliest references to the Brotherhood of the Rosary (1701) date from the beginning of the eighteenth century, and to the Brotherhood of the Rosary from 1728.[15] The Church of Nossa Senhora do Rosário dos Pretos in Luanda was destroyed during the nineteenth century.

2 Black Confraternities in Portugal

The presence in Portugal over several centuries of many individuals of African origin – a population that in the sixteenth century reached more than a tenth of the inhabitants in places such as Lisbon and the Algarve – could not fail to make an impression on Portuguese society. In terms of social organisation and artistic expression, they were distinguished by their own practices, yet one of the most original ways in which they found an outlet through which to express their own culture, at least until the nineteenth century, was through communities such as black confraternities. Black Africans quickly joined these confraternities, participating in the customary confraternal activities, without,

---

[14] Reginaldo L., *Os Rosários dos Angolas: Irmandades negras, experiências escravas e identidades africanas na Bahia setecentista* (Ph.D. dissertation, Universidade Estatal de Campinas: 2005) 22.

[15] Dos Santos Simão M., *As Irmandades de Nossa Senhora do rosário e os africanos no Brasil do século XVIII* (Master's Dissertation, Universidade de Lisboa: 2010) 36.

however, giving up their own culture. Indeed, confraternities offered a veiled space for the preservation of their values, and this generated criticism from among the more conservative clergy who were hostile to the cultural practices of black Africans. Yet black brotherhoods were clearly one of the most efficient ways for black slaves and freemen to integrate in Portuguese society, even though they were only allowed to participate as ordinary members, not as administrative officials. They generally participated in the Corpus Christi procession, although Ramos Tinhorão has questioned whether this was necessarily the reason why black Africans joined the confraternity.[16] He argues that the image of the warrior saint, São Tiago, worshipped at that time in the Church of São Domingos in Lisbon, where the altar dedicated to the Rosary was situated, would probably explain the attraction of the African population to that Lisbon church. He adds that the parallels between Santiago and the *orixá Ogum*, also a warlike deity linked to battles, iron and fire, afford clear signs of a form of religious syncretism, a subtle way of maintaining a remote cultural identity.

Confraternities participated in numerous processions that marked the Catholic religious calendar, and black Africans, as confraternal members, did indeed participate in Corpus Christi processions, as well as those of Nossa Senhora do Rosário.[17] Black Africans, though not necessarily members of the confraternity, were also involved in these processions as musicians and dancers, adding to the festivities, especially their more ludic aspects. Gianbattista Confalonieri, in his account of life in sixteenth-century Lisbon, describes the processions that took place at the time, and makes reference to that of Corpus Christi:

> Fazem muitos carros com várias representações e ornamentos, muitos mistérios também de santos, ou de aparição de diabos, ou de monstros que vão a pé (…) Na procissão, vêem-se danças de homens vestidos em diversas formas, com bastões ou arcos na mão para fazer as danças pelo caminho, e da mesma maneira há danças de mulheres negras e brancas que vão cantando com certos tambores na mão, e outras vão rodando um tambor /grande, cantando e tocando com tal rapidez, e tão desesperadas, que parecem loucas de espírito […] Primeiramente todas as

---

16   Ramos Tinhorão J., *Os Negros em Portugal* (Lisbon: 2019) 144.
17   The religious feast and procession of Corpus Christi in Lisbon dates from the thirteenth century and continues to be enthusiastically supported in modern times. In the Lisbon procession of *Corpo de Deus*, since the seventeenth century, the figure of St. George was preceded by a group of black heralds, the *pretos de São Jorge*, who played trumpets and drums; idem 160–161.

artes, conforme a sua antiguidade, levam um estandarte ou carro do seu mester com trompas, pífaros, ou tambores, bailes e danças de mulheres e homens de máscaras, de címbalos e mil charamelas.[18]

> They organise many carts with various representations and ornaments, also many mysteries of saints, or the appearance of devils, or monsters that go on foot [...]. In the procession, one sees dances of men dressed in different ways, with sticks or bows in their hands, performing dances along the route; and likewise there are dances of black and white women who go along singing with a type of drum in their hands, and others rotate a large drum, singing and playing with such rapidity, and such intensity, that they seem mad in spirit [...]. First [go] all the guilds, according to their antiquity, carrying a banner or with a cart of their trade, with trumpets, fifes, or drums, dancing and capering of women and men in masks, cymbals and a thousand shawms.

In the seventeenth century, a Castilian Capuchin missionary described how black Africans in Lisbon celebrated the feast of Our Lady of the Snows on 5 August 1633.[19] His narrative demonstrates how a degree of 'Africanisation' was acceptable to Portuguese religious authorities.

> En Lisboa ay mas de 15.000 eclavos y esclavas negros, y todos ellos y ellas se juntan dia de nuestra Señora de la nieves para hazer su fiesta, y andan cada qual en traje al uso de su tierra muchos desnudos con cinta a cabeza a un braço, al pecho, y paños de colores para esconder el culo. Algunos dellos, y de ordinario, tienen cuerpos mejor hechos y mas hermosos a vista q. no los blancos; y parece mejor un negro desnudo que un blanco, llevan arco y flechas hechos al uso de la tierra, y assi hazen una procession por

---

18   Confalonieri G., "Da Grandeza e Magnificência da Cidade de Lisboa", in Villaba y Estaña B. de – Canfalonieri G., *Por terras de Portugal no século XVI* (Lisbon: 2012) 196, 197, 204.

19   The feast of Nossa Senhora das Neves is also known as Santa Maria Maior and Salus Populi Romani. Its name stems from an ancient tradition according to which a Roman couple, who asked the Virgin Mary for council in how to use their fortune well, received the message in their dreams that the Blessed Virgin wanted a temple to be dedicated to her on Mount Esquiline that appeared covered in snow. This miraculous phenomenon happened on the night of 4–5 August, in the middle of the Roman summer: the next day, at dawn, the ground where the famous Basilica di Santa Maria Maggiore now stands, was completely covered in snow. On 12 November 1493 the Caribbean Island of Nevis was named out of devotion to Our Lady of the Snows shortly after its discovery by Christopher Columbus.

la villa, y muchos cantan, tocan gittaras, tambores, flautas y otros instrumentos al uso de su tierra, baylan con castañetes, y danças salvajes al uso de la tierra de cada uno, llevan las mugeres en la cabeza una celemina o dos, o media, conforme a lo que les dan sus amos, de trigo, o alguna otra cosa para la offrenda y con esso llegan a san Francisco da cidade, entran la ygresia baylando y cantando com danças moriscas, y dadas dos o tres bueltas por la yglesia llegan al altar a un lado adonde se canta la missa para ellos, y offrecen lo que llevan al sacerdote que se sienta alli vestido con diacono y subdiacono como dixeron la missa con dos Acolytos y todo, y al sacerdoto le besan la mano: dexando alli la offrenda se van dançando como venian y essa offrenda llegara a 60 fanegas de trigo.[20]

In Lisbon there are more than 15,000 black slaves, men and women, and they all gather on the day of Our Lady of the Snows to celebrate her feast, and each one of them goes in the costume of their land, many of them naked with a ribbon on the heads, or an arm, their chest, and colored cloths to hide their behinds. Some of them, and ordinarily, have bodies that are better proportioned and more beautiful to look at than white ones, and a naked black man looks better than a white one; they carry bows and arrows in the custom of their land, and thus they make a procession through the town, and many sing, play guitars, drums, flutes and other instruments according to their custom; they dance with castanets, and wild dances according to their custom; the women carry on their heads a bushel or two, or a half [bushel] of wheat, depending on what their masters give them, or something else to give in tribute, and with that they arrive at the Franciscan monastery of the city; they enter the church dancing and singing with Moorish dances, and, having gone two or three times around the church, they reach the altar on one side where Mass is sung for them, and they offer what they bring to the priest who sits there, attired, with a deacon and subdeacon, as Mass is celebrated with two acolytes and everything else; and they kiss the priest's hand; leaving the offering there, they dance as they came, and that offering might amount to 60 bushels of wheat.

---

20 London. British Library. Department of Manuscripts. Additional Mss. Sloane Ms. 1572 fols. 61–62: *Jornalero del año de 1633 y 1634, por um frade capuchino*; cited in Lahon D., "Esclavage, Confréries Noires, Sainteté Noire et Pureté de Sang au Portugal (XVIe et XVIIIe siècles)", *Lusitanea Sacra* (2e série) 15 (2003) 119–162, here 140. See also: Henriques I., *A Presença Africana em Portugal. Uma História Secular: Preconceito, Intergração, Reconhecimento (séculos XV–XX)* (Lisbon: 2019) www.acm.gov.pt.

The British travelers Thomas Cox and Cox Macro were astonished, and even scandalised by what they saw in a procession leaving the Lisbon monastery of the Anunciada on the first day of Lent, 1701. They noted that several black Africans participated in the procession playing a percussion instrument made from a kind of pumpkin of Angolan origin. Inside the chapel, there were many other black Africans dancing, with masks, to the entertainment of those present, even though the Holy Sacrament was on display:

> No primeiro dia da Quaresma de 1701 vi a primeira Procissão. Nela se transportavam várias imagens de Santos [...]. Vários pretos tocavam um instrumento feito de uma espécie de Abóbora; há pequenas peças de Madeira com cerca de um pé de comprimento e mais de uma polegada de largura, colocadas por cima da Abóbora, que tem uma das extremidades cortada, e ao bater com dois pauzinhos nas peças de madeira produz-se um som estranho, muito suave. Estes instrumentos já vêm feitos de Angola. Fui à capela da Anunciada, onde estavam muitos pretos a dançar para divertir as pessoas e usavam máscaras muito feias, e achei que nada podia ser mais escandaloso, numa altura em que o Sacramento estava exposto. Um dos pretos tinha um pilão e um almofariz com que marcava o tempo com os outros instrumentos.[21]

> On the first day of Lent 1701, I saw the first procession. Several figures of saints were taken in it [...]. Several black Africans played an instrument made from a kind of pumpkin; small pieces of wood, about a foot long and more than an inch wide, were placed on top of the pumpkin, which had one end cut off, and striking the pieces of wood with two sticks produced a strange, very soft sound. We saw these instruments made in Angola. I went to the chapel of the Anunciada, where there were many black Africans dancing to entertain those present, and wearing very ugly masks, and I thought that nothing could be more scandalous, at a time when the Sacrament was exposed. One of the black Africans had a pestle and mortar with which he marked time with the other instruments.

The description of this episode in the procession, as recorded by Cox, is curious. In previous years, the processional float carried two figures that represented Jesus playing cards with Santa Rosa. The presence of this float was based on the supposed appearance of Jesus to Santa Rosa in which Jesus, on

---

21 Cox Thomas – Macro Cox, *Relação do Reino de Portugal* (1701), M.L. Machado de Souza (ed.) (Lisbon: 2007) 321–322.

noticing her melancholy demeanour, decided to encourage her to play a card game in which the trump card was the ace of hearts.[22]

Cox Macro also mentioned that he attended the Corpus Christi procession, describing how, before the procession, the figures of giants roamed the streets and many women danced under arches decorated with flowers.[23]

3 The Brotherhood of Black Men at the Monastery of São Domingos, Lisbon

Most of the brotherhoods and confraternities with a membership of black Africans were created under the auspices of the Rosary of Our Lady. Their preference for confraternities of the Rosary undoubtedly stemmed from the socially open character of the statutes of these brotherhoods, that msde for an exception in a society that limited access to white people only.[24] The earliest Confraternity of Our Lady of the Rosary of Black Africans was founded in about 1520 in the church of St. Domingos, in the centre of Lisbon. This confraternity is the mother institution of the confraternities of this advocation that were established in the Portuguese kingdom and throughout its empire where white men and blacks, masters and slaves, encountered each other in shared devotional practice.[25] Like other religious brotherhoods, it aimed to protect its members, organise social gatherings and give welfare and solidarity support, as well as to take a religious figure or devotion for its spiritual practices. The Brotherhood of Black Africans was active from 1533 and brought together blacks, mulattoes and white men and women, slaves and free, thus performing a social, economic, family, moral and religious role in the life of Africans in Portugal. Greater control by the church as regards festivities celebrated among the black African community led to the prohibition of its annual celebration, according to the 1593 account of the Italian Gianbattista Confalonieri, secretary to the tax-gatherer Fabio Biondi de Montalto, who at the time lived in Lisbon: 'These Negroes used to have a solemn feast in the city once a year,

---

22 Ibidem. On playing cards in religious discourse, see: Cashner A.A., "Playing Cards at the Eucharistic Table: Music, Theology, and Society in a Corpus Christi Villancico from Colonial Mexico, 1628", *Journal of Early Modern History* 18 (2014) 383–419.
23 Cox – Macro, *Relação do Reino de Portugal* 323.
24 Fonseca, *Religião e Liberdade* 21.
25 Lahon, D., "Da Redução da Alteridade a Consagração da diferença: As Irmandades Negras em Portugal (séculos XVI–XVIII)", *Projeto História: Revista do Programa de Estudos Pós-Graduados de História*, 44 (2013) 59; https://revistas.pucsp.br/index.php/revph/article/view/6002 (consulted 8 May 2023).

with many representations and extravagant dresses, which, owing to various abuses, was forbidden' ('Estes negros costumavam fazer uma festa solene na cidade uma vez por ano, com muitas representações e vestidos soberbos, a qual, devido a diversos abusos, foi proibida').[26] These festivities were clearly organised by the Brotherhood of Black Men from São Domingos, and the ban must have followed its expulsion from the monastery in 1580; without royal support it remained banned until 1646.

Despite this, the Black Africans did not stop their daily singing and dancing. Confalonieri added the following observation: 'At the fountains, where they go to fill their pitchers with water, they can be seen all together making different festivities, such as dancing and singing in their manner; and you find men and women who seem mad, with a noise that seems to be that of a synagogue or mosque' ('Nas fontes, onde vão para encher os cântaros de água, vêem-se todos juntos a fazer diversas festas, como bailar e cantar ao seu modo; e encontram-se homens e mulheres que parecem loucos, com um estrépito que parece ser o de uma sinagoga ou mesquita').[27]

The 1565 statutes of the Confraternity of Our Lady of the Rosary of Black Africans offer some insight into how black institutions were organised [Fig. 15.3]. According to this document, slaves could not be elected to positions of responsibility in the brotherhood. References to music as part of devotional practice are found in several statutes:

> Cap. 5. Acordarão que do Domingo que vem logo passado o dia de todos os santos [...] mandarão dizer as vésperas cantadas e no dia seguinte se dira a missa cantada com ladainhas [...] Cap. 7. Nenhum escravo cativo possa ser oficial na confraria, nem mourisco branco, nem mulato, nem índio [...]
>
> Cap. 16. Na festa principal de Nossa Senhora do Rosário a procissão se fará ao domingo à tarde [...] pero cujo efeito se buscarão clérigos e virão todos os irmãos e confrades, rezando o rosário.[28]

> [Chapter 5] They agreed that from the Sunday following All Saints' Day [...], they will order that Vespers will be sung, and the following day a Mass with litanies will be sung [...]

---

26   Confalonieri, "Da grandeza e magnificência da cidade de Lisboa" 167.
27   Confalonieri, "Da grandeza e magnificência da cidade de Lisboa" 167.
28   Statutes of the Brotherhood of Our Lady of the Rosary of Black Africans dated 1565. Biblioteca Nacional de Portugal; https://purl.pt/24087.

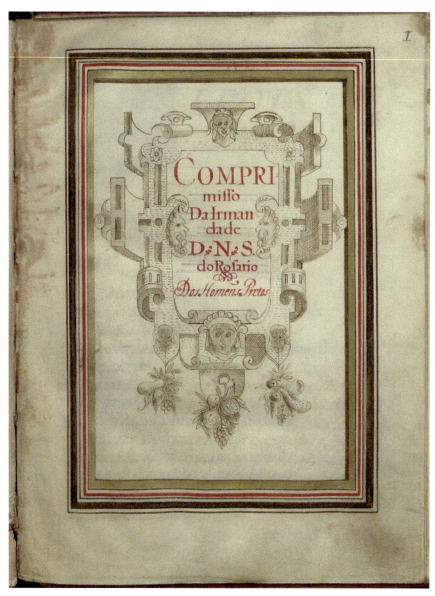

FIGURE 15.3   Statutes of the Brotherhood of Our Lady of the Rosary of Black Africans (1565). Biblioteca Nacional de Portugal: https://purl.pt/24087

[Chapter 7] No captive slave can be an official in the brotherhood, nor can a white *morisco*, nor a *mulatto* [of mixed race], nor an Indian […]

[Chapter 16] On the main feast of Our Lady of the Rosary, the procession will take place on Sunday afternoon […], to which effect, clergy will be sought, and all the brothers and confreres will attend, praying the rosary.

The tradition of festivities and representations organised by black African brotherhoods continued until much later, as is clear from the 1730 description by an anonymous author in the *Folheto de Duas Lisboas*, published by José Ramos Tinhorão. According to this source, the brotherhood of the Franciscan monastery included in its festivities a dance, theatrical performances, a banquet and a long procession through the streets of the city. This was promoted by three representatives referred to as 'kings': a 'king' of Angola, one of Mina and another of India. All these festivities were accompanied by music from *berimbaus*, gongs, marimbas, tambourines, fifes and fiddles: in all, more than three hundred instruments and dances are described.[29]

4 The Black Brotherhood of Our Lady of the Rosary in Elvas

As noted above, the presence of people of African origin in sixteenth-century Portugal exceeded a tenth of the population in regions such as Lisbon and the Algarve. The regions close to the city of Elvas in the Alentejo was the area with the largest slave population in the early modern period. Fonseca notes that a set of books belonging to the Confraternity of the Rosary of Elvas have been preserved in its archive; this is an exceptional case, since most of the documents about black African confraternities in Portugal have been lost. Nine books have survived with regard to the Brotherhood of Black Africans, a further nine of the Brotherhood of white people, and twenty-five from after the unification of the two brotherhoods.[30] This confraternity was based in the Dominican monastery in the city, and the earliest references show that it already existed in 1562. In 1590, another confraternity of the same invocation was created in the same place, but on the initiative of the nobility and other members of the urban elite. By 1670 it appeared with the designation of Confraternity of Our Lady of Rosary of white people, and so appears to have been founded as an alternative

---

29 Cited in Confalonieri, "Da grandeza e magnificência da cidade de Lisboa" 197.
30 Fonseca, *Religão e Liberdade* 38.

to the already existing brotherhood of Black Africans. This later confraternity supported five feast days throughout the year, for all of which a Mass and procession were held; these processions included music, dancing and the ringing of bells.

Although these confraternities were led by freed black men and white men, women from the African diaspora were also involved in the numerous Portuguese confraternities, even though they were not always official members. In 1657, Isabel de Matos was admitted as 'queen' of the brotherhood of Black Africans in Elvas, and two years later, in 1659, a black woman named Felónia was elected 'queen' at the same time as the 'king' and other members of the court. The custom of electing 'kings and queens', as was the case with the confraternities of Brazil and their 'kings of Congo', had the aim of raising funds and taking responsibility for the preparation of the festivities.[31] In the statutes of the rosary confraternity of Óbidos founded in 1549, it is clear that the festivities that formed part of the annual feast-day included the election of a 'king' and 'queen', with their courtiers, who then attended Mass. The black Africans who were selected to be 'kings' and 'queens' were usually slaves who roamed the streets with their music, instruments and dances, calling the attention of the inhabitants of the city and asking for alms for the festivities. In the case of the Brotherhood of Óbidos, the income collected in this way was intended to pay for a sung Mass on 8 September (Nativity of the Virgin Mary), the purchase of wax, a lunch held on that day and a sung Mass, with litanies and responses at the commemoration for deceased members.[32]

In 1677, five slaves owned by the governor of Elvas, João Furtado de Mendonça, players of shawms and other wind instruments, were admitted as members of the Rosary Confraternity of Black Africans in Elvas with the obligation to perform at the Holy Jubilee celebrations. In the 1685 procession held for Our Lady of Rosário six women danced, and there were two dances by men, accompanied by bagpipes and blind people playing barrel organs and singing.[33] As the processions passed by, the cathedral bells rang out. The Feast of the Holy Spirit of 1690 included one dance by gypsies, three by men and one by young black women. By the end of the seventeenth century, the confraternity

---

31   Roldão C., "Feminismo negro em Portugal: falta contar-nos", *Jornal Público* (2019): https://www.publico.pt/2019/01/18/culturaipsilon/noticia/feminismo-negro-portugal-falta-contarnos-1857501.

32   Fonseca J., "A Confraria do Rosário de Óbidos no século XVI: piedade, convívio e solidariedade da comunidade negra", *Lusitania Sacra* 41 (2020) 41–60.

33   Fonseca J., "Músicos escravos em Portugal e no Império português", in Pimentel M.R.P.C. – Monteiro M.R. (eds.), *Senhores e Escravos nas Sociedades Ibero-Atlânticas* (Lisbon: 2019) 179–188 (Elvas. Arquivo da Igreja. *Livro de assentos dos irmãos* fol. 204v).

charged three hundred *reais* for the entry of each member, whether free or slave, with a discount in the case of a couple; this fee could be exchanged in return for services provided to the brotherhood. With its royal license, the confraternity promoted periodic fundraising, both in the city and its surroundings. In 1677, on entry to the confraternity, Domingos, Francisco, Miguel and Pêro Furtado, four of the governor's slave musicians, gave as 'alms' a commitment to play the shawm at the celebration of the Holy Jubilee, one of the festivities organised annually by the brotherhood. In 1679, two slave captives belonging to Martim Mendes were admitted, with the duty to 'play a new instrument in the procession'. These slaves served their master in both the splendour of his domestic household and in the military ceremonies that he promoted in his official capacity.[34]

5 Final Notes

The black African population in Portugal increased significantly with maritime expansion in the fifteenth century, when many black African slaves entered the country. Throughout the kingdom, black Africans mainly joined confraternities of Our Lady of the Rosary, organising their most important festivities and displays of their culture. If the confraternities did not necessarily result in the Christianisation of black Africans, they highlighted the way in which they used an association with Portuguese roots to allow them to organise defensive strategies. It gave them the possibility to secure money to ensure the freedom of their members and to develop ways of preserving their own culture, in which music and dance constituted important elements of identity.

As Didier Lahon states:

> The history of black religious brotherhoods is that of the original conflict between two cultures: on the one hand, represented by the expanding Catholic religion, in the name of civilisation, religion and culture, and considered as the only repository of truth, and the only one that was acceptable; and, on the other, that of a culture whose beliefs, although based on a common vision of the world and the universe, are expressed

---

34 Elvas. Arquivo da Igreja de São Domingos. *Livro das Despesas de Na. Sa. do Rosário dos Pretos* fol. 7v and fol. 34v; *Livro de Assentos dos Irmãos* fol. 204v and fol. 219; cited in Fonseca, *Religão e Liberdade* 110.

in different symbolic ways on the vast African continent, but are always seen as pagan and works of the devil.[35]

By participating in religious ceremonies, black Africans introduced practices related to their music and dances that were seen as profane, but which were nevertheless appreciated by the Portuguese population while at the same time being censored by political and ecclesiastical authorities. Joana Simão, quoting Espagne,[36] has claimed that: 'The first consequence is the mix of cultural elements among or between different parties, thus one is not simply transporting those elements from one context into the other, but rather transforming them'.[37]

The villancico is generally accepted to be the most representative genre of vocal polyphony in Portugal and Spain between the 1550s and 1650s, and the *villancico de negro* is one of its most characteristic expressions.[38] Robert Stevenson refers to Francisco de Santiago (d. 1644), a Portuguese composer who was one of King John IV's favourites, and who wrote at least eighteen *villancicos de negro*.[39] Many *villancicos de negros* are preserved as part of the villancico repertory held at the Monastery of Santa Cruz in Coimbra; these works constitute a rich and original repertory of magnificent examples of the cultural exchange that took place as a result of Portuguese colonialism.[40] They reflect something of the absorption (or, at least, the use) of African elements in terms of language, text and characters as well as rhythmic patterns.

The policy of the sixteenth-century Portuguese kings was based on the hope that religion would transform foreign cultures and assimilate them into national practices. But the reality according to Norbert Elias was that 'Religion, the belief in a punitive or rewarding God never had a "civilizing" or

---

35   Lahon D., "Da Redução da Alteridade a consagração da diferença: As Irmandades Negras em Portugal (séculos XVI–XVIII)", *Projeto História* 44 (2012) 53–83, here 57.
36   Espagne M., "La Notion de Transfert Culturel", *Revue Sciences/Letters* 1 (2013) 6–14, here 6.
37   Simão Alves J.L., *The Villancicos de negros in Manuscript 50 of the Biblioteca Geral da Universidade de Coimbra: A Case Study of Black Cultural Agency and Racial Representation in 17th-Century Portugal* (Master's dissertation, Graduate College of Bowling Green State University, Ohio) 17–18.
38   Nery R. Vieira, "O Vilancico Português do Século XVII: Um Fenómeno Intercultural", in Castelo-Branco S.E. (ed.), *Portugal e o Mundo: O Encontro de Culturas na Música* (Lisbon: 1996) 91–112, here 103.
39   Stevenson R., "The Afro-American Musical Legacy to 1800", *The Music Quarterly* 54.4 (1968) 475–502.
40   Brito M. de C., *Vilancicos do Século XVII do Mosteiro de Santa Cruz em Coimbra* (Lisbon: 1983) xvii; Matta J., *Manuscrito 50 da Biblioteca Geral da Universidade de Coimbra: Vilancicos, Romances e Chansonetas de Santa Cruz de Coimbra Século XVII: Parte I* (Lisbon: 2008).

emotion-controlling effect. On the contrary, religion is always just as "civilized" as the society or class that sustains it'.[41] Black Africans brought their songs and dances to Portugal; these were once banned in 1579 because of the excesses they provoked. The use of rituals with different ethnic connotations was a common practice in Portugal, and to some extent, in Europe in general, whether in religious processions or more secular festivities. 'Moorish', gypsy and black African dances were commonly included in royal entries to cities, in commemoration of major events, such as military victories and royal weddings, as well as in the reenactment of battles with chiefs from distant kingdoms, to add to their splendour and sense of wonder. The history of Portuguese colonial expansion reveals the spread of European culture in general and Portuguese traditions in particular throughout the early modern world. This is demonstrated by the significant cultural and musical changes in religious celebrations brought about by contact with black Africans, especially through black confraternities such as that of Our Lady of the Rosary.

Nevertheless, this did not bring about a true exchange of cultures: the religious aims of the Portuguese meant that they encountered the traditions of other peoples through their evangelical endeavours so that while they related and mixed with other races, they did not adopt those elements in cultures that were in reality very different from their own or that could be incorporated in some way into their own cultural practices. In Africa, they taught the slaves to play shawms and sackbuts and to sing pieces by Morales and Guerrero. In Lisbon, they allowed some aspects of black African cultural heritage, such as their music and dances to form part of certain rituals; in this way, elements of their cultural identity survived in a particular way in the festivities of the black African brotherhoods of Our Lady of the Rosary.

Bibliography

Bejarano C. "Los esclavos negros musicos a fines del siglo XVI: una mercancia disputada", in Iglesias Rodriguez J.J. et al. (coords), *Ciudades atlanticas del Sur de España: la continuacion de un mundo nuevo (siglos XVI–XVIII)* (Seville: 2021) 337–358.

Baker G., "The 'Ethnic Villancico' and Racial Politics in 17th-century Mexico", in Knighton T. – Torrente Á. (eds.), *Devotional Music in the Iberian World, 1450–1800: The Villancico and Related Genres* (Aldershot: 2007) 399–408.

Brásio A., *Monumenta Missionaria Africana*, vol. 4: *África Ocidental (1469–1599). Suplemento aos séculos XV e XVI* (Lisbon: 1954).

---

41 Elias N., *O Processo Civilizador*, vol. 1: *Uma História dos Costumes* (Rio de Janeiro: 1994) 198.

Brásio A., *Monumenta Missionaria Africana*, vol. 15: *África Ocidental (1469–1599). Suplemento aos séculos XV e XVI* (Lisbon: 1985).

Brito M. de C., *Vilancicos do Século XVII do Mosteiro de Santa Cruz em Coimbra* (Lisbon: 1983).

Cadornega A., *História Geral das Guerras Angolanas*, 3 vols. (Lisbon: 1940–1942).

Confalonieri G., "Da grandeza e magnificência da cidade de Lisboa" (1593), in Villalba y Estaña B., *Confalonieri, Gianbattista. Por terras de Portugal no século XVI* (Lisbon: 2002).

Cox Thomas – Macro Cox, *Relação do Reino de Portugal* (1701), M.L. Machado de Souza (ed.) (Lisbon: 2007).

Elias N., *O Processo Civilizador*, vol. 1: *Uma História dos Costumes* (Rio de Janeiro: 1994).

Espagne M., "La Notion de Transfert Culturel", *Revue Sciences/Letters* 1 (2013) 6–14.

Fonseca J., "Black Africans in Portugal during Cleynaerts's Visit (1533–1538)", in Earle T.F. – Lowe K.J.P (eds.), *Black Africans in Renaissance* Europe (Cambridge: 2005) 113–121.

Fonseca J., *Escravos e Senhores na Lisboa Quinhentista* (Ph.D. dissertation, Universidade Nova de Lisboa, 2008).

Fonseca J., "Elementos para a história do associativismo dos Negros em Portugal: a Confraria de N.a Sr.a do Rosário dos Homens Pretos de Elvas", *Callipole* 17 (2009) 23–40.

Fonseca J., *Religião e Liberdade. Os Negros nas Irmandades e Confrarias Portuguesas (séculos XV a XIX)* (Lisbon: 2016).

Fonseca J., "A Confraria do Rosário de Óbidos no século XVI: piedade, convívio e solidariedade da comunidade negra", *Lusitania Sacra* 41 (2020) 41–60.

Fonseca J., (2019) "Músicos escravos em Portugal e no Império português", in Pimentel M.R.P.C. – Monteiro M.R. (eds.), *Senhores e Escravos nas Sociedades Ibero-Atlânticas* (Lisbon: 2019) 179–188.

Gabriel M. Nunes, *As Igrejas Antigas de Angola* (Luanda: 1981).

Henriques I.C., *A presença africana em Portugal, uma história secular: preconceito, integração, reconhecimento (séculos XV–XX)* (Lisbon: 2019).

Lawrence J., "Black Africans in Renaissance Spanish Literature", in Earle T.F. – Lowe K.J.P. (eds.), *Black Africans in Renaissance Europe* (Cambridge: 2005) 70–93.

Lahon D. – Neto M.C. (eds.), *Catálogo da Exposição Os Negros em Portugal – Sécs. XV a XIX* (Lisbon: 1999).

Lahon D., "Esclavage, Confréries Noires, Sainteté Noire et Pureteté de Sang au Portugal (XVIe et XVIIIe siècles)", *Lusitanea Sacra* (2ª série) 15 (2003) 119–162 https://repositorio.ucp.pt/bitstream/10400.14/4408/1/LS_S2_15_DidierLahon.pdf.

Lahon D., "Da redução da alteridade a consagração da diferença: As Irmandades Negras em Portugal (séculos XVI–XVIII)" *Projeto História* 44 (2012) 53–83.

Lowe K.J.P., "Introduction: the Black African Presence in Renaissance Europe", in Earle T.F. – Lowe K.J.P., *Black Africans in Renaissance Europe* (Cambridge: 2005) 1–16.

Lowe K.J.P., "The Stereotyping of Black Africans in Renaissance Europe", in Earle T.F. – Lowe K.J.P. (eds.), *Black Africans in Renaissance Europe* (Cambridge: 2005) 17–47.

Marques J., "A Confraria do Corpo de Deus da Cidade de Braga", in *Livro Homenagem a Lúcio Craveiro da Silva* (Braga: 1994) 223–260.

Martins I., "Igreja e colégio dos Jesuítas, Luanda, Angola", in *Heritage of Portuguese Influence/Património de Influência Portuguesa* (HPIP); https://hpip.org/pt/heritage/details/56.

Matta J., *Manuscrito 50 da Biblioteca Geral da Universidade de Coimbra: Vilancicos, Romances e Chansonetas de Santa Cruz de Coimbra Século XVII Parte I* (Lisbon: 2008).

Mkenda F. (S.J.), *Jesuits in Africa: A Historical Narrative from Ignatius of Loyola to Pedro Arrupe* (Leiden – New York: 2022); https://brill.com/display/title/60118?language=en (accessed 8/9/2023).

Nery R. Vieira, "O vilancico português do século XVII: Um fenómeno intercultural", in Castelo Branco S.E. (ed.), *Portugal e o Mundo: Encontro da culturas na música* (Lisbon: 1997) 91–112.

Rees O. – Nelson B. (eds.), *Cristóbal de Morales: Sources, Influences, Reception* Studies in Medieval and Renaissance Music (Woodbridge: 2007).

Reginaldo L., *Os Rosários dos Angolas: Irmandades Negras, Experiências Escravas e Identidades Africanas na Bahia Setencentista* (Ph.D dissertation, Universidade Estadual de Campinas: 2005).

Roldão C., "Feminismo negro em Portugal: falta contar-nos" *Jornal Público* (2019); https://www.publico.pt/2019/01/18/culturaipsilon/noticia/feminismo-negro-portugal-falta-contarnos-1857501.

Simão J.L. Alves, *The* Villancicos de negros *in Manuscript 50 of the Biblioteca Geral da Universidade de Coimbra: A Case Study of Black Cultural Agency and Racial Representation in 17th-Century Portugal* (Master's dissertation, Graduate College of Bowling Green State University, Ohio: 2017).

Stevenson R., "The Afro-American Musical Legacy to 1800", *The Music Quarterly* 54.4 (1968) 475–502.

Tinhorão J.R., *Os Negros em Portugal. Uma Presença Silenciosa* (Lisbon: 2019).

Valerio M.A., "Black Dancers and Musicians Performing Afro-Christian Identity in Early Modern Spain and Portugal", *Publication of the Afro-Latin/American Research Association* 24 (2020) 47–56.

Villalba y Estaña B., *Confalonieri, Gianbattista, Por terras de Portugal no século XVI*, (Lisbon: 2002).

CHAPTER 16

Devotional Collective Singing and the Construction of Christian Indigenous Communities: The Hospital Confraternities of the Concepción in Colonial Michoacán

Antonio Ruiz Caballero

Abstract

Studies on confraternities and pious associations of lay people in relation to music in Spain and its overseas territories is a subject that has attracted interest in recent years. In the case of Mexico, although there are a few studies on confraternities in colonial times that explore various social, ethnic, cultural and economic topics, their relationship with music and sounds is a subject that still needs attention. In this work I will focus on a specific type of associations: the hospital confraternities of the Conception in the indigenous towns of Michoacán, especially of the Tarascan or p'urhépecha ethnic group, founded in the rural areas from the sixteenth century. These associations and their spaces have been studied from various points of view. Although some of these studies have mentioned ritual and its political and social importance, due attention has not been paid to sound and musical aspects, perhaps because thus far no written musical documents have been found and because the clues are brief in other sources. The absence of written documentation is mainly due to these societies in which until a few decades ago an oral culture prevailed. As a first approach to the problem of music and sounds in the activity of these hospital confraternities in Michoacán, from the combined approach of cultural history and musicology, I will reflect on the social and cultural role that these collectives played in creating new communities and identities, as well as the role that music played in that process.

Keywords

devotional music – collective singing – colonial Mexico – Michoacán – indigenous communities – indigenous identity

Studies on confraternities and pious associations of lay people in relation to music in Spain and its overseas territories is a subject that has attracted interest in recent years. Research has generally focused on urban areas, demonstrating how these groups and the sounds associated with their activities have contributed to the development of cities and the shaping of urban soundscape, especially in the modern era.[1] In general, these studies are based on a variety of written documentation, among which there are acts of ecclesiastical chapters or civic councils, patents, constitutions, books of accounts, notarial protocols, descriptions of festivals and rituals, among others. Perhaps because of the difficulty of having access to such varied sources, it is less common to find research located in rural areas.[2]

In the case of Mexico, although there are quite a few studies on confraternities in colonial times that explore various social, ethnic, cultural and economic topics,[3] their relationship with music and sounds is a subject that still needs attention. Among the few existing studies, David Carvajal presents an overview based mainly on constitutions of Novohispanic confraternities that are preserved in the Archivo General de Indias, and Javier Marín focuses on the confraternity of Our Lady of Antigua, attached to the Metropolitan Cathedral

---

1 Diego C., "Música y religiosidad laica: el caso de las cofradías penitenciales de Valladolid durante el siglo XVI", *Revista de Musicología* 37.2 (2014) 441–460; and Robledo L., "Música y cofradías madrileñas en el siglo XVII: los esclavos del Santísimo Sacramento de la Magdalena y los Esclavos del Santo Cristo de San Ginés", *Revista de Musicología* 29/2 (2006) 481–520. For Hispanic America, see: Baker G. *Imposing Harmony: Music and Society in Colonial Cuzco* (Durham,: 2008); Baker G., "Music at Corpus Christi in colonial Cuzco", *Early Music* 32.3 (2004) 355–367; Pedrotti C.E., "Música y cofradías: una institución española transplantada a América", *Revista de Musicología* 32.1 (2009) 167–175; and Pedrotti C.E., "La periferia colonial: música de una cofradía de Córdoba del Tucumán", in Enríquez L. (ed.), *IV Coloquio Musicat. Harmonia mundi: los instrumentos sonoros en Iberoamérica, siglos XVI al XIX* (Mexico: 2009) 327–339.
2 Baker G., "Parroquia, cofradía, gremio, ayllu: organización profesional y movilidad en el Cuzco Colonial", in Bombi A. – Carreras J.J. – Marín M.A. (eds.), *Música y cultura urbana en la Edad Moderna* (Valencia: 2005) 177–190; and Alberto Díaz A. – Paula Martínez S. – Ponce C., "Cofradías de Arica y Tarapacá en los siglos XVIII y XIX. Indígenas andinos, sistema de cargos religiosos y festividades", *Revista de Indias* 74.260 (2014) 102–128.
3 Bazarte A. – García C., *Los costos de la salvación: las cofradías y la Ciudad de México (siglos XVI al XIX)* (Mexico: 2001); Bazarte A., *Las cofradías españolas en la Ciudad de México (1526–1860)* (Mexico: 1989); Bechtloff D., *Las cofradías en Michoacán durante la época de la colonia: la religión y su relación política y económica en una sociedad intercultural* (Zamora: 1996); Maquívar M.C., *Gremios y cofradías en la Nueva España* (Mexico: 1996); and Martínez P. – Von Wobeser G. – Muñoz J.G. (eds.), *Cofradías, capellanías y obras pías en la América colonial* (Mexico: 1998).

of Mexico City, where its chapel was located, and which had a special relationship with music.[4]

In this essay, I will focus on a specific type of association: the hospital confraternities of the Concepción in the indigenous towns of Michoacán, especially of the Tarascan or p'urhépecha ethnic group, founded in rural areas from the sixteenth century. These associations and their spaces have been studied from various points of view, including institutional and social,[5] architectural[6] and iconographic.[7] Although some of these studies have mentioned ritual and its political and social importance, due attention has not been paid to sound and musical aspects, perhaps because so far no written musical documents have been found and because the clues in other sources are few. But I believe that the absence of written documentation is mainly because an oral culture prevailed in these societies, until a few decades ago. As a first approach to the problem of music and sounds in the activity of these hospital confraternities in Michoacán, from the combined approach of cultural history and musicology, I will reflect on the social and cultural role that these collectives played in creating new communities and identities, as well as the role that music played in that process.

Benedict Anderson was one of the scholars who applied the concept of community in the field of cultural history in order to study the process of

---

4   Carvajal D., "La cultura sonora de las cofradías novohispanas, 1700–1821", *Temas americanistas* 27 (2011) 25–48; and Marín J., "Asistencia social, identidad peninsular y devoción mariana en una cofradía novohispana de músicos de mediados del siglo XVII", *Resonancias* 21.41 (2017) 13–33.
5   Muriel J., *Hospitales de la Nueva España: Fundaciones del siglo XVI* (Mexico: 1956) 12–13; Sánchez S., *Los Hospitales de Indios en Michoacán: el proyecto de Vasco de Quiroga y su evolución (1536–1639)* (Ph.D. dissertation, Universidad de Valladolid: 2004); Verástique B., *Michoacan and Eden. Vasco de Quiroga and the Evangelization of Western Mexico* (Austin TE: 2000); Warren, J.B., "Vasco de Quiroga, fundador de hospitales y colegios", *Missionalia hispánica* 67 (1966) 25–46; Warren J.B., *Vasco de Quiroga y sus Pueblos – Hospitales de Santa Fe* (Morelia: 1997); and Warren J.B. – Sánchez S., *Las Guatáperas. Hospitalitos y Capillas de Michoacán* (Mexico: 2007).
6   Artigas J.B., *Pueblos – Hospitales y Guatáperas de Michoacán. Las realizaciones arquitectónicas de Vasco de Quiroga y fray Juan de San Miguel* (Mexico: 2001); César M.G. – Gutiérrez A., "Espacio y funcionalidad en una institución comunal: los hospitales de Nurío, Pomacuarán, Aranza, Sevina y Turícuaro en el siglo XVII", in Paredes C. (ed.), *Arquitectura y espacio social en poblaciones purépechas de la época colonial* (Morelia: 1998) 305–336.
7   Álvarez G. *Los artesones michoacanos: los cielos historiados en tablas pintadas* (Mexico: 2000); Sigaut N. "El cielo de colores", in Paredes, *Arquitectura y espacio social en poblaciones purépechas* 269–304; and Perales R.M., "La doctrina institucional de los Austrias en el imaginario pictórico de las capillas hospitales en los pueblos fundacionales de Vasco de Quiroga: El modelo de la Inmaculada Concepción", *Liño* 26 (2020) 31–42.

shaping modern nations, but what interests me is to emphasise that according to this historian the 'imagined community' is socially constructed from the perception of a connection between its members. In this process, according to Anderson, factors such as language and other common cultural traits, shared history and the media are important, all of which contribute to the shaping of a common identity; religion could also play an important role, especially in stages prior to the emergence of nation-states.[8]

Among the cultural elements that promote the construction of collective identities are music and other sounds. R. Murray Schafer uses the term 'acoustic communities' to refer to those groups that share a common sound environment, and to those that unite the perception and recognition of that specific set of sounds as something proper to them. The acoustic community is built through the interaction of the members of the group with each other and with the sounds of their environment.[9] From this base I intend to demonstrate that the hospital confraternities were a key model of social organisation to build the new communities of indigenous Christians, and that music played a very important role in this process of community building, especially from the perspective of the collective devotional singing in which not only the listening and perception of sounds was involved, but the active participation of all members of the community in the creation of this sonic environment.

To achieve this, I will explore three main types of sources that afford clues as to the sound practices of the indigenous hospital confraternities in Michoacán: first, the brief descriptions of ritual activities in hospitals contained in seventeenth-century chronicles of the Mendicant orders; second, community devotional spaces and their iconography, dating mainly from the eighteenth and nineteenth centuries; and finally, the oral tradition linked to ritual and musical practices in today's indigenous societies, with which it is possible to establish an ethnographic analogy and draw lines of continuity. After a brief characterisation of the hospital confraternities and providing a general historical framework about their creation in Michoacán, I will dedicate three sections to reflect on each the type of sources and the insights they bring to knowledge of ritual sound practices in contexts in which the usual documents are not available for studies on music and confraternities. It is a study of the *longue durée* in that hospitals were established from the sixteenth century and that, despite undergoing transformations linked to various social and political

---

8 Anderson B., *Imagined Communities. Reflections on the Origin and Spread of Nationalism* (London – New York: 2006).
9 Schafer R.M., *The Soundscape. Our Sonic Environment and the Tuning of the World* (Rochester VE: 1994) 215–217.

processes, they had continuity during the Novohispanic and independent periods, so that some survive to the present, although their function has changed and their organisation is no longer formally conceived as a confraternity.

1   The Hospital Confraternities of the Concepción in Michoacán

In the framework of the process of conquest, colonisation and evangelisation of Mesoamerica as part of the strategies of social reorganisation of the indigenous population confraternities were introduced, according to the model that had functioned in Europe since the Middle Ages. In New Spain these associations played an important role in the strengthening of Christian religiosity through the promotion of certain devotions that were of particular interest to civil and ecclesiastical authorities: for example. the Holy Cross, which was the main symbol of conversion to the Christian faith; the Blessed Souls, through which belief into Purgatory was introduced; the Blessed Sacrament, especially in the Post-Tridentine environment that reinforced the dogma of transubstantiation; and the Marian advocations that reinforced the belief in the 'Mother of God' who, through a process of cultural hybridisation, was equated with the Mesoamerican female deities linked to the earth and fertility. The Confraternity of the Concepción stands out, at least for the bishopric of Michoacán, as the one that brought together the entire population of many indigenous towns.

According to the historian María Teresa Sepúlveda, who studied civic and religious institutions in the p'urhépecha area, the confraternities of the Concepción were the first to organise themselves in the region. She points out that, unlike religious-charitable or sacramental confraternities constituted by specific and limited groups, in those of the Concepción 'the whole people were linked through a series of religious and social obligations' ('todo el pueblo se encontraba enlazado a través de una serie de obligaciones de carácter religioso y social').[10] That is, the creation of these confraternities also contributed to social cohesion among the new Christian inhabitants of the 'pueblos de indios' (or Indian townships, as the Spanish authorities called them, in Michoacán), especially considering that people of different ethnic groups and cultures were often brought together in one place. Another function they exercised was the administration of a portion of the community's resources since they owned land, livestock or other goods that helped finance worship and mutual assistance or other tasks, such as the care of pilgrims, the sick and dying. In the

---

10   Sepúlveda M.T., *Los cargos políticos y religiosos en la región del Lago de Pátzcuaro* (Morelia: 2003) 108.

case of the confraternities of the Concepción, this social welfare activity was carried out in hospitals.

In the course of centuries of conquest and colonisation, the concept of hospital was broader than that of today. According to Josefina Muriel, one of the earliest scholars of these institutions in New Spain: 'The hospital was generally a house where all those in need were received. Therefore, sometimes they were hospitals for the poor, in other cases lodgings for pilgrims, or orphanages or nursing homes for the sick. Moreover, they could present several aspects at the same time'.[11] From the Middle Ages in Europe hospitals were institutions inspired by the concept of Christian charity, which were founded or administered by various authorities and corporations, including civic councils and ecclesiastical chapters, or religious orders, but they were also in the charge of confraternities, some of which carried out the management of the hospital as their main charitable work, hence they can be named as hospital confraternities. This is the case of the Concepción confraternities in colonial Michoacán.[12]

Hospitals established in these indigenous towns played an important role in the care of the population during the numerous epidemics that ravaged New Spain. In addition to bodily healing, hospitals were spaces where spiritual comfort and health were sought, as well as a good death, so that sacraments such as communion, confession and extreme unction were imparted. Yet it is also important to bear in mind that these institutions also carried out political activities such as the election of authorities within the hospital confraternities. These elections were held in a ritualised manner, usually on 8 December as part of the feast of the Immaculate Conception, thus bearing witness to the sacralisation of political power and, conversely, the politicisation of the communal religious space.

The original idea of creating these hospitals has been attributed both to the Franciscan friar Juan de San Miguel and to Don Vasco de Quiroga, the first bishop of Michoacán, both of whom carried out important work founding hospitals in the first decades of colonisation in this region.[13] Whoever was responsible, the institution spread successfully from the sixteenth century,

---

11   Muriel, *Hospitales de la Nueva España* 12–13: 'El hospital era en general una casa donde se recibía a todos los necesitados. Por lo tanto, en unas ocasiones eran hospitales de pobres, en otras hospederías para peregrinos, bien orfelinatos o asilos para enfermos. Además, no eran una u otra cosa privativamente, sino que podían presentar varios aspectos todos al mismo tiempo'.
12   Ibidem 13.
13   Ibidem 13.

especially in the area of p'urhépecha, both in the parishes and visits controlled by the diocesan clergy and in the doctrines administered by Franciscans and Augustinians. In 1582, the third bishop of Michoacán, the Augustinian friar Juan de Medina Rincón, wrote to the king informing him that: 'The Indians use these hospitals a lot in this province, so much so that there is hardly a town that has twenty or thirty houses that does not have a hospital and is proud of it. [...] there must be more than two hundred of these hospitals there'.[14]

Hospitals were also called 'guatáperas' or 'huatáperas', a term that is interpreted as a meeting place or community house, appropriately so because of the diversity of activities carried out there, and especially because their service involved the entire population. Fray Juan de Medina Rincón reported that: 'The way to sustain them is that all men and women by lot will serve their weeks a certain number of Indians, according to the needs of the hospital and the number of people, and will normally collect alms and carry out their work for the the hospital'.[15] The 'semaneros' (who served according to a weekly rota) were usually married couples, varied in number according to the count of inhabitants in the village, who were responsible for all the necessary tasks in the hospital, such as cleaning, care for the sick and preparation of food. Men also worked on land owned by the hospital, while in some places women spun; the proceeds from this work helped to cover the hospital's expenses.[16] As part of their extra duties, the *semaneros* took charge of cleaning and decorating the chapel, and participated in ritual activities that I will discuss further on. It should be borne in mind that, by virtue of the social and community ties established between all the inhabitants of the town through the confraternity, in addition to the ties of kinship, the *semaneros* were in fact supported by their relatives, godparents and others, so that most of the residents were involved every week in the service of the hospital, as can be seen today in some active hospitals such as Santa Fe de la Laguna.

---

14 Medina J. "Relación que su Majestad manda se envíe a su Real Consejo, del Obispo de Michoacán Fray Juan de Medina Rincón, O.S.A. (Valladolid de Michoacán, 4 March 1582. Seville. Archivo General de Indias [AGI] Mexico, leg. 374)", in Warren J.B., *Michoacán en la década de 1580* (Morelia: 2000) 44.

15 Medina, "Relación que su Majestad" 45: 'La manera de sustentarlos es que todos hombres y mujeres por su tanda van a servir por sus semanas tantos y tantas indias, conforme a la necesidad del hospital y número de la gente, y de común hacen sus limosnas y trabajan todos para el hospital'.

16 Sepúlveda, *Los cargos políticos* 117; and De la Torre E., "Algunos aspectos acerca de las cofradías y la propiedad territorial en Michoacán", in De la Torre E., *Estudios de historia jurídica* (Mexico: 1994) 139–169.

The officials were the same for both the confraternity and the hospital, demonstrating the symbiotic relationship between the corporation and the institution. Among the main positions were that of mayordomo who supervised the economic functioning and material aspect of the hospital; the prioste or steward looked after worship and spiritual aspects; while the fiscal had a managerial function and monitored the fulfillment of obligations by all members of the confraternity. Usually these formal appointments were held for one year, renewed every 8 December on the feast of the Immaculate Conception.[17] There were also other positions, which varied from village to village, some of a ritual nature and others linked to the other functions carried out by hospitals. For example, according to a description dated 1748, the positions and offices held in the hospital of Cutzio, in the region of Tierra Caliente in Michoacán were:

> prioste, mayordomo o mayordomos, escribanos, fiscal, cocinero, pendonera, casundera o copalera [quien incensaba], dos candelpanes que llevan [las candelas] en las procesiones, y cuatro guananchas que carguen la imagen; y repartidas por semanas en los cinco barrios del pueblo, las mujeres [semaneras] que necesitan para cuidar a los enfermos, hacen atole [...], y hilan y hacen mantas que se venden para agregar su importe a los demás productos pertenecientes a la cofradía.[18]

> [the] *prioste*, mayordomo or mayordomos, notary, fiscal, cook, *pendonera* [the person who carried the flag], *casundera* or *copalera* [the person who swung the censer], two *candelpanes* who carried [candles] in the processions, and four *guananchas* bore the image; and the *semaneras* or women distributed by weeks in the five neighbourhoods of the town, to care for the sick, make *atole* [...],[19] and spin and make blankets that are sold to add their contribution to the other products belonging to the confraternity.

All these actors had leading roles in the social life of hospitals, each occupying a place in the socio-political hierarchy, but it was within the framework of ritual that they participated together.

---

17   Sepúlveda, *Los cargos políticos* 154.
18   Ibidem 156. The transcript comes from the following document: Biblioteca Central del Museo Nacional de Antropología e Historia. Sección de Manuscritos, Papeles de Paso y Troncoso, Ms. s. XVIII fol. 1: 'Idea de la jurisdicción de San Juan Huetamo, extendida por persona comisionada que fue don Joseph Antonio Calderón'.
19   A drink made from maize.

2 Ritual and Sound Practices in Hospitals According to the Chronicles of the Mendicant Orders

Descriptions of the ritual life in hospitals have survived in documents such as the chronicles of the Franciscan and Augustinian mendicant orders. The first Franciscan chronicle of the Province of San Pedro y San Pablo de Michoacán was written by friar Alonso de la Rea in 1643. He describes above all the procession that took place every Saturday between the chapel of the hospital and the main church, in which four Indian women, 'the most important, with their garlands, or crowns', carried the image of the Immaculate Conception on their shoulders. Once inside the main church, a solemn Mass was sung, 'with the church being adorned with much sedge and flowers, as if every Saturday was the titular feast'. After Mass, the image was taken back to the hospital chapel 'in the same order'.[20] Thus, in the description only the sung Mass is presented as a sonic element, without further detail, but it is possible to infer that those who were engaged in solemnising the Mass were, on the one hand, the celebrant priest responsible for the intoning or singing many of the liturgical texts, and, on the other hand, the music chapel, who would have performed mainly plainchant and polyphonic music and whose performance space was primarily the choir of the main church. La Rea likewise provides no details as to what was sung or played during the procession, although there, too, priest and singers could have participated, although it is possible that, in that not strictly liturgical context, devotional songs were collectively performed, whether in Latin or the vernacular.

The same chronicle includes an account of a ritual moment of devotional character in which the protagonists would have been neither priest nor singers of the music chapel, but rather the *semaneros*. According to Alonso de la Rea, friar Juan de San Miguel established a particular custom with the foundation of the convent of Uruapan, a tradition that later spread to other towns: 'that all the *semaneros* gather at twilight in the church [of the hospital], and dividing into choirs, the women in one, and the men in another, sing the doctrine, in the melody used by the church to sing their hymns' ('que todos los semaneros a prima noche se juntasen en la iglesia [del hospital], y partiéndose a choros, las mujeres en uno, y los varones en otro, cantasen la doctrina, en el tono que la Yglesia canta sus himnos').[21] This indicates that although at first the singing of the doctrine had had an essentially mnemonic function, it was established

---

20   La Rea A., *Crónica de la Orden de San Pedro y San Pablo de Michoacán* (Mexico: 1991) 45.
21   Ibidem.

as a rule that each day it was to be sung collectively as a devotional exercise. The sung doctrine included the 'four prayers' (*Pater Noster, Ave Maria, Credo* and *Salve Regina*), as well as other contents found in the doctrine manuals or catechisms that were often versified to facilitate learning; these texts were thus learnt mainly through rhythmic recitation and collective singing.[22] In addition to the texts of Christian doctrine, La Rea indicates that at dawn 'the hymn *Ave Maris Stella*, and *Pange lingua* [...] with the "gozos" ('joys') that repeat their words' ('el himno *Ave Maris Stella*, y *Pange lingua* [...] con los gozos que repiten sus palabras') were also sung.[23] From this, it can be inferred both that these hymns previously categorised as liturgical were also sung collectively in devotional contexts, and that it was customary to sing versions in vernacular languages that translated or paraphrased the liturgical texts.

A description found in the earliest chronicle of the province of San Nicolás de Tolentino de Michoacán, written by friar Diego Basalenque in 1644, provides information on the Augustinian context. Basalenque states that in the villages administered by the Augustinian order the Marian ritual began on Friday, when a procession was held in which the image of the Immaculate Conception was carried from the hospital chapel to the church 'with music [and] singing' ('con música [y] canto'). Upon arriving at the main church, an ancient Augustinian devotion known as the 'Benedicta' was sung; this consisted of three psalms, 'with three readings of our father St. Augustine' ('con tres liciones de Nuestro Padre San Agustín'), and at the end the *Salve Regina* was sung 'with lighted candles in their hands' ('con candelas encendidas en las manos'). On Saturday, the Mass of the Immaculate Conception was sung, and then the image was taken back to the hospital, 'as it had come, with more accompaniment and music' ('con más acompañamiento y música, que había venido').[24]

When Basalenque speaks of 'accompaniment', he possibly refers to the participation of instrumentalists and so to the music chapel. No details are provided as regards whether the doctrine and devotional songs were sung, as in the Franciscan hospitals, but it is clear that there was devotional use of texts in Latin, such as the *Benedicta* and *Salve Regina*. As regards devotional practices on other days of the week, Basalenque indicates that in hospitals 'all

---

22 Ruiz A., "Encuentros culturales en Michoacán, siglos XVI–XVII: recitación rítmica en latín y canto llano en lengua tarasca, de la enseñanza de la doctrina al ámbito devocional", *Cuadernos del Seminario de Música en la Nueva España y el México Independiente* 10 (2019) 68–86.
23 La Rea, *Crónica de la Orden* 45.
24 Basalenque D., *Historia de la Provincia de San Nicolás de Tolentino de Michoacán* (Morelia: 1989) 50.

the indians of the service gather to pray and sing along to the Ave Marias [at sunset] and at dawn' ('todas las indias e indios del servicio se juntan a rezar y cantar a las Ave Marías, y al amanecer').[25]

From these two brief witness accounts dating from the 1640s, some salient points can be identified:

1. The hospital confraternities sponsored liturgical acts such as the Mass dedicated to the Immaculate Conception held on Saturdays, for which they paid the ritual specialists who took care of the sonic elements: the priest, and the music chapel usually attached to the main church. Some 'pindekuarios' (or '*pindekuas* tables') (*pindekua* means custom) also testify to this in those cases where the main festivities celebrated in these places are recorded. They include information on the type of ritual acts carried out on public feast days and on common days, which were generally those days when the ministers participated; they sometimes also mention the singers, and the payment they received for the celebration of such acts.[26]

2. The members of these confraternities, both women and men, participated actively at non-liturgical times in the collective singing of the Doctrine, devotional songs and even some Latin liturgical texts performed with a devotional function. This is potentially important since very little has been studied as regards the active participation of the confreres in singing and in the production of sounds. In the hospitals the whole town sang, because all its inhabitants participated in shifts as *semaneros* in the daily ritual life of the hospital.

3. It is very difficult to reconstruct the specific repertory that was performed in both liturgical and devotional rituals, since the descriptions are not sufficiently detailed, and no other documentation survives. Some clues can be found, however, in other sources.

3   Spaces, Iconography and Devotional Singing

In its architectural dimension the hospital was the physical place in which all the activities generated by the confraternities of the Concepción were deployed, so these acts determined their spatial distribution and hierarchy.

---

25   Ibidem 70.
26   Carrillo A. *Michoacán en el otoño del siglo XVII* (Zamora: 1993) 250.

Juan Joseph Moreno, who attributed the foundation of hospitals to Vasco de Quiroga, claimed that this prelate ordered

> que en cada pueblo se fabricase, a no mucha distancia de la Parroquia, una casa con la decencia posible, en la que hubiese separación y división de piezas, para diversos usos; unas para alojamiento de los enfermos; otras para asistencia de los que ministran; y finalmente, para unirlos más estrechamente, y con más amor a esta casa; otras para el Ayuntamiento de la República de los Indios.

> that in each village, a house be built, not too far from the parish church, with as much decency as possible, in which the rooms would be separated and divided into different spaces for various uses; some [spaces] would be for housing the sick; others for when the ministers attended; and finally, to unite them more closely, and bind them with more love to this house, others for the Council of the Republic of Indians.[27]

The hospital, and especially its chapel, should be considered as an architectural space in which, in addition to liturgical events such as the Mass, devotional acts were carried out most of the time in which the presence of priests was not necessary. These were autonomous spaces governed by indigenous authorities, with wide community participation.

While the main church – as well as the convent or the priest's house, where these existed – was the space overseen by the priests, the hospital chapel was the space that belonged to the confraternity. The image of the Immaculate Conception was the focal point of all the confraternity's activities, especially those of a ritual character, and therefore its main symbol of identity and social cohesion. It is common to find other Marian imagery in hospital chapels testifying to the fact that other festivals dedicated to the Virgin Mary were also important, among them the Assumption, the Virgin of the Rosary and, especially from the eighteenth century onwards, the Virgin of Guadalupe.

The main church, or 'Dioseo' or 'Diosio' (the 'place of God' or 'house of God') was essentially a masculine space, in both contrast to and complementary with the hospital chapel, which was also known as the 'Iurhixeo' (the 'place

---

27 Moreno J.J., *Fragmentos de la Vida y Virtudes del Illmo. y Rmo. Sr. Dr. Don Vasco de Quiroga, Primer Obispo de la Santa Iglesia Cathedral de Michoacán y Fundador del Real, y Primitivo Colegio de S. Nicolás Obispo de Valladolid* (1766). *Edición conmemorativa del IV centenario de la muerte de don Vasco de Quiroga* (Mexico: 1965) 60–61.

of the Virgin' or 'where the Virgin is kept or worshipped') and therefore identified as a feminine space. In Santa Fe de la Laguna, this male-female binomial works, because, according to its inhabitants, the main church is where the saints are (images of male entities such as the patron saint St. Nicholas and the Christ known as Lord of the Expiration); while in the hospital chapel are found the images of the Immaculate Conception, the Virgin of the Rosary and the Virgin of Guadalupe. In other p'urhépecha towns, the same scheme seems to apply, as in Santiago Nurío where the main church is dedicated to the Apostle Santiago and the hospital chapel to the Immaculate Conception. This binomial could be related to the idea of 'complementary opposites' present in the Mesoamerican cosmovision – for example, hot-cold, wet-dry, feminine-masculine, below-above, the cave and the mountain – that in pre-Hispanic times also had spatial representation in twin temples as in the case of the Templo Mayor of Tenochtitlan and others of the Mesoamerican area.[28]

Perhaps the feminine connotation of the hospital and its chapel is also explained by the prominence of women in many of the tasks necessary for how they functioned: sweeping, cooking, washing and caring for the sick. Yet women were also prominent in ritual life, since it was they who carried the Marian images in the processions and actively participated in the collective singing. It is also inferred that it was mainly women who took charge of the adornment with flowers of the images and the wooden poles (*andas*) [to support the images], as well as of changing the dress of the Virgin, as is still practiced today in several *guatáperas* of the p'urhépecha area, and other churches and chapels in Michoacán.

Inside the chapels of the *Iurhixeo* are found spaces and pieces of furniture that provide signs of the agency of different actors with regard to sonic practices. The presbytery and altar, as well as the pulpit, are the spaces where priests preached and sang liturgical texts in rituals such as the Masses of the Immaculate Conception [Fig. 16.1]. There are high choirs from which the music chapel performed plainchant and polyphonic music [Fig. 16.2]; and there are also low choirs, as in the case of the hospital chapel of Nurío, which fulfilled the same function [Fig. 16.3]. Finally, the *semaneros* and the whole community

---

28 López A. – López L., *Monte sagrado-Templo Mayor* (Mexico: 2009) 163–164. According to these authors, the idea of complementary opposites generally stems from the notion that 'everything that exists consists of the combination of two substances that, because of their varied proportions in the make-up of each being, produce diversity and movement in the cosmos' ('todo lo existente está conformado por la combinación de dos sustancias que, debido a sus diversas proporciones en la configuración de cada ser, producen la diversidad y el movimiento del cosmos').

FIGURE 16.1   Santa Fe de la Laguna hospital: chapel, presbytery and altar
IMAGE © ANTONIO RUIZ CABALLERO

sang in the nave. Other spaces, such as the atrium, were shared by all these actors, especially during processions [Fig. 16.4].

In the hospital chapels in the p'urhépecha area, it is common to find wood ceilings painted with Christian iconography, often related to the Immaculate Conception and to other Marian advocations that would be integral to the apparatus for the representation of the confraternities of the Concepción as a way of expressing their identity while reinforcing the feminine character of these spaces [Fig. 16.5]. Some hospital chapels have musical iconography, such as the images of angel musicians depicted in the apse of the chapel of the *guatápera* of Uruapan, although they are more frequently found in the main

FIGURE 16.2   Santa Fe de la Laguna: hospital chapel and high choir
IMAGE © ANTONIO RUIZ CABALLERO

churches where the chapels of singers and instrumentalists performed, as is the case of the low choirs of Nurío and Cocucho.

However, another symbol found in wood ceilings that has passed largely unremarked outside the field of iconography,[29] and which has not been sufficiently connected with the ritual context and orality, is the representation,

---

29   Perales, "La doctrina institucional de los Austrias" 31–42.

FIGURE 16.3   Nurío hospital: chapel and low choir
IMAGE © ANTONIO RUIZ CABALLERO

of images and texts related to the Loretan litany, one of the main prayers dedicated to the Virgin Mary, often reflected in the invocations of this litany in Latin, as in the ceiling of the chapel of the Immaculate Conception of Nurio [Fig. 16.6]. Elsewhere, as in the wooden ceilings of Pomacuarán, Quinceo and San Lorenzo, the words are written in Spanish. These visual representations

FIGURE 16.4   Santa Fe de la Laguna hospital: chapel and atrium
IMAGE © ANTONIO RUIZ CABALLERO

are related to devotional acts introduced after the viceregal period, such as the Rosary, which is still sung in places like Quinceo. Throughout the Catholic world, the Loretan litany was customarily sung or prayed at the conclusion of the Rosary, which would account for its representation in images and texts in painted wooden ceilings which bear witness to the collective prayer or song addressed to the Virgin Mary. Especially from the seventeenth and eighteenth centuries, this practice took root among the hospital chapels of the indigenous population in Michoacán.

The only written testimony so far located is found in a document preserved in the John Carter Brown Library dated 1853 in a p'urhépecha town called Tarejero. It is signed by José Juan Aparicio Maya, who could be a singer active in that town between the 1830s and 1850s. The document is intitled: 'Light on how to walk the Way of the Cross in the Tarascan language, with the addition of the mysteries of the most holy rosary in Castilian, and other prayers in Tarasco, and the litany of the Most Holy Virgin in Latin' ('Luz para saber andar la Via Cruz por la idioma tarasco, que van añadidos los misterios del santísimo rosario en castellano, y otras oraciones en tarasco, y la letania de ma[ría] santísima en latin'). As the title indicates, among other texts it contains

FIGURE 16.5   Nurío hospital: chapel and painted ceiling
IMAGE © ANTONIO RUIZ CABALLERO

FIGURE 16.6   Nurío hospital: chapel and detail of painted ceiling (invocation of the Loretan litany)
IMAGE © ANTONIO RUIZ CABALLERO

the Loretan litany in Latin, just after the mysteries and the salutation to the Virgin Mary.[30] The fact that this manuscript has no musical notation suggests that it was not necessary in a context in which the respective melodies were learned and memorised. Thus, both the images and the Latin text reflected in the ceilings and in this type of manuscript notebook served as facilitators of musical and ritual memory that would have reinforced the identity and social cohesion of the group through collective singing of the litany dedicated to the Immaculate Conception.

---

30   Providence RI. John Carter Brown Library. Codex Ind 34: José Juan Aparicio Maya, "Luz para saber andar la Via Cruz por la idioma tarasco, que van añadidas los misterios del santísimo rosarios en castellana, y otros oraciones en tarasco, y la letania de ma[ría] santísima en latin", fols. 30v–32r.

4   Collective Singing and Oral Tradition: Analogies and Continuities between Past and Present

Parallel to the transfer of European music in the schools annexed to the convents, where the ritual specialists were trained as singers and instrumentalists, went the transmission process of chant through memorisation based on repeated participation in devotional rituals.[31] In this way, from the sixteenth century all the members of the confraternities of the Concepción, without formal training, memorised a series of melodies and texts and sang them collectively. At this point it is necessary to present more directly data from the ethnographic record and research carried out in some indigenous communities of Michoacán, mainly p'urhépechas and nahuas, on several occasions from 2012 to the present. Although indigenous peoples have not been impervious to social and cultural change throughout history, research shows that in their ritual activities it is possible to find elements that seem to be related to those indicated by historical documentation such as the chronicles studied in this essay. It might then become possible to resort to ethnographic analogy and draw possible lines of continuity.

In some of the hospitals or *guatáperas* that still operate, as in that of Santa Fe de la Laguna, the system of *semaneros* is still in place; they come to serve these spaces that have preserved above all their community ritual function around the hospital chapel or *Iurhixeo*. They primarily take on tasks such as cleaning the hospital, decorating the chapel with flowers and candles, changing the attire of the images and preparing food for themselves and for those who attend the ritual activities on Saturday. In Santa Fe it is still the custom to perform a procession with the Marian images and, as the seventeenth-century chronicles describe, there are still four women to carry the Virgin. In this procession the women perform a song, known as *Uarhi Iurixhe* ('Lady Virgin') which they themselves describe as 'alabanza' (praise) in dedication to the Virgin of the Assumption.

The *Uarhi iurixhe* song of praise exemplifies the kind of devotional genres that were present from the early years of the colonisation process such as the devotional songs mentioned in the chronicles. Succinct analysis of this *alabanza* suggest elements of continuity. It is a text in the p'urhépecha language transcribed by Néstor Dimas from a recording that, according to his report, dates from the years 1968–1970:[32]

---

31   Ruiz A., "Paisajes sonoros devocionales: el canto colectivo en el proceso evangelizador de Michoacán, siglos XVI y XVII", in Regueiro P. (ed.), *La conquista de Tenochtitlán y las otras conquistas. Edición conmemorativa 500 años* (San Antonio: 2022) 328–366.
32   Dimas, N., *Temas y textos del canto p'urhépecha* (Zamora, El Colegio de Michoacán, Instituto Michoacano de Cultura: 1995) 308–309.

> Uarhi iurhixe santa maria
> Uarhi iurhixe santa maria
> Santa maria asunsioni
> Santa maria asunsioni
> Iarere t'u tarhatanaskare uarhi
> Angelachaksïni isï tarhatasti.[33]

The text is written in the second person, so as to address directly the image of the Virgin, establishing an emotional connection between the community (which in the past was conceived as a confraternity) and the Marian image. Although this song of praise is dedicated in particular to the advocation of the Assumption, Nestor Dimas also identifies other Marian praises that were sung in Santa Fe between 1968 and 1970, including one dedicated to the Immaculate Conception.

This text also explains in a very simple way an idea that occupied the mind of several theologians throughout the history of the Catholic Church: unlike Christ who ascended to heaven without assistance, the Virgin Mary was raised by a multitude of angels. Here is the didactic function that was also present from the first decades of the colonial period, as related by the chronicles and other narrative documents.[34] My musical transcription of this song of praise was made from another recording made in the early years of the twenty-first century, recorded on a CD made for the book *Una bandolita de oro, un bandolón de cristal. Historia de la música en Michoacán* [Ex. 16.1].[35]

This *alabanza* is performed in two parts or voices in strictly parallel diatonic thirds, a tradition of singing which I consider to be related to oral tradition polyphonies, still present in various parts of Europe, particularly those of the Western Mediterranean, from where most of the regular and secular clergy who evangelized New Spain came.[36] I believe that this song of praise is an example of the processes of transmission or transfer of European musical knowledge, in particular of the 'popular polyphony' to which the theorist Fray Tomás de Santa María referred as practised by 'men and women who do not

---

33   The free translation in Spanish reads: 'Señora Virgen / Santa María Asunción / Usted fue levantada, señora / Los ángeles la levantaron' ('Lady Virgin / Holy Mary [of the] Assumption / You were raised, lady, / The angels lifted you').
34   Ruiz, "Paisajes sonoros devocionales".
35   Martínez J.A. (ed.), *Una bandolita de oro, un bandolón de cristal: historia de la música en Michoacán* (Morelia: 2004).
36   Ruiz A. *Polifonías de tradición oral en el Pacífico Mexicano: el repertorio para Cuaresma y Semana Santa en la comunidad nahua de Santa María Ostula* (Morelia: 2023).

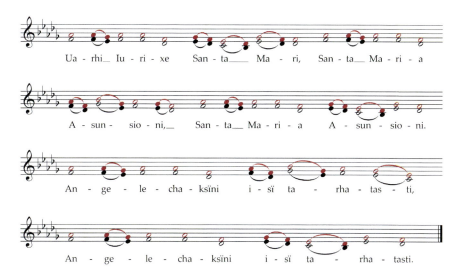

EX. 16.1   *Uarhi iurhixe* ('Lady Virgin'). Oral tradition, Santa Fe de la Laguna, Michoacan. Author's transcription

know music'.[37] At the same time it illustrates the process of cultural hybridization in which European musical practices were appropriated and transformed by the indigenous population. Although musically speaking such songs do not differ significantly from European oral polyphonies, their being sung in an indigenous language results in a completely different sonority.

A second example is provided by the Loretan litany, which weaves together the images and texts reflected in the painted wooden ceilings of the hospital chapels and the oral practices that have continuity until the present. Although there are some indications that in some p'urhépecha towns, such as Santa Fe de la Laguna and Nurío where the Loretan litany is sung, songs in Latin are still found in the oral tradition, it has not proved possible to arrange interviews or recordings with persons possessing such knowledge. So in the absence of an oral example from the p'urhépecha area, I include here the song of the Loretan litany that I recorded in 2022 in the Nahua town of Santa María Ostula, in the region known as the Nahua Coast-Sierra of Michoacán.

In 1631, when Ostula was subject to the parish of Maquilí, the priest serving there stated that he celebrated a sung Mass sporadically on Saturdays, in addition to participating in the patron saint's feast on the day of 'the Conception of

---

37 Fiorentino G., "La música de 'hombres y mujeres que no saben de música': polifonía de tradición oral en el Renacimiento español", *Revista de Musicología* 31.1 (2008) 9–39.

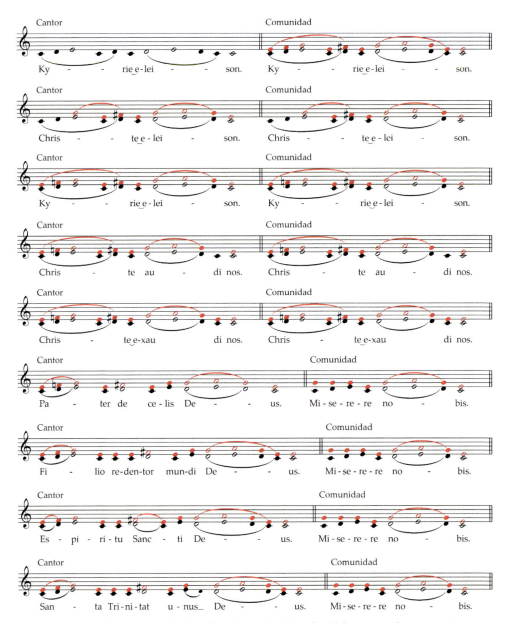

EX. 16.2A–B   Loretan litany. Oral tradition, Santa María Ostula, Michoacan. Author's transcription

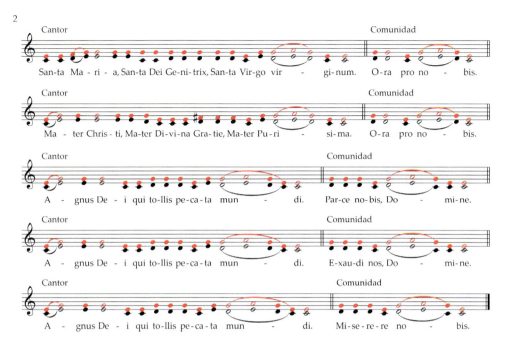

Our Lady'.[38] Although there is no data for a hospital founded in this town, it is known that in 1789 there was a confraternity of the Concepción that supported the worship of this Marian advocation with its own possessions including '100 cattle, 100 horses and 30 mules'.[39] I believe that this justifies including as an example the litany sung in Ostula, which corrresponds to a ritual context very similar to that found in the p'urhépecha area, and suggests that this was a practice shared by other indigenous ethnic groups in the bishopric of Michoacán.

Currently in Ostula the Loretan litany is sung at all Marian feasts and especially at that of the Immaculate Conception on 8 December, as well as at that of the Virgin of Sorrows (10 December), and at the feast of the Virgin of Guadalupe, present-day patron saint of the town (12 December). It is also sung at the end of the rosaries and in the Marian processions celebrated during Lent. On all these occasions, the singers sing the invocations and the whole community responds with the short and repetitive formulae characteristic of the litany: 'Ora pro nobis', etc. As in the previous example, the litany is sung in two parts, but in this case the parallelism in thirds is not strict [Ex. 16.2].

---

38   Gledhill J. *Cultura y desafío en Ostula: cuatro siglos de autonomía indígena en la costa-sierra nahua de Michoacán* (Zamora: 2004) 181.

39   De la Torre, "Algunos aspectos" 148.

Another interesting aspect, that could be a particular feature of the Ostula tradition, is that for the invocations to the Virgin Mary, the singers respond with all three invocations: 'Santa Maria, Santa Dei Genitrix, Santa Virgo Virginum / Mater Christi, Mater Divina Gratie, Mater Purisima', etc.

The litany is also a text that addresses the Virgin Mary in the second person. Although it is a text in Latin, the community of Ostula understands perfectly that it is a song dedicated to the Virgin Mary that speaks of her virtues, and therefore it is often sung before Marian images, especially in the processions that took place following the recitation of the rosary. This example also illustrates the transmission and appropriation by the indigenous population of a Latin text that was integrated into the ritual life of the Concepción confraternities and their collective devotional singing practices, contributing to the building of an acoustic community with shared sound symbols.

5   Final Reflections

To study the musical and sonic elements linked to the activity of groups such as the indigenous hospital confraternities of Michoacán, established in rural areas since the sixteenth century, it is necessary to resort to several strategies. Given the lack of detailed documentation on these aspects, especially for rural areas, it becomes essential to extend the types of sources from which it is possible to extract indications, such as spaces, iconography and oral tradition. This also requires study from a long-term perspective, since it is possible to establish an analogy between the data provided by the scarce written documentation of past centuries and the ritual-musical practices that can be recorded and observed/heard in the present, and so perhaps to identify possible continuities. Through the methodological strategies employed in this research, music can be seen as a cultural element of the first order in the social construction of the indigenous 'imagined communities' in Michoacán since the sixteenth century; above all in the p'urhépecha area, the hospital confraternities of the Concepción were a model of successful social organisation in the formation of the new 'Indian towns' following the processes of congregation.

However, beyond the interpretations that have privileged a vision of the confraternities as a means of social control by the Spanish authorities, and from the perspective of agency on the part of the indigenous peoples, it can be affirmed that the hospital confraternities in Michoacán were appropriated and controlled by the indigenous population, and that they constituted an autonomous religious, social and political space. The process of building new communities and identities should be seen as a strategy of resilience by the indigenous population, which enabled them to rebuild social ties or to establish new ones among all the inhabitants and reinforce links with existing sacred entities. Among these entities, belief in the Virgin Mary played a very important role.

Hospitals, and particularly the hospital chapel, were the physical spaces in which community and identity were built in ritual terms, and in which music played an important role: especially the collective singing of devotional use in vernacular languages and in Latin that involved indigenous agency through the active participation of women and men. The prayers sung in the second person addressed to Marian images – such as the *alabanzas* and the Loretan litany – enabled emotional bonds to be established with the Mother of God, adopted as a symbol of identity and protector of the community. At the same time, ties were established in a horizontal way, and were reinforced continuously among all members of the confraternity as an acoustic community that met to sing collectively in their hospital.

Bibliography

Primary Sources

Providence RI. John Carter Brown Library. Codex Ind 34: José Juan Aparicio Maya, "Luz para saber andar la Via Cruz por la idioma tarasco, que van añadidas los misterios del santísimo rosario en castellana, y otros oraciones en tarasco, y la letania de ma[ría] santísima en latin".

Secondary Sources

Álvarez G. *Los artesones michoacanos: los cielos historiados en tablas pintadas* (Mexico: 2000).

Anderson B., *Imagined Communities. Reflections on the Origin and Spread of Nationalism* (London – New York: 2006).

Artigas J.B., *Pueblos – Hospitales y Guatáperas de Michoacán. Las realizaciones arquitectónicas de Vasco de Quiroga y fray Juan de San Miguel* (Mexico: 2001).

Baker G. *Imposing Harmony: Music and Society in Colonial Cuzco* (Durham NC: 2008).

Baker G., "Music at Corpus Christi in colonial Cuzco", *Early Music* 32.3 (2004) 355–367.

Baker G., "Parroquia, cofradía, gremio, ayllu: organización profesional y movilidad en el Cuzco Colonial", in Bombi A. – Carreras J.J. – Marín M.A. (eds.), *Música y cultura urbana en la Edad Moderna* (Valencia: 2005) 177–190.

Basalenque D., *Historia de la Provincia de San Nicolás de Tolentino de Michoacán* (Morelia: 1989).

Bazarte A. – García C., *Los costos de la salvación: las cofradías y la Ciudad de México (siglos XVI al XIX)* (Mexico: 2001).

Bazarte A., *Las cofradías españolas en la Ciudad de México (1526–1860)* (Mexico: 1989).

Bechtloff D., *Las cofradías en Michoacán durante la época de la colonia: la religión y su relación política y económica en una sociedad intercultural* (Zamora: 1996).

Bermúdez Q. "La cofradia en la evangelización de Hispanoamerica", *Acta Académica* 45 (2009) 189–213.

Carrillo A. *Michoacán en el otoño del siglo XVII* (Zamora: 1993).

Carvajal D., "La cultura sonora de las cofradías novohispanas, 1700–1821", *Temas americanistas* 27 (2011) 25–48.

César M.G. – Gutiérrez A., "Espacio y funcionalidad en una institución comunal: los hospitales de Nurío, Pomacuarán, Aranza, Sevina y Turícuaro en el siglo XVII", in Paredes C. (ed.), *Arquitectura y espacio social en poblaciones purépechas de la época colonial* (Morelia: 1998) 305–336.

De la Torre E., "Algunos aspectos acerca de las cofradías y la propiedad territorial en Michoacán", in De la Torre E., *Estudios de historia jurídica* (Mexico: 1994) 139–169.

Díaz A. – Paula Martínez S. – Ponce C., "Cofradías de Arica y Tarapacá en los siglos XVIII y XIX. Indígenas andinos, sistema de cargos religiosos y festividades", *Revista de Indias* 74.260 (2014) 102–128.

Diego C., "Música y religiosidad laica: el caso de las cofradías penitenciales de Valladolid durante el siglo XVI", *Revista de Musicología* 37.2 (2014) 441–460.

Dimas N., *Temas y textos del canto p'urhépecha* (Zamora: 1995).

Fiorentino G., "La música de 'hombres y mujeres que no saben de música': polifonía de tradición oral en el Renacimiento español", *Revista de Musicología* 31.1 (2008) 9–39.

Gledhill J. *Cultura y desafío en Ostula: cuatro siglos de autonomía indígena en la costa-sierra nahua de Michoacán* (Zamora: 2004).

La Rea A., *Crónica de la Orden de San Pedro y San Pablo de Michoacán* (Mexico: 1991).

López A. – López L., *Monte sagrado-Templo Mayor* (Mexico: 2009).

Maquívar M.C., *Gremios y cofradías en la Nueva España* (Mexico: 1996).

Marín J., "Asistencia social, identidad peninsular y devoción mariana en una cofradía novohispana de músicos de mediados del siglo XVII", *Resonancias* 21.41 (2017) 13–33.

Martínez J.A. (ed.), *Una bandolita de oro, un bandolón de cristal: historia de la música en Michoacán* (Morelia: 2004).

Martínez P. – Von Wobeser G. – Muñoz J.G. (eds.), *Cofradías, capellanías y obras pías en la América colonial* (Mexico: 1998).

Medina J., "Relación que su Majestad manda se envíe a su Real Consejo, del Obispo de Michoacán Fray Juan de Medina Rincón, O.S.A. (Valladolid de Michoacán, 4 de marzo de 1582. AGI, México, leg. 374)", in Warren J.B., *Michoacán en la década de 1580* (Morelia: 2000) 19–65.

Moreno J.J., *Fragmentos de la Vida y Virtudes del Illmo. y Rmo. Sr. Dr. Don Vasco de Quiroga, Primer Obispo de la Santa Iglesia Cathedral de Michoacán y Fundador del Real, y Primitivo Colegio de S. Nicolás Obispo de Valladolid (1766). Edición conmemorativa del IV centenario de la muerte de don Vasco de Quiroga* (Mexico: 1965).

Muriel J., *Hospitales de la Nueva España: Fundaciones del siglo XVI* (Mexico: 1956).

Pedrotti C.E., "La periferia colonial: música de una cofradía de Córdoba del Tucumán", in Enríquez L. (ed.), *IV Coloquio Musicat. Harmonia mundi: los instrumentos sonoros en Iberoamérica, siglos XVI al XIX* (Mexico: 2009) 327–339.

Pedrotti C.E., "Música y cofradías: una institución española transplantada a América", *Revista de Musicología* 32.1 (2009) 167–175.

Perales R.M., "La doctrina institucional de los Austrias en el imaginario pictórico de las capillas hospitales en los pueblos fundacionales de Vasco de Quiroga: El modelo de la Inmaculada Concepción", *Liño* 26 (2020) 31–42.

Robledo L., "Música y cofradías madrileñas en el siglo XVII: los esclavos del Santísimo Sacramento de la Magdalena y los Esclavos del Santo Cristo de San Ginés", *Revista de Musicología* 29.2 (2006) 481–520.

Ruiz A. *Polifonías de tradición oral en el Pacífico Mexicano: el repertorio para Cuaresma y Semana Santa en la comunidad nahua de Santa María Ostula* (Morelia: 2023).

Ruiz A., "Encuentros culturales en Michoacán, siglos XVI–XVII: recitación rítmica en latín y canto llano en lengua tarasca, de la enseñanza de la doctrina al ámbito devocional", *Cuadernos del Seminario de Música en la Nueva España y el México Independiente* 10 (2019) 68–86.

Ruiz A., "Paisajes sonoros devocionales: el canto colectivo en el proceso evangelizador de Michoacán, siglos XVI y XVII", in Regueiro P. (ed.), *La conquista de Tenochtitlán y las otras conquistas. Edición conmemorativa 500 años* (San Antonio: 2022) 328–366.

Ruiz C., "Cofradías en Chile central. Un método de evangelización de la población indígena, mestiza y criolla", *Anuario de Historia de la Iglesia en Chile* 18 (2000) 23–58.

Sánchez S. "Imagen mariana y construcción de la identidad socio-religiosa en el Michoacán colonial", *Dimensión Antropológica* 55 (2012) 71–91.

Sánchez S. *Los Hospitales de Indios en Michoacán: el proyecto de Vasco de Quiroga y su evolución (1536–1639)* (Ph.D. dissertation, Universidad de Valladolid: 2004).

Schafer R.M., *The Soundscape. Our Sonic Environment and the Tuning of the World* (Rochester NY: 1994).

Sepúlveda M.T., *Los cargos políticos y religiosos en la región del Lago de Pátzcuaro* (Morelia: 2003).

Sigaut N. "El cielo de colores", in Paredes C. (ed.), *Arquitectura y espacio social en poblaciones purépechas de la época colonial* (Morelia: 1998) 269–304.

Verástique B. *Michoacan and Eden. Vasco de Quiroga and the Evangelization of Western Mexico* (Austin TE: 2000).

Verdi S., *Native Brotherhoods and Visual Culture in Colonial Quito (Ecuador): The Confraternity of the Rosary*, in Terpstra N. – Prosperi A. – Pastore S. (eds.), *Faith's Boundaries: Laity and Clergy in Early Modern Confraternities* (Turnhout: 2012) 277–299.

Warren J.B. – Sánchez S., *Las Guatáperas. Hospitalitos y Capillas de Michoacán* (Mexico: 2007).

Warren J.B. "Vasco de Quiroga, fundador de hospitales y colegios", *Missionalia hispánica* 67 (1966) 25–46.

Warren J.B., *Vasco de Quiroga y sus Pueblos – Hospitales de Santa Fe* (Morelia: 1997).

PART 4

Mapping the Contribution of Confraternities to the Urban Soundscape

∴

CHAPTER 17

Digital Cartography of the Confraternities of Granada and Their Impact on the Early Modern Urban Soundworld

Juan Ruiz Jiménez

Abstract

Following the conquest of Granada in 1492, the Crown set in motion the Christianisation of a population resistant to a change of faith that directly implied a drawn out process of acculturation. The spreading of the gospel was carried out through the rich network of sacred institutions, both secular and regular, established in an urban framework divided into twenty-three parishes. In these parishes were based the earliest confraternities of the city, fostered by the Crown and by the conquerors who settled there. In this chapter, I will present some findings from the digital cartography of the confraternities of Granada (ca. 1492–ca. 1800) I have been working on in recent years for the digital platform *Historical Soundscapes*. One of the most important aspects with regard to the dissemination of relevant data has been the creation of interactive labels to enable classification of confraternities, as well as of the most characteristic sensorial elements resulting from the cultural activities and festivities they promoted within and outside their headquarters. Moreover, reconstruction of some of their processional trajectories, drawn up through historical maps and Openstreetmap, has brought to the fore the question of occupation of public space and clarified the main ceremonial routes of the urban texture. All this helps to draw some preliminary conclusions about the sonic impact generated within confraternities' sphere of influence based on cartographic analysis.

Keywords

confraternities – Granada – digital cartography – historical soundscapes – processions

The study of cultural events in spatial terms is now well established within the field of humanities, having advanced rapidly with the use of GIS technology and the digital transformation that has generated knowledge and experimentation in what have become known as the Digital Humanities. In the disciplines of, for example, history, literature and history of art, researchers have made use of the tools and epistemological aims of cultural geography to pose new questions and develop methodological approaches that are based on the spatial representation of events and data, whether unpublished or known but reconsidered from a new perspective.[1] However, few studies in historical musicology have as yet focused on this spatial perspective or tried to integrate it into a cross-disciplinary analytical approach. To date, still fewer music historians have made use of digital tools to generate knowledge in their research through the development of new strategies in the processing of information or through new modes of presenting and disseminating results.[2]

Since the launch of the digital platform *Historical Soundscapes* on-line on 21 September 2015, the georeferencing of the urban complex of Granada (one of the original cities to be studied on the platform) has begun to be undertaken as a natural development of the various articles dedicated to the theme of the contribution of confraternitites to the city's soundscape.[3] My involvement in the research project *The Contribution of Confraternities and Guilds to the Urban Soundscape in the Iberian Peninsula, c.1400–c.1700* (CONFRASOUND), directed by Tess Knighton, led to the creation of one of the cartographical projects now found in the updated version 2.0, of *Historical Soundscapes* (launched in May 2022), with the title 'Mapping Confraternities and Their Contribution to the Urban Soundscape'.[4] Since 2020, when the CONFRASOUND project was

---

[1] On the many ways in which the terms digital humanities, spatial humanities and cultural geography overlap and their separate definitions, and on the geohumanities, see: Bauch N., "Digital Geohumanities: Visualizing Geographic Thought", *International Journal of Humanities and Arts Computing* 11.1 (2017) 1–15.

[2] Gámir A., "El giro espacial en las Humanidades Digitales y sus productos cartográficos", *Biblio3W. Revista Bibliográfica de Geografía y Ciencias Sociales* 24 (2019); Ruiz Jiménez J., "Cartografía digital de espacios sonoros: una innovadora aproximación metodológica en los estudios de Musicología Urbana", in Carrero E. – Zauner S. (eds.), *Respondámosle a concierto. Estudios en homenaje a Maricarmen Gómez Muntané* (Barcelona: 2020) 235–248. Various research projects are currently being developed, although as yet without publication of results on-line: Ferreira A. – Wohlmuth C. – Rodrigues A. – Correia N., "Plataforma Multimedia Interativa: experiencia imersiva da Paisagem Sonora Histórica de Évora", in Sá V. da – De Paula R.T., Conde A.F. – Gouveia A.C. (eds.), *Sonoridades Eborenses* (Ribeirão: 2021) 313–335; Belotti S. – Fiore A., "Maps, Music, and Culture: Representing Historical Soundscapes Through Digital Mapping", in Schwan A. – Thomson T. (eds.), *The Palgrave Handbook of Digital and Public Humanities* (Cham: 2022) 423–440.

[3] Ruiz Jiménez J. – Lizarán Rus I.J., "Historical Soundscapes (c.1200–c.1800): An On-Line Digital Platform", in Knighton T. – Mazuela-Anguita A. (eds.), *Hearing the City in Early Modern Europe* (Turnhout: 2018) 355–371.

[4] These articles can be seen on OpenStreetMap by clicking on the button labelled 'Confraternities Project', while their position on the historical maps can also be found by

included in the *Historical Soundscapes* platform, my contribution has focused on the task of the systematic cartography of the many confraternities of Granada in the different institutions in which they were based, and their liturgical and devotional activities inside and outside those churches. In this chapter, I will present the methodology underlying this study, the extent to which it has been developed over the three years of the project, the challenges it presented and preliminary analysis of results.

1   Methodology

An initial survey of the main aspects of the sensorial attributes generated by confraternal devotional activities, and the mechanisms by which they were integrated into the urban soundscape, reveals that these elements were essentially shared throughout the geographical region of Western European cultural traditions. They include: the particular topography of the specific urban nucleus; the spatial layout that generates its architecture; and the acoustic peculiar to its streets and religious, civic and private buildings that have an impact on sensorial elements of the urban context and distinguished them from other urban centres. These sensorial elements are found, presented in a more or less conventional way, in the sources studied for the identification of the urban soundscape, and which, from a physical and geographical perspective, were representative of it. At the same time, the human factor that lay behind these entities, as well as the sensorial elements integral to confraternal activity, have a key role to play in the material and distinctive character of the places in which that activity took place. Textiles, decorations, paintings, sculptures and ephemeral architecture determine these performance spaces, both interior and exterior, in a more or less transitory way [Fig. 17.1]. Candlelight, illuminations and fireworks modify natural light and, according to contemporary sources, create the illusion of the transformation of night into day. The smell of incense, perfume, flowers and aromatic herbs merge with the wide range of acoustic elements to create sensorial experiences that stimulate unique and unrepeatable emotional responses.

Confraternities form an integral part of the particular ecosystems of sacred institutions and the urban fabric in which they exert influence. Their members

---

using the search button in the window 'Cities with historical cartography', by consulting the term 'confraternities project' in the field 'types of events'. In both cases, the results will be shown on the map and in the sidebar generated by the search, which can be visualised and hidden by using the relevant icon situated in the upper left part of the screen.

FIGURE 17.1   Capilla de las Ánimas Benditas del Purgatorio.
Granada, Iglesia del Sagrario
IMAGE © JUAN RUIZ JIMÉNEZ

interact with these entities, whether trade-based or devotional, creating networks of protection, support and identity, and with those other members of the community to which they belong. These bodies thus form one of the most important focus points of sociability in the early modern period, and vie with one another in a shared territory of which they take control, whether on a sporadic or regular basis, in order to project their image and status in society and in relation to their cohabitants.

The different representations of the landscape and urban plans of Granada, drawn up from the sixteenth to the eighteenth centuries, allow the particular orography of the city, dominated by the hills of the Albaicín and the Alhambra, separated from north to south by the Darro river, to be visualised. The outline

FIGURE 17.2   Platform of Ambrosio de Vico (ca. 1600)
IMAGE HISTORICAL SOUNDSCAPES © JUAN RUIZ JIMÉNEZ – IGNACIO JOSÉ LIZARÁN RUS

of the city walls that stretched from the Puerta de Elvira to the Puerta de Bibataubín, mark the limits of urban development on the plain [Fig. 17.2].[5] Following the conquest of Granada in 1492, Isabel and Ferdinand began the complex task of rechristianisation of a population divided by the imposition of a belief system that had a direct implication for a lengthy period of acculturation. The conversion process was carried out by the rich network of religious institutions, whether lay or monastic, established within the urban complex. The city was divided into twenty-three parishes in which the earliest confraternities were based with the support of the Crown as well as of the conquistadors who settled in Granada and became members of them.[6]

This highly complex process, which lasted from 1492 to 1570, gave rise to two communities within the population that were clearly differentiated from sensorial, cultural and emotional perspectives. Over time, these two groups

---

5 Gil Sanjuan J. – Sánchez López J.A., "Iconografía y visión histórico-literaria de Granada a mediados del quinientos", *Chronica Nova* 23 (1993) 73–133; Calatrava J. – Ruiz Morales M., *Los planos de Granada 1500–1909. Cartografía urbana e imagen de la ciudad* (Granada: 2005); Espigares Rooney B., "Leer una imagen. La cartografía urbana y su conocimiento: Vista de Granada de Anton van den Wyngaerde", *Revista Letral* 15 (2015) 101–117.

6 García Pedraza A. – López – Guadalupe Muñoz M.L., "Cofradías y moriscos en la Granada del siglo XVI (1500–1568)", in Mestre Sanchis, A. – Giménez López E. (eds.), *Disidencias y exilios en la España Moderna* (Alicante: 1997) 377–392.

consolidated their position in well-defined geographical zones that were perceived in different ways by each: the *morisco* community in the Albaicín, especially on the upper part of the hill; and the Christian community on the plain of the city, which expanded into the space beyond the walled area. It is equally clear that this segregation was not absolute and that there was a high degree of porosity between these two communities, especially in contiguous areas such as the parishes of San Pedro y San Pablo, San Juan de los Reyes or San José. The expulsion of the *moriscos* from the city in 1569 led to the formation of an unequal distribution in terms of population and wealth in these two sections that had a major impact on the development of confraternities there over the following two hundred years.[7]

The chronological limit of *Historical Soundscapes* is ca. 1800 to allow a long and fluid interpretation of the early modern period. From the mid-eighteenth century, the critical approach to popular religiosity of Enlightenment thinking became more widespread and confraternities increasingly came under the control of the Crown.[8] Towards the end of the century, an anti-guild political stance also gained in strength, fomented by a series of authoritarian dictats that called for labour reform; this resulted in the abolition of the guild system during the nineteenth century and the development of new forms of trade association.[9] In the case of Granada, as in other Spanish cities, the crisis of the turn of the century was deepened by the War of Spanish Independence (1808–1814). On 18 August 1809, Joseph I published the decree by which the regular, conventual, mendicant and clerical orders were suppressed throughout Spanish dominions, with the requirement that they leave their convents within fifteen days. These were then sequestered. Granada was occupied on 29 January 1810, bringing the decree into force and having a dramatic impact on many of the regular sacred institutions in which a good number of

---

7 See Ruiz Jiménez J., "La transformación del paisaje sonoro urbano en la Granada conquistada (1492–1570)", in Rodríguez G. – Coronado Schwindt G. – Palazzo E. (eds.), *Paisajes sonoros medievales* (Mar de Plata: 2019) 139–186; García Pedraza A., "El hospital y la cofradía morisca de La Resurrección. ¿Fracaso o éxito de la política evangelizadora castellana?", *Al-Qantara* 42.2 (2021) 1–20.

8 Arias de Saavedra Alías I. – López-Guadalupe Muñoz M.L., "Debate político y control estatal de las cofradías españolas en el siglo XVIII", *Bulletin Hispanique* 99.2 (1997) 423–435; Arias de Saavedra Alías I. – López-Guadalupe Muñoz M.L., *La represión de la religiosidad popular. Crítica y acción contra las cofradías en la España del siglo XVIII* (Granada: 2002).

9 Díez Rodríguez F., "El Gremialismo de Antonio de Capmany (1742–1813). La idea del trabajo de un conservador ingenuo", *Historia y política* 5 (2001) 171–208, here 171n1.

confraternities were based: these once religious spaces were then turned into military quarters, storehouses or billeting for French troops.[10]

Once I had formulated a strategy as to the best way to contribute to the CONFRASOUND project, a workplan was devised to define the objectives and reach over the medium and longer term that, *a priori*, would not be limited by its possible continuity in a second phase after 2023. It was decided, as a priority, to establish as the main axis of activity the mapping of the different confraternities in each of the regular and secular religious institutions of the city of Granada. Other research tasks would then be structured around this central axis and developed simultaneously, including:

1. to devise a classification of confraternities according to several criteria, which subsequently generated the corresponding interactive labels on the platform. These can be complementary or distinctive, and be used in the finder (through the field 'types of events') to facilitate analytical study;
2. to undertake the complex process of georeferencing the processional routes generated by the confraternities in the urban fabric of Granada, using the same tool as for the self-guided itineraries of the *Historical Soundscapes* platform;
3. to create short articles or 'events' dedicated to the contribution of the confraternities to the urban soundscape, both as regards ritual activity in the churches of the city and in external religious displays, in which they demonstrated in public their devotional prestige, as well as displayed their wealth and social status before their cohabitants.

2   The Process of Mapping the Confraternities of Granada

The process of geolocating the confraternities of Granada is key to establishing which they were, their distribution in the places in which they carried out their liturgical acts and the areas in which they re-enacted their festive devotional activities. In order to realise this laborious process, I have relied on several primary and secondary sources that overlapped over the course of time. The first source is the monumental doctoral thesis by Miguel Luis López-Guadalupe Muñoz, with the title *Contrarreforma y cofradías en Granada. Aproximación a la historia de las cofradías y hermandades de la ciudad de Granada durante los*

---

10   Eisman Lasaga C., "Efectos que produjo la invasión francesa en los conventos de Granada", *Cuadernos de Arte de la Universidad de Granada* 22 (1991) 63–73.

siglos XVII y XVIII, completed at the University of Granada in 1992. Although it proved necessary to update its findings based on the work published during the last thirty years, this thesis is essential for an exhaustive study of the full range of Granadine confraternities in the early modern period. The various blogs dedicated to the penitential and festive confraternities of Granada written by Antonio Padial Bailón have also proved useful.[11]

For the period between the conquest of the city by the Catholic Monarchs up to the mid-seventeenth century, the chronicler Francisco Henríquez de Jorquera (1594 to after 1646) provides valuable and detailed information on the confraternities of Granada in a three-volume manuscript preserved in the Biblioteca Capitular of Seville Cathedral.[12] For the eighteenth century, the *Gazetilla curiosa o Semanario granadino* published in weekly instalments from 9 April 1764 to 17 August 1765 by the calced Trinitarian friar Antonio de la Chica Benavides, provides information on the many liturgical acts organised by the

FIGURE 17.3   *Gazetilla curiosa o Semanario granadino*. Papel XIII (Monday, 2 July 1764). Biblioteca Virtual de Andalucía
IMAGE © BIBLIOTECA DE LA FACULTAD DE TEOLOGÍA DE GRANADA

---

11   Padial Bailón A., *Hermandades de gloria de Granada* https://apaibailoni.blogspot.com/; Padial Bailón A., *La Granada eterna* https://apaibailoni.blogspot.com/.
12   Seville Cathedral, Biblioteca Capitular. sigs. 57-6-31, 57-6-32 and 57-6-33: Henríquez de Jorquera F., *Anales de Granada*, A. Marín Ocete (ed.) (Granada: 1934; reprint, with a preliminary study and new indexes by Gan Giménez P. – Moreno Garzón L. Granada: 1987).

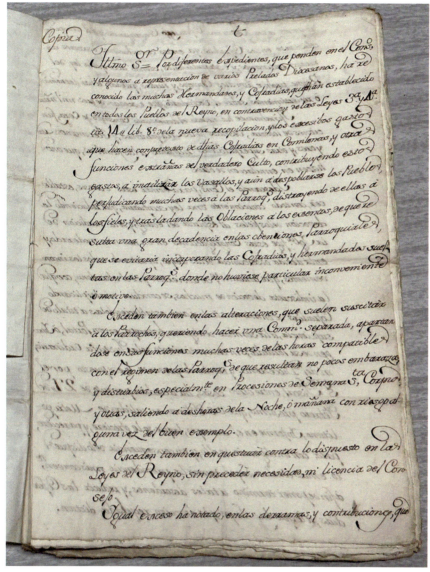

FIGURE 17.4 *Expediente* on brotherhoods in the city of Granada (1769). Archivo de la Parroquia del Sagrario leg. 28
IMAGE © JUAN RUIZ JIMÉNEZ

city's various confraternities and occasionally dedicates extended sections to relevant historical aspects which quite often offer the only source of information on them [Fig. 17.3]. A further useful documentary source, dated 1769, is the detailed account by the benefice-holders of the parish churches in Granada of the 143 confraternities active at that time in a city of 52,375 inhabitants, indicating an average of 366.25 people for each confraternity [Fig. 17.4].[13]

The cartography carried out in relation to the project is based on two historical maps of Granada, one by Ambosio de Vico (*c*.1600) and the other by Francisco Dalmau (1796), as well as OpenStreetMap. The two old maps afford topographical information for the earlier and later chronological limits of the project, although each has a specific objective, uses varied techniques and has a different mode of execution. As regards the earlier map, the architect Ambrosio de Vico affords an aerial perspective of the city. It was commissioned by Pedro de Castro Vaca y Quiñones, archbishop of Granada between 1589 and 1610, and is clearly influenced by and infused with the propagandist spirit of the Counter-Reformation. Its hidden objective was to represent the streets of Granada as a vast religious space adequate for Baroque ceremonial, as is clear from the detail with which sacred buildings are drawn, detail that is not found, with few exceptions, for the major civic buildings or private residences of the city.[14] The *Mapa topográfico de la ciudad de Granada* (1796), drawn by the Enlightenment mathematician Francisco Dalmau, is a scientific plan that reflects urban reality as well as the most advanced cartographical techniques of the time [Fig. 17.5].[15]

The overall planimetric view of the city, both past and present, afforded by the three maps is complemented by the various views of the city and of the institutions where the confraternities were based; these add to the iconographical resources related to the different brotherhoods. I have chosen to geo-reference all the locations on all three maps, with both advantages and disadvantages. The most important advantage is the possibility of achieving an up-to-date view of the whole, while a marked disadvantage is that with the Vico map some institutions, above all convents, did not yet exist at the time the map was drafted (ca. 1600), and in the case of Openstreetmap some had already ceased to exist by that time. In the individual articles dedicated to each confraternity, I have attempted to enumerate these bodies in chronological

---

13   Granada. Archivo de la Parroquia del Sagrario de Granada. Legajo 28; Arias de Saavedra Alías I. – López-Guadalupe Muñoz M.L., "Cofradías y ciudad en la España del siglo XVIII", *Studia Historica. Historia Moderna* 19 (198) 197–228, here 200.

14   López Guzmán R.J. – Gómez-Moreno Calera J.M. – Moreno Garrido A., "La plataforma de Ambrosio de Vico: cronología y gestación", *Arquitectura Andalucía Oriental* 2 (1984) 6–13; Gómez-Moreno Calera J.M., *El arquitecto granadino Ambrosio de Vico* (Granada: 1992).

15   García Pulido L.J., "Una precisa y artística representación gráfica del territorio granadino: el Mapa topográfico de la ciudad de Granada y su término de Francisco Dalmau (1819)", *Cuadernos de Arte de la Universidad de Granada* 40 (2013) 171–198.

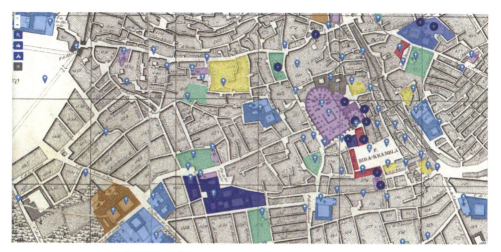

FIGURE 17.5   Topographical map of the city of Granada by Francisco Dalmau (1796)
IMAGE HISTORICAL SOUNDSCAPES © JUAN RUIZ JIMÉNEZ – IGNACIO JOSÉ LIZARÁN RUS

order, although in many cases this has proved to be mission impossible, since quite often a single reliable reference to the confraternity's existence survives, meaning that only its geolocation and an incomplete classification is possible.

A particular group of confraternities offers a distinct characteristic from the mapping viewpoint. Based in chapels in regular or secular ecclesiastical institutions where they carry out their liturgical rituals, they also maintain and celebrate their festivities before devotional images situated in the streets: crosses or images of the Virgin Mary or saints, whether painted or sculpted, before which were frequently sung polyphonic Salves, motets or other compositions by salaried or freelance musicians. Good examples of these images are those situated at the Triumph of Our Lady ('Nuestra Señora del Triunfo'), the Campo del Príncipe ('Cristo de los Favores') and the main gate of the Alcaicería that faces El Sagrario ('Virgen de la Concepción'), before which the music chapel of the collegiate church of El Salvador sang a Salve Regina every Saturday throughout the year, subsidised 'by its faithful devout' ('por sus fieles devotos') [Fig. 17.6]. Details of these devotions can easily be found at the designated locations, using the search button of the 'Location' field embedded in each map.

At the time of writing, I have completed the geolocation of all the confraternities based in the regular and secular ecclesiastical institutions of Granada, that is, scattered through the twenty-three parish churches of the city and the sixteen male and six female convents of the urban complex. The geolocation

FIGURE 17.6   Nuestra Señora del Triunfo. Alonso de Mena (1631)
IMAGE © JUAN RUIZ JIMÉNEZ

of confraternities in other, more minor institutions, whether in terms of size or endowment of priests or liturgical celebrations, such as hospitals, hermitages and niche images, is in progress. Up to 1 September 2023, I have geolocated over 230 confraternities in more than one hundred locations. The snapshot of the 1769 account shows that of the 143 active confraternities in the city, classified according to avocation, forty-four (30.76%) were Marian, twenty-eight (19.58%) were dedicated to saints, twenty-three (16.08%) to Christ, twenty

(13.98%) to the Eucharist, nineteen (13.28%) to Souls in Purgatory, seven (4.89%) had mixed advocations and two (1.39%) had other advocations.[16]

3 Labelling Confraternities and Their Liturgical and Devotional Activities

The second objective of the study of confraternities' project in the *Historical Soundscapes* digital platform has been to assign interactive labels in the fields 'Location', 'Agent' and 'Type of event' to each of the articles. These labels function basically as keywords that allow selected searches using these terms, whether in isolation or combined through the use of the operatives and/or. This offers one of the most important forms of selective retrieval of data incorporated into the platform. For the confraternities' project, individual labels have been created for each confraternity in the field 'Agent', as well as a series of more general labels that enable the classification of these brotherhoods from different perspectives in the field 'Type of event'. Given the complexity of the confraternal phenomenon, it has proved difficult to classify them without being either too reductionist or too general and confusing that it becomes an obstacle rather than a useful tool to retrieve information in a user-friendly way [Table 17.1].[17]

TABLE 17.1 Classification labels for confraternities on the *Historical Soundscapes* digital platform

confraternities with avocations of saints	confraternities of Holy Week	national confraternities	open confraternities
confraternities with allegorical avocations	penitential confraternities	ethnic confraternities	closed confraternities
confraternities with other avocations	clerical confraternities	guild confraternities	Marian confraternities
confraternities of Souls in Purgatory	confraternities of Christchild	regional confraternities	rosary confraternities
confraternities of the Blessed Sacrament	professional confraternities	hospital confraternities	

---

16 Arias de Saavedra Alías – López-Guadalupe Muñoz, "Cofradías y ciudad en la España del siglo XVIII" 202.
17 López-Guadalupe Muñoz, *Contrarreforma y cofradías en Granada* 313–323.

The labels created specifically for this project can also be combined with the general labels already in existence for the various sonic (including musical) elements, liturgical rituals, institutions or individual posts that are common to the activities organised by confraternities throughout the annual devotional or festive cycle. The cartographic visualisation of results obtained from the innumerable possible ways of filtering the information afforded by these labels opens up new analytic approaches for the greater understanding of how confraternities functioned, approaches that are complementary to traditional analytic methods.

4   The Processional Routes of Confraternities

Research into the spatial occupation of confraternities and their influence and dynamic in the urban soundscape from the viewpoint of the city as a whole, must inevitably take into consideration the processional routes as they relate to the different types of procession. As mentioned above, the *Historical Soundscapes* digital platform uses a specific tool that allows the georeferencing of any urban route, both on the historical maps and in OpenStreetMap. The institutions involved in the organisation of a particular procession, or that participated in its trajectory, can also be mapped, and can be distinguished by type using different colours for churches, male and female convents, public buildings, and so on.

However, establishing the processional routes organised by confraternities with precision is highly problematic because of four main factors:

1. absence of data provided by the sources, or, in many cases, their lack of completeness, allowing only a fragmentary recovery of processional itineraries;
2. changes in processional routes over time often making them difficult to identify except in those cases where the documentation of a particular institution is complete and offers highly detailed accounts. Such modifications are usually diachronic and permanent, or they can be caused by a particular event, in which case they are usually ephemeral in nature;
3. changes in street names over time; unfortunately, unlike other cities, there is no dedicated study of the changes in the formation and naming of the streets of Granada from 1492 to the present. This means that painstaking research is needed to locate and transfer the topographical data to the historical maps and OpenStreetMap;
4. in most cases, the historical routes cannot be transferred in full to the actual street layout of the city since this has usually undergone varied

degrees of change, and have to be significantly adapted if the processional trajectory is to be followed according to the modern street-plan. This is particularly problematic where the processional route would now have to pass through buildings erected as part of that transformation process. The penitential procession of the Confraternity of the Soledad based at the convent of Nuestra Señora de la Cabeza affords a good example of the difficulty presented by diachronic changes in its itinerary created by the transfer of its base from the convent of the calced Carmelites in the sixteenth century, as well as other changes made in the eighteenth century.[18] To date, thirteen confraternal processional routes have been georeferenced on the *Historical Soundscapes* platform.

5 Occupation of Urban Space by Confraternal Activities

The primary challenge confronting the overall study of confraternal activity in any urban complex – and the first conclusion to be drawn – relates to the extreme disparity as regards the extent of surviving documentation for individual confraternities. This can easily result in a distorted vision when the different specific aspects of its function, social welfare work and liturgical and ritual acts are compared or studied from a statistical viewpoint. The challenge becomes abundantly clear when comparison is made on the basis of those cases selected by researchers for analysis precisely because of the large and rich extant body of documentation that survives for a particular confraternity. However, even taking all this into account, the corpus of data included in the *Historical Soundscapes* digital platform relating to confraternities affords a preliminary insight into the analysis of confraternal activities and their contribution to the urban soundscape of Granada from a cartographical perspective, both inside the ecclesiastical buildings where they were based, but also in the urban complex as a whole.

Over the course of history, the confraternities were quite frequently subject to processes involving the merging and unification of brotherhoods, even, in some cases, the creation of new foundations in the heart of an existing association; in this way, they evolved into more dynamically complex

---

[18] Ruiz Jiménez J., "Procesión de la cofradía de Nuestra Señora de la Soledad y Entierro de Cristo", *Paisajes Sonoros Históricos* (2022) http://www.historicalsoundscapes.com/events/1415/granada.

macrostructures.[19] These mergers were relatively frequent between sacramental or Eucharistic confraternities or those dedicated to Souls in Purgatory or of Marian avocation. The determining factor was usually the economic situation in which the confraternities in question found themselves. The opposite situation as regards the separation of confraternities from the original matrix is also found, although less frequently and usually fairly early on in their development. In a few exceptional cases, a confraternity's activities were intermittent and disrupted to the extent that it might disappear for a while to be subsequently re-founded.[20] An additional major factor in the tracing of the history of confraternities relates to their transfer from one ecclesiastical institution to another, usually motivated by disputes between them and the members of clergy, both regular and secular, of the churches where they were based. Such disagreements often led to disapproval on the part of the clergy and even, at diocesan level, to the extent of rejection of the authorisation to make the transfer. All these circumstances generated changes in the naming of confraternities, making tracing their history highly problematic and their labelling correspondingly difficult. Systematic cartography of them can help considerably to clarify the overall view of confraternal presence in an urban centre such as Granada.

The result of this complex dynamic of confraternal activity finds expression in spatial and decorative transformations in the chapels where they resided, as well as in the ritual practices developed there, which, in some cases, can be reconstructed with some precision.[21] One of the conclusions to emerge from the work done to date is that confraternities were one of the main agents in the decentralisation of liturgical and devotional activity, and by extension of the generation of sound – and especially music – in the ecclesiastical spaces that formed their base, notably in the case of parish churches otherwise generally constrained in resources, both in terms of finance and personnel.

The distribution of confraternities and, above all, the specific status accorded each one in the urban context, was much influenced by the geographical, demographic, social and economic factors that, in a city such as Granada, present a highly distinctive character that would clearly determine

---

19 See, for example, the case of the Confraternity of Nuestra Señora del Socorro that was created in the Eucharistic brotherhood of the church of Santa Escolástica.

20 This situation occurred among the confraternities based at the church of Santa María Magdalena, see: Arias de Saavedra Alías I. – López-Guadalupe Muñoz M.L., "Las cofradías y su dimensión social en la España del antiguo régimen", *Cuadernos de Historia Moderna* 25 (2000) 189–232.

21 López-Guadalupe Muñoz M.L., *Las cofradías de la parroquia de Santa María Magdalena de Granada en los siglos XVII–XVIII* (Granada: 1992).

the development of its stability and the precariousness, or otherwise, of its economic situation.[22] Up until its expulsion in 1569, the *morisco* population was concentrated in the Albaicín and maintained a degree of equilibrium with that of the old Christians living on the city plain. The deportation of *moriscos* had a marked impact on the city's demography with a strong topographical bias that drastically affected the ecclesiastical institutions in the Albaicín. Towards mid-1571, all but a quarter of the 1200 dwellings in the Albaicín were occupied, and over half were considered to have been inhabitable, in a totally or partly ruined state, a situation that reflected the widespread impoverishment of the population that continued to live on the hill.[23] Six of the eight parish churches located in the upper part of the Albaicín had lost between 71.7% and 68.8% of their population by 1587. The most densely populated parish, that linked to the collegiate church of El Salvador, suffered a 61.4% reduction in the number of parishioners. In the mid-eighteenth century, the uneven balance in population persisted, with approximately 20% of the overall inhabitants of the city residing in the Albaicín and 80% on the city plain.[24] The document drawn up by José Antonio Porcel y Salablanca, canon of the collegiate church of El Salvador, dated 20 December 1767 and addressed to King Charles III, gives a good account of the demographic and economic transformation of the Albaicín: at that time, it was semi-deserted and poor.[25] This uneven distribution of the population and its corresponding economic resources is clearly reflected in the number and specific status of the confraternities based in the two different parts of the city.

Each confraternity had its primary relationship with the urban space within the limits of the parish (*collación*) in which it was based, and where it carried out the collection of alms, one its most important sources of income. This also applied to those confraternities based in conventual churches within a particular parish. In both cases, the confraternity was obliged to pay for the parish rights corresponding to the processions that they mounted within these ecclesiastical boundaries. There is currently no cartographic study of the exact boundaries of the twenty-three or twenty-four (depending on the date) parishes into which the city of Granada was divided, a question I hope to explore in the future, based on the different population censuses that have survived.

22   López-Guadalupe Muñoz, *Contrarreforma y cofradías en Granada* 324–325.
23   Vincent B., *Andalucía en la Edad Moderna: Economía y Sociedad* (Granada: 1985) 146.
24   Cortés Peña A.L. – Vincent, B., *Historia de Granada*, vol. III: *La época moderna. Siglos XVI, XVII y XVIII* (Granada: 1986) 59–62, 254.
25   Ruiz Jiménez J., *La colegiata del Salvador en el contexto musical de Granada* (Ph.D. dissertation, Universidad de Granada: 1992) 30.

Within parish limits, confraternities celebrated their processions with their images and other devotional artifacts on the major feasts as specified in their statutes. These processions had a strong devotional character, but were also social and ludic in nature. Through them, they reinforced ties with members of the local vicinity and, emanating out from there, with the urban space in which they cohabited. This urban space was thus transformed to create a temporary illusion that contrasted with the reality of everyday life. The reconstruction of two of the processional routes organised each year by the Confraternity of the Ánimas based in the church of Santa Ana reveals the way in which urban space was occupied. These two processions, one a commemoration of deceased members of the confraternity, with a station in the parish cemetery, and the other, with its specific visit to and station at the official site of execution and at the ossuary of San Onofre, took place around the parish church. As indicated by the surviving sources, the main objective of these two trajectories beyond the ecclesiastical space in which they were based was to foment and give expression to the devotional life of the parishioners of Santa Ana through the external display of mercy towards the families of deceased confraternity members and of compassion towards those condemned to death at the scaffold nearby in the Plaza Nueva, and those buried in the cemetery of St. Onuphrius.[26]

Two other types of procession closely connected to the confraternal sphere fit into the urban framework as delineated by the territorial boundaries that marked each parish. First, the processions that took last rites to the moribund, for which the Eucharistic confraternities were responsible. In Granada, these confraternities were found in every church, and, exceptionally, in the female Franciscan convent of Nuestra Señora de los Ángeles, probably so as to cover an area of the city that was in a relatively distant part of the parish of Santa Escolástica, where the convent was based. At a much later date, in 1801, and possibly for the same reason, the confraternity of Nuestra Señora del Destierro, based at the monastery of San Basilio situated on the left bank of the Genil River in the parish district of Nuestra Señora de las Angustias, became sacramental in nature.[27]

---

26 Ruiz Jiménez J., "Procesiones anuales de la cofradía de las Ánimas de la iglesia de Santa Ana en Granada", *Paisajes Sonoros Históricos* (2021) http://www.historicalsoundscapes.com/evento/1376/granada.

27 In its early years, the Confraternity of the Santísimo Sacramento y Nuestra Señora de Loreto, based at the convent of discalced Augustinians of Nuestra Señora de Loreto in the Albaicín, was also Eucharistic in nature.

The annual procession organised by each of these confraternities to visit the sick of the parish adopted a notably festive character, and large amounts of money were spent on them in order – once again – to rival other Eucharistic brotherhoods and to mount a display before their cohabitants living within the demarcated ecclesiastical territory. The Confraternity of the Santísimo Sacramento, based at the church of San Matías, affords a clear example of the considerable financial outlay involved by the second half of the seventeenth century. In 1682, the confraternity spent 361.5 *reales* (12,291 *maravedís*) on paying for the announcement of the celebration, which was accompanied by trumpet and drum, for two dances – one at an evening party or *sarao* and the other a gypsy dance – and on the freelance music chapel that accompanied the parade. Further expense was made on the sedge that covered the streets through which the procession passed, the wax used, the parish dues paid to the benefice-holder and priests who carried the poles of the baldachin, and to the altar boys who carried the censer and rang the handbells that announced the passing of the viaticum.[28]

The second type of procession that customarily took place within the parish boundaries was the funeral cortèges that accompanied the deceased from his or her house to the church or convent where they were to be buried. These processions formed part of the daily urban soundscape. A larger or smaller proportion of the members of the confraternity – or confraternities – to which the dead person belonged, usually took part in the cortège. Most confraternal statutes regulated in some detail the obligation on members to participate in the burial of confreres and other aspects of the ritual of death. The Confraternity of the Ánimas del Purgatorio based at the church of El Sagrario, ordained in Chapter 24 of their statutes (dated 1541, at fols. 16r–17r), that, following the demise of a member of the brotherhood, all the other members should be called to adjourn to the deceased's home, where, if necessary, two of them should participate in the wake held for the dead person. Confraternal members would also participate in the funerary procession, bearing the coffin – which was covered in the rich cloths owned by the confraternity for that purpose – on their shoulders to the parish or convent church were the deceased was to be buried. The coffin was to be preceded by a cross and two lighted candles, and led by the leader (*prioste*) and a representative of the confraternity, each holding a sceptre. Every member of the confraternity would

---

28   Ruiz Jiménez J., "Procesión de visita a los enfermos de la cofradía del Santísimo Sacramento en la collación de San Matías de Granada", *Paisajes Sonoros Históricos* (2018) http://www.historicalsoundscapes.com/evento/838/granada.

FIGURE 17.7 Statutes of the Confraternity of the Ánimas del Purgatorio based at the church of El Sagrario (1541). Biblioteca Nacional de España. MSS/18451
IMAGE © BIBLIOTECA NACIONAL DE ESPAÑA

also hold a lighted candle and accompany the widow or widower to his or her house after burial [Fig. 17.7].[29]

In other instances, the urban reach of confraternal processions went beyond parish borders and extended to different areas of the urban complex of Granada. A characteristic feature of general processions is the well-ordered and well-represented participation of the confraternities and guilds of the city. These general processions included Corpus Christi, the Taking of the City (2 January) and the Bull of Crusade, and recurred annually, while others were more sporadic in nature, motivated by especially important occasions related to natural phenomena and epidemics, as well as events connected with royalty.

The Corpus Christi route, which in the larger cities did not tend to be very extended (a characteristic common to other general processions), witnessed the highest density of confraternal and guild representation. These entities were ordered according to precedence as regards the year of foundation, and

29   Ruiz Jiménez J., "Actividad cultual de la cofradía de las Ánimas del Purgatorio en la iglesia del Sagrario de Granada", *Paisajes Sonoros Históricos* (2020) http://www.historicalsound scapes.com/evento/1203/granada.

FIGURE 17.8 Itinerary of the Corpus Christi procession in Granada
IMAGE HISTORICAL SOUNDSCAPES © JUAN RUIZ JIMÉNEZ – IGNACIO
JOSÉ LIZARÁN RUS

displayed before the co-habitants in the city, who, in turn, saw themselves represented in this way. The overall itinerary, and each of the streets and squares that comprised it, were seen as the city's principal conduits, and were chosen to heighten the importance of sporadic processions of key significance. In Granada, this route underwent a sequence of changes as a result of the itinerancy of the cathedral see in the years immediately following its foundation in 1492 until its final position was consolidated in 1561. Given the significance of this route, it has been added to the tab 'Itineraries' on the *Historical Soundscapes* digital platform, and a recreation of its soundscape has been included there [Fig. 17.8].[30]

---

30   Ruiz Jiménez J., "Procesión del Corpus Christi" *Paisajes Sonoros Históricos* (2016) http://www.historicalsoundscapes.com/itinerario/2/1; and Ruiz Jiménez J., "Recreación del paisaje

Other recurring or sporadic processions organised specifically by the confraternities of Granada occupied a more or less substantial part of the urban complex. For example, penitential confraternities were responsible for the processions held during Holy Week, and in the course of their trajectories stops or stations were made at different ecclesiastical institutions, with the cathedral becoming an obligatory station in all of them. These processions were the source of disputation with the higher echelons of the clergy who, throughout the early modern period, attempted to control and limit their excesses. Conflict also arose among the confraternities themselves, notably in confrontations caused by processions coinciding in certain streets or squares, when the question of which procession took precedence had to be resolved, together with disputes as regards the antiquity of their date of foundation.[31]

Other annual processions that went beyond the demarcated territory of a confraternity included the *via crucis* and the burial of those condemned to death organised by the Confraternity of Corpus Christi, de Misericordia y de Ánimas, based at the Hospital of Corpus Christi. The chronicler Francisco Henríquez de Jorquera provides a detailed description of the procession held on the fifth Sunday of Lent in 1614 (16 March) organised by this confraternity to give 'pious burial to the condemned to death, quartered and left by the roadside' ('piadoso entierro a los ajusticiados que hacen cuartos y ponen por los caminos'). In 1614, the boxes containing the bones of the five people condemned to execution had been placed in the Cross or *humilladero* of St. Sebastian, from where the funeral cortège was to depart and process to the confraternity's base in the hospital of Corpus Christi. The coffins were carried by the knights of the military orders, while the retinue comprised many members of the clergy, the confraternities and religious orders of the city, together with nobles, merchants and the other inhabitants. The cathedral music chapel was responsible for the accompanying music, which performed at the four stations organised along the route; in the presence of the many people present, they sang the appropriate polyphonic responsories for the soul of the condemned [Fig. 17.9].[32]

The trajectories of the *viae sacrae* of Granada connected the city with the surrounding countryside. These processions departed from various points

---

sonoro de la procesión del Corpus Christi", *Paisajes Sonoros Históricos* (2020) http://www.historicalsoundscapes.com/evento/1140/granada.

31   López Muñoz M.L., "Las cofradías de penitencia de Granada en la edad moderna", *Gazeta de Antropología* 11 (1995), article 12 https://digibug.ugr.es/handle/10481/13617. Guerrero Vílchez A., *Las cofradías de Semana Santa en Granada (1760–1960). De la Ilustración al Nacionalcatolicismo* (Ph.D. dissertation, Universidad de Granada: 2022) 39–60.

32   Ruiz Jiménez J., "Procesión de entierro de ajusticiados de Granada (1614)", *Paisajes Sonoros Históricos* (2017) http://www.historicalsoundscapes.com/evento/669/granada.

FIGURE 17.9   The route of the burial procession held for the condemned to death organised by the Confraternity of Corpus Christi, de Misericordia y de Ánimas Benditas del Purgatorio
IMAGE HISTORICAL SOUNDSCAPES © JUAN RUIZ JIMÉNEZ – IGNACIO JOSÉ LIZARÁN RUS

in the city and reached the surrounding hills, thus emphasising the uphill climb and suffering of the way to Calvary they sought to emulate: the hill of San Miguel, that of San Antonio, the field of the Martyrs, the hill of Rebites and, above all, the mountain of Valparaíso where the collegiate church of Sacromonte was built.[33]

6   The Sonic Dimension of the Devotional Activities of Confraternities

As I mentioned at the beginning of this chapter, the festive sensory elements integrated into confraternal activities, both inside and outside the ecclesiastical spaces where they were based in Granada, were for the most part standard, and comparable, to a greater or lesser extent, with those experienced in other cities. These sonic elements were usually marked by an appreciable variability year on year, according to prevailing economic factors. It was frequently the case that one person could be a member of more than one confraternity which might be based in the same or in another ecclesiastical institution. It seems likely, given the democratic way in which confraternities functioned, that this resulted in a certain degree of homogeneity, although a broader consideration of the urban soundscape suggests that many of these sensorial elements

---

33   López Muñoz M.L., "Una forma alternativa de la piedad popular: las cofradías de vía sacra en Granada", *Revista de Historia Moderna* 31 (2013) 11–31.

formed an integral part of urban festivities as a whole throughout the early modern period.[34]

From the spatial perspective, the ringing of bells was probably one of the most significant acoustic elements of confraternal activity. Bells called members to the general meetings, festive celebrations and liturgical acts they organised throughout the year. In the case of Eucharistic confraternities, bells sounded the taking of the viaticum so that members attended, unless they had a viable reason not to; and those who were unable to attend prayed at home for the souls of deceased brothers. The extent to which this ringing of bells was codified is not known: possibly it varied from one confraternity to another, or probably, as would seem to be suggested by at least some confraternal statutes, a specific bell was used by a confraternity. For the main festivities of those confraternities who were based in the convents of the city, the ringing for Vespers and Mass followed the precise regulation established by each of the religious orders in their ceremonials. A good example is provided by the *Ceremonial y processionario de los frayles de la orden de la Sanctíssima Trinidad*.[35] The ringing of bells when processions passed monasteries and convents, or went to them, was also regulated by these ceremonials.[36] It is difficult to calculate the reach and interference of these sound signals in a city such as Granada, with its proliferation of bell-towers that were often closely located to one another, and for which there is a good deal of information about their historic bells, including a precise description of those that are currently preserved in them.[37] The confraternities' handbells afforded another omnipresent sonic element, often kept and handled by the *muñidor* or fixer; these were rung both in interior spaces as well as in various kinds of procession, as has already been mentioned.

---

34   Cuesta García de Leonardo Mª.J., *Fiesta y arquitectura efímera en la Granada del siglo XVIII* (Granada: 1995) 19–48.

35   *Ceremonial y processionario de los frayles de la orden de la Sanctíssima Trinidad, y redempción de captivos, agora nuevamente corregido, y concertado con el Ceremonial Romano* (Sevilla, Juan de León: 1593) 3–8. Ruiz Jiménez J., "Regulación del tañido de campanas en los conventos trinitarios", *Paisajes Sonoros Históricos* (2018) http://www.historicalsoundscapes.com/evento/900/granada.

36   Malaga, s.d., *Ceremonial romano seráfico de los menores capuchinos de N.P.S. Francisco, según el orden de N.S. Romana Iglesia y loables costumbres de dicho Orden y especiales de esta Santa Provincia de Andalucía* (Granada, Imprenta de la Santísima Trinidad: 1721) 190. Ruiz Jiménez J., "Regulación del tañido de campanas en los conventos franciscanos capuchinos de la Provincia de Andalucía", *Paisajes Sonoros Históricos* (2023) http://www.historicalsoundscapes.com/evento/1509/granada.

37   Jiménez Díaz N., *Historia de las campanas de Granada* (Ph.D. dissertation, Universidad de Granada: 1997).

The gathering of a large group of people inevitably brought with it a degree of bustle and noise depending on a number of factors, including the space in which they had gathered, the number of people involved and the accumulated decibels produced by the sonic elements such as artillery salvos, fireworks, animals, carriages, fountains and streams, vocal and instrumental music and dancing. Other sonic elements were more specific by nature and were heard only on particular occasions and in certain types of procession. For example, one of the most distinctive sounds of processions organised by penitential confraternities, especially during Holy Week, was that of the whips with which the flagellants enacted penance. The emotional impact generated by this dull sound, multiplied rhythmically through the involvement of the 800 flagellants who usually took part in the procession by the Granada confraternity of the Soledad y Entierro de Cristo, can only be imagined. This sound would have been amplified by the narrow streets through which the procession passed.[38]

The sounds of the wooden poles with sockets that were used to support the handles of the floats and images when they stopped to rest at stations along the processional route when they were banged on the ground was a characteristic sound in those processions that used them. In Granada, a late seventeenth-century document regarding the regulation of those who held these supporting poles has been preserved for the confraternity of the Angustias. This role was assigned to the most important members of the confraternity, since the supporting poles were regarded as a symbol of prestige and power: they had to be made from the finest wood the confraternity had to hand and to have silver sockets.[39] The Confraternity of Nuestra Señora de las Tres Necesidades y Entierro de Cristo included a posse of twenty-four pole-bearers, 'with black robes and their faces covered' ('con sus túnicas negras y cubiertos los rostros'), together with twenty-four pointed flags (*gallardetes* or *flámulas*) that trailed behind them along the ground, their particular swish contributing to the soundscape.

The musical sounds of confraternal processions were very varied: different combinations of voices and instruments and musical genres mingled with the non-musical elements already described to create the soundscape of the liturgical and devotional acts organised by confraternities. While plainchant sung

---

38 Ruiz Jiménez J., "Procesión de la cofradía de Nuestra Señora de la Soledad y Entierro de Cristo", *Paisajes Sonoros Históricos* (2022) http://www.historicalsoundscapes.com/evento/1415/granada.

39 Ceballos Guerrero A., "El Cuerpo de Horquilleros de la Hermandad de Nuestra Señora de las Angustias de Granada", in *Religiosidad popular: Cofradías de penitencia* (San Lorenzo del Escorial: 2017) 241–260.

by the regular and secular clergy was an established sonic element present at all events, polyphony as performed by professional musicians contracted by brotherhoods was heard only on major feast-days and in important processions, since it represented, together with wax, the highest expenditure for the realisation of these special occasions. In Granada, the music chapels of the cathedral, the royal chapel and the collegiate church of El Salvador competed to celebrate the highest possible number of feast-days, since such celebrations brought in a substantial part of the musicians' annual income.[40]

A variable number of trumpets and drums also offered a consistent presence in all festive displays that took place in open spaces, whether in their proclamation or leading the processional entourage. Together with trumpets, wind-bands often formed part of the different kinds of procession organised by confraternities. In Granada, as occurred in other cities, there are examples of private devotional patronage of minstrel ensembles to accompany the taking of the viaticum to the moribund. In 1636, Captain Juan Álvarez de la Vega, who died in Lima, decreed in his will that the necessary funds should be set aside to hire a group of three shawms to accompany the viaticum processions 'day and night' ('de día y de noche'), in the Granada parishes of San Juan de los Reyes and San Pedro y San Pablo [Fig. 17.10].[41] On some occasions, traditional music was also present: for example, specific dances were included in different processional types organised by the confraternities of Granada resulting in a mix with – or substitution of – more cultivated music.[42]

The sacred musical genres performed during confraternities' processions were generally the same as those heard during the festive and liturgical ceremonies celebrated more generally in the ritual life of the city. Composers' names of the works that formed part of confraternal ceremonies are never mentioned in the extant sources. The musical items commonly sung at Vespers and Mass, such as litanies, multifunctional hymns, penitential psalms, and Masses, were

---

40   Ruiz Jiménez J., "Música y devoción en Granada (siglos XVI–XVIII): Funcionamiento 'extravagante' y tipología de plazas no asalariadas en las capillas musicales eclesiásticas de la ciudad", *Anuario Musical* 52 (1997) 39–75.
41   Archivo General de Indias. Contratación, leg.421A, note 2. Ruiz Jiménez J., "Dotación de tres chirimías para acompañar las salidas del Viático en iglesias de Granada (1636)", *Paisajes Sonoros Históricos* (2023) http://www.historicalsoundscapes.com/evento/1508/granada.
42   Ruiz Jiménez, "Procesión de visita a los enfermos"; Ruiz Jiménez J., "Fiestas marianas patrocinadas por la hermandad del Santo Rosario de Nuestra Señora del Triunfo en Granada (1698)", *Paisajes Sonoros Históricos* (2018) http://www.historicalsoundscapes.com/evento/803/granada; Ruiz Jiménez J., "Fiesta de la Asunción de María organizada por la cofradía de Nuestra Señora de la Asunción del granadino convento de Nuestra Señora de la Merced", *Paisajes Sonoros Históricos* 2019 http://www.historicalsoundscapes.com/evento/970/granada.

FIGURE 17.10 Sedan chairs (*sillas de mano*) used to carry the viaticum from the churches of Granada. Choir of the Royal Chapel of Granada
IMAGE © JUAN RUIZ JIMÉNEZ

selected by the city's music chapels hired for the occasion from the repertory they customarily sung and which was readily accessible in their music libraries. The composition of villancicos for feast-days celebrated by confraternities in Granada appears to have been exceptional in this period, although some seventeenth-century villancico texts have survived: for example, the *Letras* sung by the musical chapel of the Royal Chapel in 1692. These vernacular pieces were composed by the chapel master Alonso de Blas y Sandoval for the ceremony of the Forty Hours, and were commissioned by the Congregation of the Siervos del Soberano Espíritu, based at the Jesuit College of San Pablo [Fig. 17.11].[43]

---

43 Ruiz Jiménez J., "Festividad de las Cuarenta Horas organizada por la congregación de los Siervos del Soberano Espíritu del colegio jesuítico de San Pablo en Granada (1674/1692/1752)", *Paisajes Sonoros Históricos* (2015) http://www.historicalsoundscapes .com/evento/252/granada; Ruiz Jiménez J., "Festividad de la Asunción de María celebrada por el gremio de los escribanos en Granada (1693)", *Paisajes Sonoros Históricos* (2020) http://www.historicalsoundscapes.com/evento/1214/granada.

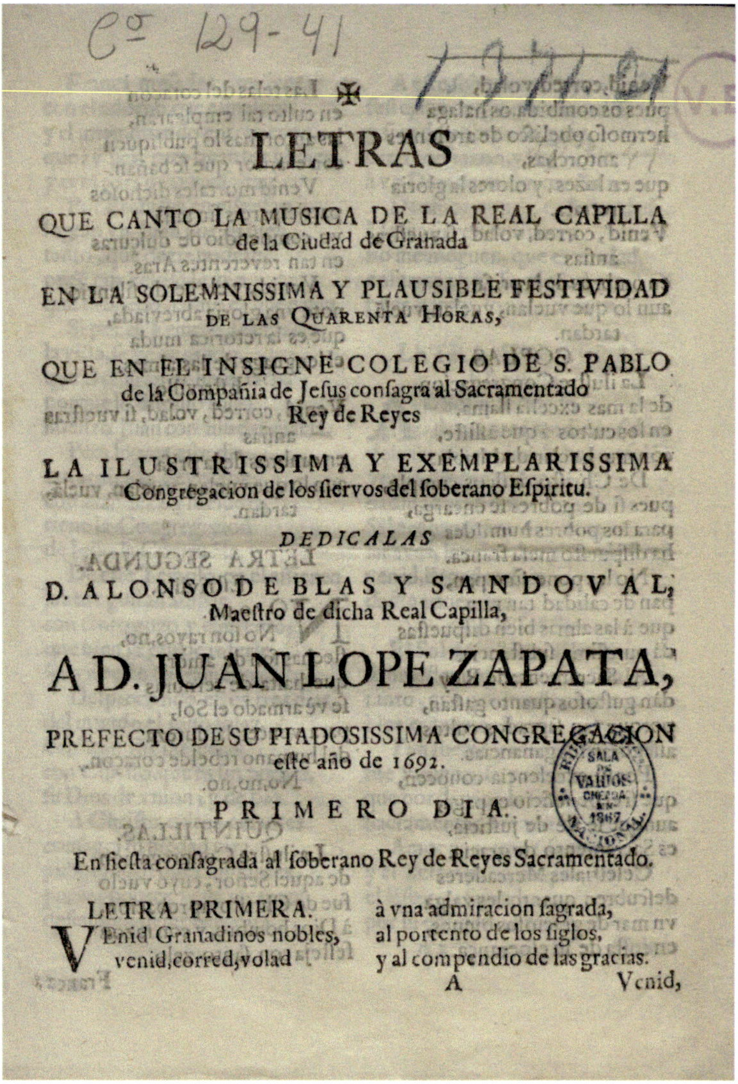

FIGURE 17.11   *Letras que cantó la música de la Capilla Real en [...] festividad de las Quarenta horas* (1692) Biblioteca Nacional de España. VE/129/41
IMAGE © BIBLIOTECA NACIONAL DE ESPAÑA

7 Conclusions

The process of researching material relating to confraternities and entering it into the digital platform *Historical Soundscapes* in the format of 'events', or micro-articles, has opened up several new perspectives on their contribution to the urban soundworld. Perhaps the most important of these new perspectives stems from digital cartographic analysis that enables the georeferencing of these entities and their liturgical, devotional and ceremonial activity within the urban fabric. Equally important is the potential this tool offers for establishing relationships between research data and for making these accessible through the interactive labels created for the platform; the impact of these materials is vastly increased by their dissemination on-line through open access and through the main types of social media on which the introduction of new content is publicised.

The writing of this essay has inevitably confronted a major difficulty: how to communicate through a fixed, written text the experience of an interactive digital project that is constantly being updated, both in content and in technological structure, which in itself represents a kind of contradiction. The snapshot of confraternal activity in Granada presented in this essay will already be superseded by the time it reaches its readership. It is impossible to avoid the limitations imposed by the static format of an analogical publication and so reflect the rich potential of cartography and iconography offered by its digital counterpart and to express the interactive dynamism, capacity for comparative analysis and retrieval of information afforded by recent and constantly developing technology. Thus, the reading of this article must necessarily be accompanied by the parallel exploration of the materials found on the original digital platform. It must be said that this necessity for researchers using DH tools to adhere to traditional publication formats is conditioned by the need to accommodate the evaluation systems that until now have served the academic world, and by its failure so far to develop adequate tools for the assessment of materials and data produced as part of digital projects such as *Historical Soundscapes*.

On the other hand, one of the errors researchers often make when developing a digital project is precisely that of treating it as if it were a traditional closed publication. Such projects rapidly fossilise so that one of their greatest strengths – that is, their open-ended nature and possibility for continued growth through addition to content and the adoption of new tools to improve possibilities of visualisation, analysis and presentation of results – is too often wasted. As with the other cartographic projects I am developing on the digital platform *Historical Soundscapes*, the data on confraternities forms part of an open-ended project, without temporal restrictions. I intend to continue adding data on a regular basis to be able to draw an increasingly precise visual geography of confraternal practice in Granada and to interrogate sonic topoi in the soundscape of other cities. This long-term growth is also key to attracting and maintaining the loyalty of the users of any digital platform. The periodic revision of its contents enables the bringing of fresh perspectives to its analytical capacity through opening up further possibilities afforded by the new DH tools used to develop the host platform.

Bibliography

Primary Sources

Ceremonial y processionario de los frayles de la orden de la Sanctíssima Trinidad, y redempción de captivos, agora nuevamente corregido, y concertado con el Ceremonial Romano (Seville, Juan de León: 1593) 3–8.

Expediente sobre hermandades de la ciudad de Granada (1769), Archivo de la Parroquia del Sagrario de Granada, leg. 28.

Gazetilla curiosa o Semanario granadino (weekly publication from 9 April 1764 to 17 June 1765).

Malaga S.d., *Ceremonial romano seráfico de los menores capuchinos de N.P.S. Francisco, según el orden de N.S. Romana Iglesia y loables costumbres de dicho Orden y especiales de esta Santa Provincia de Andalucía* (Granada, Imprenta de la Santísima Trinidad: 1721).

Secondary Sources

Arias de Saavedra Alías I. – López-Guadalupe Muñoz M.L., "Debate político y control estatal de las cofradías españolas en el siglo XVIII", *Bulletin Hispanique* 99.2 (1997) 423–435.

Arias de Saavedra Alías I. – López-Guadalupe Muñoz M.L., "Cofradías y ciudad en la España del siglo XVIII", *Studia Historica. Historia Moderna* 19 (1998) 197–228.

Arias de Saavedra Alías I. – López-Guadalupe Muñoz M.L., "Las cofradías y su dimensión social en la España del antiguo régimen", *Cuadernos de Historia Moderna* 25 (2000) 189–232.

Arias de Saavedra Alías I. – López-Guadalupe Muñoz M.L., *La represión de la religiosidad popular. Crítica y acción contra las cofradías en la España del siglo XVIII* (Granada: 2002).

Bauch N., "Digital Geohumanities: Visualizing Geographic Thought", *International Journal of Humanities and Arts Computing* 11.1 (2017) 1–15.

Belotti S. – Fiore A., "Maps, Music, and Culture: Representing Historical Soundscapes Through Digital Mapping", in Schwan A. – Thomson T. (eds.), *The Palgrave Handbook of Digital and Public Humanities* (Cham: 2022) 423–440.

Calatrava J. – Ruiz Morales M., *Los planos de Granada 1500–1909. Cartografía urbana e imagen de la ciudad* (Granada: 2005).

Ceballos Guerrero A., "El Cuerpo de Horquilleros de la Hermandad de Nuestra Señora de las Angustias de Granada", in Campos Fernández de Sevilla F.J. (ed.), *Religiosidad popular: Cofradías de penitencia* (San Lorenzo del Escorial: 2017) 241–260.

Cortés Peña A.L. – Vincent B., *Historia de Granada. III. La época moderna. Siglos XVI, XVII y XVIII* (Granada: 1986).

Cuesta García de Leonardo Mª.J., *Fiesta y arquitectura efímera en la Granada del siglo XVIII* (Granada: 1995) 19–48.

Díez Rodríguez F., "El Gremialismo de Antonio de Capmany (1742–1813). La idea del trabajo de un conservador ingenuo", *Historia y política* 5 (2001) 171–208.

Eisman Lasaga C., "Efectos que produjo la invasión francesa en los conventos de Granada", *Cuadernos de Arte de la Universidad de Granada* 22 (1991) 63–73.

Espigares Rooney B., "Leer una imagen. La cartografía urbana y su conocimiento: *Vista de Granada* de Anton van den Wyngaerde", *Revista Letral* 15 (2015) 101–117.

Ferreira A. – Wohlmuth C. – Rodrigues A. – Correia N., "Plataforma Multimedia Interativa: experiencia imersiva da Paisagem Sonora Histórica de Évora", in Sá V. da – De Paula R.T. – Conde A.F. – Gouveia A.C. (eds.), *Sonoridades Eborenses* (Ribeirão: 2021) 313–335.

Gámir A., "El giro espacial en las Humanidades Digitales y sus productos cartográficos", *Biblio3W. Revista Bibliográfica de Geografía y Ciencias Sociales* 24 (2019).

García Pedraza A. – López Muñoz M.L., "Cofradías y moriscos en la Granada del siglo XVI (1500–1568)", in Mestre Sanchis A. – Giménez López Enrique (eds.), *Disidencias y exilios en la España Moderna* (Alicante: 1997) 377–392.

García Pulido L.J., "Una precisa y artística representación gráfica del territorio granadino: el Mapa topográfico de la ciudad de Granada y su término de Francisco Dalmau (1819)", *Cuadernos de Arte de la Universidad de Granada* 40 (2013) 171–198.

Gil Sanjuan J. – Sánchez López J.A., "Iconografía y visión histórico-literaria de Granada a mediados del quinientos", *Chronica Nova* 23 (1993) 73–133.

Gómez-Moreno Calera J.M., *El arquitecto granadino Ambrosio de Vico* (Granada: 1992).

Guerrero Vílchez A., *Las cofradías de Semana Santa en Granada (1760–1960). De la Ilustración al Nacionalcatolicismo* (Ph.D. dissertation, Universidad de Granada: 2022).

Henríquez de Jorquera F., *Anales de Granada*, Marín Ocete A. (ed.) (Granada: 1934; reprint Granada: 1987, with a preliminary study and new indexes by Gan Giménez P. – Moreno Garzón L.).

Jiménez Díaz N., *Historia de las campanas de Granada* (Ph.D. dissertation, Universidad de Granada: 1997).

López Guzmán R.J. – Gómez-Moreno Calera J.M. – Moreno Garrido A., "La plataforma de Ambrosio de Vico: cronología y gestación", *Arquitectura Andalucía Oriental* 2 (1984) 6–13.

López-Guadalupe Muñoz M.L., *Contrarreforma y cofradías en Granada. Aproximación a la historia de las cofradías y hermandades de la ciudad de Granada durante los siglos XVII y XVIII* (Ph.D. dissertation, Universidad de Granada: 1992).

López-Guadalupe Muñoz M.L., *Las cofradías de la parroquia de Santa María Magdalena de Granada en los siglos XVII–XVIII* (Granada: 1992).

López-Guadalupe Muñoz M.L., "Las cofradías de penitencia de Granada en la edad moderna", *Gazeta de Antropología* 11 (1995) article 12. https://digibug.ugr.es/handle/10481/13617.

López-Guadalupe Muñoz M.L., "Una forma alternativa de la piedad popular: las cofradías de vía sacra en Granada", *Revista de Historia Moderna* 31 (2013) 11–31.

Padial Bailón A., *Hermandades de gloria de Granada* (https://apaibailoni.blogspot.com/).

Padial Bailón A., *La Granada eterna* (http://apaibailon.blogspot.com/).

Ruiz Jiménez J., *La colegiata del Salvador en el contexto musical de Granada* (Ph.D. dissertation, Universidad de Granada: 1992).

Ruiz Jiménez J., "Música y devoción en Granada (siglos XVI–XVIII): Funcionamiento 'extravagante' y tipología de plazas no asalariadas en las capillas musicales eclesiásticas de la ciudad", *Anuario Musical* 52 (1997) 39–75.

Ruiz Jiménez J., "Festividad de las Cuarenta Horas organizada por la congregación de los Siervos del Soberano Espíritu del colegio jesuítico de San Pablo en Granada (1674/1692/1752)", *Paisajes Sonoros Históricos* (2015). http://www.historicalsoundscapes.com/evento/252/granada.

Ruiz Jiménez J., "Procesión del Corpus Christi" *Paisajes Sonoros Históricos* (2016). http://www.historicalsoundscapes.com/itinerario/2/1.

Ruiz Jiménez J., "Procesión de entierro de ajusticiados en Granada (1614)", *Paisajes Sonoros Históricos* (2017). http://www.historicalsoundscapes.com/evento/669/granada.

Ruiz Jiménez J., "Procesión de visita a los enfermos de la cofradía del Santísimo Sacramento en la collación de San Matías de Granada", *Paisajes Sonoros Históricos* (2018). http://www.historicalsoundscapes.com/evento/838/granada.

Ruiz Jiménez J., "Fiestas marianas patrocinadas por la hermandad del Santo Rosario de Nuestra Señora del Triunfo en Granada (1698)", *Paisajes Sonoros Históricos*, (2018). http://www.historicalsoundscapes.com/evento/803/granada.

Ruiz Jiménez J., "Regulación del tañido de campanas en los conventos trinitarios", *Paisajes Sonoros Históricos* (2018). http://www.historicalsoundscapes.com/evento/900/granada.

Ruiz Jiménez J., "Fiesta de la Asunción de María organizada por la cofradía de Nuestra Señora de la Asunción del granadino convento de Nuestra Señora de la Merced", *Paisajes Sonoros Históricos*, 2019. http://www.historicalsoundscapes.com/evento/970/granada.

Ruiz Jiménez J., "La transformación del paisaje sonoro urbano en la Granada conquistada (1492–1570)", in Rodríguez G. – Coronado Schwindt G. – Palazzo E. (eds.), *Paisajes sonoros medievales* (Mar de Plata: 2019) 139–186.

Ruiz Jiménez J., "Cartografía digital de espacios sonoros: una innovadora aproximación metodológica en los estudios de Musicología Urbana", in Carrero E. – Zauner S. (eds.), *Respondámosle a concierto. Estudios en homenaje a Maricarmen Gómez Muntané* (Barcelona: 2020) 235–248.

Ruiz Jiménez J., "Actividad cultual de la cofradía de las Ánimas del Purgatorio en la iglesia del Sagrario de Granada", *Paisajes Sonoros Históricos* (2020). http://www.historicalsoundscapes.com/evento/1203/granada.

Ruiz Jiménez J., "Recreación del paisaje sonoro de la procesión del Corpus Christi", *Paisajes Sonoros Históricos* (2020). http://www.historicalsoundscapes.com/evento/1140/granada.

Ruiz Jiménez J., "Festividad de la Asunción de María celebrada por el gremio de los escribanos en Granada (1693)", *Paisajes Sonoros Históricos* (2020). http://www.historicalsoundscapes.com/evento/1214/granada.

Ruiz Jiménez J., "Procesiones anuales de la cofradía de las Ánimas de la iglesia de Santa Ana en Granada", *Paisajes Sonoros Históricos* (2021). http://www.historicalsoundscapes.com/evento/1376/granada.

Ruiz Jiménez J., "Procesión de la cofradía de Nuestra Señora de la Soledad y Entierro de Cristo", *Paisajes Sonoros Históricos* (2022). http://www.historicalsoundscapes.com/evento/1415/Granada.

Ruiz Jiménez J., "Regulación del tañido de campanas en los conventos franciscanos capuchinos de la Provincia de Andalucía", *Paisajes Sonoros Históricos* (2023). http://www.historicalsoundscapes.com/evento/1509/granada.

Ruiz Jiménez J., "Dotación de tres chirimías para acompañar las salidas del Viático en iglesias de Granada (1636)", *Paisajes Sonoros Históricos* (2023). http://www.historicalsoundscapes.com/evento/1508/granada.

Ruiz Jiménez J. – Lizarán Rus I.J., "Historical Soundscapes (c.1200–c.1800): An On-Line Digital Platform", in Knighton T. – Mazuela-Anguita A. (eds.), *Hearing the City in Early Modern Europe*, Épitome musical (Turnhout: 2018) 355–371.

Vincent B., *Andalucía en la Edad Moderna: Economía y Sociedad* (Granada: 1985).

CHAPTER 18

Mapping Post-Tridentine Confraternities and Processions in Sixteenth-Century Tarragona

Sergi González González

Abstract

The sonic environment on Tarragonese feast-days was clearly affected by the substantial change in the guild confraternites' work activity; the soundscape associated with daily artisanal work was transformed into a festive one. Through georeferencing, and based on data from the detailed study of the processional circuits in post-Tridentine Tarragona, it is possible to calculate the density of sonic occupation of urban space, the length of the processional circuits and the areas of the city's fabric most affected by the change of activity within urban society. Combination of different computer tools enables horizons to be broadened and results to be analysed more deeply to give a new historical vision of the urban sound ecosystem: the symbiosis between musicology and digital humanities is beginning to modify the discipline's research paradigms. With the creation of a historical and sonic map of Tarragona of the late sixteenth century and using the umbrella of sound categorisation proposed by R. Murray Schafer and the concept of acoustic community developed by Barry Truax, together with a combination of different software tools, this paper offers an overview of the general processions of Tarragona in which all the guild confraternities were, to a greater or lesser extent, involved.

Keywords

digital humanities – mapping – sound studies – urban musicology – Tarragona

Urban settings are characterised by the flow of sound, and sound waves move through cities depending on their topography, creating a communication system that, whether deliberately or not, disseminates information to the inhabitants. This chapter considers the advantages that digital cartography offers for the analysis of the flow of sound, and for the quantification of its effect on and reception by city-dwellers. I will suggest how it is possible to determine the density of sound occupancy of urban locations through mapping, and, as a result, the corresponding overall intensity of sonic experience in these spaces. This means going beyond the creation of a diagram of the processional trajectories of a city, since it is clear that sound transcends physical barriers and that its transmission held encoded information for local inhabitants. A key question here is how this information was disseminated to the general populace and to the broader ecosystem of religious processions in early modern cities. A further consideration is how, with the use of georeferencing techniques and historical cartography, the movement of processions can be represented and their acoustic components visualised in the presentation of results.

The georeferencing of processional routes draws on a technique that is already well integrated into the digital humanities which, originally developed together with Humanities Computing, combines new computing technologies with study of the humanities and social sciences.[1] The publication of the *Companion to Digital Studies* in 2004 already established the need for interdisciplinary study in the humanities, and further integration has taken place over the last decade through the development of new digital technologies. This has made possible new analytical approaches to and insight into a wide variety of data. Consequently, the experience of the digital turn has developed research methodologies that have opened up a new range of possibilities that enable large amounts of information to be analysed with great efficiency and accuracy. This in turn has led to major advances in a more nuanced understanding of historical cultural practices, dramatically widening the potential findings of historical research. Clearly, these new paradigms in methodological approaches to historical research will continue to have an increasingly important role in the field of the humanities.[2]

As Nicholas Terpstra has proposed in his introduction to the volume of essays that resulted from the DECIMA project on mapping space, sense and movement in early modern Florence:

> We describe how digitally inflected scholarship emerges and expands through technical challenges and ongoing revision. We show how emerging critical questions and expanding technical possibilities bring

---

[1] Schreiban S. et al. (eds.), *A Companion to Digital Humanities* (New Jersey: 2004). In 2016 the same editors published *A New Companion to Digital Humanities* (New Jersey: 2016).

[2] For more detailed information on the different technologies that are rapidly developing in the digital humanities, see: *The Journal of Digital Humanities* https://journalofdigitalhumanities.org/ (consulted 5 April 2023); *Debates in the Digital Humanities* https://dhdebates.gc.cuny.edu/; and the Association for Computers and the Humanities https://ach.org/ (consulted April 2023).

researchers back to the drawing board time after time. Approaches that seem feasible frequently have to be abandoned due to limits in the sources or technology. We demonstrate how digital projects can promote collaboration, allow scholars to extend their research within a field, and shift the questions and subject matter both within a particular area of research and in historical study generally. As the questions change and subject matter evolves, attention turns to how best to share findings and to whether there are new ways to bridge past and present and bring together academic creators and popular users.[3]

Terpstra's evocative words offer a succinct summary of the different processes, questions and setting out of the methodological approaches opened up by research in the digital humanities. It is also clear from the DECIMA project, and others, that one of the most useful and highly developed DH tools in recent years is digital cartography which has found favour in historical studies because of the appearance of new geographical softwares that are relatively easy to use. These are usually based on GPS (Global Positioning System), and more recently GIS (Geographic Information System) tools, available on open access, which offer the facility of creating detailed maps of the elements to be studied and the possibility of connecting data sets.[4] The technological advances provided by geographical information systems have allowed historians to create three-dimensional models of cities and historical monuments that enhance understanding of their construction and evolution over time.[5]

However, historical digital cartography and its use within the GIS system (HGIS: Historical Geographic Information System) is not exempt from a range of challenges that have to be met as research unfolds. Old maps and drawings of cities are often incomplete and imprecise, although the use of various recently developed tools can result in the creation of detailed maps. This makes it possible to show the exact position of buildings, streets and other important elements of urban topography, and also to trace how people moved and which streets were used most frequently, and in this way to present an

---

3 Terpstra N., "Introduction" in Terpstra N. – Rose C. (eds.), *Mapping Space, Sense, and Movement in Florence. Historical GIS and the Early Modern City* (New York: 2016) 19.
4 Presner T. – Shepard D., "Mapping the Geospatial Turn" in Schreiban S. et al. (eds.), *A New Companion to Digital Humanities* (New Jersey: 2016) 201–212. This study also describes how GPS and GIS can be integrated.
5 Harley, J.B., "Deconstructing the Map", *Cartographica: The International Journal for Geographic Information and Geovisualization* 26.2 (1989) 1–20.

approximation of urban space and time.⁶ The use of digital mapping tools in research today can increase the volume, extent and diversity of historical study during the early modern period and even as far back as ancient times. These technologies not only make it possible to verify and test hypotheses, but they also open up new methods to grasp the complex relationships between urban environments and many facets of societal development. The related methods enable inquiry into the creation of knowledge, the expression of social identity and the maintenance of collective memory, and provide the necessary critical framework. Modern technologies afford certain novelties, but at the same time are extensions and repetitions of an age-old and continuing conversation about the nature of social space.⁷

The DECIMA project, with its multifaceted approach to mapping the city of Renaissance Florence, falls into this line of research and provides insight into how the inhabitants experienced and related to urban space. It covers all aspects from emblematic buildings and public spaces to patterns of movement and daily life, commercial routes and density of population with reference to acquisitive power, social status and trade in the city. DECIMA creates an interactive map based on three key documents – two population census of 1551 and 1632, another relating to property of 1561 – together with the map of Florence drawn by Stefano Buonsignori in 1584. The data these sources provide is combined in a specially designed database, enabling the creation of an interactive map that allows a multidimensional approach to studying the city and its inhabitants.⁸ In the specific field of urban musicology, the digital platform *Historical Soundscapes*, launched by Juan Ruiz Jiménez and Ignacio José Lizarán Rus in 2015, has opened up new potential for research and presentation of data related to the historical urban soundscape and created a very useful tool for studying the phonosphere from new perspectives. The platform is applicable to diverse fields of inquiry, with a wide range of possibilities from serious musicological research to the teaching of music history, involving the analysis of historical space and time.⁹ Several musicological projects that involve digital cartography have also been developed in recent years, all of

---

6   Richardson, J.S., "Geographical Information Systems and Historical Research: Current Progress and Future Directions", *Journal of Interdisciplinary History* 45.1 (2014) 1–18.
7   Atkinson N., "Seeing sound", in Terpstra N. – Rose C. (eds.), *Mapping Space, Sense, and Movement in Florence. Historical GIS and the Early Modern City* (New York: 2016) 149–168, here 151.
8   For more detailed information, see the web page: https://decima-map.net (consulted 31 March 2023). Another interesting project from the viewpoint of digital cartography is MAPPINGROME: Interactive Nolli Map Website. https://mappingrome.com/ (consulted 31 March 2023).
9   http://www.historicalsoundscapes.com (consulted 24 February 2023).

which contribute to further information on sound based on the georeferencing of the various sonic activities common to early modern cities.

To study sound and space is also to analyse the relationship between the inhabitants of a city and their sonic environment. According to Barry Truax:

> The communicational significance of any sound can only be judged within its complete context in the broadest environmental, social and cultural sense. In fact, it is through context that we understand how, in a traditional acoustic environment, the inseparability of every sound from its context makes it a valuable source of usable information about the current state of the environment.[10]

Digital tools enable this three-pronged approach – environmental, social and cultural – to inform analysis of the impact of sound on urban society and thus to identify its different acoustic communities. Sound has a major communicative role to play in the creation of a deep underlying sense of community. The resulting acoustic and sensorial experience instils habits, patterns of behaviour and personal networks that are directly connected to the urban environment from which they emanate. In this way, according to Truax, all urban centres can be considered to be permeable and interchangeable acoustic communities dependent on the performative situation through which they are generated. They can be isolated, defined and broken down to facilitate detailed study, and subsequently put back together to be analysed as a whole made up of many parts. Importantly, such concepts relating to sound studies can be merged with DH technology to form what can be termed Historical Sound Studies to provide an integrated view of society-sound-space-movement-city within urban musicology.[11]

The study of sound, or its absence in silence, from an analytical perspective that permits an understanding of its role in early modern cities, requires a taxonomic classification that is far from easy to realise. R. Murray Schafer's work in the field of contemporary sound studies offers a starting-point for analysis of the sonic activities of confraternities and guilds that are the focus of the CONFRASOUND project. CONFRASOUND was a three-year Spanish government research project (2020–2023) entitled: "The Contribution of Confraternities and Guilds to the Urban Soundscape in the Iberian Peninsula, c.1400–c.1700", MINECO (PID2019–109422GB-100, I+D+i–PGC Tipo B). Through his identification of three types of sounds heard in the context of the soundscape: keynote sounds, sound signals and soundmarks. Keynote sounds refer

---

10   Truax B., *Acoustic Communication* (Westport: 2001) 12.
11   A definition of the term Sound Studies is found in Sterne J. (ed.), *The Sound Studies Reader* (New York: 2012) 4–5.

to those sounds heard more or less continuously within urban society to the extent that they do not impinge on the daily life of the city's inhabitants. If, at a certain moment and in specific circumstances, such a sound became more audible it can then be considered a sound signal that would come into sharper focus and attract attention. Schafer defined soundmarks as sounds specific to a particular community whose sonic qualities would be interpreted in a particular way by that community's members, that is, the tacit shared knowledge of an acoustic community.[12]

1   Digital Humanities and the CONFRASOUND Project

Existing research projects such as DECIMA and *Historical Soundscapes*, together with the methodologies developed through contemporary Sound Studies, including the classification of sound and the concept of acoustic communities, and combined with DH technologies such as HGIS, provide the starting-point and inspiration for the analysis of processional routes and their impact on the soundscape of early modern Tarragona undertaken as part of the CONFRASOUND project. The project's main research objective is to analyse how and in what ways confraternities and guilds contributed to the urban soundscape, and how the data obtained might be visualised through the use of digital cartography to map musical practices and their meaning for and impact on acoustic communities. This essay thus focuses on digital cartography, using old maps to localise and analyse processional routes and the density of sonic occupation of the city in order to assess their impact on the soundscape of Tarragona. Two main design bases, suitable for the project, have been used in order to combine DH tools with urban musicology: HGIS and georeferencing software [Table 18.1].

Table 18.1 presents the four software packages used for studying processional routes and their specific application in the CONFRASOUND project. QGIS is an open-access and free GIS software with a wide range of tools to facilitate visualisation, analysis and processing of spatial data. This programme, based on a straightforward system of correlation of points, enables the scaling of old maps: each point corresponds to the coordinates XY, so that the exact location can be pinpointed on *Open Street Maps*. In this way, the old map can be visualised with the modern map so that points of interest can be positioned on both maps and seen simultaneously. INSTAMAPS is a straightforward tool for drawing processional routes and for the visualisation of geographical data in an interactive and attractive way. It is compatible with different geospatial file

---

[12]   Schafer R.M., *The Soundscape: Our Sonic Environment and the Tuning of the World* (Rochester: 1994) 272–275.

TABLE 18.1 Digital cartography software used in the CONFRASOUND research project

Software	Source	Tool	Use
QGIS[a]	Foundation OSGe	georeferencing	scaling of old maps
Instamaps[b]	Servei Cartogràfic i Geològic de Catalunya	digital cartography	tracing of procesional routes
GEPHI[c]	University of Technology of Compiègne	node theory	analysis of the relationship between space and its Sonic occupation
ArcGis[d]	Esri	HGIS	data analysis

a   https://qgis.org/ca/site/ (consulted 29 March 2023).
b   https://www.instamaps.cat (consulted 29 March 2023).
c   https://gephi.org (consulted 29 March 2023).
d   https://www.esri.com/en-us/arcgis/products/arcgis-desktop/overview (consulted 29 March 2023).

formats, such as Shapefile, GeoJSON and KML, making it easy to import and export data.

Georeferencing also allows the quantification and interrelation of spaces. GEPHI is a software tool that aids network analysis in order to visualise and analyse complex relationships between people, organisations, events and artifacts. It is based on the mathematical theory of nodes which, based on a statistical system, analyses the relationships produced between the different variables selected by the user. Most uses of this application in historical research is based on the premise that historical events, people and organisations can be seen as nodes in a network. These nodes can be connected through a range of relationships, such as shared factors, political interactions, family relationships and economic profile. Through visualisation and analysis of these relationships, it is possible to discern patterns and tendencies that help to understand in a more nuanced way the history and culture of a particular region.[13]

The programme ArcGIS can handle all these areas, although a drawback of using this software is the steep learning curve required. However, once

---

13   See Bastian M. et al., "Gephi: An Open Source Software for Exploring and Manipulating Networks", *Proceedings of the International AAAI Conference on Web and Social Media* 3.1 (2009) 361–362.

mastered, the digital environment opens up a wide range of opportunities for historical musicological research. ArcGIS is a component of the Esri ecosystem that has been a pioneer in GIS, location intelligence and mapping software, and a key player in providing support for geographical study and geospatial analytics employing cutting-edge GIS technology. Armed with the appropriate DH tools, the urban musicologist working with digital cartography has to begin the process with the hunt for a historical map appropriate to the goals set by the research objectives.

2 Historical Digital Cartography of the City of Tarragona: Padre Florez's Map

Colin Rose has described the challenges that confronted the early phases of the DECIMA project:

> We faced the challenge of placing this map [Buonsignori, 1584] into Cartesian geographic space and then placing the completed data-base onto that map as a "layer" of point-based vector data.[14]

The primary decision is to select an old map that offers a reliable snapshot of the urban fabric of the city in the period to be studied, so that the location of the event(s) to be analysed can be identified with precision. The process of selection will depend on the availability of maps and take into consideration the topography and history of the city in question. Tarragona is an ancient city, relatively small in size, located on the east coast of the Iberian Peninsula on the Mediterranean coast. With a current population of 140,000 inhabitants, the city abounds in long-established traditions and practices that have survived the passage of time, having been adapted to changing aesthetic tastes. Founded over 2200 years ago, Tarragona reached the height of its importance in 218 BCE with the arrival of the Roman Empire, when it was considered to be the capital of the province Hispania Citerior. Lucius Annaeus Florus, who drew up the memoirs of the Emperor Adrian between the first and second centuries, proclaimed: 'Tarraco, civitas ubi ver aeternum est' ('Tarragona, the

---

14 Rose C., "Thinking and Using DECIMA", in Terpstra N. – Rose C. (eds.), *Mapping Space, Sense, and Movement in Florence. Historical GIS and the Early Modern City* (New York: 2016) 15–32, here 17.

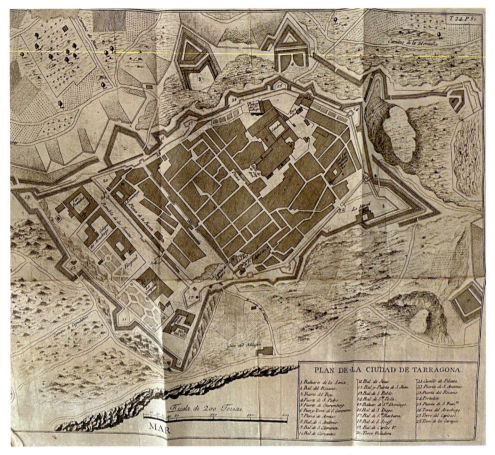

FIGURE 18.1   City plan of Tarragona by Enrique Florez (1769), in "Antiguedades Tarraconenses" in *España Sagrada* 80
IMAGE © SERGI GONZÁLEZ GONZÁLEZ

city of eternal spring').[15] The city was in effect capital of the Roman Empire during Emperor Augustus's sojourn there in the years 25 and 16 BCE, and was at that time renowned for its magnificence. One of the advantages of studying Tarragona is that its ancient nucleus and its orography has remained almost unchanged for the last seven hundred years. The old city was built over what was originally the walled area of the forum of the Tarragona province, and the

---

15   Museu Nacional Arqueològic de Tarragona. Florus, *Memoirs of Emperor Augustus*. https://www.youtube.com/watch?v=DpGoCVg6wMw.

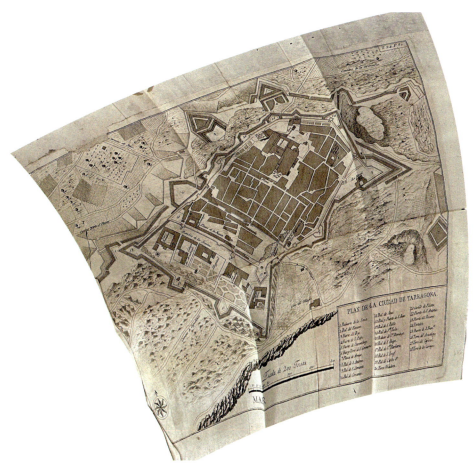

FIGURE 18.2 Enrique Florez's 1769 city plan georeferenced using QGIS
IMAGE © SOUNDSPACE

city walls continued to protect the city and define its urban space during the early modern period.[16]

Six drawings and maps, dating from 1563 to 1769, have been consulted with regard to the mapping of Tarragona during that period. The two drawings of 1563 are by the celebrated Dutch artist Anton van den Wyngaerde. These are followed chronologically by three seventeenth-century maps, the earliest of which, with the title *Tarracone*, is dated ca. 1600 and forms part of the

---

16 González González S., *Evolució del paisatge sonor del seguici festiu de la festa major de Santa Tecla a Tarragona* (Ph.D. dissertation, Universitat Autònoma de Barcelona: 2019) 24.

Anville collection (Bibliothèque Nationale de France).[17] This is followed by a map of 1643 signed by Calbet,[18] and another entitled *Plan de la ville et molle de Taragone en Catalogne assiegé par l'armée du Roy tres chrestien Louis 14 commandée par le Mariscal de la Motte et le Duc de Bregé Admiral le 22 octobre en 1644*, which seems to have been drawn in about 1659 by Sébastien de Pontault de Beaulieu.[19] The most recent map is that drawn by Enrique Florez in 1769 which was published in volume XXIV of *España Sagrada* [Fig. 18.1].[20] I have selected the Enrique Florez map, despite being from a later period, since it is the most accurate in terms of the topography of the city. Comparison of the available maps suggests that the urban design of the walled city changed little over two hundred years, so that the chronological gap does not create too many problems.[21]

The Florez map has been georeferenced, or represented in scale, and for the purposes of cartographical analysis has been used together with contemporary maps: some points are still plainly visible on both maps [Fig. 18.1]. The situation is made easier since the city gates, cathedral, bulwarks, monasteries, and major streets are all still standing. The historical map is distorted according to its proportionalities created by the georeferencing process, which has been carried out using QGIS [Fig. 18.2]. Any distortions have been adjusted through a transformation process that reshapes the image of the map to correspond with greater precision to the urban layout. Street corners and accurate assessment of distance determine the degree of distortion, which can be reduced when these variables are more precisely located.

Comparison of the georeferenced map with the original shows that the part outside the city walls beyond the urban grid, notably in the region between the wall and the sea, displays the greatest distortion. This problem has been mitigated by using several visualisation viewpoints offered by INSTAMAPS and

---

17 https://gallica.bnf.fr/ark:/12148/btv1b59702505.r=Tarracone?rk=21459;2 (consulted 1 April 2023).
18 https://gallica.bnf.fr/ark:/12148/btv1b69036389.r=Tarragona.%20Calbet?rk=21459;2 (consulted 1 April 2023).
19 https://cartotecadigital.icgc.cat/digital/collection/catalunya/id/1156/rec/3 (consulted 1 April 2023).
20 Florez Enrique, "Antiguedades Tarraconenses" in *España Sagrada*, vol. XXIV (Madrid, Antonio Marin: 1769) 80.
21 The six sources have been compared visually, and the findings are supported in Terrado Ortuño P., "Tarragona en el siglo XVII a través de la cartografía: un plano inédito de la Ciudad procedente de la Colección de Anville en la Biblioteca Nacional de Francia", *Manuscrits. Revista d'Història Moderna* 36 (2017) 57–84.

ArcGIS.[22] On the basis of the georeferenced map, it is possible to begin to analyse the sonic patterns of the processional practices of the confraternities and guilds of Tarragona.

3 The Ecosystem of Confraternities and Guilds in Early Modern Tarragona

The majority of the inhabitants of Tarragona in the medieval and early modern periods were workers dedicated to a particular trade, and as free professionals, they rendered homage to the archbishop as lord of the city.[23] While belonging to a parish, the tradespeople of the city formed guilds to gain greater power and social standing for the realisation of their activities, including trade, apprenticeship and pious deeds (often involving widows of guild members and the sick).[24] It was generally obligatory for tradespeople to become members of these groups in order to guarantee quality of production or service, development of official legislation and security through cooperation. Guilds were recognised by public, municipal and royal entities, so that the system was especially highly developed in urban centres where trade and artisanal skills were necessary and valued. In Tarragona, some of the smaller guilds formed confraternities under the avocation of their patron saint to facilitate realisation of their practices with as little hindrance as possible and to achieve greater representation in the city's social structure. They thus became guild confraternities that continued to control their working conditions and activities in addition to promoting their devotional practices.[25]

These confraternities were responsible for a number of aspects of the urban social framework, including the upkeep of their guild house and of the chapels designated to them in churches across the city; these generally became symbols of prestige that deliberately served to adorn the city. The architectural and cultural remnants of these churches can still be seen in present-day Tarragona. The Church of Nazareth in the Plaça del Rei served as the home of the Confraternity of the Sang de Jesucrist of the shoe- and espadrille-makers,

---

22 A similar situation resulted in the DECIMA project; see Rose, "Thinking and using DECIMA" 17–18.
23 For a more detailed account of the confraternal and guild structure in Tarragona, see: González González S., "Paying Homage: The Participation of Guild Confraternities in Archiepiscopal Entries into Tarragona", *Confraternitas* 31.2 (2020) 36–62.
24 Benítez Bolorinos M., *Las cofradías medievales en el reino de Valencia (1329–1458)* (Alicante: 1998).
25 González González, *Evolució del paisatge sonor* 150–155.

FIGURE 18.3   The statue of the Eccehomo (1545) in the the tympanum of the Church of Nazareth, headquarters of the Confraternity of the Sang de Jesucrist in the Plaça del Rei, Tarragona
IMAGE © SERGI GONZÁLEZ GONZÁLEZ

which was founded in 1545. In 1596, they commissioned the sculpture of the Eccehomo, which is found in the tympanum of the church, with the aim of adorning one of the entrances to the building [Fig. 18.3]. Another example is a magnificent altarpiece that was originally from the Monastery of Santa Magdalena de Belloc, which served as the headquarters of the Confraternity of Santa Magdalena of market-gardeners and was constructed between 1495 and 1504. It is now localated at the Church of Sant Llorenç, the headquarters of the Confraria of Sant Llorenç and Sant Isidre [Fig. 18.4].[26]

Guild confraternities also undertook various charitable works for the care and well-being of their members: they gave support to and looked after the sick, widows and orphans. They were also concerned with their social status. For example, towards the end of the sixteenth century, the Confraternity of the Sang de Jesucrist founded the maiden's dowry (*el dot de la ponzella*) for

---

26   Under the patronage of St. Lawrence and St. Isidor, the Confraternity of Santa Magdalena of the market-gardeners and the Confraternity of Sant Llorenç of the peasant-farmers joined together as a single confraternity in 1726. Apart from the fact that they were both involved in agriculture, the destruction of the monastery of Santa Magdalena de Bell-lloc, which was situated outside the city walls, was one of the primary causes of this union; see González González, *Evolució del paisatge sonor* 155.

FIGURE 18.4 Retable (1495–1504) in the monastery of Santa Magdalena del Belloch, headquarters of the Confraternity of Santa Magdalena of market gardeners in the church of Sant Llorenç in the Plaça de Sant Llorenç, Tarragona
IMAGE © SERGI GONZÁLEZ GONZÁLEZ

which funds were designated to orphaned girls of deceased members with few resources in order to secure marriage and thus be able to maintain their social status.[27]

The spiritual component of guild confraternities was significant in a number of ways, and helped to cement the social bonds shared by members. Members of the confraternity were required to attend all meetings, processions – notably at Corpus Christi – patron saint festivities and other celebrations held all over the city. They were also expected to take part in their church's social activities and any unusual events that occurred, including royal or archiepiscopal entries, rogations, thanksgivings, canonisations and beatifications. The confraternities' involvement in religious and devotional acts included the costs associated with memorial services, anniversaries, commemoration of the souls of the deceased and facilitating spiritual instruction. The securing of indulgences by confraternities added to their prestige and also promised their members a shorter passage through purgatory.[28]

The earliest extant references to the confraternal fabric of Tarragona date from 1321 with regard to the procession held for the arrival of the relic of St. Thecla. A total of ten confraternities, with four hundred members of the artisan class of the city took part with various visual signs to proclaim their identity as a social group; in addition to the confraternal banner, they also dressed for the occasion in different colours that symbolised their trade or artisanal activity.[29] An important document dating from the early seventeenth century indicates the number of members belonging to each confraternity, with an overall total of 925. The *Llibre del Consulat* (1617–1618), held at the Arxiu Històric de la Ciutat de Tarragona, includes the 'List of Confraternities together with the number of members of each confraternity' ('Memorial de les confraries juntament amb els confrares de la confraria'), giving the total of nineteen brotherhoods [Table 18.2].[30] The aim of this list was to take account of the men in Tarragona belonging to the militias, and for this reason it does

---

27 This pious action was common to many confraternities; for the case of Tarragona, see: Bertran Luengo J., *El mestratge de la Sang de Tarragona: Història d'una confraria. 1545–2020* (Valls: 2020).

28 Terpstra N., *Lay Confraternities and Civic Religion in Renaissance Bologna* (Cambridge – New York: 1995).

29 Barber Joseph, *Relació verdadera de la translació del Bras de la Gloriosa Verge e Invicta Protohomartyr Santa Thecla, deixebla del Apostol Sant Pau y patrona de la Ciutat, è Iglesia Metropolitana de Tarragona, Primada de las Espanyas; desde Armenia à dita Ciutat* (Tarragona, [Joseph Barber]: 1746).

30 Arxiu Històric de la Ciutat de Tarragona. Llibre d'acte del Consell 1617–1628, Sig. Top. 163.

TABLE 18.2 The confraternal ecosystem of Tarragona in the early seventeenth century

Confraternity	Guild	Members	Foundation	Statutes
Santa Magdalena	market gardeners	66	1353	1560
Sant Josep	carpenters and coopers	57	14th century	–
Sant Josep i Nom de Jesus	architects	24	–	–
Sant Pere i sant Andreu	fishermen and sailors	184	1383	1511
Sant Llorenç	farmers and labourers	200	1402	1560/1727
Nostra Senyora de la Caritat i l'arcàngel Sant Gabriel	tailors, hosiers and haberdashers	84	1383	–
Nostra Senyora de la Candela i Sant Simeó	dock workersers, stevedores and bakers	30	1483	–
Sant Miquel	weavers	33	–	–
Sant Salvador	shopkeepers and merchants	40	14th century	1653/1683/1739
Sant Ponç	ostlers, innkeepers and market stall-holders	31	16th century	–
Santa Llúcia	ropemakers	34	1568	–
Sant Antoni	wool carders	25	1514	–
Sandt Lluc	notaries and procurators	43	–	–
Santa Tecla	leather-workers and tanners	10	1500	1601
Sant Eloi	silversmiths and farriers	10	16th century	–
Sant Cosme i Sant Damià	doctors, surgeons and pharmacists	18	16th century	–
Sant Marc	shoemarkers	36	16th century	–
Sang de Jesucrist	sandal-makers and goods made of reeds	6	1545	1566/1597/1728
Sant Lluís	apprentice tailors	–	–	–

not include the Confraternity of Sant Jordi of the military and the nobility, nor that of the cathedral clergy.[31]

The number of artisans who were members of guild confraternities thus tripled between the fourteenth and early seventeenth centuries, although the population of the city was relatively low in comparison with other Mediterranean cities of the Crown of Aragon, such as Barcelona, Valencia or Naples. Tarragona was not such an important centre for commercial trade and its economy was primarily based on farming and fishing. The city also suffered a series of political and military conflicts that adversely affected population and economic growth.[32]

4 The Corpus Christi Procession in Early Modern Tarragona

It was one of the duties of confraternities to attend the processions that took place in the city, and many processions were mounted in Tarragona over the course of the year. While it is difficult to gauge their relative significance for the inhabitants of the city, each procession had some degree of importance in one way or another, whether held for a confraternity's patronal feast day or for Corpus Christi. Some twenty-seven processions associated with confraternities have been identified, several of these brotherhoods having two or more patron saints. A large proportion of these processions took place inside the cathedral, church or monastery where the confraternity was based; even so, there was always a time in the year when processions occupied urban space beyond the ecclesiastical institution. For example, the stevedores' and bakers' Confraternity of Nostra Senyora de la Candela i Sant Simeó celebrated its major feast day on 2 February, the feast of Candlemas or the Purification of the Virgin. The confraternity met in the city hall since they did not have their own building, and then processed to the chapel of Corpus Christi in the cathedral cloister, where they were based. The confraternity banner headed the procession and was followed by the dance they performed on major feast days (Corpus Christi, St. Thecla and royal entries being among the most important), accompanied by its 'música' (no further detail given). Then followed all the members of the confraternity, while the leaders (*prohomens*) of the two brotherhoods brought up the rear.[33] On 2 February, they would congregate at their

---

31   See González González, *Evolució del paisatge sonor* 154.
32   Rovira S., *L'Edat Moderna a Tarragona: una època de contrastos* (Lleida: 2011) 103–111.
33   Arxiu Històric Municipal de Tarragona. Forners.

FIGURE 18.5   The route of the early morning Candlemas procession charted on the historic map by Enrique Florez, with a transparency of 50% over an OpenStreetMap base. Software: ARGIS on line
IMAGE © SOUNDSPACE

casa early in the morning, organise the procession as previously described, and follow a brief route through the city that included parts of the Carrer Major and the Plaça dels Cols, and then climbed the steps of the Plaça de la Catedral and Carrer del Claustre before arriving at the entrance to the cloister [Fig. 18.5]. Members of the confraternity would enter and make their way to their chapel, where the liturgical ritual would begin.

As was the case with the patronal feast-day celebrations of confraternities, some other processions affected only a part of the city, such as those mounted at the level of the parish church for the taking of the viaticum to the homes of the moribund or funeral cortèges. Among the general processions that affected the city of Tarragona as a whole, there were two main types: the 'ordinary' processions celebrated throughout the year, and those held to mark 'extraordinary' events of ephemeral importance that occurred at specific and sometimes unforeseen moments. These included royal, archiepiscopal and viceregal entries, beatifications and canonisations, rogative processions to pray for divine intervention, for example, against war, plagues and drought, and those of thanksgiving when the threat or danger had passed.

In Tarragona, fourteen 'ordinary' processions were held throughout the year [Table 18.3].[34] For most of these, the confraternities were involved only in a passive sense: that is, they processed along the determined route with their banners, but usually contributed little or nothing to the urban soundscape. Their active sonic participation was restricted to the Corpus Christi procession and that mounted for the feast day of the patron saint of the city, St. Thecla, held annually on 23 September. On these occasions, the confraternities brought out their paratheatrical repesentations (*entremesos*) of various kinds, both Biblical and secular, in order to pay homage to the Eucharist and to the relic of the arm, preserved intact, of St. Thecla.[35]

TABLE 18.3 General processions in early modern Tarragona

Procession	Feast day	Chronology	Location
Purification of the Virgin	2 February	1369–1656	Cathedral – Santa Maria del Miracle – Cathedral; within the city walls; from the mid-17th century
Palm Sunday	Palm Sunday	From 1369 to the present, with modifications	From the Cathedral to St. Fructuós; within the city walls; from the first third of the 17th century

---

34 The following sources were used to develop the table: Arxiu Històric Arxidiocesà de Tarragona. Ms. 84. Consueta; Arxiu Capitular de la Catedral de Tarragona. Consueta 1656; Arxiu Històric Arxidiocesà de Tarragona. Processionale Tarraconense; Barcelona, Biblioteca de Catalunya. Ms 276; and Tomás Ávila A., *El culto y la liturgia en la catedral de Tarragona (1300–1700)* (Tarragona: 1963).

35 For more detail on the religious-ludic activities of confraternities and the ways in which they affected the soundscape of Tarragona, see: González González, *Evolució del paisatge sonor*, and González González, "Paying Homage" 36–62.

TABLE 18.3 General processions in early modern Tarragona (cont.)

Procession	Feast day	Chronology	Location
Silence[a]	Maundy Thursday	From 1589 to the mid-18th century	Followed the route of Corpus Christi
Holy Burial and Holy Thorn	Good Friday	From 1589 to the mid-18th century, and from 1932	Followed the route of Corpus Christi
Easter	Easter Day, after vespers	From 1369 until after 1656	Church of Santa Tecla la Vella – main entrance – altar – baptistery
Litanies I	Monday before Ascension Day	From 1369 to at least 1656, and from 1674 to the present	Cathedral – San Fructuós-Cathedral; stayed within the city walls
Litanies II	Tuesday before Ascension Day	From 1369 to at least 1656, and from 1674 to the present	Cathedral – Santa Maria del Miracle – Cathedral
Litanies III	Wednesday before Ascension Day	From 1369 to at least 1656, and from 1674 to the present	Cathedral – Santa Tecla la Vella – Cathedral
Translation of the Arm of St. Thecla	21 May	1321–1895	Route as for the arrival of the relic of St. Thecla in Tarragona
Corpus Christi	June	From 1330 to the present	Cathedral and through the city
Assumption of the Virgin	15 August, after Vespers	From the 15th-century to about the 19th century	Followed the route of Corpus Christi (today it takes place in the cathedral cloister)

a The 'Silence' procession may possibly have been intended to draw attention to the sounds made by penitents during the procession on Holy Thursday, such as the clinking of chains, the cracking of whips and the sound of footfall that could then be heard by those attending the procession. The ensuing soundscape must have been overwhelming, and encouraged repentance among those present, urging them to do penance; see: Bertran Luengo J., *El mestratge de la Sang de Tarragona: Història d'una confraria. 1545–2020* (Valls: 2020) 66.

TABLE 18.3 General processions in early modern Tarragona (*cont.*)

Procession	Feast day	Chronology	Location
St. Thecla	23 September	From 1321 to the present	Follows the route of Corpus Christi
Immaculate Conception of the Virgin	8 December, after Terce	From the early 16th century to 1688	Cathedral – Santa Maria del Miracle – Cathedral
Immaculate Conception of the Virgin	8 December, after Vespers	From the early 16th century to 1688	Followed the route of Corpus Christi

As is clear from earlier studies on processions in the Crown of Aragon, the Corpus Christi procession was particularly important as regards the occupation of urban space and its longevity from the fourteenth century to the present, especially so in the case of Tarragona, given the relatively small size of the city.[36] The processional circuits outlined in Table 18.3 suggest a few important locations, or nodes, that have been used to identify the urban areas occupied by the different processions.

5 Processional Circuits and Nodes in Post-Tridentine Tarragona

Just as the daily working life of urban society developed in a general way around the guilds and confraternities, the topography of cities contributed in a direct way to the formation of acoustic communities: urban spaces were defined by the sonic characteristics that stemmed from the prevalence of a particular guild in specific streets. Although urban society tended to be spatially organised in this way, central and shared spaces were also needed. The configuration of the greater part of medieval cities adhered to that of the Islamic countries of the Magreb, with a protective city wall and inside squares, mostly small but with one or more of larger size, a topography that had a considerable impact on the soundscape and one that facilitated the communication of information according to its sonic dimension.

---

36   Kamen H., *Cambio cultural en la Sociedad del Siglo de Oro. Cataluña y Castilla, siglos XVI–XVII* (Madrid: 1998) 81–85.

In Tarragona, this configuration can still be seen in the present-day layout of the city, since it has grown and developed without losing its original format. Since the districts were grouped, for the most part, according to shared artisanal activity and membership of guilds (except for the bakers whose trade is spread over the city as a whole), urban daily life hinged around work and guild. Artisans generally lived on the upper floor of their houses, and carried out their work on the ground floor, their workshops spilling out onto the streets named after their particular guild.[37] Many of the difficulties encountered when analysing early modern archival sources using historical GIS can be resolved through familiarity with the urban history of the sixteenth and seventeenth centuries. Historical cities can be mapped through the documentation found in the city archives, but it is also important to recognise the basic distinctions between how these urban areas were designed and constructed. Cities were not just places for travel, work or living in early modern societies; they also served other purposes, notably for the realisation of rituals that arose out of the necessities of their communities.[38] The extant sources help to indicate the selection of processional nodes for further georeferencing and analysis from the detailed perspective gained through HGIS, and these major ceremonial locations were primarily street crossings, squares, churches, monasteries, palaces and city gates.

The identification of processional spaces is a demanding task that requires the researcher's full attention, since it is crucial to achieve total immersion in the urban layout and be able to visualise the historical city through the superimposition of the modern city. It is often the case that the archival sources do not indicate the exact route of processions, but mention only certain aspects of the ritual to be celebrated; these can help to trace the relevant trajectories on the map. In the case of Tarragona, analysis of the ritual outlined in the *Processionale Tarraconense* (1568) as well as of other ceremonials or *consuetas*, always with reference to Florez's map, has helped to disentangle the processional routes. In addition, knowledge of the changes in street names (and the reason behind the change) is essential for recognition of the urban spaces mentioned in the archival sources.[39] Ceremonials were drawn up with the purpose of recording descriptions of particular rituals so that they could be

---

37 Arts Roca E., *Els carrers dels menestrals a la Tarragona Vella* (Tarragona: 1995).
38 Rose, "Thinking and Using DECIMA" 36.
39 On this aspect, see: Salvat Bové J., *Tarragona Antigua y moderna a través de su nomenclatura urbana: siglos XIII al XIX* (Tarragona: 1961). This study of Tarragona also refers to the importance of certain urban spaces.

FIGURE 18.6   Nodes of processional routes visualised on Florez's 1769 map, with 50% transparency over an OpenStreetMap base. Software: Instamaps
IMAGE © SOUNDSPACE

performed year after year in the same way; thus, they must be carefully interrogated through knowledge of the social history of the specific time and place and through cross checking with other sources. A data sheet needs to be drawn up from the documentary database, with the various nodes and the frequency with which these were occupied during the different processions. This accumulated information is then fed into the relevant digital tools [Fig. 18.6].

Figure 18.6 shows all the nodes and processional routes indicated by the archival sources, providing a preliminary visualisation of the density of ceremonial occupation of urban space. It can be noted that the present-day Carrer Major, originally the Roman Via Triumphalis, is the most densely occupied in terms of processions, as shown by the extra thickness of the line marking the route in comparison with that of the other streets. The Carrer de la Nau, with the second thickest line, follows closely on the Carrer Major. The Via Triumphalis was an important nexus during the imperial period of the Roman city of Tarragona, situated in the centre of the forum of the *Tarraconensis* province: straight and wide, it was flanked by the buildings and monuments that represented the power and importance of the city [Fig. 18.7].

During the Roman era, the Via Trumphalis acquired a fundamental role in the social and religious life of the city, and became the main processional route

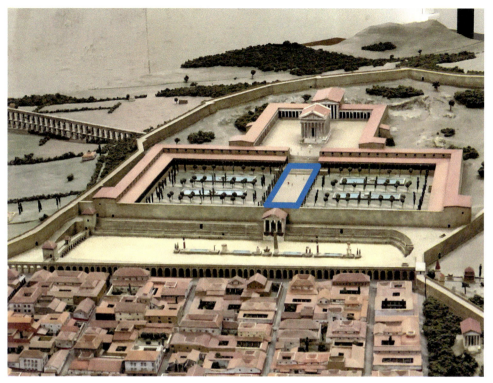

FIGURE 18.7   Via Triumphalis. From a model of the Roman Forum of the Citerior Province in Tarraco
IMAGE © SERGI GONZÁLEZ GONZÁLEZ

for the celebration of victory in war or to honour the gods. Its original route is preserved in that of the Carrer Major today, and it continues to be the space through which many modern-day processions pass. This processional trajectory has, therefore, occupied the same urban space for almost 2000 years.[40]

Georeferencing tools enable the different processions of early modern Tarragona to be grouped together according to five basic routes and the distance between their starting- and end-points to be calculated [Table 18.4].

This identification of the main processional trajectories enables analysis of shared elements of the urban soundscape, elements that might be included, or not, according to the type of processions mounted along each route.

The data sheet now includes the nodal coordinates (XY) derived from the georeferenced data thus facilitating the study of nodal mathematic theory-based studies, and improving the visualisation results. An overall visualisation of the

---

40   For more detailed analysis of the occupation of this space, see: González González, *Evolució del paisatge sonor* 29–33.

TABLE 18.4 The distances of the five main processional routes of post-tridentine Tarragona

Routes	Processions	Distance in metres
1	Candlemas/Litanies 2/Immaculate Conception (morning)	966 m
2	Palm Sunday/Litanies 1	1420 m
3	Holy Burial/Holy Thorn/Silence/Corpus Christi, Assumption of the Virgin/St. Thecla/Immaculate Conception (evening)	547 m
4	Easterday/Litanies 3	201 m
5	Translation of the Arm of St. Thecla	971 m

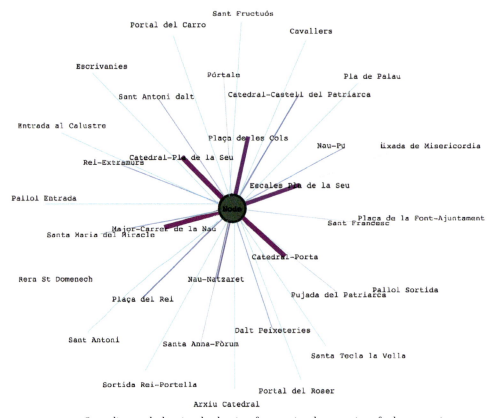

FIGURE 18.8 Centrality graph showing the density of processional occupation of urban space in post-tridentine Tarragona. Source: Gephy
IMAGE © SOUNDSPACE

density of occupancy of urban space resulting from processional activity has been obtained by using GEPHI [Fig. 18.8]. This centrality graph, which objectively confirms the data shown in Figure 18.6, indictes the density of spatial occupation through line thickness and size of the nodes: those nodes furthest from the central point of the graph saw the least processional activity. It is thus possible to link those nodes with the same density of occupation by drawing concentric circles. In this way, georeferencing and data analysis provides a direct visual representation of the relationship between occupation of urban space and the sonic density of the various spatial nodes of the city. It is thus possible to analyse the points in the city through which the greatest amount of processional activity passed and where sound accumulated throughout the year in order to gauge its impact on the urban soundscape.

6   A Bird's Ear Perspective on the Urban Soundscape of Early Modern Tarragona

Confraternities and guilds can be considered acoustic communities in the sense that they form groups of people who produce sound during their daily activities through the agency of external and corporal tools as part of their daily work. They thus contributed to a considerable extent to the urban soundscape with the creation of a wide range of sounds involving hammer blows, spinning-wheels and the tools of carpentry and stone masonry, among many others. These distinctive and characteristic sounds confirmed and projected the identity of each group. This effect was heightened in Tarragona and other cities by the grouping together of guilds by streets, their daily activities thus generating a clear sonic identity in the different quarters of the city; on non-working feast days these sounds disappeared and were replaced by others that had also been heard previously, and probably more sporadically, in the preceding days of preparations.[41] In addition to environmental and natural sounds, keynote sounds heard in urban spaces included people talking, walking and horses being ridden, among many others. Into this category also fell the daily sounds of work, which would mostly go unnoticed by the inhabitants of the city unless some specific and out-of-the-ordinary event occurred, making them more audible and transforming them into sound signals. When a general or patronal feast-day procession took place, the members of confraternities

---

41   González González, *Evolució del paisatge sonor* 175.

and guilds were obliged to cease work and attend the celebrations: to a large extent, the everyday background sound disappeared and the city soundscape was modified.

In addition to serving as a tool for building and negotiating social ties through both conventional and non-conventional behaviour, the urban soundscape functioned as a representation of the city's identity. The sound of the evening bell marked the limits of that city's legal dominance over a territory and had a considerable symbolic significance for the minds of its inhabitants. The mapping of sound networks affords insight into interaction between bodies and structures, and understanding the significance of the soundscape enables the historian to grasp in a more immediate way the complexity of urban life and its meaning for everyday experience.[42] Detailed study of various archival sources can help to reveal the soundscape of the type of processions in which confraternities participated in passive as well as active ways. For the remainder of this chapter, I will set to one side the major processions of Corpus Christi, St. Thecla and the Translation of the Arm of St. Thecla, as well as those associated with Holy Week: the Holy Burial, Holy Thorn and the Silence.[43]

The first alteration to the urban soundscape took place about a week before the procession when the main municipal trumpeter and town crier announced in the customary places, 'with a loud voice and the call of the trumpet' ('llochs acostumats a viva veu i amb so de trompeta') that the streets through which the procession was to pass should be cleaned.[44] Likewise, each confraternity had its own handbell that was rung by its own crier, the *andador*.[45] One of the duties of the *andador* was to announce the confraternity's various activities by calling members to meetings and the celebration of the feast days of its patron saint(s) or communicating important news. However, the municipal town criers and trumpeters were in charge of disseminating the information in the event that the confraternity momentarily lacked an *andador* for whatever reason. This happened in 1602 when the confraternity's chapter determined

---

42 Atkinson, "Seeing sound" 149.
43 On the Corpus Christi procession and those of St. Thecla and the Translation of the Arm of St. Thecla, see: González González, *Evolució del paisatge sonor* 121–124. The penitential nature of Holy Week processions differed significantly from others of a more festive character and their acoustic profile, characterised by wooden rattles instead of bells, together with the sound of chains and flagellation, requires a different analytical approach.
44 The texts of many town cries are found in the *Llibres del Consell de la ciudad de Tarragona* preserved in the Arxiu Històric Municipal de Tarragona.
45 The *andador* received a salary from the confraternity, among other duties, to deliver and collect messages and letters, and organise processions as well as make announcements.

that the town criers would be responsible for gathering them together, even though they would still use the confraternity's bell. Beyond specific individuals, the acoustic community's aural signatures persisted across time:

> Furthermore, we ordain and proclaim that every time and whenever the members of the confraternity are to be invited to attend a chapter meeting, a cry is made with the criers or trumpeters of this city, and the handbell that is used for this purpose, and the crier or trumpeter has to say and name the Confraternity of Nostra Senyora of the dockworkers and stevedores, and not any other name or in any other way.[46]

As can be seen from Table 18.4, the first processional route left from Tarragona Cathedral and went to the church of Santa Maria del Miracle situated outside the walls of the city and built over the ruins of the amphitheatre of the Roman province Hispania Citerior of Tarraco. The three processions that occupied this spatial trajectory were those of Candlemas or Purification of the Virgin, the second day of litanies and the morning procession of the Immaculate Conception. Geoferencing this route has enabled the distance between these two nodes to be calculated as 966 metres, and all three processions went through and returned by the same streets, meaning that its overall length was just under two kilometres [Fig. 18.9].

The processional ritual of the Purification of the Virgin began in darkness in the cathedral, and, with only a single lighted candle, the antiphon *Lumen ad Revelationem* was sung, being repeated three times while further candles were lit. This antiphon framed the singing of the Nunc dimittis (the Song of Simeon), which was followed by the verse *Obtulerunt pro eo par surturum* and the prayer *Exaudi quesumus*.[47] While the departure of the procession was being prepared, the antiphon *Adorna thalamum* was sung, and the confraternal banners were arranged according to the status of each brotherhood. While the procession followed its trajectory, the responsories *Postquam implenti sunt, Optuleruns pro eo* and *Simeon iustus* were sung, and the responses were repeated as necessary, according to its duration ('Responsum acceperat, quotquot fuerint necessaria').

---

46 Arxiu Històric Municipal de Tarragona. Forners. 10 January 1602: 'Item més, sentenciam y pronunciam que tota hora y quant se haurà de tenir y convocar confraria ho capítol, aquella se hage a cridar y convocar per hu dels corredors ho trompetas de la present ciutat, ab la campaneta que ja serveix per axò y lo tal corredor ho trompeta hage de dir y nomenar la confraria de Nostra Señora dels macips de ribera y bastaixos y no ab altre nom ni de altra manera'.

47 Arxiu Històric Arxidiocesà de Tarragona. Ms. 84. Consueta, fol. 81v.

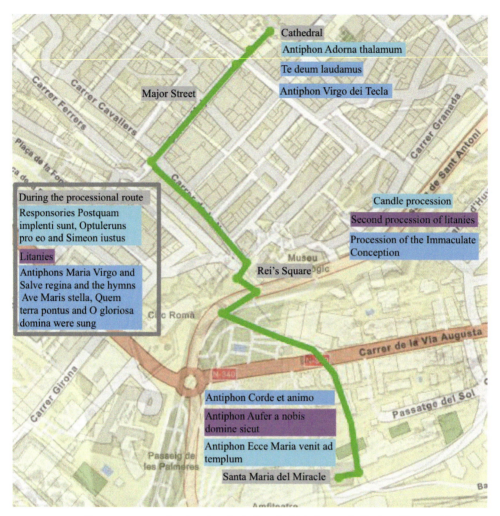

FIGURE 18.9   Tarragona: processional route 1 charted on the historic map by Enrique Florez, with a transparency of 50% over an OpenStreetMap base. Software: ARGIS on line
IMAGE © SOUNDSPACE

Once the procession reached the porch of Santa Maria del Miracle, the antiphon *Ecce Maria venit ad templum* was sung, and a procession was made inside the church before returning to the cathedral.[48]

The three litany processions followed the same liturgico-musical ritual, but with the difference of an antiphon being sung as the processions came out of

---

48   Arxiu Històric Arxidiocesà de Tarragona. Ms. 84. Consueta, fol. 82r.

their corresponding stations made along the route. Regarding the second day of the litany processions, the early fifteenth-century *consueta* specifies:

> Litanies feast-day III [...] regarding both the Mass and the procession, everything takes place as on the preceding day [Litanies feast day II], except that the procession to the church is [celebrated] according to its custom, and on entering [the church], the antiphon *Aufer a nobis domine sicut erit* is to be sung.[49]

The third procession that followed the first processional route was held on the feast day of the Immaculate Conception of the Virgin. Although the dogma of the Immaculate Concpetion was only sanctioned in Tarragona in 1854, the corresponding feast day had been celebrated there from the early sixteenth century, well before the Council of Trent.[50] For that feast day, two processions were held: one in the morning that followed the first processional route; and a second in the afternoon at the hour of Vespers, that followed the third trajectory. The first of these two processions was held once Terce had been sung, and began with the singing of the *Te deum laudamus*. On reaching the church of Santa Maria del Miracle *extramuros*, the antiphon *Corde et animo* was sung, as it was on Christmas Eve but with the variant: 'Corde et animo Christo canamus gloriam pro his sacris solemniis praecelsae Genitricis, de quo gaudit omnis mundus. Alleluia'.[51] On returning to the cathedral, the antiphons *Maria Virgo* and *Salve regina* and the hymns *Ave maris stella*, *Quem terra pontus* and *O gloriosa domina* were sung. Finally, when the procession had returned to the cathedral, the antiphon *Virgo dei Tecla* was sung.

At 1420 metres, the second processional route was the longest in early modern Tarragona and went from the cathedral to the church of St. Fructuosus, also situated outside the city walls where the forum of the Roman city had been located. This church later became a Capuchin monastery. As in the case of the first processional route, it returned the same way, and was thus 2.84 kilometres in overall length [Fig. 18.10].

---

49 Arxiu Històric Arxidiocesà de Tarragona. Ms. 84. Consueta, fol. 41r: 'Feria III letaniarum [...] omnia tam de missis quam de processione Omnia fiant sicut precedenti die continetur [Feria II letaniarum]. Excepto quod processio est ad aliam ecclesiam ut moris est eiusmodi in qua intrando dicantur illa antifona *Aufer a nobis domine sicut erit*'. The later *consueta* of 1656 modifies the antiphon to be sung by the succentor to *Maria succurre* (without Alleluia): Arxiu Capitular de la Catedral de Tarragona. Consueta 1656: 'Lunes de letanías'.

50 Tomás Ávila, *El culto y la liturgia*; and Munté Vilá J. – Tomás Ávila A., *Tarragona la tesis Concepcionista* (Tarragona: 1957).

51 Arxiu Històric Arxidiocesà de Tarragona. *Processionale Tarraconense* (1568) fol. 291.

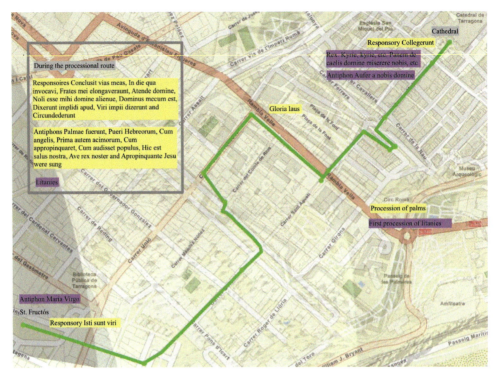

FIGURE 18.10   Tarragona: processional route 2 charted on the historic map by Enrique Florez, with a transparency of 50% over an OpenStreetMap base. Software: ARGIS on line
IMAGE © SOUNDSPACE

The two processions that followed this second route and occupied it spatially were: Palm Sunday and the first day of litanies. The Palm Sunday procession also left the cathedral after Terce, and the responsories *Conclusit vias meas, In die qua invocavi, Frates mei elongaverant, Attende domine, Noli esse mihi domine alienus Dominus mecum est, Dixerunt impii apud se, Viri impii dixerunt* and *Circundederunt* were sung, without the doxology. When the procession reached St. Fructuosus, the last responsory was *Isti sunt viri*.[52] On returning to the cathedral, and following the blessing of the palms, the antiphons *Palmae fuerunt, Pueri Hebreorum, Cum angelis, Prima autem acimorum, Cum appropinquaret, Cum audisset populus, Hic est salus nostra, Ave rex noster* and *Appropinquante Jesu* were sung. As the procession returned, the gate in the city walls through which it had to pass was closed; as it opened, from on

---

52   Arxiu Històric Arxidiocesà de Tarragona. *Processionale Tarraconense* (1568), fol. 71v.

top of a nearby tower the *Gloria laus* was sung by the cathedral choirboys in a clear emulation of angel voices. The inhabitants of Tarragona would have looked upwards to locate the sound source and so would have raised their eyes to heaven. Once at the door of the cathedral, from an iron lectern placed on a carpet, the responsory *Collegerunt* was sung, and then the entry was made into the cathedral in silence.[53]

As regards the first day of litanies, the fifteenth-century *consueta* indicates:

> Litanies feast day II [...] then the two chaplains ministering in the choir are ready in the middle of the choir to begin the litanies and go singing *Rex. Kyrie, kyrie*, etc. *Panem de caelis domine miserere nobis*, etc. With the cross and candles at the head of the procession, the litanies are sung as it moves to the main doors of the church where the procession should exit or enter, and the antiphon *Aufer a nobis domine*, etc. is sung. [...] When Mass is finished, the singers begin the antiphon *Maria Virgo*, and the other [antiphons] appropriate to the litany.[54]

This processional route, the third to depart from and return to the cathedral, was circular so that it passed through each urban space only once. It was not a particularly long itinerary at only 547 metres, but it is clear that the processions of the cycles of Holy Week, Corpus Christi and St. Thecla also took this route. The other two processions were Marian: that of the Assumption of the Virgin and of the Immaculate Conception held in the afternoon [Fig. 18.11].

Two references are found to the music to be sung in the procession on the feast of the Assumption: the first indicates that the singers were placed beside the prostrate image of the Virgin, as if they were apostles, lending a strong paratheatrical element:

---

53   Arxiu Històric Arxidiocesà de Tarragona. *Processionale Tarraconense* (1568), fol. 85v.
54   Arxiu Històric Arxidiocesà de Tarragona. Ms. 84. Consueta, fol. 40v: 'Feria II letaniarum [...] tunc duo capellani illi qui chorum ministrant sint in medio chori preparati et letaniam incipient et per viam dicant *Rex Kirie Kirie*. Etcetera. *Panem de celis domine miserere nobis* etcetera. Precedente cruce et ceroferariis ad processionem hiis qui letaniam dicunt in medio processionis ambulantibus cumque ad ianuas ecclesiae ubi processio debet venire seu ire incipient hanc antifonam *Aufer a nobis domine* etcetera. [...] Que missa finita cantores incipiant an. Maria Virgo et de ceteris aliis seu recitentur letaniam'. As in the case of the second day of litanies, a variant is found in the later *consueta* of 1656 as regards the antiphon to be sung: *Martirs tempore paschali*, probably in commemoration of the martyrdom of St. Fructuosus, St. Eulogius and St. Augurius that took place in the roman amphitheatre 259 CE: Arxiu Capitular de la Catedral de Tarragona. Consueta 1656. 'Lunes de letanías'.

FIGURE 18.11   Tarragona: processional route 3 charted on the historic map by Enrique Florez, with a transparency of 50% over an OpenStreetMap base. Software: ARGIS on line
IMAGE © SOUNDSPACE

The same day, after vespers, a procession was made around the city, in which the image of the Blessed Virgin Mary was carried, and the psalm *In exitu Israel* was sung [fol. CXII], in alternatim, with the singers representing the apostles: they did not make a station at the main altar.[55]

---

55   Arxiu Històric Arxidiocesà de Tarragona. *Processionale Tarraconense* (156), fol. 282v: 'Eodem die post vesperas fit processio per civitatem, et in ea portatur imago beate Mariae virginis, et cantatur psalmus In exitu Israel, fo. CXII. Alternatim a Choro, et cantoribus Apostolos representantes: non fit statio ad altare maius'.

POST-TRIDENTINE CONFRATERNITIES AND PROCESSIONS IN TARRAGONA   501

FIGURE 18.12   Tarragona: processional route 4 charted on the historic map by Enrique Florez, with a transparency of 50% on an OpenStreetMap base. Software: ARGIS on line
IMAGE © SOUNDSPACE

The second indication to music makes reference to the singing of the *Te Deum laudamus* before the procession began.[56]

The second procession to follow this third route was that of the Immaculate Conception held after Vespers which took place within the city walls. According to the *consueta* of 1656:

> after Compline, a procession [is held] through the city with the figure of Our Lady, and the fifteen mysteries, with copes, and with the *Te Deum laudamus* being sung in polyphony.[57]

From the minutes of the city council dated 8 December 1610, it is clear that all the city's confraternities were asked to march in the procession with their

---

56   Arxiu Capitular de la Catedral de Tarragona. *Consueta* 1656: 15 August.
57   Arxiu Capitular de la Catedral de Tarragona. *Consueta* 1656: 8 December: '[…] després de Completas proffesso per ciutat ab la figura de Na. Sra. Y los quince misteris, professó de capes, cantes lo te Deum laudeamus a cant d'orgue […]'.

banners, while those living along the processional route were reminded to clean the streets that the procession would pass through. This procession was characterised by the soundmark of three salvos sounded from the bulwarks of St. Anthony and St. Clare.[58]

The fourth processional route considered here was the shortest, the trajectory being of only 201 metres from the cathedral to the Church of Santa Tecla 'la Vella'; it returned the same way to total about 400 metres. This route was followed by the Easter Day procession and that of the third day of litanies; it left the cathedral by the main door to go to the Church of Santa Tecla 'la Vella' [Fig. 18.12]. The Easterday procession was very short and few musical indications are found, while the third day of litanies was celebrated as for the second day ('Feria IIII letaniarum [...] fieri debet sicut continetur latius feria II').[59]

7 Conclusions

This bird's ear perspective of the soundscape of Tarragona can be studied in greater detail by analysing more closely the different characteristic acoustic properties of each of the processions, a study that goes beyond the limits of this succinct chapter. Even so, these preliminary observations on the occupation of processional space in Tarragona highlight the need to research more deeply the social and devotional aspects behind the different soundmarks of the acoustic community in a way that, over time, came to form part of its sonic DNA. It is necessary to break down, disentangle and analyse closely all the parameters that might affect the urban soundscape, then to bring them back together better to understand a society that lived so directly involved in the various sounds which characterised its daily life and that permeated its everyday activities.

Urban rituals and spatial occupation are also influenced by historical continuity. Three of the four processional routes analysed in this essay pass along the present-day Carrer Major, also known as the *Via Triumphalis* in Roman times, which has long been a venue for important celebrations. Similarly, processions typically pass through or come to an end at emblematic spots within the city. For instance, three of the processional routes went past the Plaça del Rei, where the king resided when he was in Tarragona. It should be noted that processional circuits 1 and 2 had as their final stops two emblematic locations that also date back to the ancient city of Tarraco: the Monastery of Santa Maria del

---

58 Arxiu Històric Municipal de Tarragona. *Llibre del Consulat* 1609–1610, fol. 40r.
59 Arxiu Històric Arxidiocesà de Tarragona. Ms. 84. *Consueta*, fol. 41r. The 1656 *Consueta* offers no further information as regards the sonic dimension of these processions.

Mar, which is situated in the city's ancient amphitheatre, and the Monastery of St. Fructuosus, which is located in its ancient forum. It is clear that despite population changes in terms of social and religious beliefs, emblematic locations and spaces are still preserved over the passage of time.

As a result of this use of urban space, acoustic density resulting from processional activity was built up. The guild confraternities contributed to the auditory experience according to whether their daily activities were heard, or not heard, during specific processional rituals. In early modern Tarragona, since all the confraternities, whether open or closed in nature (that is, with either voluntary or conjoined members) were connected to guilds, it meant that on the days when general procession were held, their work activities ceased. This sonic transformation on procession days would have had a considerable impact on the overall urban soundscape so that what could be heard during a typical workday was completely different from what was audible on a day when all confraternity members took part in a procession. Certain keynote sounds would not have been heard, while others would have been transformed into sound signals and a range of soundmarks would have come to the fore. Thus, the change in the different types of sounds confraternities brought to the city resulted in a new way of hearing both their contribution to the processional soundscape and of hearing the city as a whole.

Within the digital humanities, digital cartography and techniques of georeferencing are opening up new frontiers for historical research into the dynamic relationship between sound and space in the urban context and into the paradigms that can be considered from new perspectives within a multidisciplinary framework.

Bibliography

Primary Sources

Barber Joseph, *Relació verdadera de la translació del Bras de la Gloriosa Verge e Invicta Protohomartyr Santa Thecla, deixebla del Apostol Sant Pau y patrona de la Ciutat, è Iglesia Metropolitana de Tarragona, Primada de las Espanyas; desde Armenia à dita Ciutat* (Tarragona [Joseph Barber]: 1746).

Florez Enrique, "Antiguedades Tarraconenses" in *España Sagrada*, vol. XXIV (Madrid, Antonio Marin: 1769).

Secondary Sources

Arts Roca E., *Els carrers dels menestrals a la Tarragona Vella*, (Tarragona: 1995).

Atkinson N., "Seeing sound", in Terpstra N. – Rose C. (eds.), *Mapping Space, Sense, and Movement in Florence. Historical GIS and the Early Modern City* (New York: 2016) 149–168.

Bastian M. et al., "Gephi: An Open Source Software for Exploring and Manipulating Networks", *Proceedings of the International AAAI Conference on Web and Social Media* 3.1 (2009) 361–362.

Benítez Bolorinos M., *Las cofradías medievales en el reino de Valencia (1329–1458)* (Alicante: 1998).

Bertran Luengo J., *El mestratge de la Sang de Tarragona: Història d'una confraria. 1545–2020* (Valls: 2020).

González González S., *Evolució del paisatge sonor del seguici festiu de la festa major de Santa Tecla a Tarragona* (Ph.D. dissertation, Universitat Autònoma de Barcelona: 2019).

González González S., "Paying Homage: The Participation of Guild Confraternities in Archiepiscopal Entries into Tarragona", *Confraternitas* 31.2 (2020) 36–62.

Harley J.B., "Deconstructing the Map", *Cartographica: The International Journal for Geographic Information and Geovisualization* 26.2 (1989) 1–20.

Kamen H., *Cambio cultural en la Sociedad del Siglo de Oro. Cataluña y Castilla, siglos XIVI–XVII* (Madrid: 1998).

Munté Vilá J. – Tomás Ávila A., *Tarragona la tesis Concepcionista* (Tarragona: 1957).

Richardson J.S., "Geographical Information Systems and Historical Research: Current Progress and Future Directions", *Journal of Interdisciplinary History* 45.1 (2014) 1–18.

Rose C., "Thinking and Using DECIMA", in Terpstra N. – Rose C. (eds.), *Mapping Space, Sense, and Movement in Florence. Historical GIS and the Early Modern City* (New York: 2016) 15–32.

Rovira S., *L'Edat Moderna a Tarragona: una època de contrastos* (Lleida: 2011).

Presner T. – Shepard D., "Mapping the Geospatial Turn", in Schreiban S. et al. (eds.), *A New Companion to Digital Humanities* (New Jersey: 2016).

Salvat Bové J., *Tarragona Antigua y moderna a través de su nomenclatura urbana: siglos XIII al XIX* (Tarragona: 1961).

Schafer R.M, *The Soundscape: Our Sonic Environment and the Tuning of the World* (Rochester: 1994).

Schreiban S. et al. (eds.), *A Companion to Digital Humanities.* (New Jersey: 2004).

Schreiban S. et al. (eds.), *A New Companion to Digital Humanities* (New Jersey: 2016).

Sterne J. (ed.), *The Sound Studies Reader* (New York: 2012).

Terpstra N., *Lay Confraternities and Civic Religion in Renaissance Bologna* (Cambridge – New York: 1995).

Terpstra N., "Introduction", in Terpstra N. – Rose C. (eds.), *Mapping Space, Sense, and Movement in Florence. Historical GIS and the Early Modern City* (New York: 2016) 1–12.

Terpstra N. – Rose C. (eds.), *Mapping Space, Sense, and Movement in Florence. Historical GIS and the Early Modern City* (New York: 2016).

Terrado Ortuño P., "Tarragona en el siglo XVII a través de la cartografia: un plano inédito de la ciudad procedente la Colección de Anville en la Biblioteca Nacional de Francia", *Manuscrits. Revista d'Història Moderna* 36 (2017) 57–84.

Tomás Ávila A., *El culto y la liturgia en la catedral de Tarragona (1300–1700)* (Tarragona: 1963).

Truax B., *Acoustic Communication* (Westport: 2001).

CHAPTER 19

Burying the Bones: Mapping the Sounds and Spaces of the Confraternity of the *Verge Maria dels Desamparats* in Early Modern Barcelona

Tess Knighton

Abstract

In Barcelona, two confraternities were primarily involved in the ceremonial mounted for the taking of the condemned to the scaffold outside the city walls and the retrieving of the bones of the dead that accumulated there for Christian burial in the parish church of Santa Maria del Pi: that of the Verge Maria dels Desamparats and that of the Purissima Sang de Nostre Senyor Jesucrist. From different points in the sixteenth century both were based at Santa Maria del Pi, being for a time united as one foundation. Their overlapping histories meant that their responsibilities varied over time, but essentially the Confraternity of the Purissima Sang took care of the spiritual and physical needs of the condemned until the execution had taken place, while the Desamparats was charged with the collection of the bones and their burial. The Purissima Sang nevertheless continued to have an important role in the procession from the Gate of St. Anthony to the parish church, even though this was organised by the Desamparats. This procession included confraternity members bearing torches and images of the Virgin and the Crucified Christ, and its itinerary was articulated by a range of sounds from bells and cries to plainchant and polyphonic singing. The boxes of bones, having been taken into the church and placed on a trestle, remained in the church overnight, watched over by members of the confraternity and clergy, until the following day a solemn Requiem Mass was celebrated and they were taken to be buried in a specified corner of the church cemetery. The trajectory followed by the cortège varied over time, being extended to take in more of the significant urban spaces or varied to accommodate special circumstances. The event presents a good example of how sound and music were used to communicate information about the progress of the ceremonial and to solemnify and enhance its meaning.

Keywords

confraternities – processions – burial ceremonies – sound studies – acoustic community

Among the charitable acts carried out by lay confraternities in the late medieval and early modern periods, those of bringing comfort to the condemned to death, accompanying them to the scaffold and taking care of the burial of their remains formed part of their more public obligations. The sombre and redemptive nature of these duties meant that they were often associated with penitential confraternities, such as those relating to the blood and wounds of Christ, thus deliberately emphasising their salvific function: contemplation of Christ's suffering on the Cross and the promise of salvation helped to comfort the condemned as they were taken to the scaffold and executed. As Kathleen Falvey has written with regard to early modern Italy: 'many [...] were penitential confraternities and their devotion to Christ's Passion took on a participatory quality that influenced their delicate mission to those facing the shame and terror of public execution'.[1] The theatrical nature of the ritual that developed around executions meant that the confraternities' involvement in the public spectacle and their work with the prisoners contributed to 'the eternal drama of salvation'.[2] This drama was played out through solemn processions, both to the scaffold, which in some places was within the city walls and in others without, and for the burial of the remains, or, at a later date, the bones that accumulated near to the location of execution. According to Nicholas Terpstra, the staging of these processions had a 'didactic, cathartic and compensatory' function, not only in that justice was seen to be done, but also, if the confraternities were successful in bringing comfort through the promise of salvation, in that the condemned person could participate in a good death and be promised a Christian burial that would ease his or her path through purgatory. The involvement of the confraternity 'guaranteed a ritual burial of the body, and the prayers and Masses to intercede for the soul'.[3] This essay analyses the sounds and spaces that characterised these rituals in early modern Barcelona to assess their intersensorial and emotional impact on the acoustic community of those who were involved, whether actively or passively, through the communication of a message of justice, repentance and salvation.

---

[1] Falvey K., "Scaffold and Stage: Comforting Rituals and Dramatic Traditions in Late Medieval and Renaissance Italy", in Terpstra N. (ed.), *The Art of Executing Well: Rituals of Execution in Renaissance Italy*, Early Modern Studies 1 (Kirksville MIS: 2008) 13–30, here 13. See also Terpstra N., "Confraternities and Capital Punishment: Charity, Culture, and Civic Religion in the Communal and Confessional Age", in Eisenbichler K. (ed.), *A Companion to Medieval and Early Modern Confraternities* (Leiden – Boston: 2019) 212–231.

[2] Terpstra N., "Introduction: The Other Side of the Scaffold", in Terpstra (ed.), *The Art of Executing Well* 1–5, here 5.

[3] Prospero M., "Consolation or Condemnation. The Debates on Withholding Sacraments from Prisoners", in Terpstra (ed.), *The Art of Executing Well* 98–117, here 102.

1   The Ritual of Earthly Justice, Burial and Salvation in Early
         Modern Barcelona

In 1536 a joint confraternity was founded in Barcelona to fulfil both the charitable and ritual aspects relating to the salvation of those condemned to death, with an all-in-one service provided by a double avocation: the Confraternity of the Puríssima Sang de Nostre Senyor Jesucrist ('Most Pure Blood of Our Lord Jesus Christ'), to comfort and accompany the condemned (*sententiats*); and the Confraternity of the Verge Maria dels Desamparats ('Virgin Mary of the Unprotected') to collect and give Christian burial to the bones of those hanged on the scaffold in the cemetery of the church of Santa Maria del Pi. The related rituals resulted in two major public processions that the confraternities used, in Nicolas Terpstra's words, 'to insert themselves as central agents in both the drama of salvation and the sanctification of urban life and space'.[4] The sparse extant documentation makes it difficult to disentangle the history of these two confraternities, but their complementary – and, at times, overlapping – roles in the realisation of these public rituals and spectacles were key to the sense of Christian reconciliation within the community, begun by the procession to the scaffold, and completed by burial of the remains of those who were executed.[5] These two processions were, according to Terpstra, 'key ritual for brotherhoods whose own profile had long rested largely on the many processions with which they commemorated saints' days, public feasts, and memorials in the brotherhood'.[6]

It is thought that both confraternities had existed separately in the city before their apparent amalgamation in 1536. The Confraternity of the Purisima Sang is believed to have been founded in 1341 at the chapel of the Peu de la Creu, located in the parish of Santa Maria del Pi, near the Portal de San Antoni.[7] They later relocated to the parish church. The origins of the Confraternity of the Desamparats remain unclear: it has been suggested that what was originally a female congregation of the 'unprotected' existed in around 1400, based at the

---

4   Terpstra, "Confraternities and Capital Punishment" 225.
5   For the situation in Valencia, see: Catalá Sanz J.A. – Pérez García P., "La pena capital en Valencia (1450–1500): Cifras, espacios urbanos y ritualidades funerarias de la Cofradía de Inocentes y Desemperados", *Revista de Historia Moderna* 39 (2021) 272–334, here 303.
6   Terpstra N., "Body Politics: The Criminal Body between Public and Private", *Journal of Medieval and Early Modern Studies* 45.1 (2015) 7–52, here 20.
7   Garrut J.M., *Notas históricas de la Real e ilustre archicofradía de la Purísima Sangre de Nuestro Señor Jesucristo* (Barcelona: 1962) 1.

Capella del Calvari in the cemetery of Montjuic.[8] It is not known whether a fully-fledged Confraternity of the Desamparats existed before, over a century later, Isabel de Josa (1490–1564), abbess of the Dominican convent established by that time at the Peu de la Creu, reached an agreement with the two confraternities, and statutes were approved in 1536 by the Bishop of Barcelona, Joan de Cardona (r. 1531–1546) with the double advocation.[9] In the foundation of the double confraternity, she was joined by other eminent figures from the city: don Enric Sentelles, Knight of the Order of Santiago; an honoured citizen, Bernat Montagut;[10] and the Valencian Gaspar Garro, then resident in Barcelona. The highly educated noblewoman Isabel de Josa, who was known for her erudition and preaching ability,[11] had met St. Ignatius de Loyola when

---

8   Martin Nicolás V., "Isabel de Josa, el impulso femenino en la fundación de la 'Confraria de la Sang' de Barcelona (1536)", in Gallego Franco H. – García del Herrero M. del C. (eds.), *Autoridad, poder e influencia: mujeres que hacen Historia* (Barcelona: 2017), vol. 2, 635–649. Saéz García M.A., *Creure, somiar, lluitar: Barcelona en femení* 1: *L'aventura spiritual d'Isabel de Josa (1490–1564)* (Ph.D. dissertation, Universitat Autònoma de Barcelona: 2018) 251. See: *Real e Ilustre Cofradía de la Virgen de los Desemparados cuya imagen se venera en el altar de su misma invocación en la iglesia parroquial de Santa María de los Reyes, o del Pino* (Barcelona: 1923) 9–10. Saéz García has suggested that the original congregation may have been related to the group of sor Sança formed in 1368 with the aim of collecting abandoned bodies and the bones of those condemned to death for Christian burial.

9   Saéz García, *Creure, somiar, lluitar* 244–254. In her Master's thesis, Saéz García reproduces the opening paragraph of the 1536 statutes, but admits that she has been unable to locate the original document which was last seen in the Arxiu particular de la Presidència de l'Audiència de Barcelona in 1922: 'En virtut de l'autoritat y decret del Rmo. Señor bisbe, e.º de Barcelona don Joan de Cardona y de son Vicari general y oficial, micer Antoni Pintor; Canonge de la Seu de Barcelona, la señora dona Ysabel de Josa les hores Abbadessa del Monestir del peu de la creu de la present Ciutat de barcelona e don Enric de Sentelles, cavaller de l'orde de Santiago, e Gaspar Garro natural de la Ciutat de Valencia habitant en Barcelona y Benet Montagut ciutedà de Barcelona, en lo any MDXXXVI instituïren y ordenaren de consentiment de dit Rmo. Señor Bisbe de Barcelona les ordinacions y capitols següents ab potestat y llibertat dada al prior y maiorals o promens de la Sacratissima Sanch de nre Señor deu Jesucrist y de la Verge Maria dels desamparats de poder aiustar y declarar altres ordinations que ben vist serà tota utilitat y profit y augment de dita Confraria …'. Cited in Saéz García M.A., "Isabel de Josa. Una insòlita dona catalana del segle XVI" (Master's thesis, Universitat Autònoma de Barcelona: 2015) 40, from Creixell J., *San Ignacio. Estudio crítico y documentada de los hechos Ignacianos relacionados con Montserrat, Manresa y Barcelona* (Barcelona: 1922) 294. This paragraph is included, with some differences, in the 1564 copy of the statutes of the Confraternity of the Purissima Sang now held in the Arxiu Històric de la Ciutat de Barcelona. Gremis Especials. Cofradía de la Purissima Sang 2B 20/2 unfoliated.

10 On this social rank, see Amelang J.S., *Honored Citizens of Barcelona: Patrician Culture and Class Relations, 1490–1714* (Princeton NJ: 1986).

11 Saéz García, *Creure, somiar, lluitar* 252–253. In his *Varia historia de Sanctas e Illlustres monges en todo género de virtudes* (1583), Juan Pérez de Moya describes Isabel de Josa's

he visited Barcelona in the 1520s, and later, in 1543 travelled to Rome with the aim of setting up a female branch of the Jesuits [Fig. 19.1]. This venture failed, but she remained in Italy to further the work with unprotected women and orphans she had already begun in Barcelona. Shortly before she moved to Rome, Isabel de Josa had asked the vicar general to ratify the double advocation so that the confraternity could continue at the church of the Peu de la Creu and receive alms there in her absence, but as she did not return to Barcelona this arrangement seems not to have endured.[12]

The inclusion of a Valencian among the founders of the Confraternities of the Purisima Sang and the Desamparats in Barcelona was probably not coincidental; according to María Ángeles Saez García, a brotherhood with the advocation of the Holy Blood had been formalised in Valencia the previous year on 15 March 1535,[13] while a Confraternity of Nuestra Señora de los Inocentes y Desamparados ('Our Lady of the Innocents and the Unprotected') had been established in that city considerably earlier in 1414.[14] The confraternity of double advocation in Barcelona shared the same patron saint, St. Matthias, as the Confraternity of Inocentes y Desamparados in Valencia, specified the same number of members at the time of its foundation, and aimed to comfort the condemned to death and retrieve and bury the bones of those executed on the scaffold.[15] These pious aims and charitable acts were of particular interest to Abbess Josa and featured in the statutes of the confraternity of double advocation she helped to found in Barcelona in 1536 which gave greater coherence and prestige to the confraternities. The division of duties between them – the comforting of the condemned in prison and the collection of the bones that accumulated at the scaffold – appear to have remained complementary, overlapping but not merging completely. It would also appear that the two confraternities did not share the same base in the parish church of Santa Maria del Pi until considerably later in the sixteenth century. At that time, separate statutes

---

preaching activities: 'Fue docta en Sagrada Scriptura. Predicaba sentada en una silla en una iglesia de Barcelona (que dizen el pie de la cruz) sermones de gran doctrina que edificava a muchos que la seguían'.

12   Saéz García, *Creure, somiar, lluitar* 252.
13   Saéz García, *Creure, somiar, lluitar* 251.
14   Catalá Sanz – Pérez García, "La pena capital en Valencia" 274; and Pérez García P., "Espacio, rito, devoción y memoria: la cofradía de Inocentes y Desamparados de Valencia (1450–1512)", in *Hommage au professeur Anita González-Raymond* (Montpellier: forthcoming). See also: Aparicio Olmos E.M., *Santa Maria de Inocentes y Desamparados en su iconografia original y sus precedentes históricos* (Valencia: 1968).
15   Catalá Sanz – Pérez García, "La pena capital en Valencia" 300, 302.

CONFRATERNITY OF THE *VERGE MARIA DELS DESAMPARATS* IN BARCELONA 511

FIGURE 19.1 Anonymous, Portait of Isabel de Josa (1490–1564). Located in the meeting room of the town hall of Vercelli. The inscription reads: VEN: ISABELLA LOSA DE CARDONA NAT: HISP: / COLLEG. FVNDATRIX OBIIT V: MARTIR: MDLCXIV / AETATIS SUAE LXXV
IMAGE © WIKIMEDIA COMMONS

were drawn up for each confraternity which reveal that while they continued to share some obligations and ceremonial activities, they also developed their own devotions and to contribute in different ways to the soundscape of the city.

2   The Confraternity of the Purissima Sang of Jesus Christ

It is likely that the Confraternity of the Purissima Sang remained at the convent at the Peu de la Creu until 1545, when it transferred to the parish church of Santa Maria del Pi.[16] From that time onwards, the confraternity continued to gain in prestige, receiving a number of papal indulgences (notably from Pope Clement VIII in 1593) and eventually being made an Archconfraternity in 1664.[17] On 17 February 1547 an agreement was drawn up between church and *prohomens* (foremen of the confraternity) in which the brotherhood was given the right to keep their vestments and ornaments in the chapter room of the church, to be buried in the tomb in the same *sala capitular* and to hold their meetings there.[18] In addition to the liturgical ceremonies and devotional events promoted by the Confraternity of the Purissima Sang, the agreement drawn up with the church of Santa Maria del Pi in 1547 specified its participation in the procession that was held on the feast day of St. Matthias (24 February), when the clergy went to the Creu cuberta ('Covered Cross') to collect the bones of those hanged on the scaffold.[19] Presumably it had been involved in this activity since at least 1536, but this penitential confraternity also took the lead in the Maundy Thursday procession in which they flagellated; the church agreed to bless their scourges before the procession.[20] The ceremonial of the Maundy

---

16   Saéz García, *Creure, somiar, lluitar* 246.
17   Arxiu Parroquial de Santa Maria del Pi. Caixa C200. Cofradia de la Purissima Sang de Jesu Christ. Batlle J., *Arxiconfraria de la Sang: notes històriques* [unpublished typescript].
18   Arxiu Parroquial de Santa Maria del Pi. Caixa C165-2: "Concordia entre la confraria de la Sanch de Jesuchrist R[ecto]r y obrers en poder de Francesch Marti notari public de Barcelona".
19   Arxiu Parroquial de Santa Maria del Pi. Cofradia de la Purissima Sang de Jesu Christ C165-2: 'Item es concordat entre les dits parts per pacte entre ells convingut que en lo dia de sanct [Matias] quant lo clero de dita sglesia aniran a la creu cuberta per portar la ossa dels sentenciats en dita sglesia dits promens he confrares de dita confraria i ab lluminaries salvo que en lo dit dia promens e confrares puguen anar devant la creu de dit clero ab lo crucifix de dita confraria e ab lluminaria'.
20   A Brotherhood of the Blood of Christ (*Hermandad de la Sangre de Cristo*) was formally established at the Augustinian monastery in Saragossa in 1554; it also held a procession with flagellation on Maundy Thursday, and took as one of its obligations to give spiritual

Thursday procession also included a mystery play of the Scourging of Christ which the confraternity mounted from at least 1592, with the figure of Christ bound to the column with two Jewish figures, one on either side ('un misteri del Açotament per anar a la processo en lo dijous sant y que la figura de Crist estigues lligat en vna columna ab dos juheus vn a cada part').[21] An inventory of the confraternity's possessions dated 1594 mentions a mystery play of the Pietà ('lo misteri de la Pietat') as well as that of the *Açotament*, and lists the forty-four black robes and eighty-five white robes for Maundy Thursday, as well as the 'Cristo gran', with its various accoutrements, and, significantly, the four robes and two hoods needed for its participation in the procession of the bones ('quatre vestes de sentenciats y dues capes').[22]

The prominent participation of the Confraternity of the Purissima Sang in both Holy Week and its duties in the ceremonial of the bones is confirmed by a copy of its *Ordinacions* or statutes dated 28 March 1564 (which makes reference to those of 1536) drawn up while it was temporarily based at the Franciscan church.[23] The confraternity had transferred their headquarters there following disagreements with the church of Santa Maria del Pi in 1561; these were only resolved in 1572. The 1564 document still makes mention of the double avocation involving the Confraternity of the Desamparats, but its focus is on that of the Purissima Sang, only making reference to its particular feasts, such as the singing of Mass ('un offici cantat') on the Feasts of the Holy Cross on 7 May (*Ordinacion* 32) and 14 September (*Ordinacion* 19), when a sermon was also preached and Vespers and Compline were celebrated liturgically. On both of these more festive occasions, the confraternity's chapel was to be decorated

---

comfort to the condemned in prison; see: Gómez Urdóñez J.L., *La Hermandad de la Sangre de Cristo de Zaragoza. Caridad y ritual religioso en la ejecución de la pena de muerte* (Saragossa: 1978) 10–12. Arxiu Parroquial de Santa Maria del Pi. Cofradia de la Purissima Sang de Jesu Christ C200 Batlle J.B., *Arxiconfraria de la Sang: notes històriques* [unpublished typescript].

21 Arxiu Parroquial de Santa Maria del Pi. Caixa C200. Cofradia de la Purissima Sang de Jesu Christ. Batlle, *Arxiconfraria de la Sang: notes històriques*.

22 Arxiu Parroquial de Santa Maria del Pi. Caixa C200. Cofradia de la Purissima Sang de Jesu Christ Batlle, *Arxiconfraria de la Sang: notes històriques*: "Inventari rebut per Francesc Clos, Pere Font, Joan Arquer y Joan Xarles promens lany present de 1594 dels promens del any pasat Pere Massons, Marti Riera, Pau Vicens y Hieronim Berenguer dels bens se son trobats en dita confraria". The 'Cristo gran' had been commissioned from the sculptor Jerónimo Xanxó in October 1545, according to Gurrut, *Real e ilustre archicofradia* [1]. During the sixteenth century it became one of the key symbols in penitential prcoessions held in Barcelona.

23 Arxiu Històric de la Ciutat de Barcelona. Gremis Especials. Cofradía de la Purissima Sang 2B 20/2.

with branches, and the choir of the Franciscan church with laurel and the smaller of the confraternity's crucifixes.[24] This statute, with its reference to the guardian and friars of the order, confirms that the 1564 copy of the confraternity's statutes was drawn up while it was resident in the Franciscan friary. As will be discussed below, it was precisely during this period of absence of the Confraternity of the Puríssima Sang that the Confraternity of the Desamparats drew up its own agreement with Santa Maria de Pi.

The 1564 statutes of the Puríssima Sang provide more details on the Maundy Thursday ceremonial, which included the preaching of a sermon on the theme of the precious blood and body of Christ at the main Mass (*Ordinacion* 28). The procession was to leave at 7PM and be attended by those who wished to flagellate as well as those who wanted to attend out of devotion; all members, men and women, should go to the chapel between 6PM and 7PM to make their preparations (*Ordinacions* 25 and 30).[25] For the flagellants, robes and scourges were supplied, and their wounds were attended to after the procession, while the devout were given a white robe and a lighted torch to carry (*Ordinacions* 27 and 29). Those who did not attend would have to pay for wax or say five *Pater nosters* and five *Ave Marias* in honour of the five wounds of Christ (*Ordinacion* 30). The confraternity's move to the Franciscan friary necessitated a change to the route of their Maundy Thursday procession which is outlined in a document dated five years later, on 11 September 1569. This stipulated that the confraternity would leave the friary between 7PM and 8PM and visit the cathedral and a select number of the parish and convent churches of the city.[26] The procession

---

24   Arxiu Històric de la Ciutat de Barcelona. Gremis Especials. Cofradía de la Puríssima Sang 2B 20/2. Statute 19: 'hagen de empaliar tota la capella de dins y de fora y enrramar aquella y posen el llorer en lo cor de la sglesia mayor ab vna creu all cap de dit llorer y se fassen vespres y completes en lo altar maior de dita sglesia hont es o sera temps dita capella y acaben dites vespres en la capella de dita confraria y paguen per charitat segons es capitulat entre dits confrares y frares qui vuy son y en lo altar maior hagen de posar lo crucifixi petit hont cremen quatre ciris per dites vespres y completes y lo dia de la festa mentres lo ofici y sermo se fara'.

25   Arxiu Històric de la Ciutat de Barcelona. Gremis Especials. Cofradía de la Puríssima Sang 2B 20/2 fol. 10v: 'Item ordenaren que lo dijous sanct tots los confrares y confraresses se apleguen en la capella de la dita confraria entre les sis y set hores de vespre y de alli partesquen en dita professo y aquella acompanyen fins dita professo sia tornada en dita capella'.

26   Arxiu Històric de la Ciutat de Barcelona. Gremis Especials. Cofradía de la Puríssima Sang 2B 20/2 fol. 15v: 'aia de fer la present volta ço es que partesca de S. Francesc entre les set y vuyt hores de vespre y vaia a Sta Maria de la Mar a S. Agosti a St Catherina deuant S. Joan a las Magdalenas a Jonqueres a S. Anna a Montision al Pi a la seu al Palau el Rey a St Just a S. Jaume a S Miquel a la merce y a S. Francesch y que esta volta se fasse per los carrers acostumats que per ninguna via no s trenque la present volta encara que donassen a dia confraria qualseuol quantitat de moneda y que ab la present ordinatio sia aguda

was not to go to other churches, such as the convent of Santa Clara, since it would became too long for the flagellants to bear and few would complete the course.

3 The Confraternity of the Desamparats

While the Confraternity of the Purissima Sang was the protagonist in the Maundy Thursday procession, the involvement of the Desamparats in that prestigious ceremony was more limited, although they were, according to their own sixteenth-century statutes, to be present at the placing of the host in the Monument in the church where they were based.[27] However, comparison of the statutes of the two confraternities reveals a certain amount of overlap in their duties towards the condemned to death and a dove-tailing of their presence and responsibilities in the related ceremonial. The statutes or *Reglaments* of the Confraternity of the Desamparats, a copy of which is held in the archive of Santa Maria del Pi, are undated, and do not specify a base in a particular church (indicating only that they can hold their meetings in any monastery or church that they choose (*Reglament* 15)), but were probably drawn up around the time that the confraternity made a formal agreement with the parish church on 19 June 1568.[28] At that time, as discussed above, the Confraternity of the Purissima Sang was based temporarily in the Franciscan monastery and the Desamparats seem to have assumed some of their responsibilities at Santa Maria del Pi; indeed, their absence may have been the driving force behind the new agreement between the church and the Confraternity of the Desamparats. It was admitted to the Chapel of St. Bartholomew and St. Barbara, and a brief summary was made of the liturgical acts that were to be celebrated by the brotherhood over the course of the year, including a Mass every Sunday, four annual feast days (of the Virgin Mary and St. Matthias), two commemorations held on the feast of St. Matthias[29] and the Conception of the

---

per trancada y anullada la anada e Sta Clara y de qualseuol altres sglesies y monestirs fora e las sus ditas anomenadas perque era gran dany de dita confraria y traball y fatiga dels disciplinats que s cansaren y se abdigauen y en lo millor dexauen la professo que com tornada a S. Francesc apenas y auia disciplinats y la dita professo anaua molt desbaratada'.

[27] Arxiu Parroquial de Santa Maria del Pi. Caixa C233 "Reglaments Desamparats" (undated; sixteenth-century hand).

[28] Arxiu Parroquial de Santa Maria del Pi. Caixa C233 "Capitulacio", dated 19 June 1568.

[29] The feast of St. Matthias was important both to the church, as the feast-day when the procession to the bones was held, and to the confraternity as its patron saint from at least 1536.

Virgin Mary (8 December), and a procession on the Feast of the Nativity of the Virgin Mary on 8 September.[30]

By at least the mid-seventeenth century, when the ceremony took place during the Octave of the Nativity, this festive procession involved a sermon and a substantial amount of music. A receipt signed by Joseph Vila, then chapel master of the parish church, mentions payment 'for the music' ('per la musica') of a total of 7*ll* 10*s*, 5*ll* for the Mass and 2*ll* 10*s* for the afternoon ('la musica de la tarde'), which presumably refers to Vespers.[31] A total of 2*ll* 6*s* was also paid to the clergy who attended on that feast day. The 'music' performed for the confraternity is not specified, but may have included instrumentalists as well as singers. From 1641, this annual celebration involved an endowment ('causa pia') by Joan de Paredes that provided dowries for two girls who were selected on the feast day.[32] The event was announced by three cries made by

---

30   Arxiu Parroquial de Santa Maria del Pi. Caixa C233 "Capitulacio": 'Als 19 de juny 1568 notari de Barcelona M. Guarnis e el R[everen]t Pau Molet [e] la comunitat del Pi firmaren la capitulatio firmada entres los confrares dels Desemperats ÿ Comunitat ab la qual foren admessos en dita Iglesia ÿ en la Capella de St Barthomeu ÿ Sta Barbara ab diferents pactes segons conte dita concordia la qual se hauia de entregar a dita comunitat copia de aquella per lo Not[ar]i sobre dit ÿ per la profeso de la festa de dita confraria ÿ per selebratio de vna missa quiscun diumenge ÿ per las quatra festes anÿals ÿ dos aniuersaris per lo que hauien de donar 18ll [?28ll] ab dos pagues pagadoras al Prior de la comunitat ÿ al obrer major de la iglesia del Pi'. The commemoration on the feast of the Conception of the BVM is also mentioned in the *Reglaments*: 'Item que lo endema de la concepcio de la verge maria cascun any puguen fer un aniversari perpetualment per les animes de tots los defuns fels en especial dels confrares e confraresses passats desta vida ab ciris encesos en les mans' (*Reglament* 16). The confraternity was involved in other processions organised by the church, such as those held in the Octave of Corpus Christi and for the Assumption of the Virgin.

31   Arxiu Parroquial de Santa Maria del Pi. Caixa C233, document dated 13 September 1662: 'Dich yo Joseph Vila preuere ÿ mestre de capella de Nª Sª del Pi auer rebut del Sʳ fabregas com a administrador de la confraria de nª Sʳª dels desemperats set lluires deu sous dich 7ll 10s ÿ son per la musica del dia feren la festa de dita confraria ço es 5ll per lo ofici ÿ las 2ll 10s per la musica de la tarde ÿ per ser la veritat fas la present rebuda de ma mia vuÿ 13 7ᵇʳᵉ de 1662. Joseph Vila preuere'.

32   Arxiu Parroquial de Santa Maria del Pi. Caixa C232, "Actes de juntes de confrares", 25 April 1641–10 September 1648. Act dated 26 May 1641: 'Item ordenan que la festa principal de Nª Sʳª dels Desemparats se fassen quiscun any lo diumenge dins la octaua de la festa de la natiuitat de nʳª Sʳ de setembre, o altre diumenge apres seguent a coneguda dels majorals de dita confraria fent celebrar en dita Iglesia de Nʳª Sª del Pi ahont es fundada dita capella y confaria lo mati offici ab molta solemnitat y sermo com se acostuma en la qual fiesta tingan de assistir tots los majorals de dita confraria y lo mateix dia de dita festa lo despres de dinar dits majorals tingan de aiuntar en lo capitol de dita Iglesia ab la consell general de dita confraria per fer extractio de quatre donselles de la bossa de la causa pia de Joan de Paredes qᵒ y de dues doncelles de dita confraria conforme altres anÿs se es acostumat fer'.

the confraternity's *andador* who assumed the role of crier among other duties, and who went round the city on horseback ('per lo andador de dita confraria tres crides anant dit andador a cauall per tota la ciutat notificant les dites extractions').

In-depth analysis of the *Reglaments* of the Confraternity of the Desamparats goes beyond the scope of this study, but it is worth noting that they are preceded by a description of the ceremony enacted for the admittance of new members which, as in other devotional confraternities, included the singing of *Veni creator spiritus*, the recitation of a number of prayers, a general absolution and a confession made on the part of the new entrant.[33] The *Reglaments* confirm that the confraternity functioned like any other brotherhood with regard to its focus on the spiritual and physical welfare of its members: supporting the sick and dying, and arranging for the funerals, including a Requiem Mass, and burial of deceased members. All members had to attend these events in black robes or dark clothing with lighted candles. Also customary were the anniversaries held for the souls of former confreres, but the confraternity also took responsibility for the burial of poor prostitutes and undertook to pray fifty *Pater nosters* and fifty *Ave Marias* for their souls.[34]

Admission was open to all decent people ('persones honestes'), and as in the equivalent confraternity in Valencia, membership was fixed at a total of 300 men, 300 women and 100 members of the clergy. The fragmentary early documentation of the confraternity makes it impossible to know whether these numbers were reached, but a list of the men attending a meeting of the confraternity on 25 April 1641 gives an idea of the range of occupations among its membership: the officials or foremen (*mayorals*) included a nobleman (Rafel Pau Vilosa), a public notary (Francesc Llunell) and a goldsmith, while the members present included a doctor-in-law, three tailors, a maker of reed-based goods (*sparter*), a maker of veils, a bookseller, a maker of silk objects (*passamaner*), a second noble, a cutler, a market-stall seller, a shoemaker, a wool carder, a market gardener, a silversmith and a printer.[35] Thus, artisans in a wide range of trades were regularly involved in meetings and the decisions taken at those reunions. Women, as in most confraternities, were not allowed to hold official or administrative positions or attend meetings;

---

[33] Arxiu Parroquial de Santa Maria del Pi. Caixa C233: "Reglaments Desemparats", fols. 10r–13r: "Rubrica com se deu rebre confrare o confraressa en lo loable confraria".

[34] Arxiu Parroquial de Santa Maria del Pi. Caixa C233: "Reglaments Desemparats": *Reglaments* 6, 8, 11–14, 21, 24–26. The main whore-house was situated within the parish of Santa Maria del Pi.

[35] Arxiu Parroquial de Santa Maria del Pi. Caixa C232, "Actes de juntes de confrares", 25 April 1641–10 September 1648, act dated 25 April 1641.

they did, however, actively participate in the confraternal processions. The *Reglaments* also indicate that members were to participate in the comforting of the condemned to death before their execution, and to take the lead in the procession collecting their bones from the scaffold.

4   Rituals of the Condemned

Private and public ritual marked the last hours of those condemned to death: from the comforting of the *sentenciat* in prison during the night before the execution and the spectacle of the procession to the scaffold. The procedure outlined in the statutes of the two Barcelona confraternities was broadly in line with practices found in Italian cities in this period.[36] As regards the support given to the condemned man in prison, the statutes of both the Confraternity of the Puríssima Sang and that of the Desamparats specify that the condemned prisoner, whether in Catalonia, Roussillon or Cerdagne should immediately become a member of the confraternity,[37] and be provided with clothing for the procession: a shirt and tunic or *sobrevesta* with the insignia of the Five Wounds of Christ and breeches in the case of the Puríssima Sang;[38] and shirt, tunic and hat in that of the Desamparats.[39] Both confraternities were to organise members and priests to go to the prison to bring spiritual comfort by carrying out instruction in Christian doctrine and celebrating Mass: the Prior is mentioned in the case of the Puríssima Sang, and 'two good and honest priests or friars' ('dos preveres o religiosos bons y onests') in that of the Desamparats. They were to spend the night with the *sentenciat*, comforting and instructing him so that he did not despair but rather wished for death and so that he would

---

36   Variants in practice and ceremonial between cities could be more or less marked; see, for example, the studies in Terpstra, *The Art of Executing Well*. These duties were also undertaken by the Valencian confraternity from 1498; see: Catalá Sanz – Pérez García, "La pena capital en Valencia" 293–294.

37   Both physical and spiritual needs were met by the confraternity, as was the case in early modern Italy; see Terpstra, "Body Politics" 12: 'They [the comforters] looked ahead pledging to bury [the condemned's] body in consecrated ground and to sing Masses for his soul as they would for any of their brothers'.

38   Arxiu Històric de la Ciutat de Barcelona. Gremis Especials. Cofradía de la Puríssima Sang 2B 20/2. *Ordinacions* 57: 'aporten una camisa o sobrevesta de la sanch de Jesucrist y uns panyos y conçerts'.

39   Arxiu Parroquial de Santa Maria del Pi. Caixa C233: "Reglaments Desemparats" fol. 16r: *Reglaments* 29: 'mirar si lo dit delat o delats auren menester camisa panyos e capell'.

go devoutly in the procession to the scaffold.[40] The priests and designated confreres were to continue to bring comfort during the procession to the scaffold; the *Reglaments* of the Desamparats specify that the Credo should be said at the scaffold, together with the prayer 'In manus tuas',[41] 'with good rhetoric and devotion that he may die with true contrition so his soul might be saved' ('ab bon stil e devotion a effecte que aquell muyra ab verdadera contrictio per que la sua anima sia salvada') (*Reglament* 30).

Other details in the *Reglaments* concerning the procession to the scaffold are sparse: the members of the Confraternity of the Desamparats carried lighted candles and stayed at the scaffold until life was extinct (*Reglament* 31), while the *Ordinacions* of the Purissima Sang mention that four red candles were to accompany the Crucifix carried before the condemned man (*Ordinacions* 54, 59), and that three lanterns were to be placed at the foot of the scaffold (*Ordinacions* 63). The statutes say little about the processional soundscape; the private susurration of catechism, prayers and liturgical texts constantly fed into the condemned person's ear was presumably drowned out by shouts, cries, gasps and weeping from the public as the macabre procession moved through the streets.[42] In Valencia, a trumpeter announced the procession, calling on the inhabitants of the city to attend,[43] and this was surely the case in Barcelona, although it is not mentioned in the confraternal statutes. Bells were also tolled to call attention to the procession and signal its duration. The anonymous Comforter's Manual studied by Nicholas Terpstra introduces a telling exegesis on the meaning of bells:

> You might say that the tolling of the bell brings you shame but again this is not true. Do you really know why the tolling of the bell is ordered? It is ordered so that each person may hear that someone is about to be

---

[40] Arxiu Parroquial de Santa Maria del Pi. Caixa C233: "Reglaments Desemparats" fol. 16r: *Reglaments* 28: 'que stiguen en la nit ab lo sentenciat confortant e instruint aquell en la sancta fe en guiza que no desespere ans vulla a la mort sanctament e ab gran devotio anar'.

[41] This prayer, from the final verse of Psalm 31, commonly formed the last words uttered at the scaffold; see: Falvey, "Scaffold and Stage" 18.

[42] These sounds are evoked in Terpstra, "Introduction" 6. The Barcelona statutes make no mention of the singing of laude, or the use of *tavolette* to distract the condemned, as was the case in early modern Italy. Nicholas Terpstra has described the use of the different senses as 'weaving a sensory cocoon' around the condemned to drown out other sensations and negative thoughts; see Terpstra, "Confraternities and Capital Punishment" 216.

[43] The description of the procession to the scaffold in Valencia includes details of the announcement made by the city trumpeter; see: Catalá Sanz – Pérez García, "La pena capital en Valencia" 296–300, and Adelantado Soriano, "La pena de muerte" 19.

executed and so that people are moved to compassion and pray for you. How many people do you think are around here who upon hearing this bell say an Our Father for your soul, or at least say 'May God forgive you'.[44]

The Comforter's Manual would seem to be referring to church bells, but the *Ordinacions* of the Confraternity of the Puríssima Sang indicate that the confraternal handbell also signalled to those in the procession that they should participate in the prayers. The *andador*, dressed in his scarlet jacket with the confraternity's insignia of the five wounds of Christ on his chest, and processing in front of the Crucifix, rang his handbell along the route and asked all those present to say a *Pater noster* and *Ave Maria* for the soul of the condemned. Following the hanging, and mounted on horseback, he rang the bell and cried to all the members of the confraternity to pray for the soul of the executed (*Ordinacions* 62, 65).[45] Presumably the *andador* used the same bell going to and from the scaffold; only one 'campaneta' is listed in the 1594 inventory of the confraternity's possessions.[46] The sounding of this handbell at ground level and amidst the movement and general hubbub of the procession may not have had the emotional impact described in the Comforter's Manual, but its meaning in the context of this penitential procession would have been clear.

5 Funerary Rites and the Burying of the Bones

As mentioned above, the 1547 agreement between the Confraternity of the Puríssima Sang and Santa Maria del Pi specified that it was to participate in the procession, organised annually by the priests, to the Creu Cuberta to collect the bones of those who had been executed and take them to be buried in the cemetery of the parish church. The confraternity's 1564 *Ordinacions*

---

44 Text cited in English translation in Terpstra, *The Art of Executing Well* 269.

45 Arxiu Històric de la Ciutat de Barcelona. Gremis Especials. Cofradía de la Puríssima Sang 2B 20/2. *Ordinacion* 62: 'que lo andador vaie ab la cota vermella ab la insignia de les sinch plagues de Jesuchrist als pits e ab la campaneta deuant lo crucifixi [...] tocant la squelleta de lloch en lloch dient ab veu publica a tothom generalment que diguen un pater noster y una Ave Maria per la anima del sententiat'; *Ordinacion* 64: 'que lo andador prengue una cavalcadura y ab la cota vestida y ab la campaneta y ab la Insignia dells sinch plagues de nostre señor Jesucrist en los pits vaie per la ciutat y per los llochs acostumats fasse una crida dient que tots los confrares y confraresses diguen les orations acostumades per la anima del sentenciat ...'.

46 Arxiu Parroquial de Santa Maria del Pi. Caixa C200. Cofradia de la Puríssima Sang de Jesu Christ. Batlle, *Arxiconfraria de la Sang*: "Inventari" [1594].

make no mention of this procession, even though contemporary descriptions all mention that its distinctive banner of the Five Wounds of Christ headed the cortège and its 'Cristo gran' processed before the main Cross of the Pi. The brief 1568 agreement between the Confraternity of the Desamparats and the church does not mention the collection of the bones and their burial, but its sixteenth-century *Reglaments* are quite detailed as to their participation (see Appendix 1). It is possible that at some point the clergy delegated responsibility for the organisational aspects of this procession to the confraternity. In general terms, all members of the confraternity, men and women, were obliged to attend the interment of the bones in the church graveyard, and to carry candles and pray for the souls of the executed as they would for the souls of departed members.[47] The confraternity owned four boxes for the collection of the bones, with linen cloths marked with the 'true cross' ('ab la vera creu') to cover them (*Reglaments* 27). *Reglaments* 34 to 45 are concerned with the 'Order and regulation that the treasurer (literally, key-holder) and foremen are to have for the burial of the bones from the Creu cuberta' ('Lo orde e regiment que lo clavari e maiorals an de tenir per la sepultura de la ossa de la creu cuberta').

During the sixteenth century, events unfolded annually around the feast of St. Matthias. The previous Sunday, the foremen and treasurer of the confraternity met to make arrangements for the procession, to determine the route to be taken and to organise who would collect alms to contribute to the cost of the wax for the cortege and burial (*Reglaments* 34, 36). The procession was announced that day with posters put up on street corners and notice being given from the pulpits of the parish churches (*Reglament* 35):

> The coming day [left blank], the praiseworthy confraternity of the Verge Maria dels Desamparats will carry, in solemn procession, the bones of the condemned to death at the Creu cuberta, and, on the feast day of St. Matthias apostle, a solemn Mass with sermon will be celebrated in the said church of the Verge Maria dels Desamparats and the bones will be buried. May it please you to accompany the said procession and to attend the said Mass and sermon and so receive the usual indulgences. The Reverent master [blank] will preach.

---

47 Arxiu Parroquial de Santa Maria del Pi. Caixa 233 Desamparats. *Reglaments* 8: 'Item que tots los confrares e confraresses sien tenguts de entrevenir a les sepultures dels desamparats e sentenciats qui seran liurats a eclesiastica sepultura e anarhi ab sos ciris e dir ses orations axi com a qual confrare e confraressa'. The other 'unprotected' included repentant prostitutes, and any bodies found abandoned in the streets.

The different elements – procession, solemn Mass, sermon and indulgences – were designed to attract as large a crowd as possible, a public desirous to witness the event and also to receive salvific benefit.[48]

On the following day (Monday), the four principal monasteries of the city (Dominican, Franciscan, Augustinian and Carmelite), and the seven parish churches of Barcelona were invited to attend; their presence was checked at the start of the formal procession from the Portal de San Antoni, and they received payment only if they were there (*Reglament* 44).[49] Arrangements were made in advance to ensure that the prior was informed that he should go to the Creu Cuberta to give absolution (*Reglament* 41), and that a deacon and subdeacon were present to assist him with the celebration of Mass (*Reglament* 42). Likewise the *clavari* and current foremen were to seek four men to carry the boxes (*Reglament* 40), and to instruct the previous year's foremen to go to the Creu Cuberta to see how many bones there would be to collect so as to determine the number of shrouds needed (*Reglament* 37); they would also ensure that the shrouding took place on the morning of the vigil of the feast of St. Matthias (*Reglament* 39). Also on the eve, the *andador* was to inform all the members of the confraternity that they should be at the Portal de Sant Antoni at 2PM to accompany the procession to the church and to witness the raising of the Cross (*Reglament* 39). On the day, the procession went to the Creu Cuberta outside the city where refreshment (*collatio*) was taken, and an absolution made before returning to the gate, where all the participants in the procession were gathered; a further *absolta* was made there, and at other, unspecified places along the route (*Reglaments* 43, 44). The confraternity officials were provided with rods (*vergues*) to clear the way for the procession, and it set off with the members of the confraternity following with their candles marked with the sign of the Cross. A group of prostitutes (*dones mundaries*),

---

48 The indulgences for attending the procession were listed at the end of the formal accounts of the procession. In 1526 these were: forty days of 'pardon' granted by the Bishop of Sigüenza and Lieutenant General of Catalonia, don Frederic de Portugal; and forty more each from the Bishop of Vich and the Vicar General of Barcelona (*sede vacante*) and don Joan de Cardona who would become Bishop of Barcelona and one of the founders of the Confraternity of the Verge Maria dels Desamparats. The total of 180 days was maintained in 1630 with a hundred granted by Cardinal Bornos and forty each by the bishops of Barcelona and Lleida. In 1658, the Archbishop of Tarragona granted eighty days and the bishops of Barcelona, Gerona and Vich forty each, making a total of 200 days.

49 In Valencia, the Confraternity of the Innocents invited the clergy from the then twelve parish churches of the city, and the same four monastic orders; see: Catalá Sanz – Pérez García, "La pena capital en Valencia" 302.

kept in check by two officials with rods,[50] was followed in turn by the female members of the brotherhood and then all other women ('e apres de ells vayen totes les confraresses e apres totes les altres dones') (*Reglament* 45). Beyond the mention of the announcement of the date and time of the procession from the pulpit, and notice given of the sermon, solemn Mass and vespers, sonic cues are absent from the *Reglaments*; however, these are found in contemporary descriptions of the procession from 1526, 1630 and 1658.

6   The Sounds of the Procession and Burial of the Bones

The *Reglaments* provide the bare bones, as it were, of the ritual of the collection and burial of the remains of those executed on the scaffold; flesh is added by a number of extant contemporary descriptions, dating from the first half of the sixteenth century until two centuries later. The earliest of these accounts, from 1526, does not specifically mention the Confraternity of the Verge Maria dels Desamparats, although its detail largely coincides with their statutes. The account is preserved in the ceremonial of the church of Santa Maria del Pi known as the 'Black book' ('Llibre negre'), into which it was copied with the intention that it serve as the model for future events of this kind (Appendix 2).[51] It confirms that the event took place at 2PM on the feast of St. Matthias and that it was announced by way of poster and pulpit; it also gives an outline of the route followed by the procession to the Creu Cuberta through the Portal de Sant Antoni and back to the parish church (discussed below). On this occasion, the description mentions seven boxes of bones carried by members of the confraternity, and it estimates the attendance by the public to have been 25,000, men and women ('ab sequela de tant poble axi homens com dones qual fou stimat en nombre de vint y cinch milia'). While undoubtedly an exaggeration, other descriptions confirm that a large number of inhabitants of the city, having been alerted in advance to the date and time of the procession, attended.[52]

---

50   The Valencian Confraternity of the Innocents also included penitential prostitutes in its procession in 1492; see: Catalá Sanz – Pérez García, "La pena capital en Valencia" 301.

51   Arxiu Parroquial de Santa Maria del Pi. Caixa B294. *Llibre negre de l'Obra* 845–847: 'E perque los actes dels passats y presents no poden axi esser notoris als sdevenidors sino ab lo exemple de la scriptura nosaltres sobredits obre[r]s de dita sglesia havem manat la present scriptura esser continuada lobre en lo qual semblants actes de nostres antepassats auem trobat esser continuats'.

52   The 1630 description refers to 'a very great number of men and women' ('grandissim numero de homens and dones') (see Appendix 3), and that of 1658 mentions a great

The 1526 description includes a few sound cues: bells were tolled as the procession set off from the Portal de Sant Antoni ('solepne toch de campanes de requiem'), and again after the Requiem Mass celebrated in the church following the procession and during the burial service proper ('ab grans tochs de campanes'). Sound and music would have had a significant role in the liturgy celebrated in the church following the procession. The boxes of bones were received in the church in front of the choir, with the celebration, by the church clergy, of Matins for the Dead followed by a general absolution. As the feast of St. Matthias in 1526 fell on a Saturday, the boxes of bones were kept in the church throughout the Sunday, surrounded by candles, and with sung Vespers for the Dead. The following day, Monday, a Requiem Mass was solemnly celebrated, with a sermon, and the boxes were taken in procession to the cemetery, where they were buried accompanied by the tolling of bells. Few members of the parish would have been unaware of the event taking place. Such records of ceremonial events typically supply little information as regards musical aspects, but an isolated set of parish accounts that survive for the year 1578–1579 confirm the involvement of the chapel master and singers of the church; they were paid 12s, while the *scolans* (acolytes) were paid 1*ll* for ringing the bells, the chaplains 4*ll* 13s for taking part in the procession and the crier of the Confraternity of the Purissima Sang 3s for the cry announcing the procession.[53] The chapel master of Santa Maria del Pi at that time was probably Joan Puig, who had been appointed to the post in September 1576 and who by June 1580 had been replaced by *mossen* Parra.[54]

---

    number of people of both genders, estimated at more than 10,000 ('un gran numero de persones de un genero y altre que s indica hi hauia passades de deu mil persones') (see Appendix 4).

53 Arxiu Parroquial de Santa Maria del Pi. Caixa B301. Llibre de comptes 1578–1579 fol. [xv]r: 'Dattes. Sentenciats: Dilluns a xxiiij de dit dia de Sta Matia donarem a lotxi per los treballs de traura la ossa dels sententiats de la creu cuberta viijs; Mes donarem al andador de la sanch de Jesuxpt per fer la crida de la professo dels sententiats iijs; Mes als capellans vingueren a la professo a r° vn sou per capella y als de les capes doble 4ll 13s; Mes al mestre de cant per ell y per los cantos 12s; Mes als scolans per los tochs han fets en part de paga 1ll; Mes per vna bossa de cuyro per portar lo xpo 5s; Mes per lo anniuersari de les animes dels sentenciats a r° de vi dines per capella y js per los de les capes y bordons y a rector per tot 2ll 2s 6d; Mes per lo compliment de dotze sous als scolans foren per la vigilia y dia que portauen los sentenciats y a compliment de 1ll 16s'. I am very grateful to the archivist of Santa Maria del Pi, Jordi Sacasas, for drawing this document to my attention.

54 Arxiu Parroquial de Santa Maria del Pi. Caixa B360. Llibre de determinacions C, fols. 43v and 60v. The document referring to Joan Puig is cited in Kamen H., *Cambio cultura en la Sociedad de Siglo de Oro: Cataluña y Castilla, silos XVI–XVII* (Madrid: 1998) 93–94.

FIGURE 19.2   The stations where polyphonic responsories (R) were sung during the procession from the Portal de Sant Antoni to the church of Santa Maria del Pi and in the church cemetery according to the 1658 description
IMAGE © SOUNDSPACE

The payment of 12s to the musicians was not a large sum, and would suggest fairly modest vocal forces were involved at that time, although sufficient to perform polyphony. Whether polyphony was sung in 1526, when the church did not have a regular chapel master or choir, is less clear. Later descriptions leave no doubt: in 1630, the responsories for the dead sung en route were performed in double-choir polyphony ('vna absolta ab cant dorgue a dos cors') and, on returning to the church, a further responsory was sung in alternatim ('una absolta a cant pla ab respostas a cant de orgue') (see Appendix 3). The 1658 description continues to refer to the responsories being sung polychorally, and gives a much clearer idea of the spaces in which these responsories were performed: at the Creu Cuberta, near to the scaffold; at the Portal de Sant Antoni; at the convent de les Jerònimes in the carrer de Sant Antoni; the Plaça de San Jaume; the Plaça nova; and on entering the church of Santa Maria del Pi [Fig. 19.2]. A further polychoral responsory was sung at the burial of the bones in the church ceremony (see Appendix 4). Although the descriptions do not specify the responsories to be sung, five texts are prescribed for funeral processions in the Barcelona Ordinary of 1568: 'Subvenite sancta Dei';

'Ne recorderis'; 'Qui lazarum'; 'Qui venturus est' and 'Libera me'.[55] Settings of these responsories were likely sung during the procession.

The singing of other liturgical texts is specified only rarely. The 1630 description mentions that on leaving the church of Santa Maria del Pi to go to collect the bones on 17 March that year, the clergy began to sing the words of psalm 5, 'Verba mea [auribus percipe domine]'. Significantly, this psalm calls on God to hear the words of the psalmist (or priest or singer), placing due emphasis on sound and the importance of listening; according to the Barcelona Ordinary, this psalm verse initiated the standard ritual for any burial procession.[56] The 1658 description refers to the boys from the general hospital and the orphanage following behind the clergy in the procession and singing the *Miserere* ('cantant lo Miserere') (see Appendix 4). Again, this was a well established practice in funerary and penitential processions in Barcelona; the boys' innocent voices were deemed to have particular intercessionary value, while at the same time they raised charity for their institutions by being paid to participate in urban ritual.[57] The 1658 account also provides more detail about the tolling of bells, which, it claims, were rung seventeen times over the three days of the procession and burial ceremony, although the text alludes only to eight specific times: once at 3PM on the eve of the procession, Saturday (7 April 1658), and once at the sounding (*toch*) of the Ave Maria; once on the Sunday morning (8 April) to announce the beginning of the prcoession; twice on the Monday morning (9 April), first thing and to call to the burial ceremony; a third time at the start of the Requiem Mass; and two more *tochs* during the burial (see Appendix 4). The tolling of bells thus cued the key moments of the ceremonial. This mid-seventeenth-century account evokes one further sonic cue, that of applause at the end of the burial service: 'the obsequies of the said deceased were brought to a conclusion with this ostentation and applause on the part of all present' ('foren acabades les obsequies de dits defuncts ab esa

---

55 *Ordinarium Barcinonense Gulielmi Cassadori Episco iussu aeditum, & in sex libros digestum, quibus ea continentur, quae potissimum ad parochi munus spectant* (Barcelona, Claudium Bornat: 1569) fol. 110v *passim*. See Knighton T., "The Soundscape of Death and Musical Experience in Early Modern Barcelona", in Sá V. – De Paula R.T. – Conde A.F. (eds.), *Paisagens Sonoras em expansão. Novas sonoridades. Novas Escutas* (Cotia – Barreiro: 2023). http://doi.org/10.17613/dsh4-mq44.

56 *Ordinarium barcinonense*, fol. 110v: 'Quant se haura de soterrar algun adulto, exint lo clero de la Esglesia ab la creu, aygua beneyta, y encenser, pera anar a la casa del defunt, lo cantor se commence lo psalm, *Verba mea*, y lo clero proseguesque aquell ab lo to seguent, y acabat dit psalm, canten dels psalms que es seguexen ab lo matex to, fins que arriben a la casa del defunt'; Knighton, "The Soundscape of Death".

57 Knighton T., "Relating History: Music and Meaning in the *relaciones* of the Canonization of St Raymond Penyafort", in (eds.) Ferreira M.P. – Cascudo T., *Música e História: Estudos em homenagem a Manuel Carlos de Brito* (Lisbon: 2017) 27–52, here 47–49.

hostentatio y aplauso de tot lo poble'). The phrase could possibly be read in a metaphorical sense, but contemporary descriptions of other major ceremonial events also mention applause.

7 Itinerary of the Procession of the Bones

Despite the relative paucity of sonic information in the surviving accounts of the ritual surrounding the procession and burial of the bones, they evoke an appropriately solemn, funereal soundscape dominated by singing of various kinds and tolling bells. It was the combination of these sounds with specific spaces in the urban topography and their calendrical repetition that the inhabitants of the city would have come to expect once they saw, and heard, the announcements for the event a few days before. The itinerary of the procession to and from the Portal de Sant Antoni followed one of the most important and lengthy ceremonial axes of Barcelona: it formed the basis for royal entries, since monarchs generally entered through that gate having spent the previous night in the Convent of Valldonzella,[58] as well as entries of other dignitaries such as bishops and papal nuncios, and relics such as that of St. Isidor the Farmer gifted to the church of Santa Maria del Pi in 1623.[59] This association of the processional route in the minds of the inhabitants of the city with extraordinary events of reception or collection must have given lustre and prestige to the confraternity's involvement; as Nicholas Terpstra has pointed out, 'The number, location, and profile of any group's spaces said a lot about its place in civic priorities and consciousness'.[60] This type of procession of collection also generally meant that the outward procession towards the gate along the carrer del Carme was often less elaborate than the return along the carrer del Hospital [Fig. 19.2], and this was the case with the procession to collect the bones, although it, unlike most reception processions, went through the city gate and beyond to the Creu Cuberta, and was a penitential rather than festive event.

At least during the sixteenth century, the procession of the bones offered a more regular spectacle in terms of the civic ceremonial calendar. The

---

58 Chamorro A., *Barcelona y el rey. Las visitas reales desde Fernando el Católico hasta Felipe V* (Barcelona: 2017).

59 Knighton T., "'Puix tot es per major aument del culto divino': El paisaje sonoro de las cofradías gremiales de Santa Maria del Pi, ss. XV–XVII", *Recòndit* 2 (2022) 81–117, here 101–106.

60 Terpstra, "Confraternities and Capital Punishment" 226.

Reglaments of the Confraternity of the Desamparats and its 1568 agreement with the parish church of the Pi both indicate that the procession was to take place annually on the feast of St. Matthias on 24 February,[61] and this is confirmed by the 1526 description in the *Llibre negre* and the set of church accounts presented in 1578–1579. However, in the seventeenth century it appears usually to have been held a month or so later: in 1607, an agreement made in a chapter meeting to hold the procession in the customary manner took place on 11 March;[62] in 1623 the procession took place on 26 March;[63] in 1630 the meeting was held on 12 March and the procession took place five days later (Appendix 3); and in 1658 the procession was held on Passion Sunday, 7 April, followed by the burial service on the Monday (Appendix 4). Reference to the customary nature of the event is consistently made in these descriptions, but it is difficult to ascertain whether the procession in fact continued to be an annual event. The minute of 11 March 1607 may possibly indicate a break of some years with its mention in the past tense: 'as the said beneficed priests well had the custom to do' ('com be o tenien acostumat de fer dits preueres beneficiats'), but this is not conclusive. Notes entered into the *Llibre negre* after the 1658 description mention that processions took place in 1688 and 1697, and there is a further description for 1709 (which took place on 15 December in the presence of the king, Archduke Charles of Austria (r. 1701–1714)) and another reference to one in 1732.[64] It may be that from the seventeenth century these processions were organised less regularly, only when there was a need to collect an accumulation of bones.

It may also be that descriptions and references were made only in response to external events, such as the presence in Barcelona of members of the royal family, that necessitated changes to the route and/or ritual of the event. For example, the discussion minuted on 26 March 1623 was triggered by the desire to change the customary route, which hitherto had kept within parish

---

61 This was also the case with the Confraternity of Innocents and Unprotected in Valencia; see: Pérez García P., "Cofradías y Germanía: la Real Cofradía de Inocentes y Desamparados (1519–1524)", in Amelang J.S. et al. (eds.), *Palacios, plazas y patíbulos: la sociedad Española moderna entre el cambio y las resistencias* (Valencia: 2018) 421–432, here 427.

62 Arxiu Parroquial de Santa Maria del Pi. Caixa B361. Llibre de determinacions 1606–1623 fol. 5r: 'per aportar los ossos dels sentenciats que estan en la creu cuberta com be o tenien acostumat de fer dits preueres beneficiats'.

63 Arxiu Parroquial de Santa Maria del Pi. Caixa B361. Llibre de determinacions 1606–1623 fol. 103v: 'per aportar los ossos dels sentenciats conforme en altres occasions tenien ben acostumat'.

64 Arxiu Parroquial de Santa Maria del Pi. Caixa B294. *Llibre negre de l'Obra* 862.

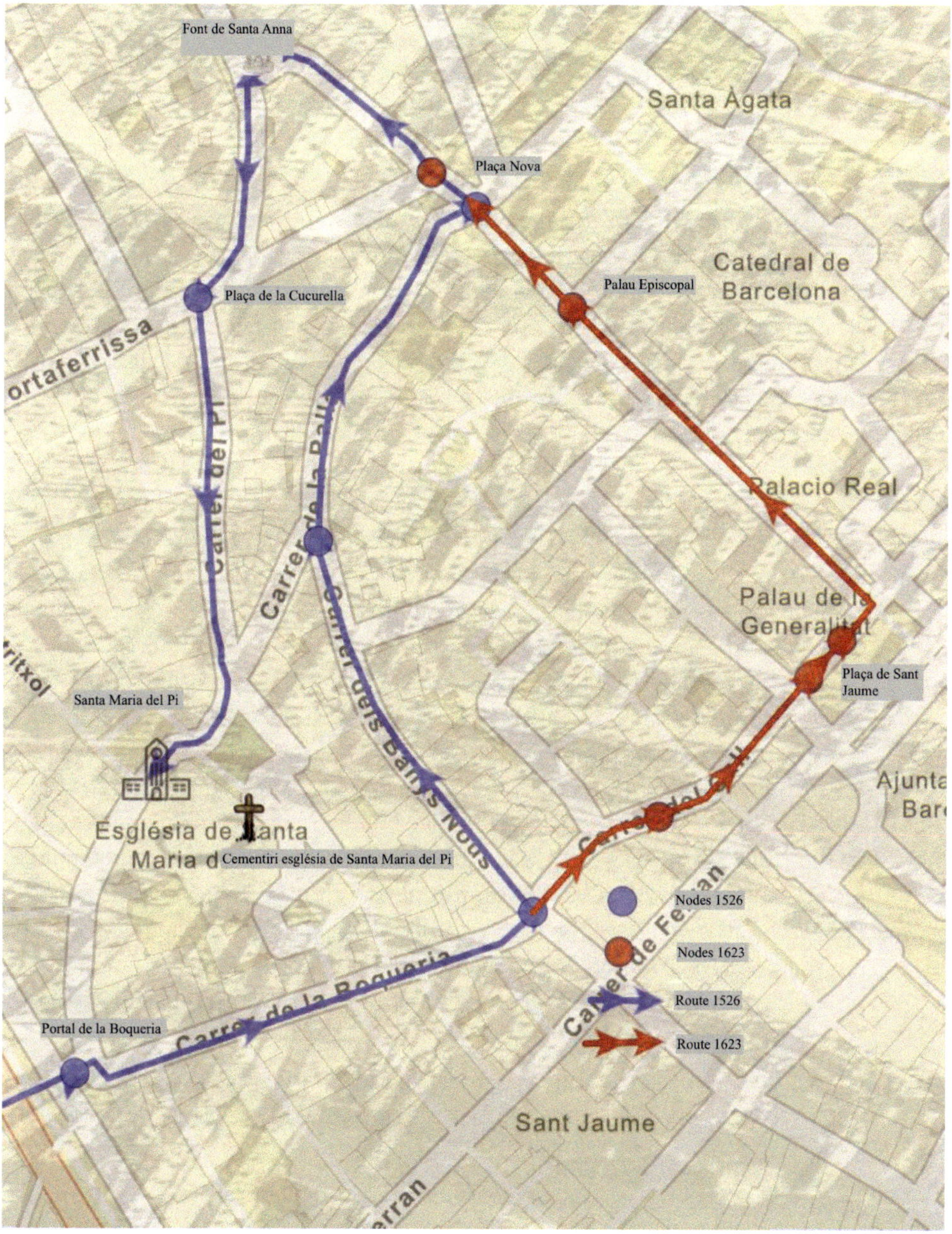

CONFRATERNITY OF THE *VERGE MARIA DELS DESAMPARATS* IN BARCELONA 529

FIGURE 19.3 The 1526 route of the procession of the bones and the change to the itinerary as minuted in the *Deliberacions* of the meeting of the community of priests of Santa Maria del Pi in 1623
IMAGE © SOUNDSPACE

boundaries, and extend it to take in the Plaça San Jaume. Thus, when the procession returned from the Portal de Sant Antoni with the boxes of bones, instead of following the customary route from the Portal de la Bocaria along the carrer dels Banys and carrer de la Palla to the Plaça Nova and round the fountain of Santa Anna to return to the church along carrer del Pi,[65] it was to go outside the parish to the Plaça de Sant Jaume and then past the episcopal palace to the Plaça Nova where it reconnected with the established route [Fig. 19.3].[66] Processing past the buildings that represented municipal and ecclesiastical governance clearly would have heightened the confraternity's profile in the civic consciousness. However, the decision was not met by universal approval ('an romput lo us antich y contra determinacio y ab gran desgust de la reverent comunitat'), and was probably taken by the confraternity, or the city council rather than the church administrators. The minute records the change, so that 'in the future the truth [behind this change] is known' ('fem esta nota per lo temps sdevenidor per que se sapia la verita').

The description of 1630 shows that once a processional route was altered, that change became absorbed into custom, since it confirms that the boxes of bones were carried to the Plaça de San Jaume, and stopped before the palace of the regional government ('devant la Diputacio') before continuing on past the episcopal palace to the Plaça Nova [Fig. 19.4]. On this occasion, it did not proceed to the fountain of Santa Anna, but rather returned by a more direct route along the carrer dels Boters. No reason is given for this slight shortening of the trajectory in 1630, although possibly it was to compensate for the extra distance covered to take in the Plaça de San Jaume. The 1630 account of the ritual was triggered by a debate as to whether the procession should deviate even more substantially from tradition to pass by the square of the Franciscan friary close to the palace of the dukes of Cardona where Maria of Austria (1606–1646), sister of Philip IV, was in residence en route to Vienna to be married to the King of Hungary, Ferdinand II.[67] This was proposed at the

---

65   This was essentially the route indicated in the 1526 description. On the importance of the Font de Santa Anna as a landmark in the parish of Santa Maria de Pi, see: Brú Turuall R., "La font de Santa Anna del Portal de l'Àngel", *Matèria* 4 (2004) 77–94.

66   Arxiu Parroquial de Santa Maria del Pi. Caixa B361. Llibre de determinacions 1606–1623 fol. 103v: 'encara que se avie acostumat en semblant professo de portar los ossos dels sentenciats exir de la parroquia ni de sos limits ans be com eran al cap de la bocaria anaue sempre la professo per los banys amunt per lo carrer de la palla a la plassa noua y rodar la font de la plassa de S*ta* Anna y tornassen per lo carrer gran del Pi Y ara an romput lo us antich y contra determinacio y ab gran desgust de la reverent comunitat perque volgueren arribar a la plassa de S*t* Jaume y devant lo palau del bisbe fem esta nota per lo temps sdevenidor per que se sapia la verita'.

67   Chamorro Esteban A., "El paso de las Infantas de la Casa de Austria por Barcelona (1551–1666)", in Serrano Martin E. (ed.), *De la tierra al cielo: líneas recientes de investigación*

CONFRATERNITY OF THE *VERGE MARIA DELS DESAMPARATS* IN BARCELONA 531

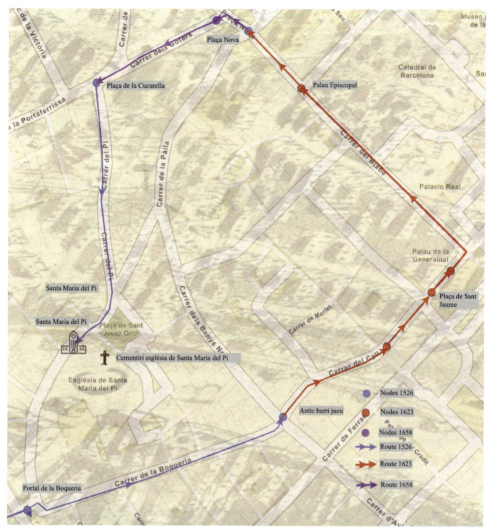

FIGURE 19.4 The route taken for the procession of the bones according to the description of 1630, including the Plaça San Jaume but returning along the carrer dels Boters
IMAGE © SOUNDSPACE

12 March meeting of the community by one of the church wardens, the soldier don Lluis Ferrer: 'given the presence of the Queen of Hungary in Barcelona at present, if they would pass in front of the palace where the said Queen Our Lady [is]' ('per quant la Reyna de vngria se trobava vuy en Barcelona que s ils

en historia moderna (Zaragoza: 2012) 495–514, here 503–507. María de Austria entered Barcelona early in February 1630 and visited the different churches of the city.

apereria passas dita professo devant el palau de dita S^ra Reyna'). The decision was taken not to do so, but at the same meeting they did agree to moving the image of the Virgin in the order of the procession (see Appendix 3).[68]

The 1658 description adheres to the route proposed in 1623: it includes the extension of the procession outside the parish to the Plaça de San Jaume as well as the loop around the fountain of Santa Anna. However, this account, copied like that of 1526 into the *Llibre negre* in order to preserve details of the ritual for posterity, also makes reference to a minor infringement of protocol in the realisation of the procession as regards the collection of the ten boxes of bones from the scaffold.[69] It usefully indicates the duration of the procession which left the church at 3PM and returned to it at 6.45PM, although the last responsory was yet to be sung inside the church, so the whole event probably lasted more than four hours, taking into account the five stations where a polyphonic responsory was sung while the bearers of the boxes of bones drew respite.

These stopping-points were spatially emblematic for the procession and for the profile of the Confraternity of the Desamparats.[70] The first *absolta* was sung at the site of the scaffold near the Creu Cuberta, outside the walls of the city, in the direction of the outlying village of Sants, approximately where the former bullring of Barcelona is situated today [Fig. 19.5]. It was a place of profound symbolism, as the site of capital punishment, serving as a warning to would-be criminals that also signalled the proximity of the city. This double function is wittily captured in Cervantes's description of don Quixote's entry by night into Barcelona, with his eponymous hero attempting to reassure the fearful Sancho Panza:

– No tiene de qué tener miedo, porque estos pies y piernas que tienta y no vees, sin duda son de algunos forajidos y bandeleros que en estos árboles están ahorcados; que por aquí los suele ahorcar la justicia cuando los coge,

---

[68]   The Valencian Confraternity of the Innocents also carried an image of the Virgin Mary in their procession of the bones, see: Catalá Sanz – Pérez García, "La pena capital en Valencia" 302.

[69]   Arxiu Parroquial de Santa Maria del Pi. Caixa B294. *Llibre negre de l'Obra* 851: 'encara que es veritat que les ditas caxas havian de star compartides desde la Creu Cuberta fins al cap devall del empedrat conforme ere costum antich lo que no saberem lo dia se feu la professo y axi se adverteig hara per una altra vegada' ('although it is true that the said boxes had to be shared from the Creu cuberta to the stoned area [of the scaffold] in accordance with ancient custom, which on the day of the procession we did not know and so we draw attention to it for when it is held again') (see Appendix 4).

[70]   Adelantado Soriano ("La pena de muerte" 18) makes this point regarding the emblematic buildings passed in the procession to the scaffold in Valencia.

CONFRATERNITY OF THE *VERGE MARIA DELS DESAMPARATS* IN BARCELONA   533

FIGURE 19.5   The route from the Portal de Sant Antoni to the Creu Cuberta
IMAGE © SOUNDSPACE

de veinte en veinte y de treinta en treinta: por donde me doy a entener que debo de estar cerca de Barcelona.

– No need to be afraid, because these feet and legs you are touching, but cannot see, undoubtedly belong to outlaws and bandits hanged in these trees; for here Justice customarily hangs them when it catches them, by the twenty, by the thirty: which gives me to understand that I must be approaching Barcelona.[71]

Cervantes's description of a nocturnal tactile encounter with the hanged at the Creu Cuberta is acutely sensorial; in daylight, the traveller entering Barcelona would have been met by a grisly sight, as well as, at times, the smell of putrefaction.

The next responsory was sung once the boxes of bones were at the Portal de Sant Antoni, where all those who were attending the procession – parish and regular clergy, confraternity members, with their emblems and lighted candles, and general public – were gathered, and the formal funeral cortège was about to begin. The Confraternity of the Desamparats erected an altar near

---

71   Cervantes, *Don Quijote de la Mancha*, II: 60; cited in Serés G., "El context històricosocial dels episodis Catalans del *Quixot*", in Riera C. (ed.), *El Quixot i Barcelona* (Barcelona: 2005) 81–91. The number of criminals hanged at the scaffold near the Creu Cuberta varied, but twenty-one bandits were hung in 1573: see García Cárcel R., "El bandolerismo catalán en el siglo XVI", in Martínez Comeche J.A., *Le bandit et son image au Siècle d'Or* (Madrid: 1991) 43–54. The numbers of hanged in Barcelona is difficult to ascertain, but in Valencia 1364 were executed in the sixteenth century, and 885 in the seventeenth, though a substantial proportion were condemned to death by the Inquisition and burnt at the stake: see Catalá Sanz – Pérez García, "La pena capital en Valencia" 274, 276.

to the portico (*porxo*) of the monastic church of Sant Antoni close by the gate [Fig. 19.6]. This funerary ceremony, with its singing of a responsory for the dead, made for marked contrast to a festive royal entry echoing to the sound of trumpets, drums and minstrels and the representation of singing angels descending from the top of the gate to present the keys of the city to the monarch, yet the emblematic entry-point served both spectacles. It was at this nodal point in the procession that the banner and crucifix of the Confraternity of the Puríssima Sang and the Confraternity of the Desamparats' image of the Virgin Mary as protector were deployed in the procession. As Nicholas Terpstra has argued, these kinds of material objects gave confraternities a quasi-intercessionary agency in civic religious ritual.[72]

The third station, according to the 1658 description, was the Jeronymite convent, known as Santa Margarida, established in the carrer de Sant Antoni from the late fifteenth century.[73] During the sixteenth century, it developed a strong profile within the city: the councillors visited the church annually on its feast day, and in 1553 the Confraternity of Booksellers chose it as their headquarters. Traditionally, the processions of the bones would have passed by the convent, but at what point it became a station, or whether it was regularly a stopping-point where a responsory was sung, is not known; it is not mentioned in the earlier descriptions. The next station mentioned in 1658 was a substantial distance away in the Plaça de Sant Jaume, which, as already noted, was the site of the city hall ('Casa de la ciutat') and the palace of the Diputació, that is the seat of government for city and province, to which the procession had been extended, beyond the parish boundaries, from at least 1623.

The singing of a responsory in the Plaça Nova took the procession back within the parish; it hosted one of the most important market squares in the city, and was the centre of activities for two of the church's other confraternities: the marketstall-holders (*Revenedors*) and market gardeners (*Hortolans*) (Fig. 19.7).[74] Both these guild or trade confraternities participated in the procession, together with the three spiritual brotherhoods based at the church: those of the Desamparats, the Puríssima Sang and the Santa Espina ('Holy

---

[72] Terpstra, "Body Politics" 21. Objects such as figures of saints or the Virgin were carried through the city so that the inhabitants could see their protector, and so that the figure would 'see' the suffering and penitence and of the supplicants and be moved to act on their behalf (idem 20).

[73] Saéz García, *Creure, somiar, lluitar* 34–35, 121–123; and Mazuela-Anguita A., *Women in Convent Spaces and the Musical Networks of Early Modern Barcelona* (New York: 2023) 60–61.

[74] Knighton, "'Puix tot es per major aument del culto divino'".

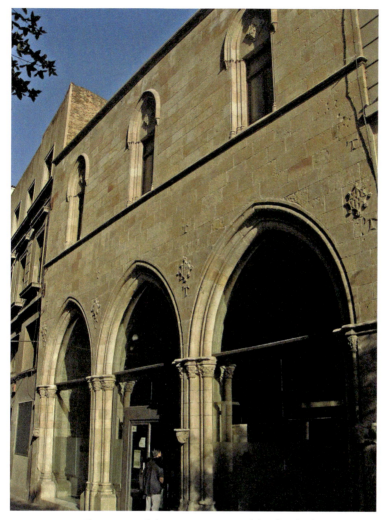

FIGURE 19.6 The remains of the *porxo* or portico of the church of Sant Antoni, Barcelona, where those participating in the procession gathered to take the boxes of bones to the parish church of Santa Maria del Pi for burial
IMAGE © WIKIMEDIA COMMONS

Thorn').[75] The 1658 description also mentions the presence of the confraternities of silversmiths (*argenters*), tailors (*sastres*) and mercers (also known

---

75 The Confraternity of the Santa Espina was founded in 1628 and became a particular focal point for devotional activity in the church of Santa Maria del Pi; see Cabré B., "La Confrària de la Santa Espina de l'Esglesia del Pi de Barcelona al segle XVII: Un nou context per un vell repertori", *Recòndit* 2 (2022) 118–143.

FIGURE 19.7   View of the Portal and Plaça Nova, Barcelona. Coloured engraving by Jean Baptiste Reville – Louis-François Couché in Alexandre Laborde, *Voyage pittoresque et historique de l'Espagne* (Paris, L'Imprimerie de P. Didot l'Aîné: 1806–1802)
IMAGE © WIKIMEDIA COMMONS

as the 'julians'), all of which contributed by carrying torches and supplying velvet or brocade cloths in black and scarlet to cover the boxes of bones (see Appendix 4).These relatively large squares, one outside the parish, one within, would have allowed many of those attending to gather within a single acoustic space, though few would have been close enough to the singers to hear the text of the responsory. Indeed, many probably heard little or nothing, bearing in mind that the 1658 description talks of more than 10,000 people in attendance and mentions that the procession stretched continuously from the Portal de la Bocaria to that of Sant Antoni ('hi havia passades de deu mil persones de tal manera que arribava lo seguiment de la professo desdel portal de la Bocaria fins lo portal de St Antoni') (see Appendix 4 and Fig. 19.5).

The final responsory was sung inside the parish church which the funeral cortège entered, according to the 1658 account, at 6.45pm:

> Y entrada en dita Iglesia dexaren alli les dites caxas al entrant del cor y posaven n[ostr]a s[enyor]a devant la taula de la obra sobra una barro o taula ab son palit y devant de ella staven les dites caxes y posades dites

> caxes y n[ostr]a s[enyor]a sobre dita taula feren altra absolta a cant de orga com les demas y alli posaren quatre atxes grogues al costat de dites caxes y feta la absolta se disgrega la dita professo.[76]

> and having entered the said church, they left the said boxes there, at the door to the choir; they placed the image of Our Lady in front of the churchwardens' table, on a wooden support, with its canopy, with the boxes in front [of the image]; and when the boxes and the image of Our Lady had been placed on the table, another responsory was sung in polyphony like the others, and there they put four yellow [tallow] torches by the said boxes, and after the *absolta*, the procession dispersed.

The boxes were not left in total silence: before the solemn Requiem Mass held in the church at 10AM the following day, the celebration of 120 Masses for the Dead in the side chapels of the parish church must have created a more or less constant susurration; some may have been chanted. A further polyphonic responsory was sung after the sermon, and the final *absolta* was sung in plainchant ('en cant pla') in the cemetery (see Appendix 4).

Although details of the order of the procession are provided in the descriptions – particularly those of 1630 and 1658 – it is difficult to establish where the singers were placed, though presumably they processed with the clergy accompanying the velvet-draped boxes, with the *minyons* singing the *Miserere* in front or behind. Together they solemnified the transfer of the bones they contained with sound. As mentioned above, material objects also moved to the step of the cortège: the banner of the Confraternity of Purissima Sang headed the procession, followed by the members of the various confraternities carrying candles and wax torches ('atxes blanques'). Then went the 'Santo Cristo' or crucifix of the Confraternity of the Purissima Sang, and the church's cross and the clergy in black vestments. The officials of the Confraternity of the Desamparats followed, bearing torches and with their image of the Virgin, carried by four members, who, when they tired, were replaced by another four (see Appendix 4). The 1658 description also mentions a canopy (*talem*) that was carried by six knights. The merchants and artisans who were members of the confraternity followed, carrying 142 torches. The Confraternity of the Desamparats clearly took the leading role in the procession, though the prestigious emblems of the Purissima Sang appear to have taken precedence; the presence of both may have reinforced the longstanding association of the two brotherhoods in the collective memory of urban ritual.

---

76   Arxiu Parroquial de Santa Maria del Pi. Caixa B294. *Llibre negre de l'Obra* (see Appendix 4).

8 Conclusions

The significance of these moving sounds and images was multi-layered:[77] the intersensory nature of the procession helped to communicate and reinforce its main messages – the redemptive power of the crucified Christ, and the mercy and protection of the Virgin Mary – to all those who attended; many would have been illiterate but nevertheless grasped the import of the occasion by these means.[78] The sights and sounds of the procession of the bones as it passed along the main ceremonial routes and by emblematic civic and religious buildings must have impressed; they were inextricably linked with the funeral cortège, but one with up to ten boxes of bones instead of a single coffin, all covered in rich drapes. Furthermore, with the participation of several confraternities and the resulting river of torches and candles, as well as the polychoral singing of responsories at the stations along the route, it represented the apotheosis of the funeral procession: only royalty and the princes of the church would have received a ceremonial valediction with a similar cathartic impact.[79] It surely did move at least some of those present to prayers, compassion and tears.

The procession held for the collecting of the bones from the scaffold outside the walls of the city represented the second and concluding part of the ritual that generated and defined the discourses relating to the bringing to justice, through capital punishment, those who committed serious crimes against society. In the prison cell and in the procession to the scaffold, those condemned to death were supported spiritually by the designated confraternities as they faced the ultimate earthly punishment. They were abjured to accept their fate and to die well, with repentance of their sins and commending their souls to God in the hope of their salvation. They were taken outside the walls of the city to die as the inhabitants of that city watched and took in the message of the macabre spectacle: only through repentance and by God's mercy could their souls be redeemed. Later, when the bones had been gathered, they

---

77 On this important aspect, see: Rihouet P., *Art Moves. The Material Culture of Processions in Renaissance Perugia* (Turnhout: 2017).

78 Adelantado Soriano V., "La pena de muerte como espectáculo de masas en la Valencia del Quinientos", in Sirera Turó J.L. (ed.), *Estudios sobre teatro medieval* (Valencia: 2008) 15–24, here 15, 20.

79 On the funeral of King Juan II in Barcelona in 1479, see Kreitner K., *Music and Civic Ceremony in Fifteenth-Century Barcelona* (Ph.D. dissertation, Duke University: 1990) 338–349; and on that of a bishop of Barcelona, see Puentes-Blanco A., *Música y devoción en Barcelona (ca. 1550–1626): Estudio de libros de polifonía, contextos y práticas musicales* (Ph.D dissertation, Universitat de Barcelona, 2018), vol. I, 409–419.

were brought back into the city for Christian burial in a dedicated tomb in the cemetery of one of Barcelona's most important parish churches, thus enacting the fulfilment of the promise of salvation. The sights, sounds and spaces of the procession of the bones emphasised its salvific function: the progress towards Christian rehabilitation and redemption. The inhabitants of the city, encouraged by the publicity that heralded these regular events, turned out in their thousands to witness and participate in a funeral cortège on a grand scale that, in turn, bore witness to the fundamental Christian doctrine of forgiveness and redemption. Mapping these processions highlights how, through time, place and sensescape, they signalled to the urban community all the potential meanings of funerary ritual, from the fundamental tenets of the Faith relating to repentance and forgiveness and the associated eschatological beliefs that equated alms-giving and indulgences with salvation, to the performance of a multisensorial experience that imprinted that message on individual minds and hearts and in the collective memory.

Acknowledgments

The research for this study was undertaken as part of the research project "The Contribution of Confraternities and Guilds to the Urban Soundscape in the Iberian Peninsula, c.1400–c.1700" [CONFRASOUND]: MINECO, Spain, PID 2019-109422GB-100. I am very grateful to Jordi Sacasas, archivist, and Albert Cortès of the church of Santa Maria del Pi for their unstinting help, and Nicholas Terpstra and Sergi González González for their assistance in the preparation of this chapter.

Appendix 1

Arxiu Parroquial de Santa Maria del Pi. Caixa C233: "Reglaments Desemparats" (undated; sixteenth-century hand) fols. 17r–18v. Statutes 34–45 relating to the procession 'of the bones' ('dels ossos'): 'Lo orde e regiment que lo clavari e maiorals an de tenir per la sepultura de la ossa de la creu cuberta'.

[fol. 17r] [34] Item que tendra lo primer diumenge o festa ans de sant Matthia los clauari e maiorals an de proposar lo que es faedor pera dita sepultura encara deuen proposar per ont ha de passar la professo dels cententiats al anar y al tornar

[fol. 17v] [35] Item que lo dit dia lo scriua de mati a de portar albarans per totes les parroquies albarans [sic] per pregar als vicaris los que vullen llegir e publicaren les trones e fan a metre altres tals per los cantons de la ciutat lo qual es del tenor seguent: –

Dia + primer vinent la loable confraria de la verge maria dels desemparats ab solemne professo portara la ossa dels cententiats de la creu cuberta e lo dia del glorios apostol sanct matia en la dita sglesia de la verge maria dels desemparats se fassa solemne offici e sermo e soterraran la dita ossa placiens acompanyar la dita processo e esser a la dita missa e sermo guanyaren los perdons acostumats. Sermonara lo R^{nt} mestre t. [blank]

[36] Item lo dit dia ques tindra lo dit capitol los dits clavari e majorals an de acompanar a quatre confrares peral dit dia de la processo los quatre bacins ço es la un pera lo capte de la creu cuberta e los tres pera la ciutat ab sos acompanyans com ne tinguen

[37] Item mes auant lo dit clavari e majorals novells an de dir als vells que en lo apres dinar vayan a la creu cuberta per veure quans cossos y aura pera mortaller aquels cossos

[38] Item lo endema lo clavari e majorals an de combidar totes les parroquies de la ciutat e los quatre monestirs ço es sanct domingo sanct francesch sanct agost e lo carme peral dia de la processo e cascuna de les dites parroquies per son salari deu auer cinc sous sis diners e cascun dels monestirs quatre sous e o qui mancara no aya res de salari

[39] Item la vespra de sanct matia lo clavari e majorals an a dir als [fol. 18r] vells que de mati vayen a mortaller los cossos donat lo drap pera los mortalles e axi matex lo dit clavari e majorals manen als andadors que de mati fassen la andada per tots los confrares e confraresses que sien al portal de sanct anthoni pera les dos hores apres dinar pera acompanyar la professo e alsa de la creu cuberta

[40] Item lo clavari a de cercar gent quatre homens per cada cos e sils trobaran per amor de deu sino donaranlos de salari lo que a ells los parexera que sia ratio y lo que se auindran

[41] Item los dits clauari e majorals feta la assignatio de portar la dita ossa de la creu cuberta diguen al prior que peral dia assignat vaja a la creu cuberta per fer la absolta segons es acostumat

[42] Item lo dit prior dels preueres que per al[g]uns confrares seran tramessos per dir misses dos de aquells puga pendre per que sien diaca e sotsdiaca pera la dita missa major e los tres fassan lo offici: –

[43] Item en lo apres dinar quan iran a la creu cuberta los dits preueres de la dita confraria ab la creu e feta per aquelles collatio e absolta en la Cruz cuberta lo dit prior tinga la caxa a vestida e faça les obsequies acostumades sobre los cossos e apres feta la dita absolutio porten los cossos a Barcelona fassen les absolucions per tots los llochs acostumats.

[44] Item los dits clavari e majorals quant los cossos seran al portal de sanct Anthoni e totes les parroquies serian alli congregades e ajustades cascuna per si fassen les absolutions acostumades e fa a mirar si hi seran totes les dites parroquies e les quatre monestirs e qui no hi sera no [fol. 18v] aja res de salari a cascuna de les dites parroquies sie tinguda de portar cis preueres pera acompanyar la processo

[45] Item los dits clavari e majorals anant voldra partir la dita processo del portal fassen donar a los andadors als conselles e als prohomens de la dita confraria les vergues acostumades per ordenar e arreglar aquella e partint la dit processo del dit portal vayan apres los dits clavari e majorals acompanyats de los confrares segons es acostumat e apres dels confrares les dones mundaries per que no fassen algunes desvariations e apres de ellas vayen dos confrares ab altres dos ciris de acompaniats sens varoles pintats de senyal de creu e ab dos consellers abs vergues e apres de elles vayen totes les confraresses e apres totes les altres dones

Appendix 2

Arxiu Parroquial de Santa Maria del Pi. Caixa B294. *Llibre negre de l'Obra* 845–847
Ceremonial for the procession of the bones, dated 24 February 1526

En lany de la Nativitat de nostre senyor .M. cinccents e vint y sis suspirats per la divina gratia los honorables obre[r]s lany present de la sglesia parochial de la verge maria del pi de la present ciutat los quales eren lo magnifich mossen Bernard Anthoni falco donzell mossen Anthoni hieronym vanover mercader Anthoni clos matalasser pere arnau gerrer introdint una obra axi sancta y meritoria com fou portar aquells ossos y cortes dels squarterats acostumen de penjar en la creu cuberta fora los murs de la ciutat en aquella part del cami real per hon se va a la vila de sanct boy aquels enpero que en terra staven y en aquells anar ab solempna processo la qual partis de dita sglesia a fi que los fos donada eclesiastiqua sepultura pera la qual cosa esser aportada a son desiyat fi fou obtenguda licençia fel Ill.ᵐ senyor don federich de Portugal per la gracia de deu Bisbe de Sigüença llochtinent general per la sacra cesarea e catholica magestad del emperador Rey y senyor nostre en tot lo principat de Catalunya comptats de Rosello y Cerdanya e nomenys per los magnifichs consellers lany present de la present ciutat los quals eren mossen Jaume salba donzell mossen galceran llul mossen francesc stela ciutadans mossen anthoni planes mercader mossen pere Gomar specier ab los quals conformes foren e unanimes lo Mag[nifica]t micer Johan Christophol faner doctor en quiscun dret e mossen Pere joan Reix notari lo mateix any obre[r]s de dita ciutat fou assignat disapte dia del glorios apostol sant matia que comptavem vint y quatre del mes de febrer del sobredit any en lo qual prevenant lo poble de cartells stampats foran posats en les cantons de las plassas e charitativament amonestats per los predicadors en las trones lo diumenge precedent parti que dita processo e lo poble anassen com de [846] fet anaren partint a les dos hores apres mix jorn ab solepne processo e solepne toch de campanes de requiem empero ab sequela de tant poble axi homens com dones qual fou stimati en nombre de vint y cinch milia se anaren per la carrera de la cucurella en la qual afrenta la casa de mosen gralla e aqui giraren al portal de la porta ferrissa e via dreta anaren a la creu cuberta exint per lo portal de sant anthoni se tornant entrar per aquell passa la processo per lo carrer del hospital y entra dret per lo portal de la boqueria fins al canto del call e per lo carrer dels banys nous arriba per lo carrer de la palla fins a la plassa nova e exint a la font de la plassa de sancta ana per la cucurella s entorna en dita sglesia per la qual volta e lochs ahont be fou vist a los sobredits obre[r]s y altres persones foren posats bassiners charitativament demanant almoyna a las charitats del poble per celebrar les exequies tals y tantes quals y quants les charitats sobredites consentiren y arribats los ossos de dits sentenciats en nombre de set caxes repartits portades ditas caxas per algunes confraries y ab propis lumns [sic] de aquellos aconpanyades e iluminades en la present sglesia foren pasades devant la porta del cor ahont per lo clero inmediadament ab molta solempnitat foren celebrades unes matines a morts y aqueles acabades una absolucio general e per que lo dia seguent era diumenge e la sglesia sens evident necesitat en semblant temps posar ni dexar no acostuma mes en pratiques la historia dominical fou feta determinacio que tot lo diumenge les caxes dels sobredits sentenciats aconpanyades de lums stigguessen en lo mateix loch ab huna que per las capellas en particular fossen celebrades algunes misses e acabades les vespres per ells ne fossen cantades altres de morts lo que axi posat en obra e [847] passat fins lo diluns ab solempne offici de requiem ab offerta general y molta celebratio de misses baixes y ab sermon specialment pera ells destinats molt honrosament foren sepultats ab grans tochs de campanes de fora la sglesia en lo cap del fossar mayor que es propinque a sol exint en hun carrer sta erecte en la paret affix ab aquell en lo qual acostuman de esser sepultades les dones del publich segons ab senyal euident de dits sentenciats sculpits en vna llosa de pedre afixa en la paret de la dita sepultura a tots los miradors pora esser notori E per quant la introduccio de les coses tals y axi meritories de si sian molt loables pero no son de tanta comendatio digues si ab lo eternitat del temps no son continuades E perque los actes dels passats y presents no poden axi esser notoris als sdevenidors sino ab lo exemple de la scriptura nosaltres sobredits obre[r]s de dita sglesia havem manat la present scriptura esser continuada lobre en lo qual semblants actes de nostres antepassats avem trobat esser continuats humilment supplicant al redemptor de natura humana y a la sacratissima y humil verge maria vulla los qui an de venir en tal manera de tal obra preterir [sic] y en aquells qui della son stats promovedors donar les la sua gratia en lo temps viuran en aquest mon y en lo altre eterna gloria Amen

    los perdons que s donaren
    als qui donaren caritat
    y acompanyare la processo
    foren

lo es per lo S^{or} visrey bisbe de çiguenca   xxxx dies
per lo vicari general y capitol de la seu sede vacante   xxxx dies

per lo R^{mo} Bisbe de Vich   xxxx dies
per lo R^{mo} don johan de cardona   xxxx dies

Appendix 3

Arxiu Parroquial de Santa Maria del Pi. Caixa B361. Determinacions E, 1623–1639
fols. 52v–53r: 'Per la professo dels sentenciats'
Ceremonial for the procession of the bones, dated 12 March 1630

Convocada la Reverent communitat en la sagristia maior en la qual foren presents lo dr Guasch, ferrer, Castells, viladecans, puig, Rosell, Garriga, Joachim, Bonostia, torres, vingues, miralles, parrassa, Rovira, Rodoli, verge, alegre, colobrans

fonch proposat per lo Dr Pau ferrer altre dels procuradors de herensies com lo dr Guasch premisser de la present esglesia los havia dit que tenia que proposar a la R^{nt} Communitat per part dels obrers com ell diria y digue dit dr Guasch com don lluis ferrer obrer militar en nom dels demes obrers li havia dit com diumenja primer vinent que contarem a 17 del present mes de mars havia assenyalat pera anar acercar los corters y ossos dels sententiats de la creu cuberta que fos servida la R^{nt} communitat de tener[h]o a be y anar ab professo com havian sempre acostumat [fol. 53r] y per quant la Reyna de vngria se trobava vuy en Barcelona que sils apareria passas dita professo devant del palau de dita S^{ra} Reyna en la plaça de St francesch y quant no ls aparegues que al manco possas dita proffesso a mes dels llochs acostumats per la Coll plassa de St Jaume a la plassa nova y carrer dels bote[r]s y tambe fonch proposat que los majorals de nostra señora dels desemparats gustarian que la Imatje de nostra S^{ra} que acostumava anar en dita proffesso no anas darrera de las caxas dels ossos dels sententiats sino en lo mitx del clero y axi vista la proposicio fonch determinat que fassa dit dia [...] dita professo y que no pase devant lo Palau de la Reyna de vngria y que s passas per los altres carrers demanaven dits obrers y que en lo del Imatje de nostra señora que se concerten ab los obrers que en dos llochs aniria molt be

[fol. 53r] dels sententiats

Diumenja a 17 de mars 1630 se feu la professo per lo soterrar y donar sepultura ecclesiastica als ossos dels miserables sentenciats qui per la justitia eran estats esquarterats la qual se feu a les tres hores despres de vespres exint per lo portal major de dita esglesia comensaren a cantar verba mea, etc. y proseguint lo cami per lo carrer del pi per las casas de Montserrat per la porta ferrissa carrer del Carme al portal de St Antoni fins ho prop lo Empedrat de la creu cuberta ahont se trobaren deu Caxas de dits ossos ab una creu de fusta havian posada per orde dels S^{rs} obrers de la present esglesia y en arribant a la primera caxa feu la R^{nt} communitat una absolta ab cant de orgue a dos cors y aquella acabada se parti la professo per lo mateix cami fins al portal de St Antoni carrer del Hospital bocaria lo call la plassa de St Jaume devant la diputatio palau del Sr Bisbe plassa nova carrer dels botes carrer del pi y torna entra per lo portal major la professo ana ab aquest orde so es que de la esglesia parti portant la pendo ho bandera [fol. 53v] negra dels confrares de la purissima sanch de Jesucrist seguint las confrarias de la present esglesia ab llums despres venia lo st crucifici de dita confraria seguint los minyons del hospital general y orfens y despres la creu maior ab la R^{nt} communitat ab los Hornaments lo domer diaca y capiscols negres en esser partida la dita professo despres de haver feta la absolta fora lo portal vn minyno [sic] del Hosptial general portava la creu devant las caxas Inmediadament en esser al portal de St Antoni tragueren la Imatje de nostra señora dels desenparats la qual estava en lo porxo devant la esglesia de St Antoni y passades totas las caxas dels morts la posaren derera acompanyada de molts confrares portant vuyt atxes devant y seguint derrera mes de cent confrares ab siris encesos en las mans y a la fi anava quatra majorals de dita confraria seguint despres va grandissim numero de homens y dones lo Ill.^{m} señor Cardenal bornos concedi a tots los qui seguirian dita professo cent dies de perdo y los Ill.^{ms} Bisbe de Barcelona y de lleyda quaranta cada hu en esser arribada dita professo en la esglesia feren una absolta a cant pla ab las respostas a cant de orgue y posaren las caxas dels morts devant la taula de la obra Ab quatra atxes posaren los obrers ab los candeleros de ferro y la Imatje de nostra señora dels desemperats la posaren ab un altar li havian posat devant la taula de dits obrers lo dilluns se digue la missa matinal de la feria y lo offici maior de Requiem per dits morts y en esser acabat lo offici los aportaren en la sepultura esta dedicada per dits en lo fossar a la part de la capella de St Joan ferense nou tochs per dits comensant lo primer [fol. 54r] a mitx die despres de vespres tocada la ave maria despres de prima lo diumenja a mitx die y encontinent parti la professo se compartiren los demes devant un toch per lo dilluns mentres se feyan las absoltas del enterro los obrers donaren a quiscun prevere dos sous per la professo ab sos dobles y sis diners al offici la communitat dona dos sous de quotidi Requiescant in pacem amen

Appendix 4

Arxiu Parroquial de Santa Maria del Pi. Caixa B294. *Llibre negre de l'Obra* 851–854: 'Enterro dels ossos de la creu cuberta
Ceremonial for the procession of the bones, dated 7 April 1658

[851] Deus dirigat verba oris [sic] mei
    A vii del mes de Abril any de la natiuitat de nostre Señor de MDClviii
    Diumenge de passio obtinguda primer llicensia del Sr Virrey del present Principat qui es lo Ex.^{m} S^r marques de Montana y dels Ill^{ms} S^{rs} consellers y obrers de la present Ciutat concedida als S^{rs} obrers desta Iglesia del Pi se ana de dita sglesia a sercar los

ossos dels miserables sentenciats que staven en la Creu Cuberta conforme ab antiqua se es acostumat sempre anarlos a sercar per donarlos terra sagrada ab professo solemna la qual parti desta Iglesia del Pi a les tres hores de la tarda per lo carrer del Pi dreta la casa del Marques de Aytona y despres per lo carrer de les cases de Monserrat Porta ferrissa carrer del Carme dret al portal de St Antoni y fins o casi al entrant del empedrat de la Creu Cuberta hahont se trobaren deu caxes sb sos llits cubertes ab draps part de eles molt ostensosos y richs (encara que es veritat que les ditas caxas havian de star compartides desde la Creu Cuberta fins al cap davall del empedrat conforme ere costum antich lo que no saberen lo dia se feu dita professo y axi se adverteig hara per una altra vegada) Los quals draps eren ço es lo hu de la confraria dels argenters de brocat, altre de la confraria dels sastres de vellut negre altre de la confraria dels hortolans del portal de St Antoni de vellut carmesi, altre de la confraria dels julians mercers de vellut negre, altre de la confraria dels revenedors de vellut carmesi, altre de la confraria dels mestres de cases y molers tambe de vellut carmesi, altre de la sanch de Jesuchrist tambe de vellut carmesi, altre de N^a S^{ra} dels Desamparats tambe de vellut carmesi, y dos de la Sta Spina a la Primera de les quals caxes hy havia una creu de fusta negre dreta ab una llanterna, y en arribant alli lo clero feren una absolta a cant dorga a dos cors, y apres de haver feta dita absolta volta la professo la dita primera caxa y sen torna vers lo dit portal de St Antoni y en haver acabat de voltar o passar la professo en continent prengueren les dites caxes diferents persones portantles al coll y aquells anaven detras de la professo ab la forma seguent Es a saber que de despres del gremial anaven los minyons dels dos hospitals ço es general a ma dreta y Orfens a ma squerra aportant la dita creu de fusta lo minyo mes gran del dit Hospital General (la qual feren posar en dites caxes los senyors obrers de dita Iglesia com es costum) y despres de eles seguien los qui aportaven les atxes que eren ab alguna de ells mes de dotze persones que per no poder tots tenirhi los muscles hi havia algunes dessota y despres anaren perseguint, y entrant per lo portal de St Antoni hahont trobaren en lo Porxet de la Iglesia de dit St Antoni Nostra Señora dels Desemparats ab un altar parat adornades [852] un manto de llana blava ab los dos minyonets y alli feren altra absolta a dos cors tambe a cant dorga, y acabada aquella tragueren nostra senyora de dit porxo, y se posa detras les dites caxes ab moltes atxes que la acompanyaven part devant y part darrera, les quals aportaven ço es la de devant los confrares y devots de nostra señora de diferents estats y las de derrera artistes y mercaders cada hu per son orde, y a fi de dita professo de totes les atxes anaven los S^{rs} mayorals de la confraria de nostra senyora dels Desemparats qui eren m^o Antoni Comes prevere beneficiat de la dita Iglesia del Pi, m^o Joseph Lledo mercader y Joseph Portaria torsedor de seda los quals anaven ab una filera ço es dit Comes al mitg, lledo a ma dreta y Portaria a ma squerra cada hu aportant una atxa, y aquells clohian la dita professo. apres ana per la carrer qui va a la plassa de Sta Anna y gira per devant la font y sen torna per lo dit carrer del Pi y entra per lo portal mayor de dita Iglesia que eren tres quarts per les set hores, y entrada en dita iglesia dexaren alli les dites caxes al entrant del cor y posaven nª sª devant la taula de la obra sobra una tumol o taula ab son palit y devant de ella staven les dites caxes y posades dites caxes y nª sª sobra dita taula feren altra absolta a cant de orga com les demes, y alli posaren quatre atxes grogues al costat de dites caxes y feta la dita absolta se disgrega la dita professo la qual Professo anava ab lo orde y forma seguent Primerament anava lo Pendo de la sanch de Jesuchrist ab algunes atxes, y despres anaven les confraries de dita yglesia parts dels confrares aportant siris y la major part atxes blanques, y despres lo s^t Christo de dita sanch de Jesuchrist ab mes atxes y despres venia la creu major tota nova que fonch la primera ixida que feu ab ornaments tots nous negres ço es tovallola de taffeta, y gremial de vellut negre y despres venia lo clero ab alguns capellans foresters que y havie cridats y despres del Clero lo gremial ço es diaca, sotsdiaca y domer qui ere lo Sr Rector de dita Iglesia ab los vestiments de vellut negre molt bons y despres dells venien los dits minyons dels Hospitals cantant lo Miserere si be al anar anaven devant la Creu y despres venien les dites caxes, y despres los dits devots, y confrares de N^{ra} S^{ra} ab atxes blanques, y despres N^{ra} S^{ra} posada dins un tabernacle ab un manto com sta dit ab corona de plata sobredorada la qual aportaven quatre devots ab vestes de bocaran [sic] ab altres quatre que aportaven una atxa cada hu devant dit Imatge de nª s^{ra} tambe altres restes axi que quant los quatre staven cansats los de les atxes aportaven n^r s^{ra}, y los que portaven n^{ra} s^{ra} pertenien les atxes y axi anaven perseguint la dita professo ab dit orde y conformitat y tambe hi havie talem que ere de vellut negre [853] Lo qual aportaven sis cauallers elegits per lo S^r don Bernat Aimerich obrer de dita Iglesia e inmediadament venien los dits artistes y mercaders per son orde cada hu ab sa atxa los quals mercaders foren convidats per lo dit S^r majoral mercader de n^{ra} s^{ra} axi que se contaren en dita professo cent quoranta dues atxes entre tots sens los ciris dels confrares, y despres de totes les atxes venia seguint la dita professo un gran numero de personas de un genero y altre que s Indica hi havia passades de deu mil persones de tal manera que arribava lo seguiment de la professo desdel portal de la Bocaria fins lo portal de St Antoni, y encara hy havia algunes persones fora de dit portal de St Antoni, les quals anaven ab molta devotio, y les demes de ells ab los rosaris a les mans als quals y a tots los qui anaven en dita professo lo Ill^m Sr Arcabisbe de Tarragona 80. dies de perdo, lo Ill^m S^r bisbe de Barcelona 40. dies, lo M^m s^r bisbe de Gerona altres 40. dies, lo Ill.^m s^r bisbe de vich ques troba en Barcelona altres 40. dies axi que en tots eren 200. dies de perdo. E mes en dita professo acaptaven los obrers y Ad.^{rs} de dita Iglesia per lo enterro y misses dels dits defuncts; y lo endema dilluns que comptaven a 8. de dit se digueren tot lo de mati misses en dita Iglesia per les animes de dits defuncts en les capelles seguints Es a saber en la capella de N^{ra} S^{ra} dels desemperats, St Miquel dels revenedors, St Isidro, S^t sepulcre de nª s^{ra} Sta spina, St. Llopart, St Miquel y St Marti, St Portacreu y St Joachim que entre totes se digueren mes de 120 misses y a les deu hores se comensa lo offici de defuncts y en comensat dit offici se ensengueren al costat de dites caxes dotze atxes grogues, y no se apagaren fins que foren enterrats los dits ossos lo qual ofici digue lo dit s^r rector, y aquels se canta a cant de orga a dos cors ab molt solemnitat y acabat lo dit offici predica lo predicador de la coresma qui ere un prevere de St Agusti, qui predica de defuncts y acabada la dita predica se ana ab la creu y clero a fer una absolta devant les dites caxes a cant de orga, y acabada aquella prengueren les dites caxes moltes persones artistes y menestrals que s trobaren en dita Iglesia y anaren despres del Clero aportant les dites caxes fins a la ecclesiastica sepultura y despres anava tambe n^ra s^ra dels desemperats, la qual aporatven quatre devots e isqueren per lo portal major y passaren per devant la creu del fossar, y rodaren dit fossar, a anaven dret a la tomba o vas que sta dedicat per los dits ossos, que es detras la capella de s^t Joan hont hi ha unes tapies ab sa porta y alli arribats feren absolta a cant pla y enterraren dits ossos en presentia de moltes persones antes de anarse de alli lo dit Clero, y sempre stigue alli la mare de deu S.^ma fins foren enterrats acompanyant los dits ossos ab les dites dotze atxes, les quals aportaren persones devotes y pies y enterrats aquells entra lo Clero y n.^ra S.^ra per lo portal qui es detras lo portal major y axi foren acabades les obsequies de dits defuncts ab [854] esa hostentatio y aplauso de tot lo poble tocant las campanes ja al dissapte y s feren desset tochs compartits a esta forma, ço es un toch al dissapte a les tres hores de la tarda, altra toch a la Ave Maria, altra toch al diumenge de mati dos tochs al dilluns de mati, un toch al entrant al offici y dos tochs quant los enterraren, Y perque conste en los sdevenedor de una tant santa y obra pia y los que vindran ne tinguen notisia plena perque ab major fer nos continuen esta obra de misericordia y del servey de deu n^r s^r Caxi com tambe lo havien trobat scrit los predecessors y haven feta la present descriptio de tot lo fet Essent obre[r]s de dita Iglesia lo present any 1658 lo dit noble s^r don Bernat Aymerich Joseph comas candeler de sera, Jaume Torrelles mestre de fer carretes y Pere Pau Ratxotxo cartayre y pera disposar y ordenar dita professo y curar tot lo necessari per aquella foren eligides y anomenats les persones seguents francesch llanoart notari y scriva major de la general governatio de Cathalunya, Pere Martir llunell notari publich de Barcelona y Saluador Cuyas gerrer anomenats per dits s^rs obre[r]s Joseph soldeuila tambe notari de Barcelona Pere Trulles notari real collegiat per scriva major de la casa de la Ciutat y t. darocha revenedor anomenats per los S^rs Ad^s de nostra señora dels desemparats sobredit darocha no y pogue asistir per estar desganat y en son loch hy asisti m^o Tomas Ballaster prevere capellaniu de dita Iglesia, lo qual hy prengue molt treball E mes posamos en memoria que se aplegaren de caritats per lo dit enterro stant a quatre lliures dotze sous y sis dines 4ll 12s y 6d ab sta forma a saber es que molts dies antes de dita professo se acapta a les portes de dita Iglesia y apres se acapta lo die de n^a s^a de mars deuant lo monestir de Nazaret tenant alli un llit ab una caxa de morts cuberta ab lo drap de n^a s^a del desemparats ab un cap de mors de sobre acaptant les dites persones elegides per dits s^rs obrers y majorals de n^ra s^a y apres se feu una acapta general per tota la present ciutat fent aquella alguns sis capellans de dita Iglesia y moltes cavallers, mercaders, artistes y manstrals [sic] quienes los S^rs obrers y A^dors de dita Iglesia y los s^rs majorals de N^a S^a ab altres sis per llur part convidats per la dita acapta precehint primera les sedules o bitllets que donaren a tots los predicadors de totes les paroquies de la present ciutat en parte en ells fossen servits notificar el auditori lo se faria una acapta general per la present ciutat per lo enterro de dits ossos. Y tambe se aplega molts dies antes de dita professo fora de dit portal de St Antoni tenant alli les caxes dels dits ossos acaptant algun dia lo andador de la capella de N^a S^{ra} dels desemperats, y altres dies alguns devots y apres se acapta per tota la professo acaptant ab bassines tots los dits S^{rs} obrers y Ad^{ros} de la Iglesia y no altres persones, y lo endema dilluns tambe se acaptan per dins la dita Iglesia fins foren enterrats los dits ossos y dos dies antes de fer dita professo se posaren per los cantons y portes de las Iglesias de la present ciutat papers stampats notificant ab lo dia se faria la dita professo y los [855] perdons que guanyarien qui anire seguint aquella. E mes notam que la caritat de dites meses que s celebraren en dita Iglesia per les animes de dits deffuncts pagaren diferents persones devotas ço es les misses de les capelles de confraries los confrares de aquelles, y en las demes capelles persones particulars.

E mes se adverteix que al dissapte al vespres vn vicari de dita Iglesia de St Antoni orde del dit Sr Bisbe ana a absolver los dits ossos en la dita Iglesia de St Antoni hahont staven retirats ab la forma que absolan [sic] los comunicats ab una vasa a la ma per lo que haver mort algu ab duelo o desafiu o altrament y per so se ana a absolver dits ossos que altrament no se ls podia dar terra sagrada.

E mes se fa nota que pagats tots los gastos de dita professo restaren sinch lliures y sis diners les quals se entregaren a M° Gabriel Torres prevere y receptor de les misses de dita Iglesia del Pi pera de aquelles ne fer celebrar vint y sinch misses de caritat de 4s per les animes de dits defuncts

Los papers de les indulgencies y altres papers son en la plica del present any de 1658. fet per mi Pere Martir llunell notari de

Barcelona
Laus deo

Bibliography

Secondary Sources

Adelantado Soriano V., "La pena de muerte como espectáculo de masas en la Valencia del Quinientos", in Sirera Turó J.L. (ed.), *Estudios sobre teatro medieval* (Valencia: 2008) 15–24.

Amelang J.S., *Honored Citizens of Barcelona: Patrician Culture and Class Relations, 1490–1714* (Princeton NJ: 1986).

Aparicio Olmos E.M., *Santa Maria de Inocentes y Desamparados en su iconografía original y sus precedentes históricos* (Valencia: 1968).

Cabré B., "La Confrària de la Santa Espina de l'Esglesia del Pi de Barcelona al segle XVII: Un nou context per un vell repertori", *Recòndit* 2 (2022) 118–143.

Catalá Sanz J.A. – Pérez García P., "La pena capital en Valencia (1450–1500): Cifras, espacios urbanos y ritualidades funerarias de la Cofradía de Inocentes y Desemperado", *Revista de Historia Moderna* 39 (2021) 272–334.

Chamorro Esteban A., "El paso de las Infantas de la Casa de Austria por Barcelona (1551–1666)", in Serrano Martin E. (ed.), *De la tierra al cielo: líneas recientes de investigación en historia moderna* (Zaragoza: 2012) 495–514.

Chamorro A., *Barcelona y el rey. Las visitas reales desde Fernando el Católico hasta Felipe V* (Barcelona: 2017).

Creixell J., *San Ignacio. Estudio crítico y documentado de los hechos Ignacianos relacionados con Montserrat, Manresa y Barcelona* (Barcelona: 1922).

Falvey K., "Scaffold and Stage: Comforting Rituals and Dramatic Traditions in Late Medieval and Renaissance Italy", in Terpstra N. (ed.), *The Art of Executing Well: Rituals of Execution in Renaissance Italy*, Early Modern Studies 1 (Kirksville MIS: 2008) 13–30.

Garrut J.M., *Notas históricas de la Real e ilustre archicofradía de la Purísima Sangre de Nuestro Señor Jesucristo* (Barcelona: 1962).

Gómez Urdóñez J.L., *La Hermandad de la Sangre de Cristo de Zaragoza. Caridad y ritual religioso en la ejecución de la pena de muerte* (Saragossa: 1978).

Kamen H., *Cambio cultural en la Sociedad de Siglo de Oro: Cataluña y Castilla, siglos XVI–XVII* (Madrid: 1998).

Knighton T., "Relating History: Music and Meaning in the *relaciones* of the Canonization of St Raymond Penyafort", in Ferreira M.P. – Cascudo T. (eds.), *Música e História: Estudos em homenagem a Manuel Carlos de Brito* (Lisbon: 2017) 27–52.

Knighton T., "'Puix tot es per major aument del culto divino': El paisaje sonoro de las cofradías gremiales de Santa Maria del Pi, ss. XV–XVII", *Recòndit* 2 (2022) 81–117.

Knighton T., "The Soundscape of Death and Musical Experience in Early Modern Barcelona", in Sá V. – De Paula R.T. – Conde A.F. (eds.), *Paisagens Sonoras em expansão. Novas sonoridades. Novas Escutas* (Cotia – Barreiro: 2023). http://doi.org/10.17613/dsh4-mq44.

Kreitner K., *Music and Civic Ceremony in Fifteenth-Century Barcelona* (Ph.D. dissertation, Duke University: 1990).

Martin Nicolás V., "Isabel de Josa, el impulso femenino en la fundación de la 'Confraria de la Sang' de Barcelona (1536)", in Gallego Franco H. – García del Herrero M. del C. (eds.), *Autoridad, poder e influencia: mujeres que hacen Historia* (Barcelona: 2017).

Mazuela-Anguita A., *Women in Convent Spaces and the Musical Networks of Early Modern Barcelona* (New York: 2023).

Pérez García P., "Cofradías y Germanía: la Real Cofradía de Inocentes y Desamparados (1519–1524)", in Amelang J.S. et al. (eds.), *Palacios, plazas y patíbulos: la sociedad Española moderna entre el cambio y las resistencias* (Valencia: 2018) 421–432.

Pérez García P., "Espacio, rito, devoción y memoria: la cofradía de Inocentes y Desamparados de Valencia (1450–1512)", in *Hommage au professeur Anita* González-Raymond (Montpellier: forthcoming).

Prospero M., "Consolation or Condemnation. The Debates on Withholding Sacraments from Prisoners", in Terpstra N. (ed.), *The Art of Executing Well: Rituals of Execution in Renaissance Italy*, Early Modern Studies 1 (Kirksville MIS: 2008) 98–117.

Puentes-Blanco A., *Música y devoción en Barcelona (ca. 1550–1626): Estudio de libros de polifonía, contextos y práticas musicales* (Ph.D dissertation, Universitat de Barcelona, 2018).

Real e Ilustre Cofradía de la Virgen de los Desemparados cuya imagen se venera en el altar de su misma invocación en la iglesia parroquial de Santa María de los Reyes, o del Pino (Barcelona: 1923).

Rihouet P., *Art Moves. The Material Culture of Processions in Renaissance Perugia* (Turnhout: 2017).

Saéz García M.A., "Isabel de Josa. Una insòlita dona catalana del segle XVI" (Master's thesis, Universitat Autònoma de Barcelona: 2015).

Saéz García M.A., *Creure, somiar, lluitar: Barcelona en femení* 1: *Laventura spiritual d'Isabel de Josa (1490–1564)* (Ph.D. dissertation, Universitat Autònoma de Barcelona: 2018).

Serés G., "El context històricosocial dels episodis Catalans del *Quixot*", in Riera C. (ed.), *El Quixot i Barcelona* (Barcelona: 2005) 81–91.

Terpstra N., "Introduction: The Other Side of the Scaffold", in Terpstra N. (ed.), *The Art of Executing Well: Rituals of Execution in Renaissance Italy*, Early Modern Studies 1 (Kirksville MIS: 2008) 1–5.

Terpstra N. "Body Politics: The Criminal Body between Public and Private", *Journal of Medieval and Early Modern Studies* 45.1 (2015) 7–52.

Terpstra N., "Confraternities and Capital Punishment: Charity, Culture, and Civic Religion in the Communal and Confessional Age", in Eisenbichler K. (ed.), *A Companion to Medieval and Early Modern Confraternities* (Leiden – Boston: 2019) 212–231.

Index Nominum

Abbate, Carlo   245, 250, 262, 265–266
Adrián (singer)   77
Adrian (Emperor of Rome)   475
Afonso, Baltasar   384
Agatha (Saint)   330*n*9, 331, 334
Aichinger, Gregor   11, 272, 294–296
Alan of Brittany   205
Alba, Duke of (Fernando Àlvarez de Toledo, Third Duke)   3, 10, 62, 66–67
Albert (Archduke of Austria)   64, 71–72, 83
Almeida Portugal, João (II Count of Asumar)   129
Althann, Maria Eva Elisabeth   254*n*22, 260
Althann, Michael Adolph von   245–249, 250, 252–254, 256, 258–263, 265, 267–268
Althann, Michael Ferdinand von   253, 263
Álvarez de la Vega, Juan   460
Alwey, Thomas   219
Ambrose (Saint)   330, 334
Andrew (Saint)   328, 385
Anglès, Pere Màrtir   117
Anhalt-Bernburg, Christian II von   246, 259, 267
Anne of Bohemia (Queen of England)   211
Anthony (Saint)   501
Antifassi, Niccolò   316
Aparicio Maya, José Juan   420
Aranda, Francisca de   75
Arbuxech, Gaspar Blay, C.O.   161*n*35
Arcimboldo, Giuseppe (painter)   254*n*20
Arco, Giovanni Vincenzo d'   256
Arnold, Georg (composer)   280
Ashmole, Elias   267–268
Ashwell, Thomas (composer)   217
Augurius (Saint)   499*n*54
Augustine (Saint)   42, 228, 286, 413
Augustus (Emperor of Rome)   476
Austria, John of   63
Auta (Saint)   382

Bach, Johann Sebastian   12
Bader, Daniel   74
Baglioni, Baccio   311
Baccio del Bianco   314*n*21
Balde, Jakob, S.J.   288–289

Baldovín   74, 77
Banchieri, Adriano   264
Bancoart, Jakob (composer)   280
Barbara (Saint)   66*n*9, 69, 294
Barter, Joan   134–135, 137, 141–142, 148
Bartholomäus von Portia (Count)   278
Bartolomé *el capón*   77
Basalenque, Diego, fray   413–414
Baumann, Jakob   294
Baussele, Hedwige van   102*n*45
Baxadonis, Dominique de   102
Beausart, Jacob de   108
Belman, Laurence   211*n*44
Benedict of Palermo (Saint)   389
Benedict XIII (Pope, Pedro de Luna)   123
Benno (Saint)   279
Berg, Adam   292
Bernard of Clairvaux   285
Bernardi, Stefano   263–266
Bidelli, Giovanni Battista   330*n*11, 353
Biondi de Montalto, Fabio   394
Blanckaert, Jan   101*n*45
Bland (citharist)   217*n*68
Blas y Sandoval, Alonso de   461
Bommaerts, Gerardo   79
Bommaerts, Baltazar   79
Bommaerts, Bernaert   79
Boniface IX (Pope, Piero Cybo Tomacelli)   207*n*23
Borja, Francisco de   123
Borromeo, Carlo (Archbishop of Milan)   12, 230, 326, 330, 346*n*45, 347, 348
Bouchet, Jean   371
Brandon, Charles (Duke of Suffolk)   218*n*78, 219–220
Briet, Philippe   267–268
Bruyn, Nicolas de   98–99, 101
Buchner, Philipp Friedrich   279
Bull, John   83
Buonarotti, Michelangelo   182
Buonsignori, Stefano   471, 475
Burigozzo, Giovan Marco   346

Caccini, Giulio   127, 312–315
Cairoli, Giuseppe   330*n*12, 353
Calbet   478

Callixtus III (Pope, Alfonso Borgia)   159
Calvi, Donato   52–53
Calvi, Lorenzo (composer)   264
Camprubí, Francesc   117
Carafa, Carlo   249*n*10, 253, 259, 261
Cardona, Joan de (Bishop of Barcelona)   509, 522*n*48, 530, 543
Carissimi, Giacomo (composer)   236
Carlier, Gilles   104*n*57
Carraresi, Bernardo di Raffaello   315
Casale, Giambattista   347
Casio, Jacomo   197*n*51
Casola, Pietro   332*n*17
Castanho, João   385
Castiglione, Giovanni Antonio   347*n*52
Castro Vaca y Quiñones, Pedro de (Archbishop of Granada)   444
Cataniis, Christoforus   327
Catherine Michaela of Spain (Duchess of Savoy)   119
Catherine (Saint)   120
Cazzati, Mauricio   280
Cecchi, Giovan Maria   309, 318–319
Cecilia (Saint)   69, 196, 281–282, 286, 378
Cendrat, Jaume   138*n*50, 150
Cervantes Saavedra, Miguel de   532–533
Chamber, Geoffrey   213, 218
Charles Emmanuel I the Great   119
Charles I (Duke of Burgundy)   104
Charles III (King of Spain)   248, 451
Charles of Austria (Archduke)   528
Charles V (King of Spain, Holy Roman Emperor)   64, 152
Charles VII (King of France)   104
Chiari, Tommaso di Stefano   323
Chica Benavides, Antonio de la   442
Chichelet, Henry   214*n*57
Chiflet, Philippe   72
Christina of Sweden (Queen)   227
Christine of Lorraine (Grand Duchess of Tuscany)   315–316
Cicognini, Jacopo   319, 320*n*34
Clare (Saint)   501
Clement VIII (Pope, Ippolito Aldobrandini)   12, 273, 512
Clerc, Richard   211*n*40
Cluts, Jean   102
Coll, Onofre   126

Collaert, Joannes   79–80
Colonere, Marguert   101
Colson, Robert   217*n*72
Columbus, Christopher   391*n*19
Comes, Juan Bautista   160*n*29
Comi, Baccio   314
Comi, Domenico   314*n*21
Compère, Loyset   344
Conan, Prince   382–383
Confalonieri, Gianbattista   390, 394–395
Conte, Francesco del   331*n*16
Conti, Carlo, Cardinal   191
Coppin, Florent   363
Cornelio   77
Cornelio, Musso (bishop)   295
Cosimo II (Grand Duke of Tuscany)   316
Cox, Thomas   393
Crane, William   214*n*60
Cremers, Franchoys   79
Cremers, Steven   79
Crescentio, Orazio   191
Crispis, Imolus de   327
Cromwell, Thomas   208, 218
Curtz, Albrecht Graf, S.J.   281
Cutler, Nicholas   219–220
Cuypere Lathomus, Grégoire   102

Dalmau, Francisco   444–445
Damiani, Pier (Saint)   330
Day, William   210*n*37, 211*n*38
De Dueñas, Alonso   77–78
De Dueñas, Bartolomé   74, 76–77, 78, 80
De Dueñas, Diego   76–77, 78
De Dueñas, Jerónimo   76–77
De Dueñas, Pedro de   76–77, 78
De Guzmán, Domingo   64
De Hoyo, Bartolomé   76
De Lovera, Juan   76–77
De Lovera, Lucas   76
De Mondragón, Cristóbal   66
De Perpiñán, Juan   77
De Pineda, Fernando   66
Del Hoyo, Juan   76–77
Denis (Saint)   6, 152–153, 154, 159, 161–162, 163–164, 166–167, 170
Delft, Joannes van   79
Dembołęcki, Wojiech   268
Des Maisons (poet)   372

INDEX NOMINUM

Dias de Novais, Paulo   383–384
Dienheim, Eberhard von (Bishop of Mainz)   294
Dietrichstein (Cardinal), Franz Seraph von   245, 261n38, 262–263, 268
Dominic (Saint)   389
Duchefeld, Reginald   211n39
Duddington, Anthony   211
Dufay, Guillaume   104n57
Duval (Duke of Dampierre), Henri   256

Eeckt, Barbara van der   108
Eligius (Saint)   184, 191–192
Erbach, Christian   294
Escobar, Francisco   77
Escolano, Gaspar   153, 163
Eugenius IV (Pope, Gabriele Condulmer)   308n2
Eulogius (Saint)   499n54
Everaert, Anthoni   74, 80

Fabri, Gerard   110
Fabri, Pierre   371
Farnese, Alessandro (Cardinal)   236–237
Fasani, Raniero   330
Felde, Nicholas   212n46
Felónia (black 'queen')   398
Ferdinand II (Emperor)   254n22, 267, 284
Ferdinand II (King of Hungary)   530
Ferdinand II (v) (King of Aragon)   152, 439, 442
Fernández Portocarrero y Mendoza, Luis Antonio (V Count of Palma del Río)   129
Fernando of Aragón (Duke of Calabria, Viceroy of Valencia)   167
Ferrand, David   364–365, 367, 369, 373–374
Ferrer, Lluís   531, 543
Festa, Costanzo   292
Figueró, Rafael   141–142, 143–144
Fineschi da Radda, Antonio   317
Florez, Enrique   476–478, 485, 489, 496, 498, 500, 502
Florus, Lucius Annaeus   475
Fontana, Giovanni Battista   315n23
Forner, Raimundo   117
Fortunatus, Venantius   312n14
Foster, John   220n89
Foxe, John   218
Francis (Saint)   256, 259, 264

Francis Xavier (Saint)   263–264, 280
Frederic de Portugal, don   522n48
Freund, Augustin   280
Fructuosus (Saint)   497–498, 499n54
Fugger, Marcus   254
Fuller, John (singer)   214
Furtado de Mendonça, João   398
Furtado, Domingos (black minstrel)   399
Furtado, Francisco (black minstrel)   399
Furtado, Miguel (black minstrel)   399
Furtado, Pêro (black minstrel)   399

Gaffurius, Franchinus   333, 344, 346
Gagliano, Giovan Battista da   311, 319–320
Gagliano, Marco da   311
Galilei, Galileo   314
Galilei, Vincenzo   127
Garro, Gaspar   509
Gas, Josep   137
Gastone, Gian (Duke of Tuscany)   240
George (Saint)   6, 117, 152 *passim*, 390n17
Getzmann, Wolfgang   293
Giacomelli, Giovan Battista ('Il violino')   315
Gigli, Giacinto   191
Gippenbusch, Jakob, S.J.   289, 291
Giralt, Bartomeu   134, 144
Giunta, Bernardo   339
Glenfeld, Roger de   203
Glymes, Elisabeth de (Countess of Salm)   102, 108n74
Gómez, Diego   76–77
Gómez, Pedro   76–77
Gonima, Manuel   137
Gonzaga (Duke of Mantua), Ferdinando   257
Gonzaga (Duke of Nevers and Rethel), Charles III   248, 249n9, 256
Gonzaga, Vincenzo (Duke of Mantua)   74
Goubaux, Francisco   79
Gouge, Richard   214
Gouveia, Francisco de   383, 385–386
Gramaye, Jean-Baptiste   253, 260–261, 268
Grandis, Vincenzo de   197n50
Gregory XIII, Pope (Ugo Boncompagni)   195n44, 197, 347
Gregory the Great (Saint)   196
Grison, Catharina   77
Grossi, Carlo   18
Guasch, Pere Joan   116, 123

553

Gucci, Raffaello   311–313, 315
Guerrero, Francisco   385, 401
Gustavus Adolphus (King of Sweden)   277, 284

Haes, Christianus   79
Halbos, Juan Baptista   79
Handel, Georg Frideric   12
Harrach (Cardinal, Archbishop of Prague), Ernst Adalbert von   250, 260
Haugenhoffer, Caspar   250–251, 260, 261*n*38, 263, 265
Haym von Themar, Johann   286–287, 291, 293–294
Henríquez de Jorquera, Francisco   442, 456
Henry IV (King of France)   359, 377
Henry VIII (King of England)   19, 220
Heymbach, Bernard   99
Heywood, Thomas   202*n*8
Hickes, Christopher   219*n*82
Hickes, Frideswide   219*n*82
Hickes, Jaspar   219*n*82
Hickes, Melchior   219*n*82
Hickes, Richard   219
Hickes, Thomas   219*n*82
Hickes, William   219*n*82
Hiesserle von Chodaw, Heinrich   250, 257*n*27, 258
Hollandre, Henri   101
Honing, William   220*n*85
Huygens, Constantijn   92*n*20

Innocent XI (Pope, Benedetto Giulio Odescalchi)   123
Isabel the Catholic (Queen of Castile)   439, 442
Isabel Clara Eugenia (Archduchess of Austria)   64, 71, 83
Isabelle of Portugal (Duchess of Burgundy)   104
Isidor the Farmer (Saint)   480*n*26

Jacob (Count of Salm)   109*n*24
Jacob (Saint)   78
Jacomelli, Giovanni Battista   315*n*23
James (Saint)   152, 207*n*25, 260
Jaume I (King of Aragon)   152–153, 164
Joan I (King of Aragon)   152, 157

John IV (King of Portugal)   400
John (Saint)   69, 329
John the Baptist (Saint)   108
Jolis, Joan   124*n*18, 150
Jordaens, Jacob   65
Josa, Isabel de   509–510
Joseph I Bonaparte (King of Spain)   440
Joseph, Karl, Archduke of Breslau   266
Juan II, King of Aragon   538*n*79
Juan de Ribera, Saint (Archbishop and Viceroy of Valencia)   152, 158, 160*n*29, 163, 165, 170
Julius II (Pope; Giuliano della Rovere)   208

Karl von Österreich, Joseph (Archduke of Austria, Prince-Bishop of Breslau)   266
Klingenstein, Bernhard   11, 272, 294

Lacerda, Agostinho de   383
Lamormaini, Wilhelm   246, 248
Lapeyra, Joseph   129*n*30
La Rea, Alonso de la   412–413
Lasso, Orlando di   278, 296–297
Lasso, Rudolph di   11, 272, 292, 296–297, 298
Lattuada, Serviliano   330
Lawrence (Saint)   328, 480*n*26
Le Vestu, Nicole   372–373
Lechner, Kaspar, S.J.   297
Legrenzi, Giovanni   280
Lemire, Adolphe   74–75, 77, 79–80
Lenzoni, Lelio   313
León, Juan de   458*n*35, 464
Leopold Wilhelm (Archduke of Austria)   267
Lescarre, Nicole   372
Lipsius, Justus   92–93, 99
Litster, John   217*n*72
Llunell, Francesc   517
Loricato, Domenico (Saint)   330
Loriente, Thomas   142
Louis XI (King of France)   99*n*35, 104
Loyola, Ignatius (Saint)   12–13, 259, 263–264, 280, 284, 509–510
Luini, Bernardino   330
Lumley, Lord   217*n*68

Macro, Cox   393–394
Magnus the Martyr (Saint)   203

INDEX NOMINUM   555

Maier, Michael   254n20
Málaga, Sebastián de   458n36, 464
Malagón (singer)   77
Malatesta, Giovanni Battista   348n54, 354
Manfredi di Guastalla, Lodovico   266
Manuel I (King of Portugal)   382n2
Marco Antonio   77
Margaret of Austria (Regent of the Netherlands)   64
Margaret of York (Duchess of Burgundy)   104
Maria of Austria (Queen of Hungary)   530
Mark (Saint)   161n32
Marot, Jean   359
Martha (Saint)   329–330, 331, 340, 348–349
Martignonus, Bernardus   327
Martín (singer)   77
Martin (Saint)   328
Mary Magdalene (Saint)   75, 79, 319, 330
Mary of Hungary (Queen of Hungary)   64
Mas, Diego   116
Matos, Isabel de   398
Matson, Leonard   217
Matthias (King of Bohemia, Holy Roman Emperor)   256
Matthias, Saint   510, 512, 515, 521–524, 528
Maximilian I (King of the Romans)   104, 279
Mayr, Erasmus   294
Medici, Gian Gastone de' (Grand Duke of Tuscany)   240
Medina Rincón, Juan, fray (Bishop of Michoacán)   410
Mei, Girolamo   127
Mena, Alfonso de   446
Mendes, António   383
Mendes, Martím   399
Michael (Saint)   254, 256, 259–260, 263–264, 265, 277
Michelangelo   182
Michiel, Marcantonio   36
Michielssen, Ignatio   79
Migliorotti, Migliorotto   312
Milleville, Francesco de (composer)   264
Millino, Benedetto   180n6
Mollazzi, Michelangelo di Jacopo   311
Mommain (musician)   373
Moncada i Gralla, Gastón de (II Marquis of Aytona)   129

Moncada i Gralla, Joan de (Archbishop of Tarragona)   129
Moncada y Benavides, Luisa Ana de (VII Duchess of Híjar)   129
Moncada y Castro, Guillén Ramón (IV Marquis of Aytona)   129
Moncada, Joan de (Archbishop of Tarragona)   129
Montagut, Bernat de   509
Monte, Philippe de   261
Morales, Cristóbal de   385, 401
Moreno, Juan José   415
Morton, John (Bishop of Ely and Archbishop of Canterbury)   201
Moscoso Osorio, María Leonor de   129
Moxet, Pere Màrtir   117
Munke, William   213, 214n54
Münnich, Johann   293–294

Narcissus (Saint)   137, 155
Navarro (singer)   77
Neander, Alexius   293
Neefs, Peter   65
Nele, John   210n38
Neri, Philip   11–12
Niccoli (castrato)   313
Nicholas (Saint)   201, 416
Nicholas V (Pope, Tommaso ParentucellI)   207n23
Nicoletti, Filippo   194n41
Niess, Johann, S.J.   297

Okeghem, Johannes   373
Oliveira de Cadornega, António   388
Onophrius (Saint)   452
Ottoboni, Pietro (Cardinal)   227

Padbrué, Thymanszoon   12
Paleotti, Gabrieli (Cardinal)   237
Palestrina, Giovanni Pierluigi da   263
Pamphili, Benedetto (Cardinal)   227
Panciatichi, Orazio (bishop)   240, 317
Paredes, Joan de   516
Paris Lodron (Archbishop of Salzburg)   266
Parra, mossén (chapelmaster)   524
Pascal, Blaise   374
Pascal, Jacqueline   374
Pasqual, Ramon   126n22

556 INDEX NOMINUM

Pătraşcu (Prince of Wallachia), Nicolae   256
Paul (Saint)   258, 280
Paul V (Pope, Camillo Borghese)   123
Pedro I (King of Castile)   154
Pere II (King of Aragon)   154
Pere IV (King of Aragon)   152, 154–156
Pérez de Moya, Juan   509n11
Peri, Jacopo   127, 319–320
Périers, Bonaventure des   371
Pesaro, Domenico da   314
Pesciolini, *cavaliere*   320–321
Peter, Saint   111, 124, 161n32, 202n4, 207n25, 277, 280
Peter of Verona (Saint)   161n32
Petrignani of Sforza, Giovanni Battista   248, 256
Phaëton, Hawel Zelensky   248n7
Phalèse, Pierre   82
Philip (Saint)   69
Philip the Handsome (Duke of Burgundy)   104n61
Philip II (King of Spain)   64, 118, 124
Philip III (King of Spain)   118, 120
Philip IV (King of Spain)   530
Philip V (King of Spain)   129, 134
Philipp Adolf von Ehrenberg (Bishop of Würzburg)   283
Philippe III the Good (Duke of Burgundy)   104
Pineda, Fernando de   66
Pinto, Manuel   383, 509n9
Pintor, Antoni   509n9
Pius V (Pope, Michele (Antonio) Ghislieri)   64, 177, 181–182, 197
Pollini, Ottavio   322
Pons, Salvador   116, 123
Pontanus, Jakob, S.J.   295
Pontault de Beaulieu, Sébastien de   478
Ponzio, Pacifico (da Ponte)   331m13, 347
Porcel y Salablanca, Antonio (canon of the collegiate church of El Salvador)   451
Porta, Costanzo   292
Puig, Joan   524
Pyson, Richard   212n46

Quiroga, Vasco de (Bishop of Michoacán)   409, 415

Ramos Tintorão, José   390, 397

Raymond of Penyafort (Saint)   118, 120, 127, 129, 138–139
Raphael   192
Raphael (Saint)   309, 314–315, 317, 320, 322
Rem, Jakob, S.J.   292
Reynold, John   219
Richard II (King of England)   211
Rifós, Rafael   117
Ripoll, Tomás   117
Robertson, Nicholas   214n60, 217n72
Robertson, Thomas   212n45, 213, 217
Robynson, John   211, 213n48
Rocetour, William   217–218
Roch (Saint)   328
Rodrigues da Silva, Diogo   388
Rolewinck, Werner   101n42
Romano, Giulio   313
Rondinelli, Camillo di Giovanni   319
Rondinelli, Giulio   319n31
Rondinelli, Orazio   319n31
Rosa (Saint)   393
Rossem, Maarten van   100
Roussel, François   192
Rubens, Peter Paul   65
Rudolf II (King of Bohemia, Holy Roman Emperor)   253, 254n20, 261
Rueda (singer)   77
Ruimonte, Pedro   82
Rumpf, Hans Georg   280

Sabbatini, Galiazzo   265
Saint German, Charles de   378
Sala, Tomás   126
San Miguel, Juan de, fray   409, 412
Sangallo, Antonio   192
Santa María, Tomás de, fray   424
Santiago. *See* James (Saint)   152, 207n25, 390, 416
Santiago Francisco de (composer)   400
Sanuto, Marin   36
Sanzio, Raphael   192
Sapiti, Niccolò   311
Savelli, Giulio, Cardinal   197n50
Schönbourn, Johan Philipp (Archbishop of Mainz)   279n27
Schweickard, Johann (Archbishop of Mainz)   293
Sebastian (Saint)   275, 284, 294, 456
Sentelles, don Enric de   509

INDEX NOMINUM

Sforza di Santa Fiora, Federico II (Duke of Segni; Prince of Genzano)   227
Sforza, Galeazzo Maria, Duke of Milan   327, 344
Sforza, Ludovico Maria, il Moro, Duke of Milan   328
Simões, Garcia   384
Simonetta, Cicco   346
Sirtori, Beniamino   348
Sixtus V (Pope, Felice Peretti di Montalto)   123–124, 197, 286
Soler, Francisco   137
Soloman, King   98
Soveral, Francisco do (Bishop of Luanda)   387
Spee, Friedrich, S.J.   291
Spínola de la Cerda, Juana   129
Sprenger, Jacob   64
Spynke, William   219n80
Stafford, Edward (Duke of Buckingham)   217
Stephen (Saint)   329
Sternberg, Adam (II) von   254n22
Sternberg, Maria Eva Elisabeth von   254n22
Stockelmans, Frederick   79
Stonzingen, Elisabeth von   254n22
Stradella, Alessandro (composer)   236
Striggio, Alessandro   265
Surià, Vicente   134n46, 149
Sylvius, Philippe Albert   101

Taverner, John (composer)   10, 200, 214–215
Távora, Francisco de   388
Tello, Doctor   126n22, 127
Testwood, Robert   219
Thecla (Saint)   482, 486–488, 492, 494, 499
Thomas Aquinas, Saint   6, 8, 116–117, 120, 123–124, 126–127, 128–129, 130–131, 134–135, 137–138, 140–141, 145–146, 147–149
Timple, Gauthier van den   102
Tomlinson, John   217n72
Tzevi, Sabbetai   19

Ulenberg, Kaspar   281
Ursula (Saint)   274n4, 284, 291, 382–383

Valls, Francesc   134–135, 136–137, 142–143, 144–145, 148
Van Dyck, Anton   65
Van Enkhuizen, Volcaart Jacobs   99n35
Van Eyck, Maria   77
Van Haecht, Godevaert   69
Varela (soldier-singer)   77
Veit Adam von Gepeckh (Bishop of Freising)   297
Verbraken, Gillibert   79
Vermeeren, Anthonis   74, 80, 82n55, 83
Vermeeren, Francisco   74
Verplancken (Verplanquen), Guilliam   75–76, 77
Vervliet, Daniel   66
Vezolo, Ercole   348n54, 354
Vicent Ferrer (Saint)   159, 162, 170
Vicent Martir de la Roqueta (Saint)   162, 164
Vico, Ambrosio de   444
Vico, Raimundo di (Cardinal)   236
Victorinus, Georg   11, 272, 288n54, 293, 296
Vigne, André de la   359
Vila, Joseph   516
Vilosa, Rafael Pau   517

Wace, Geoffrey   218n76
Wadeney, William   211n41
Waelrant, Hubert   75
Waelrant, Raymundus   74
Wallenstein, Albrecht von   277
Wendon, John   213n50
Wieseune, Daniel   99n35
Wilhelm V (Duke of Bavaria)   277
William I (King of England)   205, 375
Wolsey, Thomas (Cardinal)   214n60, 215, 217n68, 219
Wyngaerde, Anton van den   477

Xanxó, Jerónimo (sculptor)   513n22

Zarlino, Gioseffo   4, 250, 262
Zinzendorf, Count of   129

557

Index Locorum

Alfama   154
Amsterdam   18
Andechs   283, 286
Andernach   272, 281–282, 286
Antwerp   3, 10, 62 *passim*, 93, 195
Au am Inn   285
Ausgburg   272, 274, 276*n*14, 283–284, 286, 294–295
Avignon   182

Barcelona   6, 8, 116 *passim*, 155, 374, 382, 484, 506 *passim*
Belgrade   100
Bergamo   5, 25–26, 27, 32 *passim*
Bologna   2, 8, 12, 225, 229, 231–232, 237–238, 239
Bonn   282
Boston, Lincs.   10, 19, 200 *passim*
Brescia   315*n*23, 342*n*38
Brno   260
Bruges   93
Brussels   93, 105
Buda   260
Bury St Edmunds   201–202

Calais   205, 212*n*46, 218
Cambrai   105
Cambridge   214
Cocucho   418
Coimbra   400
Cologne   64, 272, 274*n*4, 275–276, 279, 281, 284, 289, 291, 382
Constantinople   249*n*9, 267
Coventry   202–203
Cremona   342*n*38
Cutzio   411

Diest   105
Dillingen   295
Donauwörth   283
Dublin   12
Durham   217

Eichstätt   280*n*31
Elvas   397–398

Esztergom   253
Evora   382
Evreux   378*n*61
Eye   220

Ferrara   232
Florence   2, 3, 7, 9, 11, 127, 140, 225, 229, 231–232, 235, 239–240, 307 *passim*, 469, 471
Frankfurt   18
Freising   297

Gerona   137, 155
Ghent   88, 93
Gran (Eztergom)   253
Granada   9, 13, 435 *passim*
Grantham   202

Higham Ferrers   214
Hildburghausen   275*n*5
Hull   214

Ingoldstadt   272, 277, 279–280, 280*n*31, 284, 287–288, 292, 295
Innsbruck   280*n*31
Ipswich   219

Landshut   278–279
Leicester   202
Leuven   5, 87 *passim*
Lima   460
Lincoln   202, 213n54
Lisbon   5, 381–382, 385–386, 389–393, 394, 397, 401
Livorno   13, 311
London   12, 202–203, 211, 218
Louth   202, 204, 220
Luanda   383–385, 387–389
Ludlow   203
Lübeck   82*n*55
Lützen   277
Lynn   202

Maastricht   100*n*38, 105
Mainz   279*n*27, 293

INDEX LOCORUM

Mantua   229, 342*n*38
Mechelen   105
Mergentheim   275*n*5
Messina   232
Mexico City   406
Michoacán   404 *passim*
Mikulov (Nikolsburg)   249, 262–263, 268
Milan   3, 12, 32, 228, 230, 232, 234, 326 *passim*
Modena   18, 229, 232, 233*n*21
Montserrat   140
Münster   276*n*10
Munich   274, 277–279, 280, 284, 292–293, 294, 296–297

Naples   232, 484
Neisse (Nysa)   266
Newark   202
Nördlingen   278, 284
Northampton   202–203
Norwich   202*n*6
Nottingham   217*n*68
Noyon   191
Nurío   416, 418–419, 421–422, 425

Óbidos   398
Olomouc   256
Oslavany   249–250, 253, 260, 262–263, 265, 268
Oxford   10, 217*n*69, 218*n*78
Oudenaarde   82*n*55

Paderborn   288
Padua   232, 314
Palermo   232
Palma de Mallorca   155
Paris   156, 378*n*61
Perugia   232
Pistoia   231*n*17
Pomacuarán   419
Prague   18, 249, 254, 256, 260

Quinceo   419–420

Römhild   275
Rome   6, 10, 11, 12, 177 *passim*, 218, 225, 227, 229, 231–232, 235–237, 239, 253*n*18, 263, 391*n*19, 471*n*8, 510

Rouen   8, 11, 105, 356 *passim*

Saluzzo   341
Salzburg   266
San Lorenzo   419
Santa Fe de la Laguna   410, 416, 418, 420, 423–425
Santa María de Ostula   425–428
Saragossa   513*n*20
Schleuzingen   275*n*5
Schmalkalden   275*n*5, 275*n*8
Seville   382, 442
Speyer   274, 293
St-Omer   105
Stuhlweissenburg   253

Tarejero   420
Tarragona   6, 9, 468 *passim*
Tattershall   213, 218*n*78
Tenochtitlan   216
Tetbury   219*n*82
Tortosa   154
Toulouse   132
Trapani   232

Uruapan   417

Valencia   6, 10, 14, 139–140, 152 *passim*, 382, 484, 508*n*5, 510, 517, 518*n*36, 519, 522*n*49, 523*n*50, 532*n*68, 532*n*70; 533*n*71
Venice   9, 10, 12, 18, 29, 32, 39, 49, 228, 231–232, 234–235, 256, 292–293, 314, 346
Vienna   3, 14, 100, 245–246, 249–250, 254, 256, 260, 262*n*41, 263, 265, 268

Wakefield   214
Warwick   218*n*78
Windsor   218*n*78
Wisbech   201–202
Würzburg   274, 279, 283–284, 286*n*51, 287–288, 293

York   205